Reach for the Stars

The Iowa High School State Wrestling Tournament

Dan McCool

authorHOUSE®

AuthorHouse™
1663 Liberty Drive
Bloomington, IN 47403
www.authorhouse.com
Phone: 1-800-839-8640

First published by AuthorHouse   7/14/2011

ISBN: 978-1-4567-6576-7 (e)
ISBN 978-1-4567-6577-4 (hc)
ISBN: 978-1-4567-6578-1 (sc)

Library of Congress Control Number: 2011908113

Printed in the United States of America

Any people depicted in stock imagery provided by Thinkstock are models, and such images are being used for illustrative purposes only. Certain stock imagery © Thinkstock.

This book is printed on acid-free paper.

"Simply put, it is what we are known for around the world."

In Iowa we live by the seasons; a time to sow and a time to reap. Hot summer days give way to cool fall nights. In the middle of the fall when the days are getting shorter, the high school wrestling season begins. After the winter solstice is upon us, wrestlers do not notice that the days are getting longer as they come out after practice and it is dark and cold. You just deal with it. Traveling the frozen highways of Iowa at sunrise on a Saturday, you will likely see a school bus full of wrestlers, coaches and cheerleaders headed to a tournament for the day. At sunset they are headed for home.

The season does eventually give way and you notice there is still a bit of sunlight after practice. Driving home, replaying the night's practice in your mind, or asking yourself if you should get another workout in later in the evening, you see some of the most beautiful sunsets you will ever see. It is warmer and you begin to get the first sense of spring. It signals that it is time for the test. An opportunity to prove if the efforts you put forth during the dark days when no one was watching can stand the light of day, the lights of our biggest stage – the Iowa State High School Wrestling Tournament.

Iowans love to watch their sons and daughters compete. We beam with pride in the accomplishments of our smartest students, our championship teams and our fastest athletes. However, few competitions compare to the way we determine our toughest wrestlers.

I have had the pleasure of watching state wrestling tournaments from across the country and I am proud to say that our Iowa tournament is on a different plane. The venue, the crowd, the pageantry, a statewide television audience and a sell-out crowd, in my opinion, make it the best in the country. Wrestling is not the most popular sport in our state, but by the standards of excellence you would have to rank wrestling near, if not at the top. Simply put, it is what we are known for around the world.

Reading Dan McCool's work you get a strong sense that the history of the Iowa State High School Wrestling Tournament is being written by the victors. One only has to look at the faces of the runners-up on the stand shortly after being defeated to get a picture of how esteemed winning a state championship is. However, that history only gives you a partial sense of the tournament's reality. Many of these young men go on to the next level and excel, taking the lessons learned from this stage to the next. In all, tens of thousands have walked away winners, achieving their goals of qualifying and placing on Iowa's biggest stage.

As a sports journalist, Dan McCool has contributed greatly to our sport and has been recognized for excellence. I am grateful that he has taken the time and given his best to what is an Iowa treasure – our State High School Wrestling Tournament.

-Jim Gibbons-

"He was always my uncle Norm."

Norman Borlaug of Cresco never won a state wrestling championship, but not every gold medalist grows up to devise a way to feed over one billion people in impoverished countries.

Thirty-eight years after placing third at 145 pounds in the 1932 state meet, Borlaug was awarded the Nobel Peace Prize. That gold medal ranks higher than a similar one from a state event, national meet or Olympiad because it signifies service to mankind.

"What he did for the world is really unfathomable when you think that he saved over a billion peoples' lives. To put it in perspective, it's like he said, 'You really can't have peace in anything until people don't worry about food,'" said Minnesota wrestling coach J Robinson, a former assistant coach at the University of Iowa. "He was a very, very humble man. I got to know him really well. We ended up having a really unique and special relationship. We didn't see each other a lot, but when we saw each other it was like seeing one of your old best friends.

"The first time I met him is when I got the job at Minnesota. I was sitting in the office and he walked in one day and introduced himself, 'Hey, I'm Norm Borlaug.' I think he was in there to see the AD or something. We talked about an hour and a half. He told me he was from Cresco, (former Minnesota coach Dave) Bartelma was his coach and how Bartelma would send him around the state and he reffed the first (high school state tournament). I had this nagging thing in my head…Borlaug, Borlaug…I'm a history major. When he left, I realized who he was. The beauty of who he was is you would have never known. If you'd have come to one of our booster parties and he was there, he'd introduce himself as Norm and he would say nothing about it."

That selfless approach was no act, according to Newton wrestling coach Bill Reed, Borlaug's great-nephew.

"He was always my Uncle Norm. My grandmother was his sister," Reed said.

At a memorial service for Borlaug at the University of Minnesota, Robinson told a gathering that he and the scientist talked about their common bond.

"We talked wrestling, how he wrestled in high school in a small town in Iowa called Cresco and had to share rides to school and practice with the three other farm families in the area," Robinson said in his speech. "He said he couldn't always get to practice because a different family drove the kids to school each day. One of the families didn't like wrestling so he couldn't get to practice one day a week, so Norm said, 'I had to work harder the other 4 days.'"

Dan Gable, an undefeated three-time state champion at Waterloo West, earned legendary status in wrestling by winning NCAA and Olympic gold medals and NCAA team championships in coaching. Gable said Borlaug is an excellent role model for selflessness.

"I look at Norman Borlaug because he was a wrestler, but he did something greater and affected the world," Gable said. "That's the way your thoughts have to be: 'How can I affect the people to be a better person, to get more out of himself?' That's what Norman Borlaug did. He is a guy that's going to live forever because when you affect the world, you live forever."

Borlaug presented himself as a simple, humble man whose DNA likely included smudges of dirt from growing a work ethic on the small farm he grew up on outside of Cresco. He became the first American to win Nobel laurels since Dr. Martin Luther King in 1964.

"I think the beauty of Norman Borlaug is what he believed in and that he spent the time. He lived in Mexico for 30 years, maybe, before he was nominated," Robinson said, "as opposed to (President Barack) Obama, who gets it for nothing. He earned it as opposed to it just being deferred upon him."

When Borlaug died in 2009, the *Wall Street Journal* described him as a person who came of age in the Great Depression – the last time widespread hunger permeated the United States – and eventually went to work easing those pangs in underdeveloped countries.

"The cool thing about him is who he was and what he did for the world, but the way in which he did it is that he set out to do something and then he lived the life that we all talk about," Robinson said. "The second part, what he did for wrestling, is that he never, ever forgot what wrestling did for him. Every time, without question, he would talk about how wrestling impacted his life, how it made him who he was, how it was a one-on-one sport.

"He would always reiterate to when he went in to talk to the Prime Minister of India and he said it was like a wrestling match, trying to get them to use this new wheat. He said, 'I went in there and I wasn't going to lose.' He did the same thing when he talked to the Prime Minister of Pakistan. They had this new wheat, this rust-resistant wheat, and it would take someone to get out there and do it."

Hard to imagine Borlaug lost in his first attempt to get into the University of Minnesota. "Norm didn't necessarily plan on coming to Minnesota, but a football player from his town (Irv Upton) was heading up to Minneapolis to go to school and suggested Norm tag along," Robinson said during his speech. "When he got to Minnesota, Norm failed his entry exam. But that Borlaug determination prevailed. Norm got into school and he wrestled anywhere from 140 pounds to heavyweight in his career as a Golden Gopher. Boy, what I wouldn't give for someone that versatile and with that much determination today."

That determination went into his work in the field.

"On the day Norman Borlaug was awarded its Peace Prize for 1970, the Nobel Committee observed of the Iowa-born plant scientist that, 'more than any other single person of this age, he has helped provide bread for a hungry world.' The committee might have added that more than any other single person Borlaug showed that nature is no match for human ingenuity in setting the real limits to growth," the *Wall Street Journal* article stated. The *New York Times* obituary for Borlaug noted, "His breeding of high-yielding crop varieties helped to avert mass famines that were widely predicted in the 1960s, altering the course of history. Largely because of his work, countries that had been food deficient, like Mexico and India, became self-sufficient in producing cereal grains."

According to the *Times* article, Gary H. Toenniessen, director of agricultural programs for the Rockefeller Foundation, said in an interview that Dr. Borlaug's great achievement was to prove that intensive, modern agriculture could be made to work in the fast-growing developing countries where it was needed most, even on the small farms predominating there.

By Toenniessen's calculation, about half the world's population goes to bed every night after consuming grain descended from one of the high-yield varieties developed by Dr. Borlaug and his colleagues of the Green

Revolution. "He knew what it was they needed to do, and he didn't give up," Toenniessen said. "He could just see that this was the answer."

Borlaug's office at Texas A & M University included a Minnesota wrestling poster. "He always carried his roots with him," Robinson said.

Borlaug had a wrestler's approach to rejoicing in his Nobel award.

"I'll be out in the field again tomorrow pulling plants," Borlaug was quoted in regards to planning a day-after celebration.

The honor afforded Borlaug the banner headline IOWA'S OWN MAN OF PEACE in the October 22, 1970 copy of the *Des Moines Register*. According to a story in that day's paper, when his wife Margaret informed him of the win, Borlaug's first thought was, "Somebody must have made a mistake."

Reed, who started wrestling in first grade in Fort Dodge, was told Borlaug wrestled in high school. But it was later that Reed learned he had a relative to really be proud of.

"My first memory of Uncle Norm…I remember the big to-do about him winning the Nobel Peace Prize in '70, that's the first I remember of grandma's brother being somebody really special," Reed said. "I had probably met him before then but it wasn't really clicking because he was just a scientist at that point in time."

Reed and Borlaug had a love of wrestling. Both made the finals of the state tournament. Borlaug had another match in the 1932 tournament after losing in the 145-pound finals to Howard McGrath of Clarion. Borlaug lost to Johnny Merryman of Fort Dodge in the wrestle-back and finished third. Reed was beaten by Brian McCracken of Bettendorf in the Class 3-A 185-pound finals in 1981. The wrestle-back for second his great-uncle went through was discontinued long before Reed made the finals.

Borlaug also played football at Cresco, teaming up with Robert Smylie, who would later serve three terms as the governor of the state of Idaho.

"From day one when I remember meeting him, he always asked me about wrestling and talked about what wrestling was going to teach me, how that was going to help me do something," Reed said. "We talked more about wrestling, but he would always remind me to make sure I was doing my studies. It wasn't always just me, it was about the sport – making sure that work ethic and that mindset that he had about wrestlers being able to do anything because of what wrestling taught you always came out."

Robinson said he had Borlaug talk to his wrestlers periodically. The message was old in years, but timeless in importance. "Norm always quoted Dave Bartelma, his college coach at Minnesota, and gives him a lot of the credit for reinforcing the lesson of hard work and dedication: "Give it the best God gave you. If you don't do that, don't bother to compete."

Robinson visited Borlaug not long before the world legend died in September 2009. "What was amazing is that our friendship transcended a lot of things because it was wrestling. There were tons of people trying to get in to see him, I mean like cabinet members and prime ministers, and I was one of the few people allowed in to see him, and it was because of his wrestling roots."

Waterloo West coach Bob Siddens remembered being impressed by meeting Borlaug at Cresco in 1994, when Borlaug was inducted into the Iowa Wrestling Hall of Fame. Joining Borlaug on the trip to his hometown was his wife, Margaret.

Siddens said he went up to Borlaug to introduce himself. "Borlaug said, 'You're Bob Siddens, the old West High wrestling coach.' That was exciting to hear this Nobel Peace Prize and Presidential Medal of Freedom winner say 'I know you,'" Siddens said. "We got talking about material things, we got talking about the athletes and he said, 'Bob, I want to tell you something. Margaret came to me one time and said "Norman, I wish you would have had a job that pays more money." And he said, 'Margaret, what do you need that you don't have?' In my way of looking at it, I never made a lot of money, but everything that I've needed, I had – six wonderful children, 14 grandchildren. There are so many things that take place and transpire."

There are discussions among wrestling fans about who the greatest wrestler was or who the greatest coach was. Robinson said there is no argument about Borlaug being the most valuable wrestler.

"You can't even compare. Because you look at wrestling, you look through very narrow glasses – Cael, Gable, Lee Kemp or any one of those guys," Robinson said, "but that's in the wrestling world. This transcends the wrestling room. You're talking about saving a billion people's lives. Most Americans can't comprehend what that's like."

Borlaug wrestled at the University of Minnesota, where he was a NCAA qualifier. His coach was Bartelma, the same man who coached him at Cresco. Reed wrestled at Iowa State, where he enrolled as a botany major. Another Cresco wrestler, Harold Nichols, was at the helm of the Cyclones' nationally known program when Reed enrolled. Having a Nobel Peace Prize-winning relative might make landing a summer internship a bit easier. There was also the thought of medical school.

"In God's plan, that wasn't His plan for me. My plan was to be a teacher and coach," said Reed, who teaches biology at Newton.

Borlaug never got to see Reed on the mat, but the talks were always about being in position for success.

""It wasn't as much what's the technique I was using, it was 'Are you working as hard as you can all the time? You've always got to do your best, always give your best effort because that's the only way you're ever going to know if you're reaching your full potential,'" Reed said. "He asked me about my favorite moves. He always liked his hammer lock. I think it's illegal (now), but he would lock on the arm, block the knee and set them, down that way. He was a farmer, he had farmer strength."

When Reed got into coaching, the discussions had a twist. "It changed from 'Are you working hard?' to 'Are your kids working hard for you, are they studying, are they getting good grades too, or are they just good wrestlers?'" Reed said.

Not every coach can introduce his charges to a world-famous relative like Reed did for a band of wrestlers when he was an assistant at Roosevelt High School in Des Moines.

"He was happy to see they were wrestling in terms of that was going to teach them work ethic, but beyond wrestling it was, 'What are you studying? Are you reading lots of books?'" Reed remembered. "Sports taught you the work ethic but you have to keep your mind fresh by reading a lot. Don't just read science because you like science, make sure you read history and lots of different things because that keeps your mind fresh too, and it broadens your perspective on things. He would never, ever let up on the education."

Nor would he quit praising the life's value of wrestling.

"I can't count the number of times when I heard him, at some point in time in his talk he would talk about what wrestling did for him, what his coach Dave Bartelma did for him and gave him the opportunities that allowed him to get to what he'd gotten to," Reed said.

With help from some wrestlers such as Borlaug, Bartelma was credited with bringing the sport to many high schools in Minnesota. A hall of fame for high school wrestling in Minnesota bears Bartelma's name. Reed said Bartelma would give the guys some money for gas and food, a map and a list of places at which they would put on demonstrations of the sport. Borlaug refereed in some of the first Minnesota high school state tournaments while still in college, according to the National Wrestling

Hall of Fame, which awarded Borlaug its "Outstanding American" award in 1992.

Reed said it's possible Borlaug would have made a good wrestling coach.

"He was a pretty good Little League coach from what I understand, the stories I heard about what he did down in Mexico," Reed said, adding that Borlaug wanted to try out with the Chicago Cubs after college. Instead, he got a forestry job that put him well west of Wrigley Field but on the right path to saving lives.

Reed remembered being with Borlaug at the annual World Food Prize presentation in Des Moines. There were meetings to attend and people who wanted to speak to him. Borlaug wished he could retire to his room and watch a baseball game on television, Reed recalled.

"I've seen it said that he is one of the 100 most important people in the last century. If you really sit and think of all the people that have been on the earth for the last 100 years, that's an amazing statement," Robinson said. "He helped people at their most basic need. He cared deeply that he invested his life, not rhetoric, but his life in putting food on people's table so they could just eat. To me, he's a remarkable man, he was a remarkable man."

People might recognize Iowa state champions such as Gable, twins Tom and Terry Brands of Sheldon and Mark Ironside of Cedar Rapids Jefferson. That's a collection of eight state titles, nine NCAA championships, four world championships and three Olympic medalists (Gable and Tom Brands won gold, Terry Brands won bronze), but Reed said Borlaug has a special kind of greatness.

"When everybody said he single-handedly fed more people than anyone else - he's credited with saving over 1-1/2 billion peoples' lives from starvation - when I get the accolades that you hang the hat on, he's one of only five people that have won the Congressional Medal of Honor, the Presidential Medal of Freedom and the Nobel Peace Prize. Obviously everybody knows about Nelson Mandela, Mother Theresa, Martin Luther King (Elie Wiesel is the other)...that's where he's at, so it's kind of a no-brainer, I think he was one the greatest people who ever lived as far as what he did.

"And it was always give, he was always giving," Reed said. "I don't feel that Uncle Norm was ever taking. I wish I could be as giving as he was sometimes. He was always working hard, but it was always to help people."

"You have your eye on one goal..."

The location of the state wrestling tournament has changed 11 times since Iowa State College's State Gymnasium played host to a state invitational on Feb. 5, 1921.

The prize has not.

"You have your eye on one goal – I want to be that state champion – and you put all of your efforts into it," said two-time Waterloo East state champion Bob Buzzard, a two-time all-American at Iowa State and member of the United States Greco-Roman team in the 1972 Summer Olympics.

Until the dual-meet state tournament started in 1987, the state finals ended wrestling season. That was the target date. "I think after you train your whole life to do that and you get to stand there and get your hand raised, you feel the satisfaction of all the hard work you put in and you realize that's what you worked for and you take it all in," said David Kjeldgaard, a three-time state champion at Council Bluffs Lewis Central.

"I've been to other state tournaments since I've been gone, other states that would say they are some of the best states in wrestling. I think the true appreciation is we have generations of people that have wrestled. A lot of states you don't have the history to it, you don't have the appreciation for it and you don't just have true wrestling fans like you have here. I think I took that for granted when I was here, I didn't understand the depth of wrestling and what it means to the state."

Those fans witnessed history in the 2011 state tournament. Two girls, freshman Cassandra "Cassy" Herkelman of Cedar Falls and sophomore Megan Black of Ottumwa, qualified at 112 pounds for the Class 3-A tournament. They became the first girls to qualify for the traditional state meet, each winning a wrestle-back match at the district tournament to secure two of the 224 spots in the large-school class.

"This just shows you can do anything if you put your mind to it,"

Herkelman told Jim Nelson of the *Waterloo Courier* following her historic win. "I've thought all year I could make it to state and the last couple of weeks I began to realize how tough it would be, but now that I made it… it surprises me too."

Black was one match away from qualifying for the 2010 state meet. She told Matt Levins of the *Burlington Hawk Eye* that she sought help right before her wrestle-back bout.

"I was just thinking, 'Please let me win.' I was praying, 'God, please let me make it.' I thank God for helping me make it," Black said.

She won by decision, but Levins reported Black had a chance to end the match by pin in the first period. "I was waiting for the ref to slap the mat, but it never happened," Black said.

While their qualifying for the state tournament drew statewide attention, what happened in the 14th match of the Class 3-A tournament put the meet in a national spotlight. Joel Northrup, a sophomore from Linn-Mar of Marion, reported to the assigned mat and said he was defaulting the match to Herkelman because of religious beliefs. Referee Eric Eckerman raised Herkelman's arm, making her the first girl to win a traditional state tournament bout without having a match. Northrup came into the state meet ranked No. 5 in Class 3-A at 112 pounds.

Northrup issued a statement about his decision, but had no other comment during the tournament. "I have a tremendous amount of respect for Cassey and Meagan and their accomplishments. However, wrestling is a combat sport and it can get violent at times. As a matter of conscience and my faith, I do not believe that it is appropriate for a boy to engage a girl in this manner. It is unfortunate that I have been placed in a situation not seen in most other High School sports in Iowa," Northrup's statement read.

Four days after the tournament ended, Northrup was on CBS's *The Early Show* to talk about his decision. He repeated his decision to default was faith-based. "(Herkelman) deserves to be out there, but I do believe that if she does wrestle, she should wrestle other girls and I should wrestle other boys," Northrup said. "I just had to stick to my convictions. It's hard for her, but I had to hold on to what I decided in fifth grade – that I wouldn't wrestle a girl."

Herkelman withheld comment until she was finished competing. When asked about Northrup's decision, Herkelman said, "He has the right to make his own choice, and he made his choice. It's not like he did what he didn't want to do. I knew it was an option. When he did it, I wasn't very surprised."

Two matches after Herkelman's initial match, Black took the mat and was pinned in the first period. She was eliminated when pinned in her consolation match later that day. Herkelman lost by decision in the quarterfinals the following day, then was eliminated from the tournament with a loss by fall. By the time they were finished competing – fueled by the controversial decision by Northrup – the girls had drawn unusual visitors such as "Good Morning America" and Rick Reilly of ESPN to the tournament.

"It's an unfortunate thing that it became such a news story, that it was such a personal and family decision that he made to default to her," said Bill Herkelman, Cassy's father. "She had no idea (about the default) up until it actually happened. She was surprised when the referee told her she didn't have to put her leg bands on. In an earlier meet, he had chosen not to wrestle her as well. We didn't know if it was going to carry through to the state tournament or not."

It was easy to find Herkelman or Black in action. Their matches had rows of photographers and video cameras documenting the action as well as the attention of most of the fans in attendance. They were escorted by security to and from their matches. "I knew it was going to be expected because, like after districts, it was already crazy. I knew it was going to be crazy here," Herkelman said.

Bill Herkelman said a train wreck of a situation never developed at state.

"It could have been a real distracting experience for her, but the way Wells Fargo Arena and the coaching staff handled it, I think she was really able to focus and do what she did this weekend," he said.

Black said it was much ado about something because only her gender differed from the other wrestlers.

"I would say it's a big deal. I wanted to make it to state just as bad as any boy. As a wrestler, I wanted to make it to state and that was my goal," Black said. "(A girl qualifying for state) was going to happen sometime, obviously, and I'm glad to be part of that. At the same time, I'm just another wrestler trying to place and make it to state just like everyone else."

Black has retooled her goals in wrestling, which has deep roots in the Black family. She said getting to state was her goal since she started in the sport in first grade. "I've always been very competitive and wanted to be the best I could be, so I set my goal here. Now I'm going to move up my goal to placing and then to winning," Black said.

The state tournament has many decorated farm kids, who considered the chores of becoming a state champion similar to the chores of keeping a farm operating. Black appreciates the work in either vein. "That's kind of what Iowa is known for. I don't think it hurt any. Farming is a tough job, everyone knows that. It definitely helped. My dad has been very supportive. He's a farmer, so being out with him from the time I was born I've wanted to be around it. I think it helps a lot," Black said.

Girls have shown improving talent in the sport, possibly a parallel of the growth of women's freestyle wrestling in the country. Women's freestyle became an Olympic sport in 2004.

The first girl to win a state tournament match in Iowa was Heather Morley of Urbandale, who scored a pin in the 2005 dual-meet state tournament. There have been other girls from Iowa participating in significant tournaments through the years. Ashley Pender of Colfax-Mingo became what was believed to be the first girl in Class 1-A or Class 2-A to qualify for districts in 2003 when she placed fourth. Class 3-A teams begin their qualification for state in a district. Cindy Johnson of West Burlington-Notre Dame was a Class 2-A district qualifier in 2004. She was believed to be the first girl in Class 1-A or 2-A to win a district match, and she finished third at 103 pounds.

Atina Bibbs of Davenport Central and Stacy Light of Lisbon met in what was believed to be the first Iowa high school match involving two girls in 1993. Bibbs also won a National Open women's freestyle championship in 1993. Quinn Vermie of Southeast Polk won the first individual championship at the first Iowa Girls' State Championship in 2000. Roni Goodale of Bettendorf won a United States Girls' Wrestling Association high school championship in 2010. Lizz Sanders of Newton was a first-team selection on Asics Tiger's 2004 high school girls' all-America team and was named to the first girls' wrestling "Dream Team" by *Wrestling USA* magazine in 2005. Tiffany Sluik of Mason City was third in a Class 3-A district meet in 2008 and has twice earned all-America honors while competing at Jamestown College in North Dakota in 2011.

If Herkelman and Black were nervous going into the state meet, they weren't alone.

Trying to achieve one's goal of gold can get nerve-wracking, regardless of the state tournament's site. Since the tournament moved to Wells Fargo Arena in Des Moines in 2006, the Iowa High School Athletic Association has 13,725 tickets for sale to the championship round and they are spoken for on Dec. 1 – the first date orders are accepted.

"It sends chills all the way throughout your body because you're not used to having that big of a crowd," said Cody Clark of Southeast Polk, who won his third Class 3-A state championship in the 2011 tournament. "You can't hear anything, the whole crowd's going crazy, you get an adrenaline rush and real bad nerves in your stomach but I just try to get off in my own little zone or something and not worry about it, stay focused on what I'm doing."

Is it a matter of life and death? Some might say that. Others have experienced an actual life-or-death situation and found out wrestling isn't quite that extreme. Justin Brower of West Lyon of Inwood qualified for his first state tournament appearance as a junior in 1998. Brower's pant leg was caught in a power takeoff and he wound up with a broken left leg and concerns of whether or not he would walk again. He was airlifted to Sioux Falls for surgery – eight pins and a plate were inserted – and then went to Minneapolis for physical therapy with a relative.

Brower came back for the 1997-98 season and never thought about using the injury and the surgery as an excuse for anything. West Lyon coach Keith Slifka met Brower halfway into a training run, and asked if he wanted a ride because Brower might be overdoing things. "He said, 'No coach, I've got (the pins) all worn down by now,'" Slifka said to the *Des Moines Register*. "I've never heard him say 'no.'"

Brower lost both of his matches in the 1998 meet.

Brower had the same goal in 1998 as the other 623 qualifiers. When the weight classes expanded to 14 in 2001, another 48 wrestlers got to work on realizing their dream.

"I think the most important thing that a young wrestler can learn is - and I think it's also true as I've applied it to my life since wrestling - within the concept of reality, you can work towards becoming the best you could ever be," said Iowa State assistant coach Eric Voelker, a two-time NCAA champion at Iowa State who did not win a high school title but was on a championship team at Dallas Center-Grimes. "I think the idea of shooting for the stars, or dreaming big, goes so against what happens to us in our minds over time. We get closed down, doors closed, options close and we quit thinking about possibilities. The odds of anything great happening then are almost gone.

When you shoot for the stars, we all know first-hand only 14 guys are going to win it out of (672). We already know the odds are against any one individual winning the tournament, but the thing that makes it great and moves the whole class ahead and the individuals rise in it is everybody going for it and we collectively make each other great. How do you cross a young wrestler over to thinking he can beat somebody he shouldn't be able to beat? We both weighed in at the same weight, both about the same age, same experience and we can make this thing happen. The question is do you want to believe you can and work for it. I think when we do shoot for the stars, everybody comes closer."

The arena floor shrinks to three championship mats on Saturday night. Three days earlier, 448 of the field of 672 wrestlers – two of the three classes – begin the tussle to the top. A third class opens competition the following morning.

"All I'm going to say is it's so special," said 1972 Olympic gold medalist Dan Gable, who won three state championships and 64 consecutive matches for Waterloo West before carving his name at the top of the tree in collegiate and international competition and coaching. "I'm not in awe of it because that's just not the way I am, but it's one of these events that, when it's done, I'm the last guy there and then all the drive home I cry because it's over."

Gable and his wife Kathy had four daughters, so he never got to take a son to the tournament like his dad Mack Gable did. These days, Gable has future competitors in tow when he visits Wells Fargo Arena in Des Moines.

"I love taking my grandkids to the Iowa state tournament now. It's the No. 1 athletic event in the state of Iowa from a standpoint of the high school," Gable said. "It's three days, four days now, you've got all of these crowds, you've got all these great wrestlers there. You take them early because they're in awe only because there's crowds and wrestlers, but you become used to it. It's almost a way of life, and I think it's a way of life with people in the state of Iowa – to go to the state tournament every year."

Whatever it is, the finals have sold out for 24 consecutive years.

"I guess the best description I could think of is it's a happening. It's an exciting time of the year and that's what people look forward to," said Dave Harty, a retired assistant executive director with the IHSAA who oversaw the state wrestling meet for over 30 years. "I think the fact it was the toughest ticket in town to get was not only exciting, but that made it appealing. People wanted to be there."

Guys who were qualified to wrestle there since 1989 had a chance to take home a piece of artwork by Tammie Ollendick. The winner of each weight class gets a giant wall chart of his bracket fully filled out, written by Ollendick in a chancery style of calligraphy. When the last of the 42 charts is handed out, she has completed writing 2,562 names. Those charts are headed for living rooms or family rooms, a work of art signifying the successful end of what became a piece of work.

"I don't think any machine could come even close to getting the enthusiasm and the importance of a kid's name being written the way she does it," said Bernie Saggau, then-executive director of the IHSAA, in a *Des Moines Register* story about Ollendick's behind-the-scenes work.

Going into the 2011 state tournament, 1,798 individuals have won 2,290 state championships since 1926. Add the tournaments in Ames and Iowa City between 1921 and 1925 and the numbers swell to 1,853 men and 2,360 championships. Another part of the event's history has been some of the host sites:

- Gable won his three championships at Waterloo's McElroy Auditorium. The mats were placed on top of a sheet of ice so the mats became hard by tournament's end. McElroy hosted between 1963 and 1969 – the first three-class tournament was in 1969 – and either Waterloo East or Waterloo West won the large-school title in six of the seven tournaments.

- Some guys remember winning state titles at West Gym, or Men's Gym, on the campus of University of Northern Iowa. In 1954, it was home to one of the milestone matches – and one of the bigger upsets - in tournament history. Simon Roberts of Davenport beat two-time champion Ron Gray of Eagle Grove, 3-1, for the 133-pound championship. Roberts became the state's first African-American state champion wrestler. It was the only loss in his final three seasons for Gray, an eventual three-time winner. Bob Steenlage of Britt became the first of the state's 19 four-time state champions there in 1962.

- State Gymnasium at Ames was home to eight state tournaments, plus five more prior to the Iowa High School Athletic Association operating the event beginning in 1926. Likely the only wrestling tournament hall of fame college basketball coach Adolph Rupp was involved in took place in Ames in 1926. Rupp was the faculty representative and Allie Morrison – who totaled three titles at Ames and Iowa City between 1923 and 1924 – was student coach.

- Waterloo West (1942-46) was the first squad to win five

consecutive state team titles. Four of those were secured at Clarion, a seven-year host. Don Bosco of Gilbertville went into the 2011 Class 1-A tournament trying to win an unprecedented sixth straight traditional championship, but finished second to Logan-Magnolia.

• Maybe the site closest associated with the state tournament is Veterans Memorial Auditorium in Des Moines. The building resembles an oversized barn, a fitting place for a sport that had strong representation from farm boys. In state meet lingo the facility is known, often reverently, as "The Barn." The place was dusty like a barn, there was a constant ring of fans milling around the six, and later eight, mats and the seating created an intimate environment that made it seem as though getting from the balcony to the floor was akin to jumping out of a hay loft. Fifteen of the four-time champions did their work there. The tournament moved across the street to its current home, Wells Fargo Arena, in 2006.

Wrestlers get attached to places. They love any place at which they won a championship, especially a fourth consecutive one. If you can't win four state titles, getting four conference championships earns you a lifetime of respect. The North Central Conference, North Iowa Conference, Northeast Iowa Conference, WaMAC Conference…say you went through four years and won the tournament annually and someone will buy your popcorn on future visits.

Nothing is quite like winning at state, and a lot of guys hold Vets in highest regard.

"After winning last year, it's almost like my holy land," Washington's Bobby Gonshorowski told the *Des Moines Register* as he prepared to win a second state championship in 1997. "All of my life, all I did was dream about winning the state title, especially after my brother won it."

Matt Gonshorowski won for Washington in 1992.

Jeff Kerber of Emmetsburg was the first wrestler to win four state titles at Vets. He said the place has an unparalleled spot in tournament history.

"To me, they'll never be able to substitute that atmosphere. I realize that time marches on and the venues have to march on too, they get outdated, but Vets was a unique atmosphere that is just very difficult to match," Kerber said. "There was an electricity, there was a personality to Vets that was very unusual and to my thinking it really fit the sport of wrestling wonderfully. It was chaotic yet it all made sense. They pulled it off with not too many hitches, rarely did you have a fight in the stands but you could have."

Prior to the final round of the state tournament a parade is staged. All of the placewinners take a lap around the floor of the arena in uniform led by a person or persons with ties to the tournament. In recent years, the theme music from the Olympic Games plays during what is known as the Grand March. One year the scorers and timers led the way, another year five guys with an undefeated career were the escorts. Other escorts have included Gov. Terry Branstad, the Gibbons brothers, the Martin brothers, the 1979 Don Bosco of Gilbertville team (the last squad to qualify its entire team for the tournament) and John Brindley, the first wrestler to win a state title in the 1926 tournament – the first run by the Iowa High School Athletic Association.

"The grand march is one of the greatest things about that state tournament," said Bobby Gonshorowski, who walked in four of them. "I remember my freshman (season) walking out – all you see are the flashes, people standing and cheering...You just want to get out there and wrestle right then and there."

Noise has also had a place in the tournament. A four-time state champion can create a lot of that noise with two standing ovations. The audience stands after the final period expires and the arm gets raised for the fourth time. They stand again when the wrestler gets his fourth gold medal. The last 18 four-timers got the double order of applause. Steenlage drew a standing ovation in 1962, and he also got an excited introduction by Herbert Graeber of Conrad, who chaired the IHSAA's Board of Control.

"This is the first time in the history of the world that a boy has gained this honor," said Graeber, who later clarified that Steenlage was the first Iowan to win four mat titles.

West Gym in Cedar Falls could rock a little. Davenport coach Jim Fox found that out in 1954, the year Roberts upset Gray.

"They tell me they had a total of 8,000 fans for the afternoon and night sessions," Fox told the *Davenport Morning Democrat*. "I'm telling you that at times Saturday night I thought they must have had 80,000 fans there. The din was terrific."

West Gym also housed Cresco ace Tom Peckham's pin over Wayne Cool of Waterloo East in the Class A 154-pound finals in 1961. A young wrestling fan named Dan Gable was trying to watch the contest among the crowd, especially since Cool was leading Peckham in the third period.

"It looked like Cool was going to upset Peckham, and that was going to be huge because (Peckham) was such a heavy favorite," Gable recalled. "There wasn't much time left and all of a sudden everybody stood up around me and I couldn't see what happened. When they sat down, the match was over and it wasn't Cool, it was Peckham who got his hand raised. I'll never forget that moment in the Men's Gym with Peckham and Cool, Waterloo and Cresco."

There were three standing ovations in the 1980 state tournament at Vets Auditorium. Iowa School of the Deaf coach Dick Pike got the first salute because he was named Class 1-A coach of the year. It was the first time the school in Council Bluffs had a qualifier (there were actually five qualifiers) and Pike, who was in the midst of being hit by the flu, had a state champion when Jackie Barron won the first of his two titles that night. The next two were for Scott Morningstar of Lisbon, who won his fourth state championship. The Lisbon fans got a head start on cheering when 105-pounder Brian Hall, Morningstar's teammate, clinched the Class 1-A team title by turning a 14-2, third-period deficit into a pin in 5 minutes, 36 seconds in the finals.

"It was the first time I ever heard the crowd, and that place just blew up," Hall said.

Fans in Vets had ringing ears prior to the 1993 finals. Dan Gabrielson of Belmond avenged a loss to Ike Light of Lisbon in the previous year's 125-pound finals by beating Light 8-5 in the 130-pound semifinals in 1993. The loss denied Light a chance to win four state titles like his brother Shane did between 1987 and 1990. Gabrielson won the semifinals match by putting Light on his back late in the third period. Gabrielson said he was too busy trying for a pin to notice the growing crescendo of cheers as the last seconds ticked away.

"I didn't hear it until after I got up. I had him on the mat and I'm looking back underneath so I can see the clock...*20, 19, 18...* by the time I had a 3-count I knew it was over but I couldn't really sense the crowd because I was still holding tight," Gabrielson said. "It was special for me, but obviously there were other people it was special for because they seemed to be erupting. It was the loudest I'd ever heard (Vets). When I listen to it on the tape, I've never seen it go crazier than it did that day."

The idea of moving the tournament out of Vets might have had some support through the years, but never from the man with the biggest say. Bernie Saggau, former executive director of the IHSAA, said he was pleased with being in Des Moines.

"If I wanted a bigger facility, I'd have moved it up to UNI," Saggau said. "I knew we could get more people in there than we could at Vets, but I liked being central. I could have put it up there, I think they'd have gone, but my school people would have been upset as hell. Here, loss of school time was never talked about. If we'd have gone there, I'd have caught a lot of static, but they would have done just as good of a job up there, maybe better, because they're wrestling people."

Saggau did bring a wrestling tournament to UNI and its 16,324-seat UNI-Dome. The dual-meet state tournament – held one week after the traditional state meet – was staged for the first time in 1987 in Cedar Falls. Beginning with the 2012 tournament, the dual-meet event will be moved to Des Moines and will be held the day before the traditional tournament starts. That move was due in part to major renovation at the dual-meet event's site in Cedar Rapids.

Bart Chelesvig became Webster City's first state champion in 1985. He has at least three memories of Vets – Chelesvig was a three-time champion and one of the nation's top recruits during his career – but one in 1986 has a special place in his heart.

"I remember a lot of little things about it. I remember warming up in the corner or the ramps," Chelesvig said. "I remember running up the ramp to go hug my mom (Nadine) after I'd won the state, and she passed away two weeks later. That's my best memory."

One wrestling person who was happy to compete at Vets was Dan Knight of Clinton. In 1987, Knight was the first of two Iowans to be named ASICS Tiger Wrestler of the Year. The other recipient was David Kjeldgaard of Council Bluffs Lewis Central in 1996.

Knight spent time growing up at 2801 N. 4th Street and at 3509 N. 3rd Street in Clinton. With a family of wrestlers, naturally there was a wrestling mat in the basement at both places. Knight could be excused for listing 833 5th Avenue in Des Moines as home. That's where Vets Auditorium is located. That's where Knight won four state titles. His older brother Steve won two championships there, and their brother Jeff won once.

"The only time I really probably got spooked was the night before (in 1984) sitting in my room before it started and realizing I was finally going to get to wrestle there," said Knight, now head coach at Bettendorf. "I'd been going there since I was 3 years old. That was home, I ran around that place every year, I was in the emergency room for falling down bleachers there. I was so comfortable in there, I knew that place inside and out and so I didn't get spooked there."

Knight's tournament record showed nothing to be scared of, unless you were the next guy to face him. He pinned nine of his 16 opponents and never won by anything less than a major decision.

Wrestlers seeking a fourth state championship tend to keep out of sight in the time between the grand march that opens the final round and the time to perform. Knight had an unusual finals evening in 1987. The grand march was to be led by Nobel Peace Prize winner Norman Borlaug, but the former Cresco state place winner was called away. Since he was trying to become the state's seventh four-timer, Knight was asked to fill in.

"They asked me if that was ok, if I didn't mind doing that, and that was fine. That was an honor I thought," Knight said.

It took Knight 28 seconds to pin Andy Price of Burlington for the Class 3-A 126-pound championship that night. Knight finished his high school career undefeated in 128 matches.

"In that finals match I just wanted to get in and get out. I didn't want any slam, anything that could go wrong go wrong. I just wanted to get a takedown, get to my halves and get out," Knight said. "I was going to pin him as fast as I could pin him. I'd wrestled him before so I knew what he had and what I was up against. I just wanted to be as quick as I could."

Jim Zalesky won two state championships at Vets for Cedar Rapids Prairie. After winning three NCAA titles at University of Iowa, Zalesky attended numerous state tournaments in several states as a college assistant and head coach.

"I've been to a lot of state tournaments scouting and recruiting and nothing beats the environment at Vets, where you could get maybe five or 10 feet from somebody you know who's going to wrestle and sit there and scream and yell and holler your lungs out, then rotate five mats over to watch another one of your wrestlers," said Zalesky, head coach at Oregon State. "The environment of Vets was something. People don't realize it was special and it's probably never going to be created again because you just don't have that environment anymore."

Wrestlers are big on getting experience. Joe Gibbons tried to drink in as much atmosphere about the tournament and "The Barn" before he became a varsity wrestler. Gibbons was the fourth four-timer, winning two titles at Waterloo Columbus and two more at Ames.

"I came down here years before I ever competed and I got used to the sights, the arena, the sounds, the crowd and how it can go in a split-second from quiet to a screaming roar where your headgear's just radiating and you can't hear anything," Gibbons said. "I was aware of my surroundings before I got there, then when I competed I wasn't scared. I had teammates that got overwhelmed by just what was going on, they couldn't concentrate and they got beat by possibly a lesser opponent because of that. Nothing beats experience, coming down, witnessing it before you get here and being committed to your technique, execution and wrestle for that moment in time, that 6-minute match."

Joe is one of four Gibbons boys who totaled 10 state championships – the most by a group of sibling wrestlers from Iowa. Jim won three titles, Tim won one and Jeff followed Joe's run by winning two. Jim and Joe were NCAA champions and they coached Jeff to all-America honors, all at Iowa State.

Joe Gibbons watched Nick Moore of Iowa City West become the 19th four-time champion at the 2010 tournament. He had an idea of what Moore was feeling.

"It's just like reliving it again. You know that he probably walked a very similar path that I walked," Gibbons said. "That's great that our sport has competitors like Mr. Moore who are committed to excellence."

Hundreds of wrestlers are committed to Vets as *the* place to house the tournament.

"Absolutely. I still get chills when I see that building," said Mike Schimp, a 1978 state champion for Belmond who had straddled life and death because of injuries sustained in a tornado 12 years earlier.

Jeff Harrison of Sloan was a three-time state champion for Westwood of Sloan. His titles came at Vets. He grew up knowing the place was special because his father, Jack, was the school's wrestling coach. When I think of (Vets), the first thing I think of is the smell and the excitement. I've been to Wells Fargo and you just don't have it there," Harrison said. "Instantly walking into Vets I get chills. Obviously that's a great facility. It feels like Vets had so much tradition. I get chills thinking about it right now."

Bob Kenny said he's experienced a state tournament that was about as far from the Iowa experience as possible. Kenny, who competed at Vets for Osage, led teams to state championships in Vets and in Wells Fargo Arena. That was a far cry from the Arizona state meet of several years ago, when Kenny coached nine qualifiers.

"It was in a high school gym, they've got these little tiny brackets up in the commons area, people are writing (bad notes) on the brackets. The officiating was so terrible. It wasn't even close. So disappointing," Kenny said.

Lewis Central's Kjeldgaard realized the family depth of Iowa's tournament once he got away from it.

"I've been to other state tournaments since I've been gone, other states that would say they are some of the best states in wrestling. I think the true appreciation is we have generations of people that have wrestled," Kjeldgaard said. "(With) a lot of states you don't have the history to it, you don't have the appreciation for it and you don't just have true wrestling fans like you have here. I think I took that for granted when I was here, I didn't understand the depth of wrestling and what it means to the state."

Harrison finished his career by winning his final match in each of his four years as a state participant. He was third as a freshman.

"Vets was good to me, I was blessed. I was 17-1 at Vets in my career, 18-0 is better," Harrison said.

"...O.K., but you're making a mistake."

The sport of wrestling grew on Bernie Saggau. Thanks to some forward thinking, Saggau helped the sport grow in Iowa.

Saggau was executive director of the Iowa High School Athletic Association between 1967 and Jan. 1, 2005. He claimed to have the same bottom line for every decision made on tournaments. Some governance was widely popular, such as playing state championship football games indoors at the UNI-Dome in Cedar Falls. Others weren't met so warmly, such as creating football playoffs, moving the state baseball tournament out of Carroll and Marshalltown to Des Moines' Principal Park (home of the Chicago Cubs' Triple-A affiliate) and relocating the boys' state soccer tournament to James Cownie Soccer Complex in Des Moines from Muscatine Soccer Complex (which soccer fans say is the state's finest facility).

"I sure wasn't perfect, but every decision I always made was what was best for kids," Saggau said.

One of his decisions seemed to be perfect for a sport. Saggau was assisting then-executive director Lyle Quinn in 1965 when he began to make overtures about moving the state wrestling tournament out of Waterloo's McElroy Auditorium, also known as the Hippodrome. The tournament had been in Black Hawk County – either Waterloo or Cedar Falls – annually since 1953. Saggau had seen what he thought was a better location.

"It may have been the second year I went up, Lyle was sitting there and I walked over and said, 'Lyle, how long is this contract? How long were you guaranteeing coming up here?' He thought the next year was the end, but we'd renew it.' I said, 'We're not coming back,'" Saggau said.

Quinn asked where he wanted to go, and Saggau said Veterans Memorial Auditorium in Des Moines. "He said, 'You'll kill wrestling if

24

you do that. You give me a good reason why you want to move it,'" Saggau said.

Saggau said he and Quinn had an agreement that Saggau be right 50 percent of the time. Moving the state wrestling meet out of the sport's Northeast Iowa hotbed – 22 of the 31 team championships between 1953 and 1969 were captured by schools in a pocket between Eldora and Waterloo and Osage and Cresco – did not fit with the 50 percent right, Saggau remembered.

"We walked downstairs, went down to the dressing room and a couple of stools had run over. Kids were walking around in there and their clothes were on the floor, the urinal was dripping over," Saggau said. "I said, 'This place isn't good enough for my sons, therefore it's not good enough for anybody else's sons. We're moving it.' (Quinn) said, 'Ok, but you're making a mistake.'"

Saggau had a supporter after the 1967 tournament when Harlan won the Class A team title. Harlan coach Dave Trotter pointed to the fact seven of the top 11 teams in that division were from Western Iowa.

"We've proved that wrestling is just as strong and just as popular out west," Trotter told the Harlan Tribune. "It's time they started thinking about moving the tourney to Des Moines or preferably Ames."

Saggau said he predicted having the tournament in Des Moines would draw a total of 25,000 people. Quinn was still not sold. "He said, 'That's one thing that's wrong with you, you do exaggerate a little.'"

Waverly referee Arlo Flege began a 30-year run of being on the whistle while the tournament was in Waterloo in 1968. Going into the 2011 tournament, no other official logged as many years ruling the mats as Flege did. He was not a fan of moving the tournament.

"I thought it was the end of wrestling because it was northeast Iowa's sport," Flege said. "It went to Des Moines that first year and God it had a crowd, I couldn't believe it."

The IHSAA staged its 1970 wrestling finals at Vets, and the *Des Moines Register*'s account detailed that a crowd of 17,000 was there for Friday's sessions and 10,000 watched Saturday night's championship round. "'I'd have given anything for Lyle to have been alive when we came (to Des Moines) and wrestled. I'd have been so proud because he would have been proud," Saggau said.

Alan Beste, who administers wrestling for the IHSAA, said people learned over time that Saggau and Harty were visionaries. "They didn't realize the foresight those two guys had to make those kinds of decisions,"

Beste said. "Dave made a lot of those kinds of decisions in the years that he was here as an administrator."

Quinn, who died in 1967, might have been giddy to know ticket demand (over 20,000 requests) has exceeded supply (11,700 seats at Vets Auditorium, 13,725 seats at Wells Fargo Arena) for the wrestling tournament's championship round. Tickets for the finals of the 2011 state wrestling tournament were sold out for the 24th consecutive year. The sellout is achieved with a Dec. 1 postmark – the first date mailed ticket requests for the event are honored at the IHSAA office in Boone.

"Taking that tournament from the Hippodrome and bringing it to central Iowa, it kind of spread wrestling in my opinion. Now it's a statewide thing. North Central and Northeast Iowa are still big wrestling communities, but there are a lot of other good programs," said IHSAA executive director Rick Wulkow, who took over when Saggau retired. "The venue was bigger, so it attracted more people. Bernie had the foresight to hire a great wrestling guy, Dave Harty, and that was one of his main charges: to coordinate, build and promote the wrestling. There isn't anybody probably in the country more knowledgeable as far as all aspects of wrestling – from coaching it to rules knowledge to officiating it – as Dave was.

"I remember the day when Bernie said to Dave and me back in the late 80's, early 90's, 'We'll never see 60,000 people again.' We've been as high as (nearly 89,000) in Wells Fargo Arena. All of those things kind of mushroomed together and it kind of grew itself. Then, our coaching is so solid. We have some of the best officials in the country – you see them working NCAA tournaments – and our wrestlers have gone on to not only national prominence but Olympic and world championships."

Mike Schimp, a state champion from Belmond, said he means no disrespect of the current tournament home of Wells Fargo Arena but he wishes the titles were still decided across the street at Vets.

"I've got a place in my heart, I wish it was still there. Nothing to do with the venue where it's at now. Wells is a wonderful, wonderful arena, nice place to have it, but it's just the historical value of Vets," said Schimp, who coached at Woodbine and at Hampton-Dumont. "Growing up, watching some of the great wrestlers I had the chance to watch go through there and a lot of history being made. A lot of people might say it, but you walk into Vets and it's even the smell of Vets. All of the people moving around, immediately that's the picture I get of Vets."

Saggau had little time initially to warm up to wrestling. He was busy with basketball.

"I was one of five guys in the country who knew a lot about basketball, so I told Lyle, 'I don't want to be around this wrestling stuff.'" Saggau said. "Lyle said, 'You gotta go up, you gotta go see the state meet.' That was the first time I ever saw wrestling, the state meet in '64."

Saggau served as chair of the National Federation of State High School Associations' basketball rules committee for eight years. "In basketball I was an expert. In wrestling I wasn't an expert but I had expert people doing it. I had the same passion for wrestling as I had for basketball."

Saggau also learned weight didn't matter.

"All the way up to Waterloo I kept telling Lyle, 'Hell, I can whip any 115-pounder up there. You get a mat, I'll show you that,'" Saggau said, adding that Quinn was indifferent. "They set up a table right on the edge of one of the mats for Mr. Quinn, and I sat next to him. The 95-pounders came out and they went at it. I turned to Lyle and said, 'Should we move the table back? I don't want those guys getting after me.' Lyle started to laugh. That was my first inkling. Then when my kids got involved…"

As Quinn's health deteriorated, he turned wrestling over to Saggau. In order to run the tournament smoothly, Saggau turned to Finn Eriksen, who had led New Hampton to a share of a team title and then coached Waterloo West to the first two of its 17 team championships. Eriksen was a respected scholar of the sport. He was also in wrestling shape long after he'd earned all-America honors at Iowa State Teachers College in 1931.

"Finn Eriksen was *the* man and he did all of our interpretations for us. Lyle had me go to one of his rules meetings and I got to know Finn. I really respected the guy, the human being," Saggau said. "I remember here Finn is, he had to be in his 60's, he's out on the mat wrestling with whoever the coach gave him. I mean they're wrestling and he's showing all the officials these holds and the coaches this stuff. I came home and I said, 'Lyle, man he knows wrestling. We can't have him on the mat like that anymore.' He said 'Why?' I said, 'My God, he could have a heart attack out there. He's not a spring chicken and he's out there.'"

About the only thing Eriksen struggled with was convincing Saggau that having mats barely separated from the ice at McElroy Auditorium would not affect the condition of the mats. Eriksen told Saggau you could drop an egg on any of those mats, and it would not break. The following day Eriksen brought an egg and dropped it. After the mess was cleaned up, the mat was put into use, Saggau said.

Otherwise Eriksen was fine, and the sport of wrestling was growing in Iowa's high schools. Saggau was looking for someone to be in the office and direct wrestling for the IHSAA. He found what he thought was a good candidate in Harty, a wrestling coach at Postville and Eagle Grove who had some administrative experience as a principal at Eagle Grove. Harty wrestled at Iowa Falls, placing third in the 1953 state tournament. As a fan, competitor, coach or administrator, Harty had seen at least a part of every state tournament from the late-1940's until 2010. He wrestled collegiately at Iowa State

"I had no vision of being with the Iowa High School Athletic Association. I hardly knew about them other than the fact of rules and regulations and rules meetings. I wanted to be a principal, maybe eventually superintendent, but I never envisioned being with the (IHSAA)," Harty said. "Bernie had contacted me later and asked of my interest. I was honored to be considered and even thought about. I talked to my wife a little bit and we decided that's what we were going to do, not knowing exactly what I was getting into. It worked out great, I had a great 35-year run.

"Bernie and I thought alike in many respects. He let me do my thing. I had to realize he was the boss, but by and large he turned that wrestling program over to me. I knew there were limitations, there were some things I would like to have done at the early times that we couldn't. I kept visiting with Bernie periodically and he was very favorable to my recommendations and respected me enough to convince the board that we should go in some of those directions – such as going from eight- to 12- to 16-man brackets, classifications as we have them, the dual-meet tournament and things of that kind – and I think it all worked for the better and I think it gave us a much better program."

After making that 25,000-fan mark, Saggau said he thought the tournament would top out with an overall crowd of no more than 70,000. That would be as good as any other state organization's wrestling tournament would draw, he said.

Wulkow said he could never imagine Saggau or Harty allowing the state tournament to be a model of mediocrity. "It would have been like a lot of other state associations' tournaments are. It's great wrestling, but there are a lot of other things that go into it. The people we bring into the hall of fame, the grand march that we have and the people that lead the grand march, statewide TV coverage that I get emails and letters about from people in all of the states surrounding us that tune in to our wrestling if they can get it. It's turned into more than just a state championship, it's a grand event.

"I tell everybody, 'It's an event, it's a happening. It's like the state fair. People put the dates of this tournament on their calendar a year in advance and by golly, they're going to be here. The eight mats, the support we get from our schools in bringing mats in and the mat companies in Iowa, everybody's bought into this thing."

Harty had not assumed his IHSAA duties yet, so Saggau was at Vets the day before the start of the 1970 tournament making sure the final details were being attended to. Saggau said he encountered Herb Gray, owner of the Hotel Fort Des Moines, who had the concessions rights at Vets. Gray was recognizable by his blue suit and white shirt, Saggau said. The question for Gray was if the concession stands were ready for good crowds.

Gray: "Bernie, you take care of the wrestling, I'll take care of the concessions."

Saggau: "Well you better be ready."

"The next morning at 11 o'clock, every concession stand was sold out and they were hustling all over town getting people to help him bring stuff up here," Saggau said. "The next day I saw him I asked, 'Herb, how did things go?' Very quietly- I never heard him swear – he said, 'Damn, I don't want to talk about it.'"

Preparation was not something Harty, like Saggau, took lightly.

"I always prided myself in details. I was a great note-taker and I kept my notes from year to year to year and expanded on them year to year," Harty said. "Where there were weaknesses, I tried to strengthen that. I think the most difficult state tournament I put on was the year we were at Ames (in 1971)."

The tournament moved to Ames in 1971 because of scheduling conflicts. The Harlem Globetrotters were booked into Vets on what would have been the night before the tournament opened. Drake had a basketball game one night. Flege, who later would serve on the IHSAA's Board of Control, said there was another reason for moving the meet. "The association didn't sew (Vets) up for the next year because they didn't know how it was going to go," he said.

Saggau said Vets would not extend the IHSAA a contract to stage the 1971 tournament, thus the brief move to Ames.

After one year at the Iowa State Armory, the state tournament has remained in Des Moines. Harty said one aspect was constant as long as he and Saggau worked together.

"Bernie wanted the best program we could put on, knowing full well we could not put on a national tournament so we had to keep it within parameters that we could operate in," Harty said. "Bernie and I never disagreed on much, and if we did Bernie understood and I understood. Once he turned it over to me, he didn't ignore it but he knew I was going to do it right so he let it go."

Saggau wanted to step away from the limelight, giving the main stage to the competitors. Saggau was not one to present the championship trophies to the teams on Saturday night. "Bernie never wanted to be in the limelight, out on the floor with the trophies, although many times we were perhaps seen in that vision," Harty said. "We thought that should be the board's position, they were the people that really ran the organization. We felt our position was to do the work and the necessary management of the association to provide good programs for kids."

Saggau learned what Harty knew well: that emotion was as much a part of the sport as wrestling shoes. Saggau was not alone in reacting to one of the more powerful moments of the tournament.

"The first night we had the grand march – and that was my baby – I stood there and clapped like everybody else and cried. It was that emotional," Saggau said. "I think in wrestling there is more emotion than in any other sport I've been attached to, that's why I like it. I'd have given anything if we had wrestling. I was at little Denison High School, I was a varsity basketball player, started as a sophomore and had a few records. I wish I had the opportunity to wrestle."

He did have the opportunity to be a wrestling parent. His son, Jeff, was a two-time state qualifier and a state runner-up at 105 pounds in Class 3-A for Boone in the 1971 tournament. Jeff Saggau was given a wrestling scholarship to University of Wisconsin, likely not generated because of the occasional training he would have with his dad in the basement.

"I got hooked on wrestling. I wrestled with my son every other night in the basement," Saggau said. "I didn't use the rules, I broke the rules every time we wrestled, and that's the only way I could stay with him. I was proud of both of my boys wrestling."

David Saggau, one of Bernie's sons, said a regular in the family basement - where the red, white and blue-colored workout mat was located - was Dave Harty. David and Jeff would occasionally drill with him and often got tips from a guy who still enjoyed teaching on the mat after he traded coaching for administration.

Bernie Saggau is now a wrestling grandfather. David's son, Bernie, is a member of the team at West Des Moines Valley. There was a concern once during the 2010-11 season that Valley was trying to pull a fast one on officials at a junior varsity tournament when they noticed the name Bernie Saggau among participants in a weight class.

For Jeff Saggau, there was not much worry about whether your dad would be there to see you wrestle Chris Larson of Urbandale for the third time that season in the 1971 state finals. Not when the group he directs is putting on the tournament.

"I hid. I stood in the background and watched it both times he was in the state tournament and died a thousand deaths. It was very competitive," Saggau said. "You hope your kid's going to win. The kid that beat Jeff in the finals, they wrestled (twice) during the season, a good little wrestler. It was just an honor to have him do it, and that gave me a feel for what parents go through, so a lot of times when I had minor problems I always put myself on the other side. I made a lot of kids ineligible over the years and they loved to wrestle. I took some out of the state tournament, and that hurt me as much as anything but I think that's what I would have gotten from wrestling, of which I got from football, basketball and track: you have a desire to do the right thing and you do it."

Two instances tested the IHSAA and Saggau in last-minute situations.

- T. J. Wilder, a 138-pound wrestler from Waterloo East, won a district championship one month after he was arrested on a charge of armed robbery. Originally, Wilder was suspended by school officials from competing in athletics because of the arrest, according to a *Des Moines Register* story. School officials reported to the IHSAA that Wilder would not compete at state, the article stated, but Wilder got an injunction against the suspension in Black Hawk County.

Wilder's spot was filled by Mike Heaford of Mason City. Heaford lost to Bruce Weisinger of Fort Madison in the first round, then Weisinger lost in the quarterfinals and Heaford could not wrestle back. Wilder filed suit in Polk County the day the tournament opened – the Class 3-A field that would have included Wilder – seeking to force the IHSAA to allow him to compete. The suit was denied. Members of the IHSAA's Board of Control held a telephone conference call the morning the tournament was to begin and unanimously adopted the recommendation that Wilder not wrestle.

31

- One of the most wrestled matches in tournament history was the Class 3-A quarterfinals 132-pound bout between John DiGiacomo of Waterloo West and Dan Anderson of Ankeny. The original contest had Anderson winning, 8-6, on a takedown with 1 second left in regulation, according to *Register* accounts. Waterloo West coach Don Huff argued that a reversal for Anderson had been waved off by the referee but was not erased from the score sheet.

The decision was made to resume the match after the first period, and DiGiacomo emerged as a 6-4 winner. A *Register* account said Anderson's father, Otis, eventually had to be escorted by police from the arena because of his prolonged disputing of the decision. Anderson told the *Register* he was not removed by the police. The next day, the second outcome of the DiGiacomo-Anderson match was discussed in Polk County District Court, as Anderson's father Otis Anderson filed suit against the IHSAA. Judge Louis Lavorato said he did not have jurisdiction to order a rematch, according to the *Register* article, but strongly urged the IHSAA to have the wrestlers go again. The final decision was to have DiGiacomo's 6-4 win stand.

DiGiacomo won the state championship and Anderson finished sixth.

Despite the occasional need to make a hard call or have the sport require a trip to the courthouse, Saggau said seeing the spectacle of Saturday night was a great part of his job. It was the final night of the season until 1987, when the addition of the dual-meet state tournament extended the season by one week.

"I think Saturday night had as much emotion for me as any tournament I ever attended," Saggau said. "I had a direct feeling because of being a parent of a wrestler and knowing what it takes to be a wrestler."

When Harty came on board, Saggau knew he had an administrator who could speak many languages: the kid wanting to excel at state, the coach who wanted the best tournament setting for his kids, the fan who wanted to see a well-organized tournament. Saggau wanted to improve keeping wrestlers safe.

"When I hired Dave, I turned wrestling to him from the standpoint of administration. I was always in the background. My biggest thing in wrestling was I wanted to protect the kids in weight cutting. We were the first state to get excited," Saggau said. "I told (the coaches), 'If we keep making kids take off weight, we're going to have our program go downhill.'

I was mentally tough when I was a kid. If my dad had told me to run through the wall or if my coach would have said, 'You're going to do this,' I wouldn't have a question, I'd just do it. Kids aren't that way today, maybe they shouldn't be."

"It was just natural for me to gravitate towards wrestling."

Dave Harty had a family growing up in Iowa Falls, but he would soon discover another association that provided him with countless friends and numerous unforgettable moments.

That new clan was wrestling. They were people with names such as Mott, Roberts, Kurdelmeier, Roethler, Yoder, Omvig, Kjeldgaard and Reiland. Harty attended a family reunion with them for over 60 years. For 35 of those years, Harty organized the party, put out the welcome mats (as many as eight of them at a time) and opened the doors to as many as 13,000 of the clan per session.

"It's amazing no matter how good, poor or average you might be, what a great camaraderie and friendship you can develop with all of those people through the years," Harty said in a 2010 interview. "As I look back now at the age I am and what I've been through, that's probably the one thing that stands out – I've met so many great people through wrestling. Kind, considerate, the kind of people that would drop what they're doing and help you if you wanted them to."

Perhaps that is why so many wrestlers, coaches, administrators and hall of fame personnel attended a memorial service after Harty passed away October 8, 2010. The 2011 tournament will be the first one since a year after World War II ended that Harty will not attend.

"There is going to be an empty chair in Wells Fargo Arena where Dave Harty should be sitting," said Alan Beste, who became administrator of the wrestling program for the Iowa High School Athletic Association after Harty retired in 2005. "It's going to be tougher than taking over the state tournament because David was always there. He may have just had his hip replaced, but he limped into the state tournament because, by God, he wanted to be there. This year without him there is going to be extremely difficult."

First and foremost, Harty loved wrestling. It got him to state. It helped him get a college degree. He got to coach it in Postville and in Eagle Grove. It landed him a job with the Iowa High School Athletic Association, with duties including overseeing the state meet. It made him all those friends.

"The other thing was my high school coach was a Mason City boy, Cecil Mott. He had just the type of temperament that gave me the incentive to want to wrestle," Harty said. "I got to know a lot of other coaches from other schools who knew him so well, that always had some kind words about those of us who were wrestling at a young age. I found there were a lot of people who cared what kind of a guy I was. It was just natural for me to gravitate towards wrestling."

A boss, coaches, wrestlers and fans of the sport gravitated towards Harty out of respect, even if they disagreed with decisions or schedules, when he was in charge of wrestling and its tournaments beginning with the 1970-71 season.

"I knew what the wrestling program was going to do, how it was going to explode on me and I thought, 'I've got to have somebody that's got more brains than I do,' but I couldn't rely on outside people," said Bernie Saggau, the former executive director of the IHSAA who hired Harty. "To have that everyday touch in the office when guys want answers, Dave had the expertise and proved to be right. Dave served on the national wrestling committee. He was recognized by the National Federation as one of the top wrestling people in the country.

"The wrestling coaches respected him. He'd been there, he'd been in the wars, he was a successful wrestling coach at a small school that wrestled big classes, he loved it with all the compassion anybody could have. The minute Dave Harty got in front of those guys, they knew in his heart what he was saying because they were communicating with him."

Before he retired from the IHSAA, Harty trained Beste in overseeing wrestling and operating the state tournament. Unlike Harty, Beste did not wrestle, but he did have Harty's experience available 24/7 by phone. "That spoke volumes that he had confidence that I could run the program, that I could do what needed to be done to pull off a successful state tournament. Yet if I had any questions, he was going to be there immediately for any assistance I needed," Beste said.

"I had an athletic training, sports medicine, health education background," Beste said. "I was a student manager in high school. I didn't wrestle at all."

Beste said he remembered the physical education teacher at his high school in Minnesota was also the wrestling coach. One unit in the PE curriculum was wrestling. "I can just vividly remember him walking by me during one of those PE classes and looking down saying, 'Beste, don't you know the object is to stay *off* your back?'"

He was an athletic trainer for wrestling at Minnesota-Morris and St. Cloud State. "Part of my student-teaching experience was with a health teacher who was also the wrestling coach at Irondale High School in Minnesota. So I went with him to tournaments partly as an athletic trainer and partly as a coach in the corner whenever he needed somebody to be the third coach, because he only had one assistant and it was a large tournament and they had three kids on the mat at once. I had exposure to wrestling, I just never wrestled."

Beste's duty in the winter when he moved to the IHSAA office in Boone in 1989 was administering swimming. Wrestling and swimming used to have their state tournaments at the same time. When the tournaments split, Beste helped Harty with the wrestling tournament. Beste said Harty was a good teacher.

"I think he was a good teacher because he was a teacher," Beste said. "He taught at the middle school level, he was an administrator. Education was his entire life, so he was able to teach. He was able to bring it down to my level, to dummy it down, so I could understand what he was talking about."

When it came time for Beste to direct the state meet on his own, there were mixed feelings.

"I was confident that I had learned enough from Dave and from sitting in on the coaches' advisory committees and those kinds of things that I could do it," Beste said, "but I can't tell you that there wasn't that shadow of a doubt in the back of my mind.

"Most of what I know I learned from Dave," Beste said.

Harty said he attended his first state wrestling tournament in Mason City. His best recollection was that it was 1947. He was in junior high then. The tournament opened on a snowy day. Merle Hamilton drove. Harty recalled staying in a hotel on Federal Avenue in Mason City. He remembered Mason City coach Howard Barker in those days having a good supply of tough guys such as future state champions Ken Meachem and Bill Oglesby and future NCAA champion Norvard "Snip" Nalan.

"He had a group of kids at that time that I think is the best overall team I'd ever seen to this day as far as from top to bottom. There weren't a lot of wrestling schools then, but on the other hand they were just tougher than nails," Harty said.

That trip to Mason City started Harty's annual appearance at the state meet. He attended at least one session of the event every year until 2010 as a spectator, competitor, coach and administrator. "Even when I was wrestling at Iowa State, our season was such that we were at home," Harty said. "Nick always had us go down to see if we could see somebody that would be willing to attend Iowa State."

Harty's mother passed away when he was 11. He said there were opportunities for him to stray from the group, but Mott helped to keep him in good standing. "I remember so much about him because he not only cared about you as a wrestler, he cared what kind of a person you were," Harty said. "I'm one of those guys that when I was younger, I could have gone as they say on the left side of the tracks rather than the right side. I had people like him who cared, and he got me in the right direction."

After placing third at 120 pounds in the 1953 tournament – he came into his only state meet appearance undefeated and with three draws – Harty attended Ellsworth Junior College and played baseball. In high school, Harty wrestled against Ron Gray of Eagle Grove, who won three state championships in four finals matches. They became teammates at Iowa State, where Gray won two NCAA titles.

"He was what I call the best technician in the business during his tenure. He was using technique that most people never thought of in those days. He was the talk of the mat all his years in college," said Harty, whose nickname growing up was "Babe." "I look back and we all know that Dan Gable was a great wrestler, but in my time Ron Gray was it, Ron Gray was the epitome that most people wanted to be like."

The idea of coaching got to Harty in his last two years of high school. He enjoyed working with kids, and he said the wrestling coaches he knew addressed him by name, not as "kid." Harty said Algona coach Leon "Champ" Martin was an influence. So was Clarion coach Dale Brand.

"I never have regretted it. I've had other opportunities where a guy could be big time and maybe make a little more money. I could have tried that, but I don't regret anything because I did what I wanted to do," Harty said. "My coaching and teaching days were much the same. I wanted to be a teacher-coach as well as a teacher in the classroom. As a coach you've got to teach. I always looked at the individual, and I knew my kids well enough. I knew their family background and I knew them individually so well that I felt very close to them. When they succeeded, I felt two things: I felt, 'Dave, you accomplished something as a coach' but, more importantly, I was there at the right time to offer some guidance and leadership to a young man that needed it, wanted it and wanted to excel."

Marv Reiland wrestled for Harty at Eagle Grove and for Chuck Patten at Northern Iowa. Reiland said they had a similarity.

"They were kind of like a second father to me as far as being a coach and the attitude they approached the sport in. I think the farther I went, the more I liked it I guess," Reiland said.

Harty said he anticipated his future was going to be as a principal or superintendent. "Bernie had contacted me later and asked of my interest. I was honored to be considered and even thought about," Harty said. "I talked to my wife a little bit and we decided that's what we were going to do, not knowing exactly what I was getting into. It worked out great, I had a great 35-year run."

Beste was worried about how long he'd be with wrestling after Saggau and Harty had him take control of weight management and communicable skin infections in wrestling.

"I didn't know how the coaches were going to accept me taking on that role and answering some of those questions during the regular season when David had been the expert for years and years and years," Beste said. "Yet Dave made it easy because we talked a lot. We sat in his office many days after the office closed and talked philosophy. Some things we agreed on, some things we didn't necessarily agree on, but he helped me learn so much."

Rick Wulkow, who followed Saggau as executive director of the IHSAA, was a Division I men's basketball referee. He said Harty taught him a lot about the sport of wrestling, and now he's a fan.

"I used to sit by Dave Harty. I didn't know a thing about wrestling and he'd tell me about different techniques and different calls by the officials. I still don't know anything about it, but at least I've become a fan and I know good wrestling when I see it," Wulkow said. "I know a good athlete, they stand out, and to see the dedication these kids put in to be the very best they can be. Their goal is to wrestle in this place, and you see the hard work that goes into it. You've got to love those kids and you've got to love the coaches for the energy and the effort they put into it. It just draws you to it."

Harty's first tournament of being in charge was in 1971, when the meet was relocated to the Iowa State Armory from Des Moines. Beginning in 1972, he ran the tournament in Des Moines – either at Veterans Memorial Auditorium or Wells Fargo Arena. The number of state qualifiers doubled to 16, the number of weight classes expanded to 14 from 12 and the number of place winners doubled to eight while Harty oversaw the state meet. The tournament expanded to four days in 2003. Harty also watched tickets to the final round sell out the first day they became available and become the hottest in town. The final round has been a sellout for nearly a quarter-century.

"I think I had a great run with the athletic association because of my love for the sport and my respect for the officials and the school administrators that run those programs," Harty said. "In turn they respected me. I never wanted to give our officials, our coaches, our athletes and our fans anything but a positive picture of our program. I wanted to have respect, myself as an individual, because I wanted respect for our program. I think I tried to treat everybody with that kind of mutual respect."

Beste said the finals of the tournament would not be such a hot ticket without Saggau deciding to hire Harty and without Harty's touch.

"He was the man for the time because the coaches and officials and the wrestling community at large had so much respect for him and that just continued to grow," Beste said. "The longer he was the administrator here in the office, I think the more people gained respect for what it was he was doing to grow the wrestling program."

Wulkow said the immediate plan is to keep the tournament at four days.

"There's a lot of people that would like to see us go back to a three-day state meet, but because of the numbers and the growth, I'm not going to have people turned away when we put two classes together and have to shut the door off," Wulkow said. "If we would have had that in Vets Auditorium, we would have had a four-day meet over there. We had sessions where we'd bring in 18-20,000 people because we had two classes wrestling at the same time in the early rounds. This facility won't allow that. What we tell people is the only way we can reduce the state tournament is to take away place finishers or reduce the number of qualifiers. That usually ends the conversation."

Saggau said his job was to give Harty a suitable place to operate as the tournament grew.

"The people that were the real kingpins – the Dave Hartys and the Bob Siddenses, those people – you could see in their eyes the excitement. All you had to do was generate a platform or a showcase for the whole state, and that was pretty easy to do," Saggau said. "I knew the secret was if you wanted to fill the place, have more wrestlers. Simple. And go one more class and bring more wrestlers in. It was an unbelievable teeter-totter with my administrators and me. I had to not say wrestling was more important than anything else, but it's important enough we've got to give it its fair shake. It's taken time away from school and it's a little different than the basketball tournament. Because we brought it along as well as we did administratively, nobody talks about loss of school time. Had we pushed it down their throat, there'd have been a war."

Harty and Saggau seemed to agree on most things. That included whose presence was needed when trophies were awarded. Members of the IHSAA's Board of Control have the fun job of giving a trophy to a pack of happy wrestlers. "We thought that should be the board's position, they were the people that really ran the organization," Harty said. "We felt our position was to do the work and the necessary management of the association to provide good programs for kids."

Even if Harty favored staying in the background, Beste said he cast a significant shadow on the sport and the tournament in the state. Harty served many years on the National Federation of State High School Association's wrestling rules committee, serving as chairman for a time.

"I think anybody who knows anything about high school wrestling in particular in Iowa knows that no one can fill Dave Harty's footsteps," Beste said. "The shadow that he cast is so much bigger than anybody even realizes, even us in the office. He had so much influence with so many people at so many levels of wrestling and they all respected him, from the National Federation of State High School Associations to the National Wrestling Hall of Fame to the wrestling coaches and officials association here in Iowa there were so many people who had so much respect for him."

Part of Harty's work was organizing the grand march.

"When it came to the Grand March, my hair used to always stand on end, no matter how many times I heard the Olympic march," Harty said. "I knew what those kids had gone through all season long for one, two, three or four years to get to the tournament let alone to get into the finals and what it meant to them.

"I wanted it to be the kind of a program that stood out in the eyes of the lay public, the moms and dads and the fans of the sport. Iowa separates itself from a lot of the states because we have the kinds of families, the moms and dads, that support great programs for kids. Without that, the programs would not prosper as they do."

Harty took notice of every part of the tournament, always looking for a way to make something run better and the tournament to run smoother.

"I always prided myself in details. I was a great note-taker and I kept my notes from year to year to year and expanded on them year to year," Harty said. "Where there were weaknesses, I tried to strengthen that. I think the most difficult state tournament I put on was the year we were at Ames. It really ended up being a darn good tournament."

Beste said he and Harty had a fondness for organization in common.

"He's the one probably who taught me, and I still do it at the state tournament. I have a notebook with me all the time," Beste said. "I'm always jotting down notes that probably don't mean anything to anybody else, but they mean something to me."

The coaches and officials were important allies, Harty said.

"Most knew I wanted the best for their program, so they knew I'd go all-out to make it that. I knew the coaches and the officials were going to back me subconsciously, because I knew what kind of program they wanted. In order to get there I needed their support, and they gave it to me. That made my work easier.

"I thought I put my heart and soul into it and my love for the sport that I couldn't give any more. Give me a bigger arena I could have made it even better, but on the other hand I worked with what I had," Harty said.

Wulkow said there are a few key reasons for the state tournament's success.

"Wrestling years ago was a north central, northeast Iowa hotbed. The tournament was at the Hippodrome (in Waterloo). It got off to a great start with a bunch of great coaches who got the right kids wrestling and taught them well. It didn't hurt to have the Dan Gables of the world come along and become heroes and role models," Wulkow said. "Taking that tournament from the Hippodrome and bringing it to Central Iowa, it kind of spread wrestling in my opinion. Now it's a statewide thing. North central and northeast Iowa are still big wrestling communities, but there are a lot of other good programs. The venue was bigger, so it attracted more people.

"Bernie had the foresight to hire a great wrestling guy, Dave Harty, and that was one of his main charges, to coordinate, build and promote the wrestling. There isn't anybody probably in the country more knowledgeable as far as all aspects of wrestling – from coaching it to rules knowledge to officiating it – as Dave was."

Harty said he was sure Iowa's tournament was special because of the wrestlers, coaches, officials and the fans. "I looked at all of the different tournaments around the country – not having attended all of them, but I do know what all of them pretty well did because I knew all those guys – and I used to chuckle inside, 'You know what? We've got the best high school wrestling program in the country, bar none.' You may get some 'Okies' and you may get an Ohio kid that is a better wrestler, but as a total program package this is by far the best. I hope I played a small part in it, maybe a large part, but I don't want to brag about that type of thing. That was my job, but it's because we had good coaches who believed in good programs, we had good athletes and officials and the fans were so knowledgeable."

Saggau thought the tournament had reached the ceiling when it drew a total crowd of 60,000 in the 1980's. That proved to be just another water mark.

"I remember the day when Bernie said to Dave and I back in the late 80's, early 90's, 'We'll never see 60,000 people again,'" Wulkow said. "We've been as high as 88,000 in Wells Fargo Arena. All of those things kind of mushroomed together and it kind of grew itself. Then our coaching is so solid, we have some of the best officials in the country – you see them working NCAA tournaments – and our wrestlers have gone on to not only national prominence, but Olympic and world championships."

"I would have rather been doing dishes."

Participants in many sports relish how they and their teammates can function as a family during the season. That family aspect seems to have no stronger ties than in wrestling. Sure, the teammates declare themselves to be a band of brothers but quite often you'll find actual brothers among those brothers. Usually those guys had older brothers who wore the same colors and set records or younger brothers who can't wait to lace up the "boots" and better their bros.

There have been father and son state champions, brother champions and twins go golden. Dig deep enough and you might find a guy whose earliest tough matches involved a big sister or two.

Tim Kelly grew up five miles west of Britt with a seemingly ideal after-school life at Paul and Marlys Kelly's house.

"There wasn't chores from the standpoint of a farm because we didn't live on a farm. When I was growing up we had snowmobiles, three-wheelers and we used to ride those all the time," Kelly said. "We'd eat and then, after we'd eat, a lot of times that's when we'd go down to the mat. I can't recall if we went down there every night, if we went down there three nights a week, but I remember we were down there quite a bit."

Karen Kelly Sankey, the oldest Kelly sibling who was three years ahead of Tim, didn't mind heading to the basement for a session. It got her out of doing the dishes, she said.

"To be honest, some of the beatings I took from her, I would have rather been doing dishes," Tim said. "She definitely got the better of me back in those early days. She and my sister Connie (1 year older), and I used to wrestle with both of them. A lot of it was (fundamentals) and once we got through all the fundamentals, the real basic stuff, we'd go live. We'd do a lot of the similar stuff they still do today – you show them a move and then go live, each person gets a chance to escape or make the takedown."

Families that didn't put a practice mat in the basement had the living room carpet as an alternative. In good weather, a wrestling mat was outside of the Don Buzzard residence in Waterloo and a good number of guys were tussling with each other.

"That was quite a little deal we had there. There were no mat clubs, there were no wrestling camps, there were a couple in Pennsylvania but we were so far from it and it was a money issue, but my dad said we could do it right here," Bob Buzzard said. "My father wasn't afraid to talk to people. He would get ol' Frankie Lane, Tom Huff, Lowell Stewart, Jim Bast, Scot Klepfer, guys from Waterloo and Cedar Falls, and invite them over. He'd say, 'We've got a workout going on tonight. When you get done with construction, come on over.' He'd give them the address where we lived and kids would drop in. It was kind of a somewhat camp."

Those early scraps in the Kelly's basement– many of them not against a sister - got a fleet of Kelly boys introduced to the sport that would become part of their DNA. Tim, Jeff, Mike, Pat and Mark Kelly combined for 14 appearances at state and five state championships (two by Jeff, two by Pat and one by Mike).

"There were two things I remember not ever thinking twice about, just kind of assuming while growing up. That was going to college and wrestling," Tim Kelly said. "It wasn't like I ever thought, 'Am I going to college or am I not going to college?' or 'Am I going to wrestle or am I not going to wrestle?' Nobody ever told us we had to, parents never said we had to. That was just part of the deal, how you make the best of yourself as a person. As long as it was ethical, law-abiding, church-going, family-oriented, it was all about what you wanted to do. It was all about you bettering yourself in life, you being the best person, a god-fearing productive member of society."

Sankey said her father, a former Britt school board member and former wrestler at Iowa State, began teaching her the sport in third grade. "I was taught this to be a good workout partner with my brother, to improve him," she said. "I was able to be a good partner. I learned the sit-outs, the takedowns, the fireman's, the cradle, switch so that it would be good competition for him."

No official word if Doug Reiter had that philosophy for his four sons outside of Gilbertville, Ia. If a brother wasn't available as a workout partner, there was likely a Reiter cousin nearby. Perhaps another future Don Bosco wrestler was a takedown away. By the time Bart Reiter put on a varsity singlet, he'd seen brothers Joe and Mack win a combined five state championships. Their brother, Eddie, was a four-time medalist. A little brother can develop quite an appetite for success seeing all of that.

"It definitely helped. It helped motivate me a lot when I was younger," Bart said. "Also having them being able to work with me helped, but I still would have done anything to win a state title."

Mack won four state titles, earning the requisite two standing ovations. Six years later, Bart made his family the first in Iowa with two four-time champion siblings.

"That was a big factor in making me want to win four titles. That's back when it was in Vets and we got to be down on the floor. Me, my dad, my brothers and my cousins…I guess our whole family was right there in the first five rows," Bart said. "Being right there in the middle of all that and talking to him afterwards, I was like, 'Man, that's definitely something I'm going to do everything I can to do.'"

Mack watched his brother win his fourth title, then gave him a hug that would be a tremendous set-up for a bodylock or similar upper-body throw.

"I've been to a lot of state tournaments now and there's few that really truly respect the state champion like you get in Iowa," Mack Reiter said. "The respect the four-timer gets with the standing ovation after his match and then on the award stand. It's a very special thing, and for us to be able to experience it twice is quite a deal."

So where does a wrestling family spend some vacation time? At the state tournament of course.

"I remember when I was very young, they used to get a babysitter that would come and stay with us while mom and dad and a group of friends of theirs would spend three or four days down there. As we got older, then we would start going. It was a real important thing," Tim said.

Karen added, "We brought food along. We stayed close so that if some of us didn't want to go to all the sessions, we didn't, but dad always did. He went to every session, 1-A, 2-A, 3-A."

About the only thing a wrestler does alone is take the mat for his or her bout. "Let's face it, when you go out for wrestling mom and dad go out for wrestling too. Your brothers or sisters go out for wrestling too. It's a total family commitment," said four-time state champion Joe Gibbons, who had two uncles, two older brothers and one younger brother win state titles.

Jake Ballweg of Waverly-Shell Rock concurred. Ballweg won three state championships for the Go-Hawks before moving to wrestle at University of Iowa. That is where his brothers, Matt and Mark, went after winning two state titles each. Their father, Tom, was a state champion in Wisconsin. Ballweg said he understands why family ties are so strong in wrestling.

"I think maybe because it's not just the athlete that feels all the emotions and experiences," Ballweg said. "It involves the whole family more because it takes so much sacrifice – the parents have to be there when the kid is cutting weight and they have to maybe not have junk food around. I think it just brings a family closer going through all those tough experiences together."

Another family had three sibling champions. Kyle, Tyler and Alex Burkle all won gold in the singlet of North-Linn of Troy Mills. Alex was the last one in the house to get a gold medal in 2009. You could get the idea it was Burkle time each year because losing hardly entered the season resume of the three. They were a combined 132-1 in their championship season. The lone loss was Kyle's in a 43-1 effort during the 2001-02 season.

"It wasn't so much the pressure of following in my brothers' footsteps," Alex Burkle told the *Cedar Rapids Gazette* after his title. "It was more proving to myself that I could actually do it. I struggled a couple of years down here and finally got the job done."

His brothers also had more words for hard work than for family business.

Kyle Burkle talked to the *Gazette* in 2002 about doing considerable routes up and down a rope. "When I am dead and can't go anymore, I climb it one more time," Burkle said.

Tyler was pleased with finishing the job in 2006. "I worked so hard for this. It feels great to finally do this," he told the *Gazette*.

Food could be a sensitive subject for the six people at the Keller household in Indianola. Eric was working his way deeply into the sport, and food stuffs might be shallow for sisters Rachel and Jennifer and brother Chris if there was a competition looming. Chris was busy with frequent youth wrestling tournaments at the time.

"When they weren't eating, nobody was eating," said Rachel Keller Tabibi.

The dieting was for Eric, she recalled. Chris was still a few years from making the varsity when she left for college. Limiting food was dad's idea, Tabibi said.

Tabibi remembered, "He had that mentality that we felt bad for him. How could we be pigging out when he's sitting in the corner sucking on ice cubes? The car trips, that's what I remember. Normally everybody stops at the gas station and hops out and loads up on junk food. We'd just get gas and drive on. Nobody was eating anything and nobody was really talking because you know what kind of a mood you're in when you're cutting weight."

Because of health issues as a young girl, Karen Kelly was not allowed to try wrestling at school. She tried out for cheerleading one year and got a varsity spot – cheering for basketball. "I turned it down because I wanted to be a wrestling mat maid, so I was a 4-year wrestling mat maid," Karen said.

Just as there never seemed to be a Britt Eagles lineup without a Kelly for a while, there was never a season for them without the presence of longtime coach Al DeLeon. A three-time Minnesota state champion and 1964 Olympic trials finalist, DeLeon was 273-138-15 as head coach at Britt. His teams won three state championships and were second at seven other meets. Pat Kelly was one of seven high school all-Americans DeLeon coached. Every Kelly boy learned about hard work and fishing through DeLeon, who was known to take wrestlers fishing in good weather.

"It was little things he would do and say to you that would make you think, 'There is nobody out there better, there is nobody out there that works harder,'" Tim Kelly said. "He was just such a convincing person, you just believed what he told you. It made people do things that they were normally not capable of doing."

DeLeon was coached to his state championships at Blue Earth by Gene Lybbert, a two-time state finalist at Cresco and an NCAA champion at Iowa State Teachers College. DeLeon was also tutored in Blue Earth by Keith Young, a three-time NCAA champion for Iowa State Teachers College who never qualified for state while growing up in Algona. DeLeon earned all-America status twice at Mankato State, where he was coached by Davenport High School product Rometo "Rummy" Macias, who started the program. For most of his coaching days in Britt, DeLeon could employ a hands-on approach to teaching technique, discipline and humility.

"He was a goer. He was firm, but he wasn't what you'd call a hard-ass," Tim Kelly said. "When he saw somebody slacking, he was all over them. When somebody would get in trouble of some sort, they would definitely get worked over, and a lot of times it was by him. If you were thinking you were pretty tough or pretty good, he'd step right in there and he'd just rip you apart."

DeLeon turned kids into champions. It was a special family moment when Jeff Kelly won the Class 2-A 145-pound state title in 1984. He would win again the following year, that time at 155 pounds in Class 1-A.

"It was a big deal. For me, I was the first one that went to state and I was the first one that placed. With that, you almost felt like the culmination of everything that my dad put into it, that the family put into it from the standpoint of working with each other, you really felt like the culmination of all that...there it is, it resolved itself. Obviously it was worth it," Tim Kelly said. "I remember being there, alongside the mats. I bet I jumped 10 feet in the air. It was a big deal."

How about the reaction of Paul Kelly? Wrestling got into his life because his parents didn't want him following after a brother who was a boxer.

"He doesn't get giddy and goofy and crazy and loud, he had such a quiet proudness," Tim said.

DeLeon was proud to have worked with Pat Kelly, who won his second state championship in 1988, had 132 career wins and was 81-0 in his last two seasons. "Pat Kelly is one of a kind. In my 26 years of coaching, I have never had a wrestler so intense, so dynamic," DeLeon told the *Britt News-Tribune*.

Speaking of intense, Steve Kelly had some high-powered support when he was competing at 152 pounds in the 1990 state tournament. Steve said he was given a medal of St. Patrick and St. Bridget blessed by Fr. Marvin Bries of St. Patrick's Catholic Church in Britt. After having surgery on his right knee, Kelly said he kept the medal on the inside of his knee brace. "I just thought maybe it would heal faster," Steve said. "I always kept it in my knee brace. It's just one of those things. I don't know if it was superstitious or what, but it gave me comfort."

If there was a protective power in the medal, Steve said he hoped it would protect his knee if an opponent cranked on it during a match. Steve reached the semifinals in 1990 before losing to eventual state champion Jeff Jens of Glenwood. Steve finished third that year.

Steve said he was not superstitious, but he understood that doing things such as warm-ups a certain way provides a comfort and relaxation to each wrestler. Steve understands now as a coach that each wrestler needs different ways to get the fire going. He said DeLeon stressed having the wrestlers write down the desire to be a state champion five times before going to bed each night. "I thought, 'That's crazy, what's that going to do?' But I'm telling you, after you do it 20 days in a row, then you start believing maybe you should be that state champ," Steve said.

After losing – and later finding – the medal, Steve said he still wears the medal. He is wrestling coach at North Iowa Area Community College in Mason City.

Doug Reiter proudly shed tears watching his sons perform at Vets and at Wells Fargo Arena. He also had a smile twice as wide as the competition floor as he collected congratulatory hugs from Don Bosco fans and from those who got to know him as their kids competed in Tulsa, Bismarck, Fargo and any other place where the challenge was stiff.

"My dad's a pretty old-school Iowa kind of guy, loves to work hard. That's how he was raised and that's how he still does it," Bart said. "That's how we look at wrestling, it's all about working hard. You've got to know the technique, but it's hard and the guys at the top are the guys who work the hardest."

If a son was not going hard enough or needed a verbal nudge, Doug Reiter could deliver like a champ. He was especially effective in Veterans Memorial Auditorium, which Mack Reiter said was a one-of-a-kind jewel for hosting the state meet. "You'll never get it again because no arena will ever built that way because it's not fan-friendly," Mack said. "It's competitor-friendly the way I look at it. You'd be hard-pressed to find a guy that didn't enjoy wrestling there.

"I'll never forget my sophomore year wrestling Dan Davilla (of Underwood) and I was getting beat. I look over and my dad, the rope was stretched against his chest because he was trying to get out there screaming at me. If it wouldn't have been in the barn, he would have been stuck somewhere. I realized, 'I better win this match or I've got to deal with him.'"

Joe Gibbons was fueled by familial success, much like Bart Reiter was.

"When I knew it could happen for me was when I was 12 years old, in sixth grade, coming down to Veterans Auditorium watching my brother, Jim, win as a sophomore in the state tournament," Joe said.

The family can share success some nights. Tim and Todd Krieger of Mason City won state championships in 1982. Their Class 3-A championships at 119 and at heavyweight came 20 years and 3 days after their dad, Herb Krieger, won the Class A 138-pound gold medal for the Mohawks in 1962.

"I didn't know until it came out in the paper. My old man never talked about what he did in wrestling, never talked about it," Tim Krieger said. "The only thing we knew was that his bracket was downstairs on the wall by a wrestling mat. It was from 1962. Until I was in high school, I didn't even know what it was. That's who he is, kind of short on words."

Tim would win two more state championships and then earn two NCAA championships at Iowa State. His brother was a senior in 1982, an all-state football player whose 56-second pin of Todd Emsinger of Burlington at heavyweight was the last of Mason City's four individual titles that night. Dail Fellin and Todd Piper were the other Mohawk champions. It wasn't enough to give the Mohawks the team title. Bettendorf broke Don Bosco's 1979 scoring record of 141 points by totaling 167 ½ with one champion – 185-pounder Brian McCracken – among 10 qualifiers. Bettendorf got a top-5 finish from each of the 10 wrestlers. Todd Krieger was hoping to get even with the Bulldogs in wrestling, since Bettendorf beat Mason City, 21-3, in the 1981 Class 4-A state football championship game. Still, he and his brother had a cool finish to the season.

"We were both undefeated state champs. I guess we didn't look at the significance of the 20 years later, we just wanted to be state champs like our old man was," Todd Krieger said. "That's what our goal was. We were a wrestling family, that's what we did."

Herb Krieger was a happy man in 1962 – he'd lost to eventual three-time state champion Mel Wieland of Cedar Rapids Jefferson in the semifinals in 1960 and in 1961 – but that February night in 1982 was a heck of an evening for a father.

"It was terrific, one of the best nights ever for me to enjoy wrestling," Herb Krieger said. "Plus we had two other state champs from Mason City. It's something you'll never forget. Very few people have the opportunity to enjoy something like that."

Herb Krieger started a youth wrestling program in Mason City with coach Jerry Ray and Pete Gribben. Todd said his dad had a good handle on things as the boys were growing up on the mat. "He was actually pretty good about the way he trained us. He hauled us around when we were little kids," Todd said. "He didn't push us super-hard, just took us to every tournament like everybody else. Once we got to high school, he turned us loose and let us go with the high school coaches."

Tim added that fatherly critiques lacked a biting touch. "He never said one disparaging word about how I wrestled. I will say that with absolute respect and gratitude. There was never one negative word about my wrestling that I heard."

There might have been a chance for the Kriegers to do their winning in the old rose and black colors of Waterloo West. That was where Bob

Siddens directed the wrestling team. Howard Barker retired as Mason City's coach when Herb Krieger was a freshman. Herb Krieger wrestled for Lowell Cook and then Cecil Mott. When Siddens visits Mason City, he always stops to visit Krieger.

"I always wanted to wrestle for (Barker), but the one I really wanted to wrestle for was Bob Siddens. I think he's one of the greatest ever," Krieger said. "West Waterloo just intimidated us when we wrestled them. He could find the right guy and he could beat me at darn near every time. I finally beat his kid (Dennis Kendall) in the state finals, but he always brought someone in. I have the highest respect for that man. What he did for wrestling was just phenomenal. I always wished that when I was in high school I could have wrestled for a guy like him because he could get it out of a kid."

Some coaches got it out of their own kids. There have been nearly 20 head coaches who watched their sons win a gold medal. One of the coaches, Royce Duncan of Pleasant Valley, is the only mentor to drape a gold medal around the neck of two sons in the same tournament. That was in 1997.

"It was real special. To our whole family it was a real special time because it just all fell into place," Duncan said. "I can remember this. Going from the motel to Vets that night, my assistant, Mark Yegge, was driving. Brandon had already beaten the No. 1 and No. 3 (wrestlers) so all he had left was the No. 6 man. Yegge said, 'I like Brandon's chances, but boy, Creighton's going to have it tough.' I said, 'You know what? There is a reason we're there.'"

Brandon Duncan beat Jake Emerick of Pella, 6-5, in the 140-pound finals. Four bouts later, Creighton Duncan pinned No. 1-ranked Jessman Smith of Southeast Polk in 1 minute 46 seconds for the gold at 171 pounds. "To be the coach of two state champions (on the same night) and they are your sons, that had never happened and it's never happened since. My wife was just so excited because she'd been a real big part of that. She was the one who kept everything together, I can say that."

After his success, Brandon had a few words for his brother. "Brandon looked up at him and said, 'You're next,'" Royce said.

Creighton and Smith had met during the season at a tournament in Iowa City and Creighton won. On the night of the state finals, Duncan had a game plan besides what his father and Yegge might have sketched for him.

"Creighton said, 'I wanna snap him, I wanna front him. If he reaches and grabs my head, I'm going to throw him,'" Royce said.

The great times didn't end that night. The Spartans won their second dual-meet state championship the following weekend. Their first team crown came in 1995.

Duncan said he attempted to make the sport fun for everyone – even his own kids. Duncan said he did not crack the whip harder on his sons or expect them to perform better than others because they were the head coach's kids. "There may have been their own set of pressure sometimes," Duncan said. "They had to do everything that was expected of them, but no more. We just had a lot of fun with it. We kept it as fun as we could."

Keeping it fun was something Duncan said he learned while wrestling at Camanche. His coach was Gerald "Buck" Stamp, and Stamp's way of doing things was something Duncan took into his coaching career, which has been at Pleasant Valley after he graduated from Northern Iowa.

That fun was included in the team's first practice after placing third in the traditional state tournament. The team tournament was dead ahead in Cedar Rapids, but the Spartans had to get something done first: a game of dodgeball.

"Virtually every boy in Iowa is interested in grappling"

They have been contesting wrestling supremacy in the state of Iowa since 1921. The Iowa High School Athletic Association has governed the meet since 1926, but Charles Mayser, athletic director and wrestling coach at Iowa State, was armed with a keen awareness of the state's stars of the day. He decided to create a wrestling tournament in Ames - only three weeks after the state's first recognized dual meet was staged.

"This pioneer enterprise in athletics promises to be even a bigger success than we had hoped," Mayser was quoted in the Jan. 13, 1921 edition of the *Cedar Rapids Republican.*

Fort Dodge beat Mason City, 24-19, in the first dual meet Jan. 15, 1921. Fort Dodge and Clarion are among the few programs in Iowa that had a team annually since 1921. According to wrestling historian Ray Arnold, Clarion's program got some coaching help from an unidentified gentleman who had done soe wrestling in carnivals. Arnold said Clarion's first coach was Jim Jones, who was also the basketball coach but knew little about grappling. All it took for Jones to get some teaching help each day was to have the carnival scrapper released from jail. Arnold said the man was released each day in time for workouts and then back in jail afterwards. There was no practice room in those days, so Clarion's wrestlers had practice outside, according to Arnold.

Mayser kept an eye on the mailbox leading up to the Feb. 5, 1921 state tournament, seeing how many of the invitations he sent to schools in the state were returned with entrants. Press accounts of the Ames tournament stated 92 wrestlers competed and 91 bouts were contested.

According to Sec Taylor, sports editor of the *Des Moines Register*, success of Iowans in the world of professional wrestling was a point for the youth of Iowa to emulate.

"Virtually every boy in Iowa is interested in grappling," Taylor wrote in the Feb. 6 edition of the state's largest newspaper. "Iowa produced the late Frank Gotch, Earl Caddock, Ed Lewis – the present champion who is to meet John Olin (in Des Moines) Feb. 18 – and many other splendid wrestlers, and as a natural consequence the youth of the state sought to emulate their heroes just as nearly every boy in Minnesota has a punching bag and boxing gloves and seeks to become a second Mike Gibbons, Johnny Tillman, Johnny Ertle or Jock Malone."

Prior to 1926, the big tournaments for high school wrestlers were at Iowa State in Ames and at the University of Iowa in Iowa City. The Ames tournament was referred to as a state championship – maybe a state invitational would be a better term – and the Hawkeyes staged the Iowa Invitational between 1922 and 1924, often weeks after the Ames tourney's completion.

The first individual state champion crowned in Iowa was Audra Liegerot of Red Oak, who pinned Walter Riley of Ottumwa for the 95-pound gold medal in 1921. Liegerot would have made any coach happy with his effort on Feb. 5, pinning all three of his opponents. Liegerot's coach, Ives Boyington, could have used a couple of those pins himself about a week earlier.

Boyington was matside for Liegerot in the Ames main event. Eight days earlier, Boyington was a fill-in for Ed Downs – promoted as the middleweight champion of South Dakota – in the main event of a pro wrestling show against Guy Elliott of Collins, Ia. at the Corning Opera House. When Downs became ill with influenza right after the weigh-in, the promoter apparently knew of Boyington and called him. The *Adams County Union-Republican* reported Boyington "has an enviable reputation among the soldiers in the war camps."

Boyington lost in two straight falls against Elliott.

The *Red Oak Express* description stated Boyington "is well known in Red Oak as a wrestler of more than ordinary ability."

He had a reputation in the Montgomery County area as a tough guy to beat. Boyington had a 50-minute draw against Homer Quimby of Craig, Mo. as the highlight of a Red Oak American Legion meeting in November of 1920. The bout was halted, according to the *Red Oak Express*, because a poorly padded mat used for the match could not protect either competitor from serious injury.

Boyington also had an exhibition match against Red Oak football coach Dwight Dyer later that month at a Rotary Club meeting. The two had demonstrated amateur wrestling moves to an audience of boys and their fathers prior to their match. While Boyington was training the Red Oak wrestlers, he had a couple of lengthy battles against an Anita, Ia. gentleman named Allanson, who was described as a champion of Iowa University. They wrestled to a 2-hour draw in Anita and later had a 90-minute draw.

Red Oak's team finished third in the 1921 team standings – the highest finish at a state tournament for a Red Oak wrestling team. Going into the 2011 state meet, Liegerot remains the only Red Oak individual to win a championship in either the invitationals or the state wrestling tournament.

Cedar Rapids High School – later known as Cedar Rapids Washington – won the 1921 team title. A highlight for the Tigers was a run of four consecutive champions by Joseph Giunta, George Carringer, Glenn Burkholder and Carringer's brother Harry. The recognized coach was Archie Peterson, but the Tigers' mentors included Jack Reynolds and Martin "Farmer" Burns, a former world champion in the "catch-as-catch-can" style. Burns beat – and later trained – future heavyweight world champion wrestler Frank Gotch of Humboldt.

"Grapplers of the Cedar Rapids team exhibited class and ability, the product apparently of expert coaching that stood out above the general class of the entries," according to an account in the following morning's *Des Moines Sunday Capital.* "The feat of placing four men in championship honors speaks for itself."

There is a piece of evidence that shows the Cedar Rapids High School team at work. About a week later, a film was shown at the Palace Theater in Cedar Rapids that showed members of the school's basketball team, swimming team and the state champion wrestlers in action. Also in the film are shots of the city's police and fire departments. The film was shown Feb. 13-16 at the theater. Nothing was said about what became of the film.

The *Register*'s Taylor was an early multi-tasker: he likely wrote his prose after he was one of the referees for the tournament at State Gym in Ames. The Chicago Tribune, which had writer Walter Eckerstall serving as a referee, called the tournament "a great success."

The lone injury was to University of Iowa athletic director E. C. Schroeder, who reportedly sustained a broken nose when he was accidentally kicked by a wrestler while Schroeder was officiating the bout.

On the eve of the 1921 tournament, the wrestlers were guests of

Iowa State at the Cyclones' meet against Nebraska. A crowd of 3,000 watched the Cyclones win. The visiting preps bunked at some of Iowa State's fraternity houses.

Taylor reported the day after the state tournament that the sport was well on its way to a long and healthy life.

"Judging by the attendance at college wrestling meets thus far this season and by the large entry list in the state wrestling meet yesterday, the amateur mat sport has arrived," Taylor wrote. "The schools and the athletes, not forgetting the professional game, will all be better off for it."

The 1921 tournament was the start of some interesting, yet largely undocumented, competitions in either Ames or Iowa City prior to the IHSAA's governance.

Winning the heavyweight championship in 1921 was Clark DeGroote of Humboldt, who apparently had the nickname "Tubby" because of his nearly 235-pound frame. It's doubtful too many folks in town used that moniker in vain. DeGroote had two challengers in the heavyweight division, and accounts of the tournament reported that both of them weighed no more than 185 pounds. DeGroote won both bouts by decision. The Iowa papers called DeGroote an impressive athlete because of his uncanny quickness as a big man. The *Chicago Tribune* account of the tournament reported him as a giant. Apparently, University of Southern California liked the skill of anyone named "Tubby" because DeGroote earned three letters as a 6-foot 1-inch, 230-pound tackle.

A young man from Davenport proved there are many ways for an athlete to make amends for a performance that didn't go as was hoped. In 1922, Davenport High School senior Paul Krasuski showed that another competition was a good antidote. Davenport won the basketball tournament in Iowa City in 1920 and in 1921. The 1922 hoops delegation seemed on its way to another big season, running undefeated through the regular season. Krasuski was the center, a big man who also was a standout tackle on the football team.

Davenport's run of basketball success – believed to be a 31-game winning streak - ended when University High of Iowa City scored an 11-10 victory on March 17, 1922. Eight days later, Krasuski won the heavyweight championship at the Iowa Invitational. He went to Iowa and played football and also wrestled. In 1923, prior to getting into the varsity competition, Krasuski won a championship in Iowa's freshman wrestling and boxing tournaments. His foray into wrestling in high school was apparently not on a whim. Krasuski was in the team photo for wrestling and for basketball – as well as for football - in the *Blackhawk*, Davenport High's annual. He was also in the Glee Club two years, in the Science Club and was a cast member in the production of three-act comedy "The Gipsy Trail."

"Davenport High School will have to wait a long time before it produces another athlete of Krasuski's caliber," was a passage in the 1922 *Blackhawk*.

Two of the better showings by a high school team regardless of tournament date were turned in at Iowa City. Waterloo East's five-man delegation that won five gold medals in the 1964 event has arguably been the best documented showing by a team since the Iowa High School Athletic Association began sanctioning the tournament in 1926. Ottumwa's performance in 1923 and Marshalltown's effort in 1924 were stunning nonetheless.

Ottumwa sent five men to the Iowa City tournament March 23, and left the next evening with five championships. That was 41 years before Waterloo East's golden showing. Bernard Booth got the success started for Ottumwa and coach F. W. Douma with a 2-minute 55-second time advantage victory over Paul Hinebaugh of Garden Grove at 95 pounds. Hubert Wilcox, Lee Franklin, Ralph Adamson and Bill Teommes joined Booth as champions. Franklin was to compete at 135 pounds, but he was three pounds overweight, according to the *Ottumwa Courier*. Franklin moved to the 145-pound division and the 10-pound difference did not faze him. Franklin won his finals bout with a nearly 4 ½-minute time advantage.

The first champion from Ottumwa was Clare Grooms, who won in 1923 after finishing second in 1921 and in 1922. Grooms was hurt in the semifinals of the 145-pound division. *The Des Moines Capital* reported Grooms spent time in the hospital at Ames until just before his finals match in 1922 against Leo Alstott of Mason City was called. "(Grooms) put up a battle with Alstott of Mason City going on the offensive most of the time but lost," according to the story.

Central City had seven individuals make the finals at the Iowa City Invitational between 1922 and 1923. Leading the way for coach Alex Evans was two-time champion Perry Mills, who won at 158 in 1922 and then dropped to 135 pounds in 1923. The story of Central City's Manley Rundall in 1922 lacked such a happy ending. Rundall reached the 175-pound finals, but had to forfeit to Roy Grimm of Boone because Rundall came down with the mumps, according to the *Cedar Rapids*

Republican and Times. Rundall didn't get individual gold, but he was a member of the championship team that finished 34 points ahead of Davenport.

Few residents of Central City might remember that championship wrestling squad, but the name of the coach remains. The school's football field is named for Evans, who was a strong supporter of all Central City athletics until his passing.

The 1924 tournament in Iowa City belonged to Marshalltown. There were nine weight classes contested, the Bobcats won eight of them and finished second at 158 pounds - James Peterson lost to Adamson, who had a 9-minute 5-second time advantage. Marshalltown won six of its championships by pin and Bobcat heavyweight Eugene Fitz was the lone entrant in his division.

The team race was just as lopsided: Marshalltown's 43 points put it well ahead of runner-up Ottumwa with 16. Apparently only four teams competed in the Iowa City meet, and one squad brought two wrestlers. Originally the tournament had seven teams accept invitations out of the 120 schools offered a spot in the event, according to the *Marshalltown Times-Republican.*

The only time the tournament at Ames followed the Iowa City competition was in 1924. It also had a lengthy tussle for the 145-pound championship. The difference? Ernie Sharp of Clarion held a 38-second time advantage over Lawrence Erickson of Boone in the fourth overtime period. Nearly 50 years later, Sharp's son Bob coached Ankeny to the Class 2-A team title in the 1971 state tournament. Ernie Sharp, who was born in Saskatchewan, was likely there because the snow kept him from touring the layout at Clarmond Country Club between Clarion and Belmond. Sharp was known to play a round any day the course was open and weather permitted.

There were some familiar schools boasting champions in the pre-IHSAA era. Clarion, Boone, Indianola, Mason City, Mount Vernon and Cherokee had winners. So did teams from Garden Grove and Sutherland, both of which fell off the state's prep wrestling map years ago. Teddy Warrington won at 105 pounds for Garden Grove in the 1922 tournament at Ames. Garden Grove consolidated in 1959 with nearby Humeston, Derby and LeRoy to form Mormon Trail High School.

Burdette Briggs remains Sutherland's lone champion, winning at 115 pounds in 1923 at Ames. Sutherland is now part of the South O'Brien school district with Primghar and Paullina. Any Sutherland kids wanting to be the next Briggs have to wrestle for Sheldon/South O'Brien.

Garden Grove sent five men to the 1923 tournament in Iowa City, all made the finals and all were second. The team placed third with 15 points, behind champion Ottumwa (25 points) and Clarion (22 points). The runners-up were Paul Hinebaugh at 95, Gerald Richards at 105, Warrington at 115, Paul Young at 125 and Norman Thomas at 145. The *Garden Grove Express* of March 29, 1923 reported that its home team fell short only in numbers to Clarion for second place.

"Had it not been for the fact that Clarion had nine men on their team, entering every class, and there were only five on our team, we would have won second. They not outclassing our men, just more points from the fact they had more on their team," was in the paper's account.

In 1924 at Ames, Eldora Training School was seven years away from tying Fort Dodge for the team championship but scored its first individual champion. William Bird took the 95-pound title in the second extra period over Bernard Johnson of Boone. The *Hardin County Ledger* reported that Bird found success despite having a left arm that could not be straightened, stemming from a childhood fracture that was not properly set.

Four decorated stars emerged during the earliest years of competition. Willis Standley (1922, 1923, 1924) and Lyle Wilson (1923, 1924, 1925) of Boone were three-time champions. Standley was also runner-up at 125 in the 1922 tournament at Iowa City. Boone's school yearbook *The Scroll* made mention of Standley's impressive habit of making quick work of opponents: "Standley, our three year champion, believes in picking up his man and pinning him before the crowd knows what is happening."

Richard Burke of Mason City won championships at Ames in 1922 and 1925. His title in 1925 came on the heels of reaching the semifinals of the 1924 Olympic Trials in New York.

Allie Morrison of Marshalltown began attracting attention to his skills in 1924, when he beat Leslie Grant of Fonda for the 125-pound championship in Ames. Morrison won that weight in the Iowa City tournament in 1924, at 125 in 1925 and was considered the student coach (he did not wrestle) in 1926, when Marshalltown won the state title. The faculty representative for that 1926 Bobcat squad was Adolph Rupp, who would later have a Hall of Fame career coaching basketball at Kentucky. Morrison in 1928 became the first Iowa boy who won a state wrestling championship to win an Olympic gold medal in the sport.

Sometimes a glowing account of one's style considers the wrestler a man among boys. Prior to 1926 and the onset of the IHSAA's rules, there were literally boys against men in some meets, according to newspaper accounts. The current restrictions of being at least in ninth grade and no older than 20 years of age were not law during the earliest years of high school wrestling in Iowa.

Fonda's team drew some attention from the *Estherville Enterprise* in 1922. The paper reported on a meet in which Fonda won six of the seven contested bouts. "They had a fast aggregation much older than the locals," the paper reported. "The boy in the 125 class said he was about 21 years of age and would quit school as soon as the wrestling season was over. Two of the boys were induced to enter school for wrestling purposes."

Fonda's 125-pound entrant in the 1922 tournament was Chester Downing, who had replaced the injured Leonard Cole. Downing lost in the second round and did not place among the top four.

One year earlier, Cedar Rapids High School got a fourth-place finish at 95 pounds from a youngster named Cook. A story in the Feb. 7 edition of the *Cedar Rapids Evening Gazette* had a passage about the boy who is believed to be Edward Cook: "This little fellow, who is but eleven years of age, won much praise for his action on the mat."

Armed with some rules that were written by Nels "N. B." Anderson of Clarion and Cleo Roberts of Ames, the IHSAA took charge of the state tourney beginning in 1926.

"Coop's Boys"

Some of the first stars in the state wrestling tournament, after the Iowa High School Athletic Association began sanctioning the event in 1926, were from a tough Fort Dodge High School pack known as "Coop's Boys."

"Coop" was Fred Cooper, who coached Fort Dodge to eight team championships – and a share of a ninth - between 1927 and 1941. There were 25 of "Coop's Boys" who won a total of 28 individual championships between John Brindley at 85 pounds 1926 and Eldon Faine in 1942.

How tough were they? The Dodgers' Andrew Pontius won the 158-pound state championship in 1927 at Ames, despite getting a case of frostbite on his ear bad enough that the ear swelled and split.

Fort Dodge's squad had a car break down 20 miles from Ames on its way to the tournament. According to the *Fort Dodge Messenger,* some of the wrestlers were picked up by passing cars and taken to Ames but there was not room for everyone. Those who remained walked an estimated 6-7 miles in an attempt to get to Boone. George Hoyer, the Dodgers' 95-pounder, and 105-pounder Randall Whinnery took their shoes and socks off after complaining of cold feet.

Two years later, Whinnery pinned four opponents in winning the 125-pound state title.

After they eventually got a ride to Boone in 1927, the remainder of the team took a train to Ames and joined their mates for weigh-ins. The Dodgers won their first of their 11 team titles by two points as Pontius was joined by 145-pounder Joe Gargano as a state champion.

"Gloom was cast over the Dodger camp by the unexpected experience but the men entered the tournament with plenty of fight and eventually won out," according to the *Messenger.*

No car breakdown or long walk in the snow could keep the Dodgers from a fine effort that weekend. Karl Haugen wrote in his *Fort Dodge*

Messenger column, "The team made an impressive appearance at Ames in their natty looking outfits with 'Dodgers' lettered across the front of their shirts. Even the Ames radio announcer was impressed and announced to the fans that the Dodgers were certainly a snappy looking outfit and evidently came from a 'hot' wrestling town."

Coop's wrestlers also shined on a national mat.

Fort Dodge competed at the National Interscholastic High School tournament at Evanston, Ill. in 1929 and 1930, finishing second in the team standings each year. Frank Gargano at 135 and Lyle Sells at 155 won national championships in 1929, along with freshman Ray Bateman of Cresco at 100 pounds. Gargano's brother Tony won the 145-pound title in 1930, when Frank moved up to 155 and lost for the first time in three years when Ken Ruggles of Ames beat him, avenging two regular-season losses. A fourth national champion from Iowa in the 1930 tournament was 165-pounder Lorne "Dutch" Simons of Cherokee.

Four of "Coop's Boys" were Gargano boys, and all four finished either first or second at state. Joe, Frank and Tony were state champions and William won a wrestle-back match in 1936 to finish second. Frank Gargano accomplished maybe the best individual effort in tournament history in 1930, when he pinned all five opponents en route to the 145-pound championship. Gargano personally scored 10 of Fort Dodge's 24 points as it won the team championship. Gargano's style on the mat was some of what Cooper was talking about after the 1929 national tournament.

Following the 1929 tournament, Cooper told *The Messenger* the style of wrestling the Iowa kids were used to was not always employed at the national tournament. "Fort Dodge and other Iowa boys are used to aggressive grappling. They will always seek a fall, if possible. Oklahoma, on the other hand, sought decisions alone. The southerners would get behind and ride till the end if they could."

Cooper's style that favored getting after someone was noticed in a *Messenger* account of the 1937 title run: "Superior aggressiveness won the crown for Coach Fred N. Cooper's squad, five points scored on first round falls more than making up for the difference between the Dodgers and (Clarion) Cowboy totals."

Three Iowa teams – the Dodgers, Ames in fourth place and Iowa Falls in fifth – finished among the top five in the 1930 tournament.

That earlier episode of the car breakdown and one wrestler's frostbitten ear was not the only flirting with danger that "Coop's Boys" experienced. Their return from the Evanston tournament in 1930 was a challenge, to put it mildly. *The Messenger* reported six Dodger wrestlers escaped injury when the car they were riding in sideswiped a car on a rain- and sleet-soaked road in Freeport, Ill. The report stated that two squad members took the train home and the others rode with Thomas Johnson, the father of one of the Fort Dodge wrestlers.

So who was "Coop?"

Examine portraits of Cooper in the school's annual *The Dodger* and one gets the idea he was a studious man complete with the spectacles and sartorial finery. When he changed into his workout clothes, Cooper became a highly successful man who was respected by his pupils. He also devised a pairing system that was employed to match wrestlers in the state tournament beginning in 1934.

"He wasn't a technician because he never really wrestled much himself, he came originally from Michigan," said Faine, who was Cooper's last Dodger state champion. "What he did was he pitted guys against each other and he'd make you wrestle two or three guys. It was one right after another and you'd feel like killing somebody. It was a matter of survival. You never got a chance to screw off, he kept pitting you against this guy, pitting you against that guy. Having a match was pretty easy after coming out of that wrestling room. The training was so damn tough."

This was a time when a kid's options were few. He could do athletics or go to work. Anyone who didn't mind being pounded by the likes of Dale Brand, the Gargano brothers, Black or Koll likely would be on the team. There was no one who could afford to pay someone to take the lumps for him, especially after the Great Depression. "We all came from a poor background. No one had any money then," Faine said.

The Cooper method might have had its finest hour in the 1933-34 season, when the Dodgers took the state team title. The 1934 *Dodger* reported that Cooper turned a green team into what he termed "the best team ever." Fort Dodge won one meet – 22-11 over Eldora Training School – that season but grew enough to win a district title and then the state title. Ken Bales, Abe Castagnoli and Floyd Messerly won individual championships. It was one of four times that three of Cooper's wrestlers would win crowns.

Cooper said Castagnoli "fulfilled my fondest hopes" but saved his highest praise for Messerly, who would become a two-time champion. In the yearbook, Cooper wrote that Messerly "is a wrestler."

Fort Dodge hosted the 1934 state meet, and Principal C. T. Feelhaver sent the financial report (a gate of over $630, the Iowa High School Athletic

Association's share of nearly $540, Fort Dodge's share of $94.68) plus a thank-you note to the IHSAA. "How do you like the gate?" Feelhaver wrote to executive director George Brown. "We enjoyed putting on the meet. We are especially happy because of the team trophy."

The Dodgers won a lot under Cooper, but also learned about class.

"If you didn't shake hands, you were going to be in big trouble. You couldn't get by with poor sportsmanship," Faine said. "He was a gentleman and he stressed the rules. He commanded a lot of respect. At that point he was probably the winningest coach in Iowa up to the time of Bob Siddens."

Faine said he caught the wrestling bug when he attended the 1939 state tournament that was held at Fort Dodge High School. That was the first wrestling competition he had seen.

"I think it was like everybody else, I was small and the only the sport I think I could have done good in was wrestling," said Faine, who was 5-5 and weighed 118 pounds. "I thought I was pretty good in junior high, so they sent me up to the high school and who do I start wrestling with but Bill Koll."

Koll was not yet the dominating wrestler whose ferocious way of bringing an opponent back to the mat led to the ban on slams, but he was a handful to contend with because of his proficiency in using the duck-under and the go-behind. He had quickness and superb agility on his side, as well as a powerful desire to succeed.

"He was very determined, he never eased up. He never goofed off and he was always serious and going full-blast all the time. He was an introverted type of guy, kind of a loner. He didn't run around, drink or smoke," Faine said.

Faine had a good strength-building job putting in ties and loading rail while working a section crew on the Fort Dodge, Des Moines and Southern Railroad. That didn't help with all ways of trying to handle Koll. "At that age I think I was stronger than Bill, but I didn't have his agility, persistence and balance and everything else," Faine said. "We had a guy named Dick Black, who was a state champion in 1940. Dick Black was one of the best high school wrestlers I'd ever seen and he pounded on Bill pretty good."

Koll got even against Black when they were in college at Iowa State Teachers College, Faine said.

During the 1940-41 season, Cooper scored two of his wins against teams coached by two of his state champions. The Dodgers beat a West Des

Moines team coached by Brindley and later beat a Clarion squad coached by Dale Brand, 21-15, as a pin by Bob Johnson at heavyweight clinched the meet. Brand would have a long, distinguished career at Clarion and the often-close duals against Fort Dodge would draw capacity or overflow crowds.

Faine's older brother was friends with Brand. Faine said he remembered Cooper talking about the toughness of Brand, who pinned his way to a 1931 state championship at 105 pounds prior to winning an NCAA championship at Cornell College and being an Olympic alternate. In later years, after Faine established a chiropractic practice in Webster City, he did some work with members of Brand's teams when the Cowboys came to town.

Siddens, a two-time state runner-up at Eagle Grove, spent one season with the Eagles before embarking on a legendary career at Waterloo West. Faine said he wrestled Siddens in high school. Faine beat a future Olympic gold medalist from Clarion named Glen Brand, a cousin of Dale Brand. Glen Brand, who was known as Junior, never forgot the match with Faine long after he struck gold in the 1948 Olympics. Faine once introduced Brand as a world champion to his son.

Faine remembered the always-humble Brand's reply: "And when I was in high school, your dad kicked my ass."

The guys tangling with varsity regulars in Cooper's practice room were pretty tough once they got a chance. Bill Koll, a future three-time NCAA champion at Iowa State Teachers College (now Northern Iowa) and Olympian, won the 135-pound state title in 1941 after teammate Dick Black won it in 1940.

Maybe the best example of running with an opportunity was Willis Kuhn, a two-time state champion who was not in the pre-season talk about the 1935-36 season and who would emerge as champion. Kuhn was behind Bill Bisacchi in the Dodgers' lineup as a junior until Bisacchi had a cold and Kuhn stepped in for the Cherokee meet. His first match was a pin in 5:20 over Kingsbury with a reverse headlock and a stepover, according to the *Fort Dodge Messenger*.

Another regular-season meet, scheduled for Feb. 14 against Eagle Grove, was called off because of a coal shortage, according to the *Messenger*. Before the Dodgers won the team title, their season included a 25 ½-7 ½ victory over Hammond, Ind., the top team from the Hoosier State.

Kuhn pinned his way to the 1936 title, including stopping Kingsbury in 3:20 in the semifinals.

The lone blemish on Kuhn's varsity record was a loss during the 1936-37 season to Maurice Morford of Clarion, who had a pair of state titles under his belt. A crowd of 1,100 attended the Jan. 29, 1937 meet in Clarion, a 20-16 Cowboys victory that was Kuhn's first setback in 13 bouts, the *Messenger* reported. Kuhn got his revenge in the semifinals, a decision over Morford that was reported to be Morford's only loss in three years.

Kuhn had a 20-1 record in his abbreviated varsity career, with 14 wins by fall.

A recap of the 1937 state tournament in the *Fort Dodge Messenger* included the following passage about Kuhn's rise: "If Fort Dodge High School has a place where the names of her athletic "immortals" are inscribed, wee Willie Kuhn, new Iowa 135-pound wrestling champion, has earned a niche in it."

The 1937 *Dodger* had a passage with Kuhn's senior picture. "Oh, it is excellent to have a giant's strength."

Faine said he wished for some of that strength when he was coming up in the Dodger practice room. He'd tangle with Koll as he waited for his chance to wear the varsity uniform. After his junior season ended below his plans, Faine was set on success as a senior.

"I was really motivated and I never eased up once. I was on fire my whole senior year," Faine said.

During the first 14 state tournaments staged by the Iowa High School Athletic Association beginning in 1926, some of the first stars not wearing a Dodger uniform emerged. Richard Cole of Ames was the first wrestler to win two state championships. He won at 115 pounds in 1926 and 1927 before moving to Iowa State, where Cole won an NCAA championship at Providence, R.I. in 1931. He must have made an impression on the folks at Brown University because Cole was named Brown's wrestling coach in 1932. Perhaps they were impressed that Cole was the first Iowa state champion to win a title in the NCAA tournament, which began in 1928.

Ames produced the IHSAA's first three-time state champion in Ken Ruggles, between 1928 and 1930. Ruggles met some tough guys on his way to the three-time champion list. Ivy Russell of Sac City took him to double-overtime before Ruggles won in 1928. In 1929, Ruggles beat eventual national high school champion Lyle Sells of Fort Dodge at 145 in the state finals. Ruggles lost at least twice in the 1929-30 season because he tangled with Frank Gargano of Fort Dodge, who moved into the 145-pound spot Ruggles vacated when he was in the 155-pound division. Gargano was a two-time champion who apparently chose not to get back to his championship weight when he entered the 1930 national tournament in Evanston. Ruggles beat him in the 155-pound finals at Evanston.

The folks in Ames were fond of Ruggles, who shined in and out of the classroom. The *Ames Tribune* reported Ruggles averaged 92 in his studies during the previous six weeks leading up to the 1930 national meet. He was also busy outside of school because Ruggles drove a truck for an Ames dairy.

Ruggles was not likely to be as popular in Sac City. Two of his championships were annexed and a third was set up by defeating Sac City wrestlers. Ruggles won a double-overtime decision over Ivy Russell in the 1928 finals at 145 and beat Lawrence Saddoris for the 155-pound crown in 1930. In 1929, prior to beating Sells at 145, Ruggles won a referee's decision over Saddoris in the semifinals. According to an account of the tournament, Saddoris had a 22-second advantage in riding time but referee B. J. Firkins awarded the match to Ruggles because of aggressiveness.

Bob Hess, a 1927 state champion for Cresco, became the first Iowa state champion to win a pair of NCAA championships when he wore Iowa State's colors in 1932 and 1933. The Cresco name was a regular locale of state champions in the 1920's and the 1930's. Blair Thomas, Albert Durfey, Dick Jones, Wallace Kent, Paul "Bo" Cameron, Don Nichols, Don Maland, Dale Hanson…the names were plentiful and so was the gold medal supply in Howard County.

In 1935, Cresco became the first program to have five state champions in a single tournament. The night opened with four Spartans (Cresco became the Crestwood Cadets in the 1960-61 season) winning state titles. Newell Ingel (85 pounds), Ed Lybbert (95), Dale Hanson (105) and Earl Hilke (115) were joined by Don Nichols at 135. Nichols is the brother of Harold Nichols, who did not win a state title but was an NCAA champion at Michigan before he started coaching at Arkansas State and then at Iowa State.

Cresco's four-in-a-row run was matched by its 1948 squad – Barney Dunneman at 118, Ray Steiger at 123, Gene Aberg at 129 and Charles Hyke at 135. It took 53 years for another team to win four straight gold medals. That was Council Bluffs Lewis Central in 2001, and the Titans set a record that year with six individual winners. The four straight were Chad Davis at 130, Brandon Mason at 135, Trent Paulson at 140 and

Travis Paulson at 145. Gabe Rostermundt at 119 and Blake Anderson at 160 completed the Lewis Central blast. Most recently, Denver-Tripoli opened the Class 2-A tournament in 2010 with championships by Dylan Peters at 103, Gunnar Wolfensperger at 112, Brandon Sorensen at 119 and Levi Wolfensperger at 125.

The IHSAA's first four-time finalist, Paul Bell of Clarion, came along in the mid-to-late '30s. After finishing second to Ingle at 85 in 1935, Bell won at 85 in 1936, at 95 in 1937 and at 115 in 1938. Ralph Goodale of Marshalltown won the heavyweight title in 1926 after winning at the Iowa City tournament in 1924, placing second at Ames in 1924 and winning at Ames in 1925.

Three future state championship coaches won titles during the 1930's – Cameron in 1931, Dave Natvig of New Hampton in 1933 and 1934 and Leon "Champ" Martin of Eagle Grove in 1939. Two-time state champion (1937 and 1938) John Roberts of Valley Junction (now West Des Moines) was recruited to University of Wisconsin by George Martin, a state runner-up for Eagle Grove in 1928, and became the first Badger wrestler to make the NCAA finals. He later won a team championship at Stevens Point (Wis.) High School and then was executive director of the Wisconsin Interscholastic Athletic Association.

One of the lasting, important parts of wrestling season was launched during the 1930's by the IHSAA. According to a story in the *Ames Tribune-Times*, the IHSAA decided on a method of getting wrestlers to the state meet. The state would have four sectionals and the top two finishers in each of the 10 weight classes would go to state. That 80-man field seems miniscule today, fitting inside six weight classes of the current format where 16 go to state in each of 14 weights in the three divisions.

The decision in 1931 was done, "in order to encourage schools having one or more individual stars and a mediocre team to enter their good men in the state competition," according to the *Tribune-Times* story.

Wrestling's growth during its early years in Iowa got high marks from Iowa State coach Hugo Otopalik, who was quoted in an 1930 *Associated Press* story. "Wrestling has taken hold in the schools and colleges as no other sport ever did," Otopalik said. "And the development of it as a sport has been more rapid than any other part of the physical education program."

Otopalik hit on the chief reasons why the sport's numbers had grown.

"Because of the opportunity it affords men who cannot enter other sports, and because it offers a thorough training in technique, sportsmanship, aggressiveness and co-ordination, wrestling has come to a more prominent place than any other sport, considering the length of time it has been established in the schools."

"I'll see you over at West High School this afternoon."

Just as Fort Dodge had been the first powerhouse of the state wrestling tournament in the late 1920's and the 30's, Waterloo West began flexing its considerable mat muscle in the 1940's. It took some time for the Wahawk program to grow into its powerful selves.

Beginning with the 1941-42 season, West High put together a run of five straight team championships. The Wahawks had an unprecedented mark until Don Bosco of Gilbertville matched it in the 2010 tournament. The Dons were denied winning a sixth straight crown in the 2011 event.

"I think it goes way back to the beginning in 1935, when West started wrestling. The principal was Bill Gibson, and he was a really strong principal that wanted every program in the school to be the best," said Don Huff, a Wahawk state champion, assistant coach and head coach who led the team to their most recent championship in 1989. "I think he hired Finn Eriksen first of all in 1935, and he coached for eight years. Starting from nothing, I think in those eight years I think he had seven or eight state champions. The last two years his teams won the state tournament."

One of Eriksen's early stars was Jim Stoyanoff, a four-time state qualifier between 1939 and 1942 who became West's first three-time state champion. He weighed in at 72 pounds as a freshman to compete at 85 pounds for the 1939 tournament. "They didn't even have tights for him, he just wore a shirt and shorts when he went out to wrestle," said Dick Hauser, a three-time state champion for West who was good friends with Stoyanoff.

Eriksen had plenty of opportunities to find good kids to fill out his lineups with, according to Hauser.

"When we started out in high school, Finn Eriksen was a PE teacher. There were three junior high schools – West Junior High, then there was

Sloane Wallace which is the one I went to and (two-time champion Leo Thomsen) went to and a third one – and he taught at all three of them so he had his pick. He'd just walk up to you and say 'I'll see you over at West High School this afternoon.' That was it."

Hauser said Eriksen did not cut an imposing figure in stature, but no one crossed him. "In size? Gosh no, but in importance around there, nobody ever talked back to him. Everybody backed him up 157 percent all the time."

Huff added, "With (Finn), I think it was discipline that he kind of demanded and, consequently, he was really respected."

At least two of his former students thought enough of Eriksen that they sent him an unusual gift from Florida. Eriksen received a 2-foot-long alligator from Dorothy and Richard Simonsen, according to a *Waterloo Courier* article. The gator became the mascot of the 1936-37 Wahawk wrestling team. The wrestlers named it Wimpy, as in the hamburger-loving sidekick of Popeye, because it was fed raw meat twice a week. No mention was made whether or not the alligator became proficient in the sport by being around Eriksen.

Hauser said learning the ropes in West's practice room was painfully great.

"I don't know whether you could say (Eriksen) did that much coaching. The guys used to come out and I can remember this so distinctly, especially with Leo Thomsen and me. All these older guys on the team and they'd just rough us around," Hauser said. "Did we learn specifically from Finn Eriksen? No, but we knew Mr. Eriksen was very dominant and he controlled things. When he told you to do something, you did it. We used to try to hide among the guys, Thomy and I, and they'd grab us and haul us out there and rough us all over, but we loved it."

Some of the veterans gave Hauser helping hands when he started his varsity career.

"I can remember very distinctly the very first varsity match I had, it was up at Cresco. I stood on the corner of the mat, they were introducing the individuals and I still had my jacket on and my long pants," Hauser said. "All of a sudden Dick Cummings and Bill Manning came running over and grabbed me, lifted me up, pulled off the pants and the jacket. About that time I had to walk out and shake hands. All I did was charge out and this guy came at me, oh shucks he was a real good wrestler. We were both the same age starting out together. We hit head on and it just happened that I got under both of his arms, bent him over and pinned him. I didn't even wrestle, I didn't even know what it was all about."

West lost only one dual meet during its five-title span. Ten men combined to win 14 individual state championships during the same time. After Eriksen stepped down to join the Navy – he would later become director of the city's physical education program - the Wahawks hired Roy Jarrard from Cherokee for the 1943-44 season. Jarrard led Cherokee to the 1939 state championship and had individual winners in 95-pounder Jimmy Stewart and 155-pounder Harry McManus, who might have used his wrestling training to survive spending nearly four years in a Japanese prison camp. At Waterloo West, Jarrard was party to impressive winning streaks for Hauser, Thomsen and Lowell Lange.

Hauser lost only once in high school. That came in the 1943 championship at 95 pounds, when Wally Hagen of Clarion pinned him. Hagen won the first of two state championships. Hauser said they were having a close scrap until Hagen ended it.

"If I remember right, we were within one or two points of each other," Hauser said. "He was tall, a lot taller than I was. I went in for a double-leg drop, grabbed both of his legs and he just walked right over me, took me over backwards and bonk, it was all over."

There was at least one other instance where Hauser could have lost. A touch of psychology helped Hauser win the Feb. 2, 1945 bout against Merle Shreve, who was known to eat at the restaurant Hauser's dad operated.

"It was really packed, they were yelling, hollering, screeching and everything else. I could remember he had me, but we were on our feet," Hauser said. "We locked up and there was only seconds to go in the whole match, we were face to face on our feet, and I said, 'Nice match Merle,' he looked up and grinned at me and I got him. I took him down, got a point for a predicament and that tied us up. We went overtime and I beat him."

The Jarrard Era got off to a roaring start. Hauser's pin of intracity rival Charles Metcalf at 105 pounds was the first of five individual titles won by West wrestlers. Joining him were Dick Cumming at 118, Bill Manning at 135, Bob Wilson at 155 and Oliver Michaelsen at heavyweight. Lange was second at 129. Had there been a win by Lange – whose grandson James Lange won a state championship in 2002 for Centerville – the Wahawks would have beaten Council Bluffs Lewis Central's 2001 team to the punch of having six winners in a single tournament.

West's quintet of gold was the first time a team had five winners since

Cresco in 1935. Going into the 2011 tournament, the 1944 West squad is one of five that crowned five champions in a tournament.

In 1945 and 1946, the story was the same: Hauser, Lange and Thomsen were West's state champions. Their victories in 1946 capped their winning streaks at 65 matches for Hauser, 51 for Lange and 27 for Thomsen.

Hauser's third championship came in a 4-3 decision at 118 pounds over Dale Nelson of Eagle Grove. Three months later, Hauser was in Eagle Grove to attend the funeral of Nelson, who died in a car-train accident near Holmes the night before he was to receive his diploma. The *Eagle Grove Eagle* reported that 700 people signed the registration book prior to Nelson's service. Also attending the service were Lange, Cornell College coach Paul Scott and Curt Stein of Gilmore City, who won the 135-pound state championship in 1946.

Scott was able to see Hauser away from the mat during a road trip that became a recruiting trip. Colleges were seeking Hauser, Thomsen and Lange for their team. "Iowa State Teachers, they really raked them in, they were sure we were going to go there. There was the three of us - me and Thomy and Lange. We had a meeting with all of them. We went out to the nationals that year with Paul K. Scott. We had a good time, and when we came back, where did we go to school? Cornell College."

Hauser and Lange were NCAA champions in 1947 – when Cornell became the first private college to win the NCAA Division I championship - and Lange also won gold in 1949 and in 1950. Thomsen was an all-American in 1947 and in 1949. Before they went to college, the three champions and their teammates had gone through the differences brought on by a coaching change at West.

"Very much so, personalities and everything. Here was a great big guy, (Jarrard) must have weighed 175-180 pounds, but he was much bigger than Finn Eriksen," Hauser said. "When Finn talked, nobody else talked. (Roy) was completely different, he wanted to be chummy with people and stuff. He'd take on the guys, they'd wrestle with him. It wasn't that way with Finn."

Jarrard was also there for the start of a successful run by the Huff family.

"I had a couple older brothers, (Charles) was 5 years older and (Dale) was 3 years older. My oldest brother, he was pretty small also and when he was a freshman was when Roy Jerrard was coach there. I think Jerrard saw him walking down the hall and said 'We need some light guys on the wrestling team and I'd like you to come out' so he said he would try it," Don Huff said. "He was pretty successful in his own right, then the next brother got started. My younger brother (Tom) and myself, we were probably in elementary school when they were wrestling. We started going up and watching them practice and they'd show us stuff at home. I got started with technique pretty early, and I had a really good partner to wrestle with at home."

Charles Huff was able to speak to the quality of future three-time state champions Eddie Kline of Mason City and Ron Gray of Eagle Grove. Kline beat Huff, 4-1, for the 95-pound championship in 1951. Gray trimmed Huff, 6-5, at 103 pounds in the 1952 finals. The Huff brothers combined for five state championships (Tom won three, Don two) and eight placings in the state meets. Dale finished third in 1954.

Charles and Dale Huff were on the first Wahawk squad coached by Bob Siddens. That 1950-51 team won the team title without crowning an individual champion. That was the first of 13 instances when the team champ had no individual champs.

Waterloo West carved its name into the wood of wrestling toughness in the state. Huff said it was basically second generation work ethic.

"A lot of the parents of that day grew up in the Depression and they knew nothing was going to be handed to them. I think they kind of passed that along to their kids," Huff said. "In junior high I got thrown around some and I had some times when I was ready to quit, feeling sorry for myself. My dad said, 'Well, if you want to be a quitter all your life, go ahead and quit.' That didn't sit very well I guess."

Hauser said there was a novel way of developing toughness in his house. The guy who was described as "122 pounds of speed" by the *Courier* during football season when he played quarterback said he could find a wrestling workout partner in his father, Herbert O. Hauser, or his brother, Herbert A. Hauser.

"What did they do? Beat the hell out of me. My brother was 7 years older than me and he wrestled up in the higher classes, 155-, 165-pound classes in high school. He was a lot taller than me," Hauser said. "There was many a time when I spent the night sleeping on the rug next to the bed. We shared a bed and sometimes he didn't want me in the bed with him. I'd say something to my mother, she'd say, 'What's the matter Richard?' and I'd say 'Herbert...' and she would say 'Well, shut up, you probably deserved it.'"

Hauser said his father went to school through seventh grade, but he was a sports fan who paid extremely close attention to wrestling. In return, Hauser said his father was well-known in wrestling circles.

Following the 1946 championship, West took a break from the top of the high school wrestling world in Iowa. The Wahawks were 24-20-1 in duals between the 1946-47 and the 1949-50 seasons. Jack Springer, Dick Barron and Dave Glenny won state championships. From the program's start in the 1935-36 season to the 1945-46 campaign, the Wahawks lost a total of 17 duals.

The Wahawk program perked back up with the arrival of Siddens in 1950.

Along with the lengthy Wahawk dominance, one of the longest championship matches in tournament history took place in 1942 when 1941's 105-pound champion Merle Roths of New Hampton and Bob Hunt of Council Bluffs Thomas Jefferson, a guy who initially wanted to make his mark as a boxer, locked up in the 112-pound finale.

Was someone going to score a touchdown? Not if either one had a say in the matter. The regulation was slightly different in 1942 than it is now.

"In those days you started on your feet, and if you stayed on your feet for 2 minutes, then you wrestled three 2-minute periods with a minute rest between the second and third period and that was 8 minutes. Otherwise, if you took your man down right away it was a straight 7 minutes," Roths said.

A boxer is used to working 2- or 3-minute periods. Hunt wasn't a big man, but he was willing to throw punches and protect his path. The boxing thing came to a sobering end one night when he was in with a boxer named Johnny Gross.

"All I know was I was doing really good beating him and all of a sudden, wham, I'm on my knees," Hunt said. "I thought, 'How'd I get down there?' I thought that was an accident. I started boxing again with him and wham, I'm on my knees again, so I quit boxing. I didn't like that."

While walking down a hallway at the school known by its alumni as TeeJay, Hunt met his high school future.

"Orville Orr was the coach at TeeJay. I was a 95-pounder walking down the hall and this big, muscular guy grabbed my arm and dragged me in. He says 'You're going out for wrestling,'" Hunt recalled. "He just more or less told you that you were going out. I never had any idea of going out. They had boxing at that time and I went out for it, so now I went out (for wrestling)."

In boxing terms, Roths-Hunt was a draw during regulation. To hear Roths recall the match, there was not going to be a wealth of scoring in the bout. "We wrestled so much alike, neither one of us could get out. I saw him wrestle through the meet, and I wanted to stay on my feet the first 2 minutes because I'd seen how good of a wrestler he was," Roths said. "Maybe he was watching me, and I don't think he tried too hard to take down either. So we stayed on our feet for 2 minutes, then we wrestled three 2-minute periods."

Perhaps an overtime would settle things. Roths was on top for 1 minute and Hunt was on top for 1 minute. Still scoreless after 10 minutes. Roths said he remembered the referee being perplexed. "So he said 'I don't know how to call it. I'm going to put it in another overtime,'" Roths said.

A second overtime session settled nothing as well. Roths said the referee was still unsure of what to do, so he chose a third overtime. That's 14 minutes without points. A fourth overtime could settle it, so the referee resumed the bout. After another points-free session, the referee finally decided to rule on a winner. Hunt got his arm raised.

"The only quibble I got was I was the (returning) champion, the champion always gets the nod. I guess the referee didn't know that," Roths said. "There was only one referee in those years too. Now they've got referees and judges running around there too. In those days just the one referee, and I guess he didn't know I was defending champion."

Hunt has one distinct memory of the contest, which landed him the first of two state titles. He won the 118-pound championship in 1943. There is no mention of whether his 1943 bout against Harold Bard of Eagle Grove went anywhere close to the 16-minute distance he and Roths fought. "It seemed like we had an awful long match, I was awful tired. I can't remember a lot about it," Hunt said.

Roths, a three-time finalist, was worn out as well. In 1942, wrestlers who lost in the finals had another match that night to determine a true second-place finisher. Roths met Mervill Angell of Osage. "I had to wrestle back for second and third, well I got beat the second match too. I had beaten (Angell) all through high school and he beat me that night because I could hardly get my arms above my head," Roths said. "That's the only time I ever wrestled overtime in my life."

In the three finals matches, Roths obviously enjoyed the 1941 match against Mickey Waterman of Oelwein because he won that. Roths said he felt strong, but he had a stern test in the semifinals that year.

"I think I could have beat heavyweight that year, I wanted to be a state champion," Roths said. "I wrestled (Duane) McCullough in the semifinals from Fort Dodge and he told me afterwards, 'My coach says if I beat Roths, I'll be a state champion.' I said, 'Well, I'll try to save you a place.' I wrestled Waterman from Oelwein and then (McCullough) came back and beat Waterman for second place. I didn't dare blink my eyes, (McCullough) was on me all the time. He was good,"

In 1940 Roths was pinned in the 95-pound finals by Grant Hunter of Council Bluffs Abraham Lincoln. The tournament that year was held in New Hampton. Roths said he made a mistake prior to the bout against Hunter. "I got a rubdown that night and I'd never had a rubdown before and I would never do that again," Roths said. "I was asleep out there. I went behind the kid right away and in 3 minutes 7 seconds I was on my back counting the lights."

Hunt knew something about getting thumped too. His first state tournament match in 1941 was against West's Stoyanoff, who was about to win the second of his three state titles. Hunt's championship in 1942 made him the first TeeJay wrestler to win under Orr's direction. "They gave me a little teeny medal about the size of a dime," Hunt recalled. "You didn't think much of it at that time. (Orr) always said if he could get one, he'd get more, and he did."

Hunt said he had his sons go to state, but the big thrill was watching his grandson, Bryce Carruthers, win a state title for TeeJay in 2004. "I taught him in my basement," Hunt said.

There were some individuals in the state tournament during the 1940's who made national and international names for themselves on the mat in later years. Gerry "Germ" Leeman of Osage won two of his three titles in the 40's, won an NCAA championship for Iowa State Teachers College (Northern Iowa) in 1946 – he was named outstanding wrestler of the tournament - and a silver medal in the 1948 Olympics at London. Bill Koll of Fort Dodge won a state title in 1941, served his county in the military and then won three NCAA titles at Iowa State Teachers College, was the first two-time outstanding wrestler (1947 and 1948) in the NCAA meet and was fifth in the 1948 Olympics. Bill Nelson of Eagle Grove won a state title in 1945, won three NCAA titles at Iowa State Teachers College and was an alternate on the 1948 Olympic team.

Glen Brand of Clarion, a 1948 NCAA champion and 1948 Olympics gold medalist, lost his only state tournament match in high school. Bill Smith of Council Bluffs TeeJay placed second in state in 1946, but he won two NCAA championships at Iowa State Teachers College and a gold medal in the 1952 Olympics. Keith Young of Algona never wrestled at state, but in 1949 he won the first of three consecutive NCAA championships for Iowa State Teachers College. Gene Lybbert was twice a runner-up in high school at Cresco, but he became a two-time NCAA champion at Iowa State Teachers College.

Russ Bush of Waterloo West, Cecil Mott of Mason City and Norvard "Snip" Nalan of Mason City never won state titles during the 1940's but they would earn NCAA titles – Bush and Mott at Iowa State Teachers College and Nalan twice at Michigan.

"There isn't anybody in the state that's going to beat you at heavyweight."

Winning a state wrestling championship at heavyweight can be a taxing thing. Just ask Bill Nelson of Eagle Grove, who won that distinction in 1945.

Nelson made the state finals at 155 pounds in 1943 and in 1944, finishing third in 1943 and second the following year. Ten pounds and one year later, Nelson had his gold medal.

"My senior year I had to wrestle heavyweight," Nelson said, adding it was the decision of coach Art Parsons. "He said, 'There isn't anybody in the state that's going to beat you at heavyweight. I don't want you to lose any weight.' He never let us cut weight."

Nelson did not gain weight as he went on to national acclaim at Iowa State Teachers College (now Northern Iowa) by winning three NCAA championships. One of those titles was at 165, the other two at 155. He did gain a spot as a distinguished member of the National Wrestling Hall of Fame in 1980 for that work, winning two AAU national championships and being an alternate on the 1948 Olympic team.

All of that winning started in Clarion, the site of the 1945 state meet. Facing three big guys – Eugene Schoeberl of Cresco, Joe Paulson of Davenport and, in the finals, Wayne Rife of Des Moines East – wore Nelson down. Nelson had beaten Rife in the Eagle Grove Invitational that season.

"I always said if (Rife) knew any wrestling, he'd have killed me," Nelson said. "When I got all through, I thought it was really an accomplishment to win the state championship (after) wrestling guys that size. Paulson was about 220 at that time, so I thought it was a great accomplishment but when I got home, I went to bed and I didn't get out of bed for about four days. Every muscle in my body was strained from wrestling him."

Nelson knew how to offset size disadvantages in matches. He could hit a side roll on anyone and he seemed to have a working knowledge of physics in relation to a match.

"When it comes to wrestling, physical strength is only as good as how you use it in the form of leverage," Nelson said in an interview with the *Des Moines Register.* "I don't think I was any stronger, I couldn't do more push-ups than anybody else, I couldn't do any more chin-ups, I couldn't run any faster. The one thing I did have was that I knew how to use the strength I had in the form of leverage."

Bill Koll, Nelson's teammate and fellow three-time NCAA champion at Iowa State Teachers College, said Nelson was deadly with the side roll. "Once he got that, you were gone," Koll told the *Register.*

Nelson also knew what it was like to wrestle in the finals and finish third. In the 1940's, the loser of the championship match would have another contest to determine a true runner-up. Today, a state runner-up has a whole season to chew on that loss and draw motivation.

"I feel that you're so deflated. You get keyed up to win the match and then you lose, now you've got to come back and you're going to be a second- or third-place finisher," Nelson said. "You don't have the same motivation. I never had the same motivation to come back and wrestle for second or third place."

"When I was a sophomore, the guy that I wrestled (Eddie Laga of Osage), it was kind of a fluky thing because he beat me in a dual meet. He was ahead of me 10-0 going into the last period and I hit him with a side roll and pinned him. It put me in the finals against (Leonard) Rohrer, and I lost to Rohrer.

"I'd wrestled Rohrer in a dual meet once, and he handled me pretty handily in the tournament. Then I had to come back and wrestle a guy named Loren Redmond, and I didn't know anything about him at all. I wasn't really psyched up to wrestle, so I ended up getting beat again."

The 1944 tournament didn't help Nelson forget his finish in the previous season.

"The following year I wrestled Bob Wilson from Waterloo twice, beat him by a couple points one time and the second time I pinned him," Nelson said. "In the finals of the state meet he waxed me, beat me pretty badly."

There may have been losses while Nelson wrestled for Parsons, but the only beef he had was a steak. That was one trade-off of having a coach who was not one to get down on the mat and get deep in technique.

"Art never got out of his street clothes in the wrestling room. He'd come in and sit in the chair and he'd say to us, 'Go ahead and warm up,' and he'd select one of us to lead the kids in warming up," Nelson said. "He'd ask a wrestler to show a move he'd just done and we'd all work on that move.

"He took over the wrestling program during the war and he told the superintendent, 'I'm going to take these boys and I'll be the wrestling coach but, when we travel, I'm going to give them a steak dinner,'" Nelson said, adding that the superintendent's protests only made Parsons suggest finding a new coach.

The coach won that battle and the Eagles had their steaks. Nelson said Parsons felt the hard work and the sacrifice the Eagles put in all week deserved a reward after they got the job done. "He was always good to us," Nelson said.

Nelson said the 1945 Eagles might have produced the school's first team championship. Harold Bard, Nelson and his brother Dale were state champions and Lewis Larsen was runner-up, but the Eagles finished third – two points behind champion Waterloo West. It hurt to lose Jack Rudey at mid-season, Nelson said.

"We'd have won the state if he stayed. He transferred. His dad worked for the power company and he transferred to Denver. He was a two-time Colorado state champion," Nelson said.

The distance between Waterloo West and Eagle Grove in the 1945 state tournament was blocked by Osage with 22 points. Osage and Eagle Grove split two dual meets and Waterloo West beat the Eagles.

That 1945 tournament included future NCAA champions Dick Hauser and Lowell Lange of Waterloo West, Bill Smith of Council Bluffs Jefferson and Nelson. Smith advanced to win a gold medal in the 1952 Olympics.

Had he been given a choice about which weight to compete at, Nelson said he probably would have tried cutting weight, "because my brother was losing weight. He was a 105-pounder and he probably cut three-four pounds to make 105, but Parsons said, 'I want you at heavyweight, that's a lot of weight to lose and I don't want you to do that' so I didn't do it."

Nelson got started in wrestling while in elementary school.

"When I was in about the fifth or sixth grade, my older brother was four years older and he'd gone out for wrestling. He wrestled four years in high school and never made the (varsity)," Nelson said. "He'd come home and my mother would give us an old quilt. In our basement, we'd take that old quilt and lay it down for a mat. Then my brother would come back from practice and he'd take Dale and me down there and show us some wrestling moves."

Nelson's wrestling career is loaded with impressive accomplishments, but his varsity record started with a loss. That's a story several of the best wrestlers can tell.

"In ninth grade, I was out for wrestling but I wasn't on the (varsity). Walt Parsons got sick, so they asked me to fill in for him. I wrestled Louis Greco from Oelwein and he pinned me in 55 seconds," Nelson said. "All the way through high school I was called Greco because I'd wrestled Louis Greco and got pinned in 55 seconds. Years later, when I coached at Osage, we played a football game at Oelwein. I talked to the Oelwein coach about the whereabouts of Greco."

The coach pointed Nelson to a police officer assigned to the game. Nelson approached and the officer was Greco, who immediately recognized Nelson.

"One match, pinned me in 55 seconds, I hadn't seen him since," Nelson said. "Maybe he'd followed wrestling, I don't know, but I walked over and he immediately shook my hand and said, 'Bill Nelson.' I said, 'The last time I saw you it only lasted 55 seconds' and he started to laugh."

Nelson had an early understanding of the value of mental preparation.

"I don't think I wrestled a match I hadn't wrestled 100 times in my mind and never lost. I didn't say I won every match, but in my thinking I always would win in preparing myself," Nelson said. "In wrestling, if you have to take time to think, it's not there anymore. I tell kids, I told my kids too, that's why you practice, that's why you do repetition, repetition, repetition in the wrestling room."

Wrestlers are impatient by nature, because they want immediate payoff for all of their hard work. Nelson said he's kept a practice room philosophy of former University of Oklahoma coach Port Robertson that stresses patience in mastering a move. Nelson said he idolized Robertson.

"'I would tell him, 'Son, have you tried it 1,000 times?' He said, 'No sir.' Well, you go back and try it 1,000 times and if you can't do it then, we'll go to something else,'" Nelson said.

Nelson coached high school teams before moving to the University of Arizona as its wrestling coach. After he retired, the Nelsons moved to the

Des Moines area and he got involved in coaching once again. This time he was a volunteer assistant to Ken Estling at Bondurant-Farrar High School. The athletes had no idea that Nelson had a rich background in wrestling, but Estling did. Estling could not invite Nelson into the practice room fast enough.

"We had a bunch of kids that had the inate ability to be good, but they were willing to work hard to be good and they had two coaches that were very knowledgable (Estling and Craig Behnke)," Nelson said. "I would throw in things to improve on what they were doing, not to say, 'My way is the right way' because that's not true."

While Nelson was with the Bluejays, they won the Class 1-A dual-meet state championship in 1997 and the Class 1-A traditional title in 1998. Those wrestlers were the same age as Nelson was when he began to master the side roll.

"It was a feeling that I had. I always knew it was there, in other words I had confidence I could use it," Nelson said. "My variation was different than Harold Nichols's, my side roll was different than Dale Bahr – and he was a great side roller. The way I always worked it, I learned to do a side roll from my stomach, from my knees, from a half-stand and from a full stand. In order to side roll, all I did was clamp the arm and when I got ready to go I was gone. It was my bread-and-butter move. As a wrestler I was adequate on my feet but never great on my feet. If I had to get a takedown then I could get a takedown, but a lot of it was off counters I would say."

Even if he did not have success, Nelson was not about to quit the sport. His father, Harry, saw to that.

"My dad worked on the railroad and would come home from off the run, as we call them, and he'd walk past the gym. You never knew when you looked up that my dad was sitting at the front door of the gym watching practice," Nelson said. "His whole philosophy was if you go out for wrestling, you're staying the whole season. 'No matter what happens, good bad or indifferent, I never had a son that's going to be a quitter.'"

Harry Nelson tried to help his son have a chance to win a second NCAA championship in 1948, when Bill had to drop out of the tournament after getting two pins and a decision. It was feared the stomachache he had was either appendicitis or an ulcer, so it was recommended that he not wrestle. Bill said his dad offered to sign papers that would absolve Iowa State Teachers College of responsibility. The school's athletic director refused to budge and Nelson was done for the season. Having won the next two years, the decision might have cost Bill a chance to win four NCAA championships 44 years before that feat was accomplished by Pat Smith of Oklahoma State in 1994.

Bill said that night in 1948, it was a stomach cramp.

Along with the success, Bill experienced unimaginable pain in losing his brother, Dale. It was 1946, the night before Dale was to graduate, when the car he was riding in collided with a train at Holmes – about five miles west of Clarion. During the 1945-46 season, Dale made a sacrifice to allow a teammate a spot in the varsity lineup. Lewis Larsen won a state championship for Eagle Grove at 123 as Dale went to 118. Dale reached the state finals at 118 pounds, but lost, 4-3, to Hauser. Three months later, Hauser was among those at Dale's funeral service.

The day of the accident, Bill and his father were sitting together by the water plant in Eagle Grove. Bill said he looked up to see Dale driving a black Ford with no passengers.

"As he came toward us, I said, 'Dad, there is Dale,' and I kept yelling at him as he went by. He went by, he had his arm out the window and I said, 'Dad, what's wrong with Dale? He's pure white. He didn't hear me yelling at him.' At 6:30 that night he was dead. My dad never got over that," Bill said.

"I didn't plan on doing as well as I did, but I'm thankful I did."

Eddie Kline considered himself a pretty good candidate to play basketball at Mason City High School in the 1949-50 season.

It was the Mohawks' wrestling program that scored in the 1950's because Kline as a wrestler became a slam-dunk success.

"I could shoot the eyes out of the bucket, but I was too small (Kline is 5 feet 2 inches tall) and I was the sixth man at the time," Kline said. "They told me to go out for wrestling. I said, 'Well, do the wrestlers get in for basketball (games)?' and he said they do, so I went out. It was tough for me because I'd played basketball and I really loved that sport and I played really tough. I could dribble, I could handle the ball really well, I could pass but the best thing I could do was I could really shoot the ball."

Apparently Kline had another skill he never got to show on varsity. "You should see him handle a football. He's a real magician. If he'd have been a little bigger, he'd have made a great back," Mason City coach Howard Barker said to the *Des Moines Register's* Bill Bryson.

By the time Kline graduated, he became the Mohawks' first three-time state wrestling champion. Kline lost his first varsity match as a sophomore but never failed to have his arm raised the rest of the time.

"I didn't plan on doing as well as I did, but I'm thankful I did," Kline said.

"Eddie, as swift, smooth and savage as a panther on the mat, is a mild-looking little chap away from the arena. He wears glasses except when he's wrestling," Bryson reported in a 1953 "Prep of the Week" feature on Kline. "He's no doubt the smallest athlete ever to gain the distinction, this sturdy and agile senior who stretches 2 inches over 5 feet."

The glasses? "I'm far-sighted. That doesn't bother me when I'm wrestling," Kline told Bryson.

Mason City won its second straight team championship in 1950, and the Mohawks added to their cache of individual titles during the decade of the 1950's. Ken Meacham, Bill Oglesby, Roger Olson and Kline combined for six gold medals. Meacham was a two-time champion, having won in 1949 as well, and was to be inducted into the Iowa High School Athletic Association hall of fame at the 2011 tournament.

Waterloo schools continued to be a dominant force in the sport during the 1950's. Beginning in 1951 to 1959, either Waterloo West or Waterloo East won a combined seven team championships. Davenport won twice, including the last single-class tournament in 1956. Iowa's tournament became a two-class event the following season, and New Hampton and Cresco split the first two Class B titles.

Kline was one of three men to win a trio of state titles in the 1950's. Ron Gray of Eagle Grove and Tom Huff of Waterloo West were the other two. Individually, some future standout coaches won state titles during this time.

- Gary Kurdelmeier won two championships for Cresco just over 20 years before he led Iowa to its first NCAA championship.
- Bob Buzzard of Waterloo East won the first of his two state titles in 1958. Buzzard was an all-American at Iowa State and later a member of the Greco-Roman team in the 1968 Olympics. He was a successful high school coach in Oregon.
- Bill Dotson won two titles for Waterloo East, was an NCAA championship at Northern Iowa and coached in Iowa high schools before moving to the University of New Mexico. His son, Charlie, was a four-time state champion in New Mexico.
- Les Anderson of Clarion won in 1954. He was a two-time NCAA champion at Iowa State (the first national champion Harold Nichols had with the Cyclones), a head coach in high school and in college, but he was best known as Nichols' assistant where the two of them forged six NCAA team titles.
- Arlin Severson of New Hampton won a title in 1957, helping the Chickasaws to their first outright team championship. Severson led his alma mater to traditional and dual-team state championships in 1990 and 1993.

Kline seemed an unlikely champion. He tried wrestling for two weeks after his hoop dream ended, but decided not to continue. "I didn't take it serious, I just went out to get in to watch basketball," Kline said.

As a sophomore, Kline told Barker he was going to get a job. Barker saw something in the diminutive fireball and did a full-court press to get Kline in a wrestling uniform. "He said, 'Your job is wrestling, you're going to be a state champion, you're coming out for wrestling,'" Kline said. "I really didn't care for it, all that hard work and all that stuff. I said, 'That's not for me' and then it was like something snapped. I just guess I wanted to win. That losing wasn't for me."

He got all the losing he wanted in his first varsity match. Bob Kain of Algona scored a 7-5 victory at 95 pounds on Nov. 24, 1950. "That's a rarity but I had a good coach," Kline said. "He said, 'You're not going to make the same mistake you did the first match.' The first match I went out too hard. I was ahead of (Kain) and all of a sudden I ran out of gas. That I can remember just like yesterday. It sticks with you when you lose."

Kline said Barker told him of a pretty good way to make sure a second loss was not happening. "After I lost that first match he said, 'Will you listen to me?' I was really down," Kline said. "He said, 'You can be a three-time state champion like I told you, but you're going to have to pay the price.' I said, 'I'll pay the price.'

"From that day on, when I went to practice, man he really crucified me. I never complained. I wanted to pay the price, I wanted to win it. If he would have told me to run through the wall, I'd have done it. I was just that stubborn, a hard-headed kid. He was absolutely a good coach and I don't think I would have gone as far as I did without him."

Kline said he lived an in-training lifestyle year-round. He would run home after practice (he lived about four miles out of town) unless the temperature was at or below 32 degrees. Once at home, he paid close attention to his diet. Kline passed on greasy food, orange juice and milk. He chose to get his rest instead of hanging with his friends on the weekend.

There may have been a perception that Kline was cocky, but he said letting down his intensity level for a second was asking for bad trouble. "You can get caught and put on your back. For three years I never slept on my back because I didn't want to get on my back. I really was conscious of getting on my back," Kline said. "I think I got on there one time, when I wrestled (Don Bernard) from Iowa Falls. I sat out and turned and he pulled me straight back. I wasn't there a split second, I turned and they gave the guy two points…then I pinned him."

Kline said Barker was able to push the right buttons to get him ready to compete. Once, Kline claimed Barker used a slightly unusual method of inspiration. An opponent had an early 4-0 lead on Kline, and the Mohawk ace said it sounded to him as though Barker was cheering for the guy to get him fired up. It worked because Kline said he pinned the guy.

"He knew when I was ready and he knew when I wasn't," Kline said. "He could get me going so easy, and I think that's what made me a three-time state champion because without that I don't think I could have done it. Everybody was gunning for me and I knew that. That made me have to be tough."

Barker liked to tell his wrestlers there was always one person better than them. Kline found his one person right away, then became that one person in 54 consecutive matches. In a *Mason City Globe-Gazette's Cub Gazette* story after his third championship, Kline said Algona's Kain was the toughest guy he faced. Right behind were Bob Lane of Waverly and Don Bernard of Eagle Grove.

"Kline is the best boy we've ever had," Barker told the *Cub-Gazette* following the tough lightweight's final championship. "He hasn't even lost a takedown all year."

He would have received far less-glowing reviews if Kline followed through on a thought in the 1951 tournament.

"This was the first time I ever thought about losing on purpose because I was all alone. I was thinking about throwing the match, then Howard said, 'Are you ready to go?' and I said yes," Kline said. "He said, 'No you're not, you're going to lose because these other guys lost? Is that your intention?' I said no. He said, 'Yes it is.' He said, 'If you go out there and lose, I'll know why you lost and you'll regret it the rest of your life.' He whapped me on the butt and I went out there and took care of business."

Kline said he never gave quitting a second thought after that.

Following his high school career, Kline said he had a scholarship offer from Dave McCuskey to wrestle at the University of Iowa. Kline said he would come to Iowa, but first he was enlisting in the Army. McCuskey said the scholarship would be waiting for him. Kline said he never got a chance to wrestle for the Hawkeyes because he injured his back in the Pan American Games tryouts.

"I had a whizzer on the guy, we were on our feet and I had him on his toes. I went to throw him and he jerked back and I was done. I was paralyzed from the waist down for like 40 minutes, 50 minutes," Kline said.

Kline said he's thought at times about the "what-if?" of wrestling in college. Barker said in 1953 the son of a butcher could find a good place in the lowest weight class at the next level. "He would be a good college wrestler in the 123-pound class," Barker said.

If he would be anything in college like he was in high school, KIine would have lived the lifestyle. Many years later, Iowa coach Tom Brands talked about the need to adopt a champion's lifestyle in order to have a chance to be a champion. It would be music to Kline's ears if he heard that speech in practice.

"It's not just going out and practicing and then going home. You've got to practice, then when you go home you've got to eat the right foods, you've got to go to bed at a regular time. It's a whole different world. I tried to tell people this and they thought I was just being funny," Kline said. "I didn't want to eat greasy food, orange juice…I never drank milk. My dad kept after me why I don't eat."

Nearly 60 years after he wrestled his way into the upper echelon of the state's list of champions, Kline has not ceased being competitive. He is a bowler who's not fond of losing a match on the alleys. Look at him and you get the idea he just might be able to out-work a lot of people as well as put on a clinic dealing with mental and physical toughness.

Why was he always on the offensive? Kline said one of Barker's favorite lines was to remind his wrestlers that there was someone better than them…perhaps in the next match.

The state wrestling tournament underwent a huge change during the 1950's as two team championships were up for grabs in 1957. The smallest 32 teams were grouped into Class B. There was seeding – an aspect today's coaches have been wanting to be employed – to put the eight wrestlers in each weight class in a match order. At this time there were 11 weight classes.

The state's first Class B champion was 95-pounder Larry Severson of New Hampton, who handed a 4-0 loss to Bill Block of Maquoketa. That started a run of New Hampton gold as Jim Carr won at 103 and Severson's brother, Arlin, took the 112-pound crown. The Chickasaws were not finished. Bob Duvall won the 165-pound championship.

Larry Severson's victory was the first state championship by a New Hampton wrestler since Sam Kramer won at 129 pounds in 1941. Merle Roths also won that night, taking the 105-pound division. That second class thing must have seemed like an excellent idea to New Hampton's fans. Beginning in 1957, they cheered on six individual champions and two Class B team titlists.

Simon Roberts of Davenport became the state's first African-American state wrestling champion in 1954. Roberts upset two-time champion Ron Gray of Eagle Grove, 3-1, in the 133-pound finals. They would meet again in college to decide the 147-pound championship at the 1957 NCAA tournament. Roberts won that match as well, becoming the first black NCAA champion.

One of the better state tournament rivalries got started in the 1959 event as Don Henry of Cresco beat Gordon Hassman of New Hampton, 2-0, in the Class B 103-pound match. Hassman turned the tables in the 120-pound finale in 1960, getting a jury decision victory over Henry. According to the *New Hampton Economist,* Hassman and Henry had 10 high school meetings including the 1960 finals. Hassman won five, Henry won three and there were two draws.

The *Economist* also reported that Henry was a "double" second cousin of Waterloo East coach Dave Natvig, who was a state champion in 1933 and 1934 at New Hampton. Natvig's teammate was Hassman's dad, Paul, a state champion in 1933 for the Chickasaws.

It did not bode well for the wrestler losing in the finals of the state tournament between 1950 and 1952. Thirteen of the 33 losers in those championship bouts were beaten in the consolation finals and placed third. Also, there were six championship matches determined by a referee's decision between 1950 and 1959.

"I didn't really know until it happened, what a kind of a history-making event that was."

Ron Gray did not strike people as state wrestling champion material when he was growing up outside of Eagle Grove.

Simon Roberts had to find something to do as a sophomore at Davenport High School after he was cut from the basketball team.

They were two guys from different worlds of Iowa who took differing routes to the sport of wrestling. They came together twice and made wrestling history, once at the state level and once on the national scale. Gray was the kid who grew up on a farm 5 miles northeast of Eagle Grove and went to country school prior to starting high school. Roberts grew up in what would now be considered the inner-city of Davenport. His high school was the biggest in the state. In the 1950's it was home to some top athletes who either wrestled for coach Jim Fox or played basketball for coach Paul Moon.

Gray didn't have the physical presence that would make someone think he was a can't-miss champion on the wrestling mat. Not even some family members gave him an endorsement early on.

"No, even though I thought he was good. He was a good wrestler, but I wouldn't have believed that (championship)," said Phyllis Cooper, Gray's sister. "I don't know how exactly I thought that, but my older two brothers were pretty good wrestlers too, and I just thought they never made it so I didn't think he ever would. He had big determination."

Betty McCart, another sister of Gray, added, "Gosh, he was little and hadn't had as much experience, but he turned out really good."

Gray didn't need the imposing build to shine.

"I don't know if there is such a thing as a natural, like in the movie, but it just was so easy for me. I don't know what it was," Gray said. "It wasn't that I knew a lot of moves specifically, my body just kind of said, 'Move here and this is the place you ought to be.' It just seemed so damned easy for me, and I never, never ran out of gas."

He could have run out of luck before he got to the 1952 state meet in Mason City. Gray was absent from school four days before the district tournament because he had the measles. He was able to compete, but lost to Don Beery of Mason City, 3-0, in the semifinals. In the wrestle-back, Gray won his way to state as a runner-up.

Bill Bryson of the *Des Moines Register* painted a wonderful description of Gray after the "cat-quick farm boy" won his third state championship in 1955: "Gray is a slender, mild-looking youngster in street clothes, a perfect model for a choirboy. Get him into those golden wrestling trunks, though, and he's a picture of controlled fury."

Roberts was a picture of some disappointment as a sophomore in Davenport in the 1951-52 school year, the same time Gray won his first state championship. Roberts had visions of playing for Moon. That was big because Davenport was so successful that a lot of guys wanted to play for Moon. Roberts was cut from the squad.

"I'd have to say the guy (who) was really instrumental in me going out for wrestling was Henry "Hank" Philmon, who placed second in state (in 1952)," Roberts said. "There was another gentleman there, Jerry Taggart, we were all neighborhood buddies. He was on the wrestling team, he was a good wrestler. At that time Davenport had a runner-up finish, Hank's team came in second two years before we won it in 1954. I think the culture was starting to develop around the wrestling program. Jim Fox came there in 1948, so the combination of the culture and the good coaching that came with that, I think I was just the benefactor of all those things coming together."

The wrestling bug bit Gray as he drew closer to graduating from Dayton Township country school in eighth grade. After school, he did chores on the family's 200-acre tenant farm and then accompanied his father on the trip into town to pick up his brothers, Bob and Bill, at wrestling practice. Ron said he would try to sneak in a workout when possible.

Not that he lacked for workouts at home. There were cows to milk, pigs and chickens to tend to. His weight-lifting consisted of shoveling manure. There was the rope hung from a windmill that he could climb. In the summer there were hay bales to throw.

"Every time I would go by that to do chores or to come in after milking the cows or going out to feed the pigs, I would climb that rope," Ron said. "I'm going to guess it was 30-40 feet high and I would not use any legs, just my arms. I think farming naturally develops some pretty good muscles. It sounds like bragging, but I think I was pretty damn strong."

So were his brothers. They were doing the same chores, plus they were tangling with teammates every day in wrestling season.

"My brother Bill was pretty damn tough and he used to kick my ass all the time. My older brother, Bob, in honesty I would have to say was just a good high school wrestler. Bill was tougher than (heck), but Bill's problem was when he got into big matches, he had problems. But he would always kick my ass," Ron said.

Many of the battles started because Bill tried to get his baby brother to milk his cows as well as the ones Ron was to do anyway. "Pretty soon we were going at it, he would beat the (crap) out of me and then I'd be so pissed off, I wouldn't milk his cows for nothing. Then my brother Bob would be the one who ended up milking his own and then Bill's. That happened quite frequently."

All three Gray boys qualified for the 1953 state tournament. Bob, who missed the 1952 tournament because of measles, lost in the first round and Bill did not get to compete because of an injury. Bob and Bill were team captains for the 1952-53 season. Bill had a tough-luck wrestling career. He placed fourth at state as a freshman, but was bothered by a dislocated elbow, measles and a back injury in his remaining years. In 1953, Bill Gray had to watch Bill Clement of Newton win the 145-pound state championship. Bill had beaten Clement during the regular season.

Dave Harty, former assistant executive director of the Iowa High School Athletic Association, said Bill Gray might have been his brother's equal in making things happen on a mat. Eagle Grove High School's yearbook, *The Eaglet,* said of Bill Gray in 1952, "This year, as in previous years, Bill was a tremendous crowd pleaser. His beautiful maneuvers often times left the crowd gasping."

"I don't know why brother Bill wasn't a champion. I swear he could have been, but maybe he didn't take it as seriously as Ron did," Phyllis Cooper said.

All of the brotherly scuffling seemed to get Ron ready for the high school scene. Ron also got a fast lesson in the aggressiveness of the sport. The Eagle Grove Invitational, Iowa's oldest regular-season tournament, was one of Ron's first varsity outings. He remembered a match against eventual winner Gary Green of Britt.

"I was kind of raw and green at the beginning, and if I remember right, the Eagle Grove Invitational was one of the first times I wrestled in high school. I can remember wrestling Green. We got on the mat, the referee said, 'Wrestle' and he smacked me hard as hell in the face. I thought, 'What the hell, this is not wrestling, you're not supposed to be doing that.' By that time he had me down on the mat. No one had ever done that to me. I thought wrestling was a fun, polite game."

Roberts said he wasn't allowed time to mope about the end of playing basketball. "I think I would have been crushed if it hadn't been for guys like Hank Philmon and Jerry Taggart. There were a couple of other guys who were neighborhood buddies that went out for wrestling," Roberts said. "If it hadn't been for their influence and their being role models that I could look up to, I might have been crushed. It might have been a life-changing experience for me, but I just transitioned right from basketball into the wrestling and it worked out really well."

Ron took some losses as a freshman in the 1951-52 season, but he avenged one of them in the state finals at Mason City, beating Beery, 6-5, for the 103-pound state championship. Ron remembered Berry as a challenging opponent. "He was real tall, I was short, 103 pounds. I could hardly touch his forehead," Ron said.

Harty said he remembered Mason City coach Howard Barker discussing Ron with Eagle Grove coach Ray Stone. Barker asked Stone what he was feeding Ron, Harty recalled. "'I don't know, but I tell you one thing I don't spoil it with my good coaching. I just let him go.'" Harty remembered Stone saying.

Roberts did not make the trip to Mason City. He was moved to varsity during the season, but Roberts was the only Davenport wrestler not to qualify for the state meet. Roberts said he read accounts of the tournament in the newspaper and waited for Hank to come home. Philmon, who is black, finished second at 145 pounds in that tournament.

Davenport had another opportunity to crown the first black state champion in 1953, but Jim McCray dropped a 4-2 decision to Jerry Salmon of Newton at 138 pounds.

Victories over Charles Huff of Waterloo West and Jim Wallace of Davenport put Ron in the 1952 finals for a rematch with Berry. It was also the start of a common occurrence up to 1959, seeing a Huff boy in the tournament. Charles was the first of four brothers to compete at state.

Eagle Grove's *The Eaglet,* noted Ron's place in program history: "Ronnie proved to be the sensation of the year. He is the first freshman in the history of Eagle Grove High School to win a state championship."

Ron said that first title changed his act. "I was kind of a cocky little shit my freshman year in high school, kind of a smartass," he said. "After that first state title, I got pretty humble. I never wanted to brag about myself, my personality changed. I really didn't like being a cocky smartass."

Betty McCart said there was no room for attitude on the farm. "Our dad didn't bring us up to brag, we were what we were and that was it. You didn't brag about it," she said.

According to Harty, Ron could have boasted about his technical skill on the mat.

"I look back and we all know that Dan Gable was a great wrestler, but in my time Ron Gray was it, Ron Gray was the epitome that most people wanted to be like," said Harty, who grew up in Iowa Falls and wrestled Ron in high school. "Ron was a good single-leg man, very good single-leg man, but what I always remember about Ron so much was he was quick and when he hit you, he hit you so low that you had nothing to defend him with. Very few guys could take him down."

The Eagle Grove yearbook painted a bright future for Ron: "Ronnie should be unbeatable in his remaining three years of wrestling."

Those wins in the 1952 state meet started Ron's undefeated streak that would annex a second championship and reach 48 matches before Roberts scored a 3-1 upset in the 133-pound championship in 1954. Roberts became Iowa's first black state wrestling champion.

In 1953, Roberts went to state in Cedar Falls but did not place. Ron won his second state championship with a 6-2 victory over Dick Heaton of Waterloo East at 120 pounds. Ron said he was not caught up in the numbers he was building.

"I was pretty naïve, just a farm kid. The furthest I had been away was Minnesota and that was just over the line," Ron said. "I just kind of took it in stride, I didn't sit around thinking about, 'Holy crap, I might be able to be a three- or four-time state champion and go on to college.'"

That trip to Cedar Falls made Roberts highly focused on another trip to state for his senior year. Unlike today, where wrestlers from distant points in the state see each other in freestyle tournaments or in regular-season tournaments, Ron and Roberts knew little about each other beyond skin pigmentation.

"I knew he had been a state champion, I knew he was a good wrestler, but I'd never seen him wrestle. I didn't watch him during the preliminary bouts," Roberts said.

One part of the match Roberts said he'll never forget took place before the first whistle. It was a classic example of the psychological impact Fox could make on one of his athletes. "Jim said to me, 'There are two people in this building who think you can win. That's you and me,'" Roberts said.

In small-town Iowa in 1954, information was not always given with sportsmanship or citizenship as the backbone.

"I'll tell you what I knew, I knew he was black. Living in a town like Eagle Grove, where blacks weren't even allowed to stay overnight as in many communities, I kept hearing these stories how they stunk, they were slippery and you couldn't hold on to them," Gray said. "I'm probably making excuses, but I ended up beating myself. I out-psyched myself against him. I'm not saying he wasn't a good wrestler because he was. I just had so many people that wrestled me and (wrestled) Simon, at least seven people came up to me afterwards and say, 'How in the hell did Simon Roberts beat you?' That's the first time I had ever wrestled a black person, and I mentally didn't have my head screwed on. But the bottom line is he beat me. Period."

Roberts got a takedown with 10 seconds left in regulation for a 3-1 victory. Roberts said he felt more relaxed preparing to face Ron than he did any other opponent. He's not sure why, but Roberts knew he was the underdog.

"What happened was it was tied, and I don't know why he did it but he tried to do a lateral drop on me," Roberts said. "I saw it coming and stepped across and his arm ended up being barred. I just kind of flattened out, turned him over and he had to wiggle to get out so I would not score any back points. That's the way the match ended. I just don't know why he tried that lateral drop because he hadn't tried it before."

Roberts said he can't remember thinking a state championship was a huge deal. "In some ways everything that developed in me happened without a great deal of thought on my part. The skills developed, the winning attitude was probably developed more by my coaches and some of my teammates. It was just one of those things that all of that took a hold of me and I just moved," Roberts said.

The initial accounts of the 1954 tournament did not mention Roberts' victory in terms other than a two-time champion being upset. It was only in follow-up stories that Roberts was mentioned as the state's first wrestling champion of color.

"I didn't really know until it happened, what a kind of a history-making event that was. It really didn't dawn on me until a few weeks after that it was a significant achievement in the sport of wrestling," Roberts said.

It was many years later – after Roberts beat Ron for the 147-pound NCAA title in 1957 and became the first black NCAA champion - when Roberts learned he had given others hope.

"I had good press coverage, the neighborhood, the black community in particular, there was a pride that they had that I had accomplished (the title)," Roberts said. "Whether I was that aware of that at the time I don't know, but I think I had Bobby Douglas tell me this: He said my winning a state championship and then the national championship was a real motivating factor for him. You just never know who's going to be looking, who's going to try to emulate what you're doing. It just really surprised me that he said that's one of the things he points to when he talks about his success."

Douglas was the first black state champion in Ohio, winning at 112 pounds in 1959 for Bridgeport High School. He also became the first black wrestler to compete in the Olympics for the United States, the first to captain an Olympic wrestling squad and the first black head coach of an NCAA Division I program. Douglas said his high school coach was forward-thinking enough to have pictures and stories about Roberts posted in the practice room.

Douglas coached 33 seasons with stops at Cal-Santa Barbara, Arizona State and Iowa State. He had a career 427-168-9 record, including a 204-75-3 mark in 14 seasons at Iowa State.

Harty said Roberts helped the sport grow in Iowa's high schools with his victory.

"It was good for the sport. The nice part of it was it happened with a great kid. Simon Roberts is a great person, a wonderful person, a great friend, a gentleman," Harty said. "At that moment, he deserved to be it because he outscored (Gray). I think it made a lot of difference, breaking that barrier, and it brought a lot more kids in. I believe."

Pete Middleton, who was one of four blacks who won state championships for Waterloo East in 1964, said Roberts made a lasting impact in the state with his state championship.

"It was based on his being able to wrestle that in Waterloo, some of the men with the Chamber of Commerce forced the high schools to bring them on," Middleton said. "I think Bob Siddens and (Dave) Natvig had a lot to do with that too. The fact that had occurred was very important to wrestling."

Ron became one of the bigger early recruits for Iowa State coach Harold Nichols, and he became a consistent winner. He was a two-time

NCAA champion, and the only thing keeping him from matching the gold medal take of his high school career was Roberts. On that night Roberts was as relaxed as ever, despite being an underdog.

"The thing I remember prior to the match out in (Pittsburgh) was he had a hell of a match with Werner Holzer of Illinois. Ron beat him 10-8, some kind of wild match," Roberts said. "When I was watching that match – I didn't watch the whole thing, but the parts I saw - I thought, 'How in the world am I going to stay with this guy?' because he was so smooth."

Roberts said he was ready for anything, including overtime, because of his time in the Iowa practice room under coach Dave McCuskey. "It's impossible not to be in shape if you were on Dave McCuskey's wrestling team," Roberts said.

Ron would have stayed home and worked on the farm if his dad had the deciding vote. Ron said his dad went to work after eighth grade, so he was not big on continuing the education even if Harold Nichols was offering a full-ride scholarship to Iowa State.

"When Harold Nichols came up to talk to me, that was the first time I started thinking, 'Maybe I should go to college,'" Ron said. "I think dad wanted me to stay on the farm and work. I didn't like that. One thing I knew was that if I went away to college, I was not going to flunk out.

"He was just getting started at Iowa State, and Iowa State prior to that had not been doing too much nationally. I was recruited by three schools – Iowa, Iowa State and either Oklahoma State or Oklahoma."

Nichols got a strong-willed young man who let his own skills tell him whether or not he'd use various moves.

"I know in high school coach Stone would show moves and everyone would watch. As far as going back and working on them, it just seemed like I didn't have to work on them," Gray said. "What I did seemed so natural and so easy that when I tried the moves I was supposed to work on, a lot of them didn't seem that natural and I didn't use them. I just did what I felt I should do. I just never even thought about losing, it wasn't in my mind. It wasn't because of my determination or something, I just didn't think anyone was going to beat me."

Ron and Roberts could have been college teammates. Ron's friend was Don Nelson, the brother of Eagle Grove state champion Bill Nelson. "I think we both kind of preferred to go to Iowa, and McCuskey invited us down. Nichols had come up a couple times to the farm and we talked. I didn't have any money and I knew my dad was not capable of helping me get through college," Ron said.

"When we went down to Iowa, that was probably my first choice, but I kept trying to talk to McCuskey about how I needed money. All he would say was, 'Ron, we'll take care of you' and to McCuskey that meant a full ride, but he would never come out and exactly say this is what we'll give you, this is what it costs. Nichols came out with paper and pencil. He said this is what it costs to go to Iowa State – your tuition, room, board, books – and laid it on the line that I wouldn't have to pay for any of that. I had his word." Ron said

Several years after their two battles, Roberts remembered Ron for one particularly admirable quality.

"That was one thing that always impressed me with Ron, he was always a gentleman. There was never any kind of hint that my being black and his being white made any difference at all," Roberts said. "He always would congratulate me on the mat and then also after we got back in the locker room. I can't remember whether it was after the state tournament or the nationals, he was sure to come over and shake my hand again. Just a super gentleman, just a super guy."

Roberts said he found such sportsmanship amazing, but it was not because of race.

"It surprised me because he was probably one of the greatest wrestlers ever to step on the mat in the state of Iowa, maybe even nationally, I don't know, but he was so humble. It was really kind of a shock."

"It wasn't one button fits all except for the respect that we developed for this guy."

Bob Siddens had his first public wrestling match as part of a pro rasslin' show at the auditorium that was across the street from the fire station in downtown Council Bluffs.

When he coached the amateur form of wrestling, Siddens made bunches of tough-minded but not always glass-smooth kids the show in the state of Iowa. Siddens would have made a poor carnival barker or Michael Buffer-like announcer because he was the mild-mannered, soft-spoken man who taught like crazy and led Waterloo West to 11 state championships between 1951 and 1977.

The son of a baker rose to the top echelon of coaching in the state with a 334-30-4 dual meet record that included one season at Eagle Grove and 27 at Waterloo West. Siddens led West to a then-state record 88 consecutive wins between the 1968-69 season and the 1975-76 campaign. He lost his first meet as head coach when Mason City beat Eagle Grove, 24-8, but the Siddens Era at West began with a 27-12 victory over Cresco. After teaching countless kids to wrestle from the top of their head to the tips of their toes and sprinkling in some nuances for each kid, Siddens is revered like few who are called coach have been, are or will be.

"It wasn't one button fits all except for the respect that we developed for this guy," said Dan Gable, an undefeated three-time state champion for West, a two-time NCAA champion at Iowa State and head coach at Iowa who led the Hawkeyes to 15 NCAA team titles.

Gable's given name is Danny Mack Gable. He is the best-known wrestler to wear West's black and old rose colors. To Siddens he's always been "Daniel."

"Daniel was probably one of the best wrestlers I ever had, but he probably wasn't the toughest. I still think of him as this little red-headed crewcut in my wrestling room," Siddens said. "I just think the world of Daniel, but I think the world of all of my wrestlers."

Bill Andrew was one of 39 men who won state titles under Siddens. Andrew got into coaching at Cardinal of Eldon and Osage, trying to emulate his mentor. He had a thought of why Siddens had such success.

"I think it's just that the way coach Siddens came across to coach everybody and to have the care for everybody. I think that's what made him special," Andrew said. "He just had that fatherly figure that you wanted to win for that guy because you knew he cared about you. You weren't just a wrestler, you were a person. I was just very blessed to have that gentleman who was such a big part of my life and still is."

The way Siddens culled success out of the Wahawks seemed unusual at the time. The coaches of the day were often shouting and demonstrative. Siddens drew attention from *Waterloo Courier* sports editor Russ L. Smith's keyboard because of his unusual animation in the 1977 state tournament when Craig Garvin's late rally secured a gold medal for Garvin and the last of West's 11 team titles under Siddens. As Garvin made the move, Siddens was jumping up and down, according to Smith's account.

"There are a lot of things that I didn't see in myself that people have said now. I guess it was just my personality. I was excited but I kept it more inside than let it go outside," Siddens said.

Siddens remembered his first wrestling match at the age of five. His opponent was twin brother Chuck and the setting was the Broadway Athletic Club in Council Bluffs, located across the street from the fire station, where the pro wrestling shows were staged. The mat had ropes around it. Siddens' father, Charles, was a fan of boxing and those wrestling cards and he knew the Council Bluffs promoter.

"(Dad) came home one day and it as the first time I ever got some gym shorts and some tennis shoes. Chuck and I got into this big ring in this big auditorium across from the fire department. We ended up starting the wrestling. We got in for about 2-3 minutes and wrestled on this mat."

Wrestling has been a part of Siddens' life for most of eight decades, but he thought there was a time he would hang up the whistle. Siddens served as athletic director at West for a time, but he had visions of being Superintendent Siddens or Principal Siddens. "I didn't think I would coach as long as I did. I had my degree in educational administration, I thought I'd end up being a principal or superintendent, but everything was so hunky dory and everything went so well that I kept coaching," Siddens said.

That was an understatement moment from Siddens' life in wrestling. Another was how he decided not to pursue an interest in going to the University of Iowa to become a dentist. Siddens attended Fort Dodge Junior College and played football for a year after graduating from Eagle Grove. Buck "Clyde" Starbeck and Dave McCuskey, the football coach and the wrestling coach at Iowa State Teachers College came through Fort Dodge. They asked Siddens if he'd like to attend. Siddens thought he could attend ISTC, play football and wrestle and then go to Iowa for dental school.

"I got sidetracked with the football and the wrestling," Siddens said. "I always say getting sidetracked was probably the best thing that ever happened to me. Didn't make a lot of money, but I ended up having some fine young lads that made me look like a respectable coach."

Siddens, who moved to Eagle Grove with his family prior to seventh grade, said the first high school wrestling meet he attended was believed to be a district tournament in Fort Dodge. Siddens hitchhiked there and remembered the Dodgers' mat had ropes around it just as the ring in Council Bluffs had. Bill Koll was there for Fort Dodge. Leon "Champ" Martin was there for Eagle Grove.

"The guy that I went over to watch was Champ Martin. Champ was one of my heroes. That probably was the very beginning of my involvement in high school wrestling," Siddens said.

In order to stay close to his favorite wrestlers and keep learning the sport, Siddens and his brother were managers for Eagle Grove coach Les Cottrill. "Basically how our wrestling came about was after practice was over, we'd go in and roll around like a couple of teddy bears," Siddens said.

Bob Siddens became a four-time state qualifier who placed second twice. He participated in the 1940 state meet as a freshman at 85 pounds – the last year for that weight class – and remembered wrestling in the 1942 state meet on a stage at Waterloo West High School. Siddens said he was talked into wrestling at 85 as a freshman, even though he had beaten eventual 95-pound state champion Grant Hunter of Council Bluffs Lincoln twice during the regular season.

"The thing that hurt me more than anything else when I didn't win state was because I always felt I let my dad down. That always bothered me. I was very close to my dad," Siddens said.

The Siddens twins enlisted in the Air Force in 1943, not long after their brother Jack was killed in action in the Aleutian Islands. "He was a colonel in the infantry. He was training at Fort Ord in California to go fight Rommel in Africa, so they sent the 17th Infantry to the Aleutians," Siddens said.

Jack Siddens was in school at Iowa at the time Nile Kinnick was there and both were Phi Beta Kappa honorees, Bob Siddens said. After they completed military service, Jack and Kinnick were going to attend law school at Iowa, Siddens said, but both died. Bob Siddens said he was training as a radio gunner on the B-17 and B-24 aircraft. He was preparing to be deployed overseas, but the atomic bomb was dropped on Hiroshima and the war was ending. Siddens said he got to play some football in Houston, playing running guard and linebacker at 160-170 pounds for the Ellington Field Ramblers.

Six years after placing second at 145 pounds, Siddens came back to Eagle Grove to begin his coaching career. He taught world history and coached wrestling at the high school and was football coach at Eagle Grove Junior College. Tom Chelesvig in 1950 became the first state champion Siddens coached. Chelesvig's son, Bart, became the first state champion for Webster City High School 35 years later.

Siddens stayed there one season. Unbeknownst to him, Siddens was being watched as the possible next coach at Waterloo West. Roy Jarrard, who had earlier coached at Eagle Grove, wanted to resign at West, and Siddens said he assumed an Iowa State Teachers College star such as Gerry "Germ" Leeman or Bill Koll would get the job. When Siddens took some Eagle Grove wrestlers to a tournament at the Waterloo YMCA in 1950, Don Blau, a West assistant coach, talked to him about the Wahawk mat job.

"I finally found out later that (former Waterloo West coach) Finn Eriksen took a very nice liking to me. He refereed some of my matches when I wrestled at Iowa State Teachers. I wasn't going to leave Eagle Grove because I really loved the place and all of a sudden I thought, 'My goodness, I shouldn't pass up an opportunity to go to West Waterloo,'" Siddens said. "I was playing golf at Eagle Grove one Sunday afternoon, and that's when the superintendents did all of the hiring. A guy by the name of Jack Logan was the superintendent of Waterloo, so he came in on a Sunday afternoon and my wife called and said Mr. Logan wanted to talk to me. I was really dumbfounded. He was very nice. He said, 'Bob, it's your job if you want it.' They weren't doing real well at that time, they had kind of slipped down. (Logan) called on Monday at noon and I said I was going to take it."

Siddens led West to its sixth team championship in his first season, despite not having an individual champion. The Wahawks repeated in 1952 as they had three qualifiers and came home with two champions – Harlan Jenkinson and John Winder – and runner-up Charles Huff. As the individual winners grew, so did the team honors. Gable said Siddens was a guidance counselor, so he knew his wrestlers, how they ticked and how he could hit the right chords with them. "Did he know how to treat the team? Yes, but did he know how to treat the individuals? Yes," Gable said.

Siddens had a name for his ability to tap into some hidden talent.

"I always said when I put on a clinic or a seminar, 'Coaching is a snowjob, but it's a sincere snowjob,'" Siddens said.

Don Huff was a two-time state champion under Siddens and later his assistant for 10 years before replacing him as head coach. In doing interviews for a book on Siddens, Huff heard stories dealing with the Siddens snowjob.

"He was very good at that, and he would do it without you even knowing it," Huff said. "Dale Anderson said Siddens told him as a senior in high school that Anderson would be a national champion."

Anderson, a two-time state champion for the Wahawks, won two NCAA championships at Michigan State.

"(Siddens) could get mad, but he didn't very often," Huff said. "He was pretty special with his I guess I call it psychology, but I think it was just him being him."

It was long before wrestling in the spring and summer became the norm, but Huff said guys worked overtime because they wanted to be the ones who helped bring home championships to West High.

"All of our friends in high school, we didn't have organized programs in the summer time, but we spent a lot of time in everybody's yard wrestling," Huff said. "Going to the swimming pool, we'd wrestle in the water and out on the grass and every place. It was pretty much ingrained in us and I think Siddens had a lot to do with that."

Success in the sport was more than just hitting more scoring holds than an opponent, Siddens said. "I'm a strong believer of the subconscious mind. That subconscious mind gets involved, the adrenaline gets involved and when that adrenaline gets involved, then you're going to beat somebody," he said.

Huff said coaching with Siddens was a great time he wished would have lingered.

"It was just a blast. It was great actually and what he said to me was,

'I'll coach the group and you do the individual coaching' which basically meant that I wrestled with the kids. I was pretty young then and I could wrestle pretty hard," Huff said. "He still got on the mat too, but that's the way he set it up. I was fine with that because I still enjoyed wrestling and had a lot of tough guys to wrestle with. I think maybe I picked up some of his characteristics. I didn't want him to quit when he retired. I wished he would have kept right on going, but he felt it was time for him to stop."

Siddens enjoyed success without spending considerable time sketching a plan for the day's drills, Huff said.

"A lot of people have asked me through the years what made him such a good coach, and I would tell them he never took a practice plan with him to the wrestling room, he didn't have a warmup. He just told the guys and they knew that when he came in the room they needed to be warmed up. This went clear back to his first year because I had one of the guys tell me the same thing."

Siddens might not want to get down on the mat to show technique these days, but he does remain active. Siddens likes to swim laps every chance he gets. To celebrate his 80th birthday, Siddens swam 80 laps that day.

Gable remembered being beached briefly by Siddens.

"He doesn't remember this, but I remember it. One time during my sophomore year when I was struggling with the weight, he walked over and told me to quit feeling sorry for myself and he picked me up," Gable said. "At that time I had a sweatshirt on and sweat pants. There were these hooks that we had jump ropes on. He put the sweatshirt right on that hook, I'm just dangling, a 95-pounder dangling from the wall. I don't know if anybody was laughing either. It wasn't a joke, it was that I needed to be straightened up a little bit. Then he picked me up and put me down. I wasn't humiliated, it just stuck with me. He basically told me to quit feeling sorry for myself and to make the moves I needed to make."

Siddens was asked about doing that. He thought one of the wrestlers had put Gable on the hook.

Gable said Siddens could handle him because he had experienced so many different personalities and wrestling styles prior to his arrival. "He was able to mix that melting pot there and be able to have a good team because of it," Gable said.

"Right away he knew when I came in that there was a void in one weight class, and the void was the smallest weight class. That was probably not my weight class, I was probably a little bigger, but he could tell already,

'I've got a kid that's disciplined, dedicated, hard-workin', big eyes.' He came up and whispered in my ear after practice, he said, 'Hey, you make this weight, you're on the team.'"

Short of the state meet, the biggest date on West's schedule was the Waterloo East meet. Those two schools have a combined 25 team championships and total 11 second-place finishes. Individually, the two schools boast 143 state titles – a state-best 87 by West, 56 for East which ranks No. 3. The series might have lost some zest in recent years, but it used to be the hottest ticket in town. Over 2,000 fans would cram into the gymnasium.

"The *Waterloo Courier* did a whale of a job. Russ Smith was awesome at that, he came down to our wrestling room and did interviews of the highlight matches. Russ had a lot to do with that I think," said East graduate Bob Buzzard.

Guys from each school were known to infiltrate tryouts for the meet in an attempt to get that morsel of scouting information that would turn the meet in one's favor. One night, the East-West meet had a group called the Disciples of Peace on hand, wound up having more than the scheduled bouts and Siddens sustained a head wound.

"Reece Wilson took an East High kid down and wanted to let him up, but the kid wouldn't come up so he swung around and took a pancake and put him down. Hell broke loose. The Disciples of Peace were trying to keep it cool, but there was a group of people in the stands that wanted to make the Disciples of Peace look bad," Siddens recalled. "When Reece Wilson pancaked this guy and went down, they came out of the stands and I got hit over the head with a chair. I had about 12 stitches in my head. My wife thought I got stabbed. It wasn't a racist thing, it was between the Disciples of Peace, who were trying to cool things off, and this other group."

Siddens said he remembered being asked if he wanted to sue anyone. He declined, saying he was just in the wrong place at the wrong time.

Seven weeks after he led West to the Class 3-A championship in the 1977 state tournament and its 14th undefeated dual-meet season, Siddens turned in his resignation from coaching wrestling at West. It was a boxed short story on page 1 of the *Waterloo Courier*.

"I have mixed feelings (about retiring) because I've enjoyed every minute of it," Siddens told Smith in a column for the following afternoon's paper. "I know I could have been enthusiastic next year."

West had talented underclassmen such as Roger DeSart, Dave Morkel and Garvin coming back from the 1976-77 squad, which Siddens said made the decision to step down difficult. "There always are going to be some good wrestlers to leave behind, and 27 years is a long time," Siddens said.

These days he's in the right place around birthday time because several of his former wrestlers drop by a local restaurant, usually at lunch time, to salute him and to catch up with each other. Those who couldn't drop in, such as Stanford University Athletic Director Bob Bowlsby, called the coach with their best wishes. Siddens also attends wrestling meets frequently, often seeing more friends and acquaintances than he does matches, and he keeps tabs on his six children and 14 grandchildren. Seeing those who wrestled for him is a special time for Siddens.

"I was just fortunate to have some fine young lads," Siddens said. "Being 85 and being an old has-been or was-been, it feels good to come in contact with those guys."

"Man, this was all worth it."

What is the difference between first and second place in a state wrestling tournament? The simple answer is that first comes with a better-looking medal.

Bob Buzzard of Waterloo East knows the margin can be measured at breakfast time.

Buzzard won Class A championships in 1958 and 1960. He finished second in 1959. The morning after in 1958, Buzzard ate well. The morning after in 1959, Buzzard's father had something else cooking.

The Buzzard name became known because future three-time state champion Dan Gable of Waterloo West worked out with Bob. Their practice in Gable's basement – on a mat that used to be in Buzzard's yard - before Gable went to Iowa State became legendary because Buzzard showed Gable that someone could get worked over like that. That was a battle of future 149.5-pounders in the 1972 Olympics. Gable was a gold medalist in freestyle, but Buzzard did not place in Greco-Roman.

In 1958, Buzzard was a 95-pound sophomore who faced Larry Bewley of Davenport High School in the finals. Buzzard scored a 2-0 victory and then scored a fine feast the next day.

"That was pretty exciting. When you look at that and you kind of go back, that Sunday you're eating steak and eggs, you're thinking about all that stuff – all the cutting weight, all the times you just didn't have a good meal, all the running and effort you put into it – and you sit there and go, 'Man, this was all worth it,'" Buzzard said, adding that his dad was the cook on Sunday morning. "That was pretty sweet, it really was. He pulled a T-bone steak out, had eggs over easy and hash browns and toast. I hadn't eaten a lot so that was pretty good eats."

The big breakfast helped Buzzard grow. In 1959, Buzzard was in the 112-pound finals against Frank Lane of Waterloo West. Championships were sorted out on Valentine's Day. Buzzard and Lane met twice during the season, with Buzzard winning both of them. In the finals, Lane won a 3-0 decision.

Buzzard, Lane and Bewley were part of a rugged 112-pound division. Russ L. Smith of the *Waterloo Courier* reported in an advance of the state meet that the 112-pound class was likely the toughest in the two-class event that year. Buzzard beat Lane twice, including a referee's decision in the district finals; and Lane had beaten Bewley, 10-1, in a dual meet. Bewley beat Buzzard, 3-1, in a dual meet. Smith hinted that Buzzard was going to have a rough time making the finals because Bewley was likely in his way in the semifinals.

Lane needed a wrestle-back win to make the state tournament field after losing by referee's decision to Buzzard in the finals of the district tournament. Buzzard's decision was 3-2 in the dual, when he got an escape early in the third period to break a tie. In the 1959 finals, Lane scored a reversal and a predicament point in the second period and then, according to Smith's account, rode Buzzard "craftily" for the remainder of the match and the decision.

"When I took second to Frankie Lane, I thought I had his number," Buzzard said. "I look back there and my dad (Don Buzzard Sr.) wasn't really upset. But I didn't know that he had things in store. That summer, I never spent one day in Waterloo. I was up to his hunting club and I was carrying five-gallon cans of diesel all day, all summer to keep the dragline running so he could dig his ponds out.

"I was even trying to get creative. He had an old Dodge truck with no bed on the back and I tied both of those gasoline cans on there and started driving across that mud flat. I sunk that thing out of sight. Oh my God, did I catch hell."

So did his opponents in the 1959-60 season, when Buzzard was at 127 pounds. Buzzard beat Jerry Millage of Muscatine, 4-0, in the finals. Buzzard gave up a total of two points in three tournament matches. His victory over Millage clinched the team championship for East. Millage was the first Muscatine wrestler to make the state finals, and the second was teammate Jay Roberts, who was second at 154 pounds that night.

"Bobby Douglas always claimed, 'You're the strongest damn guy I wrestled because your hands are so strong.' They were. Carrying gas cans across there, you're talking about a swamp bog and you drop to your knee and then you're back up and you're going again. I was literally right out there walking across the swamp. Nevertheless, that next year it was pretty easy to win," Buzzard said.

Wrestling was huge in Waterloo, with its successful roots to 1942, when Finn Eriksen's West team won the team championship. East won its first team title in 1953. Buzzard had a younger brother, Don Jr., who was also a two-time champion. They were members of five of East's eight title-winning teams.

Along with two championship programs came pretty rabid fans. Buzzard said he's yet to find a meet that will top the East-West intracity meets. "I still coach now out here at Cascade, so I've seen a lot of generations of wrestling but that was probably by far the best. Standing room only, the crowds were just into it. Back then, they even gambled on that stuff, the East-West match. There was a rash of great enthusiastic kids that went through that time era of East and West."

Buzzard said he found out about money changing hands well after the fact. It didn't cost money for him to find out who was tough and where that person was. He just asked his dad.

Don Buzzard Sr. did a lot to help East stay in the title picture. Bob said his dad would find out who was at which weight, which weight would be best for the East kid and which weight classes were stacked with talent. "The kids today, we do try to get them to work that same kind of workouts. The techniques are better today, but the kids aren't as tough. In my day, my dad said the same thing and I believed it. I believe that, those old-timers were just tough as nails," Bob said.

The elder Buzzard helped keep food on his family's table growing up in and around the Great Depression because he had a great eye for game, Bob said.

The elder Buzzard was a runner-up finisher in 1934. He kept his finish by beating Harold Nichols of Cresco in the consolation finals. Nichols would later become head coach at Iowa State and recruit Buzzard's two sons to compete for the Cyclones. Bob said he remembered Nichols recruiting him after he won the state title as a sophomore.

"I think the greatest attribute (for Nichols) to wrestling was his recruiting skills and his organization. The man never gave up on coming by in the summertime," Bob said. "If he was going to Cresco, he would stop off at Waterloo and look up two or three kids. He'd take you out and buy you ice cream, which was probably at that time illegal, but he did that just to keep you in mind.

"He did that when I was a sophomore after I won my first state title. 'I'm coming through going to Cresco. I'm a Cresco boy. I'm on a recruiting schedule and I'm just coming through, but I want to buy you an ice cream cone and let you know who I am.' We bought a wrestling mat from him and he came down and put clinics on in the summertime and helped us out."

The Buzzards were regulars at Iowa, Iowa State and State College of Iowa when those teams were facing Oklahoma A & M, which became Oklahoma State. The Cowboys' coach was Myron Roderick, who was a well-known recruiter. "I kind of knew right away that I could wrestle for an Iowa school or an Oklahoma school, but Nichols was a much better recruiter than Roderick at that time," Bob said.

College coaches weren't the only ones coming to Buzzard's house in the summer. The mat that Don Buzzard Sr. purchased from Nichols was a magnet for drawing some of the top local talent to workouts. "My father wasn't afraid to talk to people. He would get ol' Frankie Lane, Tom Huff, Lowell Stewart, Jim Bast, Scott Klepfer, guys from Waterloo and Cedar Falls and invite them over. He'd say, 'We've got a workout going on tonight. When you get done with construction, come on over.' He'd give them the address where we lived and kids would drop in. It was kind of a somewhat camp," Bob said.

"I hung out with Jim Wilharm quite a bit and hung out with Huff a little bit. I hung out with John Perry. I wrestled Frankie Lane, but I didn't really hang out with him. Back then, it was, 'That's the enemy, that's the kid I got to beat.' It was just a place to get a workout in, see a different competition, see a little different style of wrestling."

Speaking of different styles, Bob said having Dave Natvig as head coach at East was ideal for him. Natvig won two state championships at New Hampton, including the 95-pound gold medal in 1934 when Don Buzzard Sr. beat Nichols.

"Natvig was a great guy, I really liked him. He was a total opposite from my father, and I needed that," Bob said. "I needed somebody who would put an arm around you and talk to you in a low tone of voice, real easy-going. Natvig was always serious. When he talked, you listened. If you're screwing up and you did some wrong things, he'd pull you into his office and talk to you, but in a nice gentle way. We were cursing in the locker room and he just happened to hear it. He pulled me in and said, 'That's not the best language to use, I'm kind of surprised that you're using that.' I just felt about two inches high and I said, 'I won't do that again, sir.'"

Natvig didn't sugar-coat things with his wrestlers.

"When a tough kid came into town, he did not hold back," Bob said.

"He'd say, 'You're going to have to have your best day today, you're going to have to really have your tools in your tool bag. You've got a whale of a match, this kid is a tough kid, but he's not any tougher than you if you turn it on.'"

Natvig could have told a young Bob Buzzard about the need for a big effort every day when Bob worked out with Dan Carey. "I would be at the grade school and I would walk over to McKinstrey Junior High from Francis Grout (School) and I would wrestle him and I mean just get my butt kicked every night, just tossed on my ears," Don said. "My dad said, 'How do you like that wrestling?' I said, 'It's OK.'"

Bob said he got tired of being whipped by Carey, and his father said, 'Good for you.' When I got (to junior high) and Carey went to East, then wrestling got a little more fun when he was gone. My dad knew he was a good kid and would probably be a state champ because he could recognize talent pretty well. Back in our day, he'd have made a whale of a coach. He was a fired-up guy, enthusiastic. He could get on a kid, but he knew when to turn on the love for you and get you to want to compete more."

Bob said he remembered his dad having liquid amino acid that he would give to the wrestlers who wanted it. It was particularly popular with some members of East's 1964 championship squad that had five qualifiers and five champions. "It was equal to eating a steak dinner, so I always had that in my system," Bob said. "He literally babysat the (1964) kids and had their head so full of that they were going to kick tail. The final proof of the pudding was they all five won."

Along with his younger brother, Bob had some experience working out with Paul Stinson and some other folks on the 1964 team. Stinson is the only three-time state champion from East. "Paul Stinson was a pretty tough kid. I would come back from Iowa State and work out with them. Being a college guy, you'd put a thumping on them, but you could tell they were tough high school kids."

"If there was a person who defined the word coach, it's Jim Fox..."

Jim Fox of Davenport holds the distinction of being the state's only high school wrestling head coach with a state team championship to also lead a football team to a similar honor.

In 1946, one of Fox's first duties as wrestling coach at Britt was to convince skeptics that the wrestlers were not in danger of serious injury. According to the *Britt News-Tribune*, the idea of having a wrestling team was received enthusiastically by the students. There were some objections "mostly arising from the mistaken idea that it is too much a 'rough and tumble' game," the article stated.

About the only thing Fox's grapplers might have complained about was how hard they worked in practice. Guys who had Fox in their corner speak of their good fortune to have learned under Fox. They say the road to state championships was paved with life lessons.

Fox led 12 wrestlers from Davenport or Davenport Central to a total of 14 individual state championships. His first was Gene Piersall in 1949 – Piersall was one of two two-time champions Fox coached – and his last was Larry Sherman in 1963 – whose start to the championship season was slowed by an appendectomy not long after he earned all-state honors on Fox's football squad. Fox, who also officiated in 10 state wrestling tournaments, retired as head wrestling coach in 1963.

"Jim was about the most honest, straightforward person I ever dealt with in my life," said 1960 state champion Jim Leach, who served 30 years in the United States House of Representatives. "He was a classic meat and potatoes coach in the sense he was all about fundamentals. It was fundamentals in football – how you block, how you tackle, how you work as a team – and it was fundamentals in wrestling – all the discipline that goes into the sport and each move done with vigor and care.

"There is the term coach, which has huge implications in American society, far greater than most people know. If there was a person who defined the word coach, it's Jim Fox in that he was a disciplinarian who would back to the hilt anyone who performed for him. He was particularly wonderful with disadvantaged kids and with kids who did not have the greatest abilities. There are people that kind of try to take spoiled, terrific athletes and that wasn't Jim. He took any athlete and made them better. He molded teams where everybody loved him and loved each other. There was no such thing as a Jim Fox-coached team that wasn't a team with a capital T."

The first wrestling competition with Fox at the helm was Britt's competing in the annual Eagle Grove Invitational - Iowa's oldest regular-season tournament. His first dual meet as head coach was Dec. 5, 1946, when the Eagles beat Mason City 20-16. According to the *News-Tribune* account, that was Britt's first dual in 12 years and Mason City's first in four years.

Fox led Davenport High School to wrestling championships in 1954 and 1956. The 1954 championship was special because one of Davenport's two state champions was Simon Roberts, the first African-American in Iowa to win a state mat title. Roberts, who was known by virtually everyone at Davenport High as "Si", had been cut from the school's basketball team as a sophomore and won his championship two years later. Roberts said an individual who was a strong influence on his decision to try wrestling was longtime friend Henry "Hank" Philmon, who was second at 145 pounds in the 1952 tournament. Philmon is black, and would have beaten Roberts to the milestone win, but was beaten, 2-0, by Arnie Brandt of Waverly.

"I think it was a combination of knowing that (Fox) expected 100 percent out of you, hard work," Roberts said. "His practices were hard, but at the same time you could see the light at the end of the tunnel. Once he began developing that winning tradition, I think it just took care of itself."

Roberts said Fox took exception to teams that chose to not provide Roberts with an opponent because of the color of his skin.

After the 1954 tournament, Fox spoke highly of the work ethic of his wrestlers. "They worked hard all season and they were ready for this one," he said. "It is a pleasant feeling to work up to some big objective and then obtain it."

Getting through that tournament wasn't so pleasant for Fox, who said, "At times I was so nervous I didn't know where I was or who was wrestling whom."

No reports of Fox being so taken with nerves in the 1956 tournament, but his stomach likely got a workout because the team title was between his Davenport squad and Britt, where he began his coaching career. Bob Hain won his second straight heavyweight championship on a 4-0 victory over Sherwood Carter of Fort Dodge. Davenport finished with 51 points, two more than Britt.

Davenport High School became Davenport Central when Davenport West opened in the 1960-61 school year. Fox led Central to football championships in 1973, 1976 and 1983.

"I am confident that no coach has ever come out of the Quad Cities that had anything like the following of Jim Fox or influenced a quarter as many people as he did. He was *the* most influential person in the Quad Cities for a generation or two, in terms of effect on people," Leach said. "He didn't become head football coach until he'd been wrestling coach for a decade. He was always assistant coach to a guy named Butch Stouffa, who was the only coach I knew that Jim would ever speak with total deference, total awe about."

Franc Freeman, a state champion coach at Bettendorf, competed for Fox at Davenport. Freeman refused to back down from anything as a coach, but he bowed to Fox. He remembered Fox as a disciplinarian with a touch as well as someone who showed him a good reason to consider going to school before going to work. Freeman said he had post-high school plans all figured out.

"I respected coach Fox a lot. I was scared to death of him. When he barked at me, I listened," Freeman said. "I learned one thing: when he was chewing you out, he still had his arm around you. When he was making sure you were doing what you were supposed to be doing, he always touched you on the shoulder, on the hand, on the arm, maybe along side of the head. He gave you that feeling of confidence, but you had to do what he was saying to you."

Jim Craig, who learned from Fox in high school and became an NCAA champion at University of Iowa, said he's used some of Fox's methods during a long career of working with kids.

"He never really got angry at you and chewed you out for a bad performance, or a missed performance if you will," Craig said. "I don't know that I consciously thought about that, but my coaching style as a head coach was I rarely would chew the kid out after a match. I would wait until Monday when I could hit him with full double barrels. My philosophy is if I've done my job as a coach and the kid's competitive spirit is there, they're going to feel as bad about losing as I am about them losing. There is no value in me chewing them out at that point for something they feel bad about already. But Monday I don't feel so bad."

An example of the post-match care Craig cited was one of his own bouts. Craig was second at 165 pounds in 1955, losing a 3-2 decision to Jim Howieson of Clarion in a bout that was settled by riding time. "Because I lost, we lost the state tournament that year. He did not chew me out for that. I'm sure subconsciously I appreciated that and I respected him for that."

Craig said he's authored intense practices similar to what Fox did.

"He worked us hard in practice and I did the same thing when I started coaching. I was hard-nosed, pushing them to be better and I think that's the way Jim coached as well. It's also pretty much the way my college coach, Dave McCuskey, coached," Craig said.

Fox seemed to think Freeman had the goods to wrestle in college. Freeman said he was surprised to learn you could wrestle in college.

"When I was a senior, I accidentally pinned a kid from East Moline and he happened to be a state runner-up the year before. So I'm walking off the mat and coach Fox put his arm around me and said, 'What are you going to do next year?' I told him I'm going to get a job at Frank Foundry in the west end of Davenport," Freeman said. "He said, 'You ever think about going to college and wrestling?' I said, 'They wrestle in college?' I couldn't believe that.

"He set it up that we were going to go down to Frank Foundry. He knew somebody down there that was going to show us through and probably hire me when I graduated from high school, so I was all excited about that. We're walking through the plant and this one guy happened to recognize coach Fox. They made small talk and when Jim was done talking to him, we walked away. He said, 'Franc, how old do you think that guy is?'"

Freeman said he guessed the guy to be 35 or 40 years old.

"(Fox) said, 'He just graduated from high school two years ago. That's the type of work you'll be doing. It makes you old before your time.' That made me kind of think," Freeman said. "Then he started talking Iowa Teachers (Iowa State Teachers College, later known as Northern Iowa and Fox's alma mater)."

After a stint in the military, Freeman became the first member of his family – either his father's or mother's side – to go to college. Freeman was a two-time all-American for Northern Iowa, including a runner-up finish at 123 pounds in the 1962 NCAA tournament.

"I did seem to have an affinity for wrestling."

Kaye Don Young was a sports lover looking for a place to compete when he was growing up in Waterloo.

When Young got hooked up with wrestling in seventh grade, he found something he could do as well as impart to others.

"I was very, very small, I loved sports and I guess I just saw wrestling as a way to compete," Young said. "I loved a lot of other sports, but I wasn't very fast. I loved baseball, but I couldn't throw very well or very hard. I did seem to have an affinity for wrestling. The skills came relatively easy for me. Somehow I quickly had a mental grasp of it, which fortunately I was able to impart later to some of the young people I was fortunate to work with."

Little did Young know that the family was not new to wrestling. Glen Young, his father, was the state runner-up at 105 pounds for Charles City in the 1926 state tournament in Ames. That was the first tournament sanctioned by the Iowa High School Athletic Association. In that match, Richard Cole of Ames won by a coin flip after he and Glen had some overtime periods.

Kaye Young, who coached wrestling at the high school, junior college and college level during a five-decade relationship with the sport, was inducted into the IHSAA's hall of fame in 2010 – exactly 84 years after his father's runner-up finish. Glen Young did not divulge considerable information about his wrestling career, Kaye said.

"I never knew that my father wrestled until I was already wrestling varsity for Waterloo East. It was never brought up or mentioned, and I never could get much out of him," Kaye said. "I tried to validate it before. I do know that Charles City did not have wrestling for a long time. I suspect they probably dropped it during World War II maybe. My father, when he graduated, New Hampton decided they wanted a wrestling program and my father and his coach went to New Hampton a couple times a week after the season and helped them get started with their program. They went on to eventually have some very good teams. They were state champions a few times."

How did Kaye find out that his dad wrestled?

"I think he told me when I got beat in the state tournament, going home. I said something crazy like, 'I'll never wrestle again.' I was disappointed and dejected and he said, 'That isn't the way I felt about it when I got done wrestling,'" Kaye said. "I know he had a chance to go to Iowa State, and his folks didn't have any money. They had a little subsistence farm, so he never got to go to college."

When Kaye found out his hall-of-fame induction was on the same night his father was in the finals, it stunned him like a crossface from out of the blue. "My head is so filled with thought, I might not be coherent," Young said. "The first thing that comes to mind is gosh, there are a whole bunch of people I want to tell about this. Unfortunately, my mom passed away (in 2009), she was 94."

Young said his father was a good enough bowler to win a singles title in the Waterloo city tournament. He was also an avid hunter and fisherman. Young said his dad took to those activities in the same manner he went about wrestling – "Get in and do it and when you get home, you should have your limit. But you don't have to run around and tell everybody because that's what you're going hunting for."

While growing up, Young said he had no idea he came from a poor family in a poor neighborhood.

"I keep thinking 'God, you're lucky, Young, you've always had a lot of love, care and I've got a thousand aunts and uncles that looked after me. Things have fallen into place awful well for me. We were extremely poor when I was a youngster. We lived in the city limits of Waterloo, but we didn't have any running water. I didn't know I was poor because everybody I knew lived in the same kind of conditions at that time."

"Saturday night, I had to carry several pails of water in from the pump to fill the tub up. I'd let the tub set all day in the living room by the stove and by night I was able to get my once-a-week bath."

He wanted to be Saturday-night clean when he was inducted into the IHSAA hall of fame in 2010. "I'm in five other halls of fame, but these people are my peers, my professional peers. I'm a little frightened as a matter of fact," Young said.

Young said the first state tournament he remembered attending was in 1950, when he was a freshman. Mason City, the host school, won the team title and Waterloo East was second. His only trip to state as a competitor was in 1953, when he placed third at 133 pounds. That tournament was held at West Gym in Cedar Falls.

"I'll have to say that I have never been more awed by an athletic event than when they used to have the state tournament at the fieldhouse in Cedar Falls. There was just something about that, it was overwhelming," Young said.

Jack Smith and Ken Salyer were state champions for East that year. Dick Heaton was a runner-up for the Trojans. It was the year Tom Kempley of Corpus Christi High School in Fort Dodge made the 145-pound finals after finishing third in the district tournament. He got into the state meet when Bill Gray of Eagle Grove was unable to compete.

Earle Edwards won the 112-pound championship in 1953 for Northern University High of Cedar Falls. Six years later, Young was coaching at the lab school of what is now the University of Northern Iowa and led Ron Rice to the 145-pound state championship.

Two winners in the opening round of the 133-pound class in the 1953 tournament went on to be fairly well-known referees – Young and Arlo Flege of Waverly. Flege was on the whistle for an unprecedented 30 state tournaments.

One of Young's victories in 1953 was against Simon Roberts of Davenport. Roberts made history the following season by becoming Iowa's first black state champion. "I don't remember much about the match, but later on I got to know Si pretty well," Young said. "He said, 'You beat the tar out of me.' At that time, maybe, if I took him down, got an escape and took him down again, but by today's standards that wouldn't be beating the tar out of him. He sure is a nice fella. I do know one thing, he is a real gentleman.

"All I know is that he was a guy who believed in himself. I didn't know him until after he won the national championship. At that time, we didn't know anything about anybody. I had no idea he was that good until later on. Nobody knew anything about anybody else. You didn't go to summer tournaments all over the place."

Davenport coach Jim Fox was a Waterloo East graduate.

Young said Roberts was like nearly everyone he ever met in the sport throughout his career of competing and coaching. "I can count on one hand the number of really championship wrestlers that went bad, so to speak. I think it's because it's all you and it shows all the time," Young said.

"You can't escape from whatever limelight you happen to be in, you've got to live with it. Maybe it develops integrity through fear of exposure."

Not every wrestler made the bright lights of a championship. "You hear an awful lot about guys that maybe weren't standouts on the mat but were standouts in life like (Norman) Borlaug," Young said.

Borlaug wrestled at Cresco High School, his highest finish at state was third and he was awarded the 1970 Nobel Peace Prize for his efforts to develop a strand of wheat that saved over a billion people from starvation.

The bond among wrestlers is especially tight, he said. "I had never thought about that, but I would say that family ties and commitments are probably stronger in wrestling than in any other sport that I can think of," Young said. "Somehow you have to make a commitment. My wife contended that every wrestler she ever met was crazy, and I could never come up with a good argument.

"Another thing that amazed her is we could be at a dinner party or something and I'd look at someone. I'd say, 'That's a wrestler.' She'd ask how can you tell. I'd go introduce myself and ask them. At least 80 percent of the time I would be correct."

Young got into coaching after a split-schedule of classes at Northern Iowa around a stint in the military. While in the service, he wrestled for a club in San Diego and took a drive to watch one of freestyle wrestling's bigger upsets.

"I saw they were having the Olympic trials in Oklahoma. Myself and a couple other guys jumped in the car and went over to that. That was when Dan Hodge was on the cover of *Sports Illustrated* and he could beat anybody at anything," Young said. "He wound up wrestling Bill Smith in the finals of the tryouts and he hit Bill with a double-leg. Smith threw that whizzer in and flopped him. It was touch fall at that time and it was over. Then Bill didn't get to go to the Olympics that year because he was coaching high school in Rock Island, Ill. He didn't make any more money than any other coach of equal level, no more than the basketball or anybody else, but they said he was a pro."

When he got out of the service, Young had a year and a half of college remaining. He was married, so he turned to coaching rather than competing. "My senior year, the lab school had a wrestling program but they didn't have a coach. The coach was a swimming coach," Young said. "He asked me if I would come down and spend the year. That's when I coached Ron Rice. He won the state tournament that year, and we had another kid on the team, Zeke Plorins, who got second (at 154)."

Young spent seven seasons at Maquoketa and then served as interim coach at Wartburg College in Waverly prior to starting the wrestling program at North Iowa Area Community College. He coached 1976 Olympian Joe Corso as well as junior college national champions Joe Hatchett, Bob Fouts and Tom Garcia. Young led NIACC to the 1973 national team championship.

Wrestling has not been Young's only interest through the years. The father of three was also active in community theater and wrote poetry. "I was raised in a neighborhood with very, very few children. I didn't have many playmates to speak of and my youngest sibling is seven years younger than I. I just fell in love with books and movies and radio. They were my lifeline and I never got over it," Young said.

"He just called it like he saw it, and in plain words."

Ray Arnold was born too soon or else no one was smart enough to create the Internet in the 1940's, 1950's or 1960's. The bottom line is high school wrestling in Iowa never got the lasting historical message from Arnold.

He was Ray to those who read his column, "The Wristlock", in the *Wright County Monitor* at Clarion or read his historical columns in *The Predicament*, the state's publication devoted to the sport. He was Gus to those who knew him as a recovering alcoholic who drank pots of coffee daily and who wore bib overalls whether he was working on the railroad or covering wrestling. They learned he had a treasure chest of behind-the-scenes stories about the sport. Loren Parker knew Arnold as a valuable resource in a project titled "History of High School Wrestling in Iowa," which he composed in 1970 as part of seeking a Master of Science in Education degree from Drake University.

Before there were wrestling writers such as Russ L. Smith or Kevin Evans of the *Waterloo Courier* or Mike Chapman and J. R. Ogden of the *Cedar Rapids Gazette* who kept the state informed, there was Ray "Gus" Arnold the writer-historian. Had there been an Internet back then, Arnold could have written the definitive story of Iowa's high school wrestling world for all to see. Arnold attended over 40 state tournaments, seeing the event grow out of high school gymnasiums and into bigger facilities.

Arnold died of cancer in 1973.

Pat Arnold knew him as the dad who seemed to know everyone in college and high school wrestling. He had a passion for Iowa State wrestling, Cyclone coach Harold Nichols and Dan Gable, she said.

"I just remember when I was a kid going to country school, if he wasn't going on the railroad somewhere the other part of him was going to wrestling meets around the area," she said.

Arnold graduated from Clarion High School in 1935. He later wrote columns known as "The Wristlock" and "Sideline Slants" for the *Monitor.* He knew the football series between the Cowboys and opponents such as Belmond, Eagle Grove, Hampton and Iowa Falls. He reported that Clarion was one of the few schools that has had a continuous wrestling program since 1921. The Cowboys' wrestling history includes coaches such as N. B. "Andy" Anderson – who helped write some of the first rules for the sport in Iowa - and Dale Brand - a state champion at Fort Dodge and an NCAA champion at Cornell College in Mount Vernon. Clarion's first man involved with teaching the sport in Clarion who had a working knowledge of holds was a former carnival wrestler who was in jail, according to Arnold's writings. The man was let out of jail in time for practice and returned to his cell after each day's drills, Arnold reported. The coach's name wasn't recorded in writings researched from that time. Those 1921 Cowboys were a hearty bunch because Arnold reported that a lack of a practice room meant the Clarion team practiced outside.

Pat Arnold doesn't believe her father wrestled in high school. At 6 feet 1 inch, he was likely courted by the basketball team. Bill Arnold, Pat's brother, did play basketball at Clarion. Dad might have watched his games, but Pat Arnold said the winter was wrestling season for her dad. Along with his bibs, Arnold usually had his lucky red sock and his lucky crying towel when he was attending Clarion events.

"He'd always get the car in good condition because he drove everywhere. If it was a blizzard or not, he was out driving a '49 Chevy we used to go everywhere in," Arnold said. "I was very embarrassed to ride in that car, everybody had newer cars than we had, but that car would start in the winter time more than the newer ones would start."

If he didn't want to drive, Arnold had a railroad pass. He took the train to the 1965 NCAA wrestling tournament in Wyoming. On the car trips, Arnold usually had a partner.

"I wasn't in high school yet. I was probably in junior high, but I used to go to Eagle Grove, used to go to Algona. I went with him a few times to Iowa State to their meets. I loved it, I probably was the boy my dad wished he had had instead of a basketball player," Pat Arnold said.

She also one-upped her dad. Arnold said one day at school she and Anne Willemssen happened upon Nichols, Gable, Dave Martin, Chris Taylor and other Iowa State wrestlers in the girls gym doing refinishing of the wrestling mats. "If my dad would have known they were up there, I'm sure he would have been up there," Arnold said.

Dave Harty, who coached wrestling at Postville and Eagle Grove before working for the Iowa High School Athletic Association, said if he had trouble locating Clarion coach Dale Brand after a Clarion-Eagle Grove meet, he would look for Ray Arnold. That was back when the Wright County battle would draw a full house. That's full house as in people sitting on the floor right up to the edge of the mat and some perched on the basketball backboard.

Longtime Waterloo West coach Bob Siddens talked about Arnold as one of the important people of wrestling when he moved to Eagle Grove as a boy and began to get exposed to the sport.

Pat Arnold said she knew in high school that her father was popular in wrestling circles. She realized how much of an impact he made in the area when she moved back to Iowa in 1994 after being gone for 25 years. Patients did not know her when she worked at Community Memorial Hospital in Clarion, Pat said, but the mention of her father would launch people into stories about him.

Ray Arnold was a writer of matters about World War II. He also wrote a number of letters to friends in England. Pat Arnold said her dad had a grit with all of his papers enclosed. Arnold also had a yellow legal pad at the ready. He could describe with his writing anything but a boring match. Some folks learned the word "iota" or that there was such a wrestling move as a Japanese whizzer by reading Arnold's accounts. The writing style was not quite Hemingway, but wrestling fans knew what he was saying. It was similar to the days Arnold was doing broadcasts of high school wrestling meets for Marvin Hull and KRIT-FM in Clarion. The radio station signed on for the first time May 12, 1964, and it began doing reports from the state tournament in 1965. Arnold's call of matches put proper grammar on its back with terms such as "He ain't-a gonna get it did" but a listener could almost see the meet in his living room because Arnold could describe things so well.

"I remember reading some of it and he wasn't an English major or anything. He just called it like he saw it, and in plain words. It wasn't flowery or anything like that," Pat Arnold said. "When he saw whatever was going out on the mat, he was describing that in words you could understand."

The *Monitor* reported in 1968 that KRIT was the state's only radio station to do full live coverage of dual meets and tournaments. The story said it was estimated the station would do 290 hours of wrestling broadcasts dealing with high school and college during the 1967-68 season.

Arnold could have written a first-person account of a train being in a tornado. In 1966, when a twister hit Belmond, Arnold was head brakeman on a Chicago Great Western train that was in the midst of much of the storm's fury. He could also have written about his ongoing efforts to find clothing, shoes or Christmas gifts for the needy.

His writing was informative, but it could also be opinionated and the sarcasm was sometimes as subtle as a crossface across the nose. Arnold did not like his work edited, which Mary Doak of *The Predicament* learned quickly when Arnold wrote for it. "My gosh, oh he was irate. He said, 'Nobody puts a blue pencil in my work,'" Doak remembered.

Doak also remembered *Predicament* co-editor Denny Highland's stories about attending an NCAA tournament in Portland, Ore. with Arnold, including the fact Arnold usually had different colored socks on. Doak said Arnold's columns were very popular with *Predicament* readers.

Scholastic Wrestling News, a Wyoming-based publication, honored Arnold's *Wristlock* as the top weekly wrestling column in 1968.

Here are some examples of Arnold's writings. Spellings of names have not been corrected:

(1967) On stalling in high school wrestling: "Mr. Finn Erickson of Waterloo and the National Rules Committee explained the fine points of stalling. We all know the fine points – why not enforce them!"

(1968) On Olympic wrestling and television: "Wrestling fans, nation wide, are not too happy over ABC-TV and their Olympic coverage. I think every one, even wrestling fans, enjoyed the second rated basketballers showing the world we don't need our best to win a world championship. For a national TV network to show every sport or parts thereof, on even sports that have never won a gold medal and omit the free style wrestlers that have won 25 gold medals, is for the birds."

(1968) On an NCAA finals match: "The hall was furnished with fine organ music each session before the matches. The lady playing could have played during the 191 championship final as the match roughly resembled a dance. It was the poorest example of wrestling by two finalists anyone had ever looked at."

(1968) On the state tournament in Waterloo: "The "Hog Palace" was as packed as a jar of pickled-pigs' feet Friday and Saturday. The Bulging "Hippodrome" was host to over 20,000 fans."

"Rumors were prevalent that the State Meet would move to Des Moines a year early, namely next year. They locked the doors shortly after the meet began. The place was full with advance ticket holders unable to get in!"

Arnold retired to Arizona, but kept a connection to Clarion and wrestling. Pat Arnold said her dad insisted on moving to a community that began with a C and had a high school wrestling program – he and his wife moved to Chandler, Ariz.

"I knew him as dad."

New names and some familiar faces. That's a good way to describe the 1960's addition of some teams joining the familiar championship teams of Waterloo guys, Fort Dodge and Cresco at the state wrestling tournament.

Britt, Cedar Rapids Jefferson, Algona, Harlan, Humboldt and Eldora. Who were those guys? Britt had finished second twice before taking consecutive titles in 1961 and 1962. Cedar Rapids Jefferson never had a top-four finish until it won the Class A trophy in 1962. Algona was runner-up three times prior to 1966's Class A championship finish. Harlan's only wrestling championship came with a new coach in 1967, and without the benefit of a single individual champion.

Humboldt had a wrestler win a championship in 1921, but according to local information it started varsity wrestling in the 1963-64 season. The Wildcats held the gold trophy in 1968. Eldora was in its fourth season of wrestling in 1969 and had a new coach in Dick Jensen. The Tigers had yet to have an individual champion, but on March 1 they won three in a row – Dean Barnard at 154, Matt Clarke at 165 and Jim Clary at 175 – and took home the top prize in Class 1-A.

Familiar faces? Leon "Champ" Martin was a state champion for Eagle Grove in 1939 and an NCAA runner-up in 1942 for Iowa State Teachers College. He made winning a habit in Algona. Paul "Bo" Cameron won a state title for Cresco in 1931 and in 1933. Cresco's 1933 team shared the state title with New Hampton. Cameron got a title as head coach in 1962 thanks to three champions – Steve Childs, Cal Jenkins and Mel Wieland. Joe Fitch of Humboldt was an art teacher, a master with a yo-yo and a fiery motivator who had his wrestlers ready for tournament time simply by going through the tough North Central Conference schedule that included Martin's Algona boys, Dave Harty's Eagle Grove Eagles and Dale Brand's Clarion Cowboys.

Team championship trophies were being dispatched to some new locations beyond the scalene triangle of titles that was Fort Dodge, Cresco and the Waterloo schools. Those three communities housed 24 outright and two shared championships between 1926 – the first state tournament staged by the Iowa High School Athletic Association – and 1959.

You can hear different variations on how Leon Martin became known as "Champ" Martin. Some say it was his high school title – he was the third man in Eagle Grove to win a state championship. One story had Leon being re-named after his referee's decision loss to Dick DiBattista of Penn in the 175-pound NCAA finals. Martin would be "champ" four times as head coach at Algona.

"I knew him as dad," said his son Paul, a three-time champion for the Bulldogs. "Everybody in the wrestling community still calls him Champ."

ALGONA, 1966

If dual meet records counted towards a state team championship, Algona would have gotten few votes in 1966. The Bulldogs were 4-7 in duals. Algona did have a good fall, going 6-2 in football and some of those footballers provided some wrestling firepower: Larry Munger, Tom Samp, Dave Martin (the coach's son) and Tom Fitzpatrick. They helped the team finish second to a strong Britt squad at the sectional and the district. Perhaps the Bulldogs' first state title was on ice because the district tournament was too. The district tournament was at the Des Moines Ice Arena, and the state meet was on more ice at McElroy Auditorium in Waterloo. Algona sent the aforementioned four wrestlers.

"With so many good wrestlers competing in the State Meet at Waterloo, it will be necessary for all four of the locals to place first or second to have a chance for the team crown," was among the state advance in the *Algona Upper Des Moines* newspaper. "That's asking a lot – but look what happened last weekend."

Munger, Martin and Fitzpatrick won championships. Samp was second. Algona was a winner, beating Britt by 17 points.

Future wrestling stars at Algona had a cool thing to try to experience: the escort into town the day after a championship. It certainly got young Paul Martin's attention.

"Once a school wins a state championship, all of a sudden the younger kids look at that and say 'I want to be a part of that.' You came home from Des Moines, there was a little town about 10 miles south of Algona (in St.

Joseph) and the wrestlers would get on the fire truck and they'd take the fire truck and drive it 10 miles into town and there's a big parade going on," Martin said. "I always remember thinking, 'That would be neat to win the state championship as a team and be able to get on that fire truck.' My sophomore year we did that. When you're little and you see that, that's a big thing and that's what you want to do."

Dave Martin won his second individual title in 1966. That was the same tournament when Dan Gable finished his prep career with a 64-0 record and a third championship. When Dave and Paul Martin were inducted into the Iowa Wrestling Hall of Fame together in 2009, Gable made the introductory speech.

Paul Martin did not wrestle for his father on varsity. Champ resigned as head coach prior to Paul's freshman season, so Dale Bahr stepped in. Bahr was a two-time state champion for Iowa Falls and, just like Dave Martin, an NCAA champion at Iowa State. Champ came back as an assistant for the 1973-74 season and was matside when Paul capped a 90-0 run in his final three seasons with his third title and a hug from dad. "That's something I'll never forget, just one of those moments in life that you remember," Paul Martin said.

The Martins became one of the few families where the father was a state champion in Iowa and two of his sons also received gold medals.

HARLAN, 1967

Harlan's new coach, Dave Trotter, made a prophetic statement to the *Harlan News-Advertiser* at the beginning of the 1966-67 wrestling season: "I can't help but be optimistic about this squad," Trotter said. "We've got a lot of fine boys here, and if they get into their proper weights, we could have a real good year."

The Cyclones had 17 lettermen returning, so Trotter did not have to make forays into the hallways to recruit kids to practice. Apparently the boys and the weights got into a groove because Harlan was 11-0 in dual meets. It was such a good season that the *News-Advertiser* published a four-page special section with head shots of all of the wrestlers just prior to the sectional tournament. Quality can trump quantity at tournament time, and the Cyclones had to feel pretty good going into postseason with the foursome of 95-pounder Larry Kersten, Roger Hodapp at 138, Jack Gross at 165 and heavyweight Bill Larsen. They had a combined 53-0-1 mark during the regular season, the lone scratch a draw between Larsen and Roger Williams of Audubon.

Harlan's cheerleaders subscribed to truth in advertising. When the six-wrestler, two-coach delegation left for Waterloo, the cheerleaders put signs on the side of two cars that said "Next 1967 state champs. Harlan, Ia." The Cyclones finished with 31 points, seven ahead of Janesville and Algona.

Football playoffs were yet to be enacted, and the hiring of Terry Eagen as Harlan's next football coach and assistant wrestling coach was announced as the wrestlers came back to town. Harlan's townsfolk got early practice in driving to the east in 1967. Eagen led Harlan to the first Class 3-A grid championship in 1972. That game at Kinnick Stadium in Iowa City would be the start of Harlan's unprecedented 12 football state titles, 11 in the UNI-Dome at Cedar Falls since 1982 by assistant wrestling coach Curt Bladt. In 1967, the crowd that went to Waterloo was impressive. "The Cyclones performed before an estimated 400-450 Harlan fans at the Waterloo meet Saturday night in what probably marked the greatest mass exodus Harlan has ever experienced," according to an account of the state meet in the *Harlan Tribune*.

Trotter knew his way around the Waterloo-Cedar Falls area. He graduated from NU High of Cedar Falls, which was the laboratory school for Northern Iowa's teaching program.

According to the *Tribune*, five of Harlan's six qualifiers lost to eventual state champions. Gross was the only one to lose in the final round. Gross was wrestling Gary Nelson of Alden on Saturday night, and the match was ended when it was ruled Nelson could not continue after a move by Gross was determined to be an illegal slam. There was a touch of Harlan among the gold medalists. The *Tribune* reported that 138-pound winner Tom Thomas of Johnston was second cousin to Robert Jacobsen, the manager of the Vet's Building in Harlan, where the Cyclones started their tournament run by winning the sectional.

The *Tribune* reported Gross was literally cheated out of the state title by the slam ruling. It reported the senior's season record as 20-0 with "we won't count that final match a defeat!" in parentheses.

Apparently the fans at Alden planned to throw a big victory party for Nelson, but he asked for no celebration. The *News-Advertiser* quoted Iowa High School Athletic Association executive director Bernie Saggau on the decision for no celebration: "He didn't care for this special little ceremony because he didn't feel that he had won the championship outright."

Regardless of how the state meet went down, the Cyclones lived up to the promise of a good season.

CEDAR RAPIDS JEFFERSON, 1962

Had Cedar Rapids Jefferson not won its championship in 1962, the season's biggest moment would have been a sour one. Mel Wieland won two state championships and had no losses – he drew Roger Dahl of Waterloo East, 4-4, in his first varsity match as a sophomore – going into his senior season. Wieland got a big vote from a big man as the city's best wrestler as a sophomore. "He's great and only a sophomore," Cedar Rapids Washington's 315-pound heavyweight Larry Conaway, the 1960 Class A heavyweight champion, told the *Cedar Rapids Gazette.*

Wieland, who joined the varsity mid-season when 145-pounder Jim Turner graduated at semester, became the first wrestler from a Cedar Rapids high school to win a championship in a state tournament or its pre-1926 predecessor state invitational meet since Robert Kutchera won at heavyweight in the Iowa State Invitational at Ames in 1922.

In 1962, Wieland lost. A run of 53 matches without a loss ended in the district finals when Jim Evashevski of Iowa City High pinned him in 1 minute 8 seconds. Wieland won the wrestle-back, got to state and became the first three-time state champion from Cedar Rapids with a 2-1 victory over Evashevski. But when the loss happened on a snowy Saturday – a blizzard socked Cedar Rapids – there were more than a few surprised, excited folks on hand.

"He cradled me from me trying to do a kelly. I should have quit, and I figured if I got a little further under him he's going to tip," Wieland said. "He managed to lock up because I'm already under his arm trying to tip him. He just locked up and hooked my leg and, *BAM,* that was it."

The crowd went wild, Wieland recalled. "There were probably about 100 people that came on the mat and they just carried him away. I kept the article because that was most meaningful for me. My mother died shortly after that, but she told me the day would come when I would maybe lose and to accept it. And I did, I took off my bands on my ankles, I walked over to where they carried him, shook his hand and walked back. That was it, there was no huffing and puffing," Wieland said.

Evashevski remembered the suddenness of the opportunity for an upset.

"As I remember, I thought it was like a kelly where we were both on the mat. He was trying to swing under and knock my one leg out, and I caught him under the arm and turned him over," Evashevski said. "I just had him tight from that one move. It was sort of a defensive move, but I lucked into it. I was hanging on for dear life because I knew if he ever got out of that, I was going to have to wrestle really hard the rest of the match."

Evashevski, the son of University of Iowa athletic director Forest Evashevski, said Wieland had a little extra compared to most guys in those days. "He was a great, great wrestler. He not only was physically good, but he just had this assuredness that he was going to do ok on the mat that the rest of us did not have," Evashevski said.

They met four times during the 1961-62 season. Wieland won three of them. Trying to figure a way to beat him was tough on Evashevski.

"That's why I am bald today, because I worried so much about wrestling him," Evashevski said.

If the J-Hawks were rattled by having Wieland lose, they certainly didn't show it at the state tournament in Cedar Falls. Jefferson qualified seven wrestlers and six of them advanced to the final round. Wieland was joined on top of the awards podium by 95-pounder Steve Childs and Cal Jenkins at 127. The runners-up were Al Sieversten at 120, Bill Armitage at 145 and Monty Rierson at 175. The non-finalist, Ron Clark, finished fourth at 133. Jefferson finished 24 points ahead of Waterloo West.

"We didn't even have to show up for the finals, we had it won," Wieland said.

Wieland said the J-Hawks had a special mentor in Cameron, who learned the sport in Cresco from Dave Bartelma.

"To this day, I find it hard to talk about him because he was such a super guy. He struck me as a father image, he never yelled," Wieland said. "I later became a coach myself and I took what Bo had instructed me. I really think I know more moves than Bo did, but I realized that it isn't the moves that necessarily make you a good coach. It's how you interact with your athletes and how your athletes want to work for you."

HUMBOLDT, 1968

Perhaps there is a long-range dream of having a champion when a program starts. At Humboldt, a 1962 article in the *Humboldt Independent* highlighted the new mat program: "Mr. Fitch believes with a few years practice, we will have a wrestling team of which to be proud."

Perhaps Humboldt's Fitch learned something from Cameron too. The Wildcats won the Class A championship in their fifth season of interscholastic competition. Fitch packed four qualifiers for the trip to Waterloo and came home with four finalists – champions Lyle "Butch" Laird at 120, Keith Abens at 154 and Geoff Mickelson at heavyweight. Jim

Taute finished second at 103. Taute would win a state title the following season.

Abens, who won the second of his three state titles in 1968, said he got an early indication of how things got done Fitch-style.

"He taught me how to yo-yo when I was in fifth or sixth grade. He'd come in with his art cart, he was kind of a portable teacher, and he taught us all how to yo-yo," Abens recalled. "Yo-yo-ing is practice makes perfect, so you practice over and over and over. You spend hours practicing. When I was a sixth grader, I was the yo-yo champion of the Humboldt centennial.

"I learned that when you do something for Fitch, you've got to practice, practice, practice until you have it down that you can't miss it. That's how you have success."

The Wildcats didn't have time to linger at the state meet. To Fitch, it was all business, according to Abens. "One thing Fitch did with us was he wouldn't let us watch. He kept us in the locker rooms the whole time so the pressure of the tournament didn't get to us. I just remember laying in this kind of dungeon-y locker room at the Hippodrome in the dark and he kept a cool towel over my head until I had to go out and warm up,"Abens said. "I didn't see the lights of the Hippodrome until maybe 5-10 minutes before I was supposed to wrestle. Looking back it didn't hurt to do that."

Abens had an interesting tournament in 1968. He needed a late reversal to beat Larry Olson of Britt in the opening round and another late reversal to beat Mike Beaman of Greenfield. In the finals against Chuck Knutsen of Central of DeWitt, Abens needed a wake-up call and got it right away.

"The guy I had in the finals was supposed to just really wail on me because he was supposedly so much better than me, and I ended up pinning him in the first period because I got called for stalling," Abens said. "I was bushed from the semis match. I got called for stalling in the first period. The call scared me so much I went in on a double and back-heeled (Knutsen). He hit his back so hard it pinned him."

Fitch could be quick to anger because of his passion for perfection. He was also known to keep the practice intensity high around tournament time.

"One time he came in (for practice) and he was so mad, we'd either lost a match or done something he wasn't happy with," Abens recalled. "He blew his whistle, then he went to throw his clipboard like he was really enraged. He caught the clipboard on his whistle string that was around his neck and it pulled his whistle out from between his teeth and he chipped his two front teeth."

Today the idea is shorter, intense drills at tournament time. In 1968, Fitch had his own ideas.

"He would break us, basically, getting ready for the state tournament. Between district and state, we'd go to practice at 4 o'clock and we'd still be there at 7:30," Abens said. "He'd work us and work us, he had me in tears several nights in a row. I wanted to walk out of the room, but I knew I couldn't do that and hold face so I just kept going. I was literally bawling in the practice room because he drove us so hard."

Humboldt finished second in 1969. Fitch did not wrestle, but he was a student of wrestling. "He'd go to all kinds of clinics, anytime somebody was doing anything about wrestling he'd go to it," Abens said. "He'd volunteer at the Iowa State camps and such as a counselor or whatever just to be in on watching all of those college coaches teach technique and then he'd bring all that back to Humboldt."

BRITT, 1961

Britt was no stranger to top-flight wrestling. The Eagles had individuals such as Dick Govig, Dennis Foy, Alan Hiscocks, Chuck Conway and Ron Meleney who brought home state championships, but the closest they came to bringing home top team honors was a runner-up finish in 1956 and again in 1960. "Those were hellish good guys," Gene Guenther of Britt remembered.

Led by 1956 Olympics team member Kent Townley, the Eagles soared in 1961. They repeated in 1962 with Jim Craig as coach.

"I think every team dreams of that, but to me there wasn't a lot of talk," said Guenther, who was a sophomore on the 1961 championship squad. "From a coach standpoint and pumping the team up, I don't remember that. There was always encouragement. Some coaches are pretty good at the, 'rah-rah, this is our goal.' I think we knew we could do it and we had a lot of good guys."

The 1961 tournament's victory party was quieted a bit in Britt because of heavy snow and blizzard conditions the day after.

The individual accomplishment was underplayed in most newspapers, but Britt's title in 1962 had considerable attention on Bob Steenlage's successful effort to become Iowa's first four-time state champion. The Eagles were not just Steenlage in those days. Larry Lloyd and Steenlage were close friends and they won together. Not only did they win together, they posted identical match scores in the finals. Lloyd beat Bob Rosauer of New Hampton, 2-0, at 95 pounds and Steenlage beat Dan Sullivan of Corning by a similar score at 112 pounds. In 1962, Lloyd moved to 103 and beat Del Weaver of Griswold, 3-2. Steenlage made history at 120 pounds by beating Steve Balsbaugh of Perry, 3-2.

Another in-common thread was Lloyd beating Balsbaugh, 2-0, at 98 pounds in the opening round of the 1960 tournament.

Britt in the 1961-62 season was under a new coach, Jim Craig. Kent Townley left Britt, leaving a very concerned Steenlage in his wake. Townley had been coaching Steenlage since seventh grade, they knew the right buttons to push. Craig, an NCAA champion at Iowa in 1959, learned quickly the intensity to succeed that was behind Steenlage's success. Steenlage connected with Craig.

"He was like a magician leading me through a mine field," Steenlage said.

Take away the drive and Steenlage admits he would have been a wrestler, not a state champion. "I would have been mediocre at best, because I was driven," Steenlage said.

Britt had third-place finishes from Guenther at 133 and Dale Brcka at 165 to go with Lloyd and Steenlage in the finals in 1962. Lloyd opened his 1962 tournament by beating the same guy he beat for the 98-pound championship in 1961 – Bob Rosauer of New Hampton.

The Eagles were not just good in wrestling. In the pre-playoff days of the 1960's, Britt had a football coach named Steve Everett. The players called him "Skinhead" but they marveled at how he led them to success, Guenther said.

"He always seemed to know what that other team was going to do," Guenther said. "We were smaller and we were outweighed. I as a kid through junior high and high school, I never played on a losing team."

The same fortune was bestowed on Guenther's father in Clarinda. That team played football at the junior college in Clarinda, and that squad had one black athlete. A game was scheduled against a junior college in Missouri, but that team refused to play the Clarinda bunch unless the black player sat out. The decision was made to play that Missouri team with 10 players, and the Clarinda gang won the game 115-0."

"I have no reason to doubt that story," Guenther said. "I'd never known my dad to lie about anything."

That football success seemed to trickle over to the wrestling room in the winter at Britt. "It got to be such a thing that they let school out for those two days of wrestling and had it on the calendar because everybody in Britt went to the state tournament. 'There wasn't anybody left in town," Guenther said. "You were expected to win. I kind of felt like I failed my teammates (placing third) because they were all pretty good winners."

Lloyd was one of those winners. "He was a quiet kid. That was close to Bob's weight and I think they worked out a lot together," Guenther said. "When you have good competition in the room, that's when you really improve. We always seemed to have that."

For that, the Eagles had some first-place state trophies.

ELDORA, 1969

Eldora's championship season was led by a somewhat unlikely director. Jensen told the *Waterloo Courier* he did not participate in wrestling while attending Northern Iowa. He was asked about taking the wrestling job with the Tigers, replacing Bob Thurness, who was the school's highly successful football coach.

"Why am I coaching wrestling? I've always liked it," Jensen said.

It would be hard to not like coaching a team that had the "Tiger Trio" or the "Fearsome Threesome." Those were two of the nicknames given to the Tigers' powerful threesome of 154-pounder Dean Barnard, 165-pounder Matt Clarke and Jim Clary at 175. They brought a combined 77-2 record in the 1968-69 season to the state meet in Waterloo. They were the Tigers' qualifiers. They were on the front page of the *Eldora Herald-Ledger* prior to the state meet.

They were all state champions. Eldora had its first team state championship thanks to the work of the school's second, third and fourth individual state champ. Lloyd Sword at 115 pounds in 1936 was Eldora's first wrestling champ.

According to the area rankings in 1969, Milford and Greenfield were expected to be the small-school teams to beat in the first three-class tournament. Both teams led the way with six qualifiers. By the end of the first day, it became a race between Eldora and Logan-Magnolia. Whatever moniker the Eldora guys went by, they had to deal with the Johnsens of Logan-Magnolia. Rex Johnsen was an undefeated 145-pounder who seemed to pin everyone, and his brother Gale was a tough 103-pounder. Their cousin Jerry was at 154, so he might have a meeting against Barnard. By the end of the season, the Johnsens would all make the state finals and all win at least 30 matches.

Eldora got some help in the finals from an unexpected source. Gale

Johnsen had a 4-0 lead over Ron McDonald of Morning Sun, but a strong third period gave McDonald the 6-4 victory. McDonald had finished third in the district tournament, but found out the day before the event started that he would be wrestling. Kevin Newkirk of University High of Iowa City had beaten McDonald, 5-2, in the district meet but Newkirk had to withdraw from state because of a shoulder injury. McDonald was in and was golden, finishing with a 23-2-1 record.

Logan-Magnolia got its first state champion in Rex Johnsen, who capped a 33-0 senior season with a 13-6 victory over Jim Furland of Beaman-Conrad. The Panthers had a chance to win their first team championship, but Eldora's three studs would need to suddenly struggle. Barnard, who needed to win a wrestle-back in the sectional to keep his season going, struggled to score points but his second period escape was enough to seal a victory over Jerry Johnsen.

Clarke followed Barnard with an 8-0 win at 165 and Clary finished with a decision at 175. Clarke and Clary finished undefeated and Barnard lost twice. Barnard avenged one of his losses by clipping Tom Vanderloop of Alden on riding time in the district finals. His other loss was to Keith Abens of Humboldt. They finished with a combined 182-39-1 career record.

"We really didn't talk about winning the state meet a lot, but the boys really thought they could do it, especially after the district," Jensen said to the *Waterloo Courier* at the end of the tournament.

"...every time the blue ribbon was put up for grabs, he was there first."

John Robert Steenlage wanted to be known as Bob. By the end of his high school career at Britt, Steenlage became known as Iowa's first four-time state wrestling champion.

"The reason I was called Bob is because my dad's name is John and he was called Jack. Because there was some friction between my dad and I, I always preferred to stay as Bob," Steenlage said.

Steenlage is the oldest child of what he described as a dysfunctional family. Steenlage said his father John Clarence ran a bar and was an alcoholic. John and his son had an icy relationship compared to the moments he shared with his two younger sons and two daughters. Steenlage said his father passed away before they could make peace, but later the son was able to forgive his father. He realized the success could not be spelled without adversity.

"Subconsciously I wanted attention. My two younger brothers and sisters got some attention from my dad, he would maybe hold them on his lap, maybe throw them the football, hold their hand. I was like 1 ½ or 2 years old when my dad came home from the war and for whatever reason we never had that relationship," Steenlage said. "When I walked on the mat, I looked to see if my dad was there and he never was. My mom always was. I kept thinking if I get my hand raised one more time, maybe my dad will pay attention to me. I didn't understand it at all, but now it's so easy to understand because you can read books and study patterns of children that come from dysfunctional families. They like to get attention, they like to be recognized and that was the way it was."

John Steenlage never watched his son wrestle in high school. His bar sponsored Bob Steenlage's picture as part of a full-page ad in the *Britt News-Tribune* saluting the team's runner-up finish in the 1960 state tournament.

Steenlage recalled being angry as a junior when his father wanted to put up a picture of him in the bar. Nearly 50 years later, Steenlage was asked if he ever thought his father was proud of him.

"To answer your question now, I believe my dad was proud of me. He just didn't know how to express it," Steenlage said. "His wanting to hang that picture up in the bar was his way of saying 'I'm proud of you.' I interpreted it totally in a selfish way – 'You're not taking credit for what I'm doing' – so I was wrong."

Thanks to a dream involving a tractor, Steenlage as a 12-year-old told his mother, Evelyn, and his grandmother, Clara, that his goal was to be the first Iowan to win four high school state wrestling championships. Thanks to one extra second of riding time, Steenlage realized his goal on Feb. 24, 1962.

"It was two parts of a dream. One was later life, what would happen then, but in the dream I had I saw a tractor, and it was a tractor on the farm where I was working at that time – Art Nelson's between Britt and Kanawha – and I saw somebody adjusting the carburetor and the tractor ran better," Steenlage said. "The dream was, the understanding came, that human beings can change too. It's not where you start, it's where you end up. Most people are lazy on this earth. If you work hard, you can be like an overachiever.

"Just a few days after having this dream, not even understanding what goals are, I told my mom and my grandmother that my goal was to be the first person in Iowa to win the state championship four years in a row. I quickly looked at their expressions. I never saw any expression like 'This kid's crazy.' (It was) if you say that's your goal, we'll back you. They didn't really say it in words, but the expression on their faces was they got it. I never told another soul, it was between my mom, my grandmother and myself. That was my goal and I never lost sight of it. Because I wanted my dad to love me so much, I was willing to do things that most athletes would not."

One of those things was keeping enough control of Steve Balsbaugh of Perry despite a bum shoulder to score a 3-2 victory in the 120-pound finals of the 1962 state tournament. Earlier in the day, Steenlage sustained a separated or dislocated right shoulder in the semifinals while avenging his only loss of the season to Ron Barker of Osage.

Waterloo Courier sports editor Russ L. Smith watched Steenlage make history. It was the same day Smith watched future NCAA champion and

Olympian Tom Peckham of Cresco clinch a third straight title with a pin six weights later.

"Although not as invincible as Peckham appears to be, the least that can be said of (Steenlage) is that every time the blue ribbon was put up for grabs, he was there first," Smith wrote.

Officiating the Barker-Steenlage match was Iowa State coach Harold Nichols, who was aware Steenlage hurt his shoulder. Nichols told Britt coach Jim Craig something was wrong. Craig said Nichols suggested Steenlage stay at the gym and keep his shoulder limber, not go out for dinner with the team before the finals.

"(Steenlage) tried to hide it from me and I knew there was something going on, but I couldn't pinpoint it. I didn't realize it but he said he really couldn't use his injured arm that much, it was like wrestling with one arm," Craig said.

That injured arm became a concern when Steenlage left on a train a couple of days later for Fort Leavenworth to take exams for a possible appointment to the United States Military Academy at West Point. Steenlage said he believed the testing would be academic-based. When he arrived, the testing included fitness tests such as pull-ups and push-ups. Steenlage informed the officials of his injury and they said he had to do his tests or pass and have no chance at an appointment. And no chance to wrestle at West Point for LeRoy Alitz, who'd grown up on a farm near Mason City.

"I would have to say here was one of those supernatural things that happened to me. I got up there with the left hand, I did 12 left-handed pull-ups. I could not do push-ups with both hands, but did (the required) push-ups with my left hand. I tried it again that next day and never could do it again," Steenlage said.

Steenlage received his appointment and – despite four instances where he was nearly expelled from the academy – was an all-America wrestler for Alitz.

Late in the 1962 state finals, despite that bad shoulder, Steenlage was trying to prevent Balsbaugh from escaping to break a 2-2 tie.

"(Balsbaugh's) ankle would go out about 6-8 inches. I'm getting pretty scared, what am I going to do if he gets out? Just about the time he should have gotten out, his foot suddenly came back. That happened three times," Steenlage said. "Now, I realized for whatever reason I believe God was involved in that match. For some reason He wanted me to win. The match ended in a tie and he did not escape, it was 2-2."

In 1962, a wrestler earned one point for having at least 1 minute of riding time on his opponent. Steenlage had 1 minute 1 second of time against Balsbaugh. It took longer than one second to confirm that on the floor of West Gym in Cedar Falls as a crowd of 3,500 looked on.

"They had a longgggggg conference, it went on a long time," Steenlage said. "They came back and the referee came over to me, he had not a smile but it was not a frown, let me tell you that. He comes over and he said, 'Son, you've just won the state championship for the fourth time by one second.' He grabbed my (right) hand and he shoots it up in the air and pain went from here down to here (pointing to his feet). Teammates had tears in their eyes, I saw Craig, there was somewhat of an uproar and my teammates and I go out in the hallway."

The *Britt News-Tribune* reported that Nichols officiated Steenlage's championships bout as well as the semifinals.

Craig was in his first season as a varsity head coach in 1962. He was an NCAA champion at University of Iowa and wrestled in high school at Davenport for Jim Fox, who re-started the program at Britt. Steenlage's success on the mat was brought up during Craig's interview with Britt's school board.

"One of the questions they asked me was 'If you got this job, would you try to change Bob's style?' I said, 'I have a philosophy that if it's successful, why would I want to change it?' Evidently that was the right answer. They allowed me to come up there and work with him," Craig said.

Craig took over for former Iowa State wrestler Kent Townley, a member of the 1956 Olympic freestyle team. Townley had coached Steenlage since seventh grade, and the kid was not wild about losing his mentor.

Townley gave Steenlage some valuable mat time as an eighth grader. Steenlage and Bill Peterson were Townley's varsity managers then, and the junior varsity squad did not have a 95-pounder. Steenlage filled that bill, but he was too young to compete. Townley sought and received permission from the Iowa High School Athletic Association to have Steenlage wrestle exhibition matches against 95-pounders prior to the B-squad bouts.

"Townley was a genius in that way. That greatly built my confidence, it was huge," Steenlage said.

By the time he was able to compete in high school, Steenlage was working on the mental aspect.

"Whenever I walked on the mat, I had wrestled the match mentally the night before," he said. "You don't go to bed and worry about the match the night before, you wrestle the match before you go to sleep the night before.

I fell into that, so to speak, that I had that understanding, or if I didn't have the understanding I just did it so I wouldn't stay awake all night."

The mental game carried over to the match.

"When I walked on the mat every single time, I knew in my heart that I had done more push-ups, more laps, I had thrown more bales of hay, I squeezed the ball more times, I lifted the weights more times, I never skipped any practice, never smoked one cigarette, never had a drink, never was in late because I was driven. I knew I was better prepared than anybody else," Steenlage said. "It wasn't maybe, I knew it. It was like an unusual confidence because of that. I never, never panicked and most of my close matches were won in the last 5 seconds, the last 10 seconds, and I knew I was in better shape. The desire to win was so bad that when you're gasping for air, and all of the stimuli to the brain said you can't do it, the desire, the obsession to have my dad love me was greater than that pain and it was a breakthrough."

Losing coach Townley could have caused a breakdown.

"If I had not developed the ways of looking at life, that could have done me in pretty good mentally, going into my last year and my coach who has been with me this whole time left," Steenlage said. "As it turned out, bringing coach Craig in…I probably never would have won it the fourth time because of the pressure if it wasn't for his special counseling, his demeanor and the fact that I wanted to win it for him."

Craig was a father figure-protector-coach. "He was like a magician taking me through a minefield," Steenlage said.

Craig was also Steenlage's once-a-week workout partner despite a weight difference of close to 60 pounds.

"I would work out with him just to give him something big to work against," Craig said. "He and I were going hard one night in practice. He tried a double-leg takedown on me, I sprawled out on him, he still tried it and tore his back up."

Steenlage recalled, "I heard something snap in my back, but it wasn't too bad. Then I went ahead and wrestled against Osage (Ron Barker). I shouldn't have wrestled, I was in great pain and I lost 9-8. I remember all of a sudden I'm on the side of the mat and their coach very nicely turned me around and said 'There's your bench over there.' I was delirious."

"I went to Dr. David Shaw and he x-rayed me and told me I would never wrestle again. When he told me that, never once did I take him seriously. I'm not trying to be cocky about that, it was like water off a duck. I walked out that door and across the street was a chiropractor, Dr.

Peters. I went in there and 15 minutes later he took the same x-rays and said, 'You are hurt bad, but I can tell you right now you will not injure yourself (further) if you can stand the pain.' I soaked in the bathtub every single night and I was out for quite a while, got back maybe 10 days before (tournaments)."

Steenlage said part of his desire to win was to get proverbial weight off the shoulders of Craig and his wife Connie.

"Coach Craig had one of the biggest hearts of a human being you could ever have. He was living this nightmare ever since I hurt my back because he got hired with the understanding that he would not change things and he would help me get better, which he had up to that point," Steenlage said. "He made one bad judgment, not totally bad, a mistake and he gave in to it. His wife is living with it, they're almost turning gray over this whole thing. An extra motivation to win it was for them, and that was huge.

"He was so kind to me, his heart was melting and I just saw him suffering. It was worse than somebody who was waiting for his wife to have a baby and she's three weeks overdue. He was a nervous, tormented person, and I don't mean that in a bad way."

Steenlage said a rumor about him being an egomaniac began circulating in Britt late in the 1961-62 season. That sting hurt more than the back injury, he said.

"That just about did me in. I couldn't understand, I'm representing the school, why wouldn't you want me to do well? Coach Craig helped me through that. Craig kept me away from the public, kept me away from the newspapers. I knew I was like a lame duck, so to speak, physically, but my mind was OK."

Craig knew Steenlage to be a team captain with the team in mind. Once, Craig kicked a wrestler off the team after he failed to make weight – the last of several issues Craig had with him. Steenlage asked Craig to reconsider the move.

"He's given himself to the sport for several years and we think he would be an invaluable member of the team," Craig recalled Steenlage saying. "Bob did that on his own, to request it of me, and was very sincere about it. That's the type of kid he was and the type of person he is today."

Half of Steenlage's 12 state tournament victories had a margin of a takedown or an escape.

"He was pretty tough. He was a typical Britt wrestler, controlled everything. He beat a lot of guys 4-0 - take them down, ride them out, reverse them, ride them out and then ride them out in the final period. That was Britt's style. They didn't go for a lot of pins unless it really presented itself. Otherwise they preferred to control the clock," said Jack Rubendall, a wrestler from Clarion familiar with Steenlage. "I probably have the distinction of wrestling him more than anybody else and never beating him."

Rubendall recalled the district tournament in 1962, when they battled to a tie in regulation but Steenlage won on riding time.

Rubendall said he didn't have a firm grasp on the state's top individuals when he started wrestling varsity for the Cowboys. A teammate gave him a quick lesson about Steenlage in 1960.

"I remember at the Eagle Grove Invitational Roger Sebert told me, 'There's last year's state champ at 95 pounds. This year he's a sophomore, he'll probably be a two-time state champ.' Then he went on to be a three-time state champ and a four-time state champ," Rubendall said.

Steenlage did anything he could to give himself an advantage. "His dad did not follow him, and that in itself probably was a driving point for Bob, that I can do this in spite of my dad," Craig said. "He told the story about going to the local furniture store and asking if they had any mattresses left over, or old mattresses they couldn't sell, and he carried them home on his back so he could wrestle down in his basement. That's back when he was 79 pounds as an eighth grader."

The skinny kid was not afraid of throwing hay bales. He would squeeze rubber balls to strengthen his grip, he'd stay late at practice. He wanted some weights but the family could not afford them, so he made a set out of concrete with the help of Ray Peterson - the father of Britt teammate Bill Peterson - and put them on a pipe.

"It was like an addiction. It's not all good because being a child of a dysfunctional family, you can become a loudmouth and you always push yourself into a position of attention. You want to be the hit of the party. In my case, fortunately, it was directed in one narrow path – to be a success in this one area."

Steenlage's friend Larry Lloyd won the 103-pound title in 1962 as the Eagles won their second consecutive Class B team championship. One year earlier, Steenlage and heavyweight Larry Hochhaus gave Britt its first multiple champions in a state tournament.

The *News-Tribune* lauded Steenlage's historic title in 1962.

"This monumental achievement could not have come to a finer lad than Bob Steenlage. He is a fine student, a regular member of the honor roll with a 3.0 average the first semester (in 1961-62). Britt has had other state champions, several with two and three year crowns. Some have been champion wrestlers. Others have been true champions – morally sound, scholastically high, well regarded around their friends and community without distracting from their achievement. We must put Bob Steenlage at the top of the ladder. We think the community will agree," the editorial stated.

The 2012 state tournament will mark 50 years since Steenlage made history in the state. His name is in the tournament program with the other four-timers, but fans still know who Steenlage is.

"It's because Iowa is known as a wrestling state, so they follow the sport a lot so they keep track of things," Steenlage said.

"...this boy is the finest wrestler I've ever coached."

The story of Tom Peckham of Cresco and wrestling begins in fairy tale fashion. It was not Grimm's Fairy Tales, but it was not grim either.

"I started mainly because I used to fight a lot in school. They thought it would be a good place for me to take my extra energy, get me out for wrestling. Some of the coaches noticed, I liked them and they encouraged me and that's how it got started," Peckham said.

As far as his high school career goes, Peckham's story has a happy ending. It may have been late February in Cedar Falls when the man known as "Pecky" won his third straight championship, but it could have been fall. That was Peckham's favorite move if not his preferred season. Peckham won his final 76 matches, including pinning his last two championship-round opponents. The last one was future state and NCAA champion Don Parker of North Fayette of West Union in 1962. In order to gain the finals, Peckham beat 1961 state runner-up Dale Brcka of Britt, 2-0, in the semifinals thanks to a second-period reversal.

Who knew when his career would have started if no one had stepped in to try to stop him from putting up his dukes on the playground. It didn't hurt that Peckham had a kid named Flanagan in his class. The Flanagan boy's father was George "Chris" Flanagan, the wrestling coach of Cresco's powerful wrestling team.

"(Flanagan) was one of the big reasons. He had a son that was in my grade, a classmate of mine, so I used to go home with him and he'd come to my place on weekends. I got to know Chris when I was real young, he knew I was a scrapper. He took me to the Waterloo YMCA when I was in fourth grade. He did things like that, extra things. He'd pick kids out, make friends with them and develop (them)."

Flanagan did a masterful job if he developed Peckham. The style

147

Peckham employed caught the eye of a young Dan Gable, as well as many other kids in northeast Iowa. Flanagan was quoted by wrestling writer/historian Ray Arnold about Peckham's skill. "This is a hard thing to say, but this boy is the finest wrestler I've ever coached, and I've had my share of champions down through the years," Flanagan said. "He's the only wrestler I don't have to worry about when he goes out on the mat. He hasn't gotten where he is by just being a gifted wrestler as some people think. He has worked hard to become great."

Peckham said he worked hard to be able to wear that prized Cresco varsity wrestling uniform. "I remember I watched my weight, my mother cooked for me the whole summer to make 120, I couldn't wait to wrestle for Cresco, just to be on the first team," Peckham said.

All this for a guy who carded his four losses as a freshman – Don Johnson of New Hampton, Tom Huff of Waterloo West, Clyde Shirley of Charles City and Bill Block of Maquoketa – and finished with a 95-4 career record. The loss to Block was in the first round of the 1959 state tournament. The *Cresco Times-Plain Dealer* reported Peckham had been down with the flu most of the week going into what became a 4-4 referee's decision for Block.

"I was getting better. I had gotten sick a couple days before that, we'd missed a day of school. Omar Frank was with me and we got all wet, caught a real bad cold and got the flu a little," Peckham said. "When I went (to the tournament), I was just getting over the flu. I was sick, the day before I was real sick. I was kind of recovering, a little weak and oozy."

The referee in the Block-Peckham match was Iowa State wrestling coach Harold Nichols. Peckham would win an NCAA championship for Nichols and the Cyclones in 1965 and 1966. In 1959 it was just the first of a couple of "don't-look-now-but…" moments – in today's technical slang it would be an OMG moment – for Peckham and officiating.

"Coach Nichols refereed that first round match, a referee's decision. I never held it against the ref, never blamed a ref for anything, but Coach Nichols was the guy there that made the referee's decision for Block," Peckham said. "Also, when I was a senior in college, Bob Siddens refereed my match with (Fred) Fozzard of Oklahoma State when I got pinned in a dual meet. The national finals, when I was wrestling Fozzard, who walked on the mat? Bob Siddens. A lot of guys blame the ref, I never have held it against the ref. They've got to call it the way they see it."

Peckham won that 1966 title by pinning Fozzard at the Iowa State Armory in Ames. Siddens slapped the mat that day for Peckham just as he slapped it for Fozzard. If Iowans thought the method used to pin Fozzard looked familiar, they were right. Peckham used the same stuff to pin Wayne Cool of Waterloo East in a come-from-behind thriller for the 1961 state championship.

Cool was leading Peckham in the third period, when the Cresco ace turned the tables and scored a fall. Peckham had won an earlier meeting with Cool, 3-0, and was ahead, 2-0, in the finals match. "He reversed me, got a three-point near fall and almost pinned me. All I remembered was I had to pin him," Peckham said. "What I did was halfway got out, then I ended up putting a whizzer on him and he put his head down. I went right for the half-nelson, took him right over and pinned him. Actually, it was pretty similar to the (match) with Fozzard in the national finals my senior year in college. It started with a whizzer and he got his head down."

"Nichols was the referee on that one too. It was the first time I had been behind all year, first time I'd been on my back for a couple years. He was ahead 5-2 in the last period, it looked pretty bad you know. I remember tears running down Flanagan's cheeks."

Gable was at West Gym in Cedar Falls that day, but he only saw the celebratory aftermath of the fall. Fans around him stood up as the tide turned and Gable said he was too little to see the mat. He just remembered how Peckham's big move lit the place up.

"I'll never forget that moment in the Men's Gym with Peckham and Cool, Waterloo and Cresco," Gable said.

In an account of the 1961 finals, in which Cresco got championships from each of its three qualifiers, the *Waterloo Courier*'s Russ L. Smith wrote, "The Peckham-Cool match was easily the most spectacular of the finals which produced a flock of close ones....Cool rode Peckham for over a minute in the third period. Peckham was credited with a reversal before he got the referee's hand for the pin."

Gable had early dealings with Bob Buzzard of Waterloo East, and the story of how Gable got whipped by a college-age Buzzard and broke down in tears because someone was able to handle him became part of Gable lore. Gable said it wasn't Buzzard, a two-time state champion, but Peckham whose style Gable wanted to emulate.

"Bob Buzzard was a great mentor to teach me how to wrestle and to work with me, he did all that. When I watched him, he was slick and he did everything that a lot of people would like to do. The guy that I have to say that my eyes stuck on was Tom Peckham when I was a kid," Gable said. "He was from Cresco and, at that particular time, I wouldn't brag about that because of the big rivalry. Instead of that slickness so much, it was more like he got his hands on you and you couldn't get away. If he touched you, you went down. If he rode you, you went down and if he was on the bottom, he was out. It was more of a control-like situation. He got a lot of pins and that seemed like that was the most excitement in the sport. At that particular time, Buzzard had hands-on with me, but I was looking to Peckham as the style of wrestling I wanted."

Peckham said the pin was his ideal in every match. "That's the ultimate. If you pin them it means you really dominated them and you did what you wanted to do. For me it was what I was looking for," Peckham said.

Gable got into that zone as well.

"When you feel something and you experience something and you get used to it, that's a feeling you want to get to. It's like the satisfying feeling of pinning somebody as compared to beating them 25-7," Gable said. "There is a better feeling with that fall, and you just don't experience it unless you actually get it. I did get my chances to experience state wrestling but it was at a different facility."

Gable won his three state championships at McElroy Auditorium in Waterloo.

The season would end and Peckham had his version of weight training to do. He said football season got the Cresco boys excited about wrestling season. Flanagan was an assistant football coach, so he could make sure they were rounding into shape for the season.

"Us guys up in Cresco, we pitched (poop), sileage and baled hay. No weight lifting," Peckham said. "I think loading bales is the best thing ever. Square bales, stack them on a wagon behind you, it's bumpy. You develop balance and coordination. You lift them bales up and stack them and it's hot. My dad did custom baling and he'd charge 10 cents a bale, and I'd get a penny if I loaded them on the wagon.

"When wrestling was over, it was over. But the next fall we were so hungry to get back in the wrestling room, we couldn't wait to get back. That had a lot to do with it."

A boy with interest in wrestling in Cresco could find a lot of mentors. Peckham said he learned by scrapping with neighbor Don Webster.

"He lived a quarter-mile up the road from me when I was a little kid. I used to go by his place and he was a wrestler, a two-time state champion," Peckham said. "He was in high school when I was just a kid and he'd get me and we'd wrestle in the lawn. He'd rub my nose in the grass, but I loved it. He was good to me but he really worked me over. His dad took me to all the wrestling meets.

"Wrestling was big in town, it was a big thing. They used to have trouble getting guys out for basketball and Flanagan could put four teams on the floor. Sometimes we wrestled two schools at once and we'd have four teams. They just had that many guys out there."

Kids like a young Peckham had talented guys to watch. Gary Kurdelmeier won two championships and was also a heck of a football player. Don Hall was a two-time champion, Ken O'Kada, Gordon Loy, Dave Gates, Bill Murray, Jim Grover. They all brought gold medals back home. A lot of them went to Iowa State to wrestle for Nichols, a Cresco boy himself. Kurdelmeier went to Iowa and was an NCAA champion. The Iowa State connection drew Peckham.

"I just wanted to dominate, just wanted to pin them. I watched Iowa State wrestle and was pretty sold on Iowa State. A lot of guys from Cresco were going to Iowa State. I went to nationals once and watched Larry Hayes, Les Anderson, Ron Gray and those guys. For some reason I wanted to go to Iowa State, that was the only place I wanted to go," Peckham said. "Nick sent the guys home, my old teammates like the Frank boys and Don Webster. They told me, 'Nick's going to take care of you.' Everybody was trying to recruit me and I never heard from Nichols. I couldn't say no to everybody, the guys told me, but then Nick finally came up. It wasn't much of a challenge for him. He just told me what he'd do and I accepted. That was it."

By the time he went to Ames, Peckham knew about setting a goal and achieving it. He had a thing about not wanting to lose to anyone twice. One person who tried to handle him twice was Block, who moved to 127 pounds in 1960. They met in the Class B finals and Peckham had his first state title with a 4-0 victory. "That was one of my goals, I wanted to be a state champion really bad. I was pretty happy," Peckham said.

That was the end of the lightweight Peckham. He won at 154 as a junior and at 165 as a senior.

"I grew like a weed. My sophomore year at 127, I made it early in the season and we had six pounds by state time and I was having a hard, hard time making the weight," Peckham said. "I grew that much during the season, and the next season Flanagan told me to wrestle '54. I weighed about 160. I didn't cut any weight my last two years. He told me he wanted me to wrestle '54 for the team, so that's what I did my junior year."

Peckham said he loved the challenge of getting good enough to be able to whip who whipped him.

"There was a guy two grades ahead of me in school and I used to fight a lot when I was younger. This guy could whip me, I went to school and he'd whip me every day. I could feel I was gaining on him. I think he let me win because I was getting too close and he didn't want any more of it," Peckham said. "I think he gave in. I just kept after him and he wasn't a bad guy. I just couldn't stand it that he could whip me so I wound up fighting with him every day. It wasn't slugging or dirty, it was more or less wrestling. I'd make him do it. It was a challenge to me. It's no fun to beat a guy you beat easy, it's more fun to beat a guy you're not supposed to beat or one that's tough as hell. Then you feel like you did something."

Peckham had a similar challenge with Virgil Carr in practice at Iowa State, but without any scheduled fist fights. "That guy was so quick and strong on his feet, he probably took me down at will until Christmastime. I mean every night. I guess I might have been ornery or something, I loved it," Peckham said. "I wanted to get it so he couldn't take me down. I'd get him on the mat and do alright, but boy he was quick. He'd single-leg you or double-leg you, you knew it was coming but he'd still do it. Finally, by Christmastime it got a little tougher for him. If Virgil couldn't take you down, it was going to be tough for anybody to take you down. He really helped me a lot."

Was Peckham a lone wolf? Perhaps. He had a champion's quality in that he wanted to make it to the mount on his own two feet. Peckham's mount was wrestling. "I just took to it. I played football, softball or baseball, track, but I didn't have the interest. Football you've got to have the whole team cooperate if you want to win. In wrestling you could win if you paid the price," he said. "I never felt like it was a big deal because I liked going to practice."

He went to practice and competed for the Cresco Spartans until Cresco consolidated with Lime Springs, Ridgeway and Elma and the wrestling team was known as the Crestwood Cadets.

Peckham lived with his grandmother during his senior season because his parents moved to Prairie du Chien, Wis., where they were operating a zoo. "They went to a zoo there and it was closed. They had all the buildings and everything. My dad bought it, cleaned it up, restocked it. They had elephants, tigers, lions, seals, chimpanzees...I'd go up and visit, but I never stayed there."

He worked out with Omar Frank and later Russ Baker at Cresco. He'd also get an occasional workout with a Cresco boy who was at Iowa State under the tutelage of "Nick." Peckham said Flanagan was happy to have the Iowa State boys back for the holidays because it gave him a chance to learn anything new that Nichols was showing.

Peckham placed fifth for Nichols in the 1964 NCAA tournament and then rolled to his two NCAA titles. He was also party to Iowa State winning its first NCAA team championship under Nichols in 1965 in Laramie, Wyo. The outstanding wrestler honor in 1965 and in 1966 went to Yojiro Uetake of Oklahoma State, but Peckham was named Iowa State's athlete of the year in 1966. His next challenge was making the United States team in freestyle, where he placed fourth at 192 pounds.

After losing in the state tourney as a freshman getting over sickness, Peckham was healthy enough and strong enough to ward off upsets the rest of his high school career.

"I can look back and figure I should have been a four-time state champion. I was kind of disappointed in that, except it didn't bother me none. Quite satisfying, loved it, great, great fun," Peckham said.

The media that was aware of quality individuals had to consider watching Peckham wrestle as a fun assignment. "(Peckham) may be one of the state's all-time greats," said the *Waterloo Courier's* Smith. "Name a quality a great wrestler needs and Peckham has it abundantly: temperament, speed, strength, agility, confidence and balance – tremendous balance."

"Peter, your mama's here."

Timing is everything in the sport of wrestling. Hitting the right hold, getting out from underneath your opponent, having the right chemistry, having your mom watch you wrestle for the first time.

Waterloo East had the right timing – and a touch of perfection - in 1964. It's not been matched in state tournament history.

The 1964 Class AA team championship was expected to stay in Waterloo, but would it return to East High School or to West High? Some folks expected West to get its first title in five years because coach Bob Siddens' Wahawks had eight qualifiers, including 1963 state champion Dale Anderson and a sophomore kid named Dan Gable, who was getting his first taste of varsity competition at 95 pounds.

"Back in those days, the two powers were West Waterloo and East Waterloo. Actually, Bob Siddens' program probably had a little stronger background than East High in terms of state championships and so forth," said East's Don Buzzard Jr., a two-time state champion.

Waterloo East, which was coached by Dave Natvig, qualified five guys after having a tough time at the district tournament. Some of the most recent teamwork known to Paul Stinson (112 pounds in 1964), Tom Moore (120), Willie Hoosman (133) and Pete Middleton was performing in the "Colored Elks Drum and Bugle Corps." Don Buzzard Jr., whose brother Bob won a state championship for the Trojans in 1958 and in 1960, knew about having to work a little because he helped to tidy up the grounds at his family's cabin in the summer. Easy work? Hardly.

"We had a cabin up by New Hampton, Fredericka and when we were kids – of course he started with my brother first – he would drop us off at Highway 63 and you had to go about 5 miles actually to get to our cabin and we had to run to the cabin," Don Buzzard said. "When we got there, we had our chores – mow the lawn, fix the fence, cut weeds, whatever had to be done."

A dip in the nearby gravel pit was a treat. There was still the run back to Highway 63 to be picked up by dad.

Buzzard and his four teammates cleaned up at McElroy Auditorium in 1964. They all won individual championships and East won its second consecutive team championship. "We brought five men in and got five through," Natvig said to the *Waterloo Courier*. "You can't do much better than that."

While several of the East team members were in step with each other, Buzzard and Middleton got to know each other first as opponents. Don Buzzard, who was not in the drum and bugle corps, and Pete Middleton were members of opposing teams on the youth baseball fields of Waterloo. They became junior high wrestling mates at McKinstry Junior High. "It was like Mutt and Jeff, I was real tall and Don was real short," said Middleton, who was born in Wales and came to Waterloo in 1949.

As far as Millicent Mae Hendrickson-Middleton was concerned, her son should not have been wrestling. "My mother did not want me in wrestling. What brought me out was coach (George) Tesla, I was in his home room and they had intramural wrestling in junior high. I beat everybody in my weight class, including the guy that was on the wrestling team. I had nooooo experience, just from scrapping in growing up in Waterloo. I was no fancy dancy wrestler, just scrapping as best I could," Middleton said. "I did a little note to George Tesla saying that my mom had given me permission. My mother and father were divorced."

Mom discovered her son was wrestling when she came to Parents Night and talked to Tesla. She wondered why her son, who had not been a fan of school in elementary grades, was president of his home room. Pete was undefeated at the time. Middleton said his mother allowed him to continue with two provisions: that he not get hurt and that he not cut weight.

"Anytime I was cutting weight, I always hid that from her. I'd go stay at somebody else's house the night before or a couple of nights before because a lot of times I had to cut down," Middleton said. "I'd even go to my cousin's place, he was from Logan and I was from McKinstry and we were the same size, so I would go down a weight or go up a weight so as to not wrestle him. His name was Barry Hollins and I never had to wrestle him."

Middleton said he wanted to be a wrestling coach after meeting Tesla and learning the sport. He wound up as a lawyer. "Never got there. Never even came close. The civil rights movement came along and it was like I was dragged away in a wave of it."

A quintet of wrestlers would eventually capture a team championship with a wave of winning.

"We came out of (the drum and bugle corps) knowing each other. I was probably at more of an advantage because I also knew Buzzard," Middleton said. "Instead of becoming enemies, (Middleton and Buzzard Jr.) became acquaintances. We came to respect each other and depended on each other. Don was so competitive, not just as an individual wrestler but as a teammate. When he played football, he played as a part of the team. When he wrestled, he looked on it as a team."

One thing all five East High guys had in common was their ability to win the weekly tryouts staged by Natvig. "The way that coach Natvig ran those wrestling sessions, we as a whole team, whether you were a scrub or the best person in the room, you had to do a wrestle-back every week if you wanted to be on first team," Middleton said. "And nobody ever got a bye up to (varsity). It was based totally and clearly on your ability. To stay on the team, that was the thing. When you rose it was like butter and cream, your talent kept you at that level. The only thing that could torch you would be an injury."

Don Buzzard had a spot of reverence in East's wrestling lore because his state championship at 165 pounds in 1963 locked up the Trojans' sixth team championship. He also finished second at 120 pounds in 1961 as a freshman, wrestling one dual meet before he moved into the varsity spot at tournament time.

Natvig won state championships for New Hampton High School in 1933 (85 pounds) and 1934 (95 pounds). In 1934, Don Buzzard Sr. lost to Abe Castagnoli of Fort Dodge in the 145-pound finals. Buzzard secured his runner-up finish by defeating Harold Nichols of Cresco in the wrestle-back contest. Nichols later recruited Bob and Don Jr. to wrestle at Iowa State. Bob Buzzard later participated in Greco-Roman at 149.5 pounds in the 1972 Olympics.

"He said he wrestled (Nichols), but he never did tell me the score or how it came out," Bob Buzzard said of his father. "It was 'We wrestled' so that was all he ever said."

Don Jr. added, "He was vague about it. I would ask him a lot of questions...asked him about Nick. Dad did a lot of AAU wrestling, he wrestled two years at (Iowa State Teachers College), but the war came along and he never finished his college education. He came back and went into business."

Waterloo Courier sports writer Russ L. Smith reported the senior Buzzard was a basketball player at Waterloo East until he had an epiphany during a road trip to New Hampton. Following the hoops game was a wrestling meet, Smith's article stated, and Buzzard and teammate Byron Guernsey stayed to watch. "We thought we'd like this. So when we got back to school we pushed some of these old tumbling mats together and started wrestling," Don Buzzard Sr. said.

The story stated that East had its first wrestling team in the 1930's. Guernsey was East's first state champion in 1933. Buzzard was a qualifier at 145 pounds in 1933, but he lost a first-round match to eventual state champion Roger Wilcox of Eagle Grove by coin flip after two overtime periods.

Buzzard never lost his love for wrestling. He helped junior high kids learn about the sport in intramural wrestling practices. He visited Natvig's practices enough that the wrestlers considered him an unofficial assistant coach. At state tournament time in nearby Cedar Falls, Buzzard arranged to have eggs, tea and toast along with a good supply of oranges brought to West Gym so the Trojans would not have to travel for a meal.

"You either loved him or hated him because he was really tough. When he wanted something done, he went out and did it," Don Jr. said. "He expected that from my brother and me. We just grew up that way. The old story about me, once when I lost as a freshman I had to run home between the headlights. That's true."

The state tournament moved to McElroy Auditorium in Waterloo in 1963. That made it convenient Feb. 22, 1964, when Millicent Mae Hendrickson-Middleton chose to attend the state finals with daughters Millicent Elizabeth and Valerie Ann. Pete Middleton was in the 165-pound finals against Mack Anderson of Davenport Central. Buzzard was to follow at 180 pounds.

"My mother had never seen me wrestle throughout high school and, of all the matches she comes to, she comes to the last match of my high school career. That had me more nervous than having to wrestle Anderson," Middleton said. "They knew all the time they were coming, never told me anything. That day I could tell something was wrong at home, but I couldn't pick up on it. I'm in the locker room and we were at Tommy by now and somebody said, 'Peter, your mama's here.' I was so nervous, my hands were wet. That's the thing I can remember about the state tournament. Let me tell you what that did to me in terms of wrestling this guy: there was no way he was going to beat me."

Middleton won the match 2-0.

The East team of 1964 was a group of battlers who maybe weren't the greatest at keeping busy in practice, but they loved to compete. "None of us enjoyed working out. We knew we were good. If it hadn't been for old man Buzzard, there would have been no practice because we would have been faking and under the mats and call ourselves losing weight. We'd make every excuse we could," Middleton said.

Middleton called Moore a challenge for anybody. "Tommy was probably the strongest guy for his weight class and maybe three up from him. That was a bull. Here I am 4-5 weights heavier than him and he could give me a go because he was so fast and so strong. He'd give Buzzard a go," Middleton said.

Middleton learned coachability in junior high from Tesla and Mr. Buzzard. "I was coachable because of coach Tesla. He made me coachable. I've got him beating me on one side and I've got old man Buzzard beating me on the other side. You don't know wrath until you had old man Buzzard beat you five days a week, and when you got to the meet he was still beating you and that was just to get you ready to go. If he thought you were going to stray mentally, he'd stay with you like white on rice."

Stinson seemed to have a working knowledge of more than just taking someone down to the mat and pinning them. "Paul was a technician. He wrestled offensively and defensively and seemed to understand it. Stinson came from a family of boys, their daddy was a minister and they used to wrestle out on the church lot and they'd take on all comers. Paul was one of the smallest ones and he could kick anybody's butt," Middleton said.

Another part of the East program was the supply of amino acids Don Buzzard Sr. had. According to younger Don Buzzard, his dad picked up the amino acids in Ames.

"I was heavily recruited that year and Iowa State was the choice that I made verbally. I was also a pretty good football player, so I actually went to Iowa State on a football scholarship although wrestling was my main love. My dad talked to some of the football coaches and he brought all these cases home. He said, 'There are a bunch of boxes in the car, unload them and take them down to the basement.' I asked and found out they were amino acid.

"The way he had instilled this to us was that we had to take this amino acid before every practice, every meet, before every tournament.

It got to the point where it was almost a ritual, this amino acid was very important."

Middleton said he took very little because his mother worked as a nurse's aide at Allen Hospital and she had talked to a doctor about taking the amino acid. Middleton said the doctor stated that it wasn't good for the nervous system, so he shied away. "Tom took it and Willie took it religiously, a teaspoon of it," Middleton said.

Don Buzzard showed up in time for the finals. "They were like, 'Mr. Buzz, I didn't think you were going to be here, we thought you forgot about us.' The rest is history, we all won state titles," Don Jr. said.

As mentioned earlier, the Trojans did not have a fun time at the district meet. Revenge was exacted at state. Middleton said he and Stinson were the only ones to emerge from the district not too beat up.

- Stinson, who would become East's only three-time state champion, lost to Wally Reams of Charles City in the district. Stinson came back with a referee's decision over Reams in the state finals. "This was the best match of my life," Stinson told the *Waterloo Courier* after his 1964 title.

- Hoosman got beat by intra-city rival Wally Markham in the district tournament. According to Buzzard, Hoosman had enough. "My dad had to pull him out of the locker room. He put his clothes on, wasn't going to accept his medal or anything. He was going home," Buzzard said. In the state finals, Hoosman beat Markham 2-0. "We weren't too worried because Willie wanted vengeance, and when Willie wanted vengeance, he was a different wrestler," Middleton said.

Going into the final round in 1964, some of East's wrestlers were getting nervous. "The five of us were going out to warm up. My dad happened to be a little bit late that evening and Tom Moore, our 120-pound state champion, says, 'Hey Buzz, where is Mr. Buzz?' so I called him. (Moore) said, 'I can't win if I don't get my amino acid.'"

After Buzzard's dad showed up, the Trojans did their thing and Fort Dodge helped to prevent East and West finish in a tie for the team title. Kent Osboe of Fort Dodge met West's Bud Knox in the heavyweight championship. If Knox beat Osboe for the third time that season, it would be a tie. If Knox pinned Osboe, the Wahawks would have overtaken the Trojans.

Osboe won, 8-7. East won, but the Trojans were not rooting for Osboe that night.

"You know, we would not cheer against Knox. We knew Buddy," Middleton said. "A lot of those kids as teenagers, we snuck around together. Waterloo was so small. We'd meet downtown, we'd meet at shows. We'd caddy together at Sunnyside Country Club. I was shocked when Kent Osboe beat Buddy Knox, I was shocked."

Not quite as startled as when someone told him about his mother's presence, but Middleton said the outcome was a stunner.

That finals match was tough on Middleton's mother.

"My sister said (my mother's) heart was in her throat the whole match," Middleton said, adding that his mother didn't even want to watch fake pro rasslin' matches on television after that night at McElroy.

Nobody beat an East High wrestler that night. Five qualifiers, five state champions. No team since that night has crowned every qualifier as a state champion.

"We didn't talk about trying to win everything. We just believed we could win and Dave Natvig was a good coach," Buzzard said. "As time went along is where it really got to be more important and we started to realize no one's ever done this before. Lewis Central had eight qualifiers and had six champions, but no one else has ever batted 1,000."

Will East's mark be topped? "It's a record I would hope wouldn't be broken, but I think in time it certainly will. All records are broken sometime. I would talk to that team," Don Jr. said.

"It was everything that I ever expected it to be."

Mickey Mantle. Jim Brown. Dan Gable. Not bad company to keep if you're a former state YMCA swimming champion who has a jones about being a top-flight wrestler.

Gable wanted to be at the top of his game, so he watched those in the sports world who operated where he wanted to be. Mantle fit that bill in baseball. So did Brown in football.

"I don't know if I always put it up there on a pedestal. For some reason, wrestling and sports, it wasn't like I was always thinking, 'That's what I got to get to.' It was more like, 'I'm already there.' It was whatever sport I was playing, in my mind it was always like I would be at that level."

Perhaps that explains why the "little red-headed crewcut," as Waterloo West coach Bob Siddens remembers his most famous squad member, went through his three-season high school career undefeated. 64-0. He was starting to build a body of wrestling work that covered success at every phase – high school, college, international and coaching.

"I'm glad that Daniel has given the publicity and the notoriety he has. I imagine there are some people who have been jealous because he got that notoriety," Siddens said.

In 1964, 1965 and 1966 one still needed to use the term "Dan Gable" to describe him and identify him. In future years virtually everyone knew him as "Gable." On Nov. 30, 1963 Gable started on his 64-0 record by beating Dennis Severson of New Hampton 6-2.

Why wouldn't a kid want to excel in wrestling back then? Waterloo and neighboring Cedar Falls was the epicenter of high school wrestling in the state. Waterloo West and Waterloo East were multiple-time state champions. The state tournament was held in West Gym at Cedar Falls or McElroy Auditorium in Waterloo during the 60's. The large-school team championship stayed in Black Hawk County for 12 years of a 13-year span between 1957 and 1969. "When you walked in to (West Gym), it was packed. As a little kid, you got big eyes and you're watching three mats, you're watching certain people. My family was aligned growing up with East Waterloo at the beginning – we were aligned with the Buzzards."

Bob Buzzard won two state championships for Waterloo East before Gable got into high school. Buzzard's brother, Don, won the last of his two championships in 1964, Gable's sophomore season.

Why is the tournament such a big deal in Iowa?

"I think it's pretty obvious why it's a fabulous event. I don't know all of the history to it – and there is history to it, lots of it – and I don't know what the first one looked like, or the second one or the 30th or the 40th. I am familiar with the last 50 years of it, so that's a lot of history there and a lot of time span. Ever since, I can remember going to wrestling events because I'm from Waterloo, Iowa and at that time wrestling was a dominant force in the city."

Gable also aligned himself with some non-wrestlers.

"I watched all the top professional athletes in the world, Mantle, Jim Brown. My mind was always up with them," Gable said. "I didn't really understand the level differences and that's probably good. When it was time to be a competitive wrestler at the high school level that was going to go to the state championship, it wasn't really about my goal was to get there or to go there, it was part of the package."

While he watched the tournament, and some tough squads from State College of Iowa (later Northern Iowa), in West Gym, Gable never got to hit the mat for gold there. His winning was done at the same place he used to go to when the circus was in town – McElroy Auditorium, or the Hippodrome as some folks still call it today.

"They had hockey too, but I really remember it for the three state tournaments that I was in and I also remember it for the state tournament I came to before that and then I actually watched some state tournaments after that to watch some friends of mine compete," Gable said. "I drive by it I look at it and I can't believe that's where we had our state wrestling tournament. It was definitely a great wrestling venue at that time in your head. It was everything that I ever expected it to be."

For all Gable knew, everyone expected to go to state. He certainly did. "I actually got to start experiencing that situation, but my mind and focus was different then. It wasn't just trying to get there, you knew you were going to be there, it was part of the season, it was something you do like high school graduation. A lot of kids don't graduate, but I never knew that," Gable said.

He saw a neighbor boy, Bill Cannon, finish second at 95 pounds for West in the 1963 tournament. Gable remembered how Tom Peckham from Cresco pinned nearly everyone he faced. Gable did not eyeball Peckham's most memorable pin in high school – rallying from behind to deck Wayne Cool of Waterloo East in the 1961 finals at West Gym – because he could not see through the throng of fans who jumped to their feet as they saw an upset do a reversal on a dime.

In 1964, Gable got to start making his own memories.

"Once it went from UNI to McElroy Auditorium, it was a hockey rink but you didn't look at it as a hockey rink, I guess," Gable said. "It was bigger so again it was exciting. I remember it being a full house. I remember I started the team off, I was the 95-pounder. I remember the weigh-ins. You got 2 hours after weigh-ins before you'd compete. It was part of the schedule and I did my job."

The challenge at tournament time can be working through the awe factor or the shock of being in front of thousands. "That's why a lot of people can't function properly, their heads are in the stars. When their heads are up in the rafters usually your back is against the mat," Gable said.

"I think the mind is really critical in how you develop. When you're just always putting yourself in the upper level of performance, it makes things not seem so distant away," Gable said. "It puts you more in the presence to develop the necessary skills and whatever you need to be at that high level when you get to that high level. The coaches and the way I went about things prepared me for the level that was up there on a daily basis."

"When I got to go out and be on stage, it was not anything about, 'I'm glad I'm here' or 'I can't believe I'm a member of this group.' That's a coaching job to make them feel like this is where you belong if they don't feel that way or if they are in awe of it," Gable said. "When I went to the Olympic Games, I went out for the championship, I wrestled a Russian that they said they had scoured to beat me, but it didn't affect me like, 'My gosh, this is it.' It was part of the routine that I felt was normal."

Waverly referee Arlo Flege remembered Gable having an advantage over others.

"The one kid that stood out when I was officiating was Dan Gable.

What made him so good was he was so much farther ahead than other kids mentally," Flege said.

Gable's victory in the 1972 Olympics, when he did not surrender a point, became a major part of the man, the myth, the legend.

He surrendered some points in the Class A 95-pound championship match in 1964, but had the sense to keep wrestling and not panic. Gable beat Mike Reams of Charles City, 6-4.

"I didn't lose any matches in high school. I had a couple close ones my sophomore year. They really weren't so close, but all of a sudden something happened," Gable said. "Like the (1964) state finals, I'm up 4-0, 20-30 seconds to go, whatever it was. I get rolled and there's a scramble. The guy gets a reversal and a near-fall. Because I' m still wrestling, I'm going to the next move, I'm back on top and the match ends 6-4."

In his next two championship bouts, Gable shut out Denny Knudsen of Fort Dodge, 6-0, at 103 and beat Don Briggs of Cedar Rapids Jefferson, 11-2, at 112 pounds.

Dave Harty, a former assistant executive director of the Iowa High School Athletic Association, said Gable was among the elite of a host of outstanding wrestlers in the state tournament through the years.

"Today even, I say that Ron Gray, Tim Krieger and Dan Gable…there were so many, many good ones but those guys were technicians. "

Waterloo Courier wrestling writer Burke Evans referred to one of West's 1966 champions as "Phenamenal Dan Gable…" No matter how you spell it, Gable was a benchmark for the sport in Iowa.

"The state, and city, has produced numerous outstanding wrestlers. However, prior to last night, none had ever been able to go through an entire high school career without suffering at least one defeat," Evans said the morning after the Gable-Briggs match. "Even Britt's Bob Steenlage, the state's only four-time state champ, came out on the short end of the score on a couple of occasions. However, West High's Dan Gable changed all that last night."

It helped that night that Gable stayed in character, you might say.

"I didn't just prepare for that match that whole weekend, even the two hours before, one hour before. You got a routine and whatever that routine is that you do and it's good for you, you stay in it," Gable said. "I didn't really get into all that part that I think that puts pressure on you. For some reason I stayed within my present. Even though I knew what was the goal at the end, it's not like I focused so much on those goals, I focused on the every day situation going on. Because of that, it seemed like you gained more that way now that I look back at it. With that in mind, by the time you want to get to those goals you're actually built strong enough to be able to attain those type of things."

He got out of the routine once, at the 1970 NCAA tournament in Evanston, Ill. Larry Owings handed Gable his only loss in high school or varsity college competition. "I got out of the routine because of the hype, because of the atmosphere, because of going undefeated the first time for anybody from a high school or college point of view, so you get into the drama of it and you shouldn't," Gable said. "The drama was interviews and talking to people, and that just wasn't my way. It affected me, I wasn't as prepared in that particular match based on a lot of different things, but especially as I prepared in the last hour before the match.

"If you're good enough to be able to do everything that everybody else wants and still go out and do the job, hey that's pretty good. But when you're at the highest levels – state championship, national championship or the Olympic championship – usually you don't want to take a chance because your competitor is pretty darn good. With that in mind you stay within your own realm."

Gable said he never had a goal of making state. His was to win state. His was to win an Olympic gold medal, not just to make the team.

"No goals that I have have ever been down-to-the-earth bottom goals, and I think that's why I had a lot of success," Gable said. "I think it came from the YMCA when I had good people around me helping me, it came from Bob Siddens, it came from my parents, just an accumulation. Then you impact other people and hopefully they'll do the same thing."

Gable said the state tournament resembles the NCAA meet in one key aspect.

"The state tournament shows just like the NCAA tournament will, it will show unbelievable emotion, and emotion is the thrill of victory and the agony of defeat," Gable said. "If you don't think it's agony sometimes, you've just got to look at the peoples' eyes. Watch them afterwards, how much pain is going through them. Some people make it there and they handle it better, or this is better than I ever did before, but there are some that really think they were going to win that event and don't. When that happens, it's pain, it's pain in the body."

Speaking of pain in the body, Gable has a remnant in a shed on his Iowa City property of his days grappling on the Buzzards' lawn in Waterloo. It's a 12-foot by 12-foot piece of wrestling mat that was home to a lot of summer workouts involving guys from various schools.

"That was quite a little deal we had there," Bob Buzzard said. "There were no mat clubs, there were no wrestling camps. There were a couple in Pennsylvania but we were so far from it and it was a money issue, but my dad said we could do it right here."

Gable must have liked the mat as well as the competition.

"That mat the Buzzards grew up on, my dad bought from old man Buzzard. That is the mat I trained on in my basement, (Bob Buzzard) beat me up on but he also trained me there," Gable said. "I wasn't upset about him beating me up from a standpoint of he picked on me, I was mad because he beat me up. I didn't realize you could get beat up that bad. I had it in my folks' house until '81. I brought it (to Iowa City) when I built my own wrestling room in this basement. It's in my shed right now, it's up there in the corner, it's beat up, it's got a lot of cobwebs on it but I still have that old 12 by 12 that has been here since the late 50's."

That's about as long as he's been a fan of the state tournament.

"He came in with an inspiration of winning."

One of the better marriages per se in Iowa's long high school wrestling history occurred in 1972, when Bob Roethler said "I do" to the proposal of whether he'd like to be coaching the sport at Emmetsburg High School.

Roethler came close to not getting to see the conclusion of an amazing four-season run of success.

Emmetsburg's was a youthful program, just a few seasons old, when Roethler came to the Palo Alto County community from Fort Dodge St. Edmond, where he had coached for five seasons. It was during his stint with the Gaels that Roethler noticed some guys wearing E'Hawk uniforms.

"We wrestled Emmetsburg in duals and tournaments. There were kids on the team that had outstanding builds, but their technique was rather lacking," Roethler remembered. "The thing that really amazed me was you got them in the third period, they died."

There was something to be said about the E'Hawk schedule, he thought. Emmetsburg was not too far from Algona, Eagle Grove and Britt – programs with a veteran coach and a well-stocked lineup of tough guys. Teams with state team championships. Teams that were out of Emmetsburg's league, but if the E'Hawks were to get to their level they had to be on the schedule. That was one of Roethler's first orders of business with Emmetsburg Athletic Director Clint Stille.

"It was really a good marriage. It was the right program for him and he was the right guy for us," said Jeff Kerber, an undefeated four-time state champion for Emmetsburg.

It all seemed to work. The E'Hawks finished third in Class 2-A at the 1975 state tournament. Some of the guys that were part of football coach Duane Twait's first playoff team in the fall of 1974 were on that 1975 wrestling team. Things were about to get very golden for a school with colors of black and gold.

"He came in with an inspiration of winning. The first thing he did was toughen up our schedule. He said the better kids you wrestle, the better you're going to be yourself," said Rich Stillman, who would become a three-time state champion when he wasn't a standout on the football team. "He inspired all of us to work for a team goal. A good group of athletes was coming at the time, but he molded us into a great program.

"He's the one who started this, his inspiration and thoughts of setting our goals higher. We had that with Coach Twait doing that in the football program at the same time. With those two leading the programs, both of those rose to the very top."

Emmetsburg reached the finals of the Class 3-A football playoffs in 1975, then won the Class 2-A wrestling championship in 1976. The wrestling crown was the first of four in a row – one-third of Emmetsburg's 12 traditional titles. Twait won seven of Emmetsburg's nine state football championships.

Ask Roethler about the chance to have a run of four championships in succession after the quarterfinals of the 1977 tournament and he might have fixed you with a heated gaze. Perhaps he would have offered a few choice words. The E'Hawks had a rough quarterfinals in 1977, losing three matches. It was enough that Roethler sensed the run was ending. "At least I can relax now because we are out of it," he was quoted after the quarters by the *Emmetsburg Reporter*.

A strong comeback plus titles by Jeff Kerber and Stillman helped the E'Hawks win title No. 2. The *Reporter* quoted Roethler as saying the victory was super.

"I think this title was sweeter than last year because we didn't have it won by Friday and we had to come back to get it," Roethler told the paper.

Roethler's Emmetsburg teams lost only seven times and had one draw between 1972 and 1980. The number of losses matched Roethler's loss total as a high school wrestler at Central of Elkader (1959-63).

"I think Emmetsburg was something new for Bob because of the passion level. We had already laid the ground work in our little kid program," Kerber said. "When coach Roethler came here, there was quite a bit of excitement about something that hadn't been done before. We were starting to quickly open some eyes."

Kerber helped open those eyes. Starting as a skinny freshman

98-pounder, he won all 126 high school matches, got his picture in *LIFE* magazine and became the state's second four-time state champ, 17 years after Bob Steenlage of Britt set the standard. Kerber closed his career with his 100th pin.

It didn't take long for Roethler to meet the Kerbers – Jeff, older brother Mark and father John.

"The first night in Emmetsburg, I get a call at 11:30 at night. It's Mr. Kerber calling me, 'Are you the new wrestling coach? I want you over at the house right away, I want you to see my two boys,'" Roethler remembered. "I didn't know who he was or where he lived, I finally got directions from a gas station. He wakes these two young boys up and has them go downstairs…"

Jeff Kerber and Stillman were two of Roethler's aces. So were Dan Kauffman, Kevin Kauffman, Mark Kerber, Mike Van Oosbree, Mike Joynt and Jack Higley. After they won in 1976, the E'Hawks knew they wanted more and talked about their goals.

"I don't know if (the word) dynasty was in there. There was no doubt in my mind that we were going to come back and do it again the next year," Stillman said. "I knew we had a good bunch of athletes that were going to continue it. Were we going to win it every year? I knew we were going to be right there every year. Bob showed that desire and that extra push that we needed to do."

Roethler had taken another step to building a strong program: developing a youth wrestling club. "We started a little kid program that was bar none the best in Iowa," Roethler said. "We had kids coming up from Oklahoma in charter buses to wrestle in the Little E'Hawk tournament."

Mix an intense coach who insisted that no one would out-work or out-condition the E'Hawks with a group of talented athletes and you had some bruising matches – in the practice room. Roethler joked that he could have sold tickets to the tryout matches. "We'd get in the room and we were friends outside, but in the room it was competitive. You get a bunch of good wrestlers battling against each other, that improves and you get better and better," Dan Kauffman said. "Van Oosbree and I were about the same weight, so we'd switch back every year where he would go higher and I would go lower. It was team, friends and it was a battle to improve and get better."

Eventually, those teams that scored one-sided wins over the E'Hawks were getting beat.

Stillman added, "I was a die-hard athlete. I already had those same emotions with me; nobody was going to beat me, nobody was going to beat our team. He just brought that out of the kids. The group of kids were there at the right time, it was a good blend of good athletes but great coaching that we were going to take this to another level. His guidance helped open the way and showed us the way."

Kauffman, a two-time state champion, remembered Roethler as intense, but able to give as good as he got in light-hearted moments with the team. He could also make a wrestler pay for things such as not keeping his weight in check.

"He was a friend, everybody liked him. You could talk crap to him and he'd give you crap back. It wasn't being unprofessional, it was more when you're 17 and you have a coach you can have fun with, it inspires you more," Kauffman said. "He was a go-getter. In the room he made you bust your butt. I remember I came into the room way over right before sectionals, and he put me out there and lightest weight to heaviest weight twice. I had to go takedowns with everyone to make weight. By the time I got to state and I was in overtime, I wasn't even tired I was in such good shape."

Roethler's wrestlers grew loyal to the man. When Kauffman's son, Jake, won a 152-pound state wrestling championship in Arizona, it did not take long for word to get back to Emmetsburg.

"One of the first guys I called (in 2007) when my son won state here in Arizona was Roethler," Kauffman said. "I let him talk to my son because I was proud of him winning state and I knew he would be. He was my wrestling coach. I still look up to the guy for what he's done. It's a wrestling family. I was like, 'Hey coach, guess what, my son just won state. Here, say hi to him.' I was proud of him winning state and I knew (Roethler) would be too."

Dan Kauffman knew how close Roethler came to not getting that call. Kauffman and Roethler were working out Oct. 31. What happened in the practice room is a bit hazy because Roethler's account and Kauffman's account differ. Roethler said he'd been having some stout headaches, but he figured they would go away.

"I thought it was from not wearing my glasses. What happened, the bulge on the vessel on the brain was leaking blood and that's where the aneurysm occurred," Roethler said. "I had Dan Kauffman in an underhook, I was tossing him and it ruptured and I dropped right to the mat. I walked to the ambulance and spent the night in the hospital in Emmetsburg. The next day they rushed me to the hospital in Rochester. Nobody knew what it was."

Kauffman said he was trying to score on his coach, a task made more challenging by of the strength of Roethler, who could put up some prodigious pounds of weights.

"I remember I think I hit him with a headlock and I got up and got kind of excited. He laid there and he started shaking and I said, 'Oh crap,'" Kauffman said. "When you're a junior in high school, it's pretty detrimental, scary if you hit a headlock and he's shaking. You really don't know what's going on."

What happened was that Roethler, then 33 years old and a married father of a young son, was in the beginning stage of an aneurysm. He was taken to the Emmetsburg hospital and later transferred to the Mayo Clinic in Rochester, Minn.

Roethler's wife, Kathy, said her husband was administered Last Rites before the trip to Rochester. Bob Roethler knew what was going on. "I can remember riding in the ambulance up to Rochester listening to the radio 'Bob Roethler's on his way to St. Mary's Hospital in Rochester,'" Roethler said.

The *Emmetsburg Reporter* had a page one brief in its Nov. 7, 1978 issue that Roethler had an aneurysm in the tissue surrounding the brain and that he was in stable condition. Surgery was scheduled Nov. 9.

"Once they operated, I came out of the surgery just like I'm talking to you now, but then a massive stroke set in. I bled so much in the brain that the part of the brain that controls the left side didn't get blood for 8-10 hours, and that caused a stroke," Roethler said. "I remember saying, 'God, you've reached my tolerance point, I'm yours now' because it hurt. It felt like my head was on a volcano."

Roethler could not walk for two months. A lasting impact of the stroke is that Roethler's left arm and left leg are not as strong as the right side. There was a positive sign two days after Christmas 1978, when Roethler moved his left leg. He had already bucked the odds prior to moving his leg.

"My doctors told me that 50 percent of the people who have what I did die instantly, and another 25 percent die 24 hours later," Roethler said in an interview with the *Emmetsburg Democrat*. "I know I still have a long way to go, but I'm damn happy to be in that other 25 percent."

Kathy Roethler spent the first month in Rochester with her husband, then moved temporarily to Fort Dodge so she and 2 ½-year-old son Robert would be with her parents during the week. Kathy said she visited her husband on weekends and got through the lengthy ordeal because Robert was such a happy baby. "He was actually my strength," Kathy said, adding that her parents were a huge support.

Stan Peterson was appointed interim coach while Roethler was sidelined. Could the E'Hawks win a fourth consecutive state championship? That talk was trumped by whether or not Roethler would live, and if he lived, would he ever coach again?

"As far as pressure, I really think our pressure ended when Roethler had his aneuryism the first day of practice. It completely changed our season. It was no longer about fourth title or anything else, it was a bunch of young men had to grow up in a hurry because our coach is in a coma," Kerber said. "It really took a lot of pressure away because all of a sudden we started to think about the bigger things in life. At 18 years old, I would have never thought about a guy dying at 33 years old. It was helpful in a sense that we never had time to think about winning or losing or titles as much as we're going to do our best because our coach is fighting for his life."

Roethler was learning as well, but far from the practice room.

"I used to kind of feel sorry for myself, God left me this way with one arm the rest of my life, but I'd get myself in the wheelchair without help and I kind of had the run of the floor there," Roethler said. "I go into a room and here's some guy with both legs gone and an arm gone from a car-train accident and I said, 'Bob, you're going to be more ambulatory than he is.' It's an attitude thing. You've got to be positive. I don't have a physical handicap, I have an impairment and I can't use my left arm."

Kerber along with Kauffman and Van Oosbree – the quarterback on the E'Hawks' championship football team – were already considered the leaders of the band. With Roethler down, those three took on an enhanced role. "It fell on the three of us to almost become coaches. It was really, to be honest with you, a great situation because I think it was a growing-up period that we would not have had otherwise. When Roethler went down, we manned up. Not just those three, the entire team."

Roethler sat on a chair as he came back to practice leading up to the district tournament. Kauffman said it was a boost for the squad.

"It's like one of your best friends that you haven't seen for a long time or somebody that inspires you, they walk back in the room. It uplifts you and it motivates you even more to see somebody that could have died and he comes back," Kauffman said. "I don't know if we were predicted to win that year, but we knew it was going to be close. When he came in, it was another motivating factor."

The E'Hawks wound up comfortably ahead. They won the fourth straight title with 78 ½ points, 22 ahead of Sigourney, which was led by 132-pound state champion Clark Yoder.

Stillman, who is an assistant coach with the E'Hawks, said he talked with Roethler years after the run of championships. The man had one regret, Stillman said.

"He said, 'I never enjoyed it as much as I should have when we were there,'" Stillman said. "We'd go to state and win the title by 30 points and he was dissatisfied. We didn't do this good enough or we didn't do that good enough. He was always pushing us to a higher level. Even when we got to the top, he wanted us at a higher level."

Roethler resigned as head coach after the 1979-80 season, but he has remained close to the E'Hawk program. He does volunteer coaching and can help a wrestler with technique - even though he can't do the hands-on method he used before his aneurysm - and the mental approach that helped so many kids provide points to the team standings.

Bob Kenny, who led Emmetsburg/Armstrong-Ringsted to six Class 2-A traditional championships and two dual-meet championships between 2000 and 2006, said Roethler was a motivator but never an obstacle. Kenny is currently athletic director at Mason City High School.

"Bob had been there, he knew what it took, he knew hard work. His being around was a motivational piece. He led by example," Kenny said. "He'd be in the weight room and we'd be going through our circuits. He'd be there with like a 60-pound dumbbell with his one good arm and the whole time, the half-hour or 45 minutes we're lifting, he'd be pumping that thing and let it down for a little bit, then back up it would come. No matter what he did, he worked hard at it."

"He never was imposing or he'd never try to say something behind your back. No matter what it was, he had your back 110 percent. Every one of the kids he'd go to war for. If you had an E'Hawk uniform on, look out because Bob was going to be there for you. His life and his passion is wrestling as mine was for a long time. I've kind of let go of that and he hasn't. He has as much passion now as he did when he was 25 years old."

Roethler said his health scare gave him a teaching tool for the kids.

"Appreciate what you got in life when you have it because like that...," Roethler said. "You don't miss something until you lose the use of it."

During the 1970's, some guys made quickness a part of how they mapped out their immediate to short-range goals. Joe Corso, however, shifted into warp speed.

Success is food for thought to many, but Corso of West Des Moines Valley did not want to wait that hour before swimming after his goals when the decade of the 1970's got started.

Corso placed second in Class 3-A at 107 pounds in the 1970 tournament. Six years later, Corso was competing but did not place at 125.5 pounds at the Olympics in Montreal. In between those dates, Corso was a two-time junior college all-American at North Iowa Area Community College and an NCAA Division I all-American at Purdue.

"Just going to the state tournament was a big thing for me. As a sophomore, I went. I didn't go as a freshman so it disappointed me," Corso said. "By the time I got to be a sophomore, then I realized after I lost first round and I go, 'I'm coming back here and I'm going to get to the finals next year.' The next year sure enough I got to the finals. I didn't win state and I was disappointed, but to be honest with you I said it will never happen again, I'm going to come back and win it."

In 1969, Corso was the first victim for eventual Class 3-A 95-pound champion Steve Natvig of Waterloo East.

In 1971, Corso won the 112-pound championship with a 5-1 victory over Tom Lepic of Iowa City High. "I just put my blinders on. First round I had a guy (Jay Huebner of Davenport Central) that I had in the semis the year before, I pounded him in the first round. In the second round I had Jon Bagenstos from Waterloo West and we had a very close match, 4-3, and then I had Tom Lepic in the finals and I pounded him. It was about attitude, but it was a very great feeling that I could do that."

Corso was born in Italy and was adopted by a West Des Moines family. His initial athletic interest was in gymnastics.

"I did a lot of gymnastics and tap dancing. I never got into the sport until I saw a dual meet for our high school at Phenix Elementary School. They packed it in and I saw it and I said, 'This is what I want to do,'" Corso said. "I was in seventh and eighth grade at that time and I went out for the intramural wrestling team. I beat everybody and I was doing gymnastics, but I kind of found my niche at that time. I put on the blinders and went forward."

Corso said he was driven to perform in wrestling. "I enjoyed going to work out. There were a couple years I didn't like it because I was cutting so much weight, but in general when I wasn't cutting the hard weight, I loved going to practice. I loved working out, I loved going hard, I loved wrestling the competition. It was tough at first, but I found out how to win and beat any guy. I got that when I won Junior Nationals after my senior year in Iowa City."

He admits the idea of the Olympics was not on his mind when he was twice making the finals for the Tigers. International dreams had to wait for college.

"I didn't go to college to go to college, I went to college to wrestle and I got a degree. I knew I wasn't done wrestling. I really didn't get into thinking I would make an Olympic team until after my senior year in college, after I beat a two-time NCAA champ, Pat Milkovich, in the Big Tens," Corso said. "I got third in the NCAAs that year. I got a little frustrated and I decided to quit because I took sixth in the Olympic Trials. I'm going, 'All this work this year and nothing paid off for me.' I didn't realize I'd pushed myself so hard that I lost my edge. I took two weeks off and actually partied. Then I went to (DeKalb, Ill.), had a good training camp, won the Olympic Trials and all of a sudden everything started clicking."

Corso remains active in wrestling as a coach and as an official. He doesn't seem to have the answer-the-fire-alarm speed about him now, but he's teaching others to put the blinders on and go for success.

Tournaments in the 1970's featured a number of families enjoying success.

It was during those years that Lisbon's squad had a Lord in the final round. Doug Lord won the Class 1-A 132-pound championship with an 11-6 victory over Mark Schuling of Bondurant-Farrar in 1973. The following year, Lord moved up to 138 but lost in the finals, 4-0, to Marty Bussanmas of Norwalk.

Jim Lord was a freshman in 1975 and made the finals before losing, 4-0, to David Lott of Denver. That would be the last sore point because Jim beat Lott, 9-3, the following year. Jim pinned Robert Cole of Highland of Riverside at 112 and then beat Mike Blasberg of Tripoli, 28-7, at 126 pounds. Jim's point total in the 1978 finals remained the highest in a championship match going into the 2011 tournament.

The Hagen brothers of Britt added to their family's gold medal haul in the 1970's as John won two of his three championships and Brent won his three titles. Their father, Wally, was a state champion in 1943 and 1944 for Clarion. Brent Hagen also won an NCAA Division II 118-pound championship for Mankato State in 1977.

Family was a successful word during the 1970's at state. Jim Gibbons of Ames began gathering the most championships by a family – 10 – in 1975. By the end of the decade, Jim had three titles and brothers Tim and Joe added three more. Joe would get two more titles and brother Jeff won twice during the 1980's.

Gene and Duane Hunt of Algona were each two-time champions and they won consecutive crowns in 1970 and Glynn and Chuck Jones of Cedar Rapids Washington won together in 1973. The Stevenson brothers of Britt, Jeff and Mark, never won together, but they gave their family a gold medal every year between 1971 and 1975.

Brothers Eric and Mike Norris had an annual run similar to the Stevensons between 1970 and 1973. Clark and Ross Yoder of Sigourney were champions together in 1978 and Clark won the second of his three titles in 1979. Cliff and Dave Howlett of Britt won two of the family's three titles in the 1970's; Lennie and Jim Zalesky of Cedar Rapids Prairie totaled three championships and Chuck and Tim Berrier brought three titles to Urbandale. Bob and Don Erickson of Clear Lake each won a championship. So did Don and Randy Swoyer of Greenfield.

The Norris brothers must have figured the best way to win a championship was to beat a champion from the previous year. Eric Norris avenged an earlier loss to Gene Hunt of Algona, the Class 2-A 155-pound champion in 1970, with a 7-0 victory in the semifinals. Norris clinched Ankeny's team championship with a pin in the finals.

Mike Norris faced Tony Cordes of Waterloo West, the 132-pound champion in Class 3-A in 1971, in the 138-pound finals in 1972. Norris pinned Cordes, giving him a fall in all three tournament matches.

Don Swoyer and his cousin Dan were champions together for coach Larry Riley at Greenfield in 1972. The *Adair County Free Press* reported Don Swoyer was Greenfield's first wrestler in the modern era to finish a season unblemished. He was 28-0 at 138. That finish was even more impressive, according to the paper's account, because Swoyer wrestled at 119 and lost in the first round of the 1971 tournament.

Another tough pair of cousins were Henry and Ralph Reicks of Turkey Valley of Jackson Junction. Henry won the Class 2-A 98-pound championship in 1975 and Ralph took the same weight two years later. Many wrestling fans remarked about the dominance of Turkey Valley heavyweight Dick Cuvelier, who won his second straight championship in 1976 by beating Dean Phinney of Clear Lake, 7-6. Cuvelier was 53-0 in those two seasons and the only points he gave up in the 1975-76 season were what Phinney – himself a heavyweight champion in 1977 – accrued. Ralph Reicks showed the lightweight guys could also be dominating when he won his title in 1977. Ralph shut out three opponents and pinned the other.

Henry won three matches in his championship season – 3-2 against Bret Adams of Iowa Falls, 2-0 against Tracy Moore of Roland –Story and 9-2 over Roger Meyers of Glenwood. Henry's margins were not quite like his cousin's, but Henry was one of the few people that claimed a victory over Moore.

"That's the bar that I looked at."

Jeff Kerber had a role model – Dan Gable at the 1972 Olympics - in regards to doing big things on a wrestling mat. Before long, the Emmetsburg stud became a similar figure in the state of Iowa.

Kerber was an undefeated four-time state champion between 1976 and 1979. At the same time he was a member of four consecutive Class 2-A championship teams forged by coach Bob Roethler. Kerber was too young to see Bob Steenlage of Britt win his fourth title in 1962, but his work gave five Iowans within the next 10 years an extra bit of motivation to join that tight clique.

"Kerber proved it could be done again," said Scott Morningstar of Lisbon after becoming the state's third four-timer in 1980. "I didn't see Steenlage, but I saw Kerber and knew it could be done again."

Joe Gibbons, who won a pair of state titles at Waterloo Columbus and a pair at Ames, along with Greg Randall of Mount Vernon, Mark Schwab of Osage and Dan Knight of Clinton joined Morningstar as four-timers within the next 10 years post-Kerber.

Kerber made the path for a group of guys to follow, Gibbons said.

"That kind of got the ball rolling," Gibbons said. "It was like when the 4-minute mile got broken. It all of a sudden opened the floodgates up for guys like Scott Morningstar and myself, Greg Randall and Danny Knight, Jeff McGinness."

Kerber said he was branching off from a path he had been shown.

" Well, of course Dan Gable won the Olympics in '72 and I graduated high school in '79, so that was a huge name. I don't know that I ever really had a dream of being an Olympic champion. I might have said I did but I don't know if I really did, but he certainly made a lot of kids in Iowa believe that it was possible to do some special things," Kerber said. "I would say that era – Dan Gable, Ben Peterson, I remember Wayne Wells, Rick Sanders – that was the generation ahead of me that I looked at. That was more of a national scale, but with Peterson and Gable being Iowa connected, it was pretty easy to identify. That's the bar that I looked at."

Apparently John Kerber believed as well. If his son found a wrestling tournament or a camp that would challenge or educate him, John got him there. As long as there was room in the car or camper, any of Jeff's buddies were more than welcome to ride along. That the tournament was in Montana or Pennsylvania or the camp was in Ponca City, Okla. made no difference to John Kerber. All it did was get his son more than ready for high school competition. Jeff Kerber said he saw how much actions such as those by his father had advanced when he watched the 2010 NCAA tournament. Kerber's son, Justin, wrestles at Cornell University, and his teammate, Kyle Dake, won the 141-pound NCAA championship. "He didn't turn 19 until February 23rd, never redshirted, won the national title, I mean that is an amazing feat," Jeff Kerber said. "You would have never dreamt that was possible back in my era because kids weren't prepared. Now they are. I was kind of the forerunner in that, and I was fortunate that I had a dad who was willing to pay the bills and willing to seek out those opportunities."

Kerber, who started wrestling in second grade, won his first tournament as a third grader, winning the fourth grade bracket at Emmetsburg. His first title of significance was at Harlan, Kerber said.

"Then I thought I was a real big deal because they actually gave medals, not ribbons, and there were kids from other places," Kerber said.

In Iowa, Kerber ushered in a new era. No longer did guys just use single- and double-leg takedowns for their initial scoring. The chicken wing was not the exclusive partner of the half-nelson in turning an opponent. Kerber was doing variations of moves, headlocks and tilts and turks to work his way to a 126-0 high school record. Emmetsburg teammate Rich Stillman, himself a three-time champion, said Kerber helped revolutionize the sport.

"He traveled a lot to different camps as a kid growing up where a lot of us didn't have that opportunity. Jeff brought things into the room. All of us maybe didn't pick up on every one of them but we picked a handful that helped us balance out our own repertoire," Stillman said. "The one thing that Bob pushed was whatever you use, you do it to perfection. If it's two or three takedowns, you go to them and they are going to work for you. Jeff definitely brought in some new techniques that we hadn't seen and I think it very much helped everyone in the room."

Big things came from a little thing such as eyeing a t-shirt, Kerber said.

"You look back at those what they call tipping points – those critical times in your life where you make a decision that ultimately leads to future decisions – and I can remember seeing a wrestling t-shirt. I wrestled a kid at a tournament in either Harlan or Glenwood when I was in about third grade and he had a t-shirt that said 'Wapsie Y Wrestling Camp' – it was one of the few wrestling camps around and it was in Cedar Rapids," Kerber said. "We went down to that camp and that's where all the serious folks in Iowa wrestling were. We got to meet Chuck Jerkovich and Rod Earleywine and all the guys that were serious about little kid wrestling. Then we found out where the hubs of little kid wrestling were, which is Tulsa, Okla. And even the Omaha/Council Bluffs area was strong, so we pursued those opportunities. Consequently when I had entered ninth grade, I had had a lot of wrestling through summer wrestling camps, through tournaments. By the time I was in ninth grade, we had already been to Montana, Pennsylvania, California…the Gibbons family and our family used to jump in a motor home and wherever the wrestling was, that's where we went."

Pull over the mobile home or car and you were likely to find a few Gibbonses, John Thorn of Algona, some Emmetsburg guys or an Ayala from Fort Dodge. "My dad was very unselfish when it came to those opportunities and he was more excited about the folks from Iowa having a chance to compete with the Okies, the kids from Pennsylvania and that type of thing."

They even stayed close to home. "Dad and Bill Gibbons rented a gym and had a state AAU tournament so that the wrestlers could qualify for the national tournament," Kerber recalled.

As a result, Kerber was miles ahead of his fellow freshmen when the 1975-76 season began. It was as if freshmen were trying to outwit a dad who had been around the block a few times and was in top shape.

Dad was supportive, a go-getter and a trailblazer. The benefit was that when I got to ninth grade, just like (Matt) McDonough and Kyle Dake, I was ready to wrestle at that level," Kerber said. "It almost wasn't fair because I had a head start, at least compared to other ninth graders. A lot of the success I had, certainly I had to have certain skills and had to have the ability to go out and compete, but I also was fortunate enough to have a lot of experience under my belt."

Kerber won his first state title with a 1-0 victory over Jeff Hannum of Pleasant Valley. He secured a reputation for beating tough guys when he won his second crown with a 6-2 victory over Tracy Moore of Roland-Story. Moore was the 105-pound champion in 1976 and he had a 67-match winning streak halted by Kerber.

"He was stronger than a bull, very physical and a tough kid. In fact, the *Des Moines Register* picked him to beat me," Kerber said.

In his class-by-class advance of the 1977 state tournament, *The Register*'s Chuck Burdick closed the Class 2-A 112-pound weight with his pick: "With reservation, I'll pick Moore."

In the final two state meets, Kerber won by either major decision or by pin. He pinned all four foes in the 1979 tournament.

"Probably the most fun for me wasn't just being part of the Emmetsburg wrestling team. It was being part of a bigger fraternity of wrestlers that included the Gibbonses, Perry Hummel, Efonda Sproles, Lord, the Lisbon group, the Council Bluffs group, Jim Kimsey from Underwood," Kerber said. "For me, that was what was the most fun, to start to make those friendships and relationships. People that were serious about wrestling had quite a camaraderie. I wrestled those guys yet we were good friends. We trained hard, there was a kindred spirit there that wrestling has that I have never felt in other sports."

And when he won the fourth crown?

"It goes back to the fraternity of studs that I was fortunate enough to be part of. It was an accomplishment that made me worthy to be in that group," Kerber said. "The people that I had tremendous respect for, that pat on the back from them was the same pat on the back I would give them when they did something special."

After he had secured a spot in his fourth championship match, Kerber told the *Quad City Times* he planned no wild stuff when he faced the undefeated Todd Fey of Central of DeWitt.

"I'll wrestle aggressively. I'll try to get the lead early and if a pin opens up I'll go for it," Kerber said. "In a way I'll be cautious though. I won't try to do any wild rolls or other crazy things that could get me in trouble. The winning streak and the state titles mean an awful lot to me. I'm not going to do anything stupid. I'll just try to win."

Roethler said Kerber was something special. In an interview with the *Emmetsburg Democrat*, Roethler said, "Jeff Kerber is a tremendous asset to Iowa wrestling and eventually he'll probably be the same to the nation. There isn't anyone I can think of that I've seen that was better and there will never be another as far as I'm concerned. Most coaches wouldn't have a guy like Kerber in a lifetime. I was lucky."

When Kerber pinned Fey of Central of DeWitt for the 126-pound championship in 1979, Roethler had tears in his eyes.

His skill on the mat could even convert fans of other wrestlers. Jason Etherington Jr. of Algona grew up thinking Bulldog ace Paul Martin was an ideal. Martin was 90-0 and a three-time state champion in his final three years of high school wrestling. "If I remember, that's just who I wanted to be like. You want to be like that guy that wins and pins every time. Then my favorite wrestler was Jeff Kerber because that guy won everything," said Etherington, a state champion for Algona in 1983.

Kerber's amazing display of offense riveted the attention of coaches and young wrestlers to his mat. Everyone was trying to videotape his moves, and those without cameras relied on their memory banks.

"I wasn't really very creative as much as being just a pretty good copycat, a pretty good learner. It goes back to the camp experience. I spent a lot of weeks down at Myron Roderick's camp in Ponca City, Okla. I just loved it, I'd go there and stay," Kerber said. "I remember one year I was scheduled to be down there for a week and some other kids from Emmetsburg were going down the following week because of scheduling conflicts. One of them got sick or got hurt and couldn't go. I called back and said 'Could I take his spot?' I just couldn't get enough of the technique. A lot of what I was doing was learning technique from (Yoshiro) Fujita, (Yojiro) Uetake and all the guys. Myron Roderick was a trailblazer in a sense. What he did at Oklahoma State in his era was pretty remarkable and he brought in some pretty special guys. I was coming back home with a wealth of information that I had been taught, so consequently some of those techniques began to be used by myself and others.

"All the techniques were fundamentally very basic. They weren't all that fancy really, they were just different ways of doing a double-leg or a single-leg or a setup that took you into that position. I think it was an unbelievable era in wrestling because all of a sudden our kids were getting coached, they were getting taught at an earlier age."

Some of the camps were held at 2005 5th Street in Emmetsburg. That was Kerber's address growing up, and it had a two-car garage. Who needs to use the garage for cars when there is a need for practice? The Kerber family cleaned out the garage and converted it into a workout room.

"The whole thing was a mat. We parked (the cars) outside. We put a steel beam across the ceiling so there were no pillars," Kerber said. "We converted it first class, we padded the walls, we had a heater in there. When you stepped in the door, you were stepping on the mat. There wasn't an inch of floor space, there was just a little rug to step on when you came in, but it was wall-to-wall mat and the sides were padded too."

Kerber knew what he wanted when he first donned an Emmetsburg uniform. He had a workout partner in his brother, Mark, who finished third at 98 in the 1975 tournament. At the Emmetsburg kids tournament after the 1975 state meet, Kerber wrestled Jim Lord of Lisbon, who finished second at 98 in the Class 1-A state meet that year.

"I went in as a freshman expecting to win state and I fully expected to win four titles," Kerber said.

Nick Moore of Iowa City West, the 19th man to win win four titles, said expecting to have success right away in high school as Kerber did is not a bad thing.

"You can have a thought in the back of your head, 'That's what I'm going to go after.' When you come into high school, I think a lot of freshmen come in with the wrong attitude maybe. They want to be a state champion, they don't know when, they don't know how, they don't know if it's going to be until their last year," Moore said. "You've got to maybe not so much expect it, but keep it in perspective: If I have a goal to be a state champion, why don't I do it my freshman year? Then why don't I do it my sophomore year? Then why don't I do it my junior year and then why don't I do it my senior year? Coming in, if their goal is to be a state champion, how about you do it right now?"

After winning 122 matches, Kerber was ready to finish his quest for four gold medals.

"I don't think I felt that much pressure. When you've already done it three times, and I was wrestling so well at that point, I just never gave it much thought," Kerber said. "I just thought I was going to win the title. I felt more pressure when I got to college than I did all the way through high school."

Kerber, who was a three-time all-American at Iowa, watched his son win two state championships (Justin Kerber was a four-time finalist) for Emmetsburg/Armstrong-Ringsted before he went to Cornell. Justin Kerber's uncle is Randy Lewis, a three-time state champion in South Dakota, a two-time NCAA champion at Iowa and a gold medalist in the 1984 Olympics.

"He's got the double deal going, and I've heard that a lot, with his genetics it's a sure thing," Jeff Kerber told the *Des Moines Register* in a 2004 story about sons of prominent wrestlers preparing for the state tournament. "I think it does put pressure on him. Even from the time he was in second grade, he tended to have more eyes on him than most kids do."

In the same article, Justin Kerber said, "I've never wished I didn't have the name."

Jeff Kerber seemed to know nothing but winning as a high school kid, but he got a sobering life lesson as a senior when Roethler collapsed in practice because of what was found to be an aneurysm. Roethler received the Last Rites and was not expected to coach again if it did not kill him. Roethler made it back to see Kerber win his fourth title and get his two standing ovations.

"That's difficult to see because you've got a guy who is in his mid-30's, this big strong stud that you knew four months ago, a guy that can bench press 300 pounds four months ago and here he is taking very calculated steps just to get from the edge of the mat to the seat he's going to sit in. That's hard to watch, hard to understand at 18 years old," Kerber said.

Kerber said wrestling is more than just a way to collect gold medals.

"The attributes that you acquire wrestling are priceless in the real world. I don't know of too many families that haven't dealt with situations where you have to suck it up," Kerber said. "I just think life really parallels a wrestling match. You have some victories but you have some defeats, you have some times where you get your nose bloodied but you've got to push through it. I just think the sport of wrestling is tremendous preparation for life."

Kerber is now a husband, father and businessman. He looks for more than just his next practice and next pin.

"My biggest shortcoming was that when you have that kind of success, people kind of put you on that pedestal and pat you on the back all the time, pretty soon you get to thinking that you're something. That's where you need mature people that are grounded, not just in wrestling but in life, to say, 'You're a good wrestler but there is more to life than wrestling.'" Kerber said. "We're attempting to be more balanced. We're a family of faith, I believe in hard work, I think academics are important. That's why Justin's at Cornell and he's part of a great wrestling program. It's possible to do great things in wrestling and also do great things in life. To think you can't find that balance is just wrong."

Audra Liegerot of Red Oak won the 95-pound championship in the 1921 Iowa State Invitational at Ames. Liegerot pinned his way to becoming the first Iowan to win a high school wrestling state championship. Photo courtesy of Red Oak High School

Davenport High School's Paul Krasuski was a football and basketball star. A few days after his basketball team's season ended in 1922, Krasuski won the heavyweight championship in the Iowa Invitational at Iowa City. Photo courtesy of Davenport Public Schools

Norman Borlaug of Cresco placed third in the 1932 state wrestling tournament, 38 years before he was awarded the Nobel Peace Prize for his work in agriculture that prevented over 1 billion people from starving to death. Photo courtesy of Crestwood High School

A young Bob Steenlage of Britt set a goal to become a four-time state wrestling champion, but told few of his plan...

Bob Steenlage of Britt grew up to become Iowa's first four-time state champion in 1962. Five decades later, his name is still familiar with state wrestling fans in Iowa.
Photos courtesy of Bob Steenlage

Fort Dodge became the first powerhouse program in Iowa high school wrestling, under the direction of coach Fred Cooper. The Dodgers won eight outright team championships and shared a ninth title between 1927 and 1941. Photo courtesy of Fort Dodge High School

Bob Steenlage needed to get stronger in order to work toward his goal of winning four state championships. Steenlage is shown working out with some of the weights he made in high school. The weights are now in his garage. Photo by Dan McCool

Ron Gray of Eagle Grove was the first freshman state champion at his school. Gray
was a four-time state finalist and three-time champion. His runner-up finish was in
1954, when he lost to Simon Roberts of Davenport. Roberts was Iowa's first black
state champion and later became the first black NCAA champion. Photo courtesy of
Eagle Grove High School

Davenport High School won the team championship of the 1954 state wrestling
tournament. The team demonstrated some basic moves for local TV station WOC.
Center-left on the mat is Simon Roberts, the first black state champion in Iowa.
Kneeling at far right is coach Jim Fox. Photo courtesy of Simon Roberts

One of the top high school wrestlers in state tournament history is Tom Peckham
of Cresco. Peckham lost four matches as a freshman and then won three state
championships. Wrestling legend Dan Gable said Peckham's style on the mat was
what he wanted to emulate. Photo courtesy of Crestwood High School

Waterloo East qualified five wrestlers for the 1964 state tournament. The Trojans crowned five state champions and sealed the outright Class AA championship when Kent Osboe of Fort Dodge won the heavyweight title. Coach Dave Natvig (third from right) and his champions admire the team championship trophy. Photo courtesy of Waterloo Public Schools

Dan Gable of Waterloo West is likely the best-known state champion from Iowa. Gable was 64-0 and won three state championships for the Wahawks. He later won two NCAA championships at Iowa State (and took his only loss in high school and college), won a gold medal in the 1972 Olympics and coached the University of Iowa to 15 NCAA team championships. Photo courtesy of Waterloo Public Schools

Herb Krieger won a state championship for Mason City in 1962. Twenty years later, Krieger watched his sons, Tim and Todd, win state titles. Tim Krieger won three state championships before winning two NCAA championships at Iowa State. The Kriegers are one of a few Iowa families where the father and two of his sons were state champions. Photo courtesy of Mason City High School

When Bernie Saggau of the Iowa High School Athletic Association wanted a wrestling administrator, he hired Dave Harty. For over 30 years, Harty ran the state tournament. It became so popular that final-round tickets sell out the first day they go on sale. Photo by Dan McCool

Ask wrestlers from the 1970's, 1980's, 1990's and part of the 2000's where they wanted to win a state championship and the answer was Veterans Memorial Auditorium in Des Moines, also known as "The Barn." Championship night at "The Barn" was an atmosphere unmatched: The seats were filled, the Grand March induced goosebumps, the action was intense and the television cameras caught it all. Photo by Dan McCool

Two wrestling coaches and their wives wanted to see high school wrestling get more coverage in Iowa, so they started a publication called The Predicament. A test issue to see if there was interest for a statewide wrestling publication was done for the 1970 state tournament and sold for 25 cents. It was the nation's first state wrestling newspaper and remains in operation today. Courtesy of John Doak

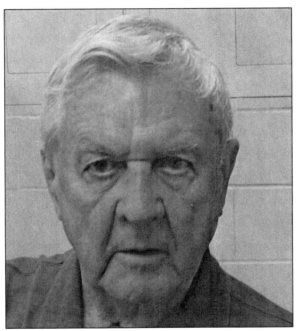

Bob Siddens hitchhiked in junior high to see his first high school wrestling competition. He never won a state championship while wrestling for Eagle Grove, but led Waterloo West to 11 team championships. Siddens was also a regular as a referee at the NCAA tournament and was a clinician at camps throughout the country.
Photo by Dan McCool

Dan Mashek wrestled for Bob Siddens at Waterloo West and for Chuck Patten at University of Northern Iowa. He took what he learned to Don Bosco of Gilbertville and to North Scott of Eldridge. Mashek retired as the leader among Iowa high school wrestling coaches with 519 dual-meet victories.
Photo by Dan McCool

Marv Reiland wrestled at Eagle Grove and returned to lead the Eagles to their first state wrestling team championship in 1974. He would lead the team to two more titles when his son, Mark, was a two-time state champion...
Photo by Dan McCool

...after winning two state titles and an NCAA championship for the University of Iowa, Mark became wrestling coach at Iowa City West, which has won two traditional team titles and five dual-meet titles. Marv and Mark are the first father and son to coach teams to traditional team championships.
Photo by Dan McCool

The sport of wrestling in Iowa's high schools is rich with family ties. Brothers watch older brothers earn a medal – or a state championship – at the state meet and want to copy or surpass sibling efforts. The Kelly family of Britt (pictured) accounted for five state championships and all six boys wrestled in the state meet. The early winners in family matches in the basement were sisters Karen (front row right) and Connie (front row middle). Photo courtesy of Karen Sankey

There have been six teams that qualified their entire lineup for the traditional state wrestling tournament since 1931, when tournaments determined the qualifiers. The most recent team was the 1978-79 team from Don Bosco of Gilbertville, which qualified all 12 wrestlers. The Dons set a record with 145 ½ points in winning the Class 1-A team title. Photo courtesy of the Iowa High School Athletic Association

Thirty years after Don Bosco of Gilbertville qualified its entire lineup for the state wrestling tournament, the Dons returned to lead the Grand March prior to the start of the championship matches. The 1979 Dons watched the 2009 Dons win their fourth consecutive Class 1-A team title and four Don Bosco wrestlers win individual championships. Photo courtesy of the Iowa High School Athletic Association

The Gibbons family of Ames and Waterloo Columbus holds the record for the most individual state championships – 10 - won by a band of brothers from Iowa. Jim Gibbons won three state titles beginning in 1975, Tim won one in 1976, Joe won state titles at Waterloo Columbus in 1978 and 1979 and then moved to Ames for titles in 1980 and 1981 and Jeff won gold medals in 1983 and 1984. Photos courtesy of Ames High School

Jeff Kerber of Emmetsburg was the second Iowa high school wrestler to win four state championships. His fourth title in 1979 came 17 years after Bob Steenlage of Britt finished his run of four in a row. Kerber's son, Justin, was a two-time state champion for Emmetsburg/Armstrong-Ringsted. Justin Kerber's second title in 2006 came 30 years after Jeff won his first title. Jeff Kerber is shown holding his 1979 gold medal in front of his son's two state championship posters. Photo by Dan McCool

Bob Darrah produced winning wrestling teams at Morning Sun, Urbandale and Des Moines Dowling/West Des Moines Dowling despite having never wrestled in high school or college. Darrah's 340-17-2 career record (.950) is best among Iowa's high school wrestling coaches for winning percentage. Darrah (left) is shown with assistant coach Ron Gray (right) encouraging Dowling wrestler Ken Lewton. Photo courtesy of Ron Gray

Mike Allen of Waterloo was the first black referee to work the Iowa high school state wrestling tournament. Allen worked 15 state tournaments, and also became a regular working NCAA tournaments. He had a non-egotistical approach to officiating: "When you get those stripes on and you had a 38 chest when you came into the arena, now you've got a 46 chest and you're going to work, you're going to miss calls." Photo by Dan McCool

Dan McCool

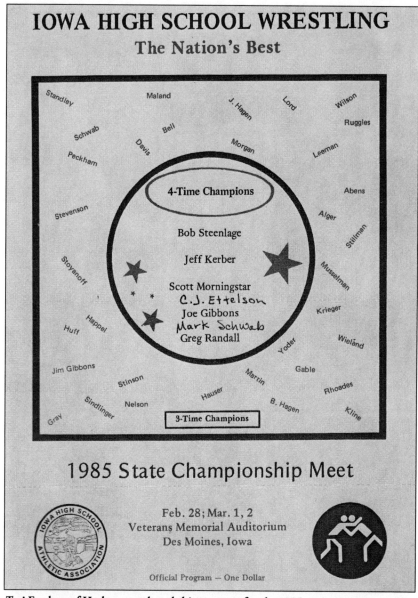

IOWA HIGH SCHOOL WRESTLING
The Nation's Best

4-Time Champions

Bob Steenlage
Jeff Kerber
Scott Morningstar
C.J. Ettelson
Joe Gibbons
Mark Schwab
Greg Randall

3-Time Champions

1985 State Championship Meet

Feb. 28; Mar. 1, 2
Veterans Memorial Auditorium
Des Moines, Iowa

Official Program — One Dollar

Teri Ettelson of Hudson purchased this program for the 1985 state tournament. Her husband, Tim, was head coach at Hudson High School. The cover dealt with the possibility that Mark Schwab of Osage might become the state's sixth four-time state champion. Ettelson added Schwab's name to the list of four-timers after he won. She also put in the name of her nearly year-old baby boy, C. J. Eighteen years later, C. J. Ettelson won his fourth state championship. Photo courtesy of Teri Ettelson

202

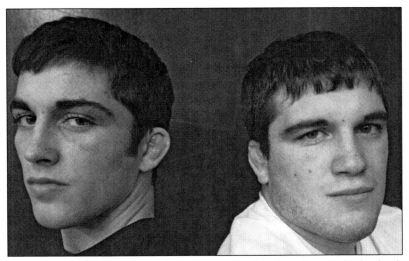

Going into the 2012 state wrestling tournament, there have been 19 high school wrestlers from Iowa who won four state championships. One family can claim two four-timers – the Reiters of Don Bosco of Gilbertville. Mack Reiter (right) won four between 2000 and 2003 and younger brother Bart (left) won four between 2006 and 2009. They combined for 344 career victories. Photo by Dan McCool

Jason Keenan of Ogden won four state championships between 1992 and 1995. He was the first state wrestling champion for coach Brian Reimers and for the Bulldogs. Keenan's only loss was the result of an injury default. Photo courtesy of Brian Reimers

Three years after Keenan finished his title run, Jesse Sundell began his quest to be a four-time champion at Ogden. Sundell won his fourth title in 2001 before moving to the college scene in an Iowa State singlet. Sundell was coached by Brian Reimers, making Reimers the only coach to lead two wrestlers to four championships. Sundell (right) is now an assistant to Reimers at Ogden.
Photo by Dan McCool

Eric Keller of Indianola was after his second Iowa state wrestling championship as a senior in 1994. His sister sent a page from a motivational calendar that mentioned lasting one second longer than the opposition makes you the winner. She also put in her own motivational words. Keller got a takedown with 1 second left to win the title that year, which helped Indianola win the Class 3-A team championship. Photo courtesy of Eric Keller

Don Bosco of Gilbertville had multiple state qualifiers for the first time in 1976, when Tom Kettman and Ray Fox joined coach Dan Mashek in Des Moines. Kettman and Fox – Don Bosco's first individual state champion - were long-time assistants under Mashek. When Kettman became Don Bosco's head coach in the 2000-01 season, Fox was his assistant. They combined for five traditional team championships and seven dual-meet state championships. Kettman resigned as head coach after the 2010-11 season. Photo by Dan McCool

The state wrestling tournament had a familiar voice asking that the mats be cleared, calling individuals to the mat and announcing individual and team champions. Ed Winger of Urbandale was the public address announcer for 31 tournaments and his "Wrestlers clear the mats. Wrestlers, let's clear the mats please" call meant the action was about to start. Winger stepped down after the 2008 tournament. Before he turned off his microphone, Winger (center) posed with current PA men John Randles of Cedar Rapids (left) and John Kinley of Gilbert. Photo courtesy of Ed Winger

Nick Ackerman of Colfax-Mingo captured the attention of state wrestling tournament
fans in 1996. The fact he placed sixth at 152 pounds in the Class 1-A tournament did
not matter. Ackerman lost his lower legs to a fast-moving form of bacterial meningitis
when he was 18 months old. After his fifth-place match ended, Ackerman was given
a standing ovation by the crowd. He made bigger news in 2001, winning an NCAA
Division III national championship for Simpson College. Ackerman is shown holding
his son, Mason.
Photo by Dan McCooll

Rick Caldwell gives encouragement to a Waverly-Shell Rock wrestler during the dual-meet state tournament. Caldwell decided to stay in Waverly after working as an assistant coach at Wartburg College, and it's been a good move all around. Caldwell led the Go-Hawks to their fifth Class 3-A traditional team championship since 2005 – their fourth in a row – in the 2011 tournament. He has also led the team to four dual-meet state championships. His 2008 squad set a state tournament record with 225 points. Photo by Dan McCool

No team in the Iowa high school state wrestling tournament cracked the 200-point mark until Waverly-Shell Rock came to Des Moines for the 2008 traditional meet. The Go-Hawks broke a tournament record with 225 points. Twelve of their 13 qualifiers placed and the Go-Hawks won the team title by 85 ½ points. "My son, when he was about second grade, would tell everybody, 'Wait 'til 2008, our team will win the state championship in 2008,'" coach Rick Caldwell said. Photo courtesy of the Iowa High School Athletic Association

"The darn thing's still going."

Iowa is well known for its first-in-the-nation political caucuses. The state holds a similar distinction for the concept of state wrestling newspapers.

What started as a 25-cent trial balloon in 1970 has grown into a publication that led the way for states showcasing their wrestling talent. Two wrestling coaches (with understanding wives) frustrated with a lack of statewide wrestling information started *The Predicament* – fittingly in 1970, when the state tournament made its move to Des Moines and Veterans Memorial Auditorium and the sport grew from the Mississippi to the Missouri.

"We decided we didn't like the coverage wrestling was getting by the Des Moines Register, not to bash the Des Moines Register but we didn't like it," said Mary Doak, wife of then-Grundy Center coach John Doak. "We decided that we could create this, so we printed a pilot issue and wrote to the people – John was coaching wrestling at the time – and we contacted all the people they knew and asked them if they would assist us, we'd like to put together an introductory issue. The coaches sent us stuff and we took 2,000 copies down so we sold them for a quarter each.

"We sat there with our mounds of paper and nobody knew who *The Predicament* was or what it was. Then we started going up in the stands and selling them. We sold enough so that we could print the very first edition, which would be about the results of the state tournament. We had enough seed money and that's how it began."

John Doak said printing that pilot paper cost just over $250. The Doaks came back from hawking their tabloid-size publication at the 1970 state tournament with $300.

Publishing a wrestling-specific paper was hardly the type of thing where the owners envisioned lavish payoffs - "It was like Christmas when you'd get a subscription order," Mary Doak said – but they were getting the sport to the state just as they wanted. The banner displayed at their table inside Vets Auditorium in 1970 is now at the National Wrestling Hall of Fame Dan Gable Museum in Waterloo.

John Doak and assistant coach Dennis Highland did the layout while their wives - Mary Doak and Bonnie Highland - did the office work, the typesetting and drove the pages 2 ½ hours to Algona to be published. Before long, the phone rang with people from other states such as future publishers Russ and Nancy Hellickson wanting to learn what the Doaks and the Highlands did. The Hellicksons began a publication titled *The Crossface* in Wisconsin while Russ Hellickson was head wrestling coach at University of Wisconsin. He later took a similar job at Ohio State.

Three owners later, *The Predicament* is still read – and in the Internet age viewed online – by fans near and far. The Doaks sold *The Predicament* to Tom and Julie Bishop of Iowa City, who sold it to Ron and Mary Seaman, who sold it to current owner Jim Steiert of State Center.

"Every once in a while I think, 'The darn thing's still going' so it's still the wrestling coaches and the fans still love it," John Doak said. "That is a very positive thing, If it wasn't worth it, it would have died."

The birth of the publication was likely at a kitchen table, where Doak and Highland likely vented about not knowing what talent throughout Iowa was possibly awaiting their Spartans at state. They knew who was hot in northeast Iowa because the *Waterloo Courier* had those bases covered, but Doak and Highland wanted more from the Register, the state's largest paper.

"We weren't trying to get anything out of it. We got some awards, but so what," Doak said. "Our motive was to get wrestling over the state of Iowa, people to know more about it. The way I look at it, there were thousands of people that had the same love for the sport as we did. We just niched into an area where it was communicated, that was the only difference."

Doak was presented a Dellinger Award – the top prize for a wrestling journalist - from Oklahoma-based Amateur Wrestling News. "The truth is I had the vision and the ideas but my wife was really the writer," Doak said. "We would talk, and as I talked she would write and then she would clean it up. She was the one who should have gotten the award."

The Predicament had an early unique touch – a front-page editorial cartoon such as those found in daily newspapers. The artist was John Butler, a lawyer and Mary Doak's father, who had taken lessons from J.N. "Ding" Darling, a two-time Pulitzer Prize-winning editorial cartoonist for the *Register.* Butler's first drawing for the new wrestling publication dealt with the path to the state tournament and the obstacles a champion had to overcome.

Coaches in the state subscribed to a package deal called bundle packs, where everyone on the team could have their own copy of *The Predicament.* With statewide listings of dual meet results in every issue, wrestlers' names were bound to be somewhere. The publication also began tracking of 50- to 100-match winners and brothers acts. A popular *Predicament* item was bumper stickers promoting the sport. "I mean, those people, those schools in Iowa picked it up…I think we made $4,000. We thought we were in hog heaven," Mary Doak said.

Despite the time constraints of teaching, coaching, refereeing and being a father, Doak wanted to see the infant publication grow some legs with a grass roots approach to covering the state, particularly the high schools.

"I'm not a quitter, I've never quit anything I've ever started," Doak said. "We guaranteed each team in the state of Iowa two dual meet coverage. They had to take the picture, they had to write the story but they got covered twice. They could pick the meets they wanted, that way they really got involved. Then we started a wrestling poll and then all of the dailies wanted our poll, so we sent the poll to them."

They also got one of the deepest, richest sources of Iowa wrestling history with columns by Ray Arnold of Clarion. "He wrote so much interesting history about wrestling. We didn't know about any of those old teams, and he had covered that and he just had volumes of stuff from years and years back. It was invaluable," Doak said.

When Dan Gable won his Olympic gold medal in 1972, *The Predicament* did a special edition. John Doak occasionally tutored Frank Gifford on the sport of wrestling because Gifford was covering the NCAA tournament for ABC Television and knew nothing about the activity. Mary Doak might have been one of the few women writing about the NCAA tournament in those days. She even crossed lines to provide coverage.

"The first year (1971) we went to Auburn to cover an NCAA and they didn't let women in the press box," Mary Doak said. "I was sitting there because I would write the stuff too, I was sitting in the press box; they came to ask me to leave. That was the whole era, that was the South."

Mary Doak grew to love the sport of wrestling. "I never attended a wrestling meet until John started coaching. I played girls' basketball so I love athletics. I loved the competitiveness (in wrestling) and I loved the courage the kids had, the sacrifices they could make. John had some great kids."

John Doak grew up in Grundy Center and was a member of a Spartans basketball team that went to state. He went to Iowa State Teachers College with an eye towards playing football but was too small, so coach Buck Starbeck put in a good word to ISTC wrestling coach Bill Koll. "In my weight was (all-American) Dick Heaton, then there was (two-time NCAA champion) Bill Weick a weight above and I couldn't beat him. I never fit in where I could make the varsity, but I learned a hell of a lot because I got beat up every night."

He also learned about wrestling as a hot spot when he was teaching and coaching in Osage. "It was good for me to be there because I found out how hot the spark of wrestling really was," Doak said.

Doak eventually returned to Grundy Center and started the wrestling program in 1961. Nine years later, he was a publisher contemplating the financial end of a new product. By the end of the first year, Doak said he felt the publication broke even and that fired them up to continue.

"By the fourth year we had about 350 colleges taking our paper for recruiting. We were the only state newspaper in the whole nation. It was just amazing how we got it going," Doak said.

Something had to eventually give, and Doak said it was a comment made one night that convinced him it was time to sell the newspaper.

"I came home one night and my two girls said 'We never get to see you anymore, Dad' and I said to Mary, 'That's it, we're selling it. The kids come first,'" Doak said. "It was fun. I can't remember dreading going to do it, I always looked forward to it. That's why when my kids hollered at me that they don't get any attention, it was kind of hard to leave it but you've got to do the right thing."

"I think anything I've done is because I believed in hard work."

Al Baxter had a teaching and coaching job at Lisbon, Iowa after he graduated in 1969 from Morningside College in Sioux City.

All he had to do was figure out where Lisbon was and if his back would allow him to teach and coach.

"I was hired on the phone by (Lisbon Superintendent) Delbert Buttry to start a football program, to be the wrestling coach and to teach K-12 boys and girls physical education and also junior high track coach," Baxter said. "I had never heard of Lisbon, and here it was 75 miles north of my hometown (Morning Sun). What a great location though – 21 miles north of Iowa City, 14 miles east of Cedar Rapids."

Baxter had injured his back lifting weights in college. When he got to Lisbon, Baxter wore a back brace for five months and absorbed 31 shots to try to alleviate the pain.

He may have been initially foggy about the location of Lisbon, but Baxter made sure wrestlers, wrestling coaches and fans of the sport knew exactly where it was: Usually on top of the Class 1-A wrestling standings. The Lions won the first five of their 14 championships during Baxter's nine-year stay. At that time there was no dual-meet state tournament, or Baxter's Lions would have added more hardware to the trophy case.

While Baxter made Lisbon a powerhouse, his high school coach was turning Dowling High School in West Des Moines into a juggernaut in the large-school class. Baxter was the first state wrestling champion Morning Sun High School produced. His coach was Bob Darrah, who later became the originator of what grew into a state-record 137-meet winning streak at Dowling.

Both hated losing and had no quarrel with working, and they got kids to approach wrestling the same way. "I think anything I've done is because I believed in hard work," Darrah said. "I always said if work will get you where you need to be to be successful, there is no reason not to be successful."

Baxter channeled Darrah when he would do weight lifting or plan practices with the Lions. "That old Bob Darrah in me. Second place? (Forget) it, we're going for first. If we had to work 10 hours a day, seven days a week to do it, that's what we're going to do," Baxter said.

If Baxter hated losing the Class 1-A team title in 1976, he found some happiness because Denny Christenson, his old Morningside teammate and longtime friend, led Belle Plaine to that championship.

Not to leave the Class 2-A field out in the cold, Emmetsburg flexed its muscle in high school wrestling in the second half of the decade of the 1970's. The E'Hawks won four consecutive team championships, managing to overcome losing coach Bob Roethler for much of the 1978-79 season because of an aneurysm, and gave the state Jeff Kerber, its second four-time state champion.

"Bob pushed us to excellence. He made us work harder than anybody else out there. We were in better shape, we worked harder and that paid off," said Rich Stillman, a three-time state champion.

Kerber added, "His passion level was very high. He's got a toughness about him that he was able to communicate to his wrestlers, that same expectation of toughness."

At Lisbon, the program was not very old and had not been very successful. Max Gradwell started the program. Baxter said it was his understanding that those wrestling practices followed basketball practice, they would see pictures of moves in a book and then work on doing those moves.

Baxter grew from the new teacher who lived with his wife and two children in an apartment behind a laundromat to a folk hero as Lisbon became a model of success. Six individuals brought a total of 10 individual championships home between 1973 and 1978, led by three-time winner Jim Lord, two-time champ Doug Englert and Scott Morningstar, who won two of his four state titles under Baxter's watch.

"All I know is according to my mom first there is God and then there is Al Baxter," said Lord, a four-time finalist who felt Baxter's wrath and won his respect. "You didn't cross Al Baxter. Anybody who probably would cross Al Baxter in that community, you got to realize their house might be burned to the ground. Everybody loved that man, the ground he walked on."

Perhaps it was because Baxter had the stories that could entertain for hours and the personality that would make every kid believe he or she could do huge things. The boys might get a pat on the back and an 'I think you could be a state champion, buddy' encouragement. And Baxter never seemed to forget a name or a face once he became acquainted with someone.

Baxter said he had 48 of the 88 boys in Lisbon High School out for football and 44 of them out for wrestling by the time he left in 1978. During the winter, Baxter could make a gem out of the roughest rocks to put on the boots, slang for wrestling shoes.

Lord said his father, Iver, bet him $10 that Lord would probably end up like his older brother. Not Doug, a state champion in 1973. Like Larry, a guy Jim Lord said was not enthused about being told what to do. "(Baxter) was everything. If not for him... I probably would have."

There were moments Lord and Baxter clashed, such as the difference between Lord wrestling at 105 pounds (Baxter's wish) and at 112 pounds (Lord's wish); junior varsity and varsity and the reason to honor loyalty; and taking care of your own business before offering an opinion on anyone else's. Lord said he once spent all night running in the streets of downtown Des Moines because he was overweight after a session at state and Baxter didn't want him to sleep without getting the weight off. Baxter always won the arguments, as well as Lord's respect. Baxter had a Lord in the state finals in six straight tournaments – from 1973 to 1978.

After Lord was second at 98 as a freshman, he wanted to jump to 112 as a sophomore. By then, Doug Englert – Lisbon's first state champion – had graduated and his backup was Jack Leonard. Baxter decided Leonard deserved something as a senior for never missing a practice, a morning run, a weight-lifting session and being on JV for three seasons, so he had 112 reserved for Leonard. Lord was going to open his sophomore season as the JV 112-pounder. Lord disagreed.

"I'm thinking, 'I was second in the state, I'm not going to junior varsity.' So I made a mistake and did not show up on time, I showed up later and I sat in the crowd, so the junior varsity wrestled and they get done he sees me sitting in the crowd. As he's walking by he looked up and yelled 'You, get in the locker room,'" Lord said.

Baxter spoke. Loudly and clearly, Lord recalled. "'You're better than the team? You're too good to wrestle on my junior varsity team?' One of the most humiliating things I'd ever been through in my life. I understand now, but then I'm 15 years old, I know everything, I'd had success, I'd bust my butt all the time and I thought that wasn't fair. He said, 'I don't care what you think, it's my way or the highway.'"

Lord said he could not let Baxter retire from Buena Vista in 2004 and move out of state without seeing him once more. Lord flew home, picked up his dad and Bob Majors (the father of Mount Vernon state champion Randy Majors) and went to Storm Lake. When Baxter was inducted into the Iowa Wrestling Hall of Fame at Cresco in 1994, Lord and Randy Majors flew home to surprise Baxter that night.

"Love the guy. There is nothing I could do in this world to repay that man for what he did for me and my family," Lord said.

When Lord began working on freestyle wrestling with a Texas boy named Brandon Slay, he made sure Slay met Baxter, who moved from Lisbon to Buena Vista College in Storm Lake. Baxter had a 376-119-5 coaching record, 12 top-10 finishes in the NCAA Division III tournament and six individual national champions at Buena Vista. He was a six-time Iowa Conference coach of the year selection. Slay went on to win a silver medal at 167 ½ pounds in the 2000 Olympics, then was given the gold when gold medalist Alexander Leipold of Germany was stripped of his award because he tested positive for steroids.

Baxter said he thought about winning state championships at Lisbon. Even dreamed about it. "I idolized Al DeLeon at Britt, the great teams he had," Baxter said. "Some of those other coaches...I'd go (to state) and think, 'If I could ever have a program like that...' and then all of a sudden the fourth year everything fell right. I was never so shocked in my life than to win state. One of the proudest days of my life, one of the happiest days of my life."

If Baxter was excited, imagine how the residents of a blue-collar town such as Lisbon reacted. Morningstar said the whole town went nuts.

When the Lion wrestlers came back from Des Moines with medals, Baxter took them to elementary classrooms to get some young minds thinking big.

Morningstar remembered when Englert won Lisbon's first state championship in 1973. "'This is Doug Englert, he is the best 112-pounder in the state of Iowa,'" Morningstar remembered Baxter saying, then pulling out a map of the state of Iowa to emphasize Englert's effort. "You're thinking, 'Wow, if he can do it, I know him, I can do it. I want to be a hero. I want to be the guy in town that everybody thinks, 'That guy is really good.' Everybody knew when he went running in the summertime,

'That's Doug Englert, he's working out to be a state champion again' and you'd think, 'Why can't we do that?'"

The man knew he got the young kids' attention. "The first-, second- and third graders, their eyes would be big as marbles," Baxter said.

Baxter could also get some extra miles out of people with some well-timed words.

"Baxter was one tough son of a bitch. I was deathly afraid of him, but I loved him," Morningstar said. "He never did anything to hurt me, but I'm telling you when he'd put his big ol' paws on your neck, and here I'm a shrimpy little 98-pounder, and he'd say, 'You're going to make him cry in front of his mom and dad and grandpa and grandma' you could beat anybody. He was just one of those motivators. He led by example."

Prior to the 1977 state tournament, Baxter was going over the tournament and what would be needed with his wrestlers. Talk turned to Morningstar, the shrimpy 98-pounder.

"'And Morningstar, hell, the way you're wrestling you can win the damn thing,'" Morningstar recalled Baxter saying. "I just went out and wrestled, whatever happened kind of happened. I was undefeated, I never even thought about it. I don't even know if I knew what my record was. When he said that I was like '(wow) he thinks I can win it.' That was one of those defining moments I'll never forget."

Morningstar won, beating 1976 state champion Gary Knutson of Lamoni, 1-0, in the quarterfinals.

Tough kids usually have experienced something akin to learning to swim. You either learn quickly or you ingest a lot of water and sink. Lord said Baxter would take him to high school freestyle tournaments in the spring and summer, sometimes trying to enter an 80-something-pound Jim Lord into the lightest weight division.

Lord also talked about spending long days and nights in Iowa City watching the early years of the Junior Nationals, a freestyle and Greco-Roman tournament involving kids from all over the country. Baxter volunteered to work the tourney and Lord rode shotgun in what he called Baxter's "piece of junk white Plymouth" to study top-flight wrestlers.

"I remember seeing Mike Land (of West Des Moines Valley) win the high school nationals. I remember watching Lee Roy Smith getting beat by Mike Land in Iowa City. I'd sit in the bleachers of the old fieldhouse all day until it was over," Lord said. "(Baxter) would take me home, drop me off... 'Alright Jimmy, tell your mother and dad I'll be by tomorrow morning.' I remember John Bowlsby (of Waterloo West) wrestling down there, Joe Zuspann (of Fort Dodge), (Mark) Harris from Algona, I used to watch all those guys from years and years ago when they wrestled down there. I remember watching Dave Schultz get beat down there."

Lord said he learned while he earned bruises along the way. At 15 he was competing in the 1976 Olympic Trials against the likes of older stars such as Jack Reinwand of Wisconsin. Two years later he entered the National Open and took a beating but loved the challenge. Lord was used to being in matches he loved but could not win. He was in elementary school and junior high when he offered to help Baxter at practice.

"I would say, 'If you let me come to practice, I'll wash the mats for you' so he would write me notes and I could get out of the last hour," Lord said. "I was allowed to come to practice when I was in elementary and junior high and I would wash the mats and scrub the side walls. I took a beating like there is no tomorrow from the kids, but Baxter let me work out with them. I started working out with the high school when I was like in sixth grade."

Lisbon didn't have the kind of training facilities associated with successful programs. "They didn't have a wrestling room so we cleaned out an art room that had a drain in the middle and a pole, a cement beam in the middle," Baxter said. "The first room we had, the custodian gave us a closet that he used. It was like 20 feet long and 14 feet wide. If you put your arms over your head, you'd hit the ceiling. They didn't have one ounce of weights in there and I had a 300-some pound set of weights and I bought some more weights. I put a bench and some weights on the stage there. We would lift weights there."

Baxter should have been accustomed to spartan equipment for practice. Darrah remembered his first practice room at Morning Sun was hardly a royal flush. "We practiced in an old rest room and for the wrestling mat we bought a cover," Darrah said. "Our first mats were made at the Fort Madison prison. When you talk about floor burns or strawberries, you could really get them on that stuff."

Darrah did not have a sterling place to work with at Dowling either. By the time he was done coaching at Dowling, facilities got better but the old boxer did enough winning and helped to create enough tough wrestlers by then that only one word was needed to identify him: Darrah. If anyone spoke of "Bobby D," it was the same guy. Still, when Darrah came to Dowling in 1969, he was not yet a deep font of knowledge.

"He knew enough to be dangerous, but I'll tell you he worked you so hard. As time wore on — we always went to clinics and we were always trying to find something – he learned a lot," said Ron Gray, Dowling's first state placewinner and Darrah's longtime assistant and eventual replacement.

Gray said Darrah had two things in his favor. "Number one, he's a tremendous motivator. He'd get you to do anything. You'd run through a brick wall for him. The second thing was it was an advantage that he didn't wrestle because, as a wrestler, sometimes I think maybe we can't do that, maybe this won't work. He never had that attitude. He didn't have the limitations that being a wrestler would necessarily impose on you in your thought process."

Lord finally understood what made Baxter tick. "Baxter was no different than Darrah, and he talked highly of Bob Darrah. I finally got to meet (Darrah) and I saw where Baxter comes from," Lord said.

Darrah had practice at Dowling in a 30-foot by 30-foot room that included a 3-foot pillar in the middle. There were also tables and chairs in the room because it served as an annex of the school lunch room that was known as "The Beanery." Gray remembered about 90 kids in practice, which limited perfecting certain technical aspects of the sport.

"We were very good mat wrestlers. We weren't very good on the feet," Gray said.

If they needed more room, the Maroons went to Holy Trinity Church's parish hall. Iowa State had lent some mats so the team could get work done on their foot skills.

"It was very cold, the snow would blow through the window, it wasn't very air-tight. Coach would mop the mat and literally there would be ice on the mat when we started practice because it was so darn cold in there," Gray said. "We got a chance to get on the feet and spread out. It was interesting at that old place."

Darrah's first coaching job was at Morning Sun in the 1958-59 school year, where he was paid $4,000 and was known to *Morning Sun News-Herald* readers as Robert Darrah. During his nine years at Morning Sun, Darrah coached basketball, football, baseball, track, started the wrestling program, taught seven classes a day and drove the south run on the bus route. One of his assistant football coaches was Bill Caldwell, the father of Waverly-Shell Rock coach Rick Caldwell.

Darrah started the Morning Sun wrestling program in the 1961-62 school year. The varsity competition began the following year, with Alan Baxter among 21 participants. When Darrah resigned after the 1966-67 season, Morning Sun had a 50-3 wrestling record and the Tigers never lost a home meet, according to the *News-Herald*. He led the football team to 6-win efforts in 1962 and in 1966.

He never wrestled in high school at Chariton or in college at Westmar. Darrah said his brother Don was on one of Chariton's first teams. He also said Westmar tried to hire him when it started a wrestling program in 1963. Darrah knew plenty about the toughness a sport like wrestling required. He did some boxing in his youth, a tough scrapper known as "Sparrow" because of his lack of size. In elementary school, he once offered to fight a taller classmate who was bullying other kids, but Darrah wanted a stipulation to make it a fair fight: the other boy had to stand in the ditch to create an eye-to-eye opportunity.

"I always liked to battle, I've always been that way," Darrah said.

There was no junior high program at Morning Sun then, but Darrah said some junior high kids interested in wrestling, such as future high school coaches Nick Hobbs and Tim Johnson, would come to practice and do managerial duties and still get in some mat time.

After his time at Morning Sun, Darrah spent two seasons at Urbandale before moving to Dowling for the 1969-70 season. His hiring at Urbandale was basically settled at a King's Food Host restaurant in Des Moines after he drove his 1954 Pontiac three hours. Darrah said he was told it might be a couple of seasons of .500 records before the feet got on the ground. The J-Hawks went 11-2 and 10-0 in those supposed marginal seasons of acclimation. Football coach Jim Williams, who became athletic director at Dowling following the death in 1969 of George Cordaro, called to see if Darrah was interested in taking over the young wrestling program at Dowling, which was still in Des Moines. The school moved to West Des Moines and became co-ed for the 1972-73 school year.

Darrah said he remembered attending a Dowling-Urbandale tournament basketball game at Des Moines North. Across the way, he noticed the enthusiasm of a multitude of boys wearing maroon sweaters with a white D sewn on. Being an all-boys parochial school at the time, Darrah liked the idea that discipline would be plentiful. Darrah said he could deal with a discipline issue rather than sending a student to the principal's office. When Williams called, Darrah said he might be interested but there was the matter of his contract at Urbandale. If a replacement was found, Darrah could leave. Gaylen Eller was hired at Urbandale and Darrah replaced Al Paone at Dowling. Paone left Dowling to accept a job at Simpson College, and 20 years later Darrah resigned at Dowling to become wrestling coach at Simpson.

Dowling won the first of its six traditional team championships in 1975, the same year 119-pounder Scott Kollings became the first Maroons wrestler to win individual gold. Dave Schreck followed Kollings to the top of the podium six weights later. If people wondered about whether or not the short, driven man knew what he was talking about, one title seemed to be the answer.

"When he won his first state championship in 1975, everybody then bought into that this guy is doing the right stuff," 1979 Dowling state champion Bob Hallman said. "Next thing you know we had Perry Hummel, who was (Dowling's) first two-time champ, then you get guys like me, (Rick) DeBartolo, (Matt) Egeland and (John) Campana and some of these guys following right behind the stars. It just kind of snowballed from there."

Be it Urbandale or Dowling, Darrah had a first-day-of-practice speech that gave everyone a clear picture of what was ahead: "This is what's going to happen, I'm going to work your butts so hard that when I get done, there might be only seven of you left and we'll give them five weights, but we'll still kick their ass because we'll win by pins. If you don't believe what I'm saying or you don't want to do what I'm telling you, get the hell out right now."

Dion Cobb remembered a different first-day speech from Darrah.

"When I went to Dowling High School, I wasn't going to wrestle. I had never wrestled before, so when I was signing up for sports I had signed up for basketball," Cobb said. "Coach Darrah took the pencil and turned it upside down and erased basketball. 'Son, I've seen you play football, I've seen you in gym class, you need to wrestle.'"

Cobb and Hallman were members of the 1978 Dowling state championship squad Cobb said is one of the best title-winning teams in tournament history. That team had state champions in Hummel and Campana as well as three future NCAA finalists in Egeland (Iowa), Hallman (Northern Iowa) and Hummel (Iowa State). They beat a Cedar Rapids Prairie team that included Barry Davis and Jim Zalesky, who combined for five state championships and later six NCAA titles at Iowa, by 34 ½ points.

"I think that team was pretty special. It was a great mix of star power and guys who were capable of beating average to good guys. We really didn't have a weak link in the squad," Cobb said. "We had great upperclassmen leadership between coach Darrah's leadership, Perry Hummel and John Campana. Those guys set a standard and an expectation that we weren't just going to compete, we were going to try to dominate and beat people as bad as we can beat them. Coach Darrah, I really believe, took the time to mine whatever wrestling potential was out of whatever kid who had any."

Darrah said that 1977-78 squad was likely the best Dowling championship squad. "If you look at what they accomplished in high school and college, it has to be the best. The 1985 team...the paper had us stop down Monday morning to pick up the trophy," Darrah said. "We lost six matches in the quarterfinals, came back and got second place....that was the year Kenny Lewton was a state champ, (Chris) Geneser placed, (Darrah's son) Matt placed, Kelly Flynn placed, (Mike) Guthrie...they were talented from top to bottom and of course '78 was too. It's hard to make comparisons."

Hallman was a wrestler Darrah could like. Hallman had wrestling excellence in his blood, with three-time state champion and two-time NCAA champion Ron Gray of Eagle Grove as a second cousin.

"The sport didn't come easily, but what I didn't mind doing was working hard. I brought the hard work to it and after a while things started paying off," said Hallman, a future NCAA runner-up at Northern Iowa. "As a freshman, I might have been the worst kid on our team, an 88-pounder. If you would have looked at records, I think I might have had the worst record of the starters and it just didn't bother me. I felt like that was what I was going to do, I did a lot of freestyling, did some camps and 3-4 short years I ended up as a state champ."

Hallman had support in setting goals from his mother, Joan, who knew well where he was coming from. State champion? It wasn't outwardly promoted, but the signals were clear.

"Bob was a doer, if he wanted to do something he worked until he got it. He had more endurance than any wrestler," Joan Hallman said. "He wouldn't even get a sweat after three periods, he beat everybody in running at UNI and Dowling and everywhere else. He ran, ran, ran and hardly ever broke a sweat. He wasn't the best wrestler but he just had a goal he was going to beat (an opponent) if he ever possibly could."

Joan Hallman said her son and his teammates had an ideal leader in Darrah.

"You can't find a better coach than Darrah," she said. "Darrah's a little bit like me – I expect something out of you and I'm going to work with you until I get it. Darrah is No. 1-plus, we're lucky we had him. He just knew there was something in a kid that he could get out of them and he worked until he got it. He could read kids."

Morningstar, who once entertained thoughts of playing basketball at Lisbon as his father, Keith, did, said only the uniform differentiated some guys from Lisbon's room and Dowling's room.

"There are so many similarities between Scott Morningstar and Jim Lord and the Dowling boys of old like Dion Cobb and Bob Hallman and Perry Hummel because they had the same guy," Morningstar said. "It all stems from Darrah and his intensity, tenacity and his never-quit attitude. It trickled down to Baxter."

Cobb said he easily could have missed being on that 1978 wrestling team. He gave consideration to changing schools after playing freshman football at Dowling. Cobb said Williams remarked that he'd had a good season and the Maroons would be thinking of possibly bringing Cobb up to varsity as a sophomore. His reason for the possible departure? Could he live up to the expectations of performance that Williams brought to the Maroons.

"I think (Williams and Darrah) had that unique ability of reaching in and providing that self-motivation and that self-confidence that if this guy believes I can do this, I can do it," Cobb said. "I really believed that the uniqueness of what was going on at Dowling at that time – even Mr. Williams' football team, they weren't the most talented, they didn't have 16 more skilled players than anybody else, they just really instilled the attitude that we could outwork anyone. Through that hard work and through holding yourself accountable to your effort and what you're really emotionally attached to, when it comes from a competitive standpoint, it's really hard to beat a conditioned, prepared, emotionally commited person to their effort. That's a tough combination to beat."

Maybe that's why Lisbon and Dowling were both tough to beat in the 1970's.

"I thought it was the coolest thing when I witnessed that."

Wrestlers are creatures of habit, from how they like to warm up for a match to what they want to eat after weighing in. If they could have the same room during the state tournament, they'd jump at the opportunity.

Greg Randall of Mount Vernon did not pay close attention to the detail, but he did have the same digs when he visited Des Moines for the tournament between 1979 and 1982. Welcome to Room 507 of the former Ramada Inn, not too far from Veterans Memorial Auditorium.

Any wrestler who checks in to that room, at which is now a part of the Choice Hotels chain, might want to see if the Randall magic is still prevalent.

That person might want to have a quiet focus on the task at hand much like Randall did. The idea is to get better each time the boots hit the mat. That's how Randall approached things. It wouldn't hurt if that person got to witness a guy winning his fourth state championship and the reverence a sell-out crowd pays him. That's what got into Randall's blood.

Randall was a four-time state champion for Mount Vernon High School, and his run of titles started Feb. 24, 1979 – the same night Jeff Kerber became the state's second four-time winner.

"I thought it was the coolest thing when I witnessed that," Randall said. "You got a standing ovation, I thought that was pretty cool and I thought to myself, 'I'm going to get one of those.'"

That happened a few times when future four-timers saw what to expect in three more seasons. Randall saw Kerber's grand finale in 1979, Mark Schwab of Osage won his first the night Randall got the standing ovation he wanted in 1982, Shane Light of Lisbon won his first title the night Dan Knight of Clinton completed his run in 1987, Jeff McGinness of Iowa City

High started towards four titles in 1990 when Light completed his career. Also, Eric Juergens of Maquoketa won his first title when McGinness got his fourth in 1993, T. J. Sebolt of Centerville's first championship was secured the night Mack Reiter of Don Bosco of Gilbertville and C. J. Ettelson of Hudson became the first four-timers to win together in 2003 and Bart Reiter of Don Bosco's first title was the night Sebolt got his standing ovations in 2006.

Fans might have assumed Randall was going to win four titles when they saw him beat John Thorn of Algona, 13-11, in the Class 2-A 98-pound finals. Freshman state champions immediately become the subject of "who's next?" discussions at the water cooler or, in recent years, Internet chat rooms. Randall beat people to those discussions, he just didn't share his views.

"We didn't really talk about it, we just worried about the next one. I probably never mentioned it to anybody about being a four-timer, I just knew in the back of my mind that's what I wanted," Randall said. "I usually kept things to myself, I just wanted to get that next title. Tim Johnson really helped me in the off-season. He got me to camps and he got me started lifting weights. Being able to do it, I was working towards that next title."

Before he became Iowa Public Television's high school and college wrestling announcer and got involved with Fellowship of Christian Athletes, Johnson was wrestling coach at Mount Vernon. He had an idea of how a tough guy goes about his business because he grew up in Morning Sun, where Hall of Fame coach Bob Darrah began his career. Johnson used to hang around Darrah's practices as a junior high student. Johnson was paired in the first state tournament wrestling match at Vets in 1970. In 1979, Johnson had a 98-pounder named Randall and a 185-pounder named Paul Hufford as state champions. Randall came into the state meet on the heels of being pinned by Jay Votroubek of Solon in the district tournament.

Johnson said it took the time to blink twice to realize he had something special in the little guy. "Talent yes, coachability was unbelievable and it came out first and foremost at the state tournament. He had a lot of talent but he followed coaching to the hilt," Johnson said. "He loved wrestling more than winning in one sense. I think that was a big part of his key because losing was just never going to get him down because he loved the sport so much. He was more mature in that area than most of us. That's somebody who loves the sport more than winning. That's a very positive trait because if you lose then and you don't love the sport more than winning, you may start quitting."

Johnson said he could learn quickly too. "Some people have to drill, drill, drill. He had this thing where he could see it and he could do it. It wasn't me that was teaching him anything except the single-leg, the double-leg and the fireman's carry," Johnson said.

An example of the coachability Johnson spoke so highly of was in the 1979 semifinals, when Randall faced Keith Colsch of Waukon. Colsch was dangerous with a cradle, so Johnson suggested takedowns, cutting Colsch loose and getting more takedowns. Randall won, 20-5, and made the finals.

"We didn't have video etc., but we knew enough about the various guys to know what their strengths and weaknesses were," Johnson said. "When Greg met (Colsch)...I just said, 'Greg, you can not be on the mat with this guy. If you can get rid of him in a second, do it, we're not going to stay on top.' This was not really recognized as a way to wrestle back then, but we weren't going to win if we let this guy cradle us."

Then came a meeting with Thorn.

"Same thing, you can't get caught in his cradle," was Johnson's instruction. "We got caught in it, but what I remember thinking is, 'Wow, this guy is coachable and he's got the talent.'"

Randall got to be well acquainted with Thorn. After the 1979 meeting, Thorn handed Randall his only loss of the 1979-80 season with a 4-2 decision in the finals of the Hudson Invitational. Randall got the payback at the right time, scoring a 5-3 decision in the 112-pound championship bout.

During the 2010-11 college wrestling season, Randall got to deal with a second generation of Thorns. Randall's Boise State team wrestled University of Minnesota in the National Duals at Cedar Falls. David Thorn wrestles at 133 for the Golden Gophers and older brother Mike is at 141. The Thorn brothers split their matches against the Broncos while John was watching in the Minnesota cheering section.

Randall came on the varsity scene when eastern Iowa was awash in talented wrestlers in the late 1970's and early 1980's. Brothers Lennie and Jim Zalesky and Barry Davis were state champions at Cedar Rapids Prairie, Jim Lord and Scott Morningstar were titlists at Lisbon, Kurt Hinschberger was a two-time champion for Belle Plaine, Scott Jehle won twice for Durant and Pete Bush was Davenport Assumption's first state champion in 1979.

Randall said he knew guys such as Lennie Zalesky and Mark Trizzino (future Iowa all-American) won Espoir Nationals championships. Zalesky and Kerber were some of Iowa's earliest Junior Nationals champions. "I thought that was the coolest thing that those guys were making world teams," Randall said. "One of my goals was to make that Espoir World team. This was when I was a sophomore in high school. I knew I had to get better and I knew I had to get bigger. I just did the right things to be able to put myself in that situation."

As a follow-up to the state championship in 1979, Randall won his first Junior Nationals freestyle title at 105.5 pounds. He won a second championship in 1982 at 132 pounds.

Johnson said Randall went about his business without fanfare and without much need for outside attention. "There was a sense that Greg was so within himself in a good way that if there was no time on the clock left, you were down by one and you were on the line, I'd rather have Greg Randall there any day than anybody else I can think of, because there was nothing messing with the task in front of him," Johnson said.

"Some people can out-think themselves, some people can out-worry themselves," Johnson added. "He just had a way of, 'I'm just doing what I do.' I think he was just plain excited his fourth time, but I don't think he was nervous."

Randall said his focus was never on piling on the titles. He wanted to be able to walk off the mat each night knowing he had added something. But keeping to his nature, Randall never told people what his reason for daily growth was.

"Whether I won two or won four, it didn't matter as long as I knew I was getting better as a wrestler. To me, it was always about being able to wrestle for any team out there," Randall said. "I always asked myself if I was in Oklahoma and at Midwest City or wherever, would I be able to start. It wasn't so much about being the best in state, I wanted to be the best in the country."

Johnson's philosophy in the Mount Vernon practice room seemed to be culled from the "dream big" train of thought. He gave an example of the thinking to the *Cedar Rapids Gazette* in 1981: "If you shoot for the stars, we tell the team, you might land on top of the barn. If you shoot for the top of the barn, you will land on top of the outhouse."

Johnson said he was assured of one thing – he would get Randall's best shot every time out.

"Because he loved the sport so much, there was no question he was not going to give his best," Johnson said. "He wasn't quirky, he wasn't a spoiled phenom, none of that, so there was never any worry that he was going to go out and be Greg Randall. He wasn't an up and down wrestler. He got caught a couple of times as a freshman because he was small, because Votroubek was a senior. When you're a senior 98-pounder you're a different animal."

Randall said he had an uncle who used to come home from wrestling practice and put his young nephews in various wrestling holds. The fun was just getting started. Johnson said Greg used to wear cut-off jeans when he was competing in youth tournaments. Greg had a workout partner in brother Steve, who was 13 months his senior and nearly identical in size. Steve won state championships in 1981 and 1982, so that made the 1982 meet very special. Both Randalls were champions - Greg's fourth that made him the fifth Iowa high school wrestler to hit quad gold. Greg won at 132, Steve followed at 138.

"We were wrestling probably ever since we were able to stand up, we didn't know it back then what we were getting into because we didn't belong to an organized club," Greg said. That changed when the family moved to Mount Vernon. "(My dad) probably noticed we were ripping up the living room carpet, so he took us to the local club in Mount Vernon. We only wrestled like on Saturdays during the season, it wasn't much, but it was fun. Both my brother and I, we were successful early."

Mike Schimp, a state champion from Belmond, remembered facing Randall in the semifinals of the 1981 tournament. Randall won, 10-4, to advance to the finals bout against Eric Strawn of Jefferson.

"He was slick. If I had to say one word about Greg Randall, he was slick. He was great on his feet. I'm not saying he was the most overpowering wrestler, he was just slick, his technique was awesome. Probably one of the best technicians I ever wrestled," Schimp said. "He had an outside kelly. I felt it coming but there was nothing I could do. I couldn't plant, I couldn't post, I couldn't sprawl. I think he took me down with it two or three times. It amazed me."

In the 132-pound finale against Doug Stumberg of Grundy Center in 1982, Greg once again followed his coach's advice.

"I just told him to go out and make history," Johnson told the *Des Moines Register* about his pre-match instruction that night. "He really deserves to be a four-time champion. He's done everything that's required to win. When he came off the mat, I told him, 'Thanks for all you've done for wrestling in the past four years.' He just said, 'You betcha.' He's a man of few words."

Greg was a man of a happy smile in a photograph the next morning in the *Sunday Register's* "Big Peach" sports section. He'd received the standing ovation he wanted since hearing what Kerber got in 1979. Like Kerber, Greg got a second ovation when he received his championship medal from Johnson. "(The grin) wasn't so much I got it done, but I was probably smiling because it was over," Greg said. "You think about it constantly, about being a four-timer or having a chance to be a four-timer. It drove me to work hard, do all of those extra workouts. It was a relief to me that it was over."

The challenge was about to resume again. It wasn't trying to be a four-time champion again, this time it was trying to live up to his confidence. Greg was going to be a member of the University of Iowa's wrestling team, but coach Dan Gable was hardly offering him the sun, moon and stars. "I knew who I had at my weight class, and it was a loaded weight class when I went there. Gable even told me that they really didn't need me," Greg said. "I said, 'That's fine with me because I'm going to make the team.' I didn't tell Gable that, but deep down inside I knew that there was nobody there that was going to stop me from making that team."

Greg became a three-time all-American and a two-time NCAA finalist for the Hawkeyes.

"I'm taking what I learned from coach Johnson and all of my coaches in the past, especially coach Gable, and I'm transferring over what I know to these wrestlers that I have (at Boise State)," Greg said.

Johnson had a proud-papa moment when he watched Greg coach 165-pounder Kirk White to become Boise State's first NCAA champion in 1999. Johnson has those proud moments anytime he is asked about coaching Randall.

"My feeling was now he knows the satisfaction that comes from coaching. I think until you've coached a champion, you haven't come the full circle and understand that feeling of coaching versus actually competing and winning a championship," Johnson said. "That gives you a sense that this can go on and on, I can continue to give and receive for a lifetime. As an athlete, once you win or don't win your final championship, sometimes you think life is over. The opportunity to understand coaching kind of allows you to see life a little bit differently. I had a smile and said, 'Now Greg understands.' I'm sure there was a richness and a reward he received from his athlete winning that's different, and even better, than him winning a championship.

"Championships run through generations. That's kind of what I felt like. I won't even be alive and perhaps (White) will be coaching another young man. There is always somebody that helped you along, so it's legacy is what you feel. You have a sense of pride for the legacy in this sport that has been established."

Johnson had a sense of excitement working with the Randall brothers.

"He had fun, worked hard and was a coach's dream. Both he and his brother were," Johnson said, adding that Greg showed a wrestler could have success without excess strain. "He showed everybody how to do this without cutting weight. He hated every minute of having to cut weight for the regionals. He went to 105.5 and won national juniors in Iowa City as a freshman. Tell me that doesn't tell you that you're good."

Greg went to 112 as a sophomore, 126 and then 132. Part of the lack of serious weight cutting might have been that he was having too much fun in other sports too. "People loved to see him play football. I was his eighth grade football coach along with another guy. He was a good baseball player, he was a good football player. He wasn't just Mr. Wrestler, that's all I do," Johnson said.

Greg said he had two pretty good wrestling coaches at Mount Vernon. Jim Bellamy, a Hall of Fame football coach, had the junior high mat program. "Tim was a great coach. He was a great motivator for me. He made sure that I needed to get where I needed to be in order to become better. Jim Bellamy was an awesome coach. He didn't know a lot of moves, but he worked us hard and made us better," Greg said.

Greg put himself in rare distinction when he won his fourth state championship, because it meant you could still count the state's four-timers on one hand. There is something about being in select company. He marvels at the fact the sport got him some lasting recognition, a college degree and a paycheck.

"I don't look at it as putting myself on a pedestal. I just keep moving forward, I don't look back at what I did even though it drives me still that I was never a national champion. It's an honor because winning those four titles has gotten me into quite a few halls of fame," Greg said. "When I look back, if I wasn't a four-timer I probably wouldn't be in any of those high school halls of fame. It was a fun experience for me, then it turned into hard work. Now I'm making a living off of it. It's incredible that I have come this far. I want Boise State to win a national title. It was fun while it was going on, there was some pressure on me but I put most of that on myself."

"All of a sudden it was like 'Maybe this guy knows what he's doing.'"

It was the classic story. School needs coach, man needs job, man has neighbor who knows priest wishes to talk to the man. Man and priest talk, man gets job, school becomes winner.

That's Dan Mashek's story and he's sticking to it.

Mashek was named wrestling coach at Don Bosco of Gilbertville, a parochial school southeast of Waterloo, in 1970. The program had one season under its belt and that produced a 5-6 record. There were no state qualifiers. Mashek's neighbor told him Fr. Kramer wanted to talk to him. "The guy knew I was looking for jobs, that I'd finished second in about three jobs so I didn't have a job. At that point in time, anything sounded good," Mashek said.

Fr. Kramer and Mashek talked.

"We hit it off pretty good," Mashek said. "He wasn't your typical priest, a lot of times (then) the people who had worked in the school had also been the basketball coach. He was very supportive of wrestling."

Perhaps Fr. Kramer knew who had shaped Mashek's wrestling knowledge. Wrestling fans in northeast Iowa knew Waterloo West's Bob Siddens was among the nation's top high school coaches. He led Mashek to a third-place finish in 1965. Those fans also knew Chuck Patten built a program at Northern Iowa that won two NCAA Division II team championships and beat some of its Division I opponents in duals. Mashek was a two-year letterman for the Panthers.

"I think I had the perfect blend. Siddens was doing things all over the United States at the time, recognized as a top high school coach. He was a good master of all, but strong in his psychological preparation," Mashek said. "Chuck Patten was as good of a technician as anybody in the United States at that time, but by his own admission it took him two years to get a handle on how to get through to guys. Siddens was probably *the* master psychologist and Chuck Patten was probably the master of technique at that point in time."

Mashek set out to help a group of kids master the sport of wrestling.

"My mindset was, coming from those two programs – they were elite programs at that day and time in Iowa high schools or NCAA Division II – having a mediocre team or being a part of it was never an option," Mashek said. "I didn't know anything else. That was just a luck of geography that I was able to work with those two guys. You start thinking that direction, and that's what eventually has led to the Don Bosco success. They don't think in terms of anything but the top tier.

"I think I always wanted to be a coach. I coached some of the Little League teams when I was 13 or 14 years old with a friend of my dad's. That had always been in my blood, but I'm just so glad that I was fortunate to be in the right place at the right time because (Siddens and Patten) had a huge influence on not my desire to be a coach so much but my ability to be a coach."

That mediocrity stuff was gone, especially after Mashek heard a kid speak poorly of the Don Bosco program. "I remember a kid at a tournament someplace saying, 'I got a Bosco kid, that will be easy' or something to that effect," Mashek said. "A couple years later it was, 'I've got a Bosco kid, he's pretty good.' Not only is it what you think but it's what other people think as well. They noticed the fact we had become a pretty decent team."

Don Bosco had its only losing record under Mashek in his second season. His string of 28 consecutive winning seasons started with a 9-2 mark in the 1972-73 season. The first of nine state championships by the Dons took place in 1979, the same year Don Bosco became the most recent program in the state to qualify its entire squad for the tournament. Mashek brought some magic to the Dons' mat.

" What he brought was Bob Siddens' theory. He started the program around the 1972 Olympics, Gable, his teammate. Anybody who was anybody could read that, see that, watch it on TV and you looked at Mashek and go, 'Wow, he was Gable's teammate,'" said Ray Fox, Don Bosco's first individual state champion and a longtime Don Bosco assistant coach. "Bob Siddens was his coach, everything that Mashek would teach us, he would always refer back to Coach Siddens, 'Wrestle from the top of your head to the tip of your toes.'

"Our whole philosophy now I think is still a lot of Bob Siddens in a lot of our kids. Siddens preached the fall, always go for the fall. We've been getting (hundreds of) falls as a team every year for about the last 10 years."

Tom Kettman wrestled for Mashek (he and Fox were the first pair of Don Bosco state qualifiers in 1976) and was Mashek's top assistant until 2000, when Mashek moved to North Scott of Eldridge, and then became head coach. Going into the 2011 tournament, Kettman had an active run of five consecutive team championships. That matched Waterloo West (1942-46) for the longest string of consecutive titles. Don Bosco finished second in the 2011 tournament. Kettman said Mashek is the reason the Dons seem to lead each season.

"He came into a non-wrestling town, set the standards – hard work is going to pay off," Kettman said. "People give me credit and there is no credit deserved there because Dan Mashek set the table. You go out for wrestling, you're going to work hard, you're going to do this, this and this. Parents didn't question why does their son have to get up in the morning to work out and why does he have to stay after to work out. Dan learned from Bob Siddens and Ray and I and everybody learned from Dan. We just kind of emulated what Dan taught us to be."

Mashek said he built the program on what he said were three key ingredients: being technically sound, being in top shape and being mentally tough.

"I think the mental aspect is what is so often overlooked in any coaching. Everybody is well aware that you coach them here on down to see their technique and see how strong they are. I think sometimes coaches get carried away with that and they forget the control center is up here," Mashek said, pointing to his head. "They have to believe in themselves, they have to believe in what we're doing to get them prepared and they have to be committed. When you get those three things, the body will follow."

It helped Mashek to not have a program with a long background. His way of producing success was going to be the benchmark and would be an excellent selling point.

"I only had about three kids who had ever been on the mat before, for part of a season here before, so the only thing they knew was what we were doing," Mashek said. "With the blessing of having two outstanding coaches to always refer back to, as far as what I had done and learned, I was able to get that to come true to them. They picked up on it. That first year, for a first-year program we went 6-6 and had a lot of success compared to what they had done the year before. All of a sudden it was like, 'Maybe this guy knows what he's doing.'"

Fox said Mashek's day-to-day workings was an early example of what became known as "tough love."

"I think a lot of it was his intensity, and you could see it in his face. Just the actual tough love. He'd beat you to death for 4-hour practices and then help you up and rub your back," Fox said. "You know he was doing it for a purpose. He really cared for all of us athletes, deeply cared for us. It was honest and genuine. As teen-age kids you can pick that stuff up, if people are genuine or not.

"I don't know if he took psychology classes in college, but he really knew how to push everybody's individual buttons, knowing their personalities. We had a kid named Corey Mills. If you didn't have a foot up his butt the entire practice he would just lay there. There were other guys he had to coddle along. He knew how to push everybody's buttons."

It might have been Mashek using an old Siddens trick. Mashek said Siddens could get more miles or harder work out of a wrestler by making a well-timed comment or two. It might have been a snowjob of sorts, but Mashek said Siddens called it a sincere snowjob.

The program's success might have spurred fans to want Mashek as mayor, but he already held that office. The title Mashek favored was coach.

"I think that's the greatest feeling in the world, to see somebody succeed and know you had a little bit to do with that. And to see the look on the face. That's the big draw to coaching for me," Mashek said.

All a future Don Bosco wrestler needed to get motivated was to visit Mashek's office at school. The walls were covered with pictures of the awards stand at state. Don Bosco guys were all over the place. On the top step were Fox, Tony Bedard, Mike Hogan, Al Francis (twice), Mills (twice), Irv Thome…guys who walked the same halls. The pictures were later moved from the office and placed on both sides of the hallway leading to the locker room and the practice room. There are also pictures of Don Bosco alums that made the stand in college.

Not getting a picture from the state meet does not mean a Don Bosco kid is out of luck. Fox remembered one instance of staying focused.

"I remember Jason Knipp in his senior year, we got back from state and he didn't place at state. He sat down in that hallway and started crying," Fox said. "I said, 'You know Jason, we got pictures of all-Americans up there. You're not going to be up there with a Bosco uniform on, but you'll still be an all-American.' He goes, 'But I'm going to Iowa State, coach. Engineering. I can't wrestle at Iowa State.' So he walked on and started, ended up transferring to Wartburg and became an all-American. Now he's got his picture on the wall. Isn't that cool? Never placed at state but he's an all-American."

The Dons' state championship team in 1979 was also a huge selling point for the program, Mashek said.

"I think anytime you break through a level or a barrier or some kind of a ceiling-type thing, I think it's huge because now people say, 'Oh, it's not just somebody in Lisbon, Iowa or Cresco, Iowa or Dowling Des Moines that can do that, we actually can do that ourselves.'"

The 1979 finish was fueled by a disappointing tournament the previous year, Mashek said.

"We took nine or 10 and we had beaten Lisbon in the district tournament. We really thought we were going to do it that year and we simply didn't wrestle very well," Mashek said. "It was a humbling experience. We mastered the dual meet level and the tournament level, we mastered the sectional and the district but we haven't mastered the state. I think it really motivated these kids to do as well as they did that next year because they remembered what happened the year before."

"I assumed that we were going to be pretty good. Having the potential to be pretty good and delivering on that potential are always two different things. I think we would have been ok, we probably would have won the state tournament. I don't think we would have had nine state placewinners had we not had that hard lesson the year before. These guys and myself, we were bound and determined we weren't going to let that happen again."

The 12-member 1979 team was reunited to lead the grand march at the 2009 state wrestling tournament. Among that group was Tony Vieth, who had to win a wrestle-back at the district meet in order to clinch the final spot.

Fox's gold medal came in 1977.

"Tell you the truth, I never really thought about being the first. We had so many good kids coming up that when it happened, I knew I was the first but it didn't really hit me that I'm the *first*. I knew it would be the first of many," Fox said. "My best friend Tony Bedard was an eyelash away that year, Steve Knebel got hurt at state, he was undefeated, I was like, 'We'll get a couple next year, we'll get a couple the year after that.' I kind of wish I was like the 28th, that would make me about 15 years younger."

The Dons had one champ at a time until 1981, when Mills, Thome and Mark Mangrich led Don Bosco to its second team championship. Don Bosco entered the 2011 tournament having had at least one state champion in 10 of the last 11 meets. The Dons failed to have a finalist in the 2011 tournament, the first time that occurred since 2004. Look at the champions and there are usually ties to earlier Dons squads, brothers or fathers – the Hogans, the Webers, the Reiters, the Thomes.

Mashek said the program benefitted from state placers or champions from a large family who had younger brothers that knew about being competitive and wanted to one-up the older brother. Mashek's brother was West's male athlete of the year in 1961. Mashek won the same award in 1965.

"It's just that motivating force that you'd like to do as well as your brother. I know it meant a lot to our parents. They never talked to a coach except to say hi or hello," Mashek said. "That was something in the back of my mind, that was part of the motivation package – you wanted to do well for yourself, your family, your school and just add it to the package which helps you creep up the ladder a little bit more."

There have been so many family ties in 37 years of coaching at the Don Bosco program, or his later years at North Scott, that Mashek has trouble finding one highlight of highlights.

"One of the things that kept me around as long as it did, my son graduated from high school in 1988, I had been coaching roughly 20 years. I was the athletic director. Those kids probably were far from the most talented but they really inspired me," Mashek said. "That might have been one of the best coaching jobs we'd ever done. We went like 9-1-1, we got to the duals and lost in the tie breaker. This group had losing season written all over it before they came in. If these guys can work that hard… that kind of rejuvenated my hunger to keep coaching. You can help some kids, you can do some things, you can put smiles on their faces. To me that's what it's all about."

Keeping the competition for varsity spots keen also helped the Don Bosco program. "If you're pretty good and you're treading water, somebody's going to catch you and get better than you are," Mashek said. "As a sophomore at West Waterloo, I was the fourth string 180-pounder going into the season and I was the varsity guy by the end of the year and got third in districts. I'll tell you, you can improve. The message was, 'Don't stand pat.'"

Fox remembered meeting Mashek, who had started a youth wrestling program at Don Bosco when Fox was in sixth grade. Fox learned about the new program a few hours after being in a scrap.

"I got in a fight on the playground with a guy, and his mom drove my school bus. On the way home the kid stood up and started walking back to me so I stood up. I thought he wanted some more," Fox said. "He goes, 'Don't hit me, they announced at school that they're starting wrestling. I think you should go out.' I went home and told my brother, he drove me to practice. I didn't know Dan Mashek, but he was the coach, he told us what was going to happen and we had a meet in two weeks. I was the very first grade school wrestler to ever wrestle at Gilbertville, 68 pounds. I had black socks, tennis shoes, gray shorts and a white t-shirt. I won 12-2. I remember coming off the mat and Mashek grabbed me - I still didn't know this guy very well - and he goes, 'You're going to be one tough son of a gun someday.' Everybody has that defining moment and right there was it for me."

Mashek had several reasons for considering, and later accepting, the teaching and coaching position at North Scott. His son, Tom, was building the program at Louisa-Muscatine and that was a shorter trip to see grandchildren from Eldridge than from Gilbertville. There was also the chance to get into the IPERS retirement program at a public school. At Don Bosco he had been a man of many hats, including athletic director, dean of students, attendance leader, janitor, teacher and coach. You do that at a small school.

"People don't realize how small the school is. I know in recent years when they were doing well, there was probably 75 boys or less in the school and 30-some of them are out for wrestling," Mashek said. "I looked down the (2008-09) roster and realized that I had either coached or taught one or both of the parents of all those kids. It's not like we had an influx of kids flocking in. Those kids and their parents, there is tremendous support in the community, kids grow up wanting to be a Don Bosco wrestler. They know it's a quality program and they know what's expected of them. They know they're going to have to work hard."

Fox said Mashek left a strong imprint on the Don Bosco program, but so did an absentee coach of sorts. "I credit Mashek for everything we've accomplished, through Bob Siddens. Our philosophy's theirs."

"I was fortunate enough to live through it."

Whoever said nothing good comes out of a tornado missed seeing Mike Schimp of Belmond wrestle as a freshman at the 1978 state tournament.

Come to think of it, Dan Gabrielson and Rich Wilson also had some head-turning efforts in the name of the Broncos on the floor of Veterans Memorial Auditorium in Des Moines. Gabrielson denied three-time state champion Ike Light of Lisbon an opportunity to become the second four-time state champion in his family. Wilson beat two-time champion Brent Hagen of Britt, who had beaten him four times during the season.

Gabrielson's win remains the only time in tournament history that a three-time champion was denied a fourth crown.

A wrestler wearing Belmond's or Belmond-Klemme's uniform has won a state championship six times. In half of them, the Broncos were not favored. Kevin Braner started the winning in 1974 and Jordan McLaughlin had the most recent success in 2004. McLaughlin pinned Tim DeBoer of Central Lyon for the Class 1-A 189-pound championship after placing third at that weight the previous winter. In between, there have been some stories that have become part of tournament lore for some longtime fans.

Schimp is known for a big 8-0 victory as a freshman at 98 pounds over John Strohman of Algona. He is likely one of the few state champions who survived a near-death experience to win a gold medal. The win came 11 years and 4 ½ months after the Belmond tornado of 1966. A partial list of the injured on page one of the Oct. 15, 1966 Des Moines Register stated that Michael Shimp, 4, was listed in "poor" condition at Community Memorial Hospital in Clarion. His 2-year-old brother, Marty, was listed in "good" condition.

"Obviously it was homecoming day and the band had just gotten off Main Street. Being back at school for about an hour, the tornado sirens went off," Schimp said. "My mom (Nancy) gathered up my brother,

239

got him halfway down the stairs and the basement was just a dug-out basement. We got halfway down the stairs and the TV was still on, so mom sent me back up to shut the TV off. Why she wanted me to shut the TV off is beyond me.

"I went back, shut the TV off – one of those old push-pull TV's – so I pulled the knob out not knowing what I had done. I had it in my hand. I remember this like it was yesterday. I turned the corner, went down the steps and I saw my mom sitting on the middle of the stairs with my brother on her lap and she had an old Montgomery Ward Christmas catalog. She was showing us pictures of Christmas gifts and things like that to keep us calm. That's about the last thing I remember as far as the tornado itself. Everything else of what happened to me was told to me in later years by my dad and my mom."

The Schimps lived one block north of Main Street, which was hammered by the storm.

"It tore our house off at the foundation," Schimp said. "Evidently, the force of the wind blew me out of my mom's arms and the only thing they can understand of what happened is that it shot me across like a torpedo and I went head-first into a block wall and down I went."

A small part of a wall landed on Marty. Nancy had sustained severe lacerations, knee injuries and a broken collarbone. "She'd seen (Marty), she didn't know where I was at, so she flipped that wall up with one hand, pulled him out and then collapsed," Mike said.

Larry Schimp came home from work and found his wife and his younger son. After sifting through some rubble, Larry found his older son. Mike was taken to a makeshift triage unit. His eyes were full of blood. He was bleeding from the nose, ears and mouth. "They were checking me over real thoroughly. I laid there and the nurses saw my hand was clenched," Mike said. "They started peeling my fingers open and there that knob was in my hand. Dad said that was one of the weirdest things they said a lot of people had heard of, that I had a hold of that and never let go of that.

"I can't remember how long I was in the hospital, I'm wanting to say a week, 10 days, about two weeks. My eyes were crossed for a couple days because of a very severe concussion. It was nip and tuck for a few days, but thanks to the doctors and everybody else who helped me, I was fortunate enough to live through it."

In order for Schimp to become a champion wrestler, he had to go back to the basement.

"I came into the sport of wrestling when I was in fourth grade. My dad was a feed salesman, and Jerry Woodin was one of my dad's customers. I had no idea what wrestling was, my dad didn't know anything about wrestling," Mike said. "The first time I ever really saw a wrestling mat, or can remember seeing a wrestling mat, was we went to the Woodins, they invited our family over for supper. Went down the basement and Tim Woodin, Jeff, Scott and Diane…I asked what is this and they said it was a wrestling mat. They started showing me what wrestling was, and from that night on it intrigued me. I fell in love with it, not knowing a thing about it. By the end of the night, I couldn't get enough of it, couldn't quit talking about it. Every weekend I'd ask dad if we could go to the Woodins so they could show me how to wrestle, and they were really good to me."

Mike grew up around fast-pitch softball, since his dad was a top area player. Larry played with two good Mason City-area teams, Butt'r Top and Poodle Club. Mike decided to try a youth wrestling tournament, and since he started small, he chose the Emmetsburg tourney. "The way I remember, it was nothing to see 800-1,200 kids come into that tournament," Mike said.

"Man, did I get my eyes opened up. It's one thing to practice wrestling, it was another thing to wrestle in it. I won one match, lost two and still was in love with it. From that point on, I don't know how many times I wrestled in that basement. Eventually it blossomed into going to more and more tournaments during the year. Anytime we had an opportunity to go, we were gone. It wasn't because anybody pushed me to do it. I just fell in love with the sport. I liked the mano a mano situation, let's step on the mat and see who can come off a winner."

Mike said he started his freshman season at Belmond at 105 pounds, but he went down to 98. His coach, John Yoder, was new that season. He may have arrived from Red Oak, but Yoder knew of Mike because Yoder grew up in Woolstock. He wrestled at Eagle Grove, had played a lot of softball and he knew Larry Schimp.

I'd heard how good this young man (Mike) was, but you never know how good somebody really is until you get to see. I was what you would say kind of leary going into this, what kind of a kid he was. But after meeting the young man the first time, you knew what kind of an individual he is," Yoder said. "He's a competitor, he knew what he wanted to do. He had a tough time making 98 back then, but once he made it he was fine. He did a great job holding it the rest of the year."

Yoder also learned of the kid's grit at the Clarmond tournament – an event shuttled between Belmond and Clarion – when Mike had to halt a match three times in the third period. Yoder said he decided one more stop and the match was over. "Mike went out and stuck him and got the job done. He won the tournament that day. You put the challenge out there and Mike met it," Yoder said.

Schimp qualified for state, but wasn't expecting to wrestle Saturday night. "I knew when I went down there I was going to compete to the best of my ability and nothing else would change. Probably that was a good way for me to think," Mike said. "I don't think either one of us knew what was going to happen that weekend. By the end of Saturday night, it was a pleasant surprise, let's put it that way."

Yoder added, "We knew who he had to beat going in. We knew Strohman was the guy, but I felt by the time we got going through the sectional and district, (Mike) was putting things together. You could see it just building each time. He did not have a close match (at state) that I recall. I still think to this day that we had (Strohman) stuck in the first period. The score ended up 8-0 and he dominated this guy, and this was a good wrestler."

Strohman was second at 98 pounds to Ralph Reicks of Turkey Valley of Jackson Junction in 1977. That might have been lost on Mike, but Marty excitedly let him know that after the championship bout in 1978. "After the finals match, Marty came running up, 'Do you know who you just beat? Do you know who you just beat?' I said, 'John Strohman, Algona.' And Marty said, 'He was the state runner-up last year.' I never looked at newspaper articles. After that, I figured that out, that I was better not knowing."

Yoder got to do what every coach yearns for: celebrating the first individual state champion he coached. "You can't describe the feeling. The jubilation you've got that you know the kid's worked many, many years as a young man. You can't really describe what it's like. He embraces you and the damn air almost comes out of you. I can remember before he took the mat I told him, 'Win or lose, you'll always be a champion in my eyes.' There was my champion."

That was not his last champion. Yoder had visions of two more in the 1990's because his son, Colby, grew up with a year-round workout partner in Gabrielson. Coach Yoder considered Gabrielson his third son. In 1993, Colby and Gabrielson were in the semifinals together. Colby was up first, tangling at 125 pounds with Brad Canoyer of Carson-Macedonia, so John was in the corner for his son's match. At 130, Gabrielson had Ike Light of Lisbon, the guy who handed him a 9-6 loss in the 125-pound finals in 1992. Belmond-Klemme assistant Mike Sinwell cornered Gabrielson's rematch with Light.

It appeared that a tough night was looming for the Broncos. Colby lost to Canoyer and Light held a 5-3 lead over Gabrielson in the third period. The moment many state tourney veterans talk about - how Vets could go instantly from its usual low clutter of noise to an earpad-throbbing crescendo - happened when Gabrielson threw Light to his back with 25 seconds left in regulation. The 5-point move gave Gabrielson an 8-5 victory, a measure of revenge and a reason not to have to watch the 1992 tape anymore.

"Every day he watched that (1992) tape between he and Ike Light, and he could not wait to get back on the mat with that young man," John said.

Gabrielson said he decided a state championship was his only goal after placing fourth as a sophomore. In the 1993 semifinals, he got in on some shots against Light but never finished them. Light finished his, including one in the third period that gave him a 5-2 lead. "I remember going down and my whole thought was, 'You have to get one,' which I thought I could get, and then just try to get it into overtime," Gabrielson said.

As it turned out, Gabrielson did not need extra periods.

"I had a pretty good tank, I trained like a madman. I don't even remember being tired before, during or after the match. He either had a cold or was just huffing bad. I could feel him kind of huffing and I shot in kind of on a scratch double, not a good one but just to get him off guard a little bit and came up," Gabrielson said. "As soon as I came up into somewhat of a body lock, he tried to do like a half headlock and get me off the mat. As soon as he did that, he kind of lost his footing. I had a body lock and I was able to elevate him. As soon as I elevated him, I had him really tight. He reaches with his left hand to ankle pick me, but I'm elevating him at the same time. As soon as he did that, I back tripped with my left leg. When he was going down, I had it so tight, my right shoulder into his chest. When we hit the mat, he tried to turn quickly but my hips were around and my right shoulder was right into his sternum. You talk about squeezing for 20 seconds. It was misdirection more than anything. It was all because of his motion that I had to trip backwards."

Light also remembered the move. "I thought I was going out of bounds. I was trying to go out of bounds but he was too tall. I tried to go out of bounds and I got caught," Light said.

Yoder was jumping up and down as Light crashed to the mat with

Gabrielson on top of him. "As soon as I heard that thud and that tremendous roar that hit that place, I was like the kid in the candy store because we got him. This guy was not going to get away from us and kid, you've come here and done what you had to do.

"There was a lot of hype to this thing because they had met the year before and they knew he was going for his fourth one. I feel bad for Ike Light that he didn't get his fourth one, but at the same time I'm not going to tell my kid to go out and lie down."

Light said he remembered the noise generated by the outcome of that match. Light said he's not watched the tape of that match very often.

"It was pretty bad when the whole place stands up and cheers. It was like that guy got a four-time standing ovation."

Gabrielson has that match on tape, but he doesn't need to watch it every day. "Every time I watch it, it looks so much like slow-motion, like how could he not fight it, but the problem is he had no points to fight it with," Gabrielson said. "I had him elevated, he was on his tip-toes. He reaches down and then I misdirection back trip him. He was going to be taken down right there, and then I was lucky enough to cast over with my right shoulder really tight and put him on his back."

There was a slight bit of public celebration as his hand was being raised, but Gabrielson eschewed too much dramatics.

"I was the type of wrestler I didn't get excited after matches. I felt kids shouldn't run, scream and jump up in the air unless they win something big. To me, if you're not the best, why are you acting like it?" Gabrielson said.

Following the match, Yoder told anyone who wanted to listen that Gabrielson was a great reason why books should not be judged by their cover.

"He's guts," Yoder said. "You look at the kid and you think you've got a fish, a long, tall string bean. As far as mental toughness and competitive edge, you aren't going to find a better one. That's why he is 33-0."

The reason Gabrielson was 34-0 had to do with his 6-3 victory over Chris Jones of Central Decatur of Leon in the finals the following night. It was the first time a Bronco wrestler had an undefeated season since Wilson was 30-0 in winning his second state title in the 1975-76 season.

Earlier on Saturday, Colby placed fifth at 125 and Light placed third at 130. Light was still a bit shocked when he talked to the *Cedar Rapids Gazette* after his final bout. Originally he did not want to wrestle in the consolation round, but went through with it for the team's sake.

"I always come to watch (consolation matches), but I never pictured myself wrestling in them," Light said to the *Gazette's* Jeff Johnson.

Lisbon won the 1993 Class 1-A championship, but the Lions and their fans were anticipating being part of a historic night. Jeff McGinness of Iowa City High and Light were trying to win their fourth championship in 1993. It had never happened before, and because of Gabrielson, it would not be until 2003 that two four-timers were crowned on the same evening. McGinness capped a 172-0 career in 1993.

"Not getting it is like cutting off one of your legs," Light told the *Gazette.*

It was Don Jones, not John Yoder, who was coaching at Belmond when the Broncos' Rich Wilson had his fifth meeting of the 1973-74 season in the Class 2-A 112-pound state championship match. The previous four outings were close, score-wise. Hagen won, 1-0, in the finals of the Clarmond tournament. He took a 5-3 decision in the dual meet. Another 1-0 match went Hagen's way in the North Iowa Conference tournament. Finally, Hagen got a 3-0 win in the district tournament.

"He was a technician, I guess I wasn't as much of one as he was, but I scouted him more than I did anybody because I had to figure him out," Wilson said. "I was just glad to be (at state). I went into that match figuring it's been close, I've got nothing to lose. I talked to my folks before and I said, 'Hey, I got at least second.' It was kind of hard to get too worried. I figured there was more pressure on him. It didn't hurt having a teammate win the match before in overtime."

Braner became Belmond's first state champion when he won the 105-pound title with a 4-4, 2-2, referee's decision over Larry Winslow of Glenwood. Braner did not have the added support of Eagle Grove fans as Wilson did. Eagle Grove and Britt were fighting it out for the Class 2-A team title that night.

Those four earlier wins were a part of Hagen's winning streak, that reached 77 matches by the time he'd reached the finals for the third time in 1974. Being in the finals was something of a Hagen family custom.

- Wally Hagen won 95-pound state championships for Clarion in 1943 and 1944. He was the only high school wrestler in Iowa to beat three-time state champion Dick Hauser of Waterloo West.
- John Hagen finished second at 95 pounds in Class A at the 1968 state tournament, then won Class 2-A titles at 95 in 1969

and at 107 in 1970. Britt was back in Class 1-A in 1971 and Hagen won at 112.

- Brent won his first championship in Class 1-A at 98 pounds in 1972 and then stayed at 98 pounds but moved to Class 2-A in 1973.

"I don't know when the first time it would have been that (I learned) my dad had been a very successful high school wrestler. He bought us a wrestling mat that we used in our basement," Hagen said. "My brother being four years older than I was, he'd come home after practice and we'd have another practice. He'd show me moves. My dad, the only thing he ever talked to us about was when you pin them, have a wide base with your legs and post your forehead. I never pinned very many, but he pinned a lot. He used a move called the keylock, that was his favorite move. It's an illegal move now."

Was there big planning and extra conditioning work done in Belmond to get ready for a possible match against Hagen at state? "I don't know if I did anything except try to get him in shape. I did have him in good shape," Jones said. "As far as me personally trying to fire him up, he was so determined that night - especially after Braner won – I didn't even say anything to him except, 'Good luck, do it.' He had a glare in his eye. I still remember that just glaring."

Wilson said his biggest problem in the earlier matches was being unable to prevent Hagen from riding his ankle. "(Jones) being from Iowa Falls, he showed me a few little tricks that he learned from Kurdelmeier."

Jones said the big key for Wilson in the state finals match was building confidence by getting a lead. Wilson led, 4-2, going into the third period. "I think Hagen got a little frustrated. He'd never been behind like that," Jones said. "The Eagle Grove people were going nuts. They were his biggest supporter and yelling for him. I think mentally he pretty well did it himself. He knew he could beat him. I think he was just determined."

"I don't even remember most of the match, to tell you the truth. I just remember the referee gave him two for a reversal that tied the match with about 20 seconds to go," Wilson said. "It wasn't a reversal, and I just rolled through and came back up on top with my crab ride. I looked over and there were 14 seconds left. I was like, 'Ain't letting go now.'"

Jones remembered how well Wilson could work his control. "Oh Christ, could he crab ride. He'd frustrate me. He'd get on me and I'd say, 'You dang leech.' I had a buddy in college who could really do this, Roger

Sebert, and I showed Wilson that early on and boy he could do it. He had the strength and he could ride."

Wilson had a 6-4 victory and a new group of fans. The Eagle Grove gang loved his contribution to the Eagles' first team championship. That blended with state titles by the Eagles' Dave Prehm and Dave Morgan. Wilson gave thanks for technical help from an unlikely source: Britt coach Al DeLeon.

"I learned a ton from DeLeon over the years. He was a great technician," Wilson said. "They always remember his fiery way of doing things on the bench, but he turned some pretty average guys into some placewinners and it was called technique. He taught me some of the basic principles of riding, probably better than anybody, at least that I understood."

Wilson said the thrill of victory gave way a few minutes after his arm was raised. "I was pretty hyped up on adrenaline. Then after I got off the mat and into the corner, I started cramping up. It was like, 'Hmmm, can't move my hand.' The adrenaline wore off," Wilson said.

Hagen was being touted as the next four-time state champion. The first one, Bob Steenlage, was from Britt and he happened to be the grand march escort in 1974. Steenlage made mention of the possibility in the *Des Moines Register* during the tournament. After the loss, Hagen said he eventually got re-energized.

"Honestly I didn't take it that hard because I guess I just didn't realize what was happening," Hagen said. "I remember I probably cried, and the next day I got up – we stayed overnight in Des Moines and we came back to Britt – and I went for a long walk. It wasn't like my life's over, it was, 'Now it's time to get going.' The only thing my dad said that summer was, 'You need to wrestle freestyle,' so I wrestled freestyle and broke my arm in two places."

Photos from the tournament for the *Belmond Independent* were provided by the *Britt News-Tribune*. Wilson's mother, Ann, usually took care of the wrestling stories and the wrestling photos that appeared each week. She was always matside, but not on March 2, 1974. "She was up in the corner. We always sat in that northwest corner. I guess she about ran people over running down the ramp afterwards," Rich said.

Jones crowned his first champion and had to wait less than an hour to repeat the process. "It was probably the most fun night of my coaching career," Jones said.

The team returned to Belmond after the tournament. Jones said he regretted not staying, possibly because he lost a lot of sleep. "They had a little rally at the high school for us (Saturday night), everybody talked and then some people came over to my house and we watched the sun come up. The next morning they had a deal out at the We 3 (Restaurant)."

Jones won a state championship in 1961 for Iowa Falls. He said it was the fourth time that season that he and Jim Richardson of Algona tangled. "We met in the finals, I beat him and of course I was happy, but it doesn't sink in until later," Jones said. "When you're a coach, it's probably a bigger deal. That was kind of fun, knowing I was going to get to do it twice."

"I never wore the banner for the blind world."

Having a blind wrestler in the state tournament was nothing new when Ray Lough of Vinton High School qualified in 1979. Whether any of those participants from Iowa Braille and Sight Saving School possessed Lough's determination was a good question.

Wayne Ball reached the semifinals of the 1951 tournament before losing by fall to Jim Harmon of Waterloo West. Ball, who was blind since he was 9 years old, won 15 in a row during the 1950-51 season before Harmon became the first man in 45 matches to pin him. Ball and Lee Creek participated in the 1950 meet for coach Lee Iverson.

Lough started wrestling at the Vinton school frequently known as Iowa School for the Blind, but he transferred to Vinton High School by the time he got attention in the opening round of the 1979 state tournament. Lough used a 5-point move in the third period to beat Bob Yilek of Belle Plaine 10-7 in the opening round of 126-pound competition at the Class 2-A tournament. He lost two 1-point matches and did not place, but Lough made a Veterans Memorial Auditorium crowd see that he did not need vision in order to battle with anyone.

"I never wore the banner for the blind world. For me it was I achieved what I'd set out to do. I got there and I won. I was a self-made success in my mind, I had achieved what I wanted to do. I never played the blind card."

Lough was the fifth of Charles and Donna Lough's nine children. His vision began to go when he was diagnosed with retinal blastoma, a form of cancer, at 2 ½ months of age. Surgery took his left eye. Radiation to try to stem the growth of the cancer all but took his other eye. He could see some colors and light until he was eight or nine, but then glaucoma set in, Donna Lough said. He saw shadows in high school, now he can tell light and dark, she said.

"There was nothing Ray was afraid to do, there was nothing he couldn't do and he wanted to do it and we let him try it," she said. "We didn't baby him, we just kind of guided him to see that he didn't get hurt. You can make a kid handicapped by not letting him do things."

The Lough-Yilek pairing was a challenge because they had worked out earlier as the teams were in postseason mode. Their mothers got to know each other because they'd pass at shift change at the Amana factory – Yilek's mother, Lucille, worked first shift and Donna Lough worked second. They knew their sons wrestled, and the Monday greeting was catching up on how the boys did at the weekend's tournaments.

Bob Yilek was a kid who thrived on speed and quickness. Ray Lough was a strong man – as a 126-pounder he would bench press 240 – who could hold his own, but made an opponent pay for a slight letup or mistake. Their matchup at state was different because the start and restarts were done with the palm-up, palm-down style employed in a match with a vision-impaired competitor. A loss of contact would result in a restart.

"It was difficult for me because of my style. My style was more using my speed and my quickness and not really tying up with an opponent," said Yilek, who recently retired as head coach at Belle Plaine. "That was a huge change for me, how you have to start with one hand up, one hand down, and his strength was unbelievable. As soon as that whistle blew, it was like 'Holy cow, what got hold of me?'"

Lough said he also had amazing reflexes, partly sharpened by his loss of vision.

"You become very in tune with your surroundings. I developed a pretty serious response ability so I worked on my conditioning and I worked on staying focused, not worrying about the other factors around me," Lough said.

How do you prepare to wrestle an opponent who is visually impaired? Yilek said some of it was psychological with the help of his coach, Al Billings.

"The preparation for me was just the fact my coach was telling me you don't have to see to wrestle. Wrestling is mostly feel. You might have some advantages where you see certain things open up, but you're going to wrestle by the feel of pressure and not pressure," Yilek said. "The only thing that was different for me was the feet part, which was a big change for me because I didn't do a lot of tying up. As far as the mat wrestling, it was pretty much a feel type of thing that you should probably become accustomed to anyway. Although, the second strength that I felt I had was the quickness from the bottom to stand up and get away, which is what happened. So I stand up and get away, what do they do? They blow the whistle and they stop and bring you back in."

Lough said it was challenging to concentrate on the bout when there are six whistles blowing at any given time, cheerleaders doing their routines and there are crowd roars. "I was so nervous. I was surprised I even was able to wrestle because I was so nervous when I went out there, almost in a panic," Lough said. "I couldn't hear a thing Rich said, not a word. I really, truly felt I was on an island by myself fighting this battle."

"I won out of sheer perseverance. I'm not sure on another given day he couldn't have beaten me, I don't know, but it was a hell of a match," Lough said, adding that the big move changed everything. "It wasn't like it just happened, I was waiting for it. I knew if things worked out, he would give me that split-second opportunity. He was like me, he was aggressive. In the third period we were both physically exhausted. I knew if I had my opportunity, I was going to take it and take it hard."

The auditorium got really noisy when Lough won. Vinton coach Rich Farmer, who was watching a promise made to Lough years before come true, was born in Belle Plaine. He swears he jumped 15 feet when Lough won. Lough didn't want to celebrate. "I felt bad for Bob because he had me beat. I knew I had won, but I knew I won barely. I didn't feel like I'd won to the point where I should be out celebrating. I didn't control that match, I didn't wrestle my match, I got caught up in wrestling Bob's style for a while and that I think hurt me," Lough said.

The Vinton fans weren't critiquing. "I came off the mat and I was just mobbed, I mean just swallowed in the crowd. I remember finding Rich and saying "I've got to get to the locker room,'" Lough said. "All those nerves had built up to the point where it was almost unmanageable. When I won, I just collapsed."

Lough lost a 4-3 match to Dave Elliott of Centerville in the quarterfinals, then lost 5-4 to Adam Davis of Atlantic in a consolation bout. Vinton's other qualifier was Jack Geiger, who lost in the first round to Al Frost of Nashua at 145 pounds.

Farmer was asked why wrestling fans without an interest in the outcome cheer for someone such as Lough or Jack Barron, who won two state titles for Iowa School for the Deaf, or Nick Ackerman, who lost his lower legs to a form of bacterial meningitis at 18 months old, placed sixth at state in 1996 and won an NCAA Division III championship in 2001.

"I think people want success for people who aren't the same as them. If they're blind or deaf or whatever, they like to see those people succeed in anything like that. With the wrestling tournament, with all of the people being kind of on our side, most of them are pretty astute as to what it takes to be a wrestler, how much work it takes to be a wrestler. Whether you're blind or deaf or whatever reason, to be able to be that successful, they can identify with that because they know how much work it takes for anybody to be a wrestler."

Farmer wanted Lough to have a chance to qualify for state and to win his first match. He didn't want to go beyond what he could immediately deal with. That's why he said if Lough would have won a gold medal, it might have been difficult to explain how that might feel. Lough wanted to get a win at state for his father, who he said was his hero. Farmer's wish might have come around the time when Farmer would visit Lough's Vinton home and get a ride from Lough on the back of a snowmobile. Lough won a sectional championship as a freshman while wrestling at Iowa Braille and Sight Saving, but fell short in the district meet.

"I think it was that freshman year, when he could start competing against the public schools and when he did win that sectional championship," Farmer said. "It might have been before that that I said, 'If you keep working Ray, I can get you to the state tournament.' I didn't realize it was going to take as long as it did. I thought we had a very good shot when he was a freshman."

Lough said the wait would not have been so long if Farmer had been his coach throughout his high school years.

"Had I had Rich for a coach for four years, I would have been there my sophomore and junior year and probably won it one of those years," Lough said. "I lost my coach and the program was seriously deficient. My brother and I were helping the other kids. It felt like it was gutted. I got to state because I myself decided I was going to do it."

Lough would have been unable to cry tears of joy if he had won a state championship. The radiation used to treat his early eye problem affected the lacrimal glands and caused Lough to be unable to produce tears.

Lough was willing to do whatever was necessary to succeed, including running steps or doing laps in the gym at school. Before his senior season, Lough used a car as a conditioning tool.

"My sister Kathy was a year older than me, we lived in the country and I had an old Galaxie my dad bought for me for $50," Lough said. "She would take me out and I would hang on to the door handle and I would run – she tried to keep it down around 6 or 7 miles an hour – for conditioning. I worked out all through the fall."

There was no plan to have Lough's style be shaped in the mold of someone else. "I never wanted to be like anybody, I wanted to be me because I was so competitive."

Lough once took an unusual measure to make sure he got to wrestle. He was once one-quarter pound overweight, so Lough said he took out a glass eye, stepped on the scale and made weight. Lough said he didn't try to pattern his wrestling style. "I never wanted to be like anybody, I wanted to be me because I was so competitive," Lough said.

He had a chance to wrestle in a national blind wrestling tournament in Washington State, but he had to pay his way there. Lough said he waxed 25 cars in a month to get the airfare, then scored four first-period pins to win a gold medal.

The Lough family moved to Vinton from Newton after Ray began attending the Braille school. Lough's brother Donald wrestled at Vinton High School and later volunteered coaching wrestling at the Braille school. Farmer knew the Braille school and some of its students. He grew up in Vinton across the street from the school. He worked at a grocery store where those students shopped and he was friends with the superintendent's son. He applied to student-teach there while attending Northern Iowa and wrestling for Chuck Patten. Farmer was offered a contract to teach there and he accepted. He did some coaching of wrestling. Farmer met an active youngster named Ray Lough and one year Farmer was his homeroom teacher.

"We had intramural wrestling when I went from kindergarten through (fourth grade). In fifth and sixth I didn't wrestle because there wasn't any program for it. Somewhere along the way he encouraged me to get back on the mat, and I was always looking for ways to compete," Lough said. "I remember I was a pretty out of control kid. I had ADHD before ADHD was ever developed. It was more just hyperactivity. My motor was running all the time, and it still does. I remember driving him crazy in home room."

Farmer and Lough bonded. They were together until Farmer moved to Vinton High School. He was an assistant coach for the 1977-78 season and then became interim head coach for the 1978-79 campaign. Lough transferred for his final two years of school. He was 12-7 as a junior, and then flourished as a senior. Never mind that Lough had to win a district wrestle-back in order to go to state. He made it. The state pairings came out and there was the match against Yilek.

"He was really worried, I remember that. He said, 'Well he knows me' and I said, 'You're just going to have to work hard.' A coach has to sometimes get into a kid's head a little bit, and I did that with Ray a little bit. I said, 'Ray, I guarantee you that if you wrestle the best you can, you will win the first match.' He believed me," Farmer said. "I just prepared him the same way we prepared him for every meet. You really had to talk to Ray, get him calmed down and get him thinking about what he could do, then you had to build him up just like you'd do with any other wrestler. He was extremely nervous going out there. I don't think he wrestled as well as I thought he would that first period, but after that he sort of settled in."

That was one of Farmer's memorable moments in coaching. Another was seeing a boy who had no muscle tone, no talent but a deep love of wrestling. He got pinned, he got pinned, he got decisioned…the same thing night after night. "The very last match he ever wrestled as a senior, he won his match. I thought he had won the Olympics, and so did everybody else and so did he," Farmer said. "Other than Ray's success, having somebody stick it out like he did and doing what he did, that's just as rewarding, to be honest, as anybody else winning any kind of tournament."

Yilek learned first-hand about preparing a wrestler with a challenge to compete.

"We had a kid with cerebral palsy. His name was Parrish Miller. He had a heart of gold and a work ethic and he hated to lose, but he walked with crutches – actually Parrish threw his crutches away basically. He didn't have balance, couldn't stand up in a wrestling stance so he wrestled down on a knee. He had (legs), but he couldn't use them to his advantage. His upper body was strong," Yilek said. "We just had a boy graduate (recently) that wrestled for us legally blind. He moved in from Vinton at the end of his sophomore year, so we had him on the wrestling mat for two seasons. Jeremy Ellis, legally blind, had to start that same way which really funked a lot of those heavyweights out because they had to do the tie-up. He competed pretty well. That experience that I had helped me in the coaching ranks, in that especially and also with Parrish, that wrestling is a lot of feel."

"With Jeremy, it was kind of hard as a coach because I was instructing and then I would have to go over and show him physically – my hands on his body – showing him the technique. It was great for me to learn that other side as well."

Yilek said Ellis knew Lough, and Lough had told him that he'd wrestled Yilek back in the day. Yilek said the fact Lough qualified for state earned him a measure of respect. Because Lough was visually impaired, that was no reason Yilek didn't want to win or feel the sting of a loss.

"I'm sure I was expected to win because I was crushed when I didn't. I've seen kids that have taken losses and you can tell they didn't expect to win because it didn't hurt," Yilek said. "I was devastated. Ray did what he had to do, I made a mistake and it cost me the match. Does it still bother me today, and that's been 31 years ago? You're darn right it does."

Yilek said his experience against Lough helped him in preparing his wrestlers for a match against an opponent that has a poor record or who is challenged. His message? Respect everyone but be ready for all things.

Lough said he thought about a career in auto mechanics. He'd been involved with repairs at his father's service station and he developed a keen enough ear that he could tune an automobile by sound. Lough owned several cars and had a race car with a friend. He decided to try law school and is currently a practicing attorney – Lough was Benton County Attorney at one time – as well as an active foster parent. His health continued to be a concern. Lough said in 2010 that he is on his third bout against cancer and he had undergone 14 surgeries since 2005.

Prior to that, Lough wanted to show he could win at least once on the state's biggest mat.

"I wanted to prove to myself and all the naysayers that I could be more successful than they. For me it was a game changer in my life in a sense that I had been successful, I had reached a goal, I had done it with style. I left my mark on the state tournament, there's no doubt about that."

"I think the toughness that wrestlers have is bigger than any physical limitations"

Mason Ackerman is too young to comprehend how magical his father's wrestling career was, both in high school and in college.

As he scurries around the family's home, Mason sees the Hodge Trophy that Nick Ackerman shared with undefeated, four-time NCAA Division I champion Cael Sanderson of Iowa State as the nation's top amateur wrestler in 2001. He sees the gold medal dad won at the NCAA Division III tournament in Waterloo, when he won the 174-pound championship wrestling for Simpson College. By defeating defending champion Nick Slack of Augsburg, he halted a 60-match winning streak. The bracket from the tournament is there. So is Nick's "outstanding wrestler" award.

Not bad for a guy who spent most of his walking years on artificial legs. A fast-moving, life-threatening form of meningitis forced doctors to amputate his legs just below the knee joint when Nick was 18 months old.

"It was amazing courage on his part to give this sport a try. He never saw himself as being a guy who didn't have legs, he didn't think that way. He said, 'That's a sports that looks like fun and I'm going to play it,'" said Ron Peterson, who coached Nick at Simpson.

In 2008, NCAA Champion magazine named Ackerman's victory over Slack the most dramatic championship victory in NCAA history. The magazine's top-10 list covered wins dating back to the 1982-83 season, which was the first year of NCAA women's championships.

Randy Lewis, a 1984 Olympic gold medalist in freestyle wrestling, was moved to tears by Ackerman's effort. "The story of Nick Ackerman has uplifted the entire sport," Lewis said in a *W.I.N.* magazine article about Ackerman's award. "When I read about it, I got emotional. I started calling people and saying, 'Have you read this story?' What other sport could do this for an athlete? Wrestling should be so proud of this guy. I've never seen anything like it. It's the best story of the year...of the decade...maybe ever....in wrestling history. Someone should make a movie of it!"

Someday Mason will hear dad tell him that hard work, mental toughness and desire can make anything possible. Mason's little brother, who was expected to arrive in March of 2011, is likely to hear the same speech. It might come in the basement wrestling room Nick is building. Wrestling teaches more than just pinning another person's shoulders to the mat, Nick said.

"What I hope to show is more of something to carry on, something to give to my sons," Nick said. "Nothing monetarily, or has any value, but one of lessons learned, that I hope you carry on that mentality, that work ethic and that desire.

"I think a lot of it comes down to the mental toughness the sport breeds. Whether it's a physical obstacle to overcome or it's a mental block you have to overcome, I think the toughness that wrestlers have is bigger than any physical limitations."

Mason and his brother will hear the story of his dad placing sixth at 152 pounds for Colfax-Mingo High School in the Class 1-A state tournament in 1997 despite not having his legs and despite breaking his left wrist in the first round of the tournament.

Nick earned a standing ovation from the crowd that was there on that Saturday afternoon to see the consolation matches. There will be mention of his first-round match, beating Clay Youngblut of Don Bosco of Gilbertville, who was ranked No. 2 by the *Des Moines Register*. The 11-9 decision was Youngblut's first loss in 39 matches. Nick reached the semifinals before losing to Andy Kiger of Audubon, then finished sixth with a 5-3 loss to Clint Jones of Bondurant-Farrar. Jones beat Ackerman five times that season.

"Iowa wrestling is such an amazing group of people. These fans know wrestling," Colfax-Mingo coach Bryan Poulter said. "The respect they showed for what they saw that day, or that state tournament, that was a huge feeling to me. I knew what it meant. When they did that, the respect they had for him was unbelievable."

Peterson added, "The people in the state of Iowa know how special wrestling is. There is no other place in the country that knows and understands and appreciates wrestling like the Iowa people do. Those people recognized that was a special moment they'd never see again probably in their lifetime. The courage and the wherewithal to stay in there, keep fighting and get on that medal stand tells you a lot about his character."

That night, Nick swapped autographs with University of Iowa wrestling coach Dan Gable.

"When I began working with him, I didn't see that he would become a high-level wrestler like he became," Poulter said. "I saw at a young age that he overcame obstacles all the time. I manage the (swimming) pool and, when he was five, I watched him take off his legs, walk on his hands to the high dive and jump off. I knew he had that kind of mentality, but I didn't think, wrestling-wise, that it was there for him like that."

Nick could have grown as tall as 6 foot 10, but a form of bacterial meningitis known as meningococcemia forced the life-saving amputation. By the time Nick took the mat in 1997, he was 4 feet 3 inches from his head to his kneecaps. Fastening his prosthetic legs made Nick look like a regular high school kid if he wore khaki pants, jeans or sweat pants.

One thing Nick learned during his time in wrestling was persistence.

"You're taught at a young age to be patient, to work hard and that success doesn't always come easily. You get that experience when you're not succeeding. You're gaining something even when you're losing," Nick said. "Knowing that there is a payday at the end, or you're working for that payday. My wife tells me I'm a pretty big optimist. I'm a fairly positive person, always try to put a positive spin on things. I think with that right attitude you can see those bright things and you don't dwell on the shortcomings or the negative."

Poulter learned quickly that Nick was going to go places.

"I can remember telling my wife early, 'I've got a special kid in my room from the standpoint of not special as in a special need, but a special ability,'" Poulter said. "I saw early that the kid didn't know he wasn't capable of something. The baggage that we had with pre-conceived ideas about what you can and cannot do, he didn't have. I knew from then that he would take himself somewhere."

Nick's brother, Nathan, was 6 feet 8 inches tall and played basketball at Simpson. Nathan scored 1,578 points and was an all-Iowa Conference selection. "I look at my brother and he was very successful in college athletics, but everything came natural to him. He had the same upbringing, the same work-hard attitude. He took it a different route.

"When he went to Simpson, he chose Simpson for the education and basketball not necessarily secondarily, but not primary. He got recruited by the Hawkeyes to play basketball, but he didn't want it to be his life. He's now a game warden in the state of Wisconsin, works hard and is successful in his own right. I don't think because I had to work harder it wasn't any better, but it did add to it. If it would have been easy, I might not have been as driven. I might not have been as persistent. I might have been happy placing sixth at state and thinking, 'There are a lot of guys that are ready to be done wrestling in high school.' That's one thing (coach) Poulter stressed: 'There's people who are ready to be done with this tournament before it started. They qualified for the tournament because they were supposed to, not because they want to be here.'"

Peterson said he met Nick through Nathan, who would walk his brother to the athletic offices on campus visits. Peterson said he originally was not sure what to think about having Nick in a Simpson singlet.

"Then I went out and watched him wrestle and thought, 'Wow, he's got some ability.' When you go to the state tournament and you see him beat the Don Bosco kid basically with no legs and a broken (wrist), it's like, 'This kid has some courage and guts. You're going to get his best every time he goes out on the mat.' We did go a little harder after him, absolutely," Peterson said.

Nick started wrestling in third grade. It was a perfectly normal thing for him to do, considering his parents found no reason for him to be treated differently just because his lower legs were gone.

"He didn't understand that there were obstacles you shouldn't get over. He thought that obstacles in front of you were things you just climb and go do," Poulter said. "He just didn't see things as barriers like I think a lot of us that take things for granted do."

As a high school senior, Nick wanted more mat time.

"I knew as soon as that state tournament was done that I wasn't ready to be done wrestling. It wasn't even an option," Ackerman said.

A couple of months into his freshman season of college, Nick seemed ready to take his headgear off for good. "When he was a freshman, he got pinned six times in a row right before Christmas and he was done, he was broke," Peterson said.

The plan was to find Nick's strengths and weaknesses and fine-tune the strengths, Peterson said. One of those strengths had to be his mental toughness.

"There was something special about in the middle of his junior year where he started talking about, 'I'm going to be a national champ,'" Peterson said. "We talk about it all the time in the room, but he started talking about it. His senior year, from the day he walked in the room, he said, 'I'm going to be a national champ.' Every day he said it.

"I didn't believe it until it was done. He kept telling us, 'I'm going to win it, I'm going to win it, I'm going to win it.'"

That last day of the 1997 state meet was special on several counts, Nick said.

"I remember like when we finished and (got) the standing ovation and thinking, 'Holy cow, there's a lot of people here. They're standing up for me.' I couldn't understand it, it wasn't something I could put my head around," Nick said. "I remember them coming up to me saying, 'We're going to go up into the stands and talk to somebody,' and they shuttled me up there and it's Dan Gable talking and asking for my autograph. Of course, I got his too. I remember (University of Iowa assistant coach) Jim Zalesky was there and (Iowa assistant) Tom Brands. Until recently, when my mom moved, I had all of their autographs that I got at the state tournament on my wall.

"The blow-up of press from that, I remember getting letters from the Iowa State football coach, Tom Harkin...I remember getting home and there's mail on top of mail from people. I guess I don't know what I thought about it at the time, but it was way bigger than I could put my head around, a 17-year-old kid."

After he earned his medal in high school, people were not ready to see his charismatic personality leave the high school wrestling scene. They remembered reading a take-out story in the *Des Moines Register* the morning of the sectional tournament. The quotes were humorous, but telling of the man in the orange and blue singlet.

"I always thought I was normal. I used to break the legs off my GI Joe guys to make them look like me, a bunch of stupid stuff like that, because I always thought I was the normal one," Ackerman said in the 1997 article.

Nick would ask Nathan if he was going to take his legs off before going to sleep.

When the school nurse told his fellow elementary students that Nick had a special disadvantage, Nick corrected her by stating he had a special *ability*: "I can take my legs off, and nobody else in the school can."

Nick was a bit nervous going into the sectional tournament. "They write a big story about you and you're supposed to be this hero of a kid that is supposed to live up to these expectations. Bigger than any of those were my own and that of my family. They were so supportive, never missed a wrestling match," Nick said.

He had to win a wrestle-back match that night to finish second and earn a spot in the district meet. Time for a steak dinner. Nick finished second at the district, clinching one of the 208 Class 1-A spots at state. "I'm looking down on Cloud 9," he said afterward.

A rite of passage for teams is to produce a state tournament T-shirt that the wrestlers, fellow students and the adult fans snap up. It can be heady stuff, especially for a first-time qualifier. "You get the shirt and you have your name on the back and your weight, living the dream as they say. As a high school kid you don't get a better feeling, in my opinion, than walking into Vets Auditorium and seeing all those people and they're all there to watch us wrestle. That's exciting."

Nick knew there would be considerable attention on him when he wrestled. He was used to that in the smaller gyms of the regular season. At state, the TV stations wanted to show him in action and everyone wanted to talk to him.

"That's something that when I walked on the mat, I could feel people watching me. Whether it's in the gym in Colfax with a couple hundred people in there or there are thousands of people at Vets Auditorium, you can feel those people watching you, wanting to do well for yourself but not wanting to let your school down, not wanting to let your coaches down, your teammates," Nick said. "Not letting myself down, that was most important. The thing that frustrated me the most was when I would lose and I would hear or I could feel – and maybe it was all self-done in my head – that, 'He has no legs but at least he's trying' mentality, which is bogus, nothing more than an excuse. I grew up without legs, I wrestled my whole life without legs. For me to wrestle with legs, I would not be any good. I thought I was the one doing the normal thing, and that's all I knew."

When Nick clinched a spot in the tournament, Poulter had trouble imagining the 152-pounder was going to bring home a medal a week later. "I thought we had a really tough draw, Youngblut from Don Bosco. I thought we were in a tough sell. I probably underrated him and thought, 'Hey, it's been a great experience, he made it to state, he was a state qualifier.' The thought of being a state placer, I will admit, was not in my mind when we went to Vets that year," Poulter said.

The idea of seeing Nick winning a medal got into Poulter's head after he taped that damaged left wrist – his left arm is shorter than his right because of surgeries – in the Youngblut match. Poulter asked Nick if he wanted to continue and Nick said yes. "I knew from then on that he was not going to be denied the highest place he could get. I probably underestimated what the total true will in his body was.

"I learned it all over again when he went to college. He felt his junior year he probably should have made nationals, but he didn't, and then his senior year making it. In my mind I wasn't thinking about (him) being a national placer and I certainly wasn't thinking about being a national champion.

"It was amazing. The emotion's running very deep. I don't want to sound selfish, but I knew I was part of it. I didn't do a lot, but I was involved in helping him believe in himself and helping him set the way. He's just such a great kid and he's meant so much for me. I was sitting right next to his mother. I'm not sure which one of us was in worse shape at the time, but it was very, very fun."

Nick found a different way to get a little extra help.

"I'd always pray a little bit before the match. I never prayed to God because I thought he's going to help that other guy out as much as he's going to help me out, so I always prayed to my grandpa and to my Uncle Dick, my dad's brother who passed away," Nick said.

Nick's effort helped a young boy from Livermore set a goal of topping his performance. Wade Satern had his right leg amputated when he was eight months old. After moving from the state of Washington, Satern started wrestling in fourth grade. After seeing Ackerman, Satern started pushing himself.

"I thought it was unbelievable. That set a goal for me to beat that, immediately when I saw it," Satern said. "What I thought of him was he had to be incredibly strong, and he was much more disadvantaged than I was if you look at it as a disadvantage. Most people would. I never did and I'm sure he doesn't."

Satern won the Class 2-A 119-pound championship in 2002, one year after Nick won his national title. Satern beat Brad Gregory of Glenwood, 7-2, in his finals bout.

Nick had fun wrestling as a kid. "You put a third grader on a wrestling mat and say, 'Grab your buddy and try to wrestle him to the ground.' That's fun," he said. "I remember crying after a match once. I'd lost, but I remember my mom telling me…the point was, it's just a wrestling match, don't make it bigger than it is."

Without legs like his opponents, Nick turned to amazing upper-body strength to level the proverbial playing field. When he was not in school or at wrestling practice, Nick had a job working with pigs. He would pick up about 200 of the 60-pound animals each day to facilitate vaccinating them. As a result, Nick developed a serious grip for that crossface cradle he loved.

"Then when it came to grabbing hold of a kid that's my size's wrist, the same size as a pig leg, that thing's not going anywhere. I'd grab my own wrist and lock that cradle up and we were along for a ride," Nick said.

Poulter said Nick seemed to blossom as a sophomore.

"It was the second half of his sophomore year when he kind of quit trying to wrestle like everybody else in the room wrestles and he went to things that worked for him," Poulter said. "He found that his arms were so long that he could crossface and go into a cradle, and that could be a ride for him because you can't be called for stalling in a pinning combination. He just developed his own style. Once he started developing a little style, then it really started taking off."

Nick was one of those guys who was happy to learn of his opponent when they shook hands to start the bout. "You always get nervous to a degree. You don't let it affect your game, but I was a big fan of not knowing anything about the person I was wrestling," Nick said. "Some folks like to study them, they like to know. I was always best not knowing and I'm thinking in hindsight that's why Coach Poulter didn't tell me about Clay Youngblut."

The state tournament did help shape today's Nick, who works as a prosthetist and who has not lost his optimism or his sense of humor. "I'm a big fan of having fun. Quality of life is most important in my book. If you don't enjoy what you're doing, it's not worth doing," he said.

"I think if I wouldn't have broken my arm in the first round and had that positive reinforcement that that pay day was there, that culmination of years and years of wrestling and without having that ah-ha, I got it. You believe in yourself but knowing you can overcome these obstacles, you can do anything then," Nick said. "That mentality carries over to my work, to my relationships, to my family. Those obstacles that seemed insurmountable when you think about it, when I think about it, a kid missing both legs with a broken arm is not going to beat the No. 2 kid in the state. But when you see it happen or when you're part of it, you think there isn't anything you can't do. Then you go taking that on through college to a national title at Simpson and into a great career as a prosthetist."

Poulter said working with Ackerman was a huge high point in his career. "For me to have an experience of what kind of attitude you can have about what you've been given, it was a life-changing event for me," Poulter said. "It made me think about my own life, the people around me and what we take for granted every day. We have this choice of what we want to go each day with, and I watched him make the choice every day that he believed in himself, he believed in what he could do and nothing was going to stop that. I learned so much more from him than what I gave him.

"It still hits me hard. As many years as I've been around wrestling, when it comes state tournament time, I can't think of a state tournament without thinking of that one. I had the privilege of coaching a state champion, Michael Bucklin, and the things involved with that were amazing, of course. But I could never get the experience I had with Nick out of my mind. It was nothing but positive, definitely."

Peterson said wrestling is one of the few sports that is equal opportunity. "Any kid, regardless of what their issues are, can compete in the sport of wrestling," Peterson said.

Confidence is a by-product of the sport, Nick said.

"I'm a very confident person. I know who I am, I know what I can do, I know what my limitations are. I think the sport of wrestling demands confidence, demands cockiness, if that's what you want to call it," Nick said. "If you're not walking on that mat thinking you're going to win… it's a mindset. When I think I know something, you better prove me wrong. You have to be humble, but all the wrestlers I know, most of them have a cocky streak in them. I don't think there's anything wrong with that. I think the only thing worse than that is somebody who doesn't believe in themselves to the point that they get walked on or they don't expect as much out of themselves."

"It was an amazing experience for us. Very inspiring."

Jackie Barron never got to hear the cacophony of noises inside Veterans Memorial Auditorium in Des Moines during the state wrestling tournament. When he got lost inside the place that resembles an oversized barn, a message board was used to get his attention rather than a public address microphone.

It didn't take long for Barron to feel the respect tournament fans had for his ability on the mat.

Barron wrestled for Richard Pike at Iowa School for the Deaf in Council Bluffs, which no longer has an interscholastic mat program. He won the first of his two state championships as a 17-year-old freshman at 119 pounds in 1980, the capacity crowd wanted to give him a standing ovation. Since he would not be able to hear the applause, the audience chose a different method: stomping their feet so Barron would be able to feel the vibration.

His sister, Stacia, was a wrestling cheerleader for the team. "I always wanted to be a wrestler too, but I was told that I couldn't because I was a girl," she said, adding that the salute to her brother was memorable.

"Oh yes, my family and I remember the ovation that Jack got in 1980 very well. It was an amazing experience for us. Very inspiring. Brought us happy tears," Stacia Barron said in an e-mail interview. "Jackie had his smile grinning from ear to ear, he was inspired. I recollected that people were standing, clapping and stomping. I didn't feel the stomping but my mother did."

Gary Bergmann, a former coach at Graettinger, said Barron's stomping ovation was his best memory of the state meet. The moment was mentioned in *Sports Illustrated*.

Jackie won his second state championship in 1983. Fifteen years later,

Tim Matthys, a deaf wrestler for Davenport Assumption, won a Class 2-A 152-pound state championship. Once again, the sport opened its arms to an individual willing to put forth the work despite being challenged.

Jack Barron Jr., or Jackie as he was known, wanted to be a basketball star similar to his father, Stacia Barron said. He lacked his father's hardcourt skill, but learned he might be inclined to succeed at wrestling. In junior high Barron had a chance to play basketball and wrestle. "Jackie won three blue ribbons in three straight wrestling tournaments during his first year of experience," said Stacia, who was her brother's workout partner at home. As his love for wrestling grew, his desire for the game of basketball was on the wane.

"He was real tall and lanky and extremely strong. He couldn't hear anything but he had a feel for where the opponent was," said Lew Massey, who watched Barron develop alongside his sons Lewie and Keith. "He had the leverage to put them over since he was so tall. His physical build was more like Abraham Lincoln, the long, really strong muscles and he wouldn't quit. He couldn't get enough of it, that's what made him so good."

Stacia said her brother fell in love with workouts in Massey's basement, even if he was exhausted at the end of the drills. Barron's father put a wrestling mat in the basement so Jackie and his brother Barry had another outlet after supper. Stacia said her father pushed his son hard, holding high expectations for the blue ribbon or gold medal. When getting a takedown against his sister remained challenging, Jack Barron offered a quarter for takedowns and reversals. Stacia won most of the quarters early, but Jackie got better as he learned more technique and was getting stronger. He was starting to beat his sister. Stacia said she wanted to stop working out with Jackie, but their father insisted she continue as a workout partner so he could keep improving his moves.

In a 1985 interview with the *Los Angeles Times* as members of the Barron family were going to compete in the World Games for the Deaf, Jack Barron Sr. explained why he wanted his children to be involved with activities: "I didn't want them to sit around and watch television. That's just a waste. That's the problem with kids and sports today. Television is such a negative influence."

Barron continued his workouts with the Masseys. If the intensity got turned up, so did Jackie's smile.

"He liked it rough, he liked the rough play, that was fun for him," Lew Massey said. "He had two sparring partners that were equally enjoying the banging around. When you started putting some technique to it, then it became fun and they couldn't get enough of it."

Barron got a late start in his freshman year of high school because he repeated both seventh and eighth grade. Stacia Barron said her father originally wanted Jackie to repeat eighth grade so he would not graduate at 17 years old. He thought it would help Jackie both academically as well as in wrestling, she said. The year Barron would be repeating eighth grade there was no eighth grade class at Iowa School for the Deaf because a lot of the students were born in a time of a Rubella epidemic, she said. The seventh graders repeated, so Jackie started the junior high cycle all over and was 16 when he started ninth grade.

The physical maturity of being older than most freshmen showed up on the high school mat. Pike said the mismatches that sometimes resulted tended to dull Barron's love of competition.

"And it was no fun for him really, unless he was going up against a really good junior – by good I mean ranked in the state - or a senior. Then he got a little more interested," Pike said. "He was wrestling at 119 pounds and he was 16 or 17 years old as a freshman, where you can throw those 15-year-old kids around like nothing when you're as good as he was."

Pike wrestled at Grundy Center for John Doak, who would later start *The Predicament,* the nation's first state publication devoted to amateur wrestling.

"I wrestled three varsity matches in my life. When I was a freshman, Grundy Center started the program and I just happened to get behind three kids who all ended up going to state two years later. I could fill in for them if one of them got hurt, but what John Doak apparently recognized in me was that I learned quickly," Pike said. "He's starting a program where nobody has wrestled, and so sometimes if he was going to teach a new move the next day he would teach it to me and then he and I would demonstrate it. I had a knack for doing and explaining things. I wasn't any good as a competitor."

Pike said he also learned instructing the sport at Lake Mills, where he assisted Bob Reece, who would later go to Linn-Mar of Marion and Clear Lake. "Bob was the best person I've ever seen for breaking down moves and teaching them," Pike said.

When Pike got to Iowa School for the Deaf, he was not fully literate in sign language even though he had a sister who had grown up in the school and was a junior when he arrived. As he began to introduce kids to the sport, Pike found himself with four veterans who got pinned in tryouts by freshmen and they quit. One of those veterans would become Pike's brother-in-law. As the youngsters found their way in the sport, they got thumped. Pike said the impressive aspect was those kids were willing to give up weekend trips home in order to compete in tournaments and take more lumps than they administered. They had their manager, Danny Miller, who to this day has a special place in Pike's heart for his amazing skills in getting everything arranged, organized and washed.

There wasn't the challenege at the Council Bluffs school that Pike had at Lake Mills. He got to tangle occasionally at Lake Mills with Mike Stensrud, the 1974 Class 2-A heavyweight state champion. Stensrud was a powerhouse in high school wrestling and, after being drafted in the second round out of Iowa State in 1979, played 11 seasons in the NFL.

"With the deaf kids, you got a lot closer. There were advantages to the fact they were right there in a closed environment and they were always together," Pike said.

They had company as the success grew.

"Any kind of success was fun. Nobody paid any attention to wrestling, nobody was following us. If the parents ever came at all, they told you what a wonderful job you were doing," Pike said. "The next year we started winning and all of a sudden there were kids wanting to come on pep buses."

Reece's skill at showing holds couldn't help Pike in the 1980 state tournament. Barron was comfortably ahead of an opponent, but was having trouble turning him. Pike suggested using a half-nelson. "He signed to me, 'What means half?' He had gotten so advanced that he forgot what a half-nelson was. So I demonstrated on my manager and he literally goes 'ohhh' and pinned him within two seconds."

There was also the matter of finding Barron in Vets. Apparently there had been a change made in regards to weigh-in times on Thursday night, according to an account in the *Council Bluffs Nonpareil.* In trying to find Barron, it was realized he could not be paged like wrestlers or individuals needing to be reunited with their squads. A message was posted on the board that stretched along the south end of the arena. The same board that would display Barron's name two nights later as a champion.

Barron completed a 31-0 freshman season with a 16-2 victory over Steve Hiller of Kingsley-Pierson. Before the finals started, Pike received a standing ovation when he was introduced as the Class 1-A coach of the year. Pike said he was aware of the unique salute to Barron, but wishes he could remember much more about the night, but he was in the throes of being really sick.

"I was sick for several days. We got up there and I got sick that night. I drove up there. I don't get the flu very often, but when I do I usually end up in the hospital. There was no way I was going to miss that tournament. The kids knew enough, 'Don't come close to him unless you have to.' Actually he wasn't the one I thought was going to win it. I thought my '55-pounder (Ricky Mortenson) was going to win it, and he got fifth."

Stacia Barron remembered watching the match matside. She and her old wrestling buddy were close, so she was looking for a good sign. That came early because Barron notched his first takedown 15 seconds into the bout. "I was so nervous. Once his opponent was on the mat, he was a lot shorter, that was when I knew that Jack would win that night. He usually beat short wrestlers pretty easy. It was more difficult with the wrestlers at his same height (6'1). There were so few of of them," Stacia Barron said.

Barron never seemed to be concerned that his opponents could hear instructions from the corner during a match while he had to look over to Pike to see what was being suggested. It was an approach people might have remembered the previous year with Ray Lough of Vinton, who was blind. Lough won his opening match and just missed placing in 1979.

"I never tried to pretend I was sighted. I just worked from the premise that you're blind and you have to overcome it. I didn't see my blindness as a big problem," Lough said. "I had to adapt the way the match started, but once it started the game was on. A lot of guys go running out there bouncing and jumping all over like they're ready to take on the world. I'd walk out cool and calm, shake their hand, the whistle blew and I'd go bang – it was like flip a switch."

Iowa School for the Deaf had never qualified a wrestler for state until the 1979-80 season. Pike had five Bobcats as qualifiers – Duane Meyer at 98, Barron, Scott Saxen at 126, LeRoy Green at 132 and Mortenson. The team won nine dual meets and claimed top honors in three of four tournaments in the 1979-80 season. "We went from having zero trophies to having 20-some in four years," Pike said.

The keyword for the Bobcats at the 1980 tournament was fun. "I was aware at the time these kids were making some of the best memories of their lives. They understood too that their ceiling for success was limited, so let's enjoy it as long as we can," Pike said.

Pike doesn't remember much celebrating of the team's performance in the 1980 tournament. He remembered there was a party after the district tournament complete with cake because it was the weekend of Pike's birthday.

In order to be prepared for all of the activity that is the state tournament at Vets, Pike took team members to the tournament in 1978 and in 1979.

"We came up two years and I paid the whole bill. I knew I had to do that because they didn't have any experience. I don't know if any of them had even seen the state tournament on TV, but I knew enough when you're traveling with kids, if you're putting them in a new experience, they're not going to be as productive generally in a new setting as they are in a familiar setting. We stayed at the Best Western in Ankeny," Pike said.

In the opening round of the 1980 meet, Barron got a pin and Meyer scored a decision. Pike said Meyer – who grew up in Britt – was a sparkplug for the squad. His brother Joey was a heavyweight on the team. "Probably the biggest motivator was my 98-pounder, Duane Meyer. Duane was the engine of this machine, he was the one who kept them all together," Pike said.

Green came close to being the school's second state champion in 1981, but he was tripped, 5-4, by David Durell of North Polk of Alleman in the 138-pound match.

Barron appeared headed for a second straight championship in 1981, but his undefeated string ended at 58 matches when Rod Hass of Woodward-Granger rallied to beat him, 7-4, at 126 pounds. Barron held a 4-2 lead, but Hass got a reversal and a 3-point near fall in the final minute, according to the *Council Bluffs Nonpareil*. Barron scored a pair of pins to finish third.

There are differing opinions about Barron's 1981 tournament performance. Pike said the loss to Hass took a lot out of Barron. Stacia Barron said her brother was grieving the loss of his beloved grandfather, who died after collapsing at the sectional tournament.

"After he lost as a sophomore, his heart wasn't in it anymore," Pike said. "I think it was, 'I've disappointed my father, I can never make up for it.'"

Stacia said, "Our grandfather had a heart attack and died during the sectional tournament a few weeks earlier. Jackie's heart and mind wasn't into it. He became a better wrestler after that."

Barron would have to wait two years before he would win another state championship at Vets. His next title would put him in exclusive company. Barron won a gold medal in the 1981 World Games for the Deaf, making him the first Iowan to claim such honors according to tournament records. The *Times* article reported that the Barron family sold its mobile home to pay for the 1981 trip to West Germany. Barron enrolled for the 1981-82 school year at Model Secondary School for the Deaf, an arm of Gallaudet College in Washington D.C. The wrestling team there competed in the National Prep School championships in Bethlehem, Pa. Barron is believed to be the only Iowan to win a national prep school title, taking the 130-pound division in 1982. Barron had a 39-0 record, among those wins 30 pins.

The outstanding wrestler in the 1982 tournament was Rico Chiapparelli of Blair Academy in New Jersey. Chipparelli would become well known to Iowa wrestling fans as a three-time all-American and 1987 NCAA champion for the Hawkeyes.

Barron came back to Iowa School for the Deaf for the 1982-83 season. He completed a 90-3 record for three seasons of wrestling for the Bobcats by pinning Mark Sexton of Rockwell City in the 138-pound finals. The finals match produced his 67th career pin.

Several years after Barron completed his career, Pike was asked how good Barron was. "I don't know because he never got a challenge. He got beat but he didn't get challenged," Pike said.

Pike remembered Barron when it came time to show new moves to the Bobcats. Barron was getting more exposure to moves through his workouts with the Masseys than his teammates.

"If I were teaching a new hold, he would decide whether or not he was going to bother learning it. He would do it, but he for himself would decide whether that was something he was interested in," Pike said. "I was a pretty good leg-riding coach. Our kids, even though they weren't the world's greatest athletes, they could throw the legs in from anywhere and weren't afraid to do it. Jackie kind of liked that, so he would do that."

Lew Massey remembered Barron having a good skill for a top-flight wrestler.

"He was a quiet kid, that may sound silly being deaf, but deaf kids are quiet too. All he needed was a couple repetitions, I hate to compare him to Lewie but you'd show them something once or twice and they might practice it once or they might wait until a match and practice it during a match, which you tell guys to never do," Massey said.

Barron and Lewie Massey were among state tournament wrestling royalty in Council Bluffs, joining Bob Hunt and Don Ryan of Thomas Jefferson, Darren Coppock of Abraham Lincoln and Adam Bendorf of Lewis Central as two-time winners. They were at the top until David

Kjeldgaard of Lewis Central won three titles between 1994 and 1996. Kjeldgaard is one of four three-time champions the Titans have produced, being joined by Travis Paulson, Brandon Mason and Jimmy Waters.

Barron died in 1995 as the result of a motorcycle accident in Tucson, Az.

"Maybe wrestling's the route we ought to go."

Every wrestler dreams of joining the rare distinction of being undefeated through four seasons of high school competition. If that was the plan of Joe Gibbons, he had the pressure of living up to such a daydream removed immediately.

Just because Gibbons lost his first high school match, it did not prevent him from becoming Iowa's fourth four-time state champion. Going into the 2011 tournament, Gibbons remains the only one of the 19 four-timers that won his medals in two different uniforms – two for Waterloo Columbus, two for Ames. Getting technical, Joe was just following a family tradition.

Joe was one of four brothers who all struck gold on the mat. He joined brothers Jim, Tim and Jeff in totaling 10 state championships. That is the highest gold medal count for one family in Iowa's tournament history. The number swells to 12 when you add their uncles, Joe and Omar Frank of Cresco, to the list of success.

"Wrestling was in my family. We don't come from big people, and my dad was smart enough to say, 'Look at your mom and dad, we're not going to be big so maybe wrestling's the route we ought to go,'" Joe said.

Beginning with Jim winning three matches at 98 pounds in 1975, the Gibbons foursome had a 40-1 record in state tournament matches. Certainly, it's one of the better familial performances in tournament history. Tim, the oldest of the boys, won a championship at 98 in 1976 when Jim moved up to 105. Joe's championship run was between 1978 and 1981 and Jeff won in 1983 and 1984. Jeff absorbed the only loss, a 9-9, 3-2 overtime setback to Steve Knight of Clinton, in the Class 3-A 105-pound championship match in 1982. That halted a run of 32 straight wins by the Gibbonses.

Joe never lost at Veterans Memorial Auditorium, but he did lose his first high school meet in Charles City. Tim Schultz, who finished second in the Class 3-A tournament at 98 pounds in 1977, handed Joe a 7-6 setback. Schultz was a senior and he was ranked No. 1 at the weight.

"I had no idea who I was wrestling that night," Joe recalled. "It was a heck of a match, but he ended up beating me so I started my career out 0-1. Actually, as the rest of the season, he went undefeated and we didn't meet again until the district finals in Waterloo. He beat me in the finals, 4-2, and he dominated the match. Very frustrating. I didn't have an answer for his toughness. A short seven days later, we're wrestling again in Veterans Auditorium on Saturday night. Because we were cross-bracketed, we were separated. We both got (to the finals), and I was able to turn the match around, the outcome, and pull off a 3-1 win."

Joe started early putting himself in position to be successful on the grand scale. He threw himself head-long into the spring and summer freestyle tournaments and found some ideal people to hang around with, work out with and wrestle with.

"It started before I came and wrestled in Des Moines at the state tournament," Joe said. "It actually happened when I was probably about 10 years old, my dad (Bill) started bringing my brothers and I down to watch some of the old West Waterloo teams that were coached by Bob Siddens. We got a chance to watch those teams compete as well as some of the Ames High teams that were wrestling down here.

"It started in kid tournaments. In the '70's, that's when it really took off in the state of Iowa – a lot of the kid tournaments that kind of erupted on the scene like Emmetsburg, Independence, Cedar Falls, Bettendorf… it started evolving. When we got into high school, that was the goal – to compete and make the team and get down to the state tournament."

Through those youth tournaments, Joe said he got to be friends with like-minded guys. "I hung out with other guys who wanted to do the same things that I did in wrestling, and that was four-time state champions like Jeff Kerber and Scott Morningstar," Joe said.

It did not hurt that the Gibbons family moved to Ames after Bill Gibbons finished law school. Iowa State was on a roll. "Iowa State was rattling off four out of five consecutive NCAA team titles…the great Dan Gable, the Dave Martins, the Chuck Jeans, the Chris Taylors, the Ben Petersons, the Carl Adams…I saw them all and that's when I really fell in love with the sport of wrestling."

Love is one thing. Confidence is another. Joe got the idea he could have success at Vets too. "When I knew it could happen for me when I was 12 years old, in sixth grade, coming down to Veterans Auditorium watching my brother Jim win as a sophomore in the state tournament."

That year, Jim clipped John Veenschoten of Des Moines Hoover 7-0 and Mike Wmaska of Bettendorf 4-3 before meeting Dan Glenn of Fairfield in the finals. There were no points in regulation and in overtime, but Jim got the victory by referee's decision.

"There was really no question who would get the decision in the championship match. The regulation match ended in a scoreless tie, as did the three-minute overtime, but Gibbons was clearly the more aggressive wrestler and nearly had a takedown in the first overtime period," according to an account of the match in the *Ames Tribune*. "No one seemed surprised when Gibbons was the unanimous choice of the three judges."

One title caused Joe to dream of four. "I thought four times when I was 12 years old and I saw (Jim) win it as a sophomore. Maybe it's a little bit of sibling rivalry, but when he did that, that's when I set the goal and I wrote it down and put it above my bed."

One season later, Tim replaced Jim as the Class 3-A 98-pound champion and Jim became the 105-pound winner. If a little brother's eyes got big watching one sibling win a gold medal, imagine the saucer size when two did it.

"Jim cleared the path and it kind of got Tim fired up to even make more of a commitment to the sport. Both my brothers won titles at 98 and 105. Boy that was really exciting because you go back to our farm outside of Ames and all of the people you care about that helped get you to that point in time – your mom and dad, your brothers, your grandparents, aunts and uncles, coaches, assistant coaches, wrestling teammates – are all there to celebrate that accomplishment. It was really exciting," Joe said.

The *Waterloo Courier* reported that Tim and Jim made history as the first brothers to win individual titles in the same tournament. The Hunt brothers of Algona (Gene and Duane) in 1970, the Jones brothers of Cedar Rapids Washington (Chuck and Glynn) in 1973, the Schmauss brothers of Cresco (Dick and Merlin) in 1960, the Huff brothers of Waterloo West (Don and Tom) and the Severson brothers (Arlin and Larry) in 1957, the Nelson brothers of Eagle Grove (Bill and Dale) in 1945 and the Gast brothers (Dick and George) in 1940 got dual golds before the Gibbons brothers did.

Those wrestlers Joe criss-crossed the state with at youth tournaments and freestyle events were some guys Joe had to beat to stay on his goal of four championships. "I grew up with all these kids and we battled. The

Paul Glynns, the Matt Egelands…the guys I competed with in the state tournament I had been competing against them for the last 5-6 years prior to that freshman year," Joe said.

Joe faced an obstacle as he was about to go into ninth grade. Ames did not allow freshmen to wrestle at the varsity level. If he was going to be the first Class 3-A wrestler to win four titles, it was not going to happen at Ames. If he wanted to stay in the Ames area, Joe would have needed to attend Nevada High School. One day he found out quickly that he was moving to Waterloo.

"I won the Tulsa Nationals in 1977. My dad and Tim and I drove in a station wagon down to Tulsa and I won it," Joe said. "As eighth grade got out, I'm out on Oakland Street, not too far from Clyde Williams Field, and I'm playing catch with my best friend. My dad comes by in a pickup truck with a flatbed full of 2-by-4's. He rolled the window down and said, 'Joe, get in the truck.'"

An hour into the trip Joe found out they were going to Waterloo. Another hour later, they were two miles from Gilbertville in the Waterloo East school district. Dad, who graduated from East, started building a house. Freshmen were not able to wrestle on varsity at East or West, but there was a chance to go parochial. Don Bosco was available in Gilbertville. In Waterloo there was Columbus High School.

"I wanted to be the first guy to (win four) in Class 3-A, so that separated me from Don Bosco," Joe said.

Regardless of classification, Gibbons had specific goals and knew some specific folks to be around.

"My goal was to become a four-time state champ, to wrestle at the college level and win a national championship," Joe said, "so I started hanging out in the summers with guys that were making that same commitment like Jim Lord from Lisbon, Jeff Kerber, Scott Morningstar of Lisbon, Greg Randall of Mount Vernon. We went around as a pack and competed and it just got us better and better. I really owe a lot of my success to their friendship and their working out with me."

Indeed they battled. Joe beat Paul Glynn of Fairfield, 1-0, in the 1978 quarterfinals and then beat Matt Egeland of West Des Moines Dowling, 4-2, in his next match.

Some of the guys Joe ran around with were farm kids, who maybe had chores to do before they could go to a tournament or were baling hay or detassling corn in between tournaments or workouts in the summer. Joe understood the importance to wrestling of farm kids.

"The whole state embraces wrestling," Joe said. "If the truth be known, wrestling got its original roots…why it was so effective in Iowa was it went back to the rural community. Hard-working families and those kids that started the programs weren't in the big cities, they were out in rural areas like Clarion, Cresco, Eagle Grove…small towns like that and the cities embraced it. That work ethic kind of transfixed itself into wrestling."

Kerber brought in a change to the sport in Iowa because he went all over to find an opportunity to improve his technique, learn new things and face top individuals. Bill Gibbons and John Kerber would take kids where the competition was. "Anytime you're on the mat wrestling, 1-on-1 and competing at that level, it's going to make you better and it's going to increase your chances of winning during the winter," Joe said.

As an example, Jim and Tim Gibbons won championships – Jim in intermediate and Tim in juniors – while Joe finished second – he competed in the midget division – in a national AAU tournament in 1973 in Missoula, Mont.

As those guys got into high school, they blazed a trail of success for the state in the national freestyle picture. Schultz might have lost a state championship bid in 1978, but he brought home a Junior Nationals 98-pound title that summer. Perry Hummel of Urbandale, who won his second Class 3-A championship for Dowling, won the 178-pound juniors championship. Kerber won a Greco-Roman championship at 123 pounds. In 1979, Randall, Tim Riley of Iowa City High and Pete Bush of Davenport Assumption were freestyle champions while Kerber at 132 and Jay Llewellyn of Cedar Falls at 165 took Greco-Roman gold. Kerber was outstanding wrestler of the tournament.

Jeff Carter of Dowling, Pat Pickford of Fort Madison and Joe Gibbons took freestyle gold in 1980 and in 1981. Joe was named outstanding wrestler of the 1981 freestyle meet. Steve Knight of Clinton and Bill Reed of Fort Dodge were Greco-Roman winners in 1981.

"Now a lot of people don't know who our national freestyle champions are in our state. It doesn't get the following, and it could be a greater accomplishment to win a national freestyle title, but everybody remembers who wins the state championship," Joe said.

Many of the good ones put themselves in as many challenging tournament settings as possible so that Saturday night at state, or even Wednesday or Thursday at state, is less likely to cause the knees to buckle.

Joe said he got himself acclimated to the Vets aura long before he wore his first varsity uniform there.

"You've got to put yourself in that situation. I came down here years before I ever competed and I got used to the sights, the arena, the sounds, the crowd and how it can go in a split-second from quiet to a screaming roar where your headgear's just radiating and you can't hear anything," Joe said. "I was aware of my surroundings before I got there, then when I competed I wasn't scared. I had teammates that got overwhelmed by just what was going on, they couldn't concentrate and they got beat by possibly a lesser opponent because of that. Nothing beats experience, coming down, witnessing it before you get here and to be committed to your technique, execution and wrestle for that moment in time, that 6-minute match."

In 1980, Joe had a choice to make. He was moving back to Ames and his dad asked if he wanted to attend West Des Moines Dowling or Ames. He picked Ames. Little Cyclone coach Jack Mendenhall was going to coach his third Gibbons boy.

"I knew coach Darrah, but Ames was my home town and I was working out with all those college guys anyway," Joe said. "It just was the easy, logical choice to go back to Ames."

Joe had a situation in his last championship match as he had in the first one – an opponent he'd faced in the district tournament one week earlier. In 1981 the finals opponent was Russ Graves of Webster City. There was also the usual pageantry and atmosphere that can make a guy forget his business.

"There was a lot of pageantry. You got the grand march, you got the induction of the hall of fame members and it's great, it's a part of the whole setup," Joe said. "I had wrestled the guy in the district finals and I had pinned him. To be honest, you never know what could happen, so I was nervous. It's good to be nervous, to have that adrenaline, and it kept me alert. I let myself get nervous."

He also let his offense go. Gibbons won the match, 13-0, and finished his high school career with a 105-5 record. The first of the two standing ovations began as referee Arlo Flege of Waverly raised Joe's arm. Like any good official, Flege liked the opportunity to be on the whistle for a historic bout.

"I kind of gloated over that. I wouldn't say that I hoped the guy won, but when he did I was very proud to be able to circle him around as a four-timer," said Flege, who worked all four of Joe's championship bouts as well as all four of Randall's and all four of Mark Schwab's.

When Joe went out to shake hands with Graves for the 1981 finale, Ames coach Jack Mendenhall had a brief chat with Flege. "Mendenhall said, 'I knew you'd be here, Arlo.' That makes you feel good," Flege said.

"I just remember Arlo Flege waving my hand in the air and I threw my other hand up with my four fingers symbolizing the four state championships. It's that moment in time and it happens so quick," Joe said. "You look around at everybody standing and clapping for you, and to accomplish that long-term goal...there's not too many times in your life where you do accomplish a long-term goal that you set out for like that. That night it went my way. All the people I cared about were in that arena that night, and to share that with them...they knew the work that I put in, they put in work. Let's face it, when you go out for wrestling, mom and dad go out for wrestling too. Your brothers or sisters go out for wrestling too. It's a total family commitment."

That family commitment continued in college as Joe wrestled at Iowa State. Joe became the first four-time champion from Iowa to win an NCAA championship by securing the 142-pound title in 1985. He was the last of 25 individuals who won an NCAA championship for the Cyclones during the Harold Nichols Era. That was the season Joe, who was named "freshman of the year" in 1982 by *Amateur Wrestling* News, set an NCAA record with 50 wins. Iowa State's assistant in 1985 was Jim Gibbons, who won an NCAA title in 1981. Jim took over as head coach when Nichols resigned after the 1985 tournament. Jim coached Joe to his fourth all-America honor in 1986. Jim coached Iowa State to its most recent NCAA team title in 1987 and he and Joe coached Jeff to all-America honors twice.

Joe grew up on wrestling mats and is now involved in private business. Some people have not forgotten the young kid.

"I kid Joe Gibbons a lot. Joe ended up being one of our sideline announcers at the high school tournament, as well as he's done some of our Big Ten wrestling meets. I kid him because just as I remember him plainly as a four-timer, I remember him as a 98-pound blond-haired, floppy-haired sort of little urchin winning his freshman title for Waterloo Columbus," said Doug Brooker, who directed Iowa Public Television's coverage of the state tournament championship round for several years.

Joe remembers being in action at a time when the state produced some strong individuals.

"I wrestled during a good era, a real strong era where a lot of guys who were wrestling in the state tournament went on and wrestled at the Division I level and had a lot of success. I look back and I'm proud of all that," Joe said.

"I knew where I was at heading into high school."

Tom Chelesvig passed a dominant wrestling gene to his son Bart dealing with being first.

Bart was a three-time state champion for Webster City High School and coach Verne Hill, becoming the first Lynx wrestler to attain such lofty status in 1985. He was part of the Class of 1987, a collection of talented wrestlers who would make their mark on the NCAA tournament and enjoy one golden Olympic moment.

Tom Chelesvig went to Eagle Grove High School after attending country school. He had four coaches in four seasons of wrestling – A. B. "Abe" Parsons, August "Pudge" Camarata, Bob Siddens and Ray Stone. While wrestling at 145 pounds in the 1949-50 season, Chelesvig became the first wrestler to win a state title with Siddens in his corner when he beat Bob Thorson of Cresco.

Bart made his name in wrestling before he ascended to the top of the award podium in Des Moines. It was a source of pride for his father and a sign of things to come for Lynx opponents.

"One thing that happened when he was a sophomore, he allowed four offensive points in the whole season. He gave up some points to let people go, but he only gave up four earned offensive points in the year, which was unreal," Tom said.

The credit for Bart's early lessons in wrestling went to his brother Russ, Tom said. Russ competed for the Lynx, but never experienced what his brother would achieve. "You have to put a lot of the credit onto Russ, working with him as a little guy and teaching him the right skills as a real young kid," Tom said. "From there he just seemed to develop and eat it right up on his own. Russ and I were always there supporting him, but he was so self-motivated it was best just to stand back and watch Russ and him do their thing."

Bart said his brother got his wrestling appetite whetted with the help of a book.

"When I was in the sixth grade, my brother gave me the book *The Legend of Dan Gable, "The" Wrestler* and that really lit a fire that I wanted to be the best, wanted to be like him. I'm sure he's done that to thousands of kids, a good influence."

Chelesvig eventually wrestled for Gable at Iowa, earning all-America honors three times.

Webster City was known athletically for its football teams, under the direction of Harley Rollinger and Dick Tighe. In wrestling, two Lynx – Keith Mourlam twice and Russ Graves – had reached the state finals but there was no gold medal. Bart said he got some early indications of where his talent level was.

"The summer tournaments were becoming more plentiful when I was coming through junior high school. That way you got a chance to wrestle the older kids and gauge where you're at. I knew where I was at heading into high school," Bart said.

He was on top of the sport in 1985 when he beat Tim Weatherman of Ballard of Huxley, 9-7, in the Class 2-A 145-pound title bout. Thirty-five years and two weeks earlier, Tom won his gold medal at 145 pounds and was carried off the mat in celebration by Bill Nelson, an Eagle Grove state champion and three-time NCAA champion.

People told Bart about his dad's accomplishment. Dad preferred to keep quiet about that part of him. "I had heard quite a bit, mostly from others. (Tony) Coltvet was always in my ear telling me about my dad. My dad didn't talk a whole lot about it, but he talked a little bit. It was more of how he loved the competition," Bart said.

Bart knew Veterans Memorial Auditorium in Des Moines. That's where wrestling's family reunion was staged. Families knew families, guys ran into former opponents from finals past. New members to the family were added each Saturday night.

"It was unbelievable, it was the greatest thing at the time because you'd set that goal. A long time in the making. I had been there so many times racing up the ramp to save seats for my family, now it was going to be me out there that everybody's going to do that for. It was quite a bit of adrenaline and quite a bit of satisfaction," Bart said.

"I remember a lot of little things about (state). I remember warming up in the corner or the ramps. I remember running up the ramp to go hug my mom after I'd won the state, and she passed away weeks later. That's my best memory. That was my second, but that was a struggle to get through the year emotionally with that. That's my best memory."

In 1986, Bart improved his winning streak to 63 matches when he won the Class 3-A 167-pound championship with a 17-2 technical fall over Aaron Chambers of Marshalltown. It was the culmination of an emotionally draining, demanding junior season. Bart's mother, Nadine, had earlier been diagnosed with cancer and she put her can-do spirit into the pages of a book entitled "When Life Hands You Lemons… Make Lemonade." By Christmas break in 1985, Nadine's condition had worsened.

"I found out on my birthday right after Christmas (Dec. 26) that she was probably not going to be around much longer. That was tough," Bart said. "It was probably fortunate that I had the wrestling going on to keep me busy. I had great support with my coaches, my teammates and friends around me. It was tough getting through practice sometimes. I'd get pretty upset over nothing, vent my anger and frustration. I was pissed at everybody for anything."

To those who know Bart, that crankiness was a tough image to picture. He was always loaded with politeness and he was a quiet kid who did not brag of his accomplishments, a model of a strong upbringing. "It seemed like he handled that real well for the age he was and the pressure you might say he had. He handled it real well," Tom said.

Nadine came to Vets for the 1986 tournament. "We wheeled her up in a wheelchair to some of the matches. She was in and out of the hospital quite a bit. I knew she wasn't going to be around for the next season, but I had no idea of how long."

After he beat Chambers, Bart ran for the balcony. "Right after the match, I ran up…right in the corner. Yeah, she just told me she was so proud of me."

Nadine died March 23, 1986, nearly one month after she got to watch Bart win his second championship and share a celebratory embrace.

Bart got his final season off to a lightning start, winning his first 12 matches by pin. He later won the Hudson Invitational and other tournaments. Bart up, opponent down. His winning streak reached 90 as Bart pinned Tim Lewis of Oskaloosa in the first round of the Class 3-A 167-pound state tournament. Ty Smith of Des Moines Roosevelt and Wade Lamont of North Scott lost, setting up Bart's third shot at a championship.

He faced Steve Sparbel of Muscatine and posted a 22-6 technical fall. He finished with a 115-7-1 record and a 93-match winning streak.

"Bart is a well-rounded athlete and has such a natural gift for the sport of wrestling," Hill told Webster City's *Daily Freeman-Journal*. "He understands what it takes to get ready for each match, and his hard work has helped to make him as good as he is."

Bart said Hill was an excellent coach for him to learn under.

"He would more or less give me any opportunity I needed. He let me go on my own a bit, but he'd point some things out here and there that would help me. He was a good mentor for me off the mat as well as in the wrestling room," Bart said. "I don't know if he had any psychology background, but he knew how to motivate, just little things about somebody that would get them moving in the right direction or give us little challenges that we'd try to strive to do a little better."

Gable spoke at Webster City's wrestling banquet. Also in attendance, according to the Webster City paper, was Iowa State assistant coach Ed Banach. Bart was a hot recruiting commodity.

"It was pretty flattering. Back then, you could recruit and call people a little earlier too. It was really flattering to have Gable, (Iowa State coach Jim) Gibbons and (Oklahoma State coach) Joe Seay all drooling over me," Bart said. "I remember being in Ames and Gibbons is asking me to sign right there in his office. I panicked and made my brother come pick (Mark) Reiland and me up."

Gable came to a Webster City-Eagle Grove wrestling meet during the 1986-87 season. That trip would give him eye time on Bart and Reiland, a two-time Class 2-A champion for Eagle Grove who was coached by his father, Marv.

"(Gable) came in when it was finally time to decide. It was after the signing date and Mark and I were down in Ames on our visit with Gibbons. We panicked and said we have to come home. Gable had heard we were going to go to Iowa State that night, so he rounded up Mark Johnson and Barry (Davis) and came up. They flew up that night and went on the hunt looking for us and ended up staying at Reilands I think," Bart said. "They got (Mark) to commit on Saturday night and they were at my place on Sunday morning. Gable said to me, 'I want to go somewhere so we can talk private.' We walked into my bedroom and he said this wasn't going to work, we need to go somewhere. So we went for a walk and I pretty much knew at that point what was going to happen. The pressure was there, but I just needed him to say, 'Quit messing around and make your decision.'

I really wanted to wrestle for the Hawkeyes, but it was real hard for me to say no to Gibbons."

Mark and Bart were regulars on that spring and summer tournament trail. They would have wrestled in the 1986 Junior Nationals, but already had reservations: they made the Junior World team and wrestled overseas. In 1987, Reiland won freestyle and Greco-Roman championships and Bart claimed a freestyle title at the Junior Nationals in the UNI-Dome at Cedar Falls.

"I and most people probably thought one of the main reasons I was at the University of Iowa was because of Bart Chelesvig. Bart was the one everybody wanted, we were going together. I'm not sure I disagreed with them at the time," Reiland said.

Bart joked that his being friends with Mark was worth extra scholarship money for the Eagle Grove champion.

Tom watched the recruiting process of his son. "We both handled it quite well. I didn't try to influence him," Tom said. "He wanted to stay in Iowa, didn't want to go anywhere but Iowa State or Iowa. I let him be the decision-maker on that. I knew Dan before anyway through Waterloo West and Bob and stuff. (Bart) fit the program quite well."

Bart's determination was handed down from his father.

"I started (at Eagle Grove) as a freshman and lost my first tryout. The fellow we had, Parsons, said, 'That was a senior you were trying out against.'"

The tryout was against Richard Amonson. "(Parsons) said, 'You surely didn't think you were going to beat a senior…' I said, 'Well, I didn't really decide that I was going to lose' and I didn't lose another tryout. We tried out again, I made the team and went from there."

Eagle Grove's school yearbook for 1948 portrayed Tommy Chelesvig as making a "splendid showing, winning as many as seven straight. He has a very bright future in wrestling."

Tom had a grand time.

"Through that four years I think I had a total of five losses. I think it was two losses as a freshman…one when I was a senior in the state tournament, when I had a shoulder out of place and broken ribs and probably shouldn't have been in there. I think the appreciation I got from it was being able to achieve something," Tom said.

He had a quality Siddens picked up on one day at practice. "Like Bob Siddens said, 'I don't think anybody could ever tire you.' He was fresh out of college and after practice was over, he and I would go another half-hour."

Siddens was a strong influence on Tom. "Out of all the coaches I had, you had to respect him so much. He was such a firm person but a humble person. Everybody has a coach they want to model themselves by, and I always thought if I could be like that it would be great because he was very tough on the mat but he was just as gentle and humble as you could get, which was a good combination. You just wanted to win for him."

Away from the mat, Tom had work to do. He developed a strong grip by milking cows.

"We farmed a pretty good-sized farm, I had an older brother and I helped my father. We had a lot of cattle feeding and hogs, so we were busy, a lot of hard work when we were little. A. B. Parsons one time said, 'For your size, you're about as strong of a kid as there was' because of the physical work we did."

Tom and Bart spent a few miles together. "My dad officiated a lot of high school stuff when I was a little kid, so I was always dragging around behind him, running around those tournaments and going to the rules clinics, but he never put any pressure on me for anything. It was all up to me."

Bart's mother joked in her book about him being a "mistake" because of the distance between Russ and him. "I wish all of my mistakes were as rewarding as he is," she wrote. Nadine's dedication to Bart in the book described him as "our pride and joy, who was responsible for many of the 'up' times during my depressive period."

He was also a benefactor of good timing. The 1987 state wrestling tournament had a sterling senior class. Among that group with Bart and Mark, who won an NCAA wrestling championship at Iowa, were Gary Steffensmeier of Fort Madison, four-time champion Dan Knight of Clinton, Travis Young of Indianola, Paul Weltha of Ames, Mike Moreno of Glenwood, Steve Hamilton of Emmetsburg, Tom and Terry Brands of Sheldon, Doug Streicher of Starmont of Strawberry Point, Greg Butteris of Lisbon, Travis Fiser of Marengo, and Jamie Cutler of West Des Moines Dowling.

Young was Simpson's first NCAA Division III champion wrestler and would be a two-time national champion. Weltha was a junior college national champion and football all-American at Iowa Central Community College in Fort Dodge. The Brands twins totaled five NCAA championships at Iowa – Tom won three, Terry two. Tom won a gold medal in the 1996 Olympics in Atlanta and Terry was a bronze medalist in the 2000 Olympics. Butteris was a national junior college wrestling champion. Steffensmeier, Knight, Moreno, Hamilton, Cutler, Streicher and Fiser were NCAA Division I all-Americans.

There were plenty of opportunities to share recruiting stories while on the freestyle circuit or while riding to LaCrosse for the Northern Plains regional tournament.

"That was a pretty phenomenal group, tough kids too," Bart said. "I can't think of too many classes out of Iowa that were that good. I would think it's pretty good. We did talk about it a little bit, but not until we were seniors, like recruiting time and 'What if we could all go to the same school?'"

The decade of the 1980's saw six four-time state champions get some or all of their gold medals between 1980 and 1989. It also had Jack Barron of Iowa School for the Deaf as a two-time state champion and some individuals who won championships for teams that no longer compete. Morning Sun totaled six individual state champions, including Jay Johnson in 1980, Earl Bryant and Jerry Malone in 1981 and Bryant in 1982. Schools such as Grundy Center – Rick Ruebel won in 1980 – and Reinbeck – Scott Beenken won in 1982 – and Gilmore City-Bradgate – Dave Tool won in 1983, Dave Vote won in 1985 – have consolidated with other districts and have different nicknames.

Bettendorf broke the state record for state tournament points with 167 ½ in 1982. The previous mark of 145 ½ was held by Don Bosco of Gilbertville in 1979. Bettendorf's 1981 squad joined Charles City, Centerville, Clinton, Dallas Center-Grimes, Glenwood and Griswold in winning the state team championship for the first time.

A new state tournament was added in 1987. The dual-meet tournament gave teams with outstanding invididuals a chance to have the other squad members join in the thrill of celebrating a team victory. The first tournament was at the UNI-Dome in Cedar Falls and Dowling, Eagle Grove and Lisbon were the first team champions.

Dowling won the first six Class 3-A dual-meet championships, a record that stood alone until 2010 when Don Bosco won its sixth consecutive Class 1-A title.

"Winning the state tournament as a team wasn't even on the radar."

Lisbon was favored to win the Class 1-A team championship in the 1984 state wrestling tournament. Having won five of the previous seven small-school titles – and finishing second in the other two – made it tough to consider any other school on top of the award stand.

So the 1984 Class 1-A championship went to…Dallas Center-Grimes. The Mustangs clipped North Tama of Traer by the thinnest margin of victory – ½ point – since the Iowa High School Athletic Association began staging the event in 1926.

"Lisbon was ranked No. 1 that year. They won probably the previous two titles if my memory serves me right," Dallas Center-Grimes coach Andy Davidson said. "It was either them or Don Bosco and Don Bosco went up to 2-A. In a pre-season meeting in November, I distinctly told (the team), 'We have the talent in this room to do something great this year. We could bring home a state trophy, there is no reason why we can't.' That was all we ever said about it. They knew I believed in them, they all nodded and the rest is history.

"We just focused on getting as many guys through as we could. With the number of guys Lisbon had ranked…I never believed in building kids up, setting them up for a fall. We just worked on small goals. What is that expression, luck is when preparation meets opportunity? It was a year that the teams were even, nobody was running away with it and it gave us an opportunity with five guys."

But a team championship?

"Winning the state tournament as a team wasn't even on the radar," said Mustang 185-pounder Eric Voelker. "We just weren't thinking that way because we had no history to think we should be shaped up that way."

The thought was similar to the members of the North Tama squad. Jeff Selby was head coach and Josh Youel was his assistant. The Redhawks had no previous state meet trophies to serve as a motivator. They also had the number of qualifiers that could fit better in a Suburban than in a school bus.

"We only qualified four, our biggest goal was bringing a trophy home, I guess," Redhawk 167-pounder Tom Kaufman said.

On Feb. 27, the Mustangs, the Redhawks and Belle Plaine's Plainsmen joined the others in starting to determine the Class 1-A champion. After the first day, Dallas Center-Grimes had the lead with 14 points, two more than Rock Valley and Monroe. Four of Dallas Center-Grimes's five qualifiers won their first bout, three by pin. Each fall carried a bonus of 2 points. The opening-round pin by Doug Schultze at 132 pounds became an important piece of the puzzle.

Day Two of the 1984 tournament saw Dallas Center-Grimes fall to sixth place. Belle Plaine held a 2-point lead over Lisbon. North Tama was 11 points behind the Plainsmen in fourth and Dallas Center-Grimes was two behind the Redhawks. In the *Des Moines Register*'s tournament account, the only mention of Davidson's team was that 105-pounder Doug Hatch ended the hopes of a second state title for Kelly Fox of Guthrie Center with a 7-1 victory. Fox won the 98-pound crown the previous year.

Voelker was *Register* writer Chuck Burdick's choice to win the 185-pound title. Pat Rule of Parkersburg beat Voelker 11-9 in the quarterfinals. Voelker's senior season got started late because of a knee injury sustained in the second-to-last football game. He had an arthroscopic surgery to repair torn cartilage, but the recovery was slowed by an infection, Voelker said. "A one-month recovery turned into three," Voelker said. "I couldn't run, maybe mid-January I could get on the bike. By that time my knee had gotten so stiff that it was terrible. Going into the state tournament that year, I had only been back three weeks. I wrestled a JV tournament in Jefferson just to see if I could do it. I hadn't practiced for two months, so I went to a JV tournament in Jefferson and it went real well. Down at the state tournament, I still was rated."

In the North Tama camp, "We didn't think too much about the team race, I know the coaches did. We were more focused on who we wrestled and what we had to do," Kaufman said. "I put myself kind of behind the 8-ball getting beat in the district. I had to go through the No. 1 and No.

2 kid in the state before I even made it to the finals, so I was more worried about that than anything else."

North Tama and Belle Plaine each had two finalists. Kaufman and 132-pounder Ken Bradley were there for North Tama. Belle Plaine had Matt Spading at 138 and Kevin Shedenhelm at 155 pounds and they were a combined 56-5 that season. Dallas Center-Grimes had Hatch, who was trying to finish 32-0 that season.

Coaches frequently say tournament championships are won in the consolation rounds. Going into the final round, Dallas Center-Grimes regained the team lead and led North Tama by one-half point and Belle Plaine by a point. Davidson said he had a pretty level-headed gang in his corner.

"That group of guys were pretty close, pretty mentally tough. There was no panic about anything," Davison said. "We had to do some damage control with Eric a little bit because he didn't expect to lose. I thought maybe that took us out of it when he got beat."

Voelker said he began pondering the possibility of a team title on the way home Friday night. On Saturday, Schultze got beat in the consolations. There was no medal for Schultze, but he did supply two bonus points with his pin in the opening round.

"I remember at the celebration for the title, we kind of made a hero out of Doug because he only won one match, but he won by a pin. We won by half a point, do the math," Davidson said.

Later in the consolations, Voelker and 112-pounder Lonnie Ferguson asked Davison if it would be possible to win the team race if they placed third and if Hatch won his finals bout.

"I said, 'We will win it if you do that.' They looked at me and went o.k., never mentioned it the rest of the day. They just went out and took care of business," Davidson said.

Hatch's 12-7 victory over Robert O'Connor of Dike gave the Mustangs a final total of 61 points. Hatch was the first individual champion for Davidson, who wrestled in high school in Indiana and became an all-American at William Penn College in Oskaloosa.

Now it was time for the Mustangs and their fans to sweat out the remaining bouts. "It's a different thing to be sitting there hoping another team loses an individual match that's not against your team," Voelker said, "but you find yourself doing it because you want to win the trophy. We had a lot of those thoughts, it was just the competitive factor."

Bradley beat Wes Andrew of Monroe 10-8 at 132 to give North Tama four more points. That got the Mustangs' attention, Voelker said, because they knew how tough Andrew was. Belle Plaine's duo lost their matches, so the team title would be decided by the outcome of the 167-pound match.

Kaufman knew his finals opponent, Jack Denholm of Parkersburg. Their Leap Year night meeting was the fourth of the season. Two of them went into overtime. All of Denholm's losses were to Kaufman; Kaufman's loss was to Denholm. The knowledge went deeper. Kaufman, Denholm, Bradley and Rule knew each other since third grade, wrestled in youth tournaments all over the place and went to each other's high school graduation parties.

But on that Saturday night at Vets Auditorium, Kaufman could clinch the Redhawks' first team title by pinning his friend. "I didn't think that with us wrestling one of us would ever pin the other," Kaufman said. "The first time I wrestled him, I beat him by 7-8 points. The second time was overtime and I won by criteria having the takedowns. In the district finals, he beat me in overtime by a point."

Kaufman had Denholm on his back in the third period, but finished with a 14-6 major decision. "He had Denholm on his back and I was sitting way up top with my wife and my family. My wife was about in tears, I was like, 'It's going to be ok' because we had a trophy locked," Davidson said. "As a high school athlete and as a coach I've been through a lot of tournaments and victories and won things by one point or half-point, but nothing nutty like that."

North Tama finished with 60 points. That meant Dallas Center-Grimes locked the school's only gold state tourney trophy in wrestling. The Mustangs have a tradition of celebrating big things with a dogpile of bodies. On Saturday night, they also got to celebrate with cake. It was Ferguson's 17th birthday and his mom and stepfather, Connie and Larry Latshaw, provided the eats.

"I just remember telling the guys, 'Calm down, we're going to win with some class. We're going to walk out like gentlemen, we're not going to put on a show.' I don't remember anything crazy," Davidson said.

Kaufman said he and his fellow North Tama seniors left a mark on the program, which is now in a sharing agreement with Gladbrook-Reinbeck.

"I guess for us second place was the best Traer has ever done. It's the only (wrestling) state trophy that school's ever won," Kaufman said. "For us as seniors, that was our No. 1 goal – to bring one trophy back. Granted, looking back, it would have been great to have the state championship..."

Voelker, now an assistant coach at Iowa State, said he has two great memories of the 1984 tournament.

"The first one is when we came to the point of realizing that we could actually win the tournament, it was a new way of thinking. It was a new reality about wrestling for me," Voelker said. "There are times when you know you have certain things you can see that are within reach of reality and it changes the way you think about possibility. Especially in looking back, it taught me to dream bigger. It let me think about bigger possibilities for the future and accepting that those were real possibilities now. That happened on Friday night.

"The other memory is the whole tournament's over, the heavyweights got done, we knew we had won. When your team goes out there and you get your picture taken with the trophy out front. That I think was like the crowning memory for me. I got a picture of that. It reminds me that great things can happen."

Voelker said Davidson was an ideal coach for the Mustangs.

"I think of several great characteristics about him. In the practice room, he would work out with us. Being one of the bigger guys, he was a workout partner for me and he would just hammer us. It wasn't really until maybe my second year at Iowa State where I would come back and put the hammer on him," Voelker said. "He was a hardcore worker, he taught us to be mentally tough. He had a great lifting program that aided in mental toughness but also just raw power. He was hardcore, very direct in practice, you might call it controlling in practice. He didn't allow people to slack off and make your own choices. If you didn't become mentally tough and physically in great condition under his leadership, there was probably not anybody else that could have gotten you there."

Davidson said he was willing to build a winner.

"You can do great things, it's like anything else, you've got to work on it," Davidson said. "Being a head coach or a successful head coach, x's and o's is only like 10 percent of it. It's motivation and passion and organization and being a student of the game, sharing your knowledge and doing the work. That's coaching. Everyone thinks it's all of this other stuff."

More great things happened for Voelker. He went to Iowa State and won NCAA 190-pound championships in 1987 and in 1989, helping the Cyclones win the team championship in 1987.

That came after the Mustangs got to celebrate with two communities of people. Word of a celebration to honor the team Sunday afternoon was spread in proper pre-Internet fashion in small towns.

"They announced it at all the churches. There was no Internet, no cell phones, no text messaging," Davidson said. "This would be the craziest thing. We met at the old Grimes school and they had a car parade. I pulled up there and I could not believe how many cars, they were just everywhere. We drove through Grimes and then Highway 44 to Dallas Center. Halfway there, I looked in the rear view mirror and told my wife to look behind. My God, it was nothing but bumper-to-bumper. Nobody counted how many cars there were, but there couldn't have been anyone home in Dallas Center. They were all in the parade. That was a good day to be a thief if you thought about it.

"I remember telling my wife and people close to me this may be the only team I ever coach to win a state championship, but I can always say I got to be around it once, particularly in Iowa where it really means a little more," Davidson said.

"You're not going to be anything with your smart aleck attitude."

Peter Anthony Bush originally viewed wrestling as a way to help him get better in football. His father John had played the game at Notre Dame (he was a member of the undefeated 1949 national championship team) and encouraged his son's football activity at Davenport Assumption. It was more than just a reason for Pete to burn off some energy after school.

Bush now covets his time spent in wrestling. He learned what the sport had to offer beyond the gold medals for winning tournaments.

He can also cherish accomplishing one of the most difficult tasks – leading your alma mater to a team championship. Bush coached Assumption to the Class 2-A team title in the 2011 traditional state tournament. The Knights won a second state championship in the dual-meet state tourney one week later.

However, before Bush made a name for himself on the mat he got some extra coaching about being successful from what he thought was an unlikely source: Assumption basketball coach Mike Loehrer. During the 1975-76 school year, Loehrer had a winless season with the Knights.

Bush had something of an obnoxious attitude.

"My freshman and sophomore year - I was at the tail end of my sophomore year - I was just a smart aleck, I didn't really deal with authority. I kind of thought I was all that, I'm not sure why I ever did, but the epiphany or the event that changed the way I felt and the way I acted towards authority was this history teacher who happened to be the basketball coach," Bush said. "I said something smart to him and he wasn't going to have none of it. He took me into the nurse's office and said, 'You're not going to be anything with your smart aleck attitude, you're hanging around people that aren't going to go anywhere and the bottom line is as long as you continue to do this, you're a joke. Until you start to realize there is something out there more than Pete Bush...'

"He went down the line and I was taking it all in. Quite frankly I was honest with myself when I was hearing those words, that I needed to change, and at that moment I felt that you know what, this is no way to live, I need to up my game a little in life and it's paid off for me up to this point."

Loehrer said he noticed a 180-degree change in Bush the next day.

Bush finished 17-10 in wrestling as a sophomore. He was about to fall in love with the sport.

"I didn't fall in love with it immediately, in fact it had kind of a love-hate relationship with me to be honest. It took me until probably my junior year in high school to really appreciate the sport and what it had to offer," Bush said. "As a seventh grader up through my sophomore year, I kind of felt like, 'Boy, this is a lot of work and I'm not necessarily sure I'm getting what I want out of it.' Sometimes it's not what you're getting out of it immediately, it's the long-range benefits that come into focus. Wrestling to me is really who I am today. I owe really my family life, my work life, my work ethic, the people I hang around with and they all stem from the fact I was in wrestling.

"I'm very proud of my discipline, I'm very proud of my ethics, I'm proud of my commitment. It really gives you a full body of work on things you can deal with in life. I just wish somehow we could get the whole country interested in wrestling, not just pockets of the country because I feel like this country is very, very desperate for a sport like wrestling, they just don't know it yet."

The new-model Bush came into his junior season of wrestling ready to make something happen. He was undefeated during the 1977-78 season. Perhaps he was going to become the Knights' first state champion wrestler. "The reason (for improvement) is I had gotten into the freestyle circuit and it really helped me with positioning and things and, of course, lifting weights along the way," Bush said.

If he had any other questions about toughness, Bush could have asked his dad. John "Jack" Bush won the heavyweight championship of the "Bengal Bouts," the intramural boxing program Notre Dame held. Pete made it to the finals of the 185-pound division and met a guy from Marshalltown named Mike Mann. The outcome: Mann won, 14-2.

When Mike Mann beat me, and I knew about him and how accomplished he was as a high school wrestler, I walked off the mat and

– I'll never forget it – I said to my coaches, 'I'll never beat that guy,'" Bush said. "My assistant coach said, 'I would never say never, because it's a very long time.'"

They wrestled again in the state freestyle finals and Mann won, 10-4.

Two years after Loehrer's verbiage in the nurse's office and one year after being whipped by Mann, Bush was ready to stake his claim for a gold medal.

"There wasn't a doubt of what I was going to accomplish. There are wrestlers out there that hope they win, there are wrestlers out there that pray and hope luck is on their side, things like that. For me it was a certainty," Bush said. "I knew after I lost in the state finals my junior year. I started that Monday preparing for my senior year. Another life/wrestling lesson is you put the work in, you prepare, the chances are you're going to get the results you're looking for. Because of the work and preparation I did in the off season, there wasn't a hint of doubt when I stepped on the mat. In fact, to be honest, I had an attitude: 'How dare this guy comes on the mat thinking he's going to take something that's rightfully mine.'"

Going into the tournament, an advance in the *Quad City Times* stated of Bush, "He has the confidence of a veteran this season, and Mike Mann, the guy who beat him last year, is now at Iowa State."

Bush ruled the Class 3-A 185-pound division with a 13-2 victory over John Schebler of Davenport Central. It was something of a painful rehearsal for Schebler, who would win the weight the following season. Bush finished 72-11 in his varsity career at Assumption.

"Until my junior year I hadn't really thought about a state championship," Bush said. "It kind of morphed itself as the season goes. You get these ideas, you get confidence in yourself, you start believing in things you didn't think were possible before."

About five months later, Bush added a 191.5-pound championship in the Junior Nationals to his credential list.

Schebler was a junior varsity wrestler until Eric Hoffmann sustained a shoulder injury that kept him out of the district tournament. According to the *Times,* Schebler was shooting pool when he got a call telling him to get to practice. Bush pinned Schebler in the district, but the Davenport Central junior qualified for state with less than 10 wins. Three more wins in Des Moines and he was in the finals against Bush.

"That's a Cinderella story if there ever was one," Central coach Banks Swan told the *Times.* "I told you the first time he wrestled that he's a tough son of a gun. Nobody listens to me though. His story is almost unbelievable."

His story did not have a happy ending. Bush finished the season 29-0.

"There was no way I was going to let him beat me," Bush said to the *Times*. "I wasn't going to let someone else be the Davenport champion."

Bush is now Assumption's wrestling coach. He can tell stories to his wrestlers about how it feels to stand on top of the award podium on the final night of the season. Bush prefers to tell them any of that spotlight requires obtaining a few bruises first.

"I tell these kids this sport necessarily isn't fun, but you sure will enjoy it. That doesn't mean immediately, that means looking back and knowing you've gone through things that a lot of people couldn't simply because you have the will to do it," Bush said. "What I alluded to earlier with the discipline, the work ethic, the good values, that's the state of Iowa. That's how we were brought up, and wrestling is a perfect complement to our lifestyle quite frankly."

Bush said a multitude of things go through your mind as you stand on the podium. "You can score touchdowns, you can hit home runs, but when you get your arm raised it's different than anything else you experienced because, quite frankly, this is an individual sport," Bush said. "The fact of the matter is when your arm is raised and you know that all of the hard work has paid off, there might be that 13,000 people there, but as far as I'm concerned it's every person in the world sitting there watching you because you've invested so much time and effort. When you get the results you're looking for, it's like anything else. Words are hard to describe it, you've got to live it in order to appreciate it."

Bush took his wrestling shoes to the University of Iowa, where coach Dan Gable had the Hawkeyes in the middle of a string of nine consecutive NCAA team championships. Bush said he was hardly the guy Gable was using to build such a powerful run. "Until I got into coaching (five seasons) ago, I didn't realize what a pill I was for Dan Gable," Bush said. "If you saw me in practice and then you watched me out on the mat, a lot of times it wasn't the same wrestler. There are people that lace them up during competition and they are able to escalate their performance. Unfortunately I would do well and then I wouldn't do so well, and there really wasn't any reason for it other than, to be honest with you, I truly questioned what I was doing up at Iowa."

Three years after he won state gold for Assumption in Des Moines,

Bush got a bigger nugget 35 miles north of the capital city by winning the 190-pound NCAA championship in 1982 at Ames. The success was culled from some tough days in the practice room. Being brought down a peg is an excellent teacher, but hardly an enjoyable experience.

"That's the beauty of it, but when you're getting humbled, you don't look at it that way. It rips your heart out," Bush said. "Wrestling teaches you coping skills. When they're not doing the right things, we need to put the hammer down to them, they need consequences. That's the way you grow. How I've developed as a coach and as a wrestler was always through my disappointments. Rarely did I learn anything from my successes."

After the 1982 NCAA tournament, Bush wrote Loehrer a thank-you note in the form of a paper for a college class. Bush indicated how important their conversation at Assumption back in the 70's became to him.

"I felt a great deal of pride," Loehrer said about the paper. "It was nice knowing I helped a young person along the way. What he told me at the time gave me a great deal of satisfaction and reinforced my belief in teaching and coaching and what I could do for others."

As a high school kid, it's easy to turn a deaf ear to authority. Why did Bush listen? "The reason why is because everything he was saying about me was true and this was about me," Bush said. "I was ready for it and I was open-minded for it. It's hard to start pointing arrows the other way when he just dressed you down and you don't have a leg to stand on."

Bush was asked if he would have not been as successful if he had kept up the hate part of his relationship with wrestling and just stayed with football.

"Unquestionably. My whole life, the foundation of it, is because I was a wrestler. My values, how I carry myself, knowing there are no shortcuts in life and, if there are shortcuts, it's going to come back and haunt you," Bush said.

"I always try to rub elbows with the successful people within this sport because they are a wealth of knowledge for me. I am always learning. In fact, probably as a coach, I talk to my kids about more what I didn't do that I should have done than what I did," Bush said. "That perks them up a little because I'm basically saying I didn't do everything right. You don't like wrestling right now? Welcome to the club, I didn't like wrestling probably 50 different times during my career. I think I've got a wealth of knowledge because of all the setbacks I had, quite frankly."

"It was really quite a challenge to do it because it was a three-ring circus."

Televising the state wrestling tournament, particularly when it was held at Veterans Memorial Auditorium in Des Moines, had to feel something like competing in the sport for Doug Brooker.

Brooker was the longtime producer of Iowa Public Television's showing of the tournament. By the time the red light came on Saturday night, Brooker had run up and down stairs, drilled on getting the best information on the participants and made sure the right preparation had been staged in order to be ready when it counted.

The state tournament went live on the Iowa Educational Broadcasting Network in 1972. The three-hour block was part of a show called "On Location." A press release sent out about the telecast stated it was the second year the meet was televised, but a check of TV listings for Feb. 27, 1971 – the date of the state finals – showed no wrestling on TV at 6:30 p.m. Brooker moved into the producer/director seat four years later.

"It was fun. It was really quite a challenge to do it because it was a three-ring circus. It's kind of like organized chaos, how do you kind of impart what's going on but still not get caught inundated with stuff and have it be too voluminous to do?" Brooker said. "After a while, we kind of developed a formula that worked as far as how we were going to cover stuff, how our floor reporters were going to report on things and when we were going to be able to do interviews and put in the team standings. It was kind of like the State Fair. On one hand you kind of loathe that it's coming because it's going to rear its head, this big obstacle to take on, but once you were into it and doing it, it was like, 'We did it, we accomplished it.' It was fun, it was a lot of fun."

In television parlance, the tournament was good theater. Holding it in a building that was seriously outdated from a technical aspect but facilitated close quarters for competitors and fans made it great theater.

There were great shots of celebration from the first seconds after the championship match ended, when a kid realized his months of work and sacrifice paid off. There were great shots of heartbreak, those first seconds after a kid realized his months of work and sacrifice weren't enough. Kids leaped into the arms of their head coach/father, fans screamed in delight or wept in defeat. Residents of the state who were not in Des Moines tuned in to see their finalist in action or their place winner shown on the award stand.

"That's what I loved about Public Television, they always gave us enough equipment and we had enough people to do it right. We had great angles there and since we weren't commercial, we didn't have to break for commercials," Brooker said. "When the mats were done, we were able to put in extra replays of the celebration and the emotion, then go right into the awards presentations. It was just nonstop spontanaeity going on, it was kind of fun to see that enthusiasm. With it being high school kids rather than professional athletes, there was just that raw emotion that was always happening."

The tournament on public television gave viewers everything but the sweat. "You saw everything from 'Wrestlers, clear the mats...' to when they turned out the lights," said Jennifer Glover Konfrst, communications manager with Iowa Public Television.

Konfrst had first-hand knowledge of the tournament's popularity. She got out of school two days and spent all day Saturday at Vets while attending Johnston High School.

Figuring which matches would be highlighted was simple thanks to a rotation plan from the Iowa High School Athletic Association. It showed four title matches in each of the three classes and chose the best heavyweight matchup or had two pick-em bouts when there were 14 weights.

"When we first started doing it, we just tried to use our editorial judgment and take what we thought was the best match," Brooker said. "For years we would say let's try to be fair geographically, let's try to be fair on the size of school, but ultimately let's put on what we think the viewers would want to see. From a television standpoint, what's most newsworthy while still trying to have some non-bias as far as in terms of school size and geography."

Naturally, the big match was whenever there was the chance to crown a four-time state champion. Eighteen of the 19 four-timers in state tournament history were on TV. Only Bob Steenlage was excluded, and that's because the final round of the 1962 tournament was not on the air.

The average tournament would have two big cameras in the balcony and four more on the main floor, Brooker said. The highlight mat had multiple cameras on it, with one each on the other two. The play-by-play announcer and the color commentator were set. A floor reporter moved where the story was: It might have been interviewing a new four-timer after the standing ovation quieted down; perhaps it was a father-son arrangement; or maybe it was the Governor of the state of Iowa or a former champion such as Dan Gable.

Brooker came to Iowa after producing and directing the Nebraska state tournament for two years. He liked the theater the Iowa tournament provided.

"That's just the beauty of the sport. It's the one-on-one with the competitors, it's the bond that the competitors have with the coaches, it's the incredible bonds the community and the families have with the wrestlers and the whole schools," Brooker said. "It was quintessential Iowa, I think, just part of the fabric of the state. Wrestling is a part of Iowa's culture and it showed up in a multitude of forms at the state tournament. The fact that it was always sold out, that added to the theater of it too."

Making Veterans Memorial Auditorium cooperate with the needs of television was maybe the biggest challenge.

"It had its own set of oddities. In most (newer) arenas they usually have camera bays where they have a place you can put up a camera on a tripod. Whether it's basketball, wrestling or whatever it is, everybody uses those common bays and that would be set up for television," Brooker said. "They didn't have those (at Vets), so it was a challenge to figure out how to put your high cameras up there and be able to cover the mats because you were going to have to put them in the seats. That's obviously going to take seats out, block people's view. People jumping up and down would shake the tripod so it wouldn't be a stable shot.

"It wasn't really set up like a lot of new arenas. Those have cable trays and they have access ways where the cables can be run through so they can hook up to the cameras conveniently. Vets being such an old auditorium, you really had to string stuff through the seats, over the rail, so it was not exactly user-friendly from a camera/cable standpoint."

There were parts of the balcony known as vomitoriums, which the online encyclopedia Wikipedia defines as "a passage situated below or behind a tier of seats in an amphitheatre, through which crowds can exit at the end of a performance." Brooker said the auditorium built a platform that would span the top of the stairwell, so people could still walk up, but there was a platform above their head.

Brooker was already doing sketch work on individuals and teams when the control truck and the equipment rolled up to Vets on Friday. Folks who left the auditorium Friday night stepping on discarded food wrappers or pages of newspapers returned Saturday morning to find thick cables taped down and the big cameras mounted like electric sentries. The arena floor was struck after the consolation matches were completed on Saturday afternoon, and the evening floor plan was completed.

"Once they re-set the arena, which happened on Saturday afternoon, then all hell kind of broke loose," Brooker said.

When Saturday night came, Brooker got busier than he'd been for the first two days.

"I'm kind of a nervous energy type. People around me might not say, 'Doug's sure having a lot of fun,' they might say 'Doug's amped up,'" Brooker said. "I was always being the producer and the director. So many details to coordinate whether it was going to the coaches breakfast in the morning to tell people who we were going to need head shots of, making sure we could get bio sheets on the finalists or dealing with Dave Harty on the setup or Siddens on the new rules. It seems I had a monster checklist of (stuff) to do. When I'm in the middle of doing that, I can't say, 'God, this is fun.' I'm stressed and worried that I haven't got all of my things off the checklist.

"But when you actually got in doing it and you were in the chair and at the end of it, it was a great meet and everybody was high-fiving each other because it was a good job. Then it's like it was all worth it. After it was over with, I'd say 'God that was fun, let's do it again.' At the beginning and when I was in the middle of it, I'm too busy getting stressed to say, 'Wow, this is fun.'"

Brooker said he had a good working relationship with Harty, who administered wrestling for the IHSAA. "I would say he was pretty easy. I would deal with Bob Siddens on getting who the referees were. I would say Dave was more a delegator. I could always work with those people because Dave endorsed me and they did whatever I needed to do."

The push each year was to surpass the previous telecast and find something to make the show memorable, he said.

"I'm always challenging myself and our other crew people to do the best they can. Collectively, that's what I like about TV, it's such a communal craft," Brooker said. "If everybody pulls together, you achieve a lot more things than in the individual parts. When the wrestling meet was going and you were seeing fantastic replays and the announcers were getting great sideline interviews with people, everyone was proud of what they were doing and I think it comes across on the tube."

The legwork Brooker put in gave him insight for great shots on Saturday night. The teamwork also provides such opportunities, he said.

"When there is that sort of outpouring of emotion, that sort of electricity in the arena, you really rely on your crew to show you what's there," Brooker said. "I remember (Emmetsburg coach) Bob Roethler was coaching Kerber and I made sure I told the camera guy I want a shot of (Roethler) and another camera guy I want a shot of Kerber. Some of the other stuff, the spontanaeity that goes on in the crowds, you rely on your crew to get the shot. It's almost like shooting ducks in a barrel sometimes. They are giving you shots, there is no bad shot, you just made sure it gets on the air. When you're doing TV, sometimes it's having enough foresight to know what shots you want, and in other times it's having enough luck to get them on while it's happening."

The post-match attention was on the competitor, Brooker said. "We'd always have a camera that followed the wrestler. Whether he plays it nonchalant and walks off or if he runs and jumps in the coach's arms, you're not going to miss it," he said. "You want to make sure you've got at least one or two angles of the wrestler. If you've got enough cameras, you can have one on the coach to see how he's reacting and that's great too."

Iowa Public Television televised the tournament for the last time in 2002. The IHSAA awarded telecast rights to Thompson Sports of Des Moines for the 2003-2006 tournaments for $10,000 annually. Iowa Public Television did not pay a rights fee during its 32-year run.

The Iowa High School Sports Network was created in 2006 and was awarded radio and television rights to all state tournaments in the state. Under the terms of the 10-year contract, the IHSAA and the Iowa Girls High School Athletic Union were each to receive $75,000 in the first year. The revenue was to increase by $5,000 each successive year. The state wrestling tournament fell under this arrangement beginning in 2007.

Brooker, who lives in the state of Washington and does producing of wrestling meets for the Big Ten Network among several projects, had some memories from his work on the tournaments despite seeing several different angles while sitting in the production truck.

"All of the four-timers were always something special," Brooker said. "We would profile those guys at the start of the evening, we would talk about it throughout the evening and then actually cover them. All of the four-timers had special meaning.

"Nick Ackerman, that was good, obviously emotional. I think it was more the unbridled joy that you'd see. It didn't always come from necessarily the four-timers. It's the thrill of victory, I guess. When I think of the state tournament, I see kids jumping into coaches arms, which is not something you see in college or international wrestling. You don't see that raw emotion. The (high school) kids aren't too cool to do that."

"I found something I really liked and couldn't get enough of it."

Perhaps the only thing Veterans Memorial Auditorium in Des Moines needed in order to be a perfect place for Mark Schwab was a pizza place. Perhaps a Godfather's Pizza outlet.

Schwab became Iowa's sixth four-time state champion while wrestling for Osage. Sixteen of his 106 career wins came at Vets. Some of his spending money for those state tournament weekends was fed to the pinball machines that used to be in a game room just off the arena floor where Schwab collected bonus points in 15 of his wins – his closest margin of victory was 9-2 in the 1983 semifinals over Brian Forgy of Winterset in 1983.

He was getting to hang out with his buddies. He could touch base with some of the dudes he got to know through competing in freestyle tournaments. He was getting to wrestle at Vets. All he needed was a few slices with the gang.

Schwab was a star trying to be a common Joe. He really could have done without the microphones, tape recorders and TV cameras that detailed his bouts, especially when he became *the* recruit of the country as a senior. Schwab won three Junior Nationals freestyle championships and one Greco-Roman title. Andrew was always close by in those summer matches, giving Schwab a familiar face and voice.

"In my mind I was just a guy who hung out with my buddies in small-town Osage and that was good enough," Schwab said. "I was never comfortable with talking to papers and all those things. I just wanted to wrestle and hang out with a couple of my buddies. I learned later on that winning four state titles made an impact."

So did his repertoire of moves and the simple fact he could determine how long a match was going to last. If the bout went the full 6-minute duration, Schwab was on the short end only once – 4-3 in his third varsity match against Dail Fellin of Mason City.

"Here's a great compliment from the greatest high school wrestling coach there ever was, Bob Siddens, who happened to be my high school coach. When Mark won his first state championship, as he comes walking off the mat, coach Siddens said to me, 'Billy, I've seen a lot of good wrestlers come through here and that Schwab is as good as any of them I've seen,'" said Bill Andrew, who was Schwab's coach at Osage.

Andrew, a state champion in 1969 for Siddens at Waterloo West, remembered getting a phone call from a fifth-grade Schwab who said, "Coach, let's go wrestle." The kid had an older brother, Mike, who won a state championship in 1981 (one year before Mark started his run) and they worked with a younger brother, Doug, who won a state title and an NCAA championship and is now head coach at Northern Iowa where Mark is an assistant.

Schwab said he began to dream about being a top-notch wrestler as a sixth grader in early 1979, after he watched Jeff Kerber of Emmetsburg become the second Iowan to win four state championships. Schwab remembered how cool he thought it was that a capacity crowd gave Kerber two standing ovations. The real work started one grade later, he said.

"I think it was that, all the people on their feet. You know when you're a kid even the people on your own high school team are heroes," Schwab said, "Now this guy is winning four state titles, pinning his guy in the finals, you know 126-0, it just was memorable."

This was the same kid who not too many years earlier could be found at youth wrestling tournaments wearing Green Devil shorts and tennis shoes. "I had fun but I didn't get obsessed about it. I think that Kerber thing was kind of the turning point where it became everything I was about."

Schwab got down to business.

"I didn't even know if I was going to be a state champion, I found something I really liked and couldn't get enough of it," Schwab said. "I loved the process, I loved running, I loved sweating, I loved the way it felt the night before tournaments, I loved the smell of the mats. At that stage of my life, I loved it. I loved every part of it."

Andrew had already become his coach. Schwab knew his phone number. About the only thing Andrew did not do was give Schwab a key to get in the wrestling room whenever the workout urge hit him. Basketball had Magic Johnson. Osage had Magic Schwab, but the kid likely would have told you his name was Mark.

"A lot of people think this kid was a natural talent. No, he really worked at it. Obviously you've got to have some talent there to do it, but Mark just lived, breathed wrestling," Andrew said. "He put himself through workouts down his basement in his home, he'd go running, he'd wrestle anybody, anytime, any place."

It was common for Schwab to log 100 matches once the high school season ended. A kid can find freestyle action almost every weekend once the Mick Pickford Tri-State tournament opens the season in Fort Madison. Some of Schwab's trips were in jeopardy of becoming one-way excursions because a ride home had not been secured. Andrew's phone number occasionally was dialed.

"He called me up one time when he was wrestling in a tournament in Hudson. 'Coach, I need a ride home,'" Andrew said. "Well, what did I do? I hopped in my car and drove the 80 miles down to Hudson to pick him up to bring him home."

Andrew found time to give to any kid who was interested in wrestling, provided he was willing to work. Andrew occasionally turned into a chauffeur for a kid willing to call him up and ask to work out. In Schwab's case, practice made damn near impossible to beat.

"Mark was one of those kids that never got out of position. He put you out of position, which made him so successful," Andrew said.

The Schwab-Andrew relationship was always tight, but it grew tighter after Fellin clipped him. "I just felt with this kid, it was going to take somebody really special to beat him, and the only way he was going to get beat is if he beat himself," Andrew said. "He did that in one match against Felin. He had beaten Dail many a time, they were great friends, that was his third match on varsity his freshman year. I met him at the middle of the mat, shook hands and I said, 'Now you're ready to listen to me, aren't you?' From then on, it was just taking off from there. It was good he got beaten that one time."

Schwab would avenge his only loss two years later by beating Fellin during a bout at the Osage Quad tournament.

By the end of his freshman season, Schwab was making a name as a must-see because his skills were usually found in guys a couple of grades ahead. Not since Kerber had a high school kid in the state of Iowa been blessed with so many moves and so many slick ways to inflict them upon an opponent. He won enough to get to wrestle in the state meet at Vets. "I remember the first time I walked in there and I couldn't believe how big it was. Vets had a smell too, and just all of the people," Schwab said. "It just felt so magical as a kid watching these guys and then, all of a sudden, next thing I know I'm there. I'm one of those guys that I used to watch."

He was barely there long enough in his first bout to get a feel for the place. Schwab pinned Chris Weyrick of Wapello in 1 minute 55 seconds. Two wins later, Schwab was face to face with Jeff Schmitz of Don Bosco of Gilbertville for the Class 2-A 98-pound championship. With Siddens and a few thousand others watching, Schwab secured his first crown with a 13-4 decision. Mike Schwab won at 98 pounds in 1981, now his brother was there in 1982. They became the first brothers to win the same weight in consecutive years since Don (1957) and Tom Huff (1958) of Waterloo West won at 112 pounds.

By the way, Dail Fellin won the Class 3-A 98-pound championship that winter.

According to the calendar, Schwab's fourth championship came 3 years, 3 days – 1,099 days - after receiving his first gold medal. Schwab had an idea it was a much quicker span when he was riding with his teammates and coaches to Des Moines in 1985. "Man, it was so great being in Osage, but it did hit me on that ride down there, I remember thinking about it and how fast it all went and this was my last time," Schwab said. "I can remember playing pinball at the hotel before the semifinal match that night and thinking 'I'm never going to do this again.'"

Schwab earned the opportunity to go for his fourth championship by beating Darron Jones of Iowa Falls. In the finals, Schwab took a page out of his memory bank and finished the way Kerber did when he started to think big: Schwab pinned Dan Sinnott of Albia in 2 minutes 40 seconds. He got the standing ovation with the pin and a second one as he received his gold medal on the award stand.

"As far as what was memorable about it? Closure to something great, a dream and efforts that were realized," Schwab said. "It was like, 'I thought about this a long time, and here I am, I did the legwork to be here and now it's here' but the legwork was the best part of it in my opinion."

Once people watched Schwab wrestle, it was easy to predict him as a four-time state champion. Schwab said the reason everything happened was because Andrew was in his corner.

"Coach Andrew was an extremely significant cog. I'm telling you, and I've said it over and over again, this guy could have coached at any level in probably any sport. He was a great psychologist and I didn't know it then, but this guy was a master motivator and he was always there," Schwab said. "You'd get there at 6 in the morning, he was already there. You're leaving at 6 at night, he's still there. You come back to sneak a workout in, some damn way he'd come back. "I've been around enough people to know that this guy really had it, he had the gift to be able to read people, know when to get on them, know when to get off them. This guy had it. It wouldn't have happened without that guy."

Andrew moved out of state to continue coaching and then get into administration, so he did not see some of the state's future four-time state champions. He still believes Schwab was one of the best the state produced. Andrew said out of Schwab's 106 wins, 100 produced bonus points. He remembered Schwab getting one of those bonus point wins as a sophomore at state, and being disappointed in himself because he thought he didn't wrestle well.

"Obviously I haven't seen the recent four-timers, but in my estimation the way he dominated people...We're going to talk about guys that pin everybody, Mark could have," Andrew said, adding that Schwab was never a showboat. "Mark would go out and say, 'Coach, I don't like to pin people in the first period, I like to wrestle. I worked too hard to get a 30-second fall.' And there were times I had to remind Mark, 'Mark, we need a fall,' that type of thing. Although he beat people 35-2 or something like that, he didn't embarrass (opponents). He wrestled, he didn't make fun of them."

Andrew never treated Schwab with kid gloves. Spending any time in the Green Devils' practice room gave a kid a good idea if someone was slacking in practice. Kids were not afraid of telling a teammate to buckle down a bit. Andrew, a driven man who coached as if he was still competing for Siddens, had no problem getting after anyone in the room.

"He would get on me, you bet he would, and there were times I needed it," Schwab said. "There were times I needed to know I didn't know as much as I thought I did or whatever it was."

Perhaps it was a little of that Siddens touch known as a sincere snowjob. "I think anybody that's had the influence of Bob Siddens probably did," Andrew said. "One of the best compliments that somebody ever paid to me, and it was paid to me by Mark Schwab. He said, 'The amazing thing about you is how you can get our not-so-good wrestlers to be good and get to the state tournament.'"

Maybe Schwab was talking about what Andrew did with Greg Fox, who never earned a varsity singlet until his senior year but learned enough in the practice room tangling with quality teammates that he was a state qualifier that season.

During Schwab's time as an assistant coach at Minnesota, he heard Olympic champion John Peterson talk about Dan Gable being a master psychologist. That made him do some reflecting. "The more I've thought about Bill Andrew, the more that term fits him as well. Great button-pusher, wasn't afraid to say whatever he had to say, whether it was a parent, whether it was the school board president, whether it was the worst wrestler on the team or the best wrestler on the team. The guy had no fear," Schwab said.

Andrew said he could do a snowjob on Schwab, telling him periodically that he was not getting out fast enough when in the down of a referee's position. All that seemed to do was irritate Schwab, who would get a reversal in less time than the nanosecond it took Andrew to suggest the move. Schwab was always seeking perfection, Andrew said.

The 2011 state tournament was 26 years after Schwab inked his name into the state's prep wrestling history. "I don't think about it much, but there is a certain time of year where it gets brought up. Like me and my buddies never sit and talk about it but usually around state tournament time some of that stuff resurfaces a little bit. I don't feel any different, but I can see where maybe it did make an impact to people."

Schwab was a two-time all-American at Northern Iowa. He made a national impact immediately, winning 49 matches as a true freshman (no redshirt) – an NCAA record that stands today – but staph infection following a knee surgery turned a promising collegiate and international career inside out. He'd placed third at the Tblisi Tournament in Russia and at the World Cup in Mongolia, but as a senior fans marveled that he was back on the mat at all. The numerous knee surgeries caused one leg to be unable to get into positions that are second nature to a grappler.

"I'm sitting thinking about what didn't happen in college, I'm not sitting thinking about that I won four state high school championships, I'm thinking about the voids that were left from my collegiate career and international career," Schwab said. "I guess there's not a lot of enjoyment if you want to be honest. I don't even think I would have known what that meant then, and that's one of the parts of it I liked about then: I didn't think a whole lot. I thought about wrestling and I dreamed about winning. I didn't dream too much in the distance, I could pretty much stay where I was at in the present or at least in the near future. Later on when I started thinking about too much forward and too much backward, that's when it's hard to be consistent, so I wish I could have kept that element of it."

Schwab was head coach at Buena Vista and at North Iowa Area Community College and was an assistant coach at Minnesota – he helped the Golden Gophers win two NCAA championships – and at Purdue. He's in his second tour as an assistant at Northern Iowa. Andrew said he's not surprised to hear college wrestlers such as Minnesota's Mack Reiter, a four-time state champion at Don Bosco of Gilbertville, favor having Schwab in their corner.

"A lot of great athletes aren't great coaches because they can't tell you what they do, because they just do it. Mark can tell you. We'd go over a match together and he would remember his entire match. I think what makes him so good and why collegiate kids like to flock to him is because he can relate that right to them," Andrew said.

Reiter said Schwab's value was more than just knowing the physical ropes. "He could put you through some workouts that will build any kind of mental toughness you could ever imagine. He had an amazing way with words to motivate you," said Reiter, a three-time all-American at Minnesota. "A lot of people say Gable was the best motivator they ever had, but Mark Schwab was my best, no doubt about it. The year I first competed as a freshman, he would send me e-mails periodically. He sent me one before the Big 10's my freshman year, boy it fired me up and I was ready to go out and tear anybody's head off. That was the best tournament I ever had in my life."

Schwab said he and Reiter had a bond of more than just being four-timers from Iowa.

"I think the bond was more that I knew a lot of people from Gilbertville and I knew Reiter's dad (Doug) to begin with and really liked the guy. I think the real bond was that I heavily recruited him and we were both from Iowa more than we were both four-time state champions," Schwab said. "I think as a wrestling coach you get a pretty good idea of what buttons to push with athletes period, but spending the year with Mack and knowing what a great competitor he was, he was the type of guy who was going to feed on that."

In high school, Schwab seemed to feed on everything wrestling and friendships as well as pizza. Schwab said he and teammate Brett Sweeney, a frequent workout partner in practice, are in communication nearly every week.

"Mark never felt like he was one of the greatest, he always wanted to be one of the guys," Andrew said.

"I think becoming a wrestler was a given."

For all of its rich wrestling history, Eagle Grove was missing a piece of the state's high school wrestling pie. There were nearly 30 individual state championships, but there was no team title.

That significant portion – which was one place out of reach six times - was finally secured in 1974. Dave Prehm and Dave Morgan won state championships, Mike Woodall finished second and Doug Korslund was third as Eagle Grove finished eight points ahead of Britt. In 1973, Britt won the most recent of its five team titles with a nine-point edge over the Eagles.

By the time Marv Reiland resigned as coach after the 1986-87 season, with three team titles to his credit, he had started to make history – he and son Mark would become the state's only father and son to coach wrestling teams to traditional championships. Mark Reiland, a two-time state champion for his father, led Iowa City West to the Class 3-A championship in 2006 and 2007. Mark's athletic director is Marv. They also combined for five dual-meet championships. Marv led Eagle Grove to the first Class 2-A dual-meet title in 1987, part of its grand slam of the sectional and district championships, the traditional title and the dual-meet crown.

"I think becoming a wrestler was a given," Mark said. "I'd been in that room since I was 4 or 5 years old. I guess I didn't envision anything any different. I just expected myself to become a wrestler."

People in Eagle Grove likely expected the Eagles to have a team championship. Lots of talent but no luck. A team title was thought to be coming in 1970, when the Eagles boasted a lineup that included eventual state champion Randy Omvig, Mike Lamer, Ralph Thomason and Kevin Reed. Lamer, who many thought was a sure-fire champion, was kicked off the team for violating what would be known now as a "good conduct" policy.

Eagle Grove's coach in 1973-74 was Marvin Reiland, better known as

Marv. He was hired for the 1970-71 season after Dave Harty – Marv's coach in high school – was hired by the Iowa High School Athletic Association. Reiland had been wrestling for Chuck Patten at Northern Iowa, earning all-America honors three times – twice in NCAA Division II, once in Division I. Did he see a state team title for the Eagles in four seasons?

"I didn't really know, I just went by what Harty had said, that there were some pretty good kids and they'll eventually be ok. I'd been away for four years, so I didn't know about any of those kids period," Marv said.

Marv Reiland was already producing at least one state champion per season. He had one qualifier in 1971, state champion Mike Morphew. Morgan started his run of three state titles in 1972 and Morgan was joined by Mike Asche as a gold medalist in 1973. Then came the team honor.

"It was sweet because it had never been done in Eagle Grove, especially after '73. Everybody said, 'Always the bridesmaid, never the bride,'" Marv said. "I don't know how many runners-up they had prior to that, they had a lot, so the fact that we finally broke the ice in '74 meant a lot to some of those guys on those earlier teams that couldn't quite get through like George McCart. (George) was a state champ himself and I'm not so sure they weren't state runner-up. It was rewarding in the fact that we were the first ones to finally get it done."

Wrestling had a high visibility in this Wright County town that had a strong economic push from the railroad as well as the surrounding agricultural aspect. "You'd see somebody from out of town or you're someplace and they'd ask where you're from. You'd say, 'Eagle Grove' and they would be like, 'Oh, you've got pretty good wrestling there don't you?' That was kind of our trademark for a long time," Marv said.

The *Eagle Grove Eagle* paid homage to the 1973-74 team: "Eagle Grove wrestlers are the best in the state of Iowa. We have known this for a long time, but last Saturday they proved it to the entire state and probably most of the nation."

The newspaper also gave a tip of the cap to the coach. "It's a great tribute to our young coach Marv Reiland. He has accomplished the most difficult task in coaching...coming back to his hometown and producing a state championship team," an editorial stated. "Certainly the victory is good for a community, the school and the individuals. It helps to shake you out of the winter doldrums, you walk just a little taller and feel like shouting from the housetops, 'I'm from Eagle Grove, home of the state wrestling champions.'"

It might have been more expecting, not proving, to be successful when Mark grew up around some of the top wrestlers the school produced.

"I enjoyed growing up when I'm four or five years old and we're competing for a state title, seeing how important it was to the community at that point," Mark said. "It kind of hooks you a little bit. Being around those guys, being around the Mike Woodalls and Dave Morgans and Dave Prehms - Woody never won a state title but Morgan wins three, Prehm wins two and (John) Schaumburg - and see the things they go through, I think you realize, 'I can do those same things.'"

Mark was a special kid, and not just because he had so many winning styles to emulate. Not every little boy gets a ride home from an out-of-town meet by a policeman. The Eagles had a road meet at Humboldt Jan. 26, 1971. The referee was going to be Bill Dotson, the former two-time state champion from Waterloo East and NCAA champion for Northern Iowa. Dotson's son, Charlie, was friendly with Mark Reiland, who often wore his own Eagle Grove wrestling uniform to meets. On nights Dotson worked an Eagle Grove meet, the crowd would be entertained between the JV and varsity meets by an exhibition contest between Charlie and Mark. Charlie Dotson would grow up to be a four-time state champion in New Mexico.

"I remember wrestling at intermissions with Charlie," Mark said, a smile breaking on his face. "I think I got beat and got left in Humboldt all in the same night. I guess I wasn't good enough, he wanted to leave me there."

There was a slight cross-up in who was bringing Mark home, so he wound up in Humboldt while the bus was steaming towards Eagle Grove. A Humboldt police officer drove Mark to Eagle Grove that night.

Marv knew having good wrestlers in those days meant only that they were in the North Central Conference. Everybody packed some quality in their lineup, they met often and frequently the last meeting was Saturday night in Des Moines. "I think you find yourself pushing kids to make them as good as they can be. It was always a big deal to go to state, and you always try to make sure – from the beginning of the year to the end of the year – that you don't lose sight of those goals," Marv said.

Wrestling was important in the Reiland circle of family. Marv's uncle, Arland Anderson, won a wrestle-back match to finish second in the 1945 state tournament. There were some matches at the Reiland family reunions with a mix of Reilands, Bruhls and Andersons on hand. Marv faced his cousin, Dwight, in a high school meet in 1966 and posted a 9-4 victory.

Mark's cousin, Brad Bruhl, won a Class 3-A state championship for Fort Dodge in 1988.

Marv's first instruction in the sport was in seventh grade, when there was a split season of wrestling and basketball. The wrestling was instructed by Ralph Rolland and Jim Murphy, who was second for Clarion in the 1951 tournament. Murphy's brother, Denny, wrestled for Clarion when Marv wrestled for Eagle Grove.

"I think it grew on me pretty quickly. Part of the reason was I wasn't very big, there was no way I was going to be a basketball player," said Marv, who was also a big fan of baseball. "My dad played softball, so I'd go play baseball all the time. When it got cold, you had to do something. We got done in the fields, so I wrestled. I could wrestle in the winter time and it didn't affect any of the work on the farm."

Marv went to state once, in 1966. He met John Houseal of Iowa City High and lost, 8-4, in the opening round. Marv said Harty in high school and Patten in college had a similar influence on him.

"They were kind of like a second father to me as far as being a coach and the attitude they approached the sport in. I think the farther I went, the more I liked it, I guess," Marv said. "It took me a while to decide what I wanted to do but, once I decided, those were my role models that I looked up to and I wanted to be like them. Coaches have a great impact on the lives of kids, and needless to say some of them need it. That's how I approached it.

"I think the thing that was different was once I got to college, I did do a little more weight training. I never really had a lot of weight training ever, hay bales, pitching (manure) and milking cows. (Patten) got me in some of that, plus he was so good at technique. He was able to take the abilities I had and develop them. I was real quick and not real overpowering, but the things I was able to do he was able to refine those and make me a pretty good college wrestler."

Could the influence of Harty and Patten make Marv a good high school coach?

"When the time came, it just so happens that's when Dave was going to Boone to assist Bernie down there and I knew this job in Eagle was going to open up again," Marv said. "I had looked at New Hampton, that was an assistant's job, and the same thing at Fort Dodge. I remember Dave saying, 'Don't get in too big of a hurry because I'll know in a month or so if this might be open.' It opened up, (Harty) put in a good word and (Superintendent) John Gannon said, 'Want to come back home, huh?'"

Harty would have been proud to watch Marv's first meet as head coach Nov. 24, 1970. Marv and the Eagles faced Don Miller's Fort Dodge Dodgers. Miller was a two-time state champion for Harty and this was his first meet as head coach. The Dodgers won, 20-19, as Dodger heavyweight Brian Woods got a second period escape to beat Denny Miller – Don's brother – 1-0 in the finale.

Mark said he was not obsessed with being great as a kid. It was more just spending time with dad and his wrestlers. "Later on, once I got into high school, then it was about me kicking somebody's (butt). Before that, I think I just enjoyed it. When your buddies are doing it and you're having fun, it makes it a lot more enjoyable," Mark said.

There were several people whose style a young boy could emulate in Eagle Grove. Mark had his eye on one guy.

"I still go back to Mike Woodall. Even though Mike was a runner-up a couple of times, his family was real close to mine. The Woodalls babysat me for ever and ever, so when I was a little kid I grew up over there so I probably looked up to Mike more than anything," Mark said. "Then he came back and was one of our assistant coaches. Obviously he probably had as big of an impact as anybody on me but, like I said, the Dave Morgans, the Dave Prehms, the Schaumburgs were all that way. Woody probably had as much influence on me as anybody, but I just wanted to be successful."

Woodall followed Marv as head coach. Woodall remembered the night in Humboldt because, as a freshman, he got to wrestle Dave Musselman, who would win the second of his three state championships that season. Musselman won, 8-0, in their match.

As an elementary wrestler, Mark remembered competing in regional tournaments. He beat a talented fellow from Minnesota named Chris Short. Several years later, in the 1987 Junior Nationals at the UNI-Dome in Cedar Falls, Mark and Short were freestyle champions. Mark also won a Greco-Roman championship that week.

Mark made the first of three straight trips to the state wrestling finals as a sophomore. The first experience lacked a pleasant ending, Mark said. Steve Hamilton of Emmetsburg beat Mark, 8-6, in the Class 2-A 126-pound title match.

"I think it was pretty devastating in the fact that I remember the last 10 seconds – I'm behind by two and I'm bawling on the mat. I'd already given up, everything in my mind was already shattered," Mark said. "I don't know how big of an impact it had on me at the time, but I remember the following year we won the state team title and dad told the story about when we got back from the state tournament the year before. When we finally got home, one of the first things I did was change clothes and go down and lift weights. I didn't think anything of it at the time. He said, 'What are you doing?' and I said, 'I guess I didn't work hard enough.'

"I think it affected me more than I wanted it to. I remember winning it the following year and thinking to myself, 'I waited a whole year for this and this is all it is?' But if I had lost, I'd have been crushed."

Marv said Mark made up for the loss with a dominating junior season. "That was a relief for him. I'm sure he had a lot of self-inflicted pressure that he put upon himself so when he finally accomplished that goal, that was fun to do," Marv said.

Beating Curt Hayek of Cedar Rapids LaSalle by technical fall for the 145-pound title in 1986, or even pinning Mike Kane of LaSalle for the 155-pound gold medal in 1987, was not the No. 1 memory of Mark's high school days.

"I think the best moment of my high school career was when we won the duals (in 1987) because everybody was there," Mark said. "It wasn't just five or six or eight individuals, but it was also the first one. We were the ones that everybody was going to compare to from then on. Both of the years I won it, the team won it but nobody else on the team won a title, so I didn't have anybody else feeling the same way I did."

Brad Gazaway reached the finals at 105 in 1986, while Dave Messerly at 126 and Rick Coltvet at 145 were runners-up for the Eagles in 1987.

As a senior, Mark said there was a matter of pressure to contend with. "All of a sudden, come tournament time, I felt like all the pressure in the world was on me. It was just a bizarre thing that I'd never really felt before," Mark said. "I remember leaving practice the night before sectionals in tears because I gave up two takedowns that night in practice and I hadn't done that all year. I was just thinking, 'What the hell's wrong with me?' I remember Dave Messerly following me out of the room, getting me and telling me, 'You're fine.'"

There were times in high school that Mark was thought to be arrogant, but he said some of that is a key to being successful on the mat.

"You need to be that way a little bit, you got to have a little bit of an attitude, a little bit of an edge. You got to have the confidence, and sometimes that's hard," Mark said. "A guy can display it but he might not think it. It's one thing to sit here and tell you that I'm good and I'm going to win, but it's quite another sometimes for me to actually think it. I think that's one of the things that helps me as a coach, because I know those kids don't always think the way they're talking and acting. You can win or lose before you even get on the mat just by the way you think."

Marv said he learned some coaching tricks through the years that he shaped with his own philosophy. There was also the desire to see his kids wrestle their way to the top of the Class 2-A field once again.

"I think over time I tried to figure out that you coach kids to their abilities. You have kids with different abilities," Marv said. "Initially when I started, I went in with the philosophy that if you can take anybody down and you can get away from anybody, you're never going to get beat. That's the way I was taught through CP. It's like anything, you taste a little bit of success and once you have that little bit of that success you want to taste it again."

Mark came along in wrestling at a time when tournaments for elementary-age kids were becoming plentiful. "I always said, 'When you get tired of going, let me know because I'm tired of taking you' because it was very time-consuming on the weekend and I had things I wanted to do too. A lot of those kids in his grade, we hauled all over the country, so when they got to be freshmen we were looking forward to them."

Marv was big on always pushing for best performances when he coached, but the years have shown him something more appreciable than draping a state champion medal around the neck of a boy. "I always look back on the relationships that were established between coach and athletes, and some of those today are as strong as ever. It doesn't matter how many trophies you have or how many medals you have, it's those things that are meaningful, that last for a long time," Marv said.

When Mark signed to wrestle at the University of Iowa, Marv began to look for a way to support his son without shirking his duties. He put aside coaching and Woodall stepped in. A job as athletic director at Iowa City West came open, so Marv applied for it and got hired. "I never had any aspirations for coaching 40 years," Marv said.

He got to watch Mark win an NCAA 167-pound championship for the Hawkeyes in 1991.

Mark had initial plans to coach wrestling in college, but he got away and started working. After a while, he missed wrestling and became an assistant at West High. His first head coaching job was at Solon, and then West High needed a head coach.

Having won at nearly every amateur level might be helpful in knowing what a wrestler needs to succeed at varying ages, but Mark said the students consider him a coach.

"I think it gives me a better perspective on it, but the kids I have anymore, some of them know, some of them don't have a clue what I did. Most of them weren't even alive when I won a national title," Mark said. "It gives me a better perspective on how to treat them. I don't think it's a perspective on their part, that they can look at me and say, 'He knows, he's done it.' I think they look at me and say, 'He's the boss and I've got to listen to him.'"

In 2006, Mark got to experience what his dad went through in 1974. Iowa City West won the first of two consecutive Class 3-A traditional championships with an 11 ½-point margin over Council Bluffs Lewis Central.

Did Mark copy his dad's coaching style? "I'd like to think I kind of decided to combine him and Gable. I had a lot of respect for (Iowa assistant and Illinois head coach) Mark Johnson. I'd like to think I took a little bit from everybody," Mark said. "I know when I first started, I took all of (Marv's) practice plans because he kept practice plans and I used them as my model. Actually, I think I took the plans from either my junior or senior year because I figured that worked."

Marv said he tried to limit how much he offered in suggestions. "Once in a while at Solon he would say something, but for the most part I tried not to intermingle. When we hired him here for the head coach, it's a little different because it's not so much a father-son, it's an AD-head coach situation. If there were suggestions I would make to him, it would be no different than I would make to any other coach," Marv said.

It was easy for the Reilands to have a seems-like-old-times moment in 2006.

"It was gratifying because, for one thing, we had never had a state wrestling championship here at Iowa City West, just like we never had one at Eagle Grove," Marv said. "He knows what that feels like as a wrestler and he hadn't had that experience as a coach. It's a great feeling as a coach. I'm not so sure it's not a better feeling as a coach than it is as a wrestler to have a team champion."

Mark has stayed active in freestyle and Greco-Roman activity for high school kids. He's currently the state director for the Iowa Wrestling Federation, which oversees all wrestling activity away from the high school season. Iowa had at least one Junior Nationals freestyle champion for 18 consecutive years – a total of 41 titles between 1971 and 1988 – but there has been talk in recent years that the state has lost some of its national juice in the wrestling picture.

"I am not really sure Iowa is lagging in top talent, but more so when depth comes into play," Mark said. "Obviously population is a major factor in the overall depth. States with very large populations like Pennsylvania, Ohio and Illinois should - and typically do - have great depth, meaning the low place winners in those states are typically better than a low place winner in (Iowa)."

Mark said the sport has taken a hit in Iowa as the agriculture picture changed. "Many families are moving away from the farms and into the city," Mark said. "It seems as though our kids are losing the work ethic and the toughness of the kids of yesteryear, and a lot can be traced to the moving away from the farms."

Oregon State coach Jim Zalesky said Iowa's history in the high school and collegiate circles means opponents still expect a rugged scrap with an Iowa kid.

"I think Iowa's always ranked up there and is always going to be. You have expectations, you have so many Iowa kids that have done well nationally that when you get to that stage you just expect it," Zalesky said. "That's one of the hardest things for a kid to overcome. You come from a state like that, you just have that advantage going into college."

"...the biggest thing we had in common was our families."

O gden is located on one of the state's more identifiable non-interstate roadways – Highway 30, which crosses the Mississippi River and the Missouri River – and on a main vein of the Union Pacific Railroad. Just about everything else in the community west of Boone runs on hard work.

Call it the cowboy way and few in town would fuss about it. Cowboys are plentiful in the Ogden area. Cowboys are in rodeo, rodeo demands toughness and a willingness to work at proficiency in the events such as bareback bronc riding or bull riding.

Perhaps it's fitting that Ogden has a unique spot among the state's 19 four-time state wrestling champions. A pair of cowboys who came from a no-frills life and shared an intense dislike of losing at anything crossed paths with a wrestling coach who learned a no-shortcut approach to the sport. Each cowboy roped four state championships. Going into the 2010-11 season, the unique touch is that Ogden coach Brian Reimers is the only coach to direct two four-timers from start to finish.

To Jason Keenan and Jesse Sundell, Reimers was part coach, part father figure.

"He was part of my family. I'd have problems at school, I'd talk to him. I'd have problems at home, we'd go talk to him. I'd have problems with wrestling, we'd go talk to him," Keenan said. "He was on a constant (communication) basis with my mom and my brothers. He was there as a coach and when it was time, it was time. But, when we were done with practice or a meet and you needed to sit and talk to somebody, he'd talk to you for 10 hours if you wanted to."

Sundell is an assistant coach at Ogden. When Reimers decides to step down from the program he started in the 1979-80 season, Sundell is expected to take over.

"It's something I'm proud of to know my coach was the first coach to coach two four-timers all four years. To even have one coach have one, that's pretty impressive," Sundell said. "For me to come back – he is the one who built the program from the start – and knowing when he steps down I'm there to take it over and knowing I'm going to be only the second coach in Ogden history, I look at it as my next challenge. I had my goals set when I was a wrestler, now I'm moving on the the next part of my career. Hoping I can keep the program where it's at, maybe build it where we're competing for state titles as a team. We'd love to have multiple four-time state champs too, to let them get the most they can out of the sport."

Keenan and Sundell had some similarities:

- Both came from a broken home.
- Their fathers took them to youth tournaments as a way to get their feet wet.
- Both lost only once during their career.
- Both loved rodeo and were battling bulls and broncs when they weren't beating opponents closer to their weight.

"We had the broken family, rodeo and everything but the biggest thing we had in common was our families. Jesse's family stuck by him 100 percent – his mother, his dad, his friends, his wrestling partners – and I had the same thing," Keenan said. "Not only that, but we had the town. The town of Ogden was amazing, they were there every time to support you. They were there, no matter where it was, cheering you on. You couldn't go to any sporting event without it being packed."

It wasn't often in front of a packed house, but Keenan said he had a key ingredient to having success in wrestling along with the support of his family.

I had a great wrestling partner in (Matt Lindholm)," Keenan said. "If we had to go in late to practice, he'd be in late to practice. If I had to cut some weight, he'd be there to help me cut weight, so I had a big group of people I could rely on."

One significant difference between Keenan and Sundell was their style on the mat. "He might have been more of an aggressor, where I was a little more methodical about it," Sundell said. "We both had that desire to win, we hated to lose. We were going to do everything we could to make sure we weren't going to get beat. Coming in, he had all the records. Coming in, my goal was that I wanted to beat all of his records. Who better to chase when you've got a four-timer who had all of these undefeated seasons, all these pins. That's what you shoot for."

Another opposite was their practice approach.

"Practice room-wise, (Keenan) was probably one of the laziest kids I had in the room, and I have a hard time with that kind of kid that wants to lay around and loaf. He would work when he needed to work but he didn't overdo it," Reimers said. "I honestly can't ever recall having to chew on Jesse about how hard he was working about anything. He was a self-motivated, never had to worry about weight cutting."

A common denominator was Reimers, who wrestled in high school at Humboldt for Joe Fitch, a renowned taskmaster.

"It's kind of funny, I honestly always envisioned myself wanting to start a program, and probably a lot of that was because I wanted to emulate the things I had been taught with Fitch. I kind of felt like I wanted to go to a program where I could have the influence of the kids from me and not have to deal with the influences from somebody else," Reimers said. "I'm pretty hard-nosed with kids. I take a real drill sergeant-type approach, not so much today as I did 15 years ago. I don't accept excuses for a lack of working hard and doing the right things. I'll never feel bad about getting after a kid that doesn't perform to the level they're capable of performing, and that includes my own kids."

Reimers spent two seasons as an assistant to Dave Ripley at Riceville. When Ogden decided to start a wrestling program, Reimers applied.

"I got an interview and actually didn't get the job. They were going to hire somebody from Cedar Falls, but two weeks after I had gotten my notice, they called me back and said he turned the job down and the job was mine if I wanted it. I said yes and we moved to Ogden," he said. "Larry Tryon was the athletic director here, he had already purchased a mat that had been used at the NCAAs at Iowa State and the uniforms, so the program was pretty much set up. All I had to do was coach it. The first year we pretty much had jv competition (1979-80)."

There had been some good wrestlers at Ogden, but no one left the mark Keenan was starting to make in the 1991-92 season. This was a kid who was confident in his abilities, but kept his confidence to himself. "When he qualified for the state tournament, he actually wrote out his bracket and he had penciled himself in as the state champion as a freshman," Reimers said. "I have it at home and I'll never give it up. His mother gave it to me."

Keenan liked finishing his task as quickly as possible. "I love to pin the guy in 30 seconds, a minute…as fast as I can. Like I've said before, you give that kid any chance, that's more of a chance you're giving him to beat you," Keenan told the *Des Moines Register*.

Keenan had 77 pins among 119 career wins. Bondurant-Farrar coach Ken Estling said Keenan could make an early finish a sound decision. "When he gets the legs in and starts cranking on your arms, he makes you want to be pinned," Estling told the *Register*.

After wrestling in his first state tournament match, Keenan came home and relaxed by painting his bedroom. "I was always the kind of person who liked to stay busy. It wasn't like I wanted to think about it constantly, I wanted to do other things. I wanted to keep my mind off of it," Keenan said. "It kept my mind off of wrestling when it didn't need to be on. I didn't want to be stressed out, I didn't want to be worried about the next day, so I always found something to do. I could turn the switch on when it was time to go and I could do whatever I needed to do."

After winning his first title with four decisions, Keenan began to put some distance between himself and opponents. He pinned eight of his last 12 foes and got a pin in the finals as a junior and as a senior.

"I always took every match, whether it was someone I'd already wrestled or someone brand new, with the same intensity," Keenan said. "We had coach Riddle as the assistant and he completely instilled in us toughness. You knew when you went out on that mat that you were going to win. You were the tougher, the more dominant, the quicker and you were going to do everything you could no matter how long it took to get it done."

Keenan said if anyone needed a refresher course in toughness, Reimers or Riddle were happy to instruct.

When Keenan won his fourth title with a pin in 40 seconds, a junior high student was taking mental notes. Sundell was starting to catch on about success at AAU tournaments. Keenan won his last 107 matches and had a 119-1 career record. His loss was by injury default, when an opponent could not continue because of an injury caused by Keenan's move.

"I didn't really know that terrible much about everything. When you're younger everything doesn't sink in as much, but as I got older about seventh grade and we started going to AAU stuff, I started seeing the bigger picture of all the stuff that was going on," Sundell said. "Maybe at that time, being a four-timer hadn't really set in. When Jason did it, I was a seventh grader at the time. Knowing him and being good friends with him, that gave me something to shoot for. I started putting in about 80-90 matches my seventh and eighth grade year. I think as an eighth grader watching the state tournament, I was like, 'That's where I want to be next year.' Having him win it I think really made it a bit more realistic. That maybe was an attainable dream if I worked hard and did the things I can do."

Keenan never seemed to worry about who his next opponent was, Reimers said. Sundell seemed to know all about his opponents. He kept records of who he'd wrestled through the years. Including youth tournaments. And Sundell was confident in his skills. He had a simple plan when filling out a goal sheet as a freshman.

"I put down 'undefeated state champ.' Coach was probably looking at it saying, 'Good expectations, but there are not many people who can do that.' That was my goal right at the start. I believed in myself that I could do it all the way through, but I think after that first year it turned my coach's eyes and some other people's eyes. Even as an eighth grader, that was my quest. I wanted to be a four-timer and everything I did up to that was kind of preparing myself.

"Coming in he had all the records. Coming in, my goal was that I wanted to beat all of his records. Who better to chase when you've got a four-timer who had all of these undefeated seasons, all these pins. That's what you shoot for."

During the time between the district tournament and state, Keenan was known to call Sundell and offer best wishes. Before he left, Keenan and Sundell could always find time to talk about wrestling or rodeo. Keenan kept up with the rodeo results of Sundell and his brother Wade – now a world-ranked saddle bronc rider.

"When someone like that has confidence in you…I remember my senior year before state, Bob Steenlage (Iowa's first four-time state champion) had called me up. He called to tell me good luck. When people like that are calling you, if you're not pumped up after stuff like that, I don't know what's going to (do it)."

Just as Sundell watched Keenan win his fourth title, Keenan was at Vets Auditorium in 2001 when Sundell pinned Chris Helgeson of Lake Mills for the Class 1-A 119-pound championship. "Jesse handled the pressure great, better than I did," Keenan told the *Des Moines Sunday Register*. "He's just so calm. There's nobody like him."

For sure, no one in Iowa with four titles had to deal with severe injury prior to the junior season as Sundell did. Sundell had yet to lose a high school match on Sept. 4, 1999, when he sustained a compound fracture of his right leg. A bull named Mr. Twister bucked Sundell off, then kicked and caused what could have been a dream-ending injury.

"The first thing that popped into my head was I'm done, this is it," Sundell said. "Once I got into the hospital and I started clearing my head a little bit, I remember the doctor came in. We were talking about when my leg was going to be ready and he said, 'Maybe by March you'll be able to start doing some stuff on it.' I was like, 'No, we've got state in February. I need to be back on the mat by December or January to be wrestling.' He said, 'There is no way you're going to do that.' I set my mind and was like 'They're not going to tell me I can't do it.'

"I remember the first part of that season: every day I was in the pool and I couldn't put any pressure on my leg. I'm doing workouts in the pool, didn't even set foot on the mat until December a little bit and it wasn't even hard. Even in January and I'm starting to come back. It was sore, but I just told myself it's not going to stop me from completing my (quest)."

One of the better verbal exchanges was between Ames surgeon Peter Buck and Doug Sundell, Jesse's father. Buck said it would take a heroic effort for Jesse Sundell to be able to wrestle as a junior. Doug Sundell's response: "You're working on a hero."

Reimers was preparing himself for someone falling short of a goal because of the injury.

"Honestly, I thought he's probably not going to win four, but he's going to win three," Reimers said. "It was a challenge every day in practice in the month of December not to get in there and want to do stuff. Finally he was cleared to do things like work on switches and stand-ups, but he couldn't do anything in contact. Once he was able to do that, it was like, 'Here we go, hang on coach because we're going to get there.' He overcame a huge obstacle, but he was always very, very focused. He knew when he came in that he could win a title as a freshman. He knew what when he did that, his next goal was to win four titles."

Sundell took his only loss in the sectionals as a senior. Mario Galanakis of Nodaway Valley of Greenfield ended Sundell's 127-match winning streak with a 3-1 victory. The following week Sundell beat Galanakis in the district.

There was a touch of superstition in Sundell. He wore a pair of socks with a Nike swoosh in matches. The only time he did not wear them, Sundell lost.

Coaching two four-time champions did not inflate Reimers's ego. "I never have been one that feels I should toot my horn, because I'm richly blessed with some good kids," Reimers told *The Register* in 2001. "While I think I probably had to play an important ingredient in that, I've had some phenomenally skilled kids that have been able to do the things necessary to win a state title."

Keenan said he got to compete in an ideal setting.

"To me, there is no other place in the world that you'd rather be doing that sport than in Iowa. To be a part of the (record book) is amazing, you almost want to do it all over again," Keenan said.

Sundell said being in select company is stunning at times.

"You look back and you can see all of these other guys that have done it and know you're a part of that. I'm still in awe at times that I'm able to be in the same class as them," Sundell said. "I'm not real big at being cocky and throwing stuff around, but it's kind of fun. First time I was at the Hall of Pride was a couple years ago and we took some wrestlers there and looked around. You hear people talk, you hear your name brought up and people actually remember you. It makes you feel good knowing that what you did people remember, and it was memorable to people besides yourself."

Sundell always gave up soda pop during wrestling season. "Whether it helped me with my conditioning or not, it would be in my head and I felt that it did so I didn't touch a pop," Sundell said. "Every year coming home from state, we had to stop and get a Dr. Pepper. The first one going down, it burnt pretty bad. That's one thing coach always remembers, stopping to get the Dr. Pepper."

Going into the 2010-11 season, Reimers has not had any more state champions, but he continues to push kids to be productive on a mat as well as in life. The wrestlers helped Reimers deal with the death of his wife, Marci, and the combat injuries his son, Seth, endured.

"Honestly I think I'm probably an average coach. I'm honored that I even had the opportunity to do that and they're part of history in wrestling in Iowa but I take as much pride in a kid like Matt Lindholm, who had an exceptional work ethic, finished fifth in the state as a senior and has gone on to be a lawyer," Reimers said. "I take as much pride in those kids as I do the kid that was a four-time state champion. Yes, I have an exceptional fondness for (Keenan and Sundell), but I doubt that any kids that's been through here would be able to say 'He made special privileges for one kid more than the other.'"

During the 1990's, wrestling fans in Iowa got used to seeing nearly two dozen state champions on top of the awards stand. Those same individuals would wrestle their way to the top of the national championship picture as well. Jeff McGinness of Iowa City High, Jessie Whitmer of Eagle Grove,

Daryl Weber of Don Bosco of Gilbertville, Mark Ironside of Cedar Rapids Jefferson, Lee Fullhart of Decorah, Eric Juergens of Maquoketa, Doug Schwab of Osage and Cliff Moore of Dubuque Hempstead went on to be NCAA Division I champions. Cory Christensen of Winterset, Dusty Rhodes of Osage, Wil Kelly of Dubuque Wahlert, Ryan Schweitzberger of Kingsley-Pierson, Andy Krueger of Sioux City Heelan, Jamie Taxted of Webster City, Ben Shane of Iowa Falls and Brian Stewart of Lisbon were NCAA Division III winners.

Rick Moreno of Glenwood was an NAIA champion and Luke Moffitt of Estherville, Todd Buckland of Des Moines Lincoln, Matt Ironside of Cedar Rapids Jefferson and Erik Josephson of Fort Dodge were junior college national champions.

In that same decade, there were some new names on top of the charts in team races. In Class 1-A, a first-time champion received the championship trophy from the IHSAA's Board of Control for six consecutive years beginning with Riceville in 1994. Columbus Junction, Riverside of Oakland, Wilton, Bondurant-Farrar and Underwood followed suit.

The run of first-timers in Class 1-A started in 1991, when Clarksville ended Lisbon's three-year run of championships. Clarksville got championships from David Stirling and Wade Kroeze to help coach Ron Peterson win his first championship. Peterson would build a second championship four years later, this time at Class 3-A Cedar Rapids Prairie.

That was a suitable going-away present for Peterson, who took over at Simpson College in 1995 after Bob Darrah resigned his duties as wrestling coach.

The most productive first-time champion in Class 1-A was Wilton in 1997. Coach Steve Shirk watched four wrestlers win a title – Matt Pasvogel and Justin Stanley at 103 and 112; Shirk's son, Ben, at 140 and Kyle Hansen at 160. The Beavers finished 61 points ahead of Wapello. Wilton is one of three Class 1-A schools to have four individual champions in a tournament since the tournament split to three classes in 1969. The others were Don Bosco of Gilbertville in 2009 and Lisbon twice – in 1982 and 1983.

Right behind in the 1990's production department was Riverside of Oakland's 1996 gang, which counted Kyle Canoyer, Steve Swope and Jimmy Rodgers as gold medalists and Daniel Klindt as a runner-up.

Class 2-A was another busy place for debut champions in the '90s. West Delaware started it in 1991, Wapello in 1992 and then a run of

Clarinda in 1994, Davenport Assumption in 1995 and Independence in 1996.

The Class 2-A field was a tough nut in the '90s. Teams might win the championship, but would not have a tassle of individual crowns. New Hampton in 1993 (Kelly Seery, Dave Morgan and Chad Utley) and Assumption in 1998 (Josh Watts, Jon Garvin and Tim Matthys) had the most individual winners of the decade. Assumption in 1995 (Ben Jobgen and Matt Gravert) and Columbus Junction in 1997 (J. D. Pugh and Jason Payne) had two individual champions.

For a short time, it seemed an even year meant a first-time Class 3-A champion would be crowned. Iowa City High was in 1992, Indianola in 1994 and Urbandale came through in 1996.

City High and Indianola used dramatics to secure a championship. Louis Pelsang got a big takedown and had a bigger grip because his 7-6 victory at 160 pounds over Ben Smith of Southeast Polk locked up the title for the Little Hawks in 1992. Pelsang was battling to maintain his grip on Smith as Smith was battling to break free and get a reversal.

Eric Keller's takedown with 1 second left in regulation over Nick Dohrmann of Iowa City West gave Indianola the championship in 1994.

Urbandale's victory seemed unlikely after a tough semifinals round, losing all four matches, but the team had a come-to-Jesus meeting when it got back to school that night. The J-Hawks had no finalists, but it was figured during that late-Friday meeting that the six placewinners could still win the team race. There were speeches by many and, by the time everyone went home, one goal in mind.

Since the state tournament became a three-class event in 1969, the 1994 tournament was the first time that the three champions – Indianola, Clarinda and Riceville - were first-time winners. That was matched two years later by the trio of Urbandale, Independence and Riverside of Oakland.

Another part of the championship picture was that five of the 13 teams in tournament history that won a championship without crowning an individual winner did so in the '90s – Wapello in 1992, Riceville and Class 3-A teams Urbandale in 1996, Cedar Falls in 1998 and Iowa City High in 1999.

Individually, the state record for career wins was broken twice in the decade of the '90s. Jeff Theiler of West Des Moines Dowling finished with three state championships and 178 victories when he graduated in 1990. That win total stood until 1999, when Blu Wahle of Underwood concluded his career with two state titles and 187 victories. Wahle, who was named after the beloved dog his dad, Curt, had growing up, lost the mark when Josh Watts of Davenport Assumption won 190 matches. That record was broken three more times. Going into the 2010-11 season, T. J. Sebolt of Centerville holds the record with 207 wins.

"I was someone who actually halfway paid attention as a kid."

Many wrestlers hear about the desire to be the best, but few had the chance to study with basically a life-long tutorial on being No. 1 like Jeff McGinness of Iowa City High enjoyed.

McGinness was an undefeated four-time state champion, one of four among 19 who got to four before they got to one (loss). The others were Eric Juergens of Maquoketa (141-0), Dan Knight of Clinton (128-0) and Jeff Kerber of Emmetsburg (126-0).

Growing up, McGinness got to spend considerable time at practice with the University of Iowa wrestling team. The Hawkeyes were winning NCAA team titles and the individuals such as Randy Lewis, Jim Zalesky, Marty Kistler, Duane Goldman, Kevin Dresser, Royce Alger and Tom and Terry Brands were winning national championships. McGinness was there because his father, Ed, was helping grow the H. A. W. K. Klub, a wrestling booster group, and got very close to the program.

"I was always around the program and they had a kids' program up in the old Fieldhouse where the Banachs, Kistlers, Davis and Zaleskys would come up and teach up on the fifth floor," McGinness said. "My dad got me involved with it just to release energy because I was kind of a troublemaker early on in school, always in the principal's office. They tried gymnastics, they tried baseball, they decided to try wrestling, given the fact they were close to it. It kind of just took. I don't remember them teaching so much of the mental aspect, the toughness or the go-go-go. I remember the technique from Rico Chiapparelli or Zalesky on specific things. That's something I learned early on – you do the technique, you listen and you try to stay focused. I was someone who actually halfway paid attention as a kid, probably more so than a lot of people, but I went in there because I wanted to wrestle live as much as possible. You'd learn two or three moves and then you'd wrestle for 80-90 percent of practice."

Even if they weren't teaching as if the room was full of college guys, McGinness got to drink in the way those Hawkeyes approached everything they did. It's a tough task for McGinness to answer the question of who was his favorite.

"It's hard to pick one, being so close to the program," McGinness said. "Randy Lewis was obviously one of my favorites, I loved watching Greg Randall wrestle, Harlan Kistler was one of my favorites, Royce Alger, Jimmy Zalesky…a lot of different people that came through the room. Every year I remember growing up, there were one or two people that I would try to pick up one or two things for my own wrestling because I really liked them. Having the benefit of going to every home meet, I was able to pick up on things."

McGinness was busy wrestling, but he wasn't quite all-in as he would be starting in late junior high. During the elementary school years, McGinness was competing in some tournaments but only a couple with significance.

"For me, it didn't really quote unquote take until probably my eighth grade year. Up until that point in time, it was 'Hey, let's go to a meet this weekend,'" McGinness said. "I didn't wrestle freestyle, didn't wrestle Greco, I wrestled only folkstyle and my dad would take me to big tournaments when I said I wanted to go. In fifth and sixth grade, I heard of the AAU and I went down there and ended up losing in the finals one year and winning in another. My seventh and eighth grade year, I sort of got wind of I need to do more. I can't just wrestle every once in a while and work out, so I started working out with Keith Mourlam and then Tom Lepic, who was the former (Iowa City) West coach."

Mourlam was a state runner-up in high school at Webster City and had been an NCAA runner-up for Iowa in 1977. Lepic was a Hawkeye letterman who left coaching for private business but still looks mat-ready.

The McGinness that became a hot topic in high school and freestyle circles arrived on the scene at the Northern Plains regional tournament in LaCrosse, Wis. "That was sort of my big breakout tournament as a kid, where it was like, 'McGinness is not just a good folkstyle guy.' I wrestled against Aaron Sieracki, Chad Kraft and then a kid named Kammerer from Pleasant Valley. That was a big tournament for me to be able to win that. Then it just grew from there."

McGinness joined City High's lineup for coach Clyde Bean as a freshman at 103 pounds. He wasn't very tall, he wasn't very broad but he also wasn't to be denied scoring points. People watching him at the Charles City Duals that season were trying to decide if he was that good or if the competition was not too strong. Most of the votes came back in McGinness's favor. He was there to dominate. Anything else would not be acceptable.

"On the mat it looked and felt like that. Off the mat, I was somebody who went to the wrestling meets and was probably flirting with the cheerleaders more than I should, and we always got in trouble. We always joke about how much grief Louis Pelsang and I gave (coach) Brad Smith my junior year," McGinness said. "It was that way as a freshman as well. Casey Hesseltine had to kind of draw me back and say, 'You need to focus a little bit more.' I was determined on the mat, but wrestling in high school was such a blast for me.

"I just loved the sport and didn't have to cut weight. It was truly a pure sport for me. In thinking back, I remember very few of my matches because I was always trained of the mindset that you don't think, you just react. When I was training with Keith Mourlam, whether it was the drilling or getting in scramble positions, you just reacted. That's why I became a very good scrambler and very good on the mat as I continued to grow and grow. Especially in college, I just reacted and didn't think.

"The unique thing about training for Keith was he could get you in shape without you even knowing it. He'd get you in shape by doing things you're not even realizing you're building your shape doing."

McGinness hammered his way to his first state championship in 1990. After a technical fall, a pin and a decision, McGinness beat Luke Swarbrick of Cedar Falls, 9-4, in the finals. That Hesseltine guy who urged him to focus more was the 171-pound state champion that night.

Three years later, another unbeaten freshman was generating talk of greatness. Juergens pinned his first state tournament opponent and won two more bouts before he clipped Jason Anderson of Council Bluffs Lewis Central, 3-2, in the Class 3-A 103-pound finals. Juergens came close to taking a loss in the second match of his career.

"Nerves were just eating me alive. I was winning, 8-2, and there was like 50 seconds left," Juergens recalled in a 1995 interview with the *Des Moines Register*. "I started letting my guard down. Before I knew it, the score was like 8-8 or 9-9. I thought I had lost at first, but we went into overtime. I got a little breath, thought about it and got the takedown. Ever since then, no matter how high up I am, I keep going because anything can happen."

Juergens beat three opponents – Chad Wickman and Casey Doyle of West Delaware and Mark Rial of Fort Dodge - who had won or would win a state championship during his four trips to state. They were part of his 141 victories. In the end, Juergens extended an olive branch to everyone he beat. "I hope nobody has any anger towards me if I beat their kid," Juergens said when asked how he hoped to be remembered after winning his fourth championship – a 17-6 decision over Mike Corsiglia of Davenport Assumption.

McGinness seemed to have the touch on the mat.

"Was I determined? Yes. Were there people that were more determined? Certainly. If you take a lot of kids and put them in the position I was, you give them the opportunities I was given, a lot of them would succeed. Granted, I might have had a few natural gifts with my flexibility and my quickness and mat awareness. I was in gymnastics once I was 3, 4, 5 for a couple years, and I think that kind of transferred over both in flexibility and general body awareness."

They don't teach the power half or the arm-bar series in gymnastics. McGinness was a good student when it came to absorbing what offensive steps would help make a match go more smoothly. That was on best display in his final three years at state. His smallest margin of victory was 12 points. He pinned eight guys and won two more by technical fall. McGinness pinned his way through the Class 3-A 130-pound division in 1993 to earn his two standing ovations.

McGinness got some early exposure to the high school practice world. As he was finishing eighth grade at South East Junior High, McGinness's dad was in contact with Bean – Ed McGinness and Jeff's uncle Jim McGinness wrestled for Bean at City High – in regard to allowing Jeff to do some working out in the room after the varsity season was done. Was there early thought of being a four-timer? Jeff said not so soon.

"I didn't even start thinking about that until my junior year," Jeff said. "Maybe part of me was thinking that, but for me I enjoyed wrestling. Did I want to be that? Probably, but I also knew a lot of things can happen. I didn't know how I was going to grow. I didn't know who was going to be at my weight. I didn't know how I was going to progress. I didn't know if I was going to continue to love the sport."

Thinking back, it seemed nearly impossible to imagine McGinness not loving the sport in high school. He was winning, the technique seemed custom-made for him to employ and he had some of his buddies going through the workouts with him. Louis Pelsang was there, Mark Mitchell was there. Not everything was all business. There might be some laughter while they were sweating.

"We had coaches that understood the importance of it too. You look at Clyde Bean, a coach that had been around long enough to coach both my uncle and my father, and I come in and win two state titles," McGinness said. "He said 'It's always been my plan to retire this year, so I'm going to retire this year.' What people don't understand about Clyde is that as good of a coach he was, he also understood that when you're screwing around, chances are that was keeping a lot of people's mind off of the intensity and focus of the wrestling."

Juergens had the same coach all four years of high school. Jeff Tampir was a slender man with a head of gradually graying hair and a voice that didn't sound as if it had yelled at years of wrestling meets. He seemed like a kid's soft-spoken uncle who wanted to see the kids achieve big things, but wasn't afraid to take them aside and deliver a few choice words about working hard or sharpening technique. Tampir pushed Juergens because he saw the quality, but he also protected him when the push for a fourth title was coming and outsiders were wanting to document his career and his brush with history.

"I wasn't expecting any of this when I started (high school). I was just hoping that by the time I was a senior, maybe I could win a championship," Juergens said.

Juergens was deceptively strong, being a long-muscled farm kid. His style on the mat was trying to emulate the Brands brothers at Iowa, who were known for a punishing attack. "They'd be up 14 points and still be going after their guy like it was a one-point match," Juergens said.

The Maquoketa ace went to Iowa, just as McGinness and the Brandses did, and he became an NCAA champion just as they did. Juergens won his championships at 133 pounds in 2000 and 2001.

Before he won NCAA titles in 1995 and 1998, McGinness was at work winning national championships. After he won the state championship as a sophomore, McGinness won a Junior Nationals championship at 114.5 pounds with a 3-2 margin over Scott Schluchter of Oklahoma. Prior to that match in Warrensburg, Mo., Schluchter was presented his award as ASICS Tiger's high school wrestler of the year. Less than one month earlier, McGinness beat Clint Musser of Ohio, 4-1, to win the 121-pound division of the Cadet Nationals in Warrensburg.

Not a bad six-month span for a kid. That kind of stuff had to make McGinness a big-time guy in the sport. It certainly was something to boast about, right? Not really, McGinness said.

"You've got to realize back then there were a lot of people saying I wasn't even the best wrestler in the state at my weight. Back then in eastern Iowa, it was all about Ike Light."

Light was a two-time Class 1-A state champion from Lisbon. Light had beaten McGinness in junior high, but they did not cross paths in high school.

"It was sort of hard for it to go to my head when you still had a lot of people questioning whether I was the best at my weight in the state," McGinness said.

With a new coach - Lisbon's Brad Smith came to City High after winning seven traditional state championships and three dual-meet titles – McGinness got to work on winning his third championship. The chatty types got to speculating that McGinness was as good as signed to wrestle at Iowa.

"Around that time was when people starting talking about with me being as close to the Iowa program and my father being as close to the Iowa program was, 'OK, he's going to come to Iowa and he's going to be a good wrestler.' In my mind, once that started, it wasn't for me training to win my next state title. It was training for that position on the Iowa wrestling team," McGinness said.

While the drive to be outstanding on the mat took serious time, McGinness never forgot his school books. His parents stressed education early, and McGinness said he never forgot their words. When he won the NCAA titles in 1995 and 1998, McGinness also earned a spot on the National Wrestling Coaches Association's academic all-America squad. That required at least a 3.0 grade-point average as well as earning a spot in the NCAA tournament.

Something else he never forgot was how impressive a pin was, especially at state. "After I won my first (title), that was always my goal, to pin my way through it. It wasn't so much pinning my way through it, but it was the, 'This is my last match here' sort of thing. Whether I pinned my way through it or not my senior year, of all the matches I wrestled, it's probably the highlight that I remembered the most. I didn't want to walk off the mat."

He pinned Rod Ergenbright of Newton in 4 minutes 36 seconds in the finals. The kid who didn't like to break out of a focused look when he competed gave up a takedown to emotion as he was on the award stand getting his fourth gold medal. Jeff Johnson of the *Cedar Rapids Gazette* led his story the next morning with, "A prep wrestling career that will be talked about for many years ended in a fitting way Saturday night."

That salute by the fans, immediately after he won the last crown and then again on the award stand, is heady stuff.

"It's so hard to put into words. You're done, you look up and you hear and you see it and you're kind of like, 'Did I really just do that over the course of four years?'" McGinness said. "No matter how good you are, some luck does come into play. My junior and senior year I wrestled up weights for fun and to get challenges. God forbid I would have bit off more than I could chew on any occasion. It was definitely an experience that I remember and wish you could live through it again."

McGinness kept things as light as possible, especially when it seemed everyone was wanting to see if he and Light could win their fourth title together – a feat never accomplished in the state. Light was upset by Dan Gabrielson of Belmond-Klemme in the semifinals, so Saturday night's spotlight was fully on McGinness. A guy needs his best buddies close by at times like that.

He had Troy Hicks, Marty Albrecht and Shane Christensen. Troy had tried wrestling for the Little Hawks but hung up his boots. Albrecht and Christianson were not wrestlers. "Shane had a whiffle ball field in his backyard. We played video games quite a bit, we scooped the loop. We all had mopeds our first two years and we'd drive all over eastern Iowa with our mopeds on roads we weren't supposed to be on, just generally doing what high school kids do."

They were in Des Moines in 1992, when the Little Hawks tipped Cedar Falls by one point for the Class 3-A team title. Smith is one of four coaches in state tournament history to have led two different teams to a state championship. Pelsang's state championship at 160 pounds locked up the title for City High. Time to have some fun.

"For me it was when I'm in the wrestling room, I'm 110 percent wrestling. When I'm on the wrestling mat, it's 110 percent wrestling. When I'm off the mat, it was not," McGinness said.

When he won that fourth championship in 1993, his mind was coming down from competition to appreciate beauty.

As exhilarating as it was to get my hand raised and 12,000 fans (watching)…in my mind I was saying, 'This is cool, there are a lot of high school girls here.' I was a high school kid, half the time I was probably focused on cheerleaders and everything else," McGinness said.

McGinness's uncle, Ken Butcher, was manager of the Hy-Vee in Ankeny in 1993. He threw a party at his house after the awards were handed out and the pictures were taken. "I had 25, 26 people from my family there, they threw me a party at his place. All I remember was I'd been invited to go to a party at one of the hotels. As fun as it was to be with my family, I wanted to go to the big party with all of the high school kids."

Ed and Jeff McGinness didn't have the experience of two intense bulls butting heads while the young bull was trying to achieve success. Jeff is thankful for the way he and his dad were able to peacefully coexist.

"For our family and for me, wrestling was a privilege, not an obligation. The other thing about it was he never tried to coach me, which allowed us to have a relationship. He was my friend off the mat. He would talk to me about certain things and I would ask him questions, but it wasn't like you hear with a lot of these parents, where they yell and scream if their kid would lose or fail to perform," Jeff said. "He also understood for me, it wasn't just about winning, it was almost like that surfer mentality: it's not whether I win the surfing competition, I want to ride that perfect wave. For me it was that when I wrestled. I wanted to ride that perfect match. When I walk off the mat and don't remember a single thing about it, you knew that was one of those perfect matches for me."

Did he ever ride a perfect match in high school? "There were parts of matches that I look back on and I'm like, I've got to go watch that tape to remember what I did," McGinness said.

He experienced the highest high in high school and in college, so he can compare the feelings. "They're completely different worlds in my mind," said.

Becoming a multiple-time champion – not to mention going undefeated – can be compared to winning an NCAA title in the work that needed to be done. In high school, McGinness did not drink, did not go to parties where smoking and drinking were present, kept close to some great friends as well as his teammates and had supportive parents who kept him grounded in reality.

"To be a three- or four-timer, you have to have so many things perfect in your life. To win a national title in college is the exact same thing, you have to have everything absolutely perfect in your life – your weight, your school, your social life. I was lucky enough to learn it before I got in the Iowa wrestling room," he said.

"No day is an easy day."

Anyone who wrestled for Bob Kenny has wondered at times why there was no such thing as slacking in his practices. Those looking for an answer can learn it just by looking at his background, and not just previous years in the sport.

"My dad taught me how to be a hard worker. He had a junkyard and he ground feed. I always physically worked very hard growing up," Kenny said. "If you weren't scooping corn fast enough or you were screwing around, you got a scoop shovel in the back of your legs or something. Loading iron, you do it as fast as you can or turning a wrench. If you're not turning fast enough, he took it away from you."

In the limited time each day that Kenny had wrestlers in his charge, they learned quickly about hard work. Kenny, who wrestled his high school at Osage, coached in Iowa at Maquoketa Valley of Delhi, Estherville and Emmetsburg. He spent a season in Arizona, but it was at Emmetsburg that Kenny left his biggest mark. The E'Hawks had already published one edition about domination during the Bob Roethler era in the 1970's. Clint Young led Emmetsburg to a pair of titles in the 1980's. The E'Hawks tallied six more championship trophies in Des Moines with Kenny, along with two dual-meet state titles. Their four-bagger between 2000 and 2003 was a run similar to one Roethler enjoyed between 1976 and 1979.

"No day is an easy day," said Jacob Naig, a two-time state champion for the E'Hawks about Kenny's workouts.

Perhaps Kenny learned the practice method from Bill Andrew, his coach at Osage, who learned his craft at Waterloo West under Bob Siddens. However he learned, Kenny practiced what had been preached.

"I've always been big on (the idea of) you've got to learn and take from everybody. I had a great coach, Bill Andrew, in high school. The biggest thing I learned from him was he'd let people wrestle the way their styles went. He took your strengths and made you good at them," Kenny said. "I had Al Baxter in college, and he's a motivational genius. When we were in there, you did not want to walk off that mat without your hand raised. Al did a nice job, plus he taught me how to treat people: 'You made a mistake, OK, you're going to get your butt chewed, but later you're also going to get a pat on the back and we'll get you pointed in the right direction so you can get better.'"

Kenny could show a move to the team, make a pointer to an individual, straighten out another individual's misdeeds and deliver high-fives within a half-hour of a workout. Like Andrew, he did not try to have a cookie-cutter squad. "I've got every style you can think of on our team," Kenny told the *Des Moines Register* prior to the final round in the 2000 state tourney. "I've got junkers, kids that are leggers, kids that are bar-armers. What you teach them is you don't say you can't do a move, you teach them that you can do that move as hard as you can. Don't give up on it."

One similarity Kenny worked into his wrestlers was to heighten the intensity with each passing round. Mark Sturm said after the quarterfinal round in the 2000 tournament the team heard Kenny. "The whole team is just kicking it in. I think we're going to be pulling away with this thing," Sturm told the *Des Moines Register*.

The E'Hawks won the team title by 19 points. In 2001, they had 154 points and won by 58. Jacob Naig saw an opportunity to better the 2001 point total in 2002 after the E'Hawks advanced nine of their 11 qualifiers through the first round. "If we get nine through (Friday), I think we'll have a really good chance of scoring more than we did last year," Naig told the *Register*.

Emmetsburg/Armstrong-Ringsted finished with 125 points, but was back in dominating fashion in 2003 with a 40 ½-point margin over Union of LaPorte City.

Kenny said he understood that not every kid's dreams come true at state. He placed fourth in the 1978 meet. Kenny also knew enough to appreciate when a wrestler reached his best or overachieved. Kenny said he got energized watching kids get something from the season, such as heavyweight Mark Hobart, who finished third in the 2004 state meet. "That look on his face of pride, that's what keeps you going. It's like a drug, you can't get enough of it," Kenny said.

He knew how hard people worked who never got the top award. Not everyone could follow a path paved in gold. Kenny said he thought about coaching the sport, but upon graduation from Osage in 1978, he and his brother worked at Kenny Brothers Body Shop in Osage. Two years later he enrolled at Buena Vista and moved to Arizona to teach and coach after graduation. Soon he was back in Osage living at home, working in a factory and helping when he could with the Green Devils program. Kenny resumed the teaching/coaching career at Maquoketa Valley for two seasons. He got to Emmetsburg by way of nine years at Estherville.

Don Cox had resigned at Emmetsburg. Kenny's Estherville squad won the sectional tournament that Emmetsburg competed in that season. Kenny said he got a phone call from Gary Kauffman, the president of the Emmetsburg School Board: "Why haven't you applied in Emmetsburg yet?"

Kenny said he had to weigh the idea of leaving a program he had helped grow. "When I started at Estherville, I had like seven kids out for wrestling. They had a really good team before the year I was head coach and after that there wasn't much left over. I got the team built up to about 30-35 kids, had good numbers then," Kenny said. "A lot of the kids I got in Estherville, we'd get them out in junior high. It wasn't much of a little kid program. It ended up to be a pretty good little kids' program, but you're 5-6 years away from having a solid team."

One difference between Estherville and Emmetsburg was the wrestling bloodline. Where there were not a lot of second-generation wrestlers in his room at Estherville, Kenny said many of the parents in Emmetsburg were used to taking their kids to youth tournaments.

"When those guys got into high school, you really didn't have to teach them the basics. You had to fine-tune them and get their head straightened on, but you knew they had the basic rules of wrestling down," Kenny said.

Kenny said he interviewed one day after Kauffman's call.

"Right away they made me feel really comfortable, the interview went well and I ended up in Emmetsburg," Kenny said. "It was a tough move for me because I was still living in Estherville and teaching in Emmetsburg because I hadn't sold my house yet. I had some kids driving by throwing stuff at my house. It was pretty ugly there for a month or so."

Kenny said he learned hard work was for everyone in Emmetsburg's practice room. On his first night of practice with the E'Hawks, the seniors came into his office. They were not happy that the varsity guys got worked and the junior varsity guys weren't quite so pushed. Their message to Kenny was simple: everyone works.

"I had great kids (at Estherville), don't get me wrong, but comments I got several times: 'You can't work them that hard, they're not college wrestlers.' I got some of those comments from working the kids so hard," Kenny said. "In Emmetsburg, it seemed like that was an expectation. Parents took pride in their kids going to be at 7:00 or 8:00 at night because they were so tired."

It was similar to what Kenny knew growing up. "Parents didn't complain in Osage, when I was growing up, about kids being tired or anything."

Kenny said he had one complaint call during his time in Emmetsburg.

One walk by the trophy case in Emmetsburg lets anyone know the football and wrestling programs excelled. Kenny was learning the wrestlers wanted to put in the work to possibly add to the hardware. "I had no idea I'd ever win a championship, none. The year we got third in '99 and had a lot of kids coming back, I thought, 'Maybe we got a shot,' but you never know," Kenny said. "I always hoped that someday I'd coach a team that would be state champions. That was kind of my goal, and ended up getting that done."

Emmetsburg had a sharing agreement with nearby Armstrong-Ringsted. During the 2000-2003 run, the E'Hawks won their first championship without an individual gold medalist. They made up for that in 2001 as Dustin Finer at 103, Naig at 112, Ryan Sturm at 160 and Travis Hinners at 189 all won championships. J. D. Naig was the E'Hawks' lone champion in 2002 and Jacob Naig got his second title in 2003. Twice the E'Hawks had seven placewinners; the other years produced six and five medalists. The E'Hawks made their move towards a championship in the semifinals and then sealed the deal with strong showings in the consolations. After holding a lead in the first round of the 2002 tournament, when the E'Hawks went 9-2, Kenny told the *Associated Press*, "The next two rounds are when you can really throw some points on the board."

There was even a touch of the other four-title run on this group because Justin Kerber finished second in 2003. Kerber's father, Jeff, became the state's second four-time state champion during the 1970's run.

J. D. Naig went on to win three NCAA Division II championships at Nebraska-Omaha and was voted outstanding wrestler of the 2007 tournament while Jacob Naig and Ryan Sturm were Division III champions at Wartburg College.

After his team won the Class 2-A dual-meet state title, Kenny said his seniors had been party to a considerable amount of athletic success during their days. The E'Hawks won the four traditional titles in Des Moines, two duals titles in Cedar Rapids, two football championships and a baseball crown. Kenny likely spoke for any coach or any participant in an area of high success when he told the *Cedar Rapids Gazette*, "It never gets old."

Kenny remembered a big positive came out of the 2003-04 season, when the E'Hawks lost Bryan Sundall to academics before sectionals. "I gave him heck pretty good for not doing well in class, but that totally changed Bryan," Kenny said. "He went from a kid that might have been a little spoiled, didn't really care about anybody but himself, had all these toys, to a kid that was focused. Became one of the best leaders I had, ended up placing the next two years. He's done well, I'm really proud of him."

The E'Hawks were usually squeezing in a team workout to prepare for the state duals in Cedar Rapids the following week while they were in Des Moines. Kenny said one trick he learned from Andrew was to make sure everyone knew what was in store at state. It was nearly impossible to find an E'Hawk thrown off or surprised by the environment at state.

"It was pretty crazy, but Bill Andrew did such a great job. We already knew what was going to happen; we knew it was going to be crowded; we knew people were going to be trying to talk to you. Everything that was going on, he brought us through it so nothing was a surprise," Kenny said. "I tried to do that through the years. There was a specific timeline when we were going to do everything. Everything was really structured and I learned that from Bill Andrew. I knew exactly what was going to happen. I knew exactly what was expected of me when I hit the mat. I was there to wrestle, not to worry about how big the place was."

After finishing second to Waterloo Columbus in 2004, Kenny brought the E'Hawks back to the top in 2005 and 2006. Kerber and Aaron Janssen were champions. All five placewinners in 2006 won their last match of the tournament. Along with Kerber was Matt Stillman, who placed fifth in 2005 (he was one of six medalists) and third in 2006. Stillman's dad, Rich, won his three championships during the first three years of Roethler's run.

The 2005 championship was clinched by Kerber's victory in the 145-pound finale. Centerville, which had champions in Pat McCaffrey and future four-timer T. J. Sebolt, held a 95 ½-93 lead when Kerber took the mat to face Nate Alber of Independence. All the E'Hawks needed was a decision to clinch. Kerber delivered an 11-2 major decision and Emmetsburg won by 2 ½ points.

"All we needed was a win, so it was nice not to need any bonus points," Kerber was quoted in an *Associated Press* account.

Kerber helped Kenny retire from coaching in fine fashion as he and Janssen added to what became Emmetsburg's 22 ½-point victory over Centerville in the 2006 tournament.

Janssen said the task was simple going into competition the day before the E'Hawks clinched the 2006 championship.

"We want to make Mr. Kenny proud of us," Janssen told the *Des Moines Register*. "I know he's proud of us, but we'd like for him to leave on a good, high note."

Kerber ended his career as a four-time finalist.

"I don't know what you call us, but I know it's been great being a part of it, whatever it is," Kerber said. "There's nothing more you could ask for, except maybe (change) that second place (in 2004)."

Kenny also learned from Andrew about outworking people. His quest to win a team championship seemed to start about as soon as the current champions headed to their school vehicle with the trophy. Kenny said he once wrote Iowa coach Tom Brands a note advising him to enjoy the NCAA championships the Hawkeyes won.

"I think that's probably what got me out of coaching, I was never satisfied," Kenny said. "A week after the state tournament, I was already trying to figure out who was going to be good next year, where my kids are going to be, what are we going to do this summer. Who needs this, who needs that. I wish I could have sat back a little longer and enjoyed, satisfied with what was happening. I don't even know if I did realize what was happening until I was done coaching."

Kenny was not satisfied in 2000, not having an individual champion. He planned to chew on that fact for months. "If you don't use it for motivation, it's going to kill you," Kenny said.

Kenny moved into administration and is presently activities director at Mason City High School. Rather than worrying about one winter sport, he keeps tabs on four seasons of activities. Does he miss the mat? "I miss the wrestling room. I miss the connections with the kids terribly. Those little things in the wrestling room that make you giggle and you go home and tell your wife about it, I miss that."

He was given a Lifetime Service to Wrestling award by the Iowa chapter of the National Wrestling Hall of Fame in the fall of 2010, about the time he was usually getting ready to start wrestling practice when he was coaching. The reason he got such an award was simple.

"I had great kids and great parents that bought into what the coaches were doing," Kenny told the *Mason City Globe-Gazette*.

"I slept on that pillow for like 10-15 years."

Can success be gleaned by sleeping on a pillow belonging to a person of success? C. J. Ettelson of Hudson would cast a vote in the affirmative for wrestling performance.

Ettelson – the C.J. stood for Christopher Jacob, but no one in wrestling called him Christopher or Chris - won four state championships between 2000 and 2003 for the Pirates. Making that individual effort sweeter were the facts the team claimed the 2003 Class 1-A team championship in the first four-day tournament, his brother, Charlie - a state finalist that year - was with him and a former next-door neighbor, Nick Beuter, won a Class 3-A state championship for Cedar Falls. The gang was definitely all there that night.

"That was real, real special celebrating that with Mack," Ettelson said. "Mack and I had grown up together. Beuter had won it that year and we won the team title. It was a very special night, really special night."

Ettelson made it special for the Hudson faithful because his 13-2 major decision provided the Pirates their 1-point margin of victory over Logan-Magnolia. The team score was tied going into the finals, and Logan-Magnolia went ahead by four when Patrick Makey won the first of his two state titles. Ettelson's win was worth five team points. When Logan-Magnolia lost in the 152-pound finals, the Pirates had their gold secured.

"The best day ever. That's all I can say," Ettelson told the *Associated Press*.

The 2003 state meet was unprecedented because Ettelson and Mack Reiter each won his fourth title, the first time two wrestlers grabbed the ultimate prize in the same state tournament.

A guy could get mighty tired celebrating that much good fortune – Ettelson said the celebrating that March 1 evening might have been off the hook if Charlie won at 130 – but Ettelson didn't have his special pillow by then.

"A funny, funny story, but when I was about 4 or 5, Danny Knight went on some Saturday tournament that my dad took him to, and he left his pillow," Ettelson said. "I slept on Danny Knight's pillow for (many) years. That was a thing I always was conscious about. My dad was always like, 'You know who's pillow that is, that's Danny Knight's pillow.' My dad gave it to me."

Knight was 128-0 and a four-time champion between 1984 and 1987 for Clinton High School. He was also one of the state's top freestyle and Greco-Roman wrestlers and named national Asics Tiger Wrestler of the Year in 1987. When Knight and his buddies were buzzing to freestyle tournaments throughout the state or at the regional level, guys piled into cars. Tim Ettelson, C. J.'s dad, was the junior division director for the Iowa Wrestling Federation in those days so he was heavily involved in the state's freestyle program. His car toted a lot of high school kids such as Knight, as well as a young son whose seeming hyperactive nature would serve him well as a high school wrestler with limitless energy.

When the Ettelsons got home from the trip Knight and his pillow had been on, a call was made to see how Knight wanted to get his pillow back.

"He knew we had it, he said 'keep it,'" said Teri Ettelson, C. J.'s mother. "Tim let him know right away and it was not a big deal."

A few years down the road, Knight was coaching at Clinton and Ettelson was wrestling at Northern Iowa. Their paths eventually crossed. "I saw him and I was like, 'A long time ago you left a pillow in my dad's car. I slept on that pillow for like 10-15 years,'" Ettelson said.

Had Ettelson had a quick finish to his senior season at state, the pillow thing would have been under a microscope. Knight won his fourth championship with a 28-second pin after he led the 1987 Grand March on a fill-in basis. Ettelson finished with a 13-2 victory over Kyle Burkle of North-Linn of Troy Mills after walking in the 2003 Grand March.

Does Ettelson believe in fate?

"I believe that I was conscious about it, so being conscious about something and making your goals to the end gain – that was the goal all grown up – so from an early age it was like 'That's his pillow, he was a four-time state champ, he was a legend, you can be there one time,'" Ettelson said. "The work I put into it was all forward to be that good and that legend. I don't know if I call it fate, but definitely it was an awareness of it at an early age of this is the goal and this is where I want to be."

His 135-pound title followed the 130-pound match between Charlie Ettelson and a young man named Dan LeClere of North-Linn, who was seeking the second of what would become four state titles. LeClere won, 6-2.

Going into the 2003 state meet, Ettelson and Reiter were featured in a story as they sought to make history. They were introduced to each other by Beuter. They were people who took the sport of wrestling seriously. They were seriously successful as a result.

"There are a lot of kids who put the same amount of time in and didn't get all the stuff," Ettelson told the *Des Moines Register*. "There was a bit of luck for both of us, but we have worked harder than everyone."

Ettelson's big wish for that Saturday night was to celebrate his title with a brother who won his. Usually an older brother would not want to acknowledge a little brother's presence, but the Ettelson boys were almost as close as identical twins. Without a brother, Ettelson said he likely would have been another kid in a singlet.

"You probably wouldn't have heard from me because most of my success was because of Chuckie. He was my partner in everything," Ettelson said. "Working out, he was the one that pushed me when I needed to be pushed. I was the one that pushed him when he needed a push. We were a team. When I didn't wanna go work out, it was Chuckie who would say, 'C'mon C.J., we gotta go.'"

Perhaps there was a bit of fate along with hard work in Ettelson's corner. Not just the pillow, this was much earlier. In 1985, the cover of the state tournament program had an image of a wrestling mat with the names of the five four-time champions – Bob Steenlage of Britt, Jeff Kerber of Emmetsburg, Scott Morningstar of Lisbon, Joe Gibbons of Waterloo Columbus and Ames and Greg Randall of Mount Vernon – listed in the inner circle and the three-time winners sprinkled throughout the rest of the mat's image. During the tournament that year, a sixth and seventh four-timer's name was written in: Mark Schwab and C. J. Ettelson.

Ettelson did not write it. He was 11 ½ months old. His mother wrote it.

"We all dream about those kinds of things for our kids, but my brothers wrestled when I was growing up, my dad wrestled before I was born, I married a wrestling coach…it was in our blood," Teri Ettelson said. "Having been around the sport, been around people who have been in the sport, all I can do is admire those people. I wanted those athletes for both boys.

"I just love the sport, I love what it does for kids, I watch them grow up and see the work ethic that it takes to be successful. You just want your kids to do their best and be their best. That's not only being a good wrestler, but being a good person too, a responsible citizen and all those things. It was one of those things where you do it and you don't think about it. One year we were looking through the pile of stuff we got – Tim's got state wrestling books since he started coaching in the '70's – and it was like 'I remember now, I wrote that on there.' It wasn't like it was a motivator in any way, but it was just one of those things where you hope and dream and somehow it came true."

Mark Schwab of Osage won his fourth title in 1985. Seventeen years, 11 months and 27 days later, Ettelson joined him. Just as mom had written.

"I wish it was prophetic. It was more just a hope and a dream," Teri Ettelson said. "It was just knowing how much the sport has meant to my family and my husband, that's the ultimate. At that point in his life, that's the ultimate, the first stage of what you hope he can accomplish."

Ettelson is and was a good person before and after he wrestled. He was extroverted enough as a kid to send pictures of Beuter, Charlie and himself in singlets doing pushups to then-Iowa wrestling coach Dan Gable. Once he put the straps up, Ettelson was admittedly not so jovial. "I'm not your friend, this is what I live for and I'm going to go out and bash someone. Afterwards, I'm the nicest kid in the world," he said.

He wrestled in such a high-octane style that keeping up with him and figuring what he would bring from an extensive supply of moves could wear down opponents. Anything he saw being done was immediately tried to see if he could use it. One of his best tools was being confident.

"One thing I hate being called is cocky. For some reason it rubs me the wrong way, maybe just because all my life I've been called cocky," Ettelson said. "I'm not cocky about things I can't back up. In my mind, anything I'm being quote unquote cocky about is confidence because when I would make claims, I could back it up. I never made goals I didn't think I could attain."

What's the old saying? It ain't bragging if you can back it up? Ettelson lost only three times in high school. He was 161-3 and won his last 149 matches in a row.

"Success is a direct relationship with work. The work you put into it, for the most part, you're going to see success in the end," Ettelson said.

He was not on a narcissistic bender at the beginning of March in 2003. The Hudson fans had booked a party room at the Hotel Fort Des Moines in which to mingle after the finals. It turned into the party room celebrating what coach Toby Bedard and the boys had accomplished. Bedard was a heavyweight known as "House" when he wrestled for Ettelson's father. Tim Ettelson assisted the Pirates of 2002-03. The title was a homegrown deal.

"He really didn't focus a lot on, 'This is my glory.' When he comes into the gathering we had back at the Hotel Fort Des Moines that night, he said, 'I've been dreaming about this all my life' and he wasn't dreaming about the four-time state championship. He was dreaming about the team. He wanted to be a part of this wonderful thing called Iowa wrestling," said Teri Ettelson.

Like thousands of other Iowa boys, Ettelson could hardly wait to compete on the biggest stage – at that time Veterans Memorial Auditorium. Lots of mats. Lots of fans. Lots of history.

"Chills. I started clapping my hands, I remember thinking, 'This is what it's about. You're going to do this,'" Ettelson said. "I got chills right now because I think of the exact day that I walked in there. I was like, 'This is my spot, my place.'"

It took Ettelson 41 seconds to get settled in his place. It was the first of four first-period falls at state. Ettelson finished with six pins, three technical falls and three major decisions among his 16 wins.

"It's all a matter of how you react. It can be overwhelming, but I'd been in so many tournaments. I'd wrestled in national tournaments two times before that and traveling all around, I was prepared for it. It wasn't overwhelming for me, that was what I lived for," Ettelson said.

Ettelson said he did not remember attending too many state tournaments as a youngster when his dad was coaching the Pirates. One match he did recall was the 1994 Class 3-A finals when Eric Keller of Indianola clinched the team title for his team with a last-second takedown on Nick Dohrmann of Iowa City West for a 9-8 championship. Moves such as Keller's winning, low single-leg shot in that would be the thing Ettelson would try to emulate and perhaps add to his repertoire.

In 2003, Ettelson was trying to get his mind around how to react to some scenarios in the finals. "Watching Chuckie wrestle and being around him all the time, I was way more nervous for his matches. When he lost, I would get way more upset than if I lost. I always had higher expectations for Chuckie than I had for myself, which was good, it was good for him,"

Ettelson said. "That night I just knew either outcome, I was going to work off it. Either a high of winning – I was going to do it back-to-back – or if he loses – I'm going to go out pissed off. I can't tell you what would have happened if he would have won."

As the final seconds ticked off the scoreboard at Vets, Ettelson was photographed on top of Burkle with two index fingers pointing skyward. The four-timers usually look worn down, as if they all four finals matches at the same time, but Ettelson seemed to treat it as a means to the end. "I don't know if I ever felt relief because I never really felt any pressure to do it from anyone but myself. This was the goal we had set, this is what we did, and I did it," he said.

The Ettelson brothers were together in college as well, wrestling for Northern Iowa. Should Teri miss the old high school days, there is a wealth of videotapes of her sons that could be viewed. She could also marvel once again at how C. J. was able to shine at a time of personal aching. "I videotaped every single match those kids wrestled, even in college, other than when my video camera broke for about the first three months of C. J.'s freshman year and I had to buy a new one," Teri said. "To see Charlie and C. J. to follow him immediately that night, whether it's my son or not, and to think what it took for C. J. to stand there and watch Charlie lose - and he was Charlie's biggest fan - and then to step up there and win the way he won. Whether that's my son or not, what does it take for focus and just determination for a kid?"

C. J. and Charlie combined for a 324-9 career record, with a total of 185 pins. They might have been nicked up a few times, but rarely did they miss a meet because of injury. That was easier on a mother, even one familiar with the sport.

"Having been around it my whole life, I wasn't worried about them getting injured. Charlie had his knee scoped when he was a freshman, but the boys went through high school pretty injury-free," Teri said. "I don't know how I would have reacted had I not grown up in the sport. I've seen a lot of moms and a lot of people out there who can't watch it. There are people who aren't around the sport and don't have people doing it who think it's the worst thing to be doing. The prayer I always said was 'Let them wrestle hard and keep them safe.'"

And that four-timer pillow? It got left in an Iowa City hotel room. Perhaps a future four-timer will claim he or she had a lucky pillow...

"That is the fastest match I ever wrestled. It seemed like it was 30 seconds long."

Wade Satern of Humboldt claims his match in the 119-pound finals of the 2002 Class 2-A state wrestling tournament was fast. Lightning fast.

According to the scoreboard, the bout against Brad Gregory of Glenwood went a full 6-minute duration. Satern won, 7-2, causing at least one grown man to cry.

"One thing you probably hear a lot, but that is the fastest match I ever wrestled. It seemed like it was 30 seconds long," Satern said. "That was crazy, I can't even explain it. It seemed like I could have wrestled for another 20 minutes. I don't know if it was mental preparation I went through or what, but it was unlike any other match I ever wrestled, and not just because it was state finals."

Satern's brother, Luke, won a Class 2-A championship for the Wildcats at 140 in 2005. Another rocket-fast match? "The opposite, it was the longest match. I got more nervous when he wrestled, 10 times more nervous than when I wrestled," Wade said.

Wade, who transferred to Humboldt from Twin River Valley of Bode before his sophomore year, got some attention because he won state as a one-legged athlete. As a freshman 103-pounder at Twin River Valley, Wade placed sixth in the 1999 Class 1-A state meet. His right leg was amputated when he was eight months old because of a defect. "I was born with a leg, and when I was born I was missing part of my knee and part of my foot and my middle finger on my right hand," Wade said.

The only attention Satern craved was the chance to improve his technique and develop new ways to score points on or turn opponents. The Saterns moved to Iowa in time for Wade to start fourth grade after living in the state of Washington. "My dad (Scott) and Dan Vote went deer hunting and they found out we had boys. Dad wrestled when he was in high school. Dad said, 'You ought to try wrestling,'" Wade said.

Scott Satern was 27-2 and placed fourth at 145 pounds for Twin Rivers of Bode in the 1973 state tournament.

The important thing, Wade said, was that no one told him "no" when he wanted to do an activity such as wrestling.

"That was just the way I was raised. You can set your goals high and nothing can stop you, no matter what the drawback is. Granted, I probably wouldn't have been a very good ice skater," Wade said.

He became a tough wrestler. Despite having a broken foot, Satern won an 85-pound national youth folkstyle championship in Kansas City in 1997 with a 2-0 victory over Travis Paulson of Council Bluffs.

Some of Wade's early training in the sport came from Bill Smith, the 1952 Olympic gold medalist, who was living around Livermore. "We just met up," Wade said. "Dad knew that he was an Olympic champion, so he contacted him to see if he'd be willing to work with me and my brother a little bit."

Wade's initial feeling about working with Smith? "I thought the guy didn't know anything because he was old. I didn't realize until I was a senior in high school that I should have been listening to him for about 12 years.

"Bill was very smart, extremely smart, and we never got into actually the mental part of it as far as how the match plays out. What Bill worked with us on is the most important stuff – the fundamentals. I was probably in sixth grade when I met Bill and I was to the point where I thought I knew all of the fundamentals. I was wanting to learn the other stuff and not wanting to put the time in to learn the fundamentals. I didn't understand at the time that fundamentals are what wins matches for you."

Wade said Smith didn't talk about his gold medal. "One big thing that really sticks out in my mind that Bill was a big, big pusher of is to establish a lead early in a match. He would jump my butt so many times because I'd take a kid down in 10 seconds and then I'd ride him out the rest of the period. He'd say, 'What are you doing? You could have taken that kid down four times.' That was my biggest weakness, being on my feet. I didn't want to be on my feet, not knowing that that's the best place I should have been."

Mike Rial of Fort Dodge, who had a youth wrestling club that Satern joined, remembered adjusting what he was teaching to the so-called normal kids to facilitate Satern's style. Rial worked with Satern from before he was 10 years old until he graduated high school.

"It actually took probably two years and watching him wrestle the kids," Rial said. "Then after we were done doing the practice, I'd say, 'Wade, let's try this.' We tried various things to make it beneficial for him. Wade was one of my favorite projects. He had a hell of a determination. His goal always was to be a state champion. Once we got into freestyle stuff, it was to be a national champion."

Wade had been focused on being successful in wrestling about as soon as he started wrestling in fourth grade. The class was learning about short- and long-term goals, he said. "I'd say by the end of the season I knew it was the sport for me. Right then I set my goals extremely high, I mean utterly high, and didn't even come close to reaching them," Wade said. "That's the way I guess I always have been. I set my goal to win three state championships. That didn't happen, but that was when I was in fourth grade."

His desire for success was ratcheted up after witnessing Nick Ackerman of Colfax-Mingo, who finished sixth at 152 pounds in the 1997 tournament. Ackerman lost both legs just below the knee joint to save his life from a form of bacterial meningitis when he was 18 months old. After that 5-3 loss in the consolations, the tournament crowd gave Ackerman a standing ovation. "That set a goal for me to beat that, immediately when I saw it," Wade said.

Ackerman grabbed some of the attention of the college wrestling world when he won the 174-pound national championship in the 2001 NCAA Division III tournament. That was the same year Cael Sanderson of Iowa State completed an unprecedented 159-0 run with his fourth championship in the NCAA Division I tournament. Ackerman and Sanderson shared the 2001 Hodge Trophy, an award given by W.I.N. Magazine to the nation's top collegiate wrestler. That success made Satern's desire to succeed on the mat go off the charts.

Rial said one of the hardest things for Wade to learn was patience. "When he would go after kids, he would stretch his body out. Honestly he only had two limbs – one leg and one arm. The other arm he could not grab. He had no grip strength at all. I feel to this day it wasn't the one leg, it's the one hand that his biggest handicap was. Once he got on top of a kid, he was tough. That kid was as strong as an old man. I used to let him get on top of me and work me, and he'd hurt me," Rial said.

"If he had the (legs) and the arm, that kid would have been a multiple-time state champion. It took him until his senior year to know how to wrestle how he should to win," Rial said.

Satern said he could use his right hand well in cupping under an armpit, but gripping an opponent with that hand like wrestlers do was much more of a challenge.

Preparing for state in 2002, the Rials delivered good luck gifts of balloons, some Gatorade and fruit baskets to members of the freestyle club. He remembered the stop to deliver Wade's goods. Wade was waiting for him with a question about an earlier tournament match. "Wade goes, 'Come in and watch this tape.' He won the match, but he felt he didn't wrestle well. He goes, 'What did I do wrong?' I looked at the tape and said, 'Wade, you didn't do anything wrong. The kids are running from you, you're chasing them, don't chase them. If you got the lead, they've got to come to you.'"

Wade's style did not have a design of waiting for much. "Mine was a style that was very, very aggressive. One of my biggest disadvantages when I was wrestling was to overextend myself when I was in the neutral position, trying to get after the guy, get hold of him," Wade said. "If I would extend myself I could be snapped down and scored on. Until I was a senior, I absolutely hated wrestling on my feet because I thought, in my mind, that was the only disadvantage I had. I wanted to get at them and I couldn't be patient enough to wait. It was just a style I wrestled, in their face all the time when we were in the neutral position."

Wade said he remembers very little about the championship match.

"The only time it really struck me about slowing down and taking it in was when I was on the (award) podium," he said. "As for the match and getting my hand raised, I don't even recall it. The only thing I remember real well from that match is that I got a takedown in about 20 seconds. I just ankle-picked him. He stood on the line and he didn't move. He had his ankle right below his head, his neck. The rest of that, it just took off."

Wade scored a three-point near fall in the first period and led, 5-0, after two minutes. He was on his way to finishing with a 22-2 record.

"It's a great feeling. There's nothing like it in the whole world," Satern told the *Humboldt Independent* after his victory. "The hard work does pay off and that's all I can credit it to. I've worked hard this whole year and finished strong. What I've had to go through, last year and the year before…it has pushed me that much further to be a state champion."

Wade qualified for state in 2001, but was sidelined by a one-point loss in the consolation bracket. In 2000, Wade did not qualify for state.

His working relationship with Rial was key to Wade's success.

"Mike Rial had a big impact on my life in general. Not only as a coach, but as a person too. I kept getting more wrestling and more wrestling since then. He would have been the coach if I could have any coach in any tournament anywhere in the world," Wade said.

What made a kid with a seemingly insatiable appetite for scrapping connect with a soft-spoken father of three wrestlers?

"Probably just his manner, the way he coached. He wasn't real intense but he could make you listen and believe him," Wade said. "You could listen and you could trust him. When Rial was at your mat, you wanted to do good for him and you wanted to win for him."

He made Rial cry on the night of Feb. 23, 2002 at Veterans Memorial Auditorium. Rial had a son, Mark, win two state championships and all three sons frequented the high school season, freestyle and Greco-Roman. Rial said he would not have been surprised to see any of his sons stand on the highest rung.

"Wade, I never dreamed he could do it because of his handicap. I thought he had the potential but I never dreamed he would do it," Rial said. "I was matside watching him and he came to me. I started bawling. It was a high, it was like one of my own kids winning a state title. They all were, kind of. He was special because he had to overcome so much to do that."

Rial said he does not remember crying when Mark won his championships.

Wade was the proverbial sponge in practices, trying to learn as much as possible, but Rial said he had a habit of trying to do too much. "After a few years he kind of learned, 'Wade, you've got to adapt to yourself.' He'd be a hell of a coach because he could learn so much," Rial said.

There are countless stories about finalists, and especially state champions, being a singlet full of nerves on the morning and afternoon of the finals. Wade said he remembered being just fine in the hours leading up to his bout. It did not hurt Wade and his nerves to experience wrestling in the Junior Nationals at Fargo, where the number of mats and the number of participants are bigger than the population of some towns in Iowa. The nerves seemed to be going away when he was a freshman or sophomore, Wade said.

"It was probably when I got the mental preparation figured out, and I never did really get it fully figured out the way I should have probably," Wade said. "That's probably when my nervousness went away. I had to have at least an hour to myself before I wrestled. By myself. Not talking. I had to have time by myself and I had to have about an hour."

As a senior at the sectional tournament, Wade said he messed around and began his preparation about 15 minutes before his match. It was the last time because he said he wrestled badly.

Wade's championship performance, and the third-place finish in Class 1-A by Andy Rousch of Wilton, in the 2002 tournament earned a congratulatory speech authored by Iowa Representative Greg Ganske – himself a former high school wrestler in Iowa - on the floor of the United States House of Representatives. During his one-minute speech,

Ganske added congratulations from Speaker of the House Dennis Hastert, a former high school wrestling coach in Illinois.

There were some talented, successful kids in Rial's club. Some of the Naig boys from Emmetsburg, the Wernimont brothers from Pocahontas as well as his sons. Rial said Wade might have been hungrier than they were, and those were some sizeable appetites.

"He needed it more than everybody else. He needed the victories, to be the best," Rial said. "Wade was definitely one of my favorites."

"You weren't getting off your back if you got on your back."

What do you do when you're ranked No. 1 in your weight class prior to ever wrestling a match?

If you are T. J. Sebolt of Centerville, you move into that spot for four years. Sebolt is the state's career leader in wins, pins and consecutive wins and he won four state championships between 2003 and 2006. He's also the first home-schooled four-timer who lost only once in 208 matches, and that occurred in Missouri.

Centerville coach Kevin Cochran said the kid who started with a state championship at 103 pounds would not strike fear in those who saw him in street clothes. You might have wondered about his hairdresser since Sebolt had this bleached-blond coif that was closer to frost-on-gold. He probably liked the tint because it was color-coordinated to the medals he loved.

"If you looked at him, he looked like a sixth grader because he was so tiny. He didn't have to cut any weight," Cochran said. "As far as the mentality, his was one of the best I've ever seen, especially at the age level he was at that first year. I think it was his 16th match of his career that he lost, so early on in the season we were trying to figure out, 'Are we as good as what we really think we are? We got beat, what do we have to do to rebound?' So there were a lot of things going on that first year that we had to make adjustments in order to obtain the goals he wanted to obtain."

In order to find Sebolt's goals, look for the sheet posted in his room. Initially he wanted to place in a state youth-level tournament. After a loss, he edited the sheet. "The next night I went to give him a kiss good night. I looked over at his board and he'd marked out 'place' and wrote 'win,'" Scott Sebolt, T. J.'s dad, told the *Des Moines Register*.

The great thing for Cochran in his first season as head coach was that he got a freshman wrestler who craved being the best. Working towards being that good was fun for Sebolt, but he needed to calm himself.

"I remember all the way up until my freshman year, my dad had always told me, 'You've been to bigger places than this,' but yet everybody would tell me how nervous you are the first time you wrestle," Sebolt said. "I didn't know what to think about it, but I remember my freshman year warming up for my first match. I'd never been more nervous in my life. There's just some feeling about it, I don't even know what it is. I was still just crazy nervous. Usually after I get the first takedown, that insane nerves would go down a little bit. I was always that person who always wanted to score and score fast."

The loss came Dec. 21, 2002. Cochran said he watched to see how T. J. handled it. "Better than I thought, if that's an easy way to put it," Cochran said. "He took it well. Just like anybody that competes, he was upset of course. I'm upset, I thought dad was going to be really upset and I think he was. (T.J.) was laying on the ground and (Scott) gave him a little kick in the foot and he told me, 'This could be the best thing for him, to realize he's not invincible.' It may have been, that's a tough question to answer."

The fact Sebolt finished with 136 career pins is special because he was a takedown artist (T. J. had 240) as a freshman. "My dad had this thing where he told me I had to take a kid down 10 times before I could pin him. For some reason I always teched them before I could pin them. I didn't start (really) pinning until my junior year."

Cochran said, "You weren't getting off your back if you got on your back, I can tell you that."

Sebolt got a scholarship to Iowa State, but he left the program. He ended up as an assistant coach at North Iowa Area Community College in Mason City and continues to help the program.

Sometimes the pin was unavoidable because Sebolt's technique was so good that an opponent seemed in a freestyle match because he was taken to a pin. Mostly a match against Sebolt was a dance where the opponent found the dips painful and repetitive and Sebolt always seemed to lead. But holding a No. 1 ranking before you don a varsity singlet? It's definitely not because of his start in the sport. It's homage to the consistent winner he became as his technique grew into his desire.

Sebolt was pinned in each of his first 27 matches when he was six years old. "I wasn't really into it. I didn't know what the rules were or anything like that, but I got pinned and I'd ask, 'Why does that kid get his hand raised?'" Sebolt told the *Des Moines Register* prior to his fourth state tournament.

He was never pinned in a high school match, so there was no need for that youthful question. The concern was Cochran's. "With really not knowing what to expect in your first year coaching, besides what you did as an assistant, and getting somebody as high-profile as (Sebolt), I felt like there was a lot of pressure on me to uphold the standards that were set upon him," Cochran said. "That was the biggest thing. I felt like if he didn't perform the way he was supposed to perform, two things could have happened: either the hype that was brought upon him was more than what was anticipated or else I didn't do the job I needed to do in order for him to achieve the success that he needed to achieve."

Sebolt was a winner without excess ego. He liked to do his business on the mat quickly and then hang around with his teammates.

"He always wanted to win when he went out there, but as far as showing cockiness or the emotion that he was that good, I never saw that coming out of him," Cochran said. "He was always prepared, stepped on the mat, tried to take care of business and walk off. The cockiness I don't feel was there in him."

Scott Sebolt didn't believe in the added theatrics. He coached his son to be good and sell his skill by wrestling. Talk was for the other guys. Technique was for winners. Mastering technique was for champions.

"I always treated every go in practice like a match. I'll be the first one to tell you if I got taken down, I was pissed. I'm talking I'd want to hit that other guy, that's how mad I'd get," T. J. said. "It didn't happen that often, but when it did, it was usually a bad day for the other guy. I'd get so emotional about it, I'd get teary-eyed sometimes because I hated being taken down that bad."

Sebolt was scrapping in practice with some tough guys. It might have been Justin Brown, a two-time state champion before he graduated. It could have been Pat McCaffrey, a transfer from Illinois (and a state champion there) who won a title in Iowa before moving out of state. Possibly he was drilling with Nick Pickerell, a longtime friend and workout partner who is one of the few wrestlers in Iowa to win a state championship at two different schools. In his case, Albia and Centerville.

Seeing T. J. against Brown in practice sold Cochran on his young kid's collection of skills. "Where I make that judgment is where we had a returning state champion in Justin Brown at 103, who is now at 112, and when I watched those two go at it in the room – we've got a senior who's physically built like a machine and this little freshman who looks like a little twig kind of – and the way they would battle is what gave me that scenario, that man, this kid's got some talent," Cochran said.

Brown spent extra time on the mat with the Sebolts. "All that kid had was grit and want," T. J. said. "He was just a rough, redneck country boy and the only thing he knew was how to be mean."

When T. J. was getting pinned as a youngster, Scott found a tough guy to help his son get some of that talent started in the sport. It was Jason Halupnick, the son of longtime Centerville coach Mike Halupnick. Jason Halupnick won a Class 2-A state title at 119 pounds in 1994. Halupnick considered giving up points to be an insult. His new pupil would learn that too. "He started coming over and working with me and I started understanding things," T. J. said.

"I kind of idolized him for a while because I would have been in first grade when I was wrestling. He treated me like a buddy, he was real cool, he'd take me around town. I thought he was my best friend for a while," T. J. said. "What happened was I tried mimicking him when I started wrestling. I'd do the same stance, move the same way as him. He'd show me a move, I'd drill it so many times, he'd make me frustrated but yet, I'd finally get that move down. I felt like I conquered the world or something."

Sebolt began conquering state championships when he beat his buddy Pickerell, 9-1, at 103 pounds. If anyone knew how Sebolt worked, it was Pickerell. They traveled to youth tournaments together, they practiced together. Eventually they won together.

"He wasn't born that good," Pickerell told the *Register* in 2006. "You have to work from the bottom to the top like he's done."

It's become common that a freshman state champion gets seemingly annointed as the next four-time champion. Cochran waited before making his judgment.

"I think there's a certain point and time once you win one, and especially at the freshman level, you think that, but I'm always of the understanding that your second one is the hardest one to win," Cochran said. "I would say most likely after his sophomore year. He won it twice at 103, probably most definitely after his junior year because he jumped up two weight classes. His body started to look different, he was growing up, you always had that doubt that somebody was going to catch up to him. After he had the tremendous success in his junior year, I felt real comfortable in the senior year."

T. J. said he got his work ethic back as a senior, working harder than ever on his craft. "I started pushing myself really hard as soon as I got into high school. I probably worked harder my freshman year than I did my sophomore year," he said. "I guess I became a little complacent, I had closer matches than I ever should have with some people."

You have to remember the loss as you pile up the wins. You have to know everyone wants to take their best shot against you. "I hate that one loss. It sticks out like a sore thumb," Sebolt said to the *Register*. "That one loss has motivated me."

Being the state's first 200-match winner wasn't quite as motivating. "I guess it's a number. No one had ever done that in the state of Iowa, that makes it a great accomplishment, but I think to him and to me it's just another number. We still had seven matches left, so it was trying to get down to that last one was what we were worried about," Cochran said. "If that stands over the next 30 years, it will probably have more meaning than it does right now, but definitely a great accomplishment."

T. J. made it through three seasons of flurried takedowns, a growing action of pinning, wrestling while he had a bout of whooping cough, a concussion as a sophomore and an injured elbow as a junior that would require post-tournament surgery. By the time he arrived in Des Moines for his last tournament, T. J. had become the first – and going into the 2010-11 season the only – Iowa wrestler to notch 200 career wins. He pinned his first two state tournament opponents in 2006, and then beat Russell Evans of New Hampton, 7-0, to gain the finals against Zach McCool of West Delaware of Manchester.

McCool was a standout baseball player after he was done with wrestling season. He wanted to score the biggest hit at the state tournament in many years.

"Everybody thinks he's an unbeatable kid, but there are people out there getting closer and closer to him. I know I'm one of them," McCool said to the *Cedar Rapids Gazette* the night before the finals. "Everybody is rooting for the underdog. I feel like I'm the underdog, so I'm going to go out there and give this huge crowd what they want."

T. J. wanted to wrestle and was growing tired of waiting for Saturday night.

"I remember waking up that Saturday morning. That was the worst wait of my life, nerves just went nuts all day," T. J. said. "I remember I was the first person on the floor of the three mats and I took my teammate, Tony Lovstuen, and I just drilled for two hours just trying to stay calm."

He still had to wait through the awards, the grand march and four championship bouts before the three-time champion would get his answer on whether or not his only goal for every season would be true. There were nerves.

T. J. liked having the control in his matches. He was concerned about things he wouldn't be able to control that night. "Especially with just the thought of, 'What if something goes wrong, what if I get caught and thrown on my back and pinned?' I wasn't afraid that he was going to be better than me - I already knew I should win this match – it was just the thought of, 'This could happen' and you can't control that," he said.

"What I do remember is that very last match he goes, 'I'm nervous as crap,'" Cochran said. "You could tell when he was focused and ready to take care of things, which was most generally most of the time."

T. J. calmed. "Once I shook hands with the kid, it all went away. I got in on a leg right away. I guess I got a little bit nervous because he defended my first takedown. Then on the second attempt I got it and boom, I was back on my game," he said.

The final score was 9-3. T. J. finally showed some emotion. He leaped into Cochran's arms as T. J. received the first Wells Fargo Arena standing ovation for a four-time champion. The kid who was usually stoic – he could grin cleverly as he and teammates would prank around – seemed to release considerable pent-up joy.

"I thought maybe that freshman year, if he won it, he'd probably show some emotion, but he took his ankle band off, shook hands, walked over and signed the card and walked over," Cochran said. "Actually I think he slapped me in the ear is what I think he did the first time. Never jumped up for the first one, never jumped up for the second one, never jumped up for the third one. During the fourth one, it was a lot of emotion and adrenaline running through my body and he said a weight had been lifted off his back."

T. J. added, "I put my arms up and pointed at my crowd. It wasn't a 'Yeah, I did it,' it was more like a 'Thank God this is over' sense of relief. It's finally over, that stress is gone, the weight off my back."

Cochran, who is now head coach at Ottumwa High School, said T. J. had two points that made him special. "One was work ethic and two was his technique. When I say work ethic, not only was he the hardest working kid in the room. He was the hardest working kid outside of the room. Now was he the most talented athlete? No, but he worked hard enough to be good enough to get where he wanted to be."

T. J. attended public school until he was in third grade before opting for a Christian-based education system administered by his mother, Kim. Would anything be different if he walked the same halls all day with his teammates? "Maybe my mindset would have been different. I was different from most other kids as far as how I worked hard or their negativity on things," T. J. said. "Every practice I had was before and after normal high school hours. We'd have 6 a.m. practices, we'd have 3:30 practice and then we'd teach little kids at night sometimes."

The Sebolts, who had a well-equipped workout center on their property outside Centerville, shared a moment just as T. J. and Cochran did on Feb. 25, 2006. "That's the first time I'd ever heard him say this, but he came sprinting down, I don't even know how he got down there, but he hugged me and said, 'I'm proud of you and I love you.' It was one of the happiest times of my life because I remember my first year, all he said to me was, 'Good job, now all you've got is a target on your head,'" T. J. said.

T. J. had food on his mind after his fourth championship. There was a Saturday night pizza party and the Centerville gang came home on Sunday.

"I've never been a kid to sleep in, never in my life, and I slept until 12:30 in the afternoon (Monday after fourth title)," T. J. said.

"We were fortunate enough to have luck on our side for both of us."

Gilbertville, Iowa is a small community east of Waterloo that relies on farming and whatever employment the non-agriculture folks find in the big city. The city fathers might not put it on their official documents, but wrestling at the parochial high school in town is a cash crop for much of the state.

Hold a tournament with Don Bosco among the teams and you'll be assured of a tidy sum at the gate and at the lunch counter because the Dons have a strong following, and those folks need some sustenance to cheer on the Dons in championship matches. A smart hotel in Des Moines at the time of the state wrestling tournament will court Don Bosco fans because they will need a considerable number of rooms and those rooms will be occupied the better part of a week. Restaurants could profit by figuring when the Dons' fans want to have meals and opening a temporary branch office in the lobby.

"Obviously we've got a lot of great tradition and a lot of guys that have done well," Don Bosco wrestler Bart Reiter said, "but I think also the fans help get the name out. I believe we have the best fans in the state."

Enough people want to watch the Dons in Des Moines that nearly 150 rooms need to be corralled. "It's a blast. It makes a little work for me but it's fun. To some people it is a little getaway, but the community is so tight, a lot of people are related, a lot of people are friends," said Scott Becker, a Don Bosco state finalist who is the program's unofficial travel agent. "We're one of those communities in Iowa where the people, when they graduate from high school, haven't moved very far away. They like the school, they like the community. You'd be amazed at how many guys that wrestled in the 70's and 80's still go down to Des Moines every year whether they got kids there or not. They're still part of it."

Family is at the heart of one Don Bosco entry in the state's wrestling record book. Mack and Bart Reiter are the state's only siblings to have four state championships apiece. Mack won his four golds between 2000 and 2003, Bart did his work between 2006 and 2009.

"That night when Bart finally won it, sharing that with my whole family and everybody respecting what we did. There have been some amazing sets of brothers go through the state of Iowa. You got to be lucky down there too. We were fortunate enough to have luck on our side for both of us. We both had close matches down there and we always came out on top. It's extremely special," Mack said.

Bart said seeing his brother receive two standing ovations as a senior motivated him to want to become a four-time champion. He is the type who finds the highest point of anything he does and does his best to ascend to that height, but the atmosphere alone that Mack won in at Veterans Memorial Auditorium did get young Bart's attention.

"That was a big factor in making me want to win four titles. That's back when it was in Vets and we got to be down on the floor," Bart said. "Me, my dad, my brothers and my cousins…I guess our whole family was right there in the first five rows. Being right there in the middle of all that and talking to him afterwards, I was like 'Man, that's definitely something I'm going to do everything I can to do.'"

Two brothers with four state championships is another story in the rich wrestling tradition at Don Bosco, which got a chance to develop that tradition when Waterloo Columbus decided not to hire a former state place winner for Waterloo West named Dan Mashek as its wrestling coach. Mashek came to Don Bosco in 1970 after the program went 5-6 under John Maehl the previous season. The Dons had one losing season and a total of 69 losses in 30 seasons with Mashek at the helm. He became the state's career wins leader among wrestling coaches at Don Bosco and finished his 37-season career with a 519-105-5 record.

The Dons were the last team to qualify an entire team for the state tournament, bringing 12 wrestlers to the 1979 meet. They also won state in 1979, the first of four traditional championships under Mashek. The Dons won a dual-meet title in 1995.

Don Bosco had 39 individual state championships won by 27 men going into the 2011 tournament. That started in 1977 when Ray Fox won the Class 1-A 119-pound title. Fox has been a longtime assistant under Mashek and Tom Kettman, who took over in 2000 when Mashek moved to North Scott of Eldridge.

The four Reiter boys competed in a total of 15 state tournaments and brought home 15 medals, including nine championship nuggets. Joe is the oldest and he won a state championship in 2000 and placed three times before he had to give up the sport as a senior because of concussions. Mack won his four, then Eddie placed four times and Bart won his four medals. The Reiter boys were raised in wrestling by their father, Doug, to appreciate hard work and embrace toughness. Once when Mack was afraid of the ball after being hit by pitches in youth games, Doug Reiter set about throwing pitches at him to prove he would not be injured by the ball while Joe held his brother's ankles to keep him from backing out.

"My dad's a pretty old-school Iowa kind of guy, loves to work hard. That's how he was raised and that's how he still does it," Bart said. "That's how we look at wrestling, it's all about working hard. You've got to know the technique, but it's hard and the guys at the top are the guys who work the hardest."

In a 2003 interview prior to the state tournament, Mack Reiter spoke of how Don Bosco's tradition was built without frills.

"You're good because of what you go through and the time you put in," Mack said to the *Des Moines Register*. "We built our tradition on the basics. Someday we'll get a flashy wrestler come in here and we aren't going to know what to do with him."

Fox said Mack Reiter showed early that he had special skills. "It was his mat savvy at that young age and his awareness of what he was doing," Fox said. "He always seemed to land on his feet. He was like a cat."

Mack Reiter said Joe's tough luck motivated him to succeed. Joe Reiter finished second at 103 pounds in 1998 and 1999 when Mack was in junior high. It was Joe's 1999 overtime loss to Nick Lee of Columbus Junction that pushed Mack to his first championship. "When I was in overtime my freshman year, the first thought in my head was, 'I remember what it felt like watching Joe lose in overtime, I'm not going to do that.' Finishing second was a hard thing to see. When I got to the finals I knew that was a painful, painful thing to watch and I didn't want to be any part of that."

Reiter beat Luke Reiland of Eagle Grove, 5-3 in overtime, for the 103-pound title. The "I'm not going to do that" line described how he won. The overtime win was his second and last regular decision at state. Mack had 10 pins – the most by any four-time champion – at state. He won by fall in seven of his last eight bouts and won the final contest by technical fall.

Mack did lose on the mats in Vets, despite his 16-0 tournament record there. In eighth grade, Reiter placed third at his weight in the AAU Nationals tournament there. "After the tourney, I'll never forget it, he said, 'I didn't think you'd ever lose in this building.' That clicked with me right there."

After beating Reiland, Mack Reiter could work towards being a four-timer.

"It was a goal. It didn't become a reality until after my first year, then it was kind of like, 'There is a chance now,' but my dad instilled that in me from the beginning," Mack Reiter said. "I was expected to be a four-time state champion. That's what I was shooting for. It wasn't to be a state champion, it was to win four."

Mack already made tournament history in 2003 when he and C. J. Ettelson of Hudson won their fourth titles. There had never been a tourney where two four-timers were feted on the same night.

Don Bosco wrestlers have done considerable damage with the pin. Mack was its best example, holding the state record of 134 career falls until fellow four-timer T. J. Sebolt of Centerville broke it three years later.

"The weird thing was with my dad, unless we were at a national tournament or a state tournament as a kid, I wasn't allowed to pin anybody," Mack Reiter said. "I couldn't. I had to tech them so I could get more mat time. Finally, my freshman year, he was like, 'Pin them whenever you want.' He turned me loose and I hit the ground running."

At first glance in high school, Mack did not cut an imposing figure. His skillful technique trumped a perceived need for bull strength in getting on an opponent. Once the action moved to the mat, Mack Reiter knew several ways to move an opponent – no matter how well he was scouted – in order to facilitate the cradle he favored. As a freshman Mack Reiter wrestled for Mashek, who would leave at the end of the season.

"He found what worked for him and his style of coaching and he hammered it. We were all taught, and we've all been brought up in the program since we were little kids, to wrestle the exact same way – wrestle hard, don't quit and when you get on top look for the fall," Mack said.

Mack Reiter said the location of his home meant he and his brothers could have easily gone to Jesup High School. That was not the family's tradition, however.

"I think it had always been (Don Bosco) was where I was going to school because of the Catholic education and wrestling just came along with it," Mack said. "My brothers and I really enjoyed wrestling and fortunately for us we were at a place where wrestling drives."

Had he gone to Jesup, Mack might not have had such a good seat as he did for the Iowa-Michigan State meet that was staged in Don Bosco's gymnasium. "I remember sitting matside for that and I remember thinking, 'This is something I want to do' and 'This is something I want to be really good at' because that was really cool."

Eddie Reiter was thought to be on the same path as Joe and Mack in regards to getting at least one gold medal. Something always jackknifed on Eddie's route and he finished with four place medals – one seventh, two fifths and one third. He didn't win gold, but Eddie did four times what few can manage after their dream is shattered: win the final match at the tournament.

"I've always felt bad for Eddie because of the way things fell," Mack said.

Bart added, "Definitely my saddest moment is when Eddie lost in his senior year. That was pretty hard."

Bart, to many observers, had some similarities to Mack, including both wear size 8 ½ shoes, signing to wrestle at the University of Minnesota (Mack was a three-time all-American for the Golden Gophers) and a love for hitting people with the cradle. That meant there was a certain expectation when he put on his boots. "We'd had similar success growing up, we'd always won the same amount so, going into high school, it was expected that he should win four state titles," Mack said.

Bart got hands-on experience about how the Reiters do toughness on the mat. He also had tough guys and champions in the practice room such as Kettman and assistants Ray Fox, Tom Hogan, Brian Frost and Cory Christensen as reference material.

"Basically every time I think about what taught me the most, what comes to mind is running halls and stuff and Ray Fox pushing us to a level we didn't know we could go to. He's one of the more motivating guys I know, especially when it comes to doing conditioning stuff in practice," Bart said. "A lot of stuff comes to mind. We would do pushups before practice and pretty much every practice he would lay down and put his legs on me while I was doing pushups.

"Our assistant coaching staff is just amazing. I wrestled with Brian Frost almost every day my senior year. There are so many guys that know so much about wrestling. There's not an area in the sport that not one of them is going to know about. (Kettman) is always there. He's a good motivator, definitely. When we're getting tired or we're wrestling live and people start to slack off, he'll yell at them. I think he sets up really good workouts for us to do."

At home, Bart understood what Mack was doing. Bart said all three brothers were teachers for him. "I knew the whole time (Mack) was beating me up and stuff and giving me a hard time, he was just trying to make me better," Bart said. "It's kind of like learning from the best to be the best."

At school, he understood what wrestling means to the Dons.

"We've got all of the pictures hanging up in the hallway of all of the state placewinners. You can tell there's just a rich tradition at Don Bosco," Bart said. "The first time I got to put on a singlet was a great moment. It truly felt like it was going to be the start to a great year and I couldn't wait for state tournament time."

Nor can anyone in town. The fever spreads to Elk Run Heights, Raymond and Jesup. "Go get a haircut and that's what is talked about. Walk into a gas station, anything like that. It's definitely the most popular thing in Gilbertville," Bart said. "It kind of reminds you of the movie *"Friday Night Lights,"* how the whole town talks about football all the time. It's like everything to everyone. It's like walking around and hearing that as a kid gets you really excited to wrestle for (Don Bosco) in high school."

Bart said he had some strong motivation for success at home, but he had plenty inside him.

"It definitely helped, it helped motivate me a lot when I was younger. Also having them being able to work with me helped," Bart said, "but from a motivation standpoint I think I still would have been motivated. It helped a little bit, but I still would have done anything to win a state title."

When his final state tournament was on the horizon, the questions about becoming the second member of his family to win four titles came with the frequency of push-ups. Bart could have sequestered himself from the print media, the TV cameras and the radio and Internet folks.

"It was more like turn it into something I love. I love the press and I love the folks talking to me about it, I tried to look at it as a positive standpoint instead of a negative. I think I would have been more nervous if I didn't talk about it."

Bart either pinned or won by technical fall in his first three tournament bouts in 2009. He would have a tough, familiar guy in the finals. Cameron Wagner lost, 3-0, to Bart in the 2007 state finals and lost, 6-1, in the 2008 quarterfinals. Actually, Bart met a Wagner in each state tourney. As a freshman he gained the finals with an 11-2 victory over Colton Wagner, Cameron's twin. Cameron Wagner and Ridge Kiley of Eagle Grove (3-2 in overtime in the 2006 quarterfinals) were the opponents when Reiter won his only four decisions at state. Reiter had seven pins, two technical falls and three major decisions.

Mack said in a 2009 interview with the *Des Moines Register,* he planned to keep the time before the finals calm in a Reiter sort of way for his little brother. "I'll just keep everything normal - challenge him to a game of ping-pong, make fun of him a little bit, beat him up every once in a while," Mack said.

The historic match was Bart's 7-1 victory. Cue the standing ovation. "When I won four, I was happy, but for him it was like almost a weight was lifted off his shoulders, like 'I'm done with that,'" Mack said.

Bart said he didn't think right away about the historical moment. "Right away was more the standing ovation stuff, it was more about me. Then I sat there and thought about it after about an hour or so and I was like 'Man, we just became the first brothers ever.'"

More importantly to Bart was the fact he was part of the tradition that is Don Bosco wrestling.

"I see tradition as meaning a lot. I would not like it at all if I wrestled for a school that had never really done anything in wrestling," Bart said. "I always want to be on a winning team, I think that makes a season so much more fun when you're not wrestling for yourself but you're wrestling for the team. I very highly doubt it. I would have worked just as hard, but it would have been hard to get as motivated without the tradition and without the same coaches. It would have been a lot harder to win four titles not going where I did."

"This team was not going to be denied. They were too good."

Good things come to those who wait. That's one of the oldest clichés in the English language, but in Waverly it became part of the best team performance in the history of Iowa's traditional state wrestling tournament.

Since the dual-meet tournament was started in 1987, the word "traditional" was put on the meet in Des Moines that involves those who get through the gauntlet of the sectionals and districts. In Class 3-A programs such as Waverly-Shell Rock, the sectionals are bypassed and the qualifying meet is the district.

The scoring record for the traditional tournament has four significant parts:

- Don Bosco of Gilbertville won the 1979 Class 1-A championship with 145 ½ points. The Dons became the last squad to qualify the entire lineup and they finished 99 ½ points ahead of Lisbon. The previous record of 111 points was set in 1977 by Class 2-A Emmetsburg.
- Bettendorf got top-five finishes from all 10 qualifiers in the Class 3-A tournament in 1982 and surpassed Don Bosco's mark with 167 ½ points. The Bulldogs finished 47 points ahead of Mason City, which had four individual champions.
- Council Bluffs Lewis Central set a record at the Class 3-A tournament in 2001 with six individual champions. The Titans accrued 188 points, finishing 81 points ahead of Iowa City High.
- Waverly-Shell Rock sent 13 guys to the Class 3-A state meet in 2008 and created the benchmark of tournament scoring. The Go-Hawks had 12 place winners (including 11 top-four

370

finishers) and became the first team in state history to crack the 200-point mark. They had 225, 85 ½ ahead of Iowa City West.

"I always underplay everything. I'm not going to be boisterous, I'm not going to be bragging about my team. I think it's unnecessary pressure on my kids, but in that year there was no question we were going to win. It was just how bad," Waverly-Shell Rock coach Rick Caldwell said of 2008.

We were intending on winning the national championship that year, that was our goal. We finally got into "The Clash," we were going to wrestle Apple Valley twice that year – a perennial top-5 team – and they beat us twice in two really close duals, so we fell short of that goal. We needed to perform, but there was no doubt with that team. When you go up and down that lineup, there was nobody in Iowa who was going to touch us. Going into it, I wasn't saying that to anybody. I wasn't even saying it to my team. But the coaching staff, we knew. We could set every record ever established: most qualifiers, most place winners, most champs, most finalists, points…we knew we could do it all. This team was not going to be denied. They were too good."

The Go-Hawks started to soar immediately. They won their first 14 matches and stayed on their pace that allowed them to win "The Clash," a tournament in Rochester, Minn. that brings together top programs from throughout the country. Waverly-Shell Rock ended the season ranked No. 4 nationally. The only team from Iowa to finish higher in a national ranking was the 2000-01 Council Bluffs Lewis Central team that was No. 3.

That 2008 Go-Hawk squad was expected to be a strong unit. The work started in 1999. Caldwell started at Waverly-Shell Rock that fall after spending the previous season at Wartburg College. The Knights won the 1998 NCAA Division III championship and Caldwell was an assistant under coach Jim Miller while finishing his master's degree. The high school needed a wrestling coach after Rick Ruebel resigned.

"To be honest, there were two main reasons we decided to stay and me to take this job. One, we loved Waverly. It was the right size town for us, about the same size as my hometown, Knoxville. We thought it would be a great place to raise a family. My son (Cody) was a kindergartner then," Caldwell said. "The second reason was I saw what was on the way. We got involved in the kids club, there were some great wrestling families and some tough little wrestlers. We started thinking about that 2008 team, they were all kindergarten through third graders at that time.

You're talking Ballwegs, Eric Thompson, Wrage, Averhoff, Kittleson, Cox, Renken, Krumweide....they were in the same room every week."

Jacob "Jake" Ballweg was a sophomore 119-pounder on that 2008 Go-Hawk squad. Ballweg won the state championship that year.

"Back when we were all kids and had fun together, I think we did look to the future," said Ballweg, who would become the school's first three-time state champion. "We made probable lineups and stuff like that – who's going to be where, who's going to grow and how big are they going to be, where are they going to fit in. It was something we looked forward to when we were little kids."

Ballweg was the third member of his family to match a gold medal with his black-and-gold uniform. Matt and Mark were both two-time champions. Their dad, Tom, was a state champion in Wisconsin. It's a challenge to imagine a Ballweg not involved in wrestling.

"I think one time back in grade school I wanted to quit. I was all mad and told them I'd never wrestle again, but I don't think that lasted too long," Ballweg said. "I think I started in kindergarten. I'm not so sure there was any way I was going to do anything else besides wrestling, being that there was so much influence in wrestling around in the house with my brothers and such. I think it was just natural that I got started in it and followed it until I was done."

Caldwell remembered his early introduction to a batch of future wrestling studs.

"Tom Ballweg and Scott Wallace were kind of running the club and they asked me to help. They started asking me to do some things on the side, like Sunday practice and extra practices for these guys. Then Rick Ruebel resigned his position and those dads really wanted me to take the job. I remember distinctly standing in my garage and Tom and Scott talking to me about this job. I decided I was going to take it," Caldwell said.

Caldwell said he got an early indication that the kids were interested in more than just burning off some energy on the weekends. "You should have seen the practices these kids had when they were six, seven, eight years old. They were intense, they were tough, their parents were motivated," Caldwell said. "My son, when he was about second grade, would tell everybody, 'Wait 'til 2008, our team will win the state championship in 2008.'

"It was the most amazing ride I've ever been on. We were fortunate enough we won it in '05 when that '08 group were freshmen. We had enough upperclassmen plus those really good freshmen – Eric Thompson was a placewinner at 215 as a freshman, Mark Ballweg was a state champ as a freshman – but all along Cody would tell everybody around town 'Wait til 2008, I'm going to be a freshman, Thompson and Ballweg's class is going to be seniors, we're going to win the state championship, you wait and see.'"

Cody, who signed to wrestle at the University of Wisconsin, could have tried telling people to watch the 2010-11 Go-Hawk squad. He and Krumweide each won their third state championship. Krumweide's major decision at heavyweight clinched Waverly-Shell Rock's fourth straight team title in the traditional meet. Cody's father resigned his coaching duties following the 2010-11 season.

"It's great that I've won three state titles, that's awesome, but it's always been bigger than me," Cody said. "It's the team aspect, and that's what I am going to remember the most – winning these titles with my team, with my friends. We're all best friends and we're working for the same goal, the state team titles, and that beats any of my individual titles. Of course I don't want to give up my gold medals, but the team aspect is so much bigger."

That team mindset was forged early, when a bunch of kids hungry to compete and to win got together.

"We were all together working out, going to tournaments, going to camps. Our coaches made it fun. We knew we had a great group of guys and we knew that once we got to high school, there was a good chance we could win titles," Cody said. "Since we were little, we loved winning. We had won AAU state titles. I remember being on dual teams together. We knew we could do something special. Just to think about that as kids, that was still in the back of our minds, but it has finally become a reality."

Waverly-Shell Rock's kids and fans enjoyed that taste of a state championship in 2005. Mark and Matt Ballweg won state championships. So did Romeo Djoumessi, a charismatic kid with muscles nearly as broad as his smile who moved to town from Cameroon to be with his older brother, Alain, who was an all-America wrestler at Wartburg and was helping to coach his brother's new team. Actually, the school had two titles to celebrate because the Go-Hawks won the state duals the following week.

As the success continued, people might have given thought to Waverly-Shell Rock being the first squad since Don Bosco in 1979 to send an entire team to state. In 2008, that would have been 14 wrestlers – two more than Don Bosco's total. "The only kid that didn't make it, I felt terrible, his name is Justin Denner. His dad, Mike Denner, is a state tournament official. His dad grew up in New Hampton, they've been in this area for 100 years. He was a two-time state qualifier and had a hammer-tough weight class."

Denner had a knee injury and finished third at district.

That 2008 performance would have been something Caldwell's father, Bill, enjoyed. Bill was a teacher and coach at Morning Sun, serving as an assistant in football under Bob Darrah, who would become well-known for wrestling achievement at Dowling. At one time, Rick was going to attend Lisbon High School to wrestle for Al Baxter. Bill died when Rick was eight years old. Rick did wrestle for Baxter, but at Buena Vista College. In high school, Rick wrestled at Knoxville.

"I think (Bill) would be extremely proud. He coached his whole teaching career, coached a lot of different places, he knows how hard it is. I'd hope he would have a smile on his face and wear our Go-Hawk gear with pride. I bet he'd never miss a meet, one of those types of dads who follow the team because he loves the sport," Rick said. "I've been a long time without my dad. I think about him quite often, about what would he think. The overwhelming thing is he'd be very proud that we've been able to get to this level and stay at this level. I know he knows this, but I hope others do too, that we've done it the right way. We do it through hard work. We do it through training, we do it through great kids and great families, a tremendous kids club. I take as much pride in that as I do our championships."

Darrah said Rick considered attending Dowling and wrestling for him. They did work together during the summer in freestyle competitions.

"Coach Darrah, I look up to that guy. He's one of the guys that really helped me, especially when I got started, about how to run a program, how to build a program, how to set expectations and get kids to buy in," Caldwell said. "I was so young, dad and I didn't talk about much of that stuff. All I do know is my dad always promised me if we were still in Wheatland, I was going to be able to go to Lisbon, where they were a wrestling powerhouse in that part of the state. He was going to make sure I had an opportunity to wrestle.

"Al Baxter, he knew me from birth. He's another guy I take a ton of information from over the years. The thing that Al Baxter did for me, that no other coach ever did, I really, honestly loved that man to my core. I would have done *anything* to make him happy. Every time I wrestled, honestly I think I wrestled as much for him as I did myself. He was a hard driver at times, he was a good technician, he was very organized, but what made him different than everybody else was the way he could motivate people. He had a knack of kids caring about him."

Rick wanted to give the Go-Hawks an opportunity for more championships after 2005. Going into the 2011 tournament, Waverly-Shell Rock was seeking its fourth straight traditional title and fourth straight dual-meet crown. The Go-Hawks had their run of gold trophies halted in the 2011 state duals.

"After you win your first one, it seems a little easier because you did it, it's doable. When I first started coaching in 1990, I really wanted to win one state championship sometime in my career," Caldwell said. "Now with dual and traditional, we've been fortunate we won nine (since 2005). The thing that's hard about it is 1, you get a target on your back, everybody wants to knock you off your pedestal; and 2, in order not to be knocked off your pedestal, it seems like every year we do a little more to prepare. Every year we take a little less time off. Every year maybe we lift a little bit more or we find a new fall running routine."

Cody said the younger wrestlers wanted to continue what a senior-heavy lineup accomplished in 2008.

"It's been crazy. Ever since my freshman year with all those great wrestlers like Mark Ballweg, Eric Thompson, Dylan Wrage, all those guys…they set the bar so high that we knew we had to do what they did and more to win, to keep the streak going," Cody said. "A lot of people after that year started doubting us as a team, losing 11 seniors out of our lineup. We wanted to prove them wrong. Having these guys push me, my dad push me. He and I don't get along all the time, but we've made it work and it's gotten a lot better over the years."

Sitting next to Rick during Cody's matches was assistant Mike Schwab, a state champion at Osage and an all-American at Northern Iowa. Schwab was known for his technique and for his constant attention to peak conditioning. "Schwab's been in my corner all four of my years. He's always been my wing man, he's my guy that I go to other than my dad. He helps me with technique, lifts, he's been a great asset to my success," Cody said.

Jake Ballweg said Rick Caldwell always found ways to motivate a talent-rich program.

"One thing about coach that sticks out the most is no matter what we did, and no matter how good we did, he made us feel like we could always do more," Jake said. "He always set the bar so high, sometimes it was almost impossible to reach it. One big thing is he always expected so much and set the bar so high, there was always more you could do. I think that made guys step it up at times and want to work harder."

Trying to build a strong program that withstands graduation takes considerable time – including time away from the family. Cody said it's helped that his mother, Kristi, was an NCAA Division I volleyball player. She understands the time requirement to succeed.

"My mom's been a huge part of my wrestling. My dad and I are gone a lot of the time for events, practices and she understands. She understands that what we're doing has reason. It's all been built up to win these titles. She knows that that is important to us and she supports us whole heartedly," Cody said. "She does the same with my sisters. They can't just play volleyball three months out of the year. She's taken them all over the country to play volleyball. She understands, she gets it. She's been at that high level of playing. She's always there cooking me meals, always there for moral support if my dad and I aren't getting along. She's been there through the thick and the thin. She's been great."

The 2008 Waverly-Shell Rock team became the measure of a program's quality, particularly at state tournament time. Ballard of Huxley in 2009 became the second team to break the 200-point mark, scoring 220 in winning the Class 2-A championship.

"I'm not a big history buff and I don't know a lot about any of the other previous great teams, but in my eyes it's probably the best team that has ever been in Iowa," Jake Ballweg said. "I think it's the best, if not one of the best teams."

Prior to 2008, Lewis Central's 2000-01 squad was considered *the* team. The Titans finished No. 3 in final national rankings and the top two teams were from prep schools, so coach Keith Massey's team had a legitimate claim as the top public school team in the country.

"I didn't know about (a record) as far as champions or not, but I had it in the back of my mind that we would be setting some records," Massey said. "At that point in time, when I had those guys coming back, I was thinking to myself, 'My job here is not to screw them up' because things were going really well. There were a lot of parents that continued to be dedicated to their sons about making sure they got to the top. It was really great to more lead than teach and coach. It probably wasn't my best coaching year – I think when Blake Anderson was a freshman and we went 17-15 was my best coaching year on getting out of them what I could."

Massey said his dad, Lew, had a lingering impact on how he approached coaching the sport. So did his college coaches, Don Briggs and Jim Miller at Northern Iowa.

"Milboy, motivationally speaking – I truly believe he lies to every one of his athletes, in a positive way, challenging them. I kind of stole that from him: 'Prove to me you can do it. I know you can do more. I know you don't think you can, but I know you can,'" Massey said. "(Briggs) really showed me number 1 organization is a key and number 2 get to know your athletes and get them to trust you to where they will absolutely run through a wall for you."

David Kjeldgaard, a three-time state champion for the Titans, said Massey had the ability to get kids to make just such a run. "It wasn't because he was coach and kind of the, 'I'm coach, do what I say.' When we worked out, he wasn't telling me what to do, he was working out with me," Kjeldgaard said. "He picked me up in the morning at 6:00 to go to a workout, he picked me up at 11:00 at night to go work out. I'd say the kids absolutely believed in him, believed in what he asked them to do. They had no reason not to by the way he lived his life, by the way he coached the kids, by the respect he treated them with. When you take a kid and get them to do things there is no way they would do on their own, to push themselves at levels it's not possible on their own, you're going to have a team that will excel beyond the normal expectations of people."

Kjeldgaard said Massey would do whatever he asked the kids to do, and he would usually beat them at it.

"Through my senior year, he would still beat me. I couldn't keep the pace that he had, and I prided myself on being able to wear anybody out," Kjeldgaard said. "I don't think he was in better shape than me, but when it came to me vs. him, one-on-one, he was not going to let me be able to beat him because he knew he had to do that, because nobody else at that point in time that I worked out with could do that."

Trent Paulson, the Titans' 140-pound champion in 2001, said the team had been working on success for a long time. "It was always in the back of our mind. We knew we had a special team. We all kind of came up together through the (Council Bluffs) Panthers wrestling program, so we all had a base from the time we started wrestling," Trent said.

When the 2000-01 season began, Massey was subdued. "Simply because you never know what's going to happen throughout the year. Injuries, sickness, somebody not cutting their weight right, a girlfriend broke up with you the night before districts and you blow the first round

– it's happened before and it will happen again. I never count my chickens before they hatch. I expect the best, train for the worst," Massey said.

The Titans' 10-man lineup at traditional state was stocked with talent: twins Trent and Travis Paulson, Brandon Mason, Anderson, Nick Hayes, Gabe Rostermundt. All went on to NCAA Division I programs. Trent won an NCAA championship and he and his brother wrestled in the World Championships in freestyle. Mason was an all-American at Oklahoma State, Hayes wrestled at Northwestern, Anderson went to Iowa and Rostermundt wrestled at Northern Iowa. Ben Moss, Chad Davis, Aaron Smith and Jon Clanton were good enough to beat anyone.

Going into state after a successful season, it was not time to put on a show. Massey never let off the "what-if" motivational button. "I kept them thinking anything can happen. That year I brought up, 'What happens if you lose first round? What happens if you get caught in a headlock and pinned? How are you going to react?' Challenging them in that way, putting the mindset of, 'We better perform at our best, otherwise bad things will happen.'"

Lewis Central put seven wrestlers into the semifinals and had its second consecutive Class 3-A team title wrapped up. The Titans earned six spots in the finals and had a chance to flirt with history. Four teams had five individual champions prior to the 2001 finals, the most recent being Waterloo East in 1964.

"I never thought of that, not until afterwards. As soon as Blake Anderson won, and we had six state champions, I was like, 'Wow, that's pretty cool,'" Massey said. "Every match I took individually. I never worried about the team title, always worried about the individual kid."

Rostermundt, who started the run of championships in 2001, called it a special time. "People are going to remember this forever almost," Rostermundt said. "This is one night for us, but it's going to last almost a lifetime."

The team was used to battling because that was the practice tempo. At match time, Trent Paulson said Massey had a simple approach: "Kick the crap out of them, and then kick them for crapping."

Massey offered each kid a chance to be outstanding, Trent Paulson said.

"He makes things optional," Paulson said in a 2000 interview with the *Des Moines Register.* "We have (running) and lifting every morning. He says you can go if you want to be a champion but, if not, you can just stay home."

Massey said the Titans could have had eight state champions in 2001. They also could have had one less champion, as Travis Paulson sustained a torn ACL and sprained MCL one week before the season started.

The impressive showing in 2001 helped Massey accomplish a goal he set for himself years earlier in the same Veterans Memorial Auditorium that his 2001 team shined in.

"Early in my career I was extremely driven to put Lewis Central on the wrestling map, simply because when I was a junior in high school, I was at the state tournament looking at my bracket and I heard somebody mention – I can't remember if it was our 12-pounder or 5-pounder - but they said, 'Alright, I got somebody from Lewis Central.' Right then, I turned to my right to my best friend, who actually went to (Council Bluffs Lincoln), and I said, 'I want to come back, coach at Lewis Central and put them on the wrestling map,'" Massey said. "My drive all throughout college of getting a job, I had to become a teacher because, in the late 80's, you didn't find any translators around. It was kind of happenstance that I was able to get a job at Lewis Central, to be the assistant coach at Lewis Central. Things just fell in place."

Lewis Central's coach – and Massey's coach - was Dick Bleth.

"When I first came back, to me he meant an authority figure who I didn't believe knew a lot of wrestling. Technically speaking, I was correct as far as all the technique and stuff like that. Little did I know how much wrestling he knew: How to run a program, unbelievable integrity. There is nobody with more integrity than Dick Bleth. He expected the best out of his athletes. The other thing he expected was if we're going to win anything, we're going to do it the right way."

Where do the Titans stand in state tourney history? Massey said Waverly-Shell Rock in 2008 is the best. "I would consider us second to those guys," Massey said.

Bettendorf was strong in Class 3-A as the decade of the 80's was beginning. The Bulldogs gave coach Franc Freeman his first team championship in 1981 and followed that up by repeating in 1982.

If Freeman had his way, the Bulldogs would have won state so many times that tournament officials would re-name the large-school championship trophy in honor of Bettendorf. Freeman started at Bettendorf in the 1964-65 season after spending two seasons coaching in Billings, Mt.

When I worked out for the first time with the Bettendorf kids, I couldn't believe how good they were compared to Montana. I came home with Sally, my wife, and said, 'Sal, we're going to win the state tournament.'

Well, we didn't even come close. We had one kid place, Tom Alex at 112 pounds."

Freeman said there was nothing wrong with setting the bar so high. "I don't think so. I always thought I was going to win the nationals three times. I thought I was going to be a state champion when I finally made the team in high school, and then got second. A lot of times we had kids that won it and they shouldn't have won. The other kid was the better kid, but our kids were just determined."

He thought the Bulldogs were going to win that team title in 1975, qualifying nine guys. Bettendorf finished second to Dowling, trailing by 3 ½ points. In 1981, the Bulldogs had state champions in Paul Glynn, Brian McCracken and Hap Peterson in edging Dowling by six points. Freeman had a feeling things would be decent in the 1981-82 season.

"We saw what we had in the room. We thought we were going to be good, but we didn't realize we were going to have 10 kids go to state," Freeman said. "That would be an unbelievable dream to have 10 kids go to state, especially to have all 10 place like they did."

The Bulldogs put on a 10-for-10 show in the first round of the 1982 tournament, and *Des Moines Register* sports writer Chuck Burdick noticed. The Bulldogs had six pins, one superior decision and one major decision among their victories.

"One couldn't help keeping an eye on the big blue and white Bulldog on the west wall of Veterans Memorial Auditorium Thursday night," Burdick wrote. "With the magic the Bettendorf Bulldogs had in the first round of the state Class 3-A wrestling tournament, you expected the Drake University mascot to turn to black and gold."

Freeman said he and assistant coach Paul Castro got increasingly surprised as the round went on. "Castro and I thought, 'We're never going to set the world on fire,' and each time another kid stepped on the mat, we won," Freeman said.

Craig Cervantes, who placed fourth in 1982, said Freeman built a powerful force that included robes – a touch Freeman copied from Iowa State's Harold Nichols. "That was kind of the mystique, the robes," Cervantes said. "For young kids, you're like, 'Wow.' When *Rocky* came out in '76, people were like, 'Hey, that's just like *Rocky* with the robes.' I know that was a big thing for a lot of the kids at the middle school."

Freeman added a touch of class with his wardrobe. The wrestlers were required to wear ties or nice sweaters with nice slacks when they went on the road. Cervantes said Freeman was dressed on the fancy level of TV character George Jefferson at meets.

Freeman knew the Bulldogs could cut an impressive figure getting ready to compete. They did that in 1982 at Vets.

"It was an honor to wear those robes and we always wore them at home, we always wore them when we had a really tough meet and of course at the district and state tournaments," Freeman said. "I got all 10 together and I said, 'I want you each to shoot two takedowns, then put your robe on and go to the next mat and shoot two takedowns. We're going to go through the entire bunch of mats.' I said, 'Don't pay attention to anybody else, don't try to get in anybody's way' and you know, the mats just cleared for the Bettendorf team."

Freeman used some interesting ways to get his wrestlers prepared for the atmosphere of the state tournament. "We had the art classes come in. I hung up three foot paper all around the room and the art classes would come in to draw in people yelling and screaming. We'd have a recording of yelling and screaming and we'd coach in that screaming and the kids would wrestle in that screaming. We invited students to come in and parents to come in and yell and scream if they wanted to," Freeman said.

Cervantes said the Bulldogs were strengthened by their willingness to compete on the mat every chance they got. It might have been in tournaments at places such as Fort Madison and Cedar Falls or in Glynn's basement. Cervantes said McCracken was going to do RAGBRAI – a week-long bicycling event in the summer that starts at the Missouri River side of the state and ends at the Mississippi River side – but he decided not to ride and finished second at the Junior Nationals in Iowa City.

Freeman noticed the 1981-82 Bulldogs were a bunch hungry for more success.

"I think those kids had a mindset that was different than any team I've coached," Freeman said. "I always thought we were going to win, even though I knew we weren't. I always thought and talked that we were the best. That team knew they were the best. They didn't rub it in. When they beat somebody, they were gentlemen and shook hands. When they got beat, they were gentlemen and shook hands and acted like state champions whether they were or weren't."

Freeman was a state runner-up in 1956 for Davenport High School and coach Jim Fox. Freeman said he tried to emulate Fox's classy style, particularly how he had an arm around his wrestler regardless of a good or bad moment. "I tried not to scream or yell at the kid in front of the other kids and parents. The Glynn brothers got popped upside the head before a match, but never in plain view," Freeman said.

The finish set a record, but Cervantes said the Bulldogs weren't overjoyed. "We had 167 ½ points, but I don't think we had the best state tournament. (Mike) Seymour beat Parry Hughes three times and ended up losing in the finals. Brian Waddell beat (1982 state champion) Steve Knight twice that season and (Jeff) Gibbons beats (Waddell) in the semis. I don't think we had our best tournament."

At Don Bosco in 1979, the Dons were hoping the bad stuff got out of their system in the 1978 state tournament. The Dons finished fifth in 1978. "I don't think there was anyone who ever thought anything big was going to come out. We had such a bad '78 state tournament, where five of us got beat in the first round. Back then you were one-and-done," said Scott Becker, Don Bosco's heavyweight on the 1982 squad.

"We had one state place winner but we had five qualifiers back, so we knew in our minds that we had a chance to win the state tournament. (Coach Dan) Mashek had drilled it from day one – we should have had it last year, we didn't do it. We're going to do whatever it takes this year to get that state tournament trophy," Becker said. "Everything just kind of fell into place. We were pretty much a junior- and senior-dominated team. We only had one freshman and one sophomore wrestling by the end of the year. As the year went on, we started doing a lot of good things and winning. We all thought we had a good chance to get quite a few guys to state. Mashek's thing was it wasn't getting to state. His goal was to win state and if you didn't have that attitude, you had to change it."

Mashek added, "It was a humbling experience. We mastered the dual meet level and the tournament level, we mastered the sectional and the district, but we hadn't mastered the state. I think it really motivated these kids to do as well as they did that next year because they remembered what happened the year before."

Don Bosco had 11 of its 12 wrestlers assured of a trip to state in the district tournament at Conrad. All that stood in the way of the Dons being the first team in 26 years to qualify its entire squad for state was a wrestle-back match for Tony Vieth at 132 pounds. Vieth scored a 3-2 decision over Mitch Moyer of Janesville and the Dons had 12 qualifiers in their 10th season of varsity competition. The other 12 state qualifiers from that district were culled from nine other schools. "The whole momentum thing got going and we went nuts," Becker said.

One of Becker's first duties after the Dons' district meet ends (he's usually doing radio reports for KWAY-FM in Waverly) is to see if that 1979 team remains Iowa high school wrestling's version of the 1972 Miami Dolphins football team – the last NFL team to go undefeated in a season.

"We would be lying to you if we don't check the districts. I know I'm not the only one that does it after sectionals to see if anybody qualified the team," Becker said. "You have a little of that idea in the back of your mind that it would still be cool if we're still the (last) one. We don't pop champagne like the Dophins, but we still take notice of that stuff."

Are the 1979 Dons among the state's best teams?

"Sometimes we get the argument we're not even the best at Don Bosco. The team (in 2009) put eight guys in the finals, and the year before we had 10 in the semifinals. That was always our argument when the younger kids would say, 'We're better than you guys,'" Becker said. "It's a different era and a different way of looking at it. I've got to say what would have happened under today's rules with the wrestlebacks. I won't ever say I think we were the greatest, I think we were one of the best.

"I think the other thing is we may be the best team. We didn't have the biggest studs but we had a team – 12 guys who all did it. 10 of the 12 guys had over 20 wins. I won't sit here and say we're the best, I think we're one of the best. You can make an argument for the Waverly team that set the scoring record, the Ballard team (in 2009) that put 10 in the finals. A couple Don Bosco teams are right there, that Bettendorf team in '82 was pretty darn good. Even go back and listen to some of the old guys - the West High teams and the (1964) East High team that brought five guys to state and had five champions."

Since the tournament field began forming through tournament competition in 1931, Valley Junction (1933), Cherokee (1935), Clarion and Waterloo West (1943) and Davenport (1953) preceded Don Bosco in qualifying the whole team. Becker looks forward to meeting the next team to do it.

"If somebody comes up and does it again, that's pretty cool because you know what it takes to do this. I'd go to the coach and give him all the props because it takes a lot of things happening to do it," Becker said.

The 1979 Don Bosco team was reunited with Mashek at the 2009 state tournament as it led the grand march prior to the finals.

"It was surreal. It was an experience you just kind of go, 'Wow, can you really believe we're doing this?' We talked about this later that night, but when we came out for the first round in Des Moines we came out not right away not late but we walked to the far mat and started warming up," Becker said. "All of a sudden I looked around and every other kid gave us the whole mat. That's one of the most vivid memories: there we are, we've got a whole mat. We're going through our normal routine as if it was a regular dual meet or a tournament. We were so relaxed because of that, this wasn't out of the ordinary."

What the Dons did in 1979 was far from ordinary.

"I think as we, in retrospect, look back when we were all in Des Moines that maybe this was even more special than we even realized," Becker said. "We didn't think we'd be the (latest). Somebody's going to do it at some point in time – there are a couple schools that were within one weight class – but it may never be done. That's one thing we take pride in, we did it. Not only did we do it, we finished off what we needed to do. It was almost like the perfect season."

"Trying to fill Dan Mashek's shoes, I was pretty nervous."

Tom Kettman wrestled for Don Bosco of Gilbertville and was one-half of history when the Dons had their first multiple state tournament qualifiers in 1976. He helped coach Dan Mashek turn the 1978-79 squad into the last team that qualified its entire lineup for the state meet.

Naturally, he would take over in 2000 when Mashek, the state's career win leader, left the little parochial powerhouse to be wrestling coach at North Scott of Eldridge.

"Trying to fill Dan Mashek's shoes, I was pretty nervous," Kettman said. "I was content, I was Dan's assistant for 19 years. Three or four times through those 19 years he told me, 'I'm getting out, get your teaching endorsement so you can take over,' or 'Before Tommy gets in high school, I'm gone,' or 'When Tommy goes to college I'm gone,' and he never left. I was content to be Dan Mashek's assistant."

Mashek, whose son Tom was a state runner-up, said Kettman was the ideal person to take over at Don Bosco.

"I don't know if I've ever come across anybody that's had a better work ethic," Mashek said. "He wasn't really crazy about it when I talked to him as I was leaving. I said, 'Tom, you're the one I trust with it. I know you, at least try it.' I had a lot of confidence in him."

Brad Smith, Ron Gray and Dale McDonough know of Kettman's concerns. They also followed a legend as head coach at a high school wrestling program in Iowa.

- Smith took over at Lisbon in the 1978-79 season after Al Baxter resigned to become head coach at Buena Vista College in Storm Lake. Baxter turned Lisbon into a Class 1-A power with five state championships between 1973 and 1978. Smith left Lisbon to follow longtime coach Clyde Bean at Iowa City High.

- Gray, the first state place winner for coach Bob Darrah at Des Moines Dowling, helped Darrah lead the Maroons to three of its four traditional state championships and its first three dual-meet titles. Darrah resigned after the 1988-89 season to coach at Simpson College in Indianola.

- McDonough became interim coach at Clarion during the 1975-76 season after longtime coach Dale Brand resigned. Brand, a state champion at Fort Dodge who won 250 dual meets in over 30 years with the Cowboys, was forced to step down because of lingering pain from an earlier auto accident.

Kettman called upon the other half of that historic 1976 pairing to help him keep Don Bosco's wrestling fortunes bright. Ray Fox was Don Bosco's first state champion in 1977 after being its first finalist in 1976.

"I knew if Ray and I put our heads together, we'd get the job done," Kettman said.

Kettman and his coaches have been successful continuing the philosophy Mashek built a powerhouse with. The Dons went into the 2011 tournament series seeking an unprecedented sixth straight traditional team championship and an unsurpassed seventh straight dual-meet championship. The run of traditional team titles ended as the Dons finished in second place, 11 ½ points behind Logan-Magnolia.

"I'm not upset about the streak being broken, I'm upset about not having that opportunity for these kids to win a state title," said Kettman, who was named 2011 Class 1-A coach of the year. "Really, we've been blessed winning one…and then winning one…and then winning one… That's kind of what we've been preaching to the kids the last couple of years. 'We're not looking at a streak, we're looking at you kids winning your state title,' Yeah, it would have been nice to win this year, just for the fact they would have won their state title. Five in a row, six in a row…sure, I'm disappointed we didn't win. We left some good kids at home that could have made a difference, but that's the way it is. We came out of a tough district. We had 18 placewinners down here, three are in the finals. That's a pretty good district."

The 2011 tournament might have been Kettman's last as head coach at Don Bosco. Kettman said on the final night of the tournament that he had not made a definite decision on whether to stay or to step down.

Outside of assistant Cory Christensen – a three-time state champion at Winterset – along with Mike Schwab – a state champion at Osage – and former assistant Jeff Bradley, the Dons have done their winning with a strong dose of homegrown coaching. Fox helps out, so does Tom Hogan – a Don Bosco state champion who later won an NCAA Division III championship at Wartburg – and state place winner Brian Frost.

"I'm really happy for them because the times when you get too many chefs in the kitchen, it tears apart a program," Mashek said. "To their credit, Tom, and to the guys themselves, they have stepped back as individuals and said, 'This is the program, we'll make a contribution any way we can.' I'm sure there is tweaking around the edges, do this a little differently, do that a little differently, but the core is the same. It's based on this idea of hard work and so on pays off."

The Dons have an enviable fan following that got started as winning did under Mashek's care. "He made it important, made it interesting, made it fun," Kettman said.

Don Bosco fans look upon the state tournament as a giant reunion. As many as 600 tickets to the finals would be sold to Dons fans until demand for the tickets got so high that sizeable ticket orders had to be reduced to try to accommodate as many orders as possible. It's one of the few reunions in Iowa that is not staged in the summer. "We always talked about the family, and just because I'm 150 miles away doesn't mean I'm out of the family. I still go back to the family reunions in Des Moines," Mashek said.

The topic is not often wrestling, but Kettman said he will touch base with Mashek periodically. They first met when Kettman was in fifth grade. "If I'm wondering about something, I'll call and talk it over with Dan," Kettman said.

There is a sense of democracy in planning workouts at Don Bosco these days. That may not have always been the case during Mashek's time. "I write up a program every day and have the assistants look it over, I have no problems with it," Kettman said, adding the coaches or the wrestlers might complain about something. "You've got to listen and see if you can justify what they're complaining about. I'm not opposed to anybody with input on anything. It may not happen that day, but it may happen the next day. Dan was one to say, 'Make sure you write up a schedule every day, have it in writing, have it in a notebook. What you don't get through, do the next day. What you think of during that day, add to it so you can add it to the next day.'"

Sometimes an opportunity develops at an unlikely time. Smith, an

NCAA champion in 1976 at the University of Iowa, found the Lisbon job that way.

"I looked forward to the challenge. The reason I found out about the job opening up, I was in the (Iowa) wrestling office and I was talking to J Robinson at the time. The phone rang and they asked if they knew anybody that was interested in a coaching position because Al was getting ready to go to the college level," Smith said. "I just happened to be there, so it was kind of like the timing. I had thought about it. I knew I wanted to coach at that point, but I didn't know if I was ready to jump in right away. I had heard of Lisbon being at the state tournament before nationals. I had seen them wrestle and I liked their style and I knew of Al Baxter."

Baxter had turned Lisbon into a showcase in the same manner a craftsman turned a block of wood into a fine heirloom on a lathe. A program that had no state qualifiers soon had individual champions, then three straight team championships. His impending departure did not sit well with at least one state champion.

"I heard some rumors that he was going. He also taught driver's ed and he told me he was leaving. That was the end of my sophomore year, and I'm telling you what, I found a corner and went in and cried. I was like, 'What do you mean? You can't go,'" said Scott Morningstar, who won the first two of his four state championships under Baxter's guidance.

Baxter said Lisbon's program had grown to the point of earning the title of dynasty. "I really think so because the thing is we won state five of the last six years I was there," he said. "They didn't have the dual-meet state championship back then. I had three, four or five teams I would have loved to have taken to the state dual meet tournament. Brad Smith won three dual-meet state championships and he won seven (traditional) championships in Des Moines. You look over the last 35-40 years, Lisbon has probably won as many state championships as anybody."

Smith knew he'd be compared, but he was ready.

"I wasn't really intimidated at all. I felt confident in what I could do. I felt I came from one of the best high school programs in the nation (Hersey High School in Arlington Heights, Ill.) and obviously one of the best collegiate programs in the nation. I felt confident in my abilities, the only thing is I had never coached a program before."

Smith, a two-time Illinois state champion, had a meeting with his future squad. He remembered most of the male enrollment of the high school was there. The cupboard was not bare, talent-wise, and the coach was energetic. Some folks had Baxter's methods engrained, but Smith wanted to do things his way.

"That took a while. When I had the kids the first year, 'Well coach Baxter didn't do it this way.' And my response right away was, 'I'm not coach Baxter, I'm coach Smith, and we're going to do things the way I feel they should be done. I have all the respect in the world for coach Baxter because he was a great coach, a great motivator and had a great program, but things are going to be done my way.' I also told them, 'There is more than one way to be successful.'"

By the middle of Smith's first season, the Lions were winning and the wrestlers were buying into his system.

Baxter scheduled Lisbon against schools from larger classifications. Smith did the same, foregoing easy wins and fattening records to get his wrestlers ready for challenges at tournament time. That's why seeing Lisbon guys on top of the award stand was no accident. Smith led 18 individuals to a total of 29 state championships in 13 seasons.

One Class 1-A opponent was not avoided on purpose. Don Bosco of Gilbertville was developing a strong program just like Lisbon. The Dons' first team championship was in 1979, Smith's first season at Lisbon. Between 1977 and 1990, Lisbon won nine Class 1-A traditional championships and Don Bosco won four.

"That was fun competing against Don Bosco, one of the highlights of every year," Smith said. "When you go to their place, it's like you got the fans right on the stage. The mat's right there, everybody's around the mat, everything's right on top of you. It's pretty intense, but that's what makes it so fun."

A guy well-connected in college circles and involved in Iowa's freestyle squad at the Junior Nationals like Smith was could have generated a few leads on coaching jobs at places much bigger than Lisbon. While he was coaching at Lisbon, Smith spent part of some Christmas breaks competing in the Midlands Open at Evanston, Ill. It was the same tournament he competed in as a member of Iowa's team.

"I didn't really want to leave and go to another high school comparable size-wise. I had an opportunity to go to University of Illinois and (coach Ron Clinton) was getting ready to retire. This was like in the middle of my career at Lisbon," Smith said. "I went out there and checked it out. At that point, I was thinking about getting my master's. And the only way to get my master's being in a collegiate program, working on that with them paying for it, and getting paid as a coach and doing camps and stuff, it would have been a big pay cut.

"In the long run it would have been an opportunity for me to become a head collegiate coach because I was still relatively young at that point. I thought about it, but I just felt I wasn't ready to leave. I was having a lot of fun – when you're winning, obviously you're having a lot of fun – and I just wanted to hold back a little bit."

Smith said Iowa City West Athletic Director Marv Reiland contacted him to see about interest in taking over the Trojans' job.

"When City High had opened up, I had been (there) because Lisbon would come and work out with City High. I knew Clyde Bean real well and (his son) Mark Bean as an official. When it opened up, I thought this was an opportunity to move to a bigger school," Smith said.

The coaching bug had found Smith while he was still competing at Iowa. He was doing camps with Dan Gable and Robinson and learned he enjoyed instructing kids. "After I felt that feeling of a state championship as a coach and as a team, I knew I was in the right spot."

Smith said he learned from Gable that you can't coach everyone the same. Smith said he had to pick his spots for when to deliver a pat on the back or a boot a few inches lower. At Lisbon and at Iowa City High, Smith said he had the state meet veterans talk to the new faces about what to expect, what to do and not do and how to prepare.

The coaching philosophy is an on-going recipe, Smith said. He has copied things learned from various sources such as former Iowa coach Gary Kurdelmeier (a two-time state champion at Cresco), Gable, (former Iowa assistant and Illinois head coach) Mark Johnson and (former Dowling and freestyle team head coach) Bob Darrah. "I'll take anything out of anybody. If I think it's going to effect me to be a better coach, help my program and help our kids, I'm all for that because I'm open-minded," Smith said.

He might have borrowed some things learned from Terry McCann, a former Iowa NCAA champion and 1960 Olympic gold medalist. McCann coached wrestling for the Mayor Daley Youth Foundation in Chicago, and Smith worked out there in the off-season. Smith said McCann was responsible for him getting to Iowa and coach Kurdelmeier, McCann's former teammate. Kurdelmeier never saw Smith in action, but took McCann's suggestion to bring Smith to campus.

When City High won the Class 3-A traditional title in 1992, Smith became the third of four coaches in tournament history to win a championship at two different schools. Finn Eriksen led New Hampton to a share of the 1933 title and won the first two of Waterloo West's state-best 17 championships. Roy Jarrard won at Cherokee in 1939 and at Waterloo West between 1944 and 1946.

After Smith won at City High, Ron Peterson added a title at Cedar Rapids Prairie in 1995 to a championship his Clarksville team won in 1991.

"My feeling is a state title is a state title," Smith said. "A lot of people feel a 3-A team is going to be dominant over a 1-A team, head-to-head, which in some cases might be true. But I know I had some teams at Lisbon that won state titles that I feel could have beaten the 3-A state title team."

Smith said he doesn't see the turnouts now that he did when he was at Lisbon, when it seemed nearly all of the boys were on the team. That makes him appreciate the kids who complete their career in undecorated fashion.

"Numbers in wrestling throughout the state I have seen decline, and the reason that's happening is kids just don't want to work," Smith said. "The kids that do stick it out - my kids that have gone through my program, never won a state medal, a state championship or never made the state meet - those guys that were out four years, that came and busted their butt day-in and day-out, those are the guys I respect because they're hanging in there. Those guys have gone on to be real successful people."

During his career at City High, Smith coached three 100-match winners - his sons Jake, Cody and Colton. "With my boys coming through this practice room, the other kids in the room at the same time never saw me favor my kids or coach my kids more or yell at my kids more," Smith said. "What I tried to do as a wrestling coach was to be their wrestling coach when we're in the practice room and treat them like everybody else. Once we left the practice room, I became their dad. We watched tape and stuff at home, but besides that, sitting around the dinner table we wouldn't talk about wrestling much."

Watching one of your athletes winning a state championship can be painful, as Smith found out in 1988 when Brian Krob won the Class 1-A 145-pound championship. Smith said he wasn't ready for the celebratory burst by Krob and wound up in a chiropractor's office. There are also the affirmation moments, such as when City High's Zach McKray won the Class 3-A 135-pound title in 2005. Mitch Mueller of Iowa City West had beaten McKray during the season, but a narrow loss at the Mississippi Valley Conference tournament told Smith that McKray had a chance.

In the state semifinals, McKray upset Mueller, 2-1. A string of six losses to Mueller had been cut. "Matches like that make it all worthwhile. That's one of the highlights of my coaching career," Smith said.

Dale Brand had many highlights during his coaching career, most of it spent at Clarion. Brand arrived in the 1940-41 season after coaching football, baseball and wrestling at Tripoli. He developed a reputation for long, tough practices that were more about live wrestling than extensive work on specific technique. His teams were comprised of tough guys who maybe didn't have natural skills other than an ability to fight for as long as necessary.

Phil Brand, one of Dale's six sons, said his dad grew up in Fort Dodge during the Great Depression. Dale didn't have much money, but he had a love of competition and a desire to excel. It was that fight-for-everything mindset that helped Dale pin his way to a state title in 1931. Dale took it to Cornell College in Mount Vernon, where he was an NCAA champion; and then into coaching. He developed state champions such as Les Anderson, Mel Waldon, Larry Willis, Larry Benson, Russ Paulsen and Randy Smith.

Dale was a social studies teacher at Clarion. One of his courses was government, and since he was required to memorize the Constitution in high school, he gave students at Clarion a clear understanding of amendments as well as the preamble. The students were known by their last name, and that was the same for those who wrestled for him. Phil said he and his four brothers who wrestled for their dad were called by their last name at school, but he knew their first name at home.

Dale McDonough was hired at Clarion for the 1973-74 school year to teach junior high science and to be an assistant coach in football, baseball and wrestling as well as coach junior high track. He had just graduated from Northwestern College in Orange City.

"When I interviewed for the job, my first interview was with the entire school board," McDonough said. "Dale was not in town that night, but they said, 'We want you to come back again. We want Dale to meet you before we decide to offer you the job.' I knew right then that Dale had a lot of clout within the community, and rightly so because of the long history and what he had accomplished in the sport of wrestling."

McDonough returned to Clarion to meet Brand. "It was funny when I did meet Dale. In my mind driving over there to meet him, I pictured this big guy in my mind. Then Dale pulls up, not very tall, stocky...we sat in the car for a little bit and he said, 'As far as I'm concerned, we're OK.' and it probably lasted 10-15 minutes."

McDonough went to Schaller High School, which started a wrestling program when he was a senior. He had done wrestling as part of physical education class at school and he occasionally traveled to Storm Lake to watch some friends compete. McDonough's first experience of varsity competition in the sport was at college, where he originally intended to play football. Russell King was an assistant football coach as well as the Red Raider wrestling coach. King talked McDonough into coming out for wrestling.

The interview in Clarion, which had one of the charter high school wrestling programs in 1921, was an eye-opener for McDonough. "Coming from northwest Iowa, not in a wrestling mecca area, it was definitely new to me as far as that whole atmosphere and the importance of wrestling in the school system," he said.

The two coaches had at least one thing in common: both Dales enjoyed fishing. Dale Brand's skill at catching catfish while growing up in Fort Dodge provided meals for his family. Phil said his dad kept that love of catfishing as an adult, usually in the river by Rutland, when he was not teaching, hunting or managing the community swimming pool in the summer.

McDonough, who moved into an apartment just east of Brand's house, said he and Brand were on the same page when it came to getting better in practice. "I liked that attitude, where you have to push yourself to perform at a certain level. When he spoke, the kids responded and that's what I admired about his abilities and his technique. The man was amazing. He'd be walking around the room and he'd pick something out on a kid and correct him. He just had a coaching style that was very unique," McDonough said.

"Dale was one that when he did his coaching, he didn't do a lot of drilling or teaching technique. He observed more as kids were wrestling and if they executed the move wrong or didn't execute it properly, that's when he did his correcting and coaching. When I took over, one of the things I implemented was running. I had the kids run before practice and sometimes after practice. We didn't really agree on that, that was not something he had done, but that was something I felt they needed to have was some endurance as well. Dale's conditioning part was wrestling, which I agreed with 100 percent, but I was looking at it and saying I want the kids to have some longer endurance."

McDonough became interim head coach in January 1975. Dale Brand had been injured in an automobile accident earlier, and lingering pain from his injuries was affecting his ability to coach in his usual manner. According to the *Wright County Monitor,* Brand told the team after recording his 250th victory with the Cowboys in a meet against Clear Lake that he was going to retire immediately.

McDonough's first meet as head coach was a 34-24 victory over Humboldt on Jan. 17, 1975.

"There was really no discussion initially. I think Dale was intending to continue coaching as long as he possibly could. As long as he was physically able to be a part of the program, he was going to continue, so there was no initial discussion," McDonough said. "He didn't say much during football season or anything like that, but wrestling season started and you could just tell he wasn't comfortable. He was always in somewhat constant pain with his arm and finally he told me. One day after practice he said, 'I think I'm going to give it up.'"

Taking over the program drew mixed feelings for McDonough. "I welcomed the opportunity because I knew he'd still be there, but it was a scary situation too, to take over a storied program like that with the expectations that were there," McDonough said. "Fortunately, we were sitting with a room full of excellent kids too, so anybody could have coached those kids and been successful."

McDonough was coaching at Clarion through the 1978-79 season before he got into private business. He later became a wrestling referee and caught himself reminiscing about his start as a head coach as he worked meets.

When I was still refereeing, I'd see some of these young coaches that became head coaches at a young age and I'd be thinking, 'That guy's not old enough to be a head coach,' and then I'd think back that I was in that same boat," McDonough said, adding he understood both sides of the coach-referee debates at meets and tournaments.

"As an official you always think you're right, but you know you screw up. You miss a call every now and then, maybe some nights more than others," McDonough said, "but I can say I experienced both sides. As a coach, when I would give the referee heck for what I thought was a bad call - now I'm the one making the call and the coach chews my rear end about it, fine, we'll talk about it but the decision was made. If I messed up and it's something that can be corrected, we'll correct it."

McDonough worked 12 state tournaments as an official after he left coaching.

When Darrah left coaching at Dowling in 1989, finding the Maroons' next wrestling coach was as simple as athletic director John Hayes asking one question to assistant Ron Gray.

"I thought it would be scary as hell, but kind of neat to follow him," Gray said. "When they were going to announce that coach Darrah was going to Simpson, John Hayes, God bless him, said, 'Do you want it?' I said, 'Yeah' and he said, 'You got it.' That was it."

It seemed like a simple task. Darrah led Dowling to seven state championships – four traditional and three dual-meet – and left the school with an active 79-meet winning streak. The state record was 88 by Waterloo West. Dowling was 161-1 from 1979 to 1989. Some of the victories were against Apple Valley, Owatonna and Simley High School of Minnesota, Columbus, Neb. and Vermillion, S.D. – all powers at the time. In the 2010-11 season, Apple Valley, which is coached by former Oelwein wrestler Jim Jackson, was ranked No. 1 nationally among high school teams.

"When you throw that in, you think, 'Boy, that's pretty scary,'" Gray said. "It didn't bother me. I knew we were going to have some tough bouts because we had Apple Valley and Simley that we're going to run across as well as anyone else in the meantime. I never wanted to see it end, but I'm a realist too. It's going to end sometime, and we got beat by a good team."

Charles City halted what became a state-record 136-meet winning streak by beating the Maroons, 32-24, Jan. 4, 1992 at the Comet Duals. "It was a fun ride," Gray said that night.

Gray's ride with Dowling wrestling started as a freshman in 1969. "I finally got someone my own size to whup on instead of people bigger. I was always small," Gray said. "I walked into Dowling as a freshman at 4-11 and 85 pounds, so in the neighborhood you got some thumpings. It was nice to have someone your own size for a change.

"I was second-string freshman team. You didn't have much knowledge. It was fun, the one-on-one and the combativeness of it. You didn't have much back then, no cable, you didn't have Internet, you didn't have cell phones. I had an older brother that was a swimmer (Bill) and another older brother (Tom) that wrestled, so my twin brother (Don) and I decided we were going to try wrestling."

Gray said he learned that Darrah might not have always been deep in technical knowledge, but he was an unbelievable motivator with an intense desire to succeed and a willingness to work at his goals. That could have explained how Dave Schreck lost to Les Cottrell from Indianola several times in the season and beat him in the 1975 state finals.

"I laugh because (Darrah) said the greatest match in the world is when you win, 4-3, but the guy is crawling off the mat puking in a barf bucket," Gray said.

Gray was Dowling's first state placer, then its first collegiate all-American when he placed third at the 1975 junior college nationals for Black Hawk Junior College. He also qualified at 134 pounds for the NCAA Division I tournament while wrestling at Illinois State. Gray beat Ken Mallory of Montclair State, 11-10, in the opening round. Mallory was the NCAA Division I champion in 1978 and was a three-time Division III winner.

Gray finished college at Drake and was helping Lonnie Timmerman coach the Bulldogs. Gray ran into Darrah as the Bulldogs were getting ready to face Iowa State. Darrah encouraged him to seek Dowling as a place to do his student teaching and left saying, "I'll see you in the room tomorrow."

"I've been there ever since. He still had that command over you, you know?" Gray said. Dowling won state that year (1978).

"I think we worked well together. He didn't have the experience of wrestling and I did. I believed in his philosophy. I had my own little quirks. Being a wrestler, I think I did things and showed some things on top of what he did. We got along really well, we still go out to eat," Gray said. "Our philosophies complemented each other. He had things that were good for the kids, I had some things that could help out. I think it was a great combination."

A change was on the horizon.

"Between the state tournaments in 1989, (assistant coach) Mike Skoglund and I knew something was up because we'd go to a place to eat and he'd be in another booth talking to people. Quite honestly, to this day, he has never told me he's leaving Dowling, but we had our suspicions," Gray said.

Gray won two traditional titles and three dual-meet titles as Dowling's coach.

"Iowa is a wrestling state. To win a state championship in arguably one of the toughest wrestling states in the nation, and to have kids in the school that perform and succeed like that, it's truly exciting," Gray said. "You can't help but be very proud of the kids, the program and the parents that helped push all that through. Success sells itself. If you're having success, people want to do it and they're not afraid to work hard."

Things began to change at Dowling in the mid-'90s, Gray said.

"To ask kids to work hard like those kids did in the past, it's tough for kids to want to do that. There's not many around the state who want to do that anymore, and I think we got caught up in part of that," Gray said. "To get the kids to do what he asked them to do and to do that for me got to be quite a challenge. Kids were different, still great kids, you can't coach a kid today like you did 25 years ago. Mentally, kids couldn't handle a lot of that."

Gray said there were stick-it-out types such as Ronnie Gomez, who won very few matches as a freshman but turned in a big performance, as did Jesse Reeves, when the Maroons beat Cedar Falls in the semifinals on the way to winning the 1991 state duals tourney. There were the step-up individuals such as Shane Broderick, a junior varsity 160-pounder, who stepped in when Pat Kraber could not wrestle and finished third at state at 171 pounds.

There were some good moments, but some of the Dowling mystique had chipped away.

"I love Ronnie, a great kid, but he wasn't mean enough, tough enough," Darrah said.

Gray's contract to coach wrestling was not renewed after the 1999-00 season. After winning an appeal to get his job back, Gray quit coaching wrestling in the 2005-06 season. He continues teaching at Dowling.

"(Wrestling) was just not as much of a priority for kids by then," Gray said.

"People would say, 'That's the state tournament guy.'"

The voice seemed to emanate from deep inside Veterans Memorial Auditorium or Wells Fargo Arena in Des Moines for three or four days every February – and sometimes into March – for 31 state wrestling tournaments. Its clarity made it seem as if your dad somehow commandeered the public address microphone. Yet, no matter how easily the voice grabbed your attention, the manners were always present.

"Wrestlers, clear the mats. Wrestlers, let's clear the mats, please."

With that, Ed Winger of Urbandale was opening another session of the state tournament. That introduction became a goosebump-inducing, often-imitated, not-to-be-missed staple of the tournament.

"Isn't it amazing how that creates a certain amount of excitement?" asked Dave Harty, the assistant executive director of the Iowa High School Athletic Association, who hired Winger for the 1978 state tournament. Darry Chiles and Rex Hight of Greenfield were stepping away from the microphone. Harty had heard Winger's work at Urbandale High School, particularly at the high school's annual invitational wrestling tournament.

"When those guys decided to kind of bow out, I knew that I needed to come up with a good announcer," Harty said. "I made an inquiry of Ed then. I said, 'Ed, would you think you would be interested in something like that?' He said he would be, so that's how we took off on that."

The fans got to know Winger by voice, and some knew the face that went with the voice. "That wasn't crazy, that was identification. I'd go places and people would say, 'That's the state tournament guy.' That would make me feel good," he said.

Perhaps they knew him because his voice left an indelible mark on their lives.

"When you hear his voice say, 'Wrestlers, clear the mats...,' that's an awesome feeling. Every single kid that walked into that state tournament, he said their name many, many times. It's kind of a personal thing. You hear him say your name and your town to Mat 6, it's a pride thing and it just sticks with you," Urbandale Coach Mike Moreno said.

"You hear him announcing the names of those wrestlers and these schools, announcing these great match-ups, it just goes hand in hand. Everybody who's ever wrestled in it knows. We have that common bond of him personally saying our names."

Winger said Harty did a good job making sure the tournament had few hiccups.

"At times he was fun to work for. At times he was pretty sticky. It wasn't bad, it was just making sure the tournament ran smoothly and everything was going good," Winger said. "He'd pretty much leave it to us to keep things going without him having to interfere. He just knew we were there, we were doing our job and he didn't have to worry about it."

Winger said he looked forward to three or four days of calling names to mats, waiting for the table workers to wave a flag to indicate he could send the next match there, giving team scores twice a session for each of the three classes and, of course, delivering his signature line. Winger said he patterned his call after the famous start to the Indianapolis 500 auto race – "Gentlemen, start your engines."

"I was happy to be a part of it. I was looking forward every year to coming into the tournament, doing the tournament, getting it done, feeling like, 'I did a good job, I hope.'" Winger said. "I just enjoyed the whole thing. I enjoyed it when I made the first call to start the tournament. At the end of the deal, the last year or two, it was tiresome. I still felt I could do it. I told Dave I'd quit when I was ready if they would let me."

Winger said in a 2008 interview with the *Des Moines Register* that he needed three things for a tournament: plenty of water, throat lozenges and 7-Up.

When he started calling the tournament to order, Winger watched over as many as six mats. That number grew to eight. The tournament was three days when he started, then it grew to four days in 2003.

Vets Auditorium gave the tournament an extra touch of atmosphere, Winger said. "I think the closeness of it. Everything was right there and everybody knew what was going on. That was 'The Barn' and that was the place to wrestle. It was not received with open arms by many (after moving from Waterloo in 1970), but that has changed."

The preparation for the tournament got easier once computers could be programmed to print out the bout sheets. Prior to that, Winger said he and tournament co-workers Darl Weaver, Gaylen Eller and Shannon Waddell, along with their wives, would get together one night to do the bout cards by hand. Once the computer era began, Winger said his biggest step of preparation was checking the list of state qualifiers to see if he faced any challenging names to pronounce. Winger had experienced co-workers such as Eller, Waddell and Dave Kaus helping him take care of issues. Also available was Joyce Lindahl, an administrative assistant with the IHSAA, who could seemingly answer any question or solve any puzzle.

"I have a saying (that) if I pronounce a name and nobody hits me, I must be close," Winger said in a 2008 interview with the *Register*.

Doug Brooker, longtime producer/director of Iowa Public Television's coverage of the state wrestling tournament finals, put Winger in select company among P.A. talent. "I kind of associate Ed Winger at the high school tournament with Bob Sheppard at Yankee Stadium. This is because I am a Yankees fan. (Winger) was the guy you always heard. Just a very distinctive voice and easy to work with from a television standpoint," Brooker said.

Winterset wrestling coach Gary Christensen mentioned Jim Duncan, Iowa's legendary track and field public address voice, when discussing Winger in a 1994 interview with the *Register*.

"He's kind of like Jim Duncan was at the Drake Relays," Christiansen said.

Ask a wrestler who competed during the 31 tournaments Winger was working and that voice is high on their list of memories. Winger, who wrestled in high school at Des Moines North, was a mystique to some of those high school guys.

"I didn't know he actually lived in town. I thought he just lived in Vets and that's what he did. I never saw him outside," said Urbandale's Moreno, who wrestled in the tournament for Glenwood.

Winger called Moreno's name as a 126-pound freshman, a 126-pound sophomore who placed fifth, a 132-pound junior who placed third and a 132-pound senior who won a Class 2-A state championship. Winger also called Moreno's name as a state champion coach when his Clarinda Cardinals won the Class 2-A team championship in 1994.

"I had no idea what Ed really looked like. You see all those guys up on that podium all those years and you don't ever identify the face. I knew him by his voice," Moreno said. "He's like (radio disc jockey) Wolfman

Jack. I still don't know what Wolfman Jack looked like, but I know what his voice sounds like and I can identify him. When I met (Winger), it was like, 'You need to speak so I can recognize you.'

"I remember walking in as a freshman and hearing his voice – it's a distinctive voice he has – and calling my name. The nerves and the excitement and everything built up you associate with that voice. Everybody who hears that voice still gets a little nervous when they hear it. You get butterflies like, 'It's time to go.' It's like Pavlov's dog."

Winger also called Moreno's son, Michael, in his first two trips to state for Urbandale, but he stepped down before Michael Moreno was called the Class 3-A 171-pound state champion in 2010.

Jim Zalesky heard Winger call his name as a state champion twice while wrestling at Cedar Rapids Prairie. Zalesky heard the voice as an assistant and then head coach at Iowa.

"When you're wrestling you probably don't even know Ed Winger's name, but you get to realize it as time goes on and you realize it more when the guy's not doing it. All of a sudden, where's that voice at? Year after year after year it just sticks in your mind, and all of a sudden…you don't realize it or appreciate it until the voice is gone," Zalesky said.

He added, "I remember '…clear the mats…' more than anything. That's the first time I heard it. Anymore, you go to the national tournament or any big state tournament and that's the one command you hear. It's time to wrestle and say, 'Clear the mats.' People realize that probably gets kids more fired up than anything, that one command to clear the mats. It's go time."

Mike Moreno remembered thinking how cool it was that Urbandale's wrestling team had the state tournament's voice do the P.A. at J-Hawk dual meets and tournaments. The team's invitational tournament in January is known as the Ed Winger Classic.

When the first round of the state tournament opened, veteran coaches made a steady path to the head table to say hello to Winger. At the start of the session, it was simple to figure out which mat your son and classmate would be wrestling on as long as he was at the first weight class. After calling the first six or eight bouts, the rest of the competition is plugged in on the first available mat. When the tournament was in Vets, wrestlers warmed up in the basement and came up about the time Winger called them as "in the hole." When they moved on to "on deck" status, the wrestlers and coaches were ready to move. And the call they waited for – "On mat (insert one through six or eight) right now…" – started them doing a crosscut saw move through a moving mosh pit of folks circling on the outside of the mats.

"Part of the fun was coming up from the basement, that voice… fighting the crowds, trying to get through the ropes and get to your mat," said Iowa City High Coach Brad Smith, who had Winger call his wrestlers from Lisbon and from City High and call him a state champion at both schools.

Winger worked six state tournaments as a table worker before he got behind the microphone. Was he worried about handling the chore of keeping the tournament running smoothly as he told wrestlers and coaches from Ackley to Woodward where to go?

"No, I wasn't concerned because I thought I could do it," Winger said. "The last year I was a little concerned because of my health, whether or not I could do the job to the point that I wanted to. I figured it was time to quit when I didn't feel I could do it."

Winger stepped down after the 2008 state tournament at Wells Fargo Arena. He had called the names of thousands of wrestlers, including his sons Doug and David. Prior to his final session of work, Winger and his wife Connie were recognized as he walked the length of the three finals mats to take his place at the head table. The sold-out crowd gave a standing ovation to the Wingers, the same way they saluted any of the 17 four-time state champions Winger announced.

"It was stirring. That was something. It was about like calling a four-time state champion," Winger said. "(The grand march) was another high point for me, to watch those kids march around and know how many times they had to wrestle to get that far. That was fun."

So was calling a four-timer's name, Winger said. "In fact, it was very emotional for me when I announced them on the stand as a four-time state champion. I would even choke up. I just knew in my own mind what they did go through to achieve this. It was something that really, really got to me. Those were some of the nice things that happened to me, the ability to announce a four-time state champion."

Winger did not use an extra flourish when announcing the likes to Jeff Kerber of Emmetsburg, Greg Randall of Mount Vernon and Shane Light of Lisbon as champions for the fourth time. "Harty would say, 'Keep it down, don't do a lot of embellishment. Announce the kid and his achievement, that's it,'" Winger said.

A couple of other high points were calling Robert Cole of North as the Class 3-A 171-pound state champion in 1996 – North's other state champion was Jack Welch in 1970 – and identifying his beloved Urbandale team as the Class 3-A team champion in 1996.

What does a good public address man need to do at the state tournament? "He needs to be on the ball for all of the things to happen," Winger said. "Be ready to adjust to them and try to keep everything going smoothly and make sure you don't get too many mistakes. Once in a while, I'd wrestle with a name…"

The first state tournament Winger attended was in 1971 at Iowa State Armory in Ames. His sons grew up doing youth wrestling tournaments, but part of the reason for attending that year was his daughter was dating a member of the Urbandale team.

Winger said former Urbandale Athletic Director George Long got him started doing the public address duties at school events.

As Harty was retiring from his duties with the IHSAA, he wanted to make sure a good P.A. talent was ready for the day when Winger would inform the office he was turning off his microphone. John Kinley of Gilbert assisted Winger, then teamed with John Randles of Cedar Rapids to handle the calls.

Was it difficult for Winger to step back? "Not really, because I felt that I was at the point, health-wise, that I really wasn't feeling that sure in myself," Winger said, adding that a four-day schedule got to be taxing in his final years with the microphone.

"The first year, I missed it. As my health has been a problem, I have not missed it that much. I still of course keep track of everything. I haven't gone back down to state because of health," Winger said.

Mike Moreno said Winger's talent at the microphone won't be topped.

"No disrespect to the people who are following him, but I don't think that there will be that somebody with the longevity that he's had. Just the excitement he brought, his tone. I don't know if it will be matched. I guarantee you there's a lot of former wrestlers out there that would agree," Mike said. "There might be somebody good, very good in their own way, but it's not going to match him. I hope there is somebody good, but they're not going to be Ed Winger.

"He was always very clear, concise and just very distinct. There's not a guy out there who has been to the state tournament or who has wrestled that doesn't imitate him. He should have trademarked that thing because it's used all the time."

"I was very familiar with a tackle. A tackle was a double-leg drop."

Wrestling became a sport of choice for Mike Allen of Waterloo because of its correlation to the sport of football.

Do a takedown? That's just like dropping a ballcarrier on the gridiron, and a student such as Allen at Waterloo East High School in the 1960's knew how to tackle. That was a basic skill of football, and football coach Howard Vernon demanded perfection in the fundamentals of the game. That's one reason why East became synonymous with success every fall.

Doing the basics well made Allen's name synonymous with 35 years of outstanding officiating in wrestling matches. He was the first African-American to work the Iowa state tournament as a referee and worked 15 tournaments. Allen became a regular at the major college tournaments, including 23 NCAA Division I tournaments. First he was an official, then he became head official at meets such as the Pac-10 tournament and the Midlands. He received a lifetime service to officiating award from the National Wrestling Hall of Fame in 2007. Allen retired his whistle in 2009.

Years before, Allen wanted to be a football star – his older brother, Willie, was a high school football all-American at East – and needed something to do in the winter.

"After football season was over, you'd go into either basketball or you'd go into wrestling, and I went into wrestling basically because I couldn't shoot any baskets," Allen said. "I was very familiar with a tackle. A tackle was a double-leg drop. I watched the high school wrestlers at the time. When I was in seventh grade, we had some guys at East High School – Don Buzzard, Paul Stinson, Tommy Moore…that was the thing to do, to wrestle. They were really good and we followed them around."

Allen was pretty good until tournament time rolled around.

"I was basically a pretty good wrestler, but an out-of-shape wrestler. I was more of a football player, but I really wanted to be a better wrestler," Allen said. "I got into wrestling just because my friends were wrestling. It was a transition. It's kind of embarrassing to even talk about this, but I never lost a high school (dual meet) match, but I would lose at sectionals and districts.

"Shape. It was shape. I was not in the best shape for wrestling, and it was not because I wasn't working hard in practice. Back in those days, we were doing more cutting than we were conditioning. The coaching was there, Dave Natvig was a heck of a good coach and we had a good wrestling room. We knew a lot about things. The high school coaches sent down skills to the junior high coaches for us to know, so when we came into East High School it was ride, baby ride. We'd hit that outside single and we'd hit that double."

After wrestling and playing football at Ellsworth Junior College and then wrestling at Northern Iowa, Allen began officiating. He found the timing ideal. Allen wanted to officiate wrestling like a good referee does a boxing match – stay on the outside with a sharp eye and come in only when necessary. A stalemate in wrestling was like a clinch in boxing. He found coaches working who wanted their kids to stop wrestling only after the final horn sounded. If they felt the need for Allen to intercede, they'd tell him. Loudly.

"When I was officiating up at UNI, (Panther coach) Chuck Patten used to yell at me to warn his kids for stalling," Allen said. "Bill Dotson was at Charles City, and I would do Charles City matches. He would say, 'Make them wrestle.' My situation was that I was at the right time in regards to they wanted someone that was not necessarily trying to engineer and get so much involved.

"Sometimes people seem to forget that the wrestling in the state of Iowa, when I decided to go into officiating - with Gary Kurdelmeier, Harold Nichols and Dick Walker - was taking that to a new level altogether in regards to conditioning."

Allen stood out on the mat for more than his muscular stature. He was a fan of coaches who favored conditioning because Allen liked a busy pace on his mat. If a team faced a visiting opponent that had a habit of stalling, it was smart money to assume Allen would be on the whistle.

"They liked the idea that I kept the action going. I didn't really keep the action going, I kept the possibility of the action going," Allen said. "I made sure that you were not going to go out of bounds and think that you would stay out of bounds. How I'd deal with that was that I made sure I'd walk them back (to a restart). The high school coaches and the college coaches liked that idea that I stayed away, but if you thought you were going to go ear-to-ear…I used to break certain near-fall situations as a stalemate because of a lack of activity."

Guys who wore officiating stripes got an invitation to work the state tournament if they had enough recommendations from coaches. Allen said he got his first invitation in 1976 or 1977. "I got a lot of votes, but I was doing at least 42 meets a year. Wednesday was church night and Sunday was Sunday, they were the only nights off.…things just went well. People like Kevin Evans and Russ Smith (of the *Waterloo Courier)* saw a person that basically felt I was never…I always wanted to be a gentleman on the mat way before I ever heard about Bobby Jones. I felt it was necessary to be in shape. Rules interpretation was no problem. It was be where you need to be without being Hollywood."

That "Hollywood" stuff was frowned upon by one of Allen's favorite critics – his mother.

"My mother was just outstanding in caring for people. I always wanted to please her. She meant a lot to me," Allen said. "She was just an outstanding person. She would do anything for anybody, and it really bothered us as kids the way she would treat everybody. She always said that there is something good in everybody," Allen said, adding that his mother's classy nature reminded him of former presidential candidate Shirley Chisholm.

Allen was among the officials who worked well at state despite never wrestling at state. It didn't hurt to have two key people at the Iowa High School Athletic Association in Boone watch him work.

"When we first started officiating, all I wanted was a sectional or to get a district. To this day, I don't know how but my first year I got a sectional, a district, a state tournament and a finals," Allen said. "Dave Harty saw me work and Bernie Saggau saw me work too. They felt I was not a risk-taker. I felt good about it and very scared. When I used to officiate, I didn't eat that day because of nerves. It's one thing nerve-wracking to be on that mat by yourself and it's nerve-wracking secondly knowing if you make a mistake you've got two choices – change the mistake or stick with the mistake. You shouldn't be nonchalant about that."

Allen was nonchalant about nothing when he was on the whistle.

"If you're putting on the stripes because of you, then you got a problem. The best official is a non-existent official. He starts it, he watches the wrestlers do their thing, makes sure there are no illegal holds and makes the calls," Allen said. "When you get those stripes on and you had a 38 chest when you came into the arena, now you've got a 46 chest and you're going to work, you're going to miss calls. You're not going to be in position to prevent injury. You had a 38 chest when you came in, have a 38 chest when you leave. The officiating is a whole lot better now than when I first started out."

Allen said he had good mentors as he grew in officiating. The key, he said, was to surround himself with good people and to have his eyes and his ears open. Allen paid attention to Gene Luttrell and his way of working a match. He noticed how Mike Exline always had his arm raised high as he indicated points so as to insure all spectators a chance to see. He remembered how Bob Siddens handled people with dignity. One lesson learned: "Whether I was right or whether I was wrong, always treat people with respect."

In at least one instance, Allen said he kept the respect treatment while losing weight. He was contracted to work an Iowa State-Oregon State meet in Ames. Oregon State's coach at the time was Dale Thomas, who grew up in Marion. Thomas seemed to believe his team never got a break when it came to Iowa, and he told Allen as much before the meet.

"I bet I lost 22 pounds," Allen said. "After it was over, I'm signing the book and he says, 'Fella, come here a minute. I'm going to tell you right now young man, you screwed us both.'"

The next night Oregon State wrestled at Northern Iowa and Allen was working. He said Patten wanted to experiment with the idea of using two referees, so Luttrell joined him. "If you can be fair, you will be OK. I'll never forget Dale Thomas for that," Allen said, adding that he made sure to greet Thomas when they were at future tournaments such as the Pac-10 Conference meet together.

Allen also recalled working his first state tournament in Iowa.

"It didn't mean very much until the finals because there was a black basketball referee named (Ed) Hightower, and I always knew the good job he did. When I finally got the tournament, I had so many friends down there. Arlo Flege, I knew Bob McNeil at the time, Mike Exline was down there," Allen said. "I didn't realize the color significance until everyone would talk about it, that I was the first. So many people were helping me to get there and they knew who I was that it felt like being at home.

"I was representing more than just Mike. I got a son and a daughter, my mother and my father, and at the time I was married. I had to make sure I was not average because perception can go positively or negatively. By being a negative or bad official – at that point in time being the only black official in the state of Iowa and one of a few on the national level – that probably wouldn't allow too many of the other black officials to get the kind of meets (I had). I always felt like I was always in the spotlight, but I was more concerned about my son, Victor, and my daughter, Denise, because so many times the peer pressure....one of the things you have to admit, when I made a bad call, it wasn't, 'Who is that guy?' They always knew."

Allen said he wanted to work a sectional and a district tournament because of the perceived attachment those assignments had.

"If you did a sectional and a 3-A district, most of the time you were going to get the state tournament. The question was when you walked on the mat at Vets, with 15,000 people in there, eight mats, wall-to-wall people. You wanted to make sure you did the best for the kids. That's what I thought about at the time. I don't think I had the credibility that an Arlo Flege had at the time, and I don't think I had the credibility that Mike Exline had at the time. Then I got the finals – when we did it, we worked all three days – so I felt like as I was growing, Gene Luttrell was helping me. Bob Siddens was out there as I was growing."

His name grew quickly, according to longtime friend Phil Caldwell, a former assistant coach at East.

"When you are the only man of color, people recognize that quickly and you associate a name with the person," Caldwell said. "He and I are probably best friends. He happened to draw my son one time in a wrestling match. The reason I knew how fair Mike was, he was trying to withdraw from that match but he got stuck with it. I didn't agree with his calls, but it was a fair match and he treated everybody the same. I watched the way he always conducted himself out there. He was very professional with it, he didn't let friendship get in the way, he didn't let the buddy-buddy systems that sometimes exist get in the way. He was very well known for not letting a wrestler stall, he was quick to call stalling and he got well known for that."

As his name grew in officiating, the distance to a meet got longer. He was working meets in Madison, Wis., Champaign-Urbana, Ill. or Tempe, Ariz., rather than calling a meet in Gilbertville, Waterloo, Waverly or Cresco, Iowa. "I used to tell him all the time, 'Mike, they know you are fair and you are consistent. When you have a consistency with what you're doing, then you get good at it and people start calling for the best.' And that's what happened," Caldwell said.

Caldwell said there were two reasons why Allen shined as an official.

"One was he had a no-nonsense attitude, but he had integrity. People knew of his involvement in the schools and kids and stuff. Kids spot things quickly. If you are fake, a kid will spot it. If you're not sincere, a kid will spot it. His integrity stood out a lot," Caldwell said. "A lot of times he and I won't agree on stuff, but I know when he stands for something, he won't back down, and I admire him for that. His honesty, his integrity and his fortitude really stood out for him because he wouldn't back down and they knew that. Sure, he'd make a call and not everybody was going to agree with that, but he stood by what he said and that's what stood out about him to me."

Allen spoke previously about being at the top of your game. He was asked how often he was at that point during his career.

"I don't think I was ever at my best. Let's put it this way, I was not afraid to call an edge call," he said.

"When you've got Brad Smith as your coach, and you had Al Baxter, you never give up."

Brian Hall's method of winning a state wrestling championship is not likely to be found in a how-to guide. Hollywood might like it. Writers composing a far-out tale of a wrestling match could struggle matching Hall's real-life situation.

It gets mentioned here because of a blend of some amazing comebacks and great finishes at Iowa's state wrestling tournament. Hall's tremendous comeback sealed the Class 1-A team championship for Lisbon in 1980.

There have been periodic close finishes since team races became contested in 1921 at Ames. The closest margin was in 1984, when Dallas Center-Grimes tripped North Tama of Traer by one-half point. On 14 other occasions, the difference between the best and the second-best trophy was a single point. If there is one program closely associated with tight finishes it's Waterloo West, the state's most decorated program. The Wahawks won five of their 17 team titles by one point.

Hall said he never worried about being in tight matches or being behind because one truth in the wrestling gospel according to Lisbon coaches Al Baxter and Brad Smith was that losing was not an option.

"When you've got Brad Smith as your coach, and you had Al Baxter, you never give up," Hall said. "I guess I never once thought I was going to get beat, even being down. That was a mentality we had back in those days too."

But a 14-2 hole against Roy Keough of Nora Springs-Rock Falls seemed too much to climb out of that night. Especially since Hall fought back from a 5-1 deficit to beat Marty Davis 7-6 in the semifinals.

"That Roy Keough, one thing after another, whatever he had worked. He kept on turning me and turning me. No one had ever done that to me, I just couldn't believe it," Hall said.

"I couldn't believe it" or a variation thereof has been said countless times during and after matches at the state tournament. Perhaps it was a buzzer-beating takedown. Maybe it was a 4- or 5-point move seemingly out of nowhere. Sometimes it was a victory by a wrestler who had been beaten multiple times by the man he conquered in the finals. Whenever and however it happens, fans are bound to be talking about the great finishes for a long time. At least one coach uses an amazing finish as a teaching tool three decades later. Guys like Eric Keller, Jim Zalesky and Craig Garvin will never forget their finish.

"I talk about that Brian Hall match with my guys here still. In the long run, you want to teach kids that there always is a chance, not to give up, keep battling. It takes one situation, one flurry to take a guy, and if you get him on his back, don't let him up," said Iowa City High coach Brad Smith, who replaced Baxter at Lisbon in time to be in the corner of the Hall-Keough bout.

Smith said Hall had a weapon if the opportunity presented itself. "Brian Hall was in a situation where he had one move - a lateral drop. The guy got in position where he shouldn't have been and we took advantage of it," Smith said.

Hall remembered adhering to the 'don't let him up' part against Keough. "I had some pretty good shots that I relied on most of the time, but I had good hips and could throw. I set the move up real good, I hipped into him three or four times to make him push back. He pushed back and I threw him right into Smith's lap. He was out of bounds, I was inbounds and I picked him up and set him right back inbounds and to this day I still think I was touching the mat through his chest."

Hall's win followed a come-from-behind 7-6 state title at 98 pounds for the Lions' Brett Stoneking, who charged back from trailing 4-2 with a 3-point near fall and a reversal. The win by Hall clinched the team title that night – Smith's first as a head coach. Three matches after Hall, Scott Morningstar won his fourth state championship. Smith had a lot to celebrate that night, and he got a little air time as well after Hall's bout.

"I jumped about 8 feet in the air. Doing a lateral drop and pinned him, that was pretty awesome," Smith said.

Keller was one of four Indianola wrestlers in the Class 3-A finals of the 1994 tournament. He won a 103-pound state championship two years earlier. Keller wanted a second title, particularly after finishing third at 112 as a junior in 1993. "My goal, my dream had always been to be a three-time state champ at that point," Keller said.

In order to win a second title, Keller had to beat Nick Dohrmann of Iowa City West in the 119-pound finals. Dohrmann was going to wrestle at Iowa, so there were folks chatting him up as the winner that year. "Maybe some of it was being naïve or stupidity but I always felt like I was going to win," Keller said.

Dohrmann's path to the finals included a 12-7 victory in the quarterfinals over Jeff Bellows of Council Bluffs Lewis Central, who was ranked No. 1 at his weight. Bellows, who had an 86-match winning streak halted, had beaten Keller in the 1993 tournament.

"I showed up (thinking), 'I'm going to win this thing, I'm going to beat everybody by 15 points.' It took me a lot of years before I could say I got second," Dohrmann said.

Thanks to a low-level takedown with 1 second left in regulation, which resembled something from the arsenal of Oklahoma State star John Smith, Keller scored a 9-8 victory.

"A miracle had to happen. He needed a low single to get something to happen on the whistle and he got it. I always know he's never out of a match," Indianola coach Wes Creason said.

When reminded that the winning move resembled a John Smith shot, Keller replied, "Johnny would be proud," while he made no attempt to wipe a smile off his face. The victory clinched the first Class 3-A team title for Indianola. There was no stopping the Indians once they held a 16-point lead after the semifinals.

"We refer to it in Indianola as being 'on the juice,'" Creason said.

Juiced or not, Keller had to try a favored move against Dohrmann if he wanted a second piece of gold.

"The low single, that was a shot I always loved. John Smith was one of my favorite wrestlers when I was growing up, watching him hit low singles," Keller said. "The low single, the way he did it, was just perfection. I did spend a lot of time working on low singles, but to hit that low-level shot and to sweep the ankles out the way it did – it had to go that way, it couldn't have gone any other way – and the way I hit that was just instinct."

Dohrmann, now head coach at Wilton High School, said the Keller match still gets discussed. "People ask me what I remember about that match. I remember two takedowns - the first and the last. He got the first and took me to my back and he got the last," Dohrmann said.

That late takedown occurred soon after a restart when the wrestlers went out of bounds.

"I didn't think he was going to score, but I didn't think I had it won," Dohrmann said. "I figured, 'Three seconds, I'll put my foot on the line, I'll move it forward and I'm going to wrestle every second of the match.' It just so happened he came up there, I had my foot on the line first and he knew exactly what to do. He just circled up and…"

They became some of the more famous seconds in recent tournament history.

"Walking back to that line I didn't really think 'I'm doing this or doing this.' I walked back to that line thinking 'I'm going to win this' but instinct took over," Keller said. "To do it in that fashion the way it happened, I didn't even know what was going on. I was just elated, so many emotions. It's weird because I never even allowed myself to think like, 'What if that wouldn't have worked?' It just never occurred to me to think about what if I would have won just one state title?"

Keller had a three-point near fall in the first period and tried in vain to get more back points in the third period. He favored getting the job done early. "I knew I could save my mom and dad a lot of gray hairs that way," Keller told the *Des Moines Register* after the match.

Days before the tournament started, Keller received a good-luck note from his sister, Rachel, who was living in California. Included was a note from what appeared to be a desktop calendar collection of motivational comments. The note she sent was dated Feb. 19 – one week prior to the night of the finals – and proved to be amazingly prophetic. "Grind it out. Hanging on just one second longer than your competition makes you the winner," was the original comment. Rachel Keller added her own motivation: "You have been grinding it out and hanging on three seconds longer your whole life, so you will always be a winner to me…"

That passage and the sister's addition is posted on Keller's second state championship wall chart.

Eric Keller noticed the words on his sister's mailing after the dust from the tournament had cleared. "I never thought about it until after this whole thing. It was insane, so crazy. Just the fact that she used the 'three seconds…your whole life' and it went down like that."

Rachel Keller Tabibi said she chose the words because they fit how her brother went about his business. In late February 1994, she was a student at University of Northern Iowa – about 2 hours from Vets Auditorium.

"It wasn't really a self-filling prophecy, but it kind of just sums up Eric. He's kind of a fly-by-the-seat-of-his-pants, last-minute guy and he's going to go after it and do whatever he can to make it work in his favor,"

Tabibi said. "I can picture myself still standing there, even though seeing that time on the clock, knowing it was not over and he was going to win because that was his time. No doubt, no doubt, I knew it.

"I just remember racing back and forth daily from UNI to Vets to go to the tournament. My sister (Jennifer) and I joke about the car that we had - it didn't have any heat in it."

Eric Keller said he had a lot of good heat in the support of his father, Rich, who wrestled at Leon for future Hall of Fame coach Jack Mendenhall. "He was always there to support, always there to push me along but he never crossed the line," Eric Keller said. "I always had that confidence, the confidence coming from him, 'Hey man, I know you can do it.'"

Keller is coaching at Wartburg and has two sons of his own. Will he coach their Little League baseball teams like Rich Keller did? That remains to be seen, but he knows who he will emulate when he's raising his sons.

"I've thought a little about it because people say, '(They're) going to wrestle.' My goal, and this is not just wrestling but fatherhood and everything else, is to do it just like my dad did. Just to instill in them, 'Hey man, I'm with you, no matter what. And if you don't win, I'm still there.' He was always there to lift you right back up. That's what I want to be."

Dohrmann said he uses the experience of that championship match in coaching.

"I've done drills, three-second drills. We'll do three seconds on the line, how are you going to do it? I use my own experience to teach the kids I work with. I say, 'Hey, three seconds on the line, it can be done.' We do it with underneath too – three seconds on the line, can you get out in three seconds? Can you get out with two seconds?

"It's the old try. If you do it and it doesn't happen, you've got to tell the kid, 'Let's say we go back and do that match with three seconds 100 more times. He may only get it one time, but (Keller) did it when he needed it.' That's what you try to teach kids. Sure, three seconds on the line, you've got to get out. In practice you're going to fail it more than you're going to get it, but once you get it once, you know if you get in that big match, 'I've done it in practice and I can do it again.'"

In 1978, Jim Zalesky of Cedar Rapids Prairie believed he could win the Class 3-A 145-pound championship. All he needed was to make up for trailing Dick Marshall of Southeast Polk 5-0. In the final 15 seconds of the bout, Zalesky turned Marshall for a title-clinching 3-point near fall and an 8-6 victory.

"You just try to find a way to win. It's a thing wrestling breeds, a never-give-up attitude," Zalesky said. "A lot of that came from the coaches, maybe it goes back to that environment of Lisbon, Mount Vernon and Prairie, guys working out together and you get a lot of coaches preaching like (Lisbon coach Al) Baxter and (Prairie coach) Ron James to keep wrestling."

Prior to the state meet, it was common for Lisbon, Mount Vernon and Prairie wrestlers to practice together. Prairie had Zalesky and Barry Davis – future three-time NCAA champions and college head coaches – while Mount Vernon had Randy Majors – a future NCAA all-American – and Lisbon had Scott Morningstar – a future four-time state champion – and Jim Lord – a four-time finalist and three-time state champion. Baxter and James were neighbors in Lisbon, so coming up with practice plans was as simple as going to each other's house and going over details. Zalesky said having a go in practice with Lord was the kind of challenge a championship-minded wrestler craved.

"You always say you're a product of your environment. Well that environment was unbelievable with a lot of guys that wanted to win the state," Zalesky said. "If you know Jim Lord, you know he's the kind of guy who's going to try to kick your ass no matter how much time is left."

Time was running out on Prairie's bid to win a second Class 3-A state championship in 1995. Everything came down to the heavyweight finals, when Prairie's Trent Hynek faced Chad Deal of Council Bluffs Lewis Central. Prairie led Lewis Central, 76 ½-71, going into that bout. A pin by Deal would give the Titans the title by one-half point and tie them with Dallas Center-Grimes in 1984 for the closest margin of victory.

Hynek scored a 4-1 victory for the clincher as the Hawks gave coach Ron Peterson a sweet going-away present. Peterson was taking the job of wrestling coach at Simpson College, and he left being one of four coaches in state tournament history to have won a state championship at two different schools. Peterson led Clarksville to the Class 1-A title in 1991.

On at least one occasion, trickery helped produce a title-clinching victory. That was in 1926, the first year the Iowa High School Athletic Association ran the tournament. Ralph Goodale was Marshalltown's heavyweight and he faced Clarence Anderson of Fort Dodge in the finals. Goodale was familiar with the finals, winning the 175-pound title at the 1924 Iowa City Invitational and at the 1925 state invitational in Ames. Goodale also was apparently smitten with a young lady and Marshalltown faculty advisor Adolph Rupp, a future Hall of Fame college basketball coach, knew it.

According to a *Des Moines Register* story about Rupp's involvement with the championship, Rupp pretended to have a telegram from Goodale's sweetheart. "Tell him if he doesn't win the heavyweight championship, not to bother coming to my house for dinner Sunday," was the alleged note. Goodale got the fall in 48 seconds and Marshalltown got the team championship.

Marshalltown and Boone tied for the team title in the 1925 invitational. An overtime victory by Marshalltown heavyweight Eugene Fitz forged the tie, and the Bobcats won a coin flip for the first-place trophy.

Winning by a late pin is not limited to the final round. Ted Tuinstra of Des Moines East was tabbed as the favorite to win the Class A heavyweight championship in 1962. Jim Casey of Iowa City High did not get the message because he built an 8-2 lead over Tuinstra during the first round of competition. Tuinstra came back and pinned Casey with 5 seconds remaining. He got that state championship two matches later with his second straight 3-1 decision, this one against Bob Hartliep of Waterloo West.

Tuinstra, who passed away in 2011, was the most recent of East's three individual state champions.

Bob Siddens of Waterloo West boasts the most team championships won by a coach with 11. His first title came in 1951 – his first season at West – without the benefit of an individual champion. His last came through a big finish by Craig Garvin at 132 pounds in 1977.

Garvin used what *Waterloo Courier* sports editor Russ L. Smith described as a "freestyle-type hip toss" to score five points and defeat Al Melchers of Fairfield, 8-4, for the Class 3-A 132-pound championship. A highlight of the finish, according to Smith's story, was the uncharacteristic celebrating by Siddens. The story reported Siddens to be jumping up and down as Garvin held Melchers for the 3-point near fall.

That was a smashing end to the Wahawks' tournament for Siddens, who the *Courier* reported was involved in an automobile accident the day before the tournament started.

The Wahawks got their one-point titles in 1945, 1952, 1955, 1965 and 1971. Heavyweight Bud Knox clinched the 1965 championship by beating Dale Stearns of Chariton, 2-1, in the finals. That helped ease the memory of the 1964 state tournament for Knox. Waterloo East went five-for-five in the tournament, but West could have forced a tie if Knox got a pin in beating Kent Osboe of Fort Dodge for the third time that season. Osboe

416

won, 8-7, and arguably the best state tournament showing by a team was preserved.

An equally exciting end to Eagle Grove's bid for its second state team championship in eight years was the reward to anyone who stayed late on championship night in 1982. The Eagles held a 104 ½-100 ½ lead, so they could live with Emmetsburg heavyweight Doyle Naig beating Jon Vrieze of Forest City in the finals. They could tolerate an 11-point victory. It would have been just ducky if Vrieze won.

Their allegiance was clearly defined by the crowd's chants. Eagle Grove fans and any outside supporters were rooting for Vrieze. Emmetsburg fans and their friends chanted "Stick him" to Naig.

Naig got the fall in 5 minutes 22 seconds and Emmetsburg locked up its first championship since 1979 – when the E'Hawks completed their run of four consecutive titles. The E'Hawks finished with 106 ½ points, two more than the Eagles.

New Hampton fans could have taken notes at the 1982 tournament on how to handle a drawn-out championship round. Actually it was a winner-take-all situation in 1993 for New Hampton and West Lyon of Inwood. New Hampton had individual titlists in Kelly Seery at 112 and David Morgan at 135, but in order to beat West Lyon they would need Chad Utley to come through at 189 pounds. Utley faced Chad Koedam of West Lyon.

Utley won, 5-2, and the Chickasaws had their fifth outright championship, their sixth of at least a tie. New Hampton shared the 1933 title with Cresco.

That was the last time two teams shared the traditional team title. Osage and Humboldt shared the Class 2-A championship in the 1992 dual-meet state tournament. The Class 3-A team race at the 2011 traditional tournament could have ended in a tie. Iowa City West finished with 150 points, but lost two points for conduct unbecoming. Waverly-Shell Rock won its fourth straight team title as heavyweight Cody Krumweide delivered a 10-0 major decision over Bettendorf's Brody Berrie and vaulted the Go-Hawks from third to first. Krumweide's win gave the Go-Hawks 152 points. If Berrie would have won and West was not penalized the team points, Bettendorf and West would have tied.

In 1993, West Lyon held an impressive 11-point lead over New Hampton going into the final round. The Wildcats could have put it out of reach with Terry Zuraff's victory at 119 pounds, but Carlisle's Doug

Titus refused to cooperate. Titus won, 6-5, to set up the finish. Koedam was West Lyon's other finalist.

New Hampton won by one point. "We knew going into the finals that we could win, so it was kind of disheartening to finish second when you had a good feeling you could finish first," West Lyon coach Ty Seaman told the *Lyon County Reporter*. "I'm sure in a week or two everyone will feel real good about how they did."

That good feeling had to wait. West Lyon and New Hampton met the following Saturday in the the Class 2-A finals of the dual-meet state tournament. Utley beat Koedam again, this time 3-2, as New Hampton posted a 29-18 victory.

Some of the other one-point finishes included:

- Davenport Assumption edging New Hampton for the Class 2-A crown in 1999. Jon Garvin won his second state title for the Knights, avenging his only loss (8-3 at the Osage Duals) by beating Ryan Sturm of Emmetsburg/Armstrong-Ringsted. New Hampton had three individual champions, and could have won the title if Jason Reicks scored at least a technical fall over Rex Gray of Clarke of Osceola at 171 pounds. Reicks won, but only by a 4-2 decision and the Knights became the first Class 2-A squad to win consecutive championships since Eagle Grove in 1986 and 1987.

- The same year the Knights won a nail-biter, Iowa City High won the Class 3-A in even tougher methods. The top-ranked Little Hawks, who dropped to eighth place after the semifinals, charged back through the consolation round and finally clinched the crown when Ryan Fulsaas of Decorah beat Mike Novak of Cedar Rapids Prairie, 16-5, in the heavyweight finals. A pin by Fulsaas would have caused Decorah and City High to share the title. "I was so nervous I had to walk around the auditorium," said City High coach Brad Smith, whose team won without an individual state champion.

- Bondurant-Farrar, Columbus Junction and Postville were all in position to win the Class 1-A championship in 1998. Bondurant-Farrar wound up the winner because of Tim Cory's major decision at 135 pounds, which put the Bluejays one point ahead of Columbus Junction. Rob Hoback won a championship at 145 for Columbus Junction, and could have forged a tie with a major decision. He was ahead, 11-3, after two periods but wound up with an 11-9 victory. Postville would have tied for the lead if Brent Meyers got a pin at 171 pounds, but he lost, 15-7, to Jed Vanlengen of Janesville.

- How important are consolation points? Ask the 1986 Charles City squad. The Comets trailed Marshalltown by 13 points after the semifinals, but they outscored the Bobcats, 21-4, in the consolation bracket. Marshalltown cut the lead to one with Dave Manchon's state championship at 98 pounds, but lost its other two finals matches. Charles City lost its two finals matches.

There have been several great finishes to the team race, but there is a limit to how long they can be dwelled upon before book deadlines interfere. Maybe there is a book of nothing but great team races in the works somewhere.

"If you're good at something, you don't have to tell anybody."

Jim Guyer wanted to be good enough in wrestling that his fellow students at North Fayette High School in West Union would applaud his effort.

Guyer and his two sons, Jym and Lance, heard that applause a total of four times during their wrestling careers. Jym won two championships while Jim and Lance each won one.

Jim remembered the applause in school the day North Fayette wrestlers Bob Trautman and Don Parker won first-round matches in the 1962 tournament in Cedar Falls. Trautman beat Jim Miles of Cedar Rapids Prairie, 9-3, at 138 pounds and Parker pinned Bill Cozzalino of Camanche in 2 minutes 51 seconds at 165 pounds. Parker would become North Fayette's first state champion the following season.

In 1962, the results were relayed to the school by a telephone call from coach Blake Brown. The students who did not go to Cedar Falls got the results over the PA system.

"I was a freshman and (Parker) was a junior. I was in my seventh period class and the coach had called back and said they had won their matches. This was right before school got out and I remember everybody just applauding," Guyer said. "I was a little freshman. I'd gone to a country school so I was really a naïve kid, had never wrestled before, but I did wrestle that year. (The applause) just excited me and I thought to myself right then, 'I want to be down there so they can call back and say, "Jim Guyer won his first match" and imagine the applause. That was really something for me."

Parker would become a two-time NCAA Division II national champion at Northern Iowa, Trautman and Guyer were all-Americans for the Panthers.

The Guyers, the Martin family of Algona, the Hagens of Clarion and Britt, the Woods of Centerville and Chariton, the Hinschbergers of Belle Plaine and the Kriegers of Mason City…they all know the feeling of an Iowa state champion who had two of his sons win a title. The Ballweg family of Waverly knew an interstate version of that story. Tom Ballweg was a state champion in Wisconsin. Three of his sons – Matt, Mark and Jake – won a total of seven Class 3-A state titles for Waverly-Shell Rock. The stories are likely not embellished as the years go on. They might be little more than, "Yes, I won it." The best evidence could be seeing the filled-out weight bracket dad competed in. The record book lists them by surname but does not indicate fathers and sons.

"He may have (told us) and I just don't remember it, but it would be very unlike him to go back and tell us how good he was when he wrestled or what he did," Paul Martin said of his father, Leon "Champ" Martin. "That just wasn't his style at all. His theory always was, 'If you're good at something, you don't have to tell anybody. They'll figure it out, they'll know it.' I just really doubt if he would have ever dwelled much on what he did. He'd be more inclined to try to motivate us."

Gary Wood said he approached wrestling the way Kermit Wood approached life.

"My dad believed if you're going to do something, you better do it right and you work hard at it. Anything worth having is worth working for," Gary said. "He grew up in a tough situation, and we just grew up to be tough."

In the end, the applause dad heard is similar to what his sons heard. It was likely louder for the second generation because the crowd numbers were bigger, but hearing that cheering is a monster motivator. You just hope no one drops the ball. When Guyer opened the 1965 tournament at McElroy Auditorium in Waterloo, he pinned Ted Gere of Greenfield in 3 minutes 5 seconds at 154 pounds. That applause Parker got in school never happened for Guyer. Brown forgot to call the school.

"I thought about it at the time. This so disappointed me because the coach forgot to call back. I can't tell you how devastated I was after that first match," Guyer said. "For three years, I wanted that to be me. I was the only one there. I didn't know it at the time but he told me later he'd forgotten to call."

Brown made it up to his wrestler later.

"I'd ridden down with the coach in his own personal car. This is something that would never happen in this day and age," Guyer said, "but he let me and the kids who went down with me take his car out on Friday night, so we went to the movies in Waterloo."

Guyer won his championship with a 6-5 victory over Jason Smith of Ankeny, who took his first loss in 15 matches. Smith led, 4-2, after two periods and got a takedown in the third period for a 5-3 lead. A reversal tied the score, and Guyer's riding Smith for nearly all of the second period paid off because Guyer's victory was secured by 1 minute 17 seconds of riding time. Anything more than a minute in advantage time scored a point. "Back then we could stall," he said with a laugh.

That North Fayette applause Guyer missed Friday showed up Saturday night.

"We rode back on the pep bus, so I got a big thrill when I got on the pep bus after the match on Saturday night. Then I got the big applause, it all made up for it," Guyer said.

Guyer said he remembers more the time leading up to the finals match than he does the bout. Smith was an African-American whose physique cast an imposing figure.

"I'm a kid from northeast Iowa who'd probably never seen three black men in person in my life. My perception at that time was black people were supermen, unbeatable," Guyer said. "This kind of psyched me out I guess. I can remember watching him warm up. If you remember Jason, and through college too, he was kind of a funky guy, and he was wearing these old swaddly clothes and that's basically all I remember."

Guyer said he learned a lesson from Brown that he used as head coach at his alma mater a few years later. "When I was a freshman, one night (Brown) told me I was going to be a state champ. That's another thing I'll never forget," Guyer said. "I used that when I was coaching. You've got to tell kids, you've got to make them believe."

Did Brown see something? "I don't know because technically I always figured I was always the third- or fourth-best wrestler on the team," Guyer said. "I still think that today, but for some reason it never surprised me that I did it. Part of it is because he told me I was going to be."

Guyer said he also remembered little things about that night in 1965, such as Class AA 145-pound champion Phil Henning of nearby Decorah buying him an ice cream bar.

Guyer must have used Brown's line on his son, Jym. The younger Guyer won Class 2-A titles in 1986 (155) and in 1987 (167) with dad in the corner. By the time Lance won at 190 pounds in 1998, dad had resigned as head coach. Just because the Guyer boys were the wrestling coach's sons, they did not live and breathe the sport. Both were outstanding football players for the Hawks.

"I didn't want them to feel any pressure. I wanted them to go to the kid tournaments, but I would make them earn money to go and beg to go," Jim said. "I wanted them to want it. They're both very mentally tough and I think that's why. We never talked about (wrestling) at home unless they brought it up, even when I was coaching my own."

There was an element of surprise in each son's championship, Jim said.

"It was a kind of a surprise that (Jym) won it as a junior. There was a kid named (Rick Bigalk) from Cresco, who had placed fourth the year before and had actually pinned Jimmy in the sectional or district. He was back at his weight," Jim said. "We really didn't expect to be a state champ that year because Bigalk had handled him so overwhelmingly as a sophomore. That was a big surprise."

Lance decided he was not going to sweat controlling his weight as a senior, so he wrestled at 189 – about four pounds above his natural weight – in his championship season.

"He had started the year maybe ranked sixth or seventh and he'd jumped two weights. He decided he wasn't going to cut any weight…so he was small. He beat some good kids early on and he jumped in the ratings, but we still didn't know," Jim said.

Lance cleared a hurdle by beating 1997's 160-pound champion, Drew Bouwman of West Lyon of Inwood, 6-3, in the quarterfinals. Lance beat Nick Paulsen of Atlantic, 5-2, in the championship bout.

Jim laughingly remembered one little thing from each of his sons' title match: Henning never bought them an ice cream bar.

"I just can't imagine what my life would have been like without wrestling. It's just meant so much to me, and not just my kids," Jim said. "Some of my very most admired kids were not the ones who won, but the ones you knew never would but stuck it out and worked hard. Some of them never made varsity, but those are the type of kids you really have to admire. Not everybody has the talent and most of them, when they find out somewhere along the line they don't have the talent, most of them will give it up."

The Guyers decided to differentiate between father and son when James Jr. came along, thanks in part to television. The Waterloo television station, KWWL, had a weatherman in those days named Jym Ganahl.

"He spelled his name that way and we thought that would be kind of cool, so that's where that came from."

Jym has three daughters, but Jim might have a chance to watch another Guyer win a state title. Lance and his wife, former University of Iowa basketball player Kristie Faulkner, had a baby boy.

Gary Wood was not the baby of his family, but he had to watch his step when he watched his brother, Kermit Jr., in wrestling practice at Chariton. Gary got invited to practice by Chariton coach Bill Marsole, but he was under Kermit's threat of kicking his kiester if he got in the way of the varsity guys. "I knew it was a long walk home to be limping the whole way home," Gary said.

That toughness Kermit Sr. preached helped in odd ways. Gary was once put through a wall at the family's house after moving to Centerville. Another time there was an attempt to throw him out of a second-floor window while he was scrapping with a neighbor boy.

When the Woods moved to Centerville, there was no junior high wrestling program as Gary was coming through. He started on the basketball team – "We only lost one junior high basketball game the whole time," he said – but continued his desire to wrestle. In eighth grade, Gary occasionally worked out with the varsity Big Reds.

"I knew that's what I wanted to do, so I started as a freshman with not one bit of experience. Just a little bit watching it and a little bit playing around with it," Gary said.

After qualifying for the district meet as a freshman and sophomore, Gary placed fifth at 126 pounds as a junior. "I never went to a state tournament until I was a sophomore in high school. I went and watched it and thought, 'That's what I want to do.'"

Any other thoughts? "It was like a big barn, it could hold a lot of hay," Gary said.

Gary knew he wanted a state title as a senior. No Centerville wrestler had done that since the program started in 1967.

"I did a lot of extra things to try to be good. I did a lot of extra running, but also do a lot of hard labor," Gary said. "My dad would have a rock pile and I'd shovel it all up and move it, then move it back just to keep active. He kept me busy."

Gary beat Lyle Clabaugh of South Hamilton of Jewell, 13-3, in the 132-pound championship match. Gary said he expected to meet Clabaugh much earlier in the tournament. Dave Howlett of Britt was eyed as the man to beat. Howlett was the 126-pound state champion in 1973. Wood beat Howlett, 7-3, in the first round.

"What was strange was having to wrestle who I wrestled first round. I wasn't expecting that. I was expecting to wrestle Clabaugh and not Howlett, first round. Then I had to wrestle (John) Reicks from Turkey Valley – he was the only kid that took me down all year," Gary said. "After that, back then you'd weigh in and then you could eat up, well I felt pretty good come the finals. I hit an outside carry right off the bat and put (Clabaugh) right to his back for 5 points. After that, I knew I had things pretty much in control. He reached, I hooked his arm and did the outside carry to a 5-point move. I legged a lot, I'd put the legs in, hammer on you, tire you out."

Alex Paul of the *Centerville Iowegian* called Wood "a one-man bombshell for coach Larry Casey throughout his four-year career."

Casey has a special place in Gary's high school memories. "I had a coach who never wrestled a day in his life, but he went to the Air Force Academy and he did a lot of (research). He had an uncanny knack of getting the very best out of every student-athlete he ever worked with. He was like that in the classroom too," Gary said.

Gary said winning the state title was a ground-breaking moment for the Centerville program. "It broke the ice, then other people thought they could do it," Gary said. "It's just like at Chariton. Ron Poush was Chariton's first state champion (in 1964), but it was (1997) before Chay won it. Then after Chay won it, Taylor won it then after that (Clint) Sellers and (Avery) Fuhs....once the ice is broken, then people think this is achievable."

Gary went to college at William Penn College in Oskaloosa. He learned to hit holds with vigor and finish quickly by working out with bigger teammates such as 177-pounder Andy Davidson and 190-pounder Mike Burggraff. It worked because Gary won an NCAA Division III 150-pound championship for the Statesmen in 1979.

"I guess I was always self-motivated. I really wanted to be good at it," Gary said. "That's the way it was when I was coaching, I wanted to be good at it. Now I work bird dogs and I don't do things half-ass, I like to be the best at it."

After college, Gary wanted to coach. "I was one of those people – I could watch a move, pick it up and do it. I wanted to relay that on," he said. He coached in high school at Chariton

For all of the enjoyment he got in being Centerville's first state champion, Gary got more from watching Chay and Taylor reach the same spot their father did. "I just enjoyed watching them wrestle," Gary said. "I was coaching at Simpson, so I was not always able to get to their meets. We'd break down film and figure what to work on, concentrate on things at tournament time. They both had a real intense attitude. Chay was an all-state football player as well. I thought, in my mind, he was a better wrestler, but he pursued football for a while. They all had that attitude that if you're going to beat me, you better beat me because I'm going to battle with you."

Like father, like sons. The attitude went too far once, when Chay got kicked out of the state tournament for fighting, but those instances were rare.

"It feels good to have your children win it. Wrestling is important to us. I think they learned a lot about dealing with things in life," Gary said, adding he learned what his mother went through attending his matches in high school. "You don't realize what the parents have to go through until you sit back and watch it. Watching my own two, there is a lot of stress on parents. It's neat to watch those families. It brings a closeness to their families, something they can never take away. Sometimes I think you need a little luck too, because you've got to stay healthy. I've had kids who came up sick before sectional or district or they get injured. There are too many variables that can happen."

State was also an opportunity for Chay and Taylor to keep their uncle in line. Glen Wood of Oskaloosa, Gary's younger brother, worked 17 state tournaments as a referee.

The state tournament was a regular event for the Hagen family, partly because Britt had some good wrestlers. Wally Hagen ran a grocery store in Britt that had a big picture window – a great place to hang pictures of the Britt wrestlers for all to see as they walked or drove by.

As the 1967-68 season dawned, it was time for Hagen to put a picture of his son in the window. John was a 95-pound freshman. That was a big weight for the Hagen family. Wally was the only high school wrestler to beat three-time state champion Dick Hauser of Waterloo West and he won a state championship for Clarion at 95 in 1943 and 1944.

"He didn't bring it up to me much, but I saw his scrap books so I kind of asked him about it," John said. "Dad wasn't one to brag."

When the family moved to Britt, Wally put a wrestling mat in the basement. Another mat appeared in his backyard during the summer. After all, it was a wrestling neighborhood. The Stevenson brothers lived two houses away, and they would win five state championships. Britt coach Al DeLeon lived nearby, and he would lead the Eagles to three team championships.

John reached the state finals as a freshman before losing to Ted Derscheid of Clarion. John then set a goal and went to work on it.

"I would say I had a goal and that was to be a three-time state champion. My father was a two-timer and as a senior he had a problem and didn't win it," John said. "In order to do that, I had to work hard. I wasn't the strongest guy, I wasn't the fastest guy, but I was probably one of the smartest guys wrestling. I never did anything that would put myself in jeopardy. I didn't make too many mistakes."

He never lost again in high school after Derscheid pinned him. John went his last 84 matches without a loss, the blemish being a draw with eventual state champion Steve Natvig of Waterloo East as a sophomore. "I did have a big fear of losing. It was more losing than winning. I think that's kind of common in a lot of successful athletes, it's the thought of losing that kind of bothers a guy," John said.

John's first championship was at 95 pounds and came 25 years after his dad's last title. There was not the usual family celebration with hugs and kisses. "My family was not huggers. We just kind of looked at each other and basically shook hands with dad," John said. "I'm not even going to say I ever hugged my mother, other than when she got older. Mom was never a real demonstrative person, she or my dad."

Wally did pass some moves on to his son, but not his favored keylock. That became illegal.

"Dad taught me the switch, which was my signature move. That's basically all I ever needed in high school was the switch," John said. "He taught me a half-nelson, which I didn't use much. He taught me how to ride a guy, and that's one thing I was pretty good at. Most times when I wrestled a guy, they never got their stomach off the mat."

John said the Hagen family ranks among the top producers in the state.

"Back in our day, it wasn't like there was a four-time champion every year like there is now. When you were a three-time champion, that was a big deal back then," John said. "You were up there with Gable and all the guys that won it. When you got a father and two sons that win eight titles, two seconds and a semifinal, I feel we're right up there with anybody else in the family names in the state."

The third member of the Hagen gang was four years behind John.

Brent would run the family's string of finals appearances to eight in a row. He won in 1972, 1973 and in 1975. He was second in 1974.

Brent remembered his dad as a big supporter of the sport. "He was pretty humble about it, but he really encouraged wrestling. He had a true love for the sport. That was before they started these little kid tournaments. We always went to the Britt wrestling meets or the Clarion meets. I was pretty young when we moved from Clarion to Britt, but he always kept us around the sport," Brent said.

He had a good practice partner as he was learning the sport. "My brother being 4 years older than I was, he'd come home after practice and we'd have another practice. He'd show me moves," Brent said. "My dad, the only thing he ever talked to us about was when you pin them, have a wide base with your legs and post your forehead.

"(John) helped me tremendously though by every day he'd come home from practice and I'd want to have practice. We had an Iowa State-Oklahoma State meet almost every night in our basement and he would let me do moves. Finally when I got a little too cocky he would just pound on me."

Brent went out a winner in 1975, beating Jim Makey of Guthrie Center, 4-1, at 112 pounds. That started a pretty good night for the Eagles, who qualified three guys and had three state champs – Hagen, Duane Cook at 119 and Mark Stevenson at 145. Britt was second to Lisbon that year.

"I couldn't say that even going through the process that I knew the significance of what the Hagen family was doing, what my brother had done, what I was doing," Brent said. "It was just kind of expected of us. Coach DeLeon never talked about just going to state, it was all about winning state and he never really talked about that until the week before the sectional tournament. I knew more that my mom in her senior year was the state tournament queen than I knew that my dad had won two state titles.

"I honestly didn't even know Britt had a four-time state champion, that's how focused I was. I just was focused on winning. I hated losing so bad, that was probably my main motivation."

Brent, like John, said the family name is strong in Iowa high school wrestling circles. "I think it's a pretty good deal when you've got three people that have eight titles among them and that for eight years in a row there was a Hagen in the state finals," he said. "I had the best possible dad to have as a wrestler because he loved the sport so much that he would have helped me in any way. His other main focus was during the season, your coach is going to coach you. He was always there for support. My mom was there to kick me in the butt if I felt sorry for myself."

Mary Lois Hagen didn't like how some people reacted to losing.

"I wrestled my first dual meet as a freshman against Clear Lake and I get pinned. I made a mistake in the first period and in the second period I tried to come back and I got pinned. I literally cried the whole meet," Brent said. "When I walked in the house, my mom grabbed me by the ear, 'Son, you're probably going to get beat again. If you cry like that, you're not going to ever wear a singlet again because I'm not going to have a son of mine let that guy beat you twice.' He beat me on the mat and beat me again because I showed it, so we didn't show much emotion."

Brent only lost four times in his high school career.

In Algona, Paul Martin did very little losing. When your father – best known by his moniker "Champ" - has won two of his four team championships and your older brother, Dave, has two state championships and an NCAA title by the time you get into high school, people expect you to be cut of a similar cloth.

Paul was one of two freshmen in the 1971 tournament and he finished with a 19-9 record. He never lost again, winning 90 in a row and three state championships.

"I played football all four years of high school, but wrestling was definitely my first love. That's basically because I grew up in a wrestling family: dad was a coach, both of my older brothers wrestled," Paul said. "There wasn't any real pressure put on us to be wrestlers, but that's what we grew up around. I always wanted to wrestle for Algona and I think it evolved from there."

"Champ" coached Dave and Bob on varsity, but he retired before Paul moved up. Dale Bahr, a two-time champion from Iowa Falls and an NCAA champion at Iowa State, was Paul's coach and sometimes workout partner.

"To have a guy like Dale Bahr as a workout partner…he was bigger when I first started but by the time I was a senior we were pretty close in size. That's a huge advantage to have somebody like that as your coach that not only can teach you but can be a workout partner," Paul said. "Dale was an outstanding mat wrestler. He had a side roll, he could wrestle with the best of them, as far as the side roll. In fact, it was a move that I used quite a bit in college.

"I think any wrestler that's had success is going to tell you that you're only as good as the workout partners. Mark Harris was future Division I all-American, we had some good kids but to have somebody like Dale Bahr, that was better than I was obviously, and to have to strive to be able to take him down or hold him down or get away from him, that's a huge advantage."

Paul had no worries about wrestling for his father. "Champ" was Bahr's assistant when Paul was a senior. "If we did something wrong or he thought we could do something better, he'd let us know but it wasn't like, 'If I don't do this move right or if I don't win a match, my dad's going to come down hard on me.' It wasn't that at all, I would have loved to wrestle for him."

The third title afforded Paul generous applause from the crowd. There had been one four-time champion at that time and 18 others had won three since 1926. "The fans in Iowa are tremendous wrestling fans. I do remember a four-timer was (almost) unheard of and a three-timer, there weren't very many, so when you win your third title, even people that may not like you as a wrestler or don't like your school, those people stand up and it's a big deal. To do that with my dad in the corner, that was a big thing."

Paul passed on working again with Bahr at Iowa State – when Bahr left Algona, "Champ" returned as head coach – or training at Iowa with Dan Gable – Dave's college roommate – when he went to college. Dave was an assistant coach at Oklahoma State.

"People from Iowa that have had some success in the wrestling world generally go to Iowa and Iowa State, there's very few people that don't go to one of the state schools for obvious reasons," Paul said. "Quite frankly when it came right down to it, I went to Oklahoma State because that's where my brother was. And at that time, at the weight class I was at, Chuck Yagla was at Iowa, Pete Galea was at Iowa State and Oklahoma State really didn't have somebody coming back. I knew I could start there immediately. I wrestled four years at Oklahoma State. Back then, you wanted to go somewhere where you could wrestle for four years. That coupled with the fact my brother was down there, that's pretty much why I went there."

Paul was a three-time all-American in Stillwater, including an NCAA runner-up finish at 167 in 1978.

Kurt Hinschberger started wrestling in Belle Plaine, but a family move put him in Bob Darrah's practice room at West Des Moines Dowling for one season. Once he returned to Belle Plaine, Kurt started working on building an impressive family name in the sport.

Kurt won a Class 1-A championship in 1978 and a Class 2-A title in 1979 for the Plainsmen. Recently retired Belle Plaine coach Bob Yilek was Hinschberger's teammate. "Kurt and I were best friends going through high school. Kurt moved in and we became friends and hung out. Obviously we wrestled together," Yilek said, adding that he didn't qualify for state as a sophomore but went to Des Moines as a spectator and stayed with the Hinschbergers.

"Kurt was 119, I was 126 so obviously you know the rest of the story," Yilek said. "We were workout partners day-in and day-out and he was my ride to school in the morning, so we spent a lot of time together."

Yilek remembered Hinschberger as a disciplined kid who had an advantage once he got some points on the board. "Once he scored his points, it was pretty much a done deal," Yilek said.

Hinschberger married an older sister of twins Kurt and Kevin Shedenhelm of Belle Plaine. The Shedenhelm brothers wrestled at Northern Iowa. When the Hinschbergers had children, they passed along a good championship gene. Shanna was a member of a state champion relay team. Dustin was a state champion wrestler in 2002 and Drew won a title on the mat in 2009. Dustin later was a dominating wrestler in NCAA Division III, winning three championships for Wartburg.

"Our family is really competitive. We like being successful at what we're going to do and we work hard," Dustin said.

One of Yilek's assistant coaches during his time as head of the Plainsmen was Kurt Hinschberger. "It was really kind of neat that I not only was his teammate, now he and I were going to coach together and we were going to coach his sons. Having the opportunity to help Kurt coach his boys was really a neat experience for me, and having a good high school friend as one of my assistants – we kind of shared the same philosophy – was really kind of special in my coaching career."

Dustin said he didn't need dad harping at him in high school about being in uniform on Saturday night at Vets Auditorium. He had a good idea of its coolness already committed to memory.

"I think as a kid, you grow up and you go to the state tournament and you watch that state finals match all the time. It's just burned into your mind, you picture yourself wrestling in the finals with that many fans. You picture yourself winning that match and seeing your fans go crazy down there," Dustin said. "Having a dad that won two state titles was motivating for me, just because I wanted to live up to those same goals. I wanted to win state titles. Having him in the house, he kind of put you down the right path and kind of directed you where to go. He never forced you to do anything but recommended if your goal is to win a state title, this is probably what you need to be doing."

Yilek said there was a quality that made it easy to identify the bloodline of Dustin and Drew. "The styles were a little bit different, but the same work ethic, the same motivation. That was developed as they were going through," Yilek said.

At Mason City, Herb Krieger gave his sons, Todd and Tim, an opportunity to learn the sport of wrestling by helping to start a youth program. "Hopefully they would be competitive, I didn't know how far they would go," Herb said. "I guess you always hope they'll do great, but I felt that I wanted them to be competitive when they got out there. That was my main objective, and then down the road, hopefully if they do good… which worked out, they both prevailed."

Tim said the best part was how dad gave him room to grow without harsh criticism.

"He never said one disparaging word about how I wrestled. I will say that with absolute respect and gratitude. There was never one negative word about my wrestling that I heard," Tim said.

Todd said dad was happy to become a fan as his sons reached high school. "He was actually pretty good about the way he trained us. He hauled us around when we were little kids. He didn't push us super-hard, just took us to every tournament like everybody else. Once we got to high school he turned us loose and let us go with the high school coaches."

Twenty years and three days after Herb won his state championship – he'd lost in the semifinals to Mel Wieland of Cedar Rapids Jefferson in 1960 and in 1961 – Tim and Todd won state championships. Mason City was second to Bettendorf in the 1982 Class 3-A tournament.

"It was terrific, one of the best nights ever for me to enjoy wrestling," Herb said. "Plus we had two other state champs from Mason City. It's something you'll never forget and very few people have the opportunity to enjoy something like that."

Todd said his dad was not one to point out his accomplishment.

"We had a little room down below and he had his state championship bracket there. We saw that," Todd said. "Maybe as little kids, when we were going to little kid tournaments, he might have showed us that stuff but I never remember him talking about it as we were older."

Tim added, "My old man, that's who he is, kind of short on words."

The media caught on to the accomplishment quickly, Todd recalled.

"It got to be a big deal afterwards. The next day the papers were calling. Then we realized it was kind of cool," Todd said. "Maybe everybody was talking about it beforehand but they sure never brought it to us, which I suppose was by design."

When Herb gave way to Mason City coach Jerry Ray, Tim and Todd said they got to work with a man who was good in his forward thinking.

"There were other good coaches, but he was light-years ahead of a lot of people back in the day. He was a big fitness guru. We were doing interval training back in the 80's," Todd said. "A lot of people hadn't even heard of that back then. His demeanor just kind of fit everybody. He wasn't a guy that raised his voice, he was just one of those cool, calm guys that fit in good with all of us. We were really lucky."

Ray said, "It's a system that you've got to get the kids to buy into, and certainly they did after much implementation. Once they bought into it, they weren't sure what was happening to their bodies during those sessions because we would peak them so much at times. It made sense to me to use the kind of things that would get the kids in shape and hopefully peak at the right time at the end of the season."

Tim said Ray had an amazing rapport with the Mohawks.

"In my mind, I can't tell you how good Jerry Ray was. He didn't care about individual records or titles, he just cared about the kids having a great experience and he cared about them getting better as wrestlers," Tim said. "He was always researching training. It wasn't just come in and make your eyes bleed, he did interval training. He was so far ahead of his time. I went to Iowa State...I took what Jerry had taught me and kind of did my own stuff."

Practice was fun, Tim said, especially considering the alternative. "Going to wrestling practice was fun, easy compared to working for the old man. It was vacation," Tim said.

"He did not wrestle like a freshman."

The Etherington family joined a modest club at the 2010 state wrestling tournament when Jesse Etherington was one of Charles City's four qualifiers. Membership does not always mean everyone wins a state championship, but it speaks well of the bloodline.

Does that surname ring a bell? Algona fans know it for championships. Jason won the Class B 133-pound championship in 1960. His son, Jason Jr., won a Class 2-A title at 119 pounds in 1983. Jesse is Jason Jr.'s son, and he placed fourth in Class 2-A at 125 pounds as a freshman in 2010. Jesse's bid to get another medal at state in 2011 was rejected because he was beaten twice in the district tournament.

They are not the first family to have three generations of qualifiers, but the elder Jason would love to cheer a third-generation state champion as soon as the 2012 tournament. Bud Legg, information director for the Iowa High School Athletic Association, said his office is not aware of three generations of gold medalists in an Iowa wrestling family. Some of the three-generation qualifiers include the Gasts of Osage (Dick, Bruce and Ben), the Luederses of Clinton and Northeast of Goose Lake (Bob, J. D. and Eric, Cole and Spencer), the Kriegers of Mason City (Herb, Todd, Tim and Clint), the Fleges of Waverly, Waverly-Shell Rock and Cedar Rapids Prairie (Arlo, Stacy and Jayden) and the Sharps of Clarion and Ankeny (Ernie, Bob and Ryan). There are likely many more, but a cross-search of tournament opening rounds since 1921 has yet to be undertaken.

Jayden Flege qualified for the Class 3-A state tournament for Prairie in 2011. His first-round opponent? Spencer Derifield of Waverly-Shell Rock. Jayden's father, Stacy, wrestled for Waverly-Shell Rock and grandfather, Arlo, wrestled for Waverly High School and then served on the Waverly-Shell Rock school board for 27 years. Arlo also served on the Iowa High School Athletic Association's Board of Control – which sets up rules and policies for high school athletes in the state – for several years.

Jason Etherington Sr. was a proud grandpa at the 2010 tournament.

"I'm really proud of what the kid accomplished. When he qualified for the state tournament that felt just awesome," Jason Sr. said. "I was amazed. The ending of his season just blew me away, it really did. He did not wrestle like a freshman."

Jason Jr. was similarly impressed. "It was pretty cool. It was a long time coming. Like I said, both of my boys started when they were 4 ½. Even now, you still think about it and go, 'Wow.' I never even had a winning record (as a freshman). It was probably a little more for my dad than me, a lot of pride there."

Jesse said he knew early in life how big getting to wrestle at state was.

"I've known that my whole life, ever since I was little. I knew my dad and grandpa always talked about state wrestling. We never talked about the season wrestling, just down at state, all of the experiences down here," Jesse said. "My dad was talking about how the guy calls your name and when he says, 'Wrestlers clear the mats…' he'd tell me how much of an adrenaline rush it is."

Ed Winger, whose commanding "Wrestlers, clear the mats…" opened every session of competition, stepped away from the public address microphone after the 2008 tournament. "It was kind of sad when I heard he was retired from doing it," Jesse said.

Jesse wants to hear his name called several times at a state tournament.

"Since they both won it, they know what it's like to wrestle through the whole tournament and do well each match. We've talked about winning it before. That's my goal," Jesse said.

Jesse also learned that grandpa really did know his way around a wrestling mat. Jason Sr. helped his grandson get ready for an AAU tournament. The elder Etherington recalled, "When I left, he told Jason, 'You know for an old guy, grandpa can still shoot pretty good.'"

The start of the Etherington championships came one year after Jason Sr. got a lesson on how quickly fortunes can change in a wrestling match. In 1960, Jason Sr. had only a draw marking his nine regular-season matches, according to the *Algona Upper Des Moines* newspaper. He was described by the paper as "unheralded as a wrestler until mid-season a year ago." With a 7-4 victory over Jim Deutsch of New Hampton in the Class B tournament, he was praised for scoring 12 points and placing the Bulldogs ninth as their lone qualifier. "His one-man point finish at the state is listed as one of the finest performances of all-time," the paper reported.

In 1959, Jason Sr. was pinned in the Class B 127-pound finals by Joe Frank of Cresco. It was during that match that Jason Sr. had his first idea he might be championship material.

"I'm leading Joe Frank and I'm in the down position. All of a sudden it dawned on me, it just hit me like a ton of bricks, 'Holy cow, what am I doing here? This is the state finals. If I win this match, I'm a state champion,'" he said. "Until that minute, that second, it hadn't really occurred to me that I might be a state champion. I was just out having a great time. I was in my own little zone and having a ball. I lost that focus for an instant, and that's when he stuck a cradle on me and pinned me. Only time I got pinned in my life."

One aspect of the 1960 tournament Jason Sr. found pleasing was beating Omar Frank, Joe's brother, 5-3, in the first round. In the finals, Deutsch had a guy in his corner who would become a partner of Jason Sr.'s in radio broadcasts of Algona meets in later years – Fritz Nielsen. Prior to the match, Jason Sr. got some advice from Algona coach Champ Martin.

"I remember Champ telling me Deutsch had one of those suicide cradles. He said, 'Whatever you do, don't pull your arm out.' The guy stuck that cradle on me about halfway through the match and my first reaction – my arm came right out. As it's coming out, I'm thinking, 'Oh my God, I ain't supposed to do this,'" he said. "I fought it off. I lost a three-point near fall and in those days that was next to being pinned. I caught myself in time, was able to fight my way out and get a reversal, got him on his back and got those points back. Went on to win the match without a lot of problem, but I do remember that one move."

His toughness got shaped from a tough sophomore season. "As a sophomore I basically had a mediocre year. I was probably a little better than .500 and I attribute that to the fact we had a lot of seniors at my weight, 120, and they just kicked my tail from one end of the mat to the other," Jason Sr. said. "When I got through that year, as a junior things started perking. Those guys got out and apparently I must have learned something because I only lost that one match in the state finals."

Jason Sr.'s second child was a boy who was named for his father. Any question about him loving wrestling was answered within two years.

"I remember taking him to his first wrestling match when he was in the neighborhood of 1 ½-2 years old. We're sitting in the old Algona gym at the scoring table, he's sitting next to me. He's got his hands folded on the table and his chin on his hands. He was just mesmerized. He sat there the whole varsity meet and he hardly moved. It was amazing," the elder Jason said. "He was into wrestling at an early age. I could roll around with him on the floor and show him (things). He couldn't wait to get into the kiddie tournaments, and you had to wait until fourth grade in those days. He wanted to go to every one he could."

After a while, his son's experience level increased and so did dad's thoughts of big things. "It was probably in that period of time that I started thinking 'Maybe this kid could be a state champ. That would really be neat to have a son be a state champion too,'" Jason Sr. said.

The younger Jason doesn't remember the early nights in Algona's gym. He does remember when dad was doing radio for wrestling meets and tournaments such as the Eagle Grove Invitational. "I remember getting ready Saturday mornings for the tournaments. We'd get ready and we'd go to Fritz Nielsen's and they'd have their coffee and talk about the day that's ahead of them," Jason Jr. said. "We'd head to Eagle Grove and sit in the gym all day long. It was 10:00 til 8:00 that night and wrestling, wrestling, wrestling.

"I was a kid, I enjoyed doing other things, but I always knew I was going to wrestle. I didn't get started until I was in fourth grade. Both of my boys started when they were 4 ½ years old."

By that age, Jason Jr. had his future plans mapped out. In an article about the 1983 tournament, it was reported that the Etheringtons asked Jason what he wanted to be. His response? To be a state champion and a race car driver.

"My dad announced the races too, so I'd get carted off to the races every weekend in the summer. I wanted to drive a car. He did some for Algona, did some for Alta, Boone…early on he was going all over using his voice to earn a buck here and there. I was always at the track, and in the winter time we were always at the wrestling meet."

Gene Schattschnatter of Algona in his No. 56 car was a favored driver. "I think I would go to the pits a lot and he would be there," Jason Jr. said.

He also knew what dad accomplished in high school.

"I learned that early on because I would look at his tournament card. I would look his card and picture myself," Jason Jr. said. "I wrote Jr. after his name on each line, so his state tournament card has Jason Etherington Jr. I would kick my kid's butt if he did that to mine."

The younger Jason expected to have his own bracket one day. "There was never a doubt in my mind that I wouldn't be one. It just never crossed my mind and I don't know why I felt like that. It could have not happened just as easily," Jason Jr. said.

Jesse wants his own too. "The card is way better than the medal. I think that proves you're a state champion. The card has your name written on it as a champion. That's been a big thing for our family," he said.

Father and son spent a lot of time with wrestling – going to Algona meets and Iowa State meets (Jason Sr. used to do public address work at Cyclone meets), watching the college meets on television and just talking about the sport. Dad also taught his son how to make maple syrup, including tapping into the tree. Grandpa also taught syrup-making to Jesse.

"It was a wrestling community. Champ Martin was dad's coach and he was a big name. It was a big deal. I don't think there was another sport in Algona that won any titles," Jason Jr. said.

Algona was home to two successful winter-sport coaches – Champ, who coached four state championship teams, and basketball's Howard "Howie" Stephenson, who led the Bulldogs to four state appearances, including a third-place finish in 1964.

A young wrestling fan growing up in Algona had several guys to aspire to be on the mat, such as brothers Gene and Duane Hunt, Mark Harris and Paul Martin, who is Champ's son and a three-time state champion. "He would always get a pin, he was so smooth. I was pretty young when I was watching him, but I remember he was smooth and he would end up with a pin almost every time," Jason Jr. said of Martin. "It was like he was a college wrestler and they were high school wrestlers, he made them look that silly. If I remember, that's just who I wanted to be like. You want to be like that guy that wins and pins every time. Then my favorite wrestler was Jeff Kerber because that guy won everything."

Jason Sr. remembered Champ Martin being polished in making a guy's attack better.

"I had a switch that I could switch anybody from down until I got the one guy that stopped my switch. I was dumbfounded at that point and couldn't get much going," Jason Sr. said. "The next night in practice, Champ comes up and said, 'Jason, for you this week, the switch is illegal.' It was like tying one arm behind your back with your favorite move. You can't do it, so you learn real quick. I learned how to do the sit-out, the stand-up, the side roll and do all of those other things I learned that week. Things like that, Champ was really very good at."

If the elder Jason got nervous while his son wrestled, he masked it because he and Nielsen were broadcasting Algona's meets on radio. Dad called the action when his son finished fifth in the 1982 tournament. In 1983, the final call was a state championship contest.

"The butterflies were really rolling. Being on the radio, I had to keep my head about me and not get too carried away and get shouting like a regular fan," Jason Sr. said. "All through his high school years, most of the time I was on the radio. It really was probably better for me than being an average fan dad in the stands because I'd have probably gone wild."

Jason Jr. faced a familiar opponent for the 119-pound championship. He wrestled Mike Schwab of Osage in the consolation round of the 1982 meet and slipped away with a 4-3 victory. When they met for the gold medal in 1983, Jason Jr. won, 10-2.

"It was kind of a blur. I wish I had one more trip down there, to go down and enjoy it a little different," Jason Jr. said. "When I was down there as a junior, it was you weigh in, you eat, go and you wrestle. I didn't get to enjoy the atmosphere quite as much."

The bout was shown on television, so Jason Jr. can watch it if the spirit moves him. He does remember just before the bout started. "I remember approaching the bench to get my ankle band and (Schwab) was standing next to me. I remember thinking, 'Second's not that bad.' It was like a split-second thought that went through my mind, then I'm like. 'Heck with that, I'm going to get first.' I grabbed my ankle band, put it on and away we go."

Jason Jr. never got to enjoy the atmosphere as a wrestler again. He sustained an ankle injury that caused him to default out and not qualify for state in 1984 as a senior. "If I had that sprained ankle in the middle of the season, I probably would have been down for three weeks. But you don't have that time (at districts)," he said.

He went to state, but not through the wrestler's entrance. Jason Sr. was also there doing radio. "It was really heartbreaking when he tore his ankle up and couldn't wrestle (at state) in his senior year. That just killed me," the elder Etherington said.

Still, they did get to share one special moment at state. Jason Sr. said there was no awards stand ceremony when he won his state title.

"It's really a lot of pride and an accomplishment your son does that you feel like you were a part of. Having been there, I knew what I was talking about. We had a good father-son rapport. It gives you the goose bumps standing there watching your son walk up to the top and getting that gold medal," Jason Sr. said.

"We don't think there has ever been a third generation state champion, so that's pretty cool," Jesse said. "Winning a state title, always having that thought in your mind. I keep doing this to get better, to win the state title, a third generation state championship."

"It's always just wrestling. All we did, every single one of us."

Thanks to the Internet, wrestling fans in all points of the world who know the right address can listen to matches in Iowa's state tournament. If they can wait a few minutes, those fans can access match results on the Iowa High School Athletic Association's website.

It seems so long ago that people had to wait for a phone call or the next morning's newspaper to see how a kid's match went.

What if you're in Okinawa, Japan, your brother is on the mat at Veterans Memorial Auditorium in Des Moines and the radio station your mom is doing play-by-play on does not have live streaming on the Internet? What about if you're in Iraq and it's match time at state?

If you are Sara Hildreth Higgins, you stay up late and wait for the cell phone to ring.

Higgins was in the Air Force and stationed overseas when it was state tournament time in 2003 and 2004. Big deal? The tournament is a big deal to Sara's family because her dad is Tom Hildreth, the longtime Rockwell City and Rockwell City-Lytton coach. Her mom, Theresa, was on the air on KTLB-FM. Her older brother, Ryan, was a two-time qualifier and her younger brother David was a three-time qualifier. Ryan and David qualified together in 2001. Sara was a statistician for her dad's team until she graduated in 2002. Anne replaced her sister as a statistician. Everybody worked.

"It's always just wrestling. All we did, every single one of us," Sara said. "I think (doing stats) was my way of fitting into the family. Growing up with Ryan and David wrestling, I played sports, but (wrestling) was what I was always at because that's where our family was always at. My dad would never let me wrestle. I tried. I did (want to wrestle) at times, I actually was really good. I used to beat both of my brothers when I was

441

younger. When I got old enough, my mom and dad would not let me join wrestling, which I can understand."

Theresa said state was exhilarating and nerve-wracking for the Hildreth gang. "It was a highlight of the season. There were a lot of sleepless nights and sick stomachs leading up to it because it was the culmination of the whole year," she said. "(2001) was the season Ryan was a senior and David was a freshman. David qualified first, and I'll never forget that feeling and the prayers of, 'Please, please let his older brother qualify.' Once Ryan qualified, it was like this huge weight was just lifted."

In 2003, Sara was surprised to find her first duty station was Okinawa. That made getting back for the state tournament a little challenging. "I left for basic training two weeks after I graduated high school. I guessed I always assumed that I wouldn't leave the country," Sara said. "When you join the Air Force, you get what's called the 'Dream Sheet.' You put the list of locations where you want to go. My list consisted of Midwestern states because I wanted to be close to home. I had David and Anne and I wanted to be a big sister to them. I was kind of a homebody at first, so when I got through basic training and into my school, and I found out I was going to Okinawa, Japan, it was quite a shock."

Sara started going to state while in the womb. "My first state tournament was 1984 and I had Ryan in my arms and I was a month and a half from delivering Sara," Theresa said. "We took the kids that qualified and we were there for the whole time. That was really a tough one, being pregnant and having a 16-month-old. I really appreciated the coaches' wives' room."

A few years later, Sara started to remember the trips. "Probably when I was 8 or 9 is the memory I have of the beginning of it. I just remember getting all dressed up. I had blonde hair, so my mom would let me put blue stuff in my hair and write on my cheeks, stuff like that," Sara said.

The tournament's constant action served as a babysitter of sorts for Theresa. "It wasn't until when Ryan was in seventh grade that we started bringing the kids with us. They could kind of take care of themselves," she said, "I started doing radio probably in 1992 or '93 – I did radio for eight or nine years – and they would go with me. We'd get there early and we'd get the seats right behind on press row where the radio setup was. They'd sit behind me and watch while I broadcast."

When she was overseas, Sara was matside because Rockwell City fans such as Superintendent DeWayne Cross and his wife Cathy called her cell phone and narrated the match to her. Sara also got videotapes of the matches sent to her.

"She wanted it. It was killing her that she couldn't be there," Theresa said of the calls. "She hadn't missed a wrestling tournament in years. It killed her that she wasn't getting to watch David wrestle."

Sara remembered a cast of callers in 2003. "I talked to so many people on the phone that year. The Internet wasn't as advanced as it is now back in '03, but mom and I had very good calling cards. Mr. Cross called me, I know I talked to Cathy Cross too, my sister, my mom was doing radio, Ryan did a lot for me too. It was definitely difficult, but we made it work as much as we could."

Theresa said the calling card allowed for calls to Okinawa to cost about six cents per minute. The time difference between Des Moines and Okinawa is 14 hours, so the morning alarm sometimes rang soon after the cell phone did. The choice was sleeping or listening to a sibling's chance at a state championship.

"That would have been an easy call. There are two things in Okinawa I stay up for, and that's family and Hawkeyes," Sara said. "If I have to wake up to hear about David's wrestling match or watch an Iowa Hawkeye football game, that's what I have to do."

Communicating is still cheap for mother and daughter. Sara has a telephone service using high-speed Internet that has the same 712 area code she grew up in. As mom is ready to go to work each day, she can say good night to the mother of two overseas without excessive bills. If that doesn't work, they can Skype. Sara is a civilian employee for the Air Force and her family was working in the fall of 2010 on moving back to the United States.

Mother and daughter did have an opportunity for in-person chat a few days before the 2004 state tournament. They met in Baltimore when Sara was en route to Okinawa after being in Iraq. Theresa flew to Des Moines the day before the tournament started. David won his first two matches, but got beaten in the semifinals by Mitch Norton of Nashua-Plainfield. The semifinals was when Sara got to take calls again after getting settled.

David finished third at 140 pounds as a senior after finishing fourth at 135 the year before. Had he won state in 2003, David might have caused a slight panic overseas. "That would have been amazing. Even for him to place fourth was amazing. I'm sure that entire camp that I was at knew that he placed fourth in the Iowa state tournament. If he would have won, I don't know what I would have done. It was pretty exciting," Sara said.

Sara listened to the calls hoping to hear a magic word: Williams. David learned a move that combined a takedown and a cradle called a

"Williams." He pinned several opponents with it, so big sis knew what she wanted to hear.

"I remember every second I'm praying and hoping while listening to him to just do it. Every time he's pinned them in seconds," Sara said. "That's all I wanted to hear most of the time. Of course it didn't happen always, but I always felt so guilty and so bad for not being there for him and for my sister all throughout the rest of their high school. Being on the phone and at least listening made me feel a lot better trying to support him and at least knowing how it ended up. It was good to have that opportunity to be on the phone."

The wait could shorten her patience. "I probably get more nervous than my mom does. If I would have to wait to hear how he was doing....I get super-nervous. There was one instance I know I called and they were like, 'No, he's not up yet. Call back in 10 minutes' and I almost missed the match. I think I talked to my grandfather on that day," Sara said.

There was little phone interaction between Sara and David at tournament time. "David is a man of few words. I don't think he talked to anybody during those tournaments except dad," she said. "I think I talked to him after, but during he needed to stay focused. I'm sure he didn't want to talk to his big sister. One thing David always could do is focus very well."

Sara said going to sleep in Okinawa or Iraq after the matches wasn't a very good alternative to the atmosphere being at state provided. "It was my greatest time of year. We got to live in a hotel, but we also got to experience wrestling," Sara said. "To this day, if anybody asks me my favorite sport... absolutely wrestling 100 percent."

Wrestling has been as much a part of the family as having the change of seasons.

"There's nothing I would change. It was the glue of our family. We all knew how to cope with the moods of the coach, the kids helped one another," Theresa said. "To this day, when everybody's together, it's a topic of conversation and they laugh. To this day, they still think they've got to wrestle on the middle of my living room floor. It's a good thing that Sara and Anne were not allowed to wrestle because they would have kicked somebody's butt. The girls did wrestle with the boys in this house, but that was not allowed outside the house. They knew how tough wrestling practice was."

Sara hopes to pass the sport to her children. Perhaps her daughter Hailey will do statistics like mom and Aunt Anne did. She hopes Connor follows his grandfather and his uncles. "I'm hoping he takes it and runs and continues on the Hildreth tradition," she said.

HONEST, COACH

Coaches hear some amazing excuses for tardiness at practice if they stay in the business long enough. Cars won't start, cell phone died, a friend borrowed the car and it ran out of gas or the car had gas but the tires were flat.

How about, "We stopped to rescue an elderly couple from their car in a deep ditch, then we drove them home, then we got a tractor to pull their car out and then we drove the car back to their house."

Bedford coach Gail Christensen heard that excuse as the Bulldogs got ready to practice for sectionals week in 2001. Michael Irvin, who was Bedford's senior 189-pounder, and Jared Gray, the senior 215-pounder, were on their way to practice when something caught their eye.

"It was an old couple that had been stranded. They slid off the road, they said some wildlife had jumped out at them and they'd spun off into the ditch," Irvin said. "It was one of those situations where you sure couldn't leave them. It was a pretty deep ditch. We walked down in there and saw there was no way they were getting out.

"They had just been to town to buy groceries that day, so we took all their groceries out and we carried the lady and the older fellow out and carried them up. Then we ended up taking them back to their place, which was like 10-15 miles away. We came back and got a tractor and pulled their car out and took it back to them later in the day."

The whole process of doing the good deed made them terribly late for practice. When they got to school, the boys told Christensen about the whole chain of events that took about four hours. And he didn't buy it.

"He just cussed at us. We told him our story and he didn't believe it," Irvin said. "We had a little extra practice afterwards and got a workout in. A couple days later, he found out from one of the cops that it actually did happen."

Christensen said, "It was a heroic thing they had done."

Originally, Christensen said the details sounded too good to be true. Christensen is known throughout southwest Iowa as "Eddard" and rarely gets addressed by his given name at meets or tournaments or when chatting with fellow coaches in the area.

"At that point and time, yeah, because you didn't think it would come out of their mouths to say that," Christensen said. "They're two good kids, but it was surprising to me and it was true."

The guys passed their efforts off as doing what they were taught to do.

"It was just one of those things where you just do it, we do around (Bedford)," Irvin said. "It happened and I hope that if it would have been the other way around somebody would have helped us out too. My parents raised me that way, you do it because it's the right thing to do. There were consequences, but that's just the way it worked. I figured Eddard would have to get over it."

Irvin finished second in the Class 1-A tournament and Gray placed third at 215. That showed that being late once for practice didn't hurt them.

"I had to commend the two boys for their effort and I never doubted them again," Christensen said.

THE CHAMP LIVES HERE

Terry Parham Jr. won the Class 3-A 152-pound state championship as a junior in 1997 for Glenwood High School. Parham grew up in nearby Pacific Junction, and a family friend, Jack Marshall, hatched an idea that people should know where he was from. That's how a sign posted at two ends of town came into being.

"He said 'How many state champions have there ever been from Pacific Junction?'" according to Terry Parham Sr. "Of course we found a couple more, but we approached the city with the idea that if we bought one – actually there were three – would they purchase the other two. I thought it was a little gaudy at first, it kind of embarrassed the son, and when he comes back to town and they're still up. He's had bigger accomplishments according to him."

The other two state champions from Pacific Junction, who are mentioned on the sign, are state discus champion Jim Holmes in 1979 and state hurdles champion Craig Prindle in 1989. Both competed for Glenwood.

The cost was about $240 per sign. Terry Jr. saw them after earning all-America honors wrestling at Air Force Academy. He sees them when he comes back from nearly 10 deployments overseas with the Air Force. When they first went up, father and son had a discussion.

"He said, 'Dad, do you think people in town don't know me?' I said, 'I want the people coming into town to know you.'"

The younger Parham, who was 38-0 in his championship season, was a bit embarrassed by the sign, but he learned it could help when playing a game called "Give one interesting fact about yourself."

"Not many people have their name on the 'welcome to city X' sign," Terry Jr. said. "Wrestling 160 high school matches and easily as many off-season matches in high school, I can recognize most any Iowa town based on a previous opponent's hometown.

"I always felt a sense of privilege growing up in a small town in the middle of America. I don't use the term privilege as in wealth or access to many fancy things, but in the meaning I had the opportunity to make what I wanted out of my life."

One thing he wanted to make was a state championship. When he beat Brannon Hilton of Indianola, 3-1, it was mission accomplished. Parham was denied a second title in 1998, when Andy Harrison of West Des Moines Valley beat him, 7-1, in the 160-pound finale. That championship night at Vets was pretty cool in the Parham household.

"I was very proud of it. I don't think there's any thrill that a father could get better than in the old barn watching his kid win a state championship. I was in Albany, New York when he won his all-American (honor) by beating a kid from Iowa. Since Iowa didn't recruit him, that was kind of nice. That was a tearful event too. Even the high school tournament now when I watch it, it's pretty emotional.

"Iowa wrestling is the best in the country. If you can win in Iowa, I think you can win anywhere."

Father and son shared a golden moment on the floor of the auditorium.

"'You never cease to amaze me' is what I told him," Terry Sr. said. "That's the way it's always been. When the odds were down....in eighth grade when he won an AAU state championship, I took him and I didn't think he was going to be a state champion at that age, but of course he did. He's always amazed me with just about everything – grades, ability... just a little bit of everything."

The son never ceased to listen to his dad's instruction.

"While he was definitely beaming with pride after my win, my father was certainly not the coddling type. I rarely got pep talks growing up. What I really got was reality checks. What I learned about my personal goal-setting style from my father was that no one besides yourself can set goals for you," Terry Jr. said. "While one might say he set the bar low in terms of achievement, he always set the bar high in terms of personal pride and losing and winning with class.

"I think I took a lot of his personality, in that I was always going to do things on my terms. No amount of outside pressure could motivate me anymore than my own personal internal drive could. I have seen many young men turned off and burned out by a sport because of their father putting too much pressure on them to succeed at a sport. I often offer up my father's style as a model to my friends who are now fathers of young boys. I think that is probably the greatest compliment a dad can receive."

FAMILY CALL

The folks in and around Charles City knew Wendell Williams as a teacher and coach who had a distinctive speech pattern. He was doing broadcasts of Charles City wrestling meets over KCHA-FM after he stepped away from coaching the Comets.

Williams was better known by his initials or Double. He never had a more unique call of a match than in the Class 3-A 160-pound championship bout of the 1989 state tournament. That match had Curtis White of West Des Moines Dowling against Steve Williams of Charles City. Steve is Wendell's son.

Previous White-Williams matches were not pretty. One-sided they were, and in White's favor. White had even spoiled a big day for Williams at the Comet Duals, when Williams handed Willy Short of Inver Grove Heights (Minn.) Simley High School a rare loss. This was the last go.

"What I remember very clearly was that Todd Kirkland came downstairs before that match and basically got me in the right mindset for that match," Steve said. "He had been ranked No. 1 or No. 2 for like three years straight and he never got to the finals. Todd and I grew up together, we were actually neighbors when we were in fourth grade. We wrestled our whole lives in practice. Todd had already lost his chance to win a state title and he came downstairs before the match and had a good talk with me. Basically, his conversation was this is your last chance, this is it and don't have any fear. I pretty much already accepted second place. I had very low expectations for the finals, but after Todd talked to me, he really got my adrenaline pumping."

Williams said a key moment occurred right away in the finals match. "At the beginning of the match, when Curtis first shot in on me, I threw him out of bounds and I'd never been able to move him because he's so strong. I give all the credit to Todd Kirkland because without him I probably would have never won that match."

Williams did not strike people as the champion wrestler type. His brother, Dave, wrestled for the Comets but never won gold. However, Dave won a silver medal in Greco-Roman at the Junior World tournament and later wrestled for Northern Iowa – where his father was an all-America football player.

"Obviously my goal was a state title, that's your goal right?" Williams said. "I'll be honest, in my sophomore and junior year I didn't really see that in my future. I wasn't the dominating wrestler my entire life, it was more kind of peaking at the right time."

The pinnacle of that peak was the final minute of his finals match. Wendell was trying to describe the match, but he was getting sidetracked by the thought his son was seconds away from a huge upset. He became less understandable as the time ticked away. By the time the match ended, Wendell was shouting, laughing, possibly weeping and trying to inform the listeners that his son was a state champion. It was one of the better proud-papa moments of the tournament's history.

"I actually had not heard a thing about it until I watched the tape. Somebody brought over the videotape after the match, we sat down at home and watched it. I got a good chuckle out of listening to him," Steve said, adding he could decipher what dad was saying. "Fortunately for me, I had heard his mumbling talk my whole life because that's just the way dad talked, so I understood every word. It's a classic.

"That's one of the really cool things about it, you get to hear dad going through what a dad's going through."

A videotape of the match with Wendell's radio call dubbed in was a hit when coaches and wrestlers came to Charles City that summer for the annual North-South all-star meet.

Wendell passed away in 1999. Steve can hear his dad's voice anytime he wants because he has a copy of the tape and watches it often.

"That's why I still have the tape and that's why I still watch it. It's nice to hear his voice. I love the part where the real him comes out in the end part of that tape. It's pretty funny stuff," Steve said. "For me, obviously it's a memory of my father. If they want to know who my dad was, which they will hear about him, I play that tape and then they can hear a little bit about who he was. A lot of it is getting rid of the non-believers that a skinny kid like me won the Iowa state title. I have to show them video proof."

That match is good for reaffirmation, Steve said. "I still think about it to this day when I think about life. When you feel like you can't do something, I still rewind to that day," he said.

A KEY TO SUCCESS

Jeff Harrison of Westwood of Sloan had plans to be a four-time state champion. He wrote it as a goal while in kindergarten at elementary school in Salix. Harrison's father, Jack, was Westwood's wrestling coach, so it was easy to imagine his son setting a goal to succeed on the mat. "I had that set in me from a very young age that I was going to succeed at everything I did," Jeff said. "I couldn't wait to wrestle, and my dad wouldn't let me wrestle in tournaments officially until I got into second grade. I loved it. I couldn't wait every weekend to go to a different place to wrestle."

His dream of achieving his goal for high school got dashed when Jeff placed third at 103 pounds as a freshman. "I didn't like how the freshman year turned out at all. Maybe that's a lot of the reason why my last three years went so well and the confidence I had about matches," Jeff said. "It seems like if you're in high school, confidence is about 80 percent of a win. You go out there and smack somebody in the head, take them down...I grew up watching Hawkeye wrestling and you could just tell. The Brands brothers could break somebody instantly. Takedown, takedown, shoving them out of bounds and that person was thinking, 'Man, get this over with.' You've got a lot of kids out there who could potentially give you pretty dang good matches and they just fold. That's where the little mental edge takes over."

Chad Shook, who had been Jack Harrison's assistant, became Westwood's head coach when Jeff was a freshman. Jeff was in fourth grade when he first met Shook.

"My class was so bad and they gave him all of the guys that were just out there to terrorize the world. He had us pouting in the corner," Jeff said. "He's a huge guy and if he started yelling at us, it wasn't long before the tears started flying for most of the class. As soon as you started crying, he'd send you into the Shook Pouting Corner."

Jeff and Shook had reason to consider pouting on the afternoon of the 1998 state finals. They went to eat at a Fazoli's restaurant in Des Moines, several miles from Veterans Memorial Auditorium. Jeff's match against Scott Burns of Pleasantville was not the highlight 112-pound bout that night, but Jeff joked that maybe going into overtime would get him some airtime.

"I liked to get him all riled up," Jeff said. "By the time we get out to the car, you should have seen the look on his face. He's in panic mode. Then I'm like '(Crap)!' All of our families, all of the other wrestlers, they're all at Vets."

Shook locked the keys in the school's Chevrolet Suburban.

"We're in Fazoli's, we eat, the lady's handing out breadsticks and everything else. Life is good, kinda got his mind off that finals match for a little while," Shook said. "We come out and it was like, 'Jeff, you're not going to believe this. There are the keys in the ignition.'

"This is a day when not everybody had cell phones. We called and called and called and could not find a locksmith. We finally found one. It was getting to the point to where we needed to go, and we needed to go *now*. I was actually looking for things to throw through the window of the Suburban because the locksmith hadn't shown up yet."

Jack and Rita Harrison showed up. They too looked at the out-of-reach keys. The locksmith finally showed up.

"He pulled up, no big deal. He's got this little wedge, pounds it in there, sticks a little deal down the door, pops it open, that was it," Shook said. "It took him 10 seconds. I don't remember how long we waited. I don't remember if we waited 30 minutes, I don't remember if we waited an hour. It seemed like we were there for three days."

Even the normally unflappable Jeff was getting uncomfortable with the long wait. "I used to have to pry him off of the Nintendo in the hotel room to get him to his state finals match," Shook said. "He was in no hurry to get there. He was starting to sweat this one. It was literally getting to that time."

Jeff remembered, "I was getting pretty nervous as it was, and I was going to be right away the second match," Jeff said. "We finally got hold of somebody at Vets, we were going to have them come back and get us and I would have missed the Grand March probably. We got there and I got down there as they were getting ready to walk out."

Jeff locked up his first championship with a 2-0 margin in overtime after he and Burns finished regulation tied, 1-1.

"It was funny afterwards, but it wasn't funny at all before," Shook said of the lock-out. "I have never locked the keys in any vehicle under any circumstances since that day. It is forever etched in my memory. You can't really ever put into words what that feels like.

"I was so embarrassed. If memory serves me correctly, I paid the locksmith in cash and I never even turned in a receipt to the school because I felt like such an idiot."

THE LOSS IN A WIN

John Newmeister of Cedar Rapids Washington won the Class AA 154-pound state championship in 1966. Judging by his 23-0 record, no one was surprised to see him get the gold medal. Newmeister did sustain one loss that season.

Newmeister lost a tooth cap to a forearm during a 1-0 victory in the first round of the state meet. According to the *Cedar Rapids Gazette,* in order to prevent the uncomfortable feeling of air hitting a nerve, Newmeister used chewing gum to fill the space. He later went to the dentist for some emergency work, the *Gazette* reported. The teeth didn't keep Newmeister from winning, 9-1, in the finals. He gave up one point in the state meet.

BUSY MAN

Don Henry of Cresco and Gordon Hassman of New Hampton had a well-documented series of matches during their careers. In 1960, Henry put in a long opening day of the state meet. After winning his opening-round 120-pound match, 4-2, over Dick Hunter of Jesup, Henry got in a car and went to Mason City to join classmates in performing a one-act play at a speech contest. He then drove back to Cedar Falls and won his semifinals match before losing to Hassman by referee's decision.

TAKE A HIKE

There is much to see in Des Moines, and those opportunities come in handy if anyone needs a break from the wrestling at the state tournament. Shopping, fine dining, multiplex movies…even a slice of pie.

In 1977, a first-time visitor to the state tournament accompanied the state qualifiers from his school. It was the only way his father would allow him to attend the then-three-day event. The kid was given a press pass by Tom Bishop, then-publisher of *The Predicament,* so he shot pictures throughout the tournament. That trip got him out of school for two days, which was a very cool thing. The first day was uneventful, but Friday got to be a day to remember. The two qualifiers each made Saturday night's finals. The tricky part was the time between the quarterfinals and the semifinals.

After they won in the quarters, the wrestlers went back to the hotel with the coaches. Their passenger was somewhere in Vets, so they had him paged. Vets was so old-school that it didn't bother to post what directions the exits were, in case someone was told to meet at a certain entrance. After being inside Vets, newbies might as well have been blindfolded and spun around as if trying to break a piñata. Directions were useless. The kid was a fast learner. About 90 minutes later, that entrance was found. The ride was long gone.

Fearing that word would get back to his father about missing the ride, he decided it was best to get to the hotel with his bag of school-owned photographic equipment as quickly as possible. The hotel was located at the bottom of an off-ramp from Interstates 35 and 80 on the north part of Des Moines. That walk built up an appetite, but there was likely not enough time to have a sit-down meal. He grabbed a slice of strawberry pie and completed the walk to the hotel. That pie was going to be tasty. He got back to the room just as the team was heading back to Vets for the semifinals. After two bites – and tremendous rounds of laughter by the coaches - the pie went into the trash. Not a good idea to eat pie in front of wrestlers who still had to make weight that night.

Prior to the finals, a sewer line cracked in the wing of the hotel the team was staying at. He was blamed for causing the rotten-eggs aroma, but he swore innocence. The team had to move to a different part of the hotel that day.

The final results were mixed; one state champion, one runner-up. The worst part of the evening came when the guy got his new down jacket stolen during the finals. The temperature outside that night was arguably 10 degrees colder than on a clear January midnight north of the Arctic Circle. The reception he would face at home without that new coat was expected to be even chillier.

He survived the long walk, the early dismissal of a tasty-looking piece of pie, a chilly, shirt-sleeved dash in the parking lot and parental displeasure to one day write a book about the state tournament.

CHAMPIONSHIP BOUTS SINCE 1921
(Date of championship round in parentheses) Some tournaments included a wrestle-back round for a true second place

1921 (February 5)

95-Audra Liegerot, Red Oak pinned Walter Riley, Ottumwa, 4:28.

115-Elmer Garber, Leon beat Richard Burke, Mason City.

125-Robert Bingaman, Indianola pinned Lester Harms, Geneva 4:35.

135-Joseph Giunta, Cedar Rapids High School beat Charles Cunningham, Boone .

145-George Carringer, Cedar Rapids High School Leo Alstott, Mason City .

158-Glenn Burkholder, Cedar Rapids High School beat Clare Grooms, Ottumwa .

175-Harry Carringer, Cedar Rapids High School beat Clifford Meyers, Odebolt .

Hwt-Clark DeGroote, Humboldt beat Darrell Fisher, Garden Grove.

1922 (February 11 at Ames)

95-Ben Phillips, Marshalltown beat William Daly, Mason City.

105-Teddy Warrington, Garden Grove beat Walter Riley, Ottumwa.

115-Richard Burke, Mason City beat Harold Boyvey, Boone.

125-Willis Standley, Boone beat Harold Saylor, Mason City .

135-Ray Peasley, Cedar Rapids High School beat Francis McCarron, Oelwein.

145-Leo Alstott, Mason City beat Clare Grooms, Ottumwa .

158-Glenn Burkholder, Cedar Rapids High School beat James Blair, Mason City (4 OT).

175-Roy Grimm, Boone beat Elmer Kingery, Knoxville.

Hwt-Robert Kutchera, Cedar Rapids High School beat Don Thompson, Red Oak.

1922 (March 25/University of Iowa Invitational)

95-Francis Hockensmith, Boone beat Clarence Clark, Central City.

105-Darrell Sawyer, Central City beat Waytne Rohlf, Davenport.

115-Joe Sams, Clarion pinned Virgil Welch, Davenport 5:53.

125-Thomas Kearns, Central City pinned Willis Standley, Boone 5:19.

135-Harold Vogel, Davenport beat Irwin Douglas, Ames.

145-Robert Smola, Central City pinned Milton Scheppele, Dubuque 2:38.

158-Perry Mills, Central City beat Roy Fletcher, Davenport.

175-Roy Grimm, Boone won by medical forfeit over Manley Rundall, Central City.

Hwt-Paul Krasuski, Davenport pinned Donald Henderson, Central City 4:13.

1923 (February 10 at Ames)

95-Lyle Wilson, Boone beat Bruce Church, Cresco.

105-William Daly, Mason City beat Clarence Shertz, Iowa Falls.

115-Burdette Briggs, Sutherland beat Fred Tompkins, Mason City.

125-Willis Standley, Boone beat Harold Stotser, Iowa Falls.

135-Raleigh Fisher, Council Bluffs beat Ray Morris, Boone.

145-Clare Grooms, Ottumwa beat Bob Michaels, Fort Dodge.

158-Donald Blair, Mason City beat Wilmer Adamson, Boone.

175-Philip Foster, Mason City beat Roy Grimm, Boone.

Hwt-Archie Midkiff, Mount Vernon beat John Chester Acher, Fort Dodge.

1923 (March 24/ University of Iowa Invitational)

95-Bernard Booth, Ottumwa beat Paul Hinebaugh, Garden Grove.

105-Elmer McClelland, Clarion beat Gerald Richards, Garden Grove.

115-Hubert Wilcox, Ottumwa beat Teddy Warrington, Garden Grove.

125-Carroll Wilson, Clarion beat Paul Young, Garden Grove.

135-Perry Mills, Central City pinned Alvin Bargmann, Davenport 2:40.

145-Lee Franklin, Ottumwa beat Norman Thomas, Garden Grove.

158-Ralph Adamson, Ottumwa beat Claude Lang, Carlisle

(Wrestle back: Leland Wilson, Clarion beat Lang by coin toss for second place).

175-Bill Teommes, Ottumwa beat Ora White, Clarion.

Hwt-Archie Midkiff, Mount Vernon beat Glenn Schutt, Clarion.

1924 (February 16/University of Iowa Invitational)

95-Leo Jacobson, Marshalltown pinned Howard Long, Belle Plaine, 5:19.

105-Ben Phillips, Marshalltown pinned Walter Martin, Belle Plaine, 2:10.

115-Theodore Hesmer, Marshalltown pinned Hubert Wilcox, Ottumwa, 9:58.

125-Allie Morrison, Marshalltown pinned Hessel Sauers, Ottumwa, :27.

135-James Noid, Marshalltown beat Lee Franklin, Ottumwa.

145-Edward Feld, Marshalltown pinned Earl Andrews, Belle Plaine, 4:01.

158-Ralph Adamson, Ottumwa beat James Peterson, Marshalltown.

175-Ralph Goodale, Marshalltown pinned Frank Pillard, Anamosa, 9:41.

Hwt-Eugene Fitz, Marshalltown was sole entrant.

1924 (February 23 at Ames)

95-William Bird, Eldora Training School beat Bernard Johnson, Boone.

105-Lyle Wilson, Boone beat Clarence Shertz, Iowa Falls.

115-Willis Standley, Boone pinned Darrell Ridout, Iowa Falls 1:49.

125-Allie Morrison, Marshalltown beat Leslie Grant, Fonda.

135-Charles Seaman, Cherokee beat Dwyer Moe, Fort Dodge.

145-Ernie Sharp, Clarion beat Lawrence Erickson, Boone.

158-Ralph Adamson, Ottumwa beat Lytle Jones, Boone.

175-Randall Ewalt, Boone beat Ralph Goodale, Marshalltown.

Hwt-Glenn Schutt, Clarion beat Paul Yegge, Boone.

1925 (February 28 at Ames)

95-Glenn Cable, Eldora Training School pinned Tom McCrary, Carroll 4:03.

105-Lyle Wilson, Boone pinned Melvin Akers, Iowa Falls 5:28.

115-George Perrin, Cherokee beat Francis Hockensmith, Boone.

125-Allie Morrison, Marshalltown beat Harold Morris, Boone.

135-Ray Morris, Boone beat Bruce Rogers, Ottumwa.

145-Richard Burke, Mason City beat Carroll Wilson, Clarion.

158-Ernie Sharp, Clarion beat Albert Pederson, Cresco.

175-Ralph Goodale, Marshalltown pinned Willard Adams, Mason City 4:55.

Hwt-Eugene Fitz, Marshalltown beat Clarence Casey, Cherokee.

Beginning in 1926, the Iowa High School Athletic Association was in charge of the tournament.

1926 (February 20)

85-John Brindley, Fort Dodge beat Thomas Wright, Eldora Training School (time advantage 2:08).

95-Victor Michaelosky, Eldora Training School beat William Cunningham, LeMars (time advantage 1:45).

105-Richard Cole, Ames beat Glen Young, Charles City (won by coin flip).

115-Blair Thomas, Cresco beat Sam Trowbridge, Marshalltown (time advantage 2:06).

125-Merle Foster, Marshalltown beat Lloyd Conley, Cherokee (time advantage 2:03).

135-Chuck Seamon, Cherokee pinned Earl Hingst, Eldora Training School 6:24.

145-Frank Nockles, Carroll pinned Ernest Byoure, Cherokee 6:14.

158-Carroll Wilson, Clarion beat James Edwards, LeMars (time advantage 3:20).

Hwt-Ralph Goodale, Marshalltown pinned Clarence Anderson, Fort Dodge :48.

1927 (February 19)

85-Albert Durfey, Cresco beat Merle Dennis, Eldora Training School (time advantage 1:51).

95-Tommy Stevens, Cherokee beat Gordon Rosenberg, Iowa Falls (decision after 2 OT periods).

105-Charles Albert, Eldora Training School pinned Frank Chickering, Ottumwa 4:06.

115-Richard Cole, Ames beat Tom McCrary, Carroll (time advantage 3:14).

125-James Lucas, Eldora Training School beat Tommy Rhodes, Fort Dodge (decision after 4 OT periods).

135- Bob Hess, Cresco pinned Phillip Brockert, Eldora Training School 5:11.

145-Joe Gargano, Fort Dodge pinned Tom Murray, Cresco, 1:06.

158-Andrew Pontius, Fort Dodge pinned Ted Demplewolf, Cresco 3:44.

Hwt- Lester Hall, Iowa Falls beat Everil Merkley, Sac City (time advantage 4:04).

1928 (February 18)

85-Paul Thomas, Cresco beat Ivan Love, Cherokee (time advantage 5:59).

95-Robert Strever, Clarion pinned Albert Durfey, Cresco 3:13.

105-Gordon Rosenberg, Iowa Falls beat John Davis, Eldora Training School (decision after 2 OT periods).

115-Dick Jones, Cresco beat Dan Caraway, Mount Vernon (time advantage 5:52).

125-Wallace Kent, Cresco beat Willard Minkle, Fort Dodge (decision after 2 OT periods).

135-Bert Dull, Cherokee beat George Martin, Eagle Grove (time advantage 3:36).

145-Ken Ruggles, Ames beat Ivy Russell, Sac City (decision after 2 OT periods).

158-Ross Stanley, Eldora Training School beat Hodge "Guy" Morrison, Marshalltown (time advantage 3:02).

Hwt-Charles Sergeant, Marshalltown beat Albert Hallman, Eldora Training School (time advantage 3:12).

1929 (February 23)

85-Wallace Johnson, Fort Dodge pinned Marion Shane, Iowa Falls 6:45.

95-Tommy Stevens, Cherokee beat Ray Bateman, Cresco.

105-Albert Durfey, Cresco beat Victor Strever, Clarion.

115-Jim McCurdy, Ames beat Orvin DeWalle, Cresco (decision after 2 OT periods).

125-Randall Whinnery, Fort Dodge pinned Bruce Warner, Iowa Falls 5:55.

135-Frank Gargano, Fort Dodge beat Don Strever, Clarion.

145-Ken Ruggles, Ames beat Lyle Sells, Fort Dodge.

158-Hodge "Guy" Morrison, Marshalltown beat Ivy Russell, Sac City.

Hwt-Charles Sergeant, Marshalltown pinned Dutch Simons, Cherokee 7:25.

1930 (March 1)

85-Roland Lillie, Carroll beat Clarence Johnson, Fort Dodge.

95-Marion Shane, Iowa Falls beat Howard Wildman, Cresco.

105-Marion Hoskins, Iowa Falls beat Ralph Harrison, Carroll.

115-Jim McCurdy, Ames beat John Champlin, Iowa Falls.

125-Earl Kielhorn, Cherokee beat Earl Shane, Iowa Falls

135-Andrew Kovacivich, Eldora Training School beat Tony Gargano, Fort Dodge.

145-Frank Gargano. Fort Dodge pinned Charles Brown, Ames 4:36.

155-Ken Ruggles, Ames beat Lawrence Saddoris, Sac City.

Hwt-Dutch Simons, Cherokee beat Melvin Hall, Fort Dodge.

1931 (February 28)

85-Clarence Johnson, Fort Dodge pinned Raymond Hamilton, Iowa Falls 6:42.

95-Paul Cameron, Cresco beat Richard Kinsella, Eldora Training School.

(Wrestle-back: Lawrence Hamilton, Iowa Falls beat Kinsella for second place).

105-Dale Brand, Fort Dodge pinned Maurice Kenyon, Perry 4:48.

(Wrestle-back: Dell Inman, Ames beat Kenyon for second place).

115-Ralph Harrison, Carroll pinned Marion Hoskins, Iowa Falls 5:40.

(Wrestle-back: Charles Chrisman, Eldora Training School beat Hoskins for second place).

125-William Nelson, Ames beat Bob Larson, Fort Dodge.

135-James Champlin, Eldora Training School beat Orvin DeWalle, Cresco.

(Wrestle-back: Clyde Perrego, Eldora Training School beat DeWalle for second place).

145-Ralph Aman, Eldora Training School beat Ralph Ruggles, Ames

(Wrestle-back: Richard Poundstone, Clarion beat Ruggles for second place).

155-Tony Gargano, Fort Dodge beat William Shepherd, Eldora Training School.

165-Earl Turnure, Eldora Training School beat Myron Walsh, Clarion.

Hwt-Lorren "Dutch" Simons, Cherokee beat Bernard Doerning, Graettinger.

1932 (February 27)

85-Max Parmelly, Fort Dodge beat Rex Croft, Iowa Falls.

(Wrestle-back: Billy Prehm, Eagle Grove beat Croft for second place).

95-Don Mailand, Cresco pinned George Vujnovich, Valley Junction, 5:02.

(Wrestle-back: Fred Fryman, Eldora Training School beat Vujnovich for second place).

105-Lawrence Hamilton, Iowa Falls pinned Kenneth Ferguson, Valley Junction 5:18.

(Wrestle-back: Richard Kinsella, Eldora Training School beat Ferguson for second place).

115-Charles Chrisman, Eldora Training School beat Meril Thomas, Clarion.

125-Ralph Harrison, Carroll beat Dale Brand, Fort Dodge.

135-Robert Larson, Fort Dodge beat Joe Tallman, Clarion.

(Wrestle-back: Charles Carran, Cherokee beat Tallman for second place).

145-Howard McGrath, Clarion pinned Norman Borlaug, Cresco 2:21.

(Wrestle-back: Johnny Merryman, Fort Dodge beat Borlaug for second place).

155-Floyd Corrington, Cherokee beat Paul Hassman, New Hampton.

165-William Shepherd, Eldora Training School pinned Duane Barrett, Carroll 5:18.

(Wrestle-back: Gilmore Passick, Valley Junction pinned Barrett in 5:28 for second place).

Hwt-Bernard Doerning, Graettinger pinned DeWalt Gibson, Perry 2:11.

(Wrestle-back: John Whinnery, Fort Dodge pinned Gibson, :25 for second place).

1933 (February 18)

85-Dave Natvig, New Hampton beat Edward Erway, Eldora Training School.

95-Don Nichols, Cresco pinned Jack Gleason, New Hampton 6:30.

105-Don Maland, Cresco beat Joseph Loucks, Cherokee.

115-Paul Cameron, Cresco beat Richard Kinsella, Eldora Training School.

125-Francis Whalen, New Hampton beat Marvin Gustafson, Clinton.

135-Byron Guernsey, Waterloo East beat Abe Castagnoli, Fort Dodge.

145-Roger Wilcox, Eagle Grove beat Charles Carran, Cherokee.

155-Paul Hassman, New Hampton beat Willard Sharp, Clarion (decision after 2 OT periods).

165-Floyd Corrington, Cherokee beat Floyd Messerly, Fort Dodge.

Hwt- Cliff Peck, Cherokee beat Clarence Wright, Clinton.

1934 (February 24)

85-Dale Hanson, Cresco beat Dick Larson, Fort Dodge (time advantage 5:17).

(Wrestle-back: Billy Prehm, Eagle Grove beat Larson for second place).

95-Dave Natvig, New Hampton beat Max Parmelly, Fort Dodge.

(Wrestle-back: Edward Erway, Eldora Training School beat Parmelly for second place).

105-Ken Bales, Fort Dodge beat Earl Hilke, Cresco (time advantage 3:10).

(Wrestle-back: Eddie Stewart, Burt beat Hilke for second place).

115-Earl Thomas, Cresco pinned Jack Gleason, New Hampton 3:10.

(Wrestle-back: Don Madole, Fort Dodge pinned Gleason, 2:15 for second place).

125-Don Maland, Cresco beat Glenn Osman, Eagle Grove (time advantage 6:17).

135-Scott Fisher, Eagle Grove beat Carl Wooten, Council Bluffs Jefferson (time advantage 6:25).

145-Abe Castagnoli, Fort Dodge beat Don Buzzard, Waterloo East (time advantage 2:53).

155-Roger Wilcox, Eagle Grove beat William Harthorn, Eldora Training School (time advantage 4:28).

165-Floyd Messerly, Fort Dodge beat Jack Lukehart, Eagle Grove (time advantage 5:52).

(Wrestle-back: Joe Tallman, Clarion beat Lukehart for second place).

Hwt-Don Gugler, Council Bluffs Jefferson beat Gaylord Hill, Eagle Grove (time advantage 1:54).

(Wrestle-back: Harold Leake, Mason City beat Hill for second place).

1935 (February 23)

85-Newell Ingle, Cresco beat Paul Bell, Clarion.

95-Ed Lybbert, Cresco pinned George Karamitros, Mason City (pin in overtime, time unavailable).

(Wrestle-back: Tom Prehm, Eagle Grove beat Karamitros for second place).

105-Dale Hanson, Cresco beat Walt Leewright, Mason City (referee's decision).

115-Earl Hilke, Cresco beat Ray Miller, New Hampton (time advantage 4:48).

(Wrestle-back: Kenneth Bales, Fort Dodge beat Miller for second place).

125-Maurice Morford, Clarion beat Victor Brown, Eldora Training School.

135-Don Nichols, Cresco beat Roger Isaacson, Fort Dodge (time advantage 5:04).

(Wrestle-back: Stanley Corrington, Cherokee pinned Isaacson, 2:16 for second place.)

145-Marvin Farrell, Luverne beat Russell Woolver, Valley Junction (time advantage 3:21).

(Wrestle-back: Harry Hamilton, Cherokee beat Woolver for second place, time advantage 1:47).

155-Cliff Berry, Eldora Training School beat Leroy Mott, Mason City (time advantage 3:03).

(Wrestle-back: Lloyd Gulling, Cherokee beat Mott for second place, time advantage 3:00).

165-Floyd Messerly, Fort Dodge pinned Charles George, Cherokee 4:50.

(Wrestle-back: Howard Matson, Eagle Grove pinned George, 5:25 for second place).

Hwt-Walter Ponte, Eldora Training School beat Harold Leake, Mason City (time advantaghe 1:59).

(Wrestle-back: Donald Johnson, Fort Dodge beat Leake for second place, time advantage 1:53).

1936 (March 7)

85-Paul Bell, Clarion beat Paul Macek, Fort Dodge.

95-Irvin Kressley, Waterloo East beat William Kirstein, Clarion.

(Wrestle-back: Herman Luchsinger, Valley Junction beat Kirstein for second place).

105-Louis Pazzi. Valley Junction pinned Clair McOllough, Clarion, 2:39.

(Wrestle-back: Ray Hollar, Waterloo East pinned McOllough, 5:40 for second place).

115-Lloyd Sword, Eldora High School beat Robert Muhl, Fort Dodge.

125-Willis Kuhn, Fort Dodge pinned William Haynes, Waterloo West 4:00.

(Wrestle-back: Kenny Kingsbury, Cherokee beat Haynes for second place).

135-Maurice Morford, Clarion beat Gerrold Johnson, Osage.

(Wrestle-back: Bernard Soppe, Waterloo West pinned Johnson, 1:24 for second place).

145-Tom Rumeliote, Mason City pinned Franklin Brown, Clarion 5:46.

(Wrestle-back: William Gargano, Fort Dodge pinned Brown 1:58 for second place).

155-Charlie George, Cherokee pinned Mike Rajevich, Clinton 5:25.

(Wrestle-back: Mickey Castagnoli, Fort Dodge beat Rajevich for second place).

165-Lloyd Gulling, Cherokee beat Walter Ponte, Eldora Training School.

Hwt-Phil Strom, Fort Dodge beat Manley Wilcox, Perry(OT).

(Wrestle-back: John McLaren, Valley Junction beat Wilcox for second place).

1937 (February 27)

85-Albert Leeman, Osage beat Grant Tuttle, Cresco

(Wrestle-back: Jake Thorson, Fort Dodge beat Tuttle for second place).

95-Paul Bell, Clarion beat Leonard Bateman, Cherokee.

(Wrestle-back: Paul Macek, Fort Dodge beat Bateman for second place).

105-Bill Kirstein, Clarion beat Gaylord Bales, Fort Dodge.

(Wrestle-back: Irvin Kressley, Waterloo East beat Bales for second place).

115-Orin Thompson, Mason City beat Delbert Jensen, Waterloo West.

(Wrestle-back: Vic Wilcox, Waterloo East pinned Jensen for second place, time unavailable).

125-Einer Lindholm, Waterloo East pinned Orlando Calicchia, Mason City 7:53.

(Wrestle-back: Lloyd Sword, Eldora High School beat Calicchia for second place).

135-Willis Kuhn, Fort Dodge beat John Ball, New Hampton.

(Wrestle-back: Maurice Morford, Clarion beat Dave Porter, Waterloo West for second place).

145-Roger Isaacson, Fort Dodge beat Al Fliger, New Hampton.

(Wrestle-back: John Connolly, Cresco beat Fliger for second place).

155-John Roberts, Valley Junction beat Tom Rumeliote, Mason City.

165-Dean Campbell, Clarion beat George Rajevich, Clinton.

Hwt-John McLaren, Valley Junction beat Don Martin, Eagle Grove.

1938 (February 26)

85-Dean McOllough, Clarion beat Fred Christen, Waterloo West.

95-Albert Leeman, Osage beat Grant Tuttle, Cresco.

105-Paul Macek, Fort Dodge beat Leonard Bateman, Cherokee.

(Wrestle-back: John McGee, New Hampton beat Bateman for second place).

115-Paul Bell, Clarion beat Gaylord Bales, Fort Dodge.

125-Orin Thompson, Mason City beat Bill Kirstein, Clarion.

135-Bob Muhl, Fort Dodge beat Einar Lindholm, Waterloo East.

145-Dale Penn, Waterloo West beat Harold Weiska, Burt.

155-Tom Rumeliote, Mason City beat Ronnie Hudgins, Eagle Grove.

165-John Roberts, Valley Junction pinned Leonard Culbert, Cresco 1:17.

Hwt-Bill Bennett, Valley Junction beat Robert Penaluna, Waterloo West.

(Wrestle-back: Don Sharp, Clarion beat Penaluna for second place).

1939 (February 25)

85-Milan Macek, Fort Dodge won by injury default over Orval Bakken, Algona.

(Wrestle-back: Franklin Searcy, Cresco beat Don Beazley, Council Bluffs Lincoln for second place).

95-Jimmy Stewart, Cherokee pinned Tom Whitty, Clarion 4:05

(Wrestle-back: Melvin Bernard, Eagle Grove beat Whitty in OT for second place).

105-Gerald Leeman, Osage beat Grant Tuttle, Cresco.

115-Jack Wilcox, Waterloo West beat Carl Bergin, Iowa Falls.

125-Hugh Roberts, West Des Moines beat Raymond Deane, Cresco.

(Wrestle-back: Art Lynn, Waterloo East beat Deane for second place).

135-Leo Blanchet, Gilmore City beat Leo Sealock, Council Bluffs Jefferson.

145-Max Burke, Des Moines East beat Dean Carlson, Fort Dodge.

(Wrestle-back: Keith Strahorn, Iowa Falls beat Carlson for second place).

155-Harry McManus, Cherokee pinned Roger Claseman, Clinton 6:55.

165-Leon Martin, Eagle Grove pinned Vince Gebel, New Hampton 5:00.

(Wrestle-back: Stanley Simons, Cleghorn beat Gebel in OT for second place).

Hwt-Gordon Steele, Cherokee beat Harold Zell, Waterloo East.

(Wrestle-back: Bud Rademacher, Osage pinned Zell, 1:23 for second place).

1940 (February 24)

85-Jim Stoyanoff, Waterloo West beat Grant Tuttle, Cresco.

(Wrestle-back: Leland Christenson, Cherokee beat Tuttle for second place).

95-Grant Hunter, Council Bluffs Lincoln pinned Merle Roths, New Hampton 3:07.

105-Walter Oldham, Clarion beat Gus Kavars, Mason City.

115-Gerald Leeman, Osage beat Charlie Pickett, Waterloo West.

(Wrestle-back: Don Roderborn, Fort Dodge pinned Pickett, 4:36 for second place).

125-Jack Wilcox, Waterloo West pinned Mike Balherne, Waterloo East 4:29.

135-Dick Black, Fort Dodge pinned Kenny Harris, Osage 4:24.

145-Alfred Schultz, Eldora Training School pinned Hurschel O'Brien, Mason City 2:13.

155-Dick Gast, Osage beat Clarence McCullough, Des Moines Roosevelt.

(Wrestle-back: Donald Kirby, Gilmore City beat McCullough for second place).

165-George Gast, Osage beat Dick Geppert, Council Bluffs Jefferson.

Hwt-Harold Zell, Waterloo East pinned Clayton Bailey, Fort Dodge 4:11.

(Wrestle-back: Gordon Steele, Cherokee beat Bailey for second place).

1941 (March 1)

95-Jim Stoyanoff, Waterloo West beat Leland Christenson, Cherokee.

105-Merle Roths, New Hampton beat Mickey Waterman, Oelwein.

(Wrestle-back: Duane McCullough, Fort Dodge beat Waterman for second place).

112-Walter Oldham, Clarion pinned Glen Behrens, Osage, 1:40.

(Wrestle-back: Garth Lappin, Cresco beat Behrens for second place).

118-LuVerne Klar, Osage pinned Franklin Searcy, Cresco, 4:38.

123-Gerald Leeman, Osage pinned Pete Stasi, Oelwein, 5:50.

129-Sam Kramer, New Hampton beat Ralph Thomas, Council Bluffs Jefferson.

135-Bill Koll, Fort Dodge beat Harold Kramer, New Hampton.

(Wrestle-back: Doyle Shaver, Cresco beat Kramer for second place).

145-Henry Geilenfeldt, Algona pinned Bruce Lefler, Fort Dodge, 6:04.

155-Bob Johnson, Fort Dodge beat Clarence McCullough, Des Moines Roosevelt.

Hwt-Ray Carlson, Fort Dodge beat Bob Geigel, Algona.

(Wrestle-back: Fred Mulhern, Mason City beat Geigel for second place).

1942 (February 28)

95-Ronald Kelly, Eldora Training School pinned Hilton Wilcox, Mason City, 5:58.

105-Jim Stoyanoff, Waterloo West beat Felix Diaz, Oelwein.

(Wrestle-back: Keith Cantwell, Waterloo East beat Diaz for second place).

112-Bob Hunt, Council Bluffs Jefferson beat Merle Roths, New Hampton, 4 OT (referee's decision).

(Wrestle-back: Mervill Angell. Osage beat Roths for second place).

118-Richard Ditsworth, Algona beat Jim Weir, Oelwein.

123-Charles Nelson, Gilmore City pinned Bill West, Waterloo East, 3:51.

(Wrestle-back: Glen Behrens, Osage beat West for second place).

129-Eldon Faine, Fort Dodge pinned Bob Schaeffer, Eldora Training School, 5:35.

(Wrestle-back: Barney Ball, New Hampton beat Schaeffer for second place).

135-Bob Gamble, Mason City beat Doug Neve, Council Bluffs Jefferson.

(Wrestle-back: Bob Siddens, Eagle Grove beat Neve for second place).

145-Walter Parsons, Eagle Grove beat Floyd Reagan, Waterloo East.

(Wrestle-back: Gordon Landswerk, Cresco beat Reagan for second place).

155-Harvey Clemmensen, Waterloo West beat Louis Greco, Oelwein.

Hwt-Del Perrin, Cherokee beat Bob Geigel, Algona.

1943 (February 27)

95-Wally Hagen, Clarion pinned Richard Hauser, Waterloo West, 5:25.

105-LeRoy McGrew, Belle Plaine beat John Leo, Oelwein.

112-Felix Diaz, Osage beat Leonard Slaughter, Waterloo West.

118-Bob Hunt, Council Bluffs Jefferson beat Harold Bard, Eagle Grove.

(Wrestle-back: Mervill Angell, Osage beat Bard for second place).

123-Charles Nelson, Gilmore City pinned Darrell Hickenbottom, Clinton, 3:55.

(Wrestle-back: Lowell Lange, Waterloo West beat Hickenbottom for second place).

129-Duane Hanson, Oelwein beat Kenneth Tuttle, Hampton.

135-Neal Johnson, Waterloo West beat Roger Ratcliff, Cresco.

145-Gordon Landswerk, Cresco beat Ken Carlson, Fort Dodge.

(Wrestle-back: Bob Siddens, Eagle Grove won second place by forfeit).

155-Leonard Rohrer, Clarion beat Bill Nelson, Eagle Grove.

(Wrestle-back: Loren Redman, Clinton beat Nelson for second place).

Hwt-Harry Linderbaum, Cresco beat Oliver Michaelsen, Waterloo West.

(Wrestle-back: James Claggett, Eagle Grove won second place by injury default).

1944 (February 26)

95-Wally Hagen, Clarion beat Dick Holst, Council Bluffs Jefferson.

105-Dick Hauser, Waterloo West pinned Charles Metcalf, Waterloo East, 4:37.

112-George McCart, Eagle Grove beat Ed Steinhoff, Fort Dodge.

118-Dick Cumming, Waterloo West beat Tommy Cummings, Osage.

123-Alec Kloberdanz, Osage beat Dick Evans, Clarion.

(Wrestle-back: Bernard Hayden, Fort Dodge beat Evans for second place).

129-Mervill Angell, Osage beat Lowell Lange, Waterloo West.

135-Bill Manning, Waterloo West beat John Schwab, Osage.

(Wrestle-back: Robert Larson, Eagle Grove beat Schwab for second place).

145-Virgil Counsell, Osage beat Lloyd Callopy, Eagle Grove (OT).

(Wrestle-back: Kenneth Schmoker, Fort Dodge beat Callopy for second place).

155-Bob Wilson, Waterloo West beat Bill Nelson, Eagle Grove.

Hwt-Oliver Michaelsen, Waterloo West beat Joe Paulsen, Davenport.

(Wrestle-back: Leonard Rohrer, Clarion beat Paulsen for second place).

1945 (February 24)

95-Dominic Aversa, Oelwein pinned Jack Springer, Waterloo West, 5:41.

(Wrestle-back: Gaylord Rich, Council Bluffs Jefferson beat Springer for second place).

105-Dale Nelson, Eagle Grove beat Glenn Angell, Osage.

112-Dick Holst, Council Bluffs Jefferson beat Charles Metcalf, Waterloo East.

118-Dick Hauser, Waterloo West pinned Denmar Cope, Davenport, 1:18.

(Wrestle-back: Arland Anderson, Clarion beat Cope for second place).

123-Tom Cummings, Osage pinned James Nares, Davenport, 1:14.

(Wrestle-back: Lewis Larson, Fort Dodge beat Nares for second place).

129-Leo Thomsen, Waterloo West pinned Paul Ridone, Council Bluffs Jefferson, 6:08.

135-Harold Bard, Eagle Grove beat Dick Barker, Osage.

(Wrestle-back: Bob Appleby, Waterloo West beat Barker for second place).

145-Lowell Lange, Waterloo West beat John Schwab, Osage.

155-Harry Horn, Osage beat Jerome Rohrer, Clarion, referee's decision.

(Wrestle-back: Kenneth Carlson, Fort Dodge beat Rohrer for second place).

Hwt-Bill Nelson, Eagle Grove beat Wayne Rife, Des Moines East.

(Wrestle-back: Joe Paulsen, Davenport beat Rife for second place).

1946 (February 23)

95-Virgil Rink, Clarion beat Dick Lewis, Council Bluffs Jefferson, 2-0.

105-Manuel Macias, Davenport beat Frank Altman, Osage, 4-1.

(Wrestle-back: Dominic Aversa, Oelwein beat Altman, 1-0, for second place).

112-Carroll Martin, Clarion beat John Harrison, Fort Dodge, 7-2.

118-Dick Hauser, Waterloo West beat Dale Nelson, Eagle Grove, 4-3.

123-Lewis Larson, Eagle Grove beat Bill Smith, Council Bluffs Jefferson, 2-0.

129-Leo Thomsen, Waterloo West beat Al Lau, Oelwein, 4-1.

(Wrestle-back: George McCart, Eagle Grove beat Lau, 4-1, for second place).

135-Curt Stein, Gilmore City beat Bob Appleby, Waterloo West, 5-3.

(Wrestle-back: Ed Maakestad, Osage beat Appleby, 2-1, for second place).

145-Lowell Lange, Waterloo West beat John Schwab, Osage 2-0.

155-Harry Horn, Osage beat Merle Mikelson, Clarion 2-0.

(Wrestle-back: Ken Gangestad, Eagle Grove beat Mikelson, 4-2, for second place).

Hwt-Joe Paulsen, Davenport beat Roy Hutchinson, Fort Dodge, 2-0.

(Wrestle-back: Jerome Rohrer, Clarion beat Hutchinson, 4-3, for second place).

1947(February 22)

95-Dick Barron, Waterloo West beat Kenneth Anderson, Osage 6-4.

105-Edward Nelson, Eagle Grove beat Dick Lewis, Council Bluffs Jefferson 8-5.

(Wrestle-back: Gene Lybbert, Cresco beat Lewis, 1-0, for second place).

112-Frank Altman, Osage beat Harry Dexter, Davenport 2-1.

(Wrestle-back: Marvin Cervene, Fort Dodge beat Dexter, 1-0, for second place).

118-Jack Springer, Waterloo West beat Walter Furler, Council Bluffs Jefferson 2-0 (OT).

(Wrestle-back: Robert Wilson, Clarion beat Furler, 9-2, for second place).

123-John Rowen, Clarion beat Don McCormick, Gilmore City 6-5.

129-Don Miller, Waterloo East beat John Campbell, Davenport 4-1.

(Wrestle-back: Bill Connell, Council Bluffs Jefferson beat Campbell, 1-0 (OT) for second place).

135-Glenn Angell, Osage beat Dan Gallery, Waterloo West 2-0.

(Wrestle-back: Dick Cibert, Fort Dodge beat Gallery, 6-4, for second place).

145-Don Ryan, Council Bluffs Jefferson beat Leonard Morphew, Eagle Grove 2-0.

155-Jerry Rohrer, Clarion pinned Dick Sherwood, Waterloo East 4:04.

(Wrestle-back: Walter Ohl, Oelwein beat Sherwood, 6-4, for second place).

Hwt-Joe Paulsen, Davenport beat Merle Wilson, Clarion 2-1.

1948 (February 20)

95-Jack Turk, Clarion beat Bob Lewis, Davenport 10-6.

(Wrestle-back: Dean Ketelson, Osage beat Lewis, 4-3, for second place).

105-Don Lahr, Eagle Grove beat Richard Burkeholder, Fort Dodge 3-1.

112-Ed Nelson, Eagle Grove beat Phillip Duggan, Davenport 2-0.

(Wrestle-back: Gene Lybbert, Cresco beat Duggan, 7-3, for second place).

118-Barney Duneman, Cresco beat Tom DiBlasi, Council Bluffs Lincoln 7-3.

(Wrestle-back: Bob Wilson, Clarion pinned DiBlasi, 5:44, for second place).

123-Ray Steiger, Cresco won by injury default over Harold Dexter, Davenport.

(Wrestle-back: Bob Wirds, Iowa Falls won second place by forfeit).

129-Gene Aberg, Cresco beat Dick Hurst, Waterloo West 1-0 (OT).

135-Charles Hyke, Cresco beat Gerald Mayberry, Maquoketa 5-2.

145-Don Miller, Waterloo East beat Bill Waddell, Newton 4-0.

155-Don Ryan, Council Bluffs Jefferson beat Walter Ohl, Oelwein 6-3.

165-Dave Glenny, Waterloo West beat Bernard Lammers, Newton 3-0.

(Wrestle-back: Ed Southard, Clarion beat Lammers, 4-2, for second place).

Hwt-Merle Wilson, Clarion pinned Carl Olson, Osage 3:33.

(Wrestle-back: John McChesney, Waterloo West beat Olson, 2-0, for second place).

1949 (February 19)

95-Dale DeSart, Cresco beat Willard Blake, Davenport 4-0.

(Wrestle-back: Frank Patterson, Fort Dodge pinned Blake, 3:41, for second place).

105-Gene Piersall, Davenport beat Frank DiBlasi, Council Bluffs Lincoln 3-2.

(Wrestle-back: Norvard Nalan, Mason City beat DiBlasi, 3-0, for second place).

112-Dean Shunkwiler, Mason City beat Roger Hansen, Cedar Falls 4-3 (OT).

(Wrestle-back: Bill Butcher, Waterloo East beat Hansen, 2-0, for second place).

118-Ed Nelson, Eagle Grove beat Derald Morse, Clarion 2-0.

(Wrestle-back: Ray Rucker, Cresco beat Morse, 2-0, for second place).

123-Ken Meachem, Mason City beat Keith Angell, Osage 3-2.

129-Ray Steiger, Cresco beat Bill Wilcox, Waterloo East 5-1.

135-Wes Sterner, Waterloo East beat John Campbell, Davenport 10-0.

(Wrestle-back: Tom Chelesvig, Eagle Grove won second place by forfeit).

145-Stan Davis, Waterloo East beat Phil Haring, Fort Dodge 3-1.

(Wrestle-back: Bill Ogelsby, Mason City beat Haring, 1-0, for second place).

155-Dave McKinley, Council Bluffs Lincoln beat Joe Vokaty, Cresco 6-1.

(Wrestle-back: Don Bailey, Osage beat Vokaty, 1-0, for second place).

165-Melvin Peed, Fort Dodge beat Roger Mohs, Cresco 3-2 (OT).

(Wrestle-back: Bob Nusser, Council Bluffs Jefferson beat Mohs, 6-1, for second place).

Hwt-Mel Waldon, Clarion beat Jim Burright, Waterloo West 3-1 (OT).

1950 (February 18)

95-Dale DeSart, Cresco beat Dick Kain, Algona 4-2.

105-Charles Boerjan, Osage beat Dick Goetz, Davenport 3-0.

112-Gene Piersall, Davenport beat Norvard Nalan, Mason City 6-0.

118-Maurice Comisky, Osage beat Dean Shunkwiler, Mason City 5-4 (OT).

123-Paul Fisher, Algona beat Beauford Haizlip, Council Bluffs Jefferson 2-0.

129-Ken Meacham, Mason City beat Roger Chapman, Waterloo East 4-1.

135-Wes Sterner, Waterloo East beat Howard Blount, Clinton 8-1.

145-Tom Chelesvig, Eagle Grove beat Bob Thorson, Cresco 2-1.

(Wrestle-back: Stan Davis, Waterloo East pinned Thorson, 6:13 (OT), for second place).

155-Bill Ogelsby, Mason City beat Phillip Haring, Fort Dodge 3-1.

165-Bob Musser, Council Bluffs Jefferson beat Vic Jass, Iowa Falls 5-3.

Hwt-Dick Schmidt, Independence beat Herb Hess, Cedar Rapids Wilson 1-0.

(Wrestle-back: Vernie Bierl, Clarion beat Hess, 2-1, for second place).

1951 (March 3)

95-Eddie Kline, Mason City beat Fred Metz, Newton 4-1.

(Wrestle-back: Chuck Huff, Waterloo West beat Metz, 4-2, for second place).

105-Dick Govig, Britt beat Dick Kain, Algona 3-1.

112-Monte Black, Algona beat Frank DiBlasi, Council Bluffs Lincoln 4-2.

(Wrestle-back: Charles Boerjan beat DiBlasi, 4-0, for second place).

118-Carl Hernandez, Oelwein beat Wayne Sovereign, Cresco 3-2.

(Wrestle-back: Jim Murphy, Clarion beat Sovereign, 2-0, for second place).

123-Dean Lufkin, Newton beat Dean Ketelson, Osage 3-3 (referee's decision).

129-Paul Fisher, Algona beat Paul Woodard, Cresco 7-6.

135-Ralph Rieks, Iowa Falls beat Ron Bemus, Waterloo West 4-2.

(Wrestle-back: Howard Blount, Clinton beat Bemus, 4-0, for second place).

145-Jerry Seeber, Osage beat Jim Harmon, Waterloo West 5-3.

155-Elmer Bradley, Traer beat LaVerne Gunderson, Osage 6-5.

(Wrestle-back: Harlan Jenkinson, Waterloo West beat Gunderson, Osage, 2-0, for second place).

165-Wayland Blake, Eagle Grove beat John Winder, Waterloo West 3-2.

Hwt-Dick Wade, Des Moines East beat Dick Burns, Carroll 3-2.

1952 (March 1)

95-Eddie Kline, Mason City pinned Earle Edwards, NU High, 4:52.

(Wrestle-back: Gary Klemesrud, Osage beat Edwards, 3-1, for second place).

103-Ron Gray, Eagle Grove beat John Beery, Mason City, 6-5.

(Wrestle-back: Charles Huff, Waterloo West beat Beery, 4-0, for second place).

112-Dick Govig, Britt pinned Leon Lopez, Davenport 2:38.

120-Don Hall, Cresco beat Bob Kain, Algona, 2-1.

(Wrestle-back: Gene Plath, Mason City beat Kain, 5-2, for second place).

127-Dean Lufkin, Newton beat Darrell Miller, Iowa Falls 3-1.

133-Bob Trauffer, Davenport beat Dick Kain, Algona 6-6 (referee's decision).

138-Ralph Rieks, Iowa Falls beat Dick Goetz, Davenport 1-1 (referee's decision).

145-Arnie Brandt, Waverly beat Alan Bailey, Osage, 2-0.

(Wrestle-back: Henry Philmon, Davenport beat Bailey, 2-1, for second place).

154-Harlan Jenkinson, Waterloo West beat Dean Hiscocks, Britt 4-0.

165-John Winder, Waterloo West beat Ken Salyer, Waterloo East 2-1.

Hwt-Ron Shirley, Bettendorf pinned Gaylen Peckham, Cresco, 5:51.

(Wrestle-back: Lorne Willadsen, New Hampton beat Peckham, 2-1, for second place).

1953 (February 28)

95-Jack Koehn, Waterloo West beat Jerry Demro, Charles City 2-1 (OT).

103-Eddie Kline, Mason City pinned Bill Leeman, Osage 3:13.

112-Earle Edwards, NU High (Cedar Falls) beat Larry Moser, Waterloo West 4-3.

120-Ron Gray, Eagle Grove beat Dick Heaton, Waterloo East 6-2.

127-Don Hall, Cresco beat Gordon Cranston, Cedar Falls 4-2.

133-Darrell Miller, Iowa Falls beat George Nord, Clinton 5-2.

138-Jerry Salmon, Newton beat Jim McCray, Davenport 4-2.

145-Bill Clement, Newton beat Tom Kempley, Fort Dodge Corpus Christi 5-2.

154-Jack Smith, Waterloo East beat Dick Formanek, Tama 3-0.

165-Ken Salyer, Waterloo East beat David Weiss, Clarion 3-0.

Hwt-Gary Kurdelmeier, Cresco pinned Dave Shakespeare, Cedar Rapids Roosevelt 5:04.

1954 (March 6)

95-Vince Garcia, Davenport beat Tom Turk, Clarion 2-0.

103-Les Anderson, Clarion beat Kaye Slocum, Cedar Rapids Roosevelt 4-2.

112-Don Bernard, Eagle Grove pinned Dick Hansen, Britt 3:27.

120-Earle Edwards, NU High (Cedar Falls) beat Gary Green, Britt 2-0.

127-Gary Klemesrud, Osage beat Clint Lau, Oelwein 2-1.

133-Simon Roberts, Davenport beat Ron Gray, Eagle Grove 3-1.

138-Gordon Moser, Waterloo West beat Dick Heaton, Waterloo East 2-0 (OT).

145-Del Rossberg, Waterloo West beat Bill Meffert, Cedar Rapids Franklin 4-0.

154-Ron Meleney, Britt beat Bob Ihlfeld, Davenport 5-0.

165-Arnie Nelson, Audubon pinned Jim Newsome, Des Moines East 2:40.

Hwt-Gary Kurdelmeier, Cresco pinned Joe Funk, Algona 1:59.

1955 (March 5)

95-Dan Carey, Waterloo East beat Dennis Friedrichs, Fort Dodge 3-2.

103-Orlo Ottosen, Osage pinned Vince Garcia, Davenport 2:47.

112-Dee Brainerd, Fort Dodge beat Larry Moser, Waterloo West, 1-1 (referee's decision).

120-Roy Andrews, Waterloo East beat Les Anderson, Clarion 5-1.

127-Jerry Mark, Iowa Falls beat Jim Larick, Clarion 2-1.

133-Tom Winder, Waterloo West beat Gene Bahr, Iowa Falls 7-4.

138-Ron Gray, Eagle Grove beat John Hiscocks, Britt 2-0.

145-Del Rossberg, Waterloo West beat Gaylord Peter, Cresco 5-4.

154-Bob Ihlfeld, Davenport pinned Ron Roberts, Cresco 5:53.

165-Jim Howieson, Clarion beat Jim Craig, Davenport 3-2.

Hwt-Bob Hain, Davenport beat Dick Schilling, New Hampton 2-1.

1956 (March 3)

95-Don Huff, Waterloo West beat Ron Booth, Mason City 6-4.

103-Jim Klepfer, Cedar Falls beat Don Carey, Waterloo East 3-1.

112-Don Webster, Cresco beat Morris Barnhill, Davenport 4-2.

120-Dee Brainerd, Fort Dodge beat Francis Freeman, Davenport 6-1.

127-Chuck Conway, Britt beat Jim Barton, Davenport 1-0.

133Ken O'Kada, Cresco beat Merle Stottlemeyer, Clinton 2-1.

138-Tim Blount, Clinton beat John Hiscocks, Britt 2-1 (OT).

145-Jim Bunning, Waterloo West beat Bill Riebsamen, Britt 6-3.

154-Gerald McDonald, Waterloo East beat Bob Landau, Waterloo West 8-3.

165-Alan Hiscocks, Britt beat Virgil DeVary, Mason City 5-4.

Hwt-Bob Hain, Davenport beat Sherwood Carter, Fort Dodge 4-0.

1957 (February 23)

CLASS A

95-Tom Huff, Waterloo West beat Banks Swan, Davenport 5-4.

103-Tom Nordyke, Waterloo West beat Herb Schnee, Dubuque 6-1.

112-Don Huff, Waterloo West beat Daryl Hamlin, Waterloo East 5-0.

120-Jay Hollins, Waterloo East beat Jerry Walker, Cedar Rapids Wilson 4-3.

127-Dave Jensen, Charles City beat Jim Sanford, Fort Dodge 6-2.

133-Bill Dotson, Waterloo East beat Mike Bewly, Davenport 10-1.

138-Larry Hayes, Des Moines Lincoln beat Jerry Springer, Waterloo West 2-0.

145-Virgil Carr, Waterloo East beat Don Matson, Mason City 5-2.

154-Gerald McDonald, Waterloo East beat Merle Stottlemeyer, Clinton 6-1.

165-Roger Olson, Mason City beat Bob Elliott, Davenport 2-0.

Hwt-Jim Hoosman, Waterloo East pinned Tom Greene, Council Bluffs Lincoln 1:59.

CLASS B

95-Larry Severson, New Hampton beat Bill Block, Maquoketa 4-0.

103-Jim Carr, New Hampton beat Frank Reed, Iowa Falls 4-0.

112-Arlin Severson, New Hampton beat Harold Thompson, Osage 4-0.

120-Don Webster, Cresco beat Morris Wilson, Clarion 4-0.

127-Gordon Loy, Cresco beat Gene Ritchmond, New Hampton 5-0.

133-Chuck Conway, Britt beat Ken Penaluna, Hampton 4-2.

138-Jack Stifler, Waverly pinned Doug Morford, Clarion 5:20.

145-Bob DaVitt, Audubon beat Wayne Howard, Eagle Grove 4-2.

154-Bob Wall, Iowa Falls beat Lynn Hassman, Waverly 5-4 (riding time).

165-Bob Duvall, New Hampton beat Duane Hansen, Britt 3-1 (OT).

Hwt-Jan Schwitters, Iowa Falls pinned Jerry Wedemeier, Waverly 3:37.

1958 (February 15)

CLASS A

95-Bob Buzzard, Waterloo East beat Larry Bewley, Davenport 2-0.

103-Lloyd Grandon, Cedar Falls beat Trino Gomez, Bettendorf, 8-7 (OT).

112-Tom Huff, Waterloo West beat Howie Finneman, Mason City 6-2.

120-Herb Schnee, Dubuque beat Mike Nissen, Mason City 3-1.

127-Jay Hollins, Waterloo East pinned Gary Miller, Waterloo West 5:22.

133-Alan McElhose, Waterloo West beat Jim Sanford, Fort Dodge 4-2.

138-Jerry Springer, Waterloo West beat Mike Natvig, Decorah 5-3.

145-Bill Dotson, Waterloo East beat Cecil Ritter, Bettendorf 5-1.

154-Virgil Carr, Waterloo East beat Terry Isaacson, Dubuque 3-1.

165-Dave Church, Fort Dodge beat Wayne Powers, Des Moines Tech 5-2.

Hwt-Joe Chezum, Fairfield beat Sherwyn Thorson, Fort Dodge 4-2.

CLASS B

95-Dick Bernard, Eagle Grove beat Don Henry, Cresco 2-0.

103-Frank Reed, Iowa Falls beat Merlin Schmauss, Cresco 6-1.

112-Dennis Foy, Britt beat Joe Fox, Osage 9-5 (OT).

120-Morris Wilson, Clarion beat Ed Fox, Osage 2-0.

127-Dave Gates, Cresco beat Ron Betts, Oelwein 5-0.

133-Carroll Flatebo, Eagle Grove beat Monte Briner, Waverly 2-0.

138-Francis Bjustrom, Algona beat Jim Chelesvig, Eagle Grove 5-3.

145-Bill Murray, Cresco beat Ron Rice, NU High (Cedar Falls) 1-0.

154-Jim Grover, Cresco beat Mike Seller, Algona 1-0.

165-Larry Schultz, Eagle Grove beat Dennis Schwitters, Iowa Falls 3-1.

Hwt-Jeremy Wedemeier, Waverly beat Roger Watkins, NU High (Cedar Falls) 5-4 (OT).

1959 (February 14)

CLASS A

95-Jim Barman, Waterloo East beat Fran Augustron, Waterloo West 2-0.

103-Lowell Stewart, Waterloo West beat Lowell Husome, Cedar Falls 4-0.

112-Frank Lane, Waterloo West beat Bob Buzzard, Waterloo East 3-0.

120-Tom Huff, Waterloo West pinned John Rinderknecht, Cedar Rapids Washington 3:30.

127-Tom Gesell, Waterloo East beat Jon Perry, Waterloo West 3-0.

133-Scot Klepfer, Cedar Falls beat Jim Bast, Waterloo West 2-1.

138-Larry Kay, Charles City beat Larry Pederson, Fort Dodge 2-1.

145-Ed Winborn, Davenport Central beat Cecil Ritter, Bettendorf 3-2.

154-Bob Grant, Charles City beat Roy Frantz, Iowa City High 3-1.

165-Steve Machovec, Iowa City High beat Ralph Walthers, Davenport Central 6-3.

Hwt-Dan Grimm, Des Moines Roosevelt beat Chauncey Carr, Waterloo East 2-0.

CLASS B

95-Bob Steenlage, Britt beat Ron Jones, Iowa Falls 2-1.

103-Don Henry, Cresco beat Gordon Hassman, New Hampton 2-0.

112-Merlin Schmauss, Cresco beat Larry Sagers, Maquoketa 6-2.

120-Larry Willis, Clarion beat Ed Fox, Osage 3-2.

127-Joe Frank, Cresco pinned Jason Etherington, Algona 3:41.

133-Jim Boerjan, Osage beat Mike Harman, New Hampton 2-1.

138-Vern Cutsforth, New Hampton beat Monte Briner, Waverly 2-1.

145-Ron Rice, NU High (Cedar Falls) pinned Alex Egorenko, Cresco 3:47.

154-Virgil Reiter, Perry beat Zeke Plorins, Cedar Falls 5-4.

165-Dick Duvall, New Hampton beat Sid Severson, Clarion 9-3.

Hwt-Larry Hochhaus, Britt beat Roger Schilling, New Hampton 5-0.

1960 (February 20)

CLASS A

95-Bill Duff, Waterloo East beat Jim Bleakley, Newton 6-6 (jury decision).

103-Jim Barman, Waterloo East pinned Dick Coleman, Council Bluffs Jefferson, 3:05.

112-Al Robinson, Waterloo East beat Steve Weeker, Iowa City High 8-0.

120-Clyde Shirley, Charles City beat Larry Bewley, Davenport Central 10-9.

127-Bob Buzzard, Waterloo East beat Jerry Millage, Muscatine 4-0.

133-Paul Mayo, Grinnell beat Gary Harold, Cedar Falls 8-4.

138-Jim Leach, Davenport Central beat Dick Cool, Waterloo East 6-1.

145-Mel Wieland, Cedar Rapids Jefferson beat Bob Borden, Davenport 3-2.

154-Don Westcott, Iowa City High beat Jay Roberts, Muscatine 4-1.

165-Mike Gordon, Charles City beat Roy Frantz, Iowa City High 5-4.

175-George Thompson, Davenport Central pinned Larry Warnke, Waterloo West :29.

Hwt-Larry Conaway, Cedar Rapids Washington beat Steve Caldwell, Iowa City High 5-3.

CLASS B

95-Dick Schmauss, Cresco beat Quentin Rohrer, Eagle Grove 12-1.

103-Bob Steenlage, Britt beat Rich Leichtman, New Hampton 4-0.

112-Merlin Schmauss, Cresco beat Roger Sebert, Clarion 6-4.

120-Gordon Hassman, New Hampton beat Don Henry, Cresco 0-0 (jury decision).

127-Tom Peckham, Cresco beat Bill Block, Maquoketa 4-0.

133-Jason Etherington, Algona beat Jim Deutsch, New Hampton 7-4.

138-Dave Randall, Osage beat Monte Briner, Waverly 3-0.

145-Alex Egorenko, Cresco beat Larry Hibbs, New Hampton 3-1.

154-Larry Hochhaus, Britt beat George Hartley, Waukon 9-3.

165-Paul Smith, Britt beat Virgil Reiter, Perry 5-4.

Hwt-Bob Campbell., Iowa Falls beat Ken Buhr, Cresco 7-2.

1961 (February 18)

CLASS A

95-Anthony Jensen, Fort Dodge beat Kelly Donham, Iowa City High 6-5.

103-Paul Miller, Waterloo East beat Bob Highland, Fort Dodge 4-0.

112-Don Henry, Cresco beat Trino Gomez, Bettendorf 1-0.

120-Dick Patterson, Fort Dodge pinned Don Buzzard, Waterloo East :39.

127-Dave Saddler, Waterloo East beat Bill Hanaman, Mason City 2-1.

133-Omar Frank, Cresco beat Otto Fiei, Davenport Central 4-1.

138-John Kessler, Davenport Central beat Ron Kenworthy, Clinton 3-2.

145-Mel Wieland, Cedar Rapids Jefferson beat Bob Borden, Davenport Central 1-0.

154-Tom Peckham, Cresco pinned Wayne Cool, Waterloo East 5:07.

165-Gary Langan, Bettendorf beat Charles Butler, Waterloo East 5-4 (OT).

175-Roy Frantz, Iowa City High beat Clarence Sharp, Des Moines East 3-0.

Hwt-Dave Fobian, Cedar Falls beat Terry Hummell, Waterloo West 1-1 (jury decision).

CLASS B

95-Larry Lloyd, Britt beat Bob Rosauer, New Hampton 2-0.

103-Bob Mayo, Grinnell pinned Russ Miller, Jesup 1:50.

112-Bob Steenlage, Britt beat Dan Sullivan, Corning 2-0.

120-Dick Hunter, Jesup beat Roger Sebert, Clarion 5-2.

127-Jerry Brown, Jesup beat Larry Arthur, Clarion 3-1.

133-Don Jones, Iowa Falls beat Jim Richardson, Algona 10-8.

138-Tom Thompson, Janesville beat Ken Shaner, Alden 7-6 (OT).

145-Dennis Krull, Britt beat Jerry Seiler, Algona 2-0.

154-Dick Austin, Waverly-Shell Rock beat Dale Brcka, Britt 4-3.

165-Stan Saunders, Janesville beat Dennis Bahr, Iowa Falls 3-2.

Hwt-Roger Schilling, New Hampton beat Leonard Ackerman, Waverly-Shell Rock 2-1.

1962 (February 24)

CLASS A

95-Steve Childs, Cedar Rapids Jefferson beat Dick Hutchinson, Bettendorf 2-1.

103-Paul Miller, Waterloo West beat Jeff Hubner, Davenport Central 2-0 (OT).

112-Bill Smith, Des Moines Roosevelt beat Obie Saddler, Waterloo East 4-2.

120-Jack Boltz, Davenport West beat Alan Sieversten, Cedar Rapids Jefferson 4-2.

127-Cal Jenkins, Cedar Rapids Jefferson beat Randy Lewis, Cedar Falls 4-2.

133-Dave Saddler, Waterloo East beat Roger Lane, Waterloo West 3-2.

138-Herb Krieger, Mason City beat Dennis Kendall, Waterloo West 3-1.

145-Ron Noah, Charles City pinned Bill Armitage, Cedar Rapids Jefferson 2:53.

154-Mel Wieland, Cedar Rapids Jefferson beat Jim Evashevski, Iowa City High 2-1.

165-Glen Mitchell, Davenport Central beat Gary Langan, Bettendorf 7-4.

175-LaVern Alters, Davenport West pinned Monty Rierson, Cedar Rapids Jefferson 4:30.

Hwt-Ted Tuinstra, Des Moines East beat Rob Hartliep, Waterloo West 3-1.

CLASS B

95-Kendall Miller, New Hampton beat Steve Woodley, Estherville 3-0.

103-Larry Lloyd, Britt beat Del Weaver, Griswold 3-2.

112-Rich Leichtman, New Hampton beat Bill Blazek, Tama 4-0.

120-Bob Steenlage, Britt beat Steve Balsbaugh, Perry 3-2 (Riding time).

127-Bob Rausenberger, Iowa Falls beat Clyde Barnhart, Chariton 7-1.

133-Bob Patton, Algona beat Darrell Brown, Jesup 4-0.

138-Ken Shaner, Alden beat Dave Bahr, Iowa Falls 3-0.

145-Dick Wilkes, Osage beat Russell Sill, Manchester 8-2.

154-Dennis Wegner, Wapsie Valley beat Nick Nichols, Clarion 4-3.

165-Tom Peckham, Cresco pinned Don Parker, North Fayette (West Union) 4:34.

Hwt-Jim Homan, Waverly-Shell Rock beat Jim Siebiska, Grinnell 2-0.

1963 (February 23)

CLASS A

95-Steve Childs, Cedar Rapids Jefferson beat Bill Cannon, Waterloo West 2-0.

103-Paul Stinson, Waterloo East beat Jon Winger, Cedar Rapids Jefferson 3-0.

112-Anthony Jensen, Fort Dodge beat Obie Saddler, Waterloo East 5-2.

120-Dale Anderson, Waterloo West beat John Bleakney, Newton 2-0.

127-Al Sievertsen, Cedar Rapids Jefferson beat Willie Hoosman, Waterloo East 2-0.

133-Dick Conly, Carroll Kuemper beat Jack Deere, Bettendorf 3-1.

138-Dave Cherry, Des Moines Lincoln beat Rich Wellman, Des Moines Roosevelt 2-2, 1-0 OT.

145-Burt Mericle, Des Moines Tech beat Doug Woods, Iowa City High 5-4.

154-Richard Bleakley, Cedar Rapids Washington beat Gary Mitskoff, Des Moines Roosevelt 9-7.

165-Don Buzzard, Waterloo East beat John Rate, Iowa City High 4-0.

180-Monty Rierson, Cedar Rapids Jefferson beat Steve Moss, Iowa City High 1-0.

Hwt-Larry Sherman, Davenport Central pinned Jim Hoffman, Cedar Rapids Washington 5:35.

CLASS B

95-Bruce Woolsey, Waterloo Orange beat Chuck Moen, New Hampton 3-0.

103-Kendall Miller, New Hampton beat Mike Schmauss, Cresco 4-0.

112-Chuck Joergenson, Cresco beat Don Hutchinson, Algona 4-3.

120-Gary Johnson, New Hampton beat LeRoy LaRue, Clarion 9-3.

127-Bob Rausenberger, Iowa Falls beat Ron Tope, North Fayette (West Union) 3-1.

133-Bill Rex, Central Decatur beat Gary Watts, Clarion 3-2 (OT).

138-Tim Vipond, Algona pinned Ron Stoskopf, Decorah 3:52.

145-Dale Bahr, Iowa Falls beat Dick Moeller, Wapsie Valley 5-2.

154-Don Miller, Eagle Grove pinned Vinnie Kopacek, Britt 5:39.

165-Don Parker, North Fayette (West Union) beat Ron Pyle, Eagle Grove 4-2.

Hwt-Glenn Pitkin, Britt beat Jon Lambi, Greenfield 1-0.

1964 (February 22)

CLASS AA

95-Dan Gable, Waterloo West beat Mike Reams, Charles City 6-4.

103-Tyrone Orr, Davenport Central beat Allen Millen, Cedar Rapids Washington 3-1.

112-Paul Stinson, Waterloo East beat Wally Reams, Charles City 1-1, 1-1 (referee's decision).

120-Tom Moore, Waterloo East beat Jim Frei, Davenport Central 5-2.

127-Dale Anderson, Waterloo West pinned Rich Mihal, Cedar Rapids Jefferson 1:54.

133-Willie Hoosman, Waterloo East beat Wally Markham, Waterloo West 2-0.

138-Ed Heene, Waterloo West beat Bill Harrold, Charles City 2-0.

145-Dick Bason, Des Moines Lincoln beat Dennis Lyall, Des Molines Tech 5-2.

154-Bob Bream, Iowa City High beat Tom Horton, Fort Dodge 2-0.

165-Peter Middleton, Waterloo East beat Mack Anderson, Davenport Central 2-0.

180-Don Buzzard, Waterloo East beat Floyd Shade, Des Moines Tech 3-0.

Hwt-Kent Osboe, Fort Dodge beat Bud Knox, Waterloo West 8-7.

CLASS A

95-Danny McKenzie, Urbandale beat John Spence, Waterloo Orange 2-1.

103-Mike Schmauss, Cresco beat Steve Woodley, Estherville 4-0.

112-Gary Tourtelotte, Clarion beat Bob Ewoldt, Algona 3-2.

120-Lorri McLaughlin, Hampton beat Dave Mayberry, Maquoketa 2-0.

127-Ron Poush, Chariton beat Joe Wiewel, Manchester 4-2.

133-Dennis Miller, Algona beat Terry Eckerman, Cresco 4-1.

138-Bill Rex, Central Decatur pinned Gary Watts, Clarion 3:57.

145-Dale Bahr, Iowa Falls beat Carl Aegler, Cresco 6-3.

154-Russell Sill, Manchester beat Reg Wicks, Decorah 1-0.

165-Don Miller, Eagle Grove beat Duane Nosbisch, New Hampton 4-0.

Hwt-Wade Winters, Bondurant-Farrar beat Dick Hardon, Tama-Toledo 4-1.

1965 (February 20)

CLASS AA

95-Wiley Lodge, Waterloo East beat Mike Austin, Mason City 4-0.

103-Dan Gable, Waterloo West beat Denny Knudsen, Fort Dodge 6-0.

112-Paul Stinson, Waterloo East beat William Ellis, Perry 9-2.

120-Paul Austin, Mason City pinned Dennis Nixt, Charles City 1:35.

127-Mel Freeman, Davenport West beat Bruce McClintock, Waterloo West 4-2.

133-John Powers, Davenport Central beat Curtis Cooper, Cedar Falls 4-3.

138-Rich Mihal, Cedar Rapids Jefferson beat Dave Borden, Davenport Central 2-1.

145-Phil Henning, Decorah beat Allen Mohr, North Scott 4-2.

154-Frank Spinka, Cedar Rapids Jefferson won by injury default over Wilson Thomas, Davenport Central.

165-Kim Rhoades, Cedar Falls beat Verlyn Strellner, Tama-Toledo 4-0.

180-Pete Kohl, Cedar Rapids Washington beat Tim Blackman, Des Moines Tech 6-1.

Hwt-Bud Knox, Waterloo West beat Dale Stearns, Chariton 2-1.

CLASS A

95-Bob Mueller, Osage beat Gene Casey, Griswold 4-2.

103-Roy Seymour, Camanche beat Jim Byrnes, Osage 7-1.

112-Gary Tourtelotte, Clarion beat Ervin Nelson, Britt 2-1.

120-Pat Hannon, Urbandale beat Arnold Fett, Audubon 5-1.

127-John Haub, Rockwell City beat Lindy Peterson, Britt 2-0.

133-Norbert Kisley, Osage beat Chuck Dewey, Britt 5-4.

138-Dennis Miller, Algona beat Dave Jahnel, Osage 4-1.

145-Dave Martin, Algona beat Steve Rosengren, Logan-Magnolia 4-1.

154-Jim Guyer, North Fayette (West Union) beat Jason Smith, Ankeny 6-5 (RT).

165-Al Baxter, Morning Sun beat Shelby Johnson, Johnston 1-0.

Hwt-Steve Klein, Alden beat Tom Fitzpatrick, Algona 3-2.

1966 (February 26)

CLASS AA

95-Dennis Knutson, Decorah beat Bill Knight, Iowa City High 5-0.

103-Don Eggenberg, Muscatine beat Gary James, Chariton 5-4.

112-Dan Gable, Waterloo West beat Don Briggs, Cedar Rapids Jefferson 11-2.

120-Marty Dickey, Waterloo West beat Henry Vasey, Des Moines Lincoln 2-0.

127-Tony Stevens, Waterloo East beat Jim Neighbors, Fort Dodge 8-6.

133-Steve Noah, Charles City beat Don Yahn, Clinton 7-4.

138-Phil Sherburne, Waterloo West beat Dennis Brown, Waverly-Shell Rock 6-1.

145-Tim Shade, Des Moines Tech beat Dave Borden, Davenport Central 3-2.

154-John Newmeister, Cedar Rapids Washington beat Mannie Holmes, Waterloo East 9-1.

165-Kim Rhoades, Cedar Falls pinned Frank Thomas, Davenport Central 3:53.

180-Don Gillespie, Des Moines Roosevelt beat Rod Reifsteck, Cedar Falls 3-2.

Hwt-Ed Huffman, Ames beat Curt Meyer, Iowa Falls 3-1.

CLASS A

95-Steve Funk, Osage beat Doug Trees, Greene 2-0.

103-Jerry Schropp, Cedar Rapids Prairie beat Mike McKenzie, Urbandale 3-2.

112-Larry Munger, Algona beat Mike Matern, Britt 2-0.

120-Stan Slessor, Reinbeck beat Steve Hanson, Council Bluffs Lewis Central 8-4.

127-Joe Carstensen, Camanche beat Tom Samp, Algona 8-8, 1-0 OT.

133-Wayne Lewis, Ankeny beat John Haub, Rockwell City 0-0, 2-0 OT.

138-Frank Havick, Oakland beat Mike Halupnick, North Tama 3-2.

145-Larry Benson, Clarion beat Mike Snodgrass, Mount Vernon 5-2.

154-Dave Martin, Algona beat Ron Crooks, Nashua 3-1.

165-Jason Smith, Ankeny pinned Miles Huck, Waterloo Orange 3:03.

180-Dave Grant, Britt beat Chuck Hubbard, Monticello 4-0.

Hwt-Tom Fitzpatrick, Algona beat Bill Larsen, Harlan 2-1.

1967 (February 25)

CLASS AA

95-Dennis Vanderhorst, Ottumwa beat Jim Gillespie, Council Bluffs Lincoln 5-3.

103-Norm Wilkerson, Ottumwa beat Joe Coty, Mason City 5-0.

112-Henry Ramirez, Davenport West beat Bob Doughman, Council Bluffs Jefferson 3-1.

120-Bernie Graser, Waterloo West beat Ken Stockdale, Eagle Grove 4-3.

127-Landy Waller, Cedar Rapids Washington beat Doug Moses, Waterloo West 2-1.

133-Tony Stevens, Waterloo East beat Bill Stopperan, Cresco 5-2.

138-Mark Meyerhoff, Waterloo West beat Milton Neal, Davenport Central 4-0.

145-Keith Abens, Humboldt beat Don Horton, New Hampton 4-2.

154-Bob Heene, Waterloo West beat Dennis Doederer, Iowa City High 5-2.

165-Kim Rhoades, Cedar Falls beat Joe Hatchett, Cedar Rapids Washington 0-0, 0-0 (referee's decision).

180-Frank Thomas, Davenport Central pinned Frank Guthrie, Tama-Toledo 2:59.

Hwt-Roger Collins, Iowa City High beat Steve Exline, Cresco 1-0.

CLASS A

95-Don McCune, Central (DeWitt) beat Stuart Lang, Janesville 5-4.

103-Paul Graham, Sigourney beat Doug Trees, Greene 2-0.

112-Len Liston, West Sioux beat Paul Tonn, Jesup 8-5.

120-Tim Dillon, Hampton beat Johnnie Wilson, Greenfield 7-2.

127-Steve Claude, Algona beat Jerry Blank, Vinton 4-2.

133-Mike Nason, West Marshall beat Terry Eyberg, Oakland 2-1.

138-Tom Thomas, Johnston beat Tom Gresham, Pleasant Valley 2-0.

145-Clint Young, Algona beat Mick Snodgrass, Mount Vernon 1-1, 0-0 (referee's decision).

154-Gerald Malacek, Belle Plaine beat Chuck Knutsen, Central (DeWitt) 6-4.

165-Gary Nelson, Alden won by disqualification (slam) over Jack Gross, Harlan.

180-Leonard Thompson, Janesville beat Clark Allen, Greene 4-0.

Hwt-Rex Smith, Waterloo Orange beat Rick Maehl, Elkader 6-4.

1968 (March 2)

CLASS AA

95-Dave Nicol, Cedar Falls beat Dennis Vanderhorst, Ottumwa 12-6.

103-Duane Krebs, Cedar Falls beat Steve St. Clair, Cedar Rapids Kennedy 5-2.

112-Bill Knight, Iowa City High beat Jack Blake, Cedar Falls 3-1.

120-Lee Johnson, Cresco beat Dave Moses, Waterloo West 1-0.

127-Larry Bolanos, Fort Madison beat Keith Brown, Fort Dodge 2-2 (referee's decision).

133-Todd Rhoades, Cedar Falls pinned Tom McCluskey, Clinton 2:55.

138-Charles Heene, Waterloo West beat Duane Vance, Charles City 9-3.

145-Brad Havig, Osage beat Bill Stopperan, Cresco 5-2.

154-John Evashevski, Iowa City High beat Bill Barnard, West Des Moines Valley 10-4.

165-Dave Hackett, Waterloo West beat John Everett, Mason City 2-1.

180-Steve Wearth, Ames beat Keith Burchett, Harlan 4-3.

Hwt-Brian Homan, Waverly-Shell Rock pinned Bill Larsen, Harlan 5:18.

CLASS A

95-Ted Derscheid, Clarion pinned John Hagen, Britt 3:40.

103-Paul Graham, Sigourney beat Jim Taute, Humboldt 5-0.

112-Doug Trees, Greene pinned Donnie Wilson, Greenfield 5:56.

120-Lyle Laird, Humboldt beat Paul Havick, Oakland 9-4.

127-Jerry Bothwell, Tri-Center (Neola) beat Tom Swanson, Mount Ayr 3-2.

133-Mike Nason, West Marshall beat Bob Cox, Urbandale 5-3.

138-Larry Taylor, Algona beat Lynn Pitts, Ankeny 4-2.

145-Ron Gresham, Pleasant Valley beat John Showalter, Hampton 3-1.

154-Keith Abens, Humboldt pinned Chuck Knutsen, Central (DeWitt) 1:55.

165-Gerald Malacek, Belle Plaine beat Keith Flugge, Riceville 6-1.

180-Paul Zander, Tripoli pinned Dennis McDonald, Morning Sun 5:58.

Hwt-Geoff Mickelson, Humboldt beat Logan Harms, Tripoli 6-0.

1969 (March 1)

CLASS AAA

95-Steve Natvig, Waterloo East beat Doug Davis, Iowa City High 1-1, 1-0 OT.

103-Dave Nicol, Cedar Falls beat Dennis Vanderhorst, Ottumwa 9-0.

112-Don Williams, Des Moines Tech beat Bob Kertsen, Harlan 1-0.

120-Dave Moses, Waterloo West beat Mike Bostwick, Iowa City High 5-1.

127-Lee Johnson, Cresco beat Jon Robken, Cedar Rapids Washington 3-0.

133-Bill Andrew, Waterloo West beat Dick Ingvall, Cedar Rapids Jefferson 1-1, 1-0 OT.

138-Jeff Cox, Harlan beat Steve Barnes, Iowa City West 3-2.

145-Jordan Smith, Dubuque Senior beat Dan Holmes, Fairfield 4-3.

154-Steve Strellner, Tama beat Jack Welch, Des Moines North 7-4.

165-Rich Binek, Waterloo West beat Rick Parsons, Cedar Falls 5-0.

175-Reece Wilson, Waterloo West beat Jeff Elgin, West Des Moines Valley 1-1, 1-1 (referee's decision).

Hwt-Henry Banke, Cedar Rapids Jefferson beat Chuck Blaskovich, Des Moines Roosevelt 3-2.

CLASS AA

95-John Hagen, Britt beat Kelly Bast, Urbandale 4-2.

103-Rick Schropp, Cedar Rapids Prairie beat Rich McMahon, Corning 6-4.

112-Jim Taute, Humboldt beat Dan McCune, Central (DeWitt) 4-4, 0-0 (referee's decision).

120-Al Zach, Cedar Rapids Prairie beat Stu Slater, Storm Lake 7-0.

127-Bill Fjetland, Eagle Grove beat Rob Claude, Algona 7-2.

133-Cliff Howlett, Britt beat Tom Steffen, LaPorte City 9-2.

138-Bruce Gast, Osage beat Jim Huerter, Anamosa 4-3.

145-Larry Taylor, Algona beat John Showalter, Hampton 6-5.

154-Keith Abens, Humboldt beat Phil Bode, Algona 8-0.

165-Duane Hunt, Algona beat Terry Lessmeier, Fort Dodge St. Edmond 4-0.

175-Marv Palmer, Corning beat Bruce Bennett, Algona 7-6 (riding time).

Hwt-Al Borkowski, Audubon beat Glen Richardson, Urbandale 4-3.

CLASS A

95-Steve Burkholder, WACO (Olds) beat Joel Fye, Pekin 2-0.

103-Ron McDonald, Morning Sun beat Gale Johnsen, Logan-Magnolia 6-4.

112-Jon Moeller, Gladbrook beat Tom Cross, Wapello 4-3.

120-Doug Trees, Greene beat Martin Eyberg, Oakland 8-2.

127-David Sielaff, Alden beat Mike Yeager, Milford 5-1.

133-Roger Buchholz, Tripoli beat LeRoy Noltensmeier, Reinbeck 7-6.

138-Gene Wadle, Southeast Warren beat Griff Norton, Wilton 3-2.

145-Rex Johnsen, Logan-Magnolia beat Jim Furland, Beaman-Conrad 13-6.

154-Dean Barnard, Eldora beat Jerry Johnsen, Logan-Magnolia 1-0.

165-Matt Clarke, Eldora beat Leroy Crooks, Nashua 8-0.

175-Jim Clary, Eldora beat Dave Suter, Rock Valley 10-4.

Hwt-Wayne Gregg, Ballard pinned Bill Ehlers, Midland (Wyoming) 4:36.

1970 (February 28)

CLASS AAA

98-Mitchell Taylor, Waterloo East beat Scott Miller, Cedar Falls 4-3.

107-Greg Hutchinson, West Delaware beat Joe Corso, West Des Moines Valley 8-5.

115-Tim Taylor, Council Bluffs Lincoln pinned John Tabat, Fort Dodge 4:55.

123-Rod Harp, Waterloo West beat Russ Winegardner, Cedar Rapids Kennedy 9-2.

130-Dan Rowray, Cedar Rapids Jefferson beat Aaron Doolin, Cedar Rapids Washington 4-3.

137-Mark Fox, Waterloo West beat Dave Mulcahy, Cedar Rapids Washington 3-2.

145-Jerry Siefert, Ames beat Sy Bassett, Cedar Rapids Washington 1-0.

155-Jack Welch, Des Moines North beat Clark Beltz, Cedar Rapids Jefferson 2-1.

165-Gary Menefee, Cedar Rapids Washington beat Mike Ott, Cedar Falls 1-0.

175-Fred Penrod, Davenport West pinned Larry Readout, Marshalltown 5:54.

185-Charles Smith, Cedar Rapids Washington beat Dan Schmitt, Dubuque Wahlert 4-4, 2-1 OT.

Hwt-Jim Waschek, Cedar Falls beat Tom Bribriesco, Davenport West 7-5.

CLASS AA

98-Dave Musselman, Humboldt beat Tony Jennings, Corning 9-0.

107-John Hagen, Britt beat Gary Moore, Osage 4-0.

115-Rick Danford, Marion beat Tracy Funk, Osage 4-3.

123-Duane Doughan, Britt beat Randy Nigg, Hampton 3-2 (riding time).

130-Dennis Milbrandt, North Fayette (West Union) beat Denny Cooper, Clear Lake 6-5.

137-Chuck Berrier, Urbandale beat Bob Gittins, Perry 1-1, 1-1 (referee's decision).

145-Eric Norris, Ankeny beat Andy Fairlie, Cedar Rapids Prairie 9-0.

155-Gene Hunt, Algona beat Joe Smith, Ankeny 11-5.

165-Duane Hunt, Algona beat Bill Varner, Decorah 11-3.

175-Paul Cote, Decorah beat Les Simpson, Algona 1-0.

185-Randy Omvig, Eagle Grove beat Gene Harmegnies, Chariton 4-2.

Hwt-Dan Dubishar, Cedar Rapids Prairie beat Al Borkowski, Audubon 1-1, 1-0 OT.

CLASS A

98-Jim Peacock, Greenfield beat Terry Crawford, Winthrop 5-2.

107-Joel Fye, Pekin beat Ron McDonald, Morning Sun 6-4.

115-Lonnie Underhill, LDF (LeGrand) beat Randy Neuendorf, Tripoli 11-4.

123-Martin Eyberg, Oakland beat Steve Blasberg, Tripoli 9-1.

130-Mike Bentley, Coon Rapids beat Dan Swailes, Belle Plaine 2-1.

137-Harold Reed, Adel beat Rick Reinicke, Dike 6-4.

145-Dave Martin, Adel beat Steve Adam, Pekin 7-2.

155-Kenton Moss, Carson-Macedonia pinned Paul Marsden, Eldora 4:23.

165-Gary Schmidt, Jesup beat Kurt Odle, Wapello 12-1.

175-Scott Sickles, Janesville beat Merlin Neer, Southeast Warren 6-0.

185-Terry Carritt, West Harrison beat Ken Buskohl, Dike 12-3.

Hwt-Bernie Draper, Johnston pinned Kevin Kimm, Iowa Valley :25.

1971 (February 27)

CLASS AAA

98-Tom Danner, Dubuque Wahlert beat Larry Dawson, Southeast Polk 2-1.

105-Chris Larson, Urbandale beat Jeff Saggau, Boone 3-2.

112-Joe Corso, West Des Moines Valley beat Tom Lepic, Iowa City High 5-1.

119-Karl Waller, Cedar Rapids Washington beat Ivan Musselman, Fort Dodge 4-1.

126-Rod Harp, Waterloo West beat Dedric Doolin, Cedar Rapids Washington 3-0.

132-Tony Cordes, Waterloo West beat Dan Rhoades, Cedar Falls 6-3.

138-Ken Snyder, Waterloo Columbus beat Theodis Craig, Davenport Central 6-1.

145-Chuck Berrier, Urbandale beat Steve Marcus, Southeast Polk 7-0.

155-Jim Rizzuti, Urbandale beat Stan Peterson, Estherville 2-0.

167-Steve Hwerum, Estherville beat Dave Staska, Urbandale 4-2.

185-John Schoeneman, Ames beat Waynbe Leistikow, Waterloo West 9-2.

Hwt-Eric Barker, Marshalltown beat Jerry Wilson, Iowa City West 6-5.

CLASS AA

98-Dennis Cline, Decorah beat John Wilson, Clarion 10-6.

105-Dave Musselman, Humboldt beat Tony Jennings, Corning 5-0.

112-Tim Swain, Corning beat Bob Erickson, Clear Lake 2-0.

119-Stuart Newman, Perry beat Scott Huse, Nevada 2-0.

126-Randy Moore, Perry beat Randy Hickman, Corning 2-1.

132-Rod Evans, Glenwood beat Mike Norris, Ankeny 5-2.

138-Steve Moore, Carlisle beat Dean Ellison, Anamosa 4-2.

145-Russ Paulsen, Clarion beat Tom Dougan, Iowa Falls 4-0.

155-Eric Norris, Ankeny pinned Dan Kubik, North Tama 2:32.

167-Dave Kluever, North Scott beat Mike Anderson, Belmond 4-0.

185-Mike Morphew, Eagle Grove beat Steve Fitzpatrick, Algona 4-3 (riding time).

Hwt-Dan Dubishar, Cedar Rapids Prairie beat Tim Roosa, Clarion 3-2.

CLASS A

98-Dan McKee, Stuart-Menlo beat Richy Nelson, Britt 2-0.

105-Murray Fenn, Carson-Macedonia beat Mike Crawford, Winthrop 1-1 OT (referee's decision).

112-John Hagen, Britt beat Warren Burkholder, WACO (Olds) 6-2.

119-Jeff Stevenson, Britt beat Mike McDonough, Eddyville-Blakesburg 6-4.

126-Craig Christensen, Woodbury Central beat Paul Swenson, Britt 5-4.

132-Ted Wallace, Greenfield beat Tim Zinger, Wilton 5-0.

138-Denny Finken, Tri-Center (Neola) beat Leon Edsen, Ida Grove 7-1.

145-Cliff Howlett, Britt beat Tyrone Kruger, George 4-0.

155-Ted Gunderson, Beaman-Conrad beat Steve Essick, Norwalk 9-0.

167-Bob Kampe, Camanche beat Gary Schmidt, Jesup 5-2.

185-Brian Tracy, Greenfield beat Terry Carritt, West Harrison 3-0.

Hwt-Kevin Marshall, Adel pinned Greg Bruns, Denver 4:33.

1972 (February 26)

CLASS AAA

98-Mike Gallagher, Cedar Rapids Jefferson beat Tom Hinrichsen, Clinton 4-4, 6-1 OT.

105-Dave Cunningham, Waterloo East beat Keith Mourlam, Webster City 3-1.

112-Chris Larson, Urbandale beat Chuck Jones, Cedar Rapids Washington 4-3.

119-Dave Leon, West Des Moines Valley pinned Gary Bentrim, Cedar Rapids Jefferson 3:35.

126-Brad Suma, Cedar Rapids Jefferson beat Joe Zuspann, Fort Dodge 11-9.

132-Bill Kunnerth, Ames beat Robert Pratt, Waterloo West 3-3, 3-1 OT.

138-Mike Norris, Ankeny pinned Tony Cordes, Waterloo West 2:30.

145-Bruce Wilson, Waterloo West beat Chuck Yagla, Waterloo Columbus 6-4.

155-Terry Jensen, Waterloo West beat Mike Ratliff, Cedar Falls 3-1.

167-Tom Ball, New Hampton beat Roy Middleswart, Indianola 6-2.

185-Scott Justice, Ankeny beat Rod Seiler, Indianola 3-0.

Hwt-Bob Fouts, Waterloo West pinned Mike Kissinger, Burlington 4:28.

CLASS AA

98-Dave Morgan, Eagle Grove beat Randy Nielsen, Algona 3-3, 2-1 OT.

105-Jack Fliehler, Starmont beat Randy Williams, Nevada 8-2.

112-John Wilson, Clarion beat Dan McCart, Eagle Grove 6-3.

119-Larry Bergman, Turkey Valley beat Stuart Newman, Perry 2-2, 5-0 OT.

126-Dave Musselman, Humboldt beat Steve Delanty, Council Bluffs Lewis Central 3-0.

132-Paul Martin, Algona beat Dave Linn, Humboldt 5-2.

138-Bernie Hanson, Humboldt beat Steve Harvey, Creston 9-4.

145-Dave Zidlicky, Decorah pinned Dave Askvig, Clarion 3:06.

155-Craig Faldet, Decorah beat Bill Harris, Carlisle 12-7.

167-Gene Hunt, Algona beat Mike Stark, Linn-Mar (Marion) 3-0.

185-Bill Benskin, Saydel pinned Bill Fredericks, Osage 1:57.

Hwt-Tim Roosa, Clarion beat Rob Boelkes, Hampton 2-2, 6-0 OT.

CLASS A

98-Brent Hagen, Britt beat Brian Blasberg, Tripoli 6-5.

105-Dan McKee, Stuart-Menlo beat Richy Nelson, Britt 6-2.

112-Ken Gordon, Pleasantville beat Mark Stevenson, Britt 6-3.

119-Mike McGivern, Iowa Valley (Marengo) beat Dave Howlett, Britt 5-2.

126-Dan Swoyer, Greenfield beat Mark Schuling, Bondurant-Farrar 6-4.

132-Jeff Stevenson, Britt beat Allen Fausch, Noth Polk 2-1.

138-Don Swoyer, Greenfield beat Jeff Ulch, Gladbrook 6-4.

145-Bruce Gayken, Britt beat Ron Lilly, Greenfield 6-1.

155-Ed Herman, Johnston beat Jon Sundell, Odebolt-Arthur 1-0.

167-Dave Fox, Johnston pinned Doug Peters, Columbus Junction 3:04.

185-Lloyd Zander, Tripoli beat Randy Terpstra, North Mahaska 4-1.

Hwt-Mike Furne, Durant beat Chuck Blaine, Gladbrook 1-0.

1973 (February 24)

CLASS AAA

98-Don Finnegan, Ames beat Tom Hinrichsen, Clinton 7-7, 5-1 OT.

105-Paul Vornbrock, LeMars beat Marion Ray, Cedar Rapids Washington 6-4.

112-Glynn Jones, Cedar Rapids Washington beat Keith Mourlam, Webster City 7-0.

119-Chuck Jones, Cedar Rapids Washington beat Dan Wilkerson, Ottumwa 3-2.

126-Gary Bentrim, Cedar Rapids Jefferson beat Jim Kinney, Ames 11-1.

132-Don Cacek, Cedar Falls beat Milton Manning, Waterloo East 8-3.

138-Don Zimmerman, Cedar Rapids Jefferson beat Merrill Norris, Indianola 2-0.

145-Mike Norris, Ankeny beat Bill Edmondson, Urbandale 15-10.

155-Tony Cordes, Waterloo West beat Curtis Craig, Davenport Central 7-5.

167-Dana Sutherland, Cedar Falls beat Howard Johnson, Cedar Rapids Jefferson 5-0.

185-Pat Wright, Bettendorf beat Brian Stuckey, Ames 3-1.

Hwt-John Bowlsby, Waterloo West beat Mike Kissinger, Burlington 2-0.

CLASS AA

98-Brent Hagen, Britt beat Dean Digman, Dyersville Beckman 3-0.

105-Dave Morgan, Eagle Grove beat Dick Perez, Hampton 2-0.

112-Mike Howard, Creston beat Dan McCart, Eagle Grove 2-2, 4-2 OT.

119-Mark Stevenson, Britt beat John Wilson, Clarion 0-0, 3-0 OT.

126-Dave Howlett, Britt beat Mike Woodall, Eagle Grove 1-0.

132-Bill Allan, Council Bluffs Lewis Central beat Steve Dummett, Britt 7-2.

138-Paul Martin, Algona beat Ken Peterson, Pleasant Valley 12-0.

145-Bernie Hanson, Humboldt pinned Robert Broulik, Mount Vernon 1:23.

155-Mike Asche, Eagle Grove beat Randy McPherrin, Corning 3-0.

167-Tom Ball, New Hampton beat Rich Wedmore, South Tama 6-0.

185-Randy Smith, Clarion beat Bill Harris, Carlisle 4-2.

Hwt-Kory Krebs, Nevada beat Mike Stensrud, Lake Mills 3-2.

CLASS A

98-Mike Draper, Grundy Center beat Chuck LeGrand, Lisbon 3-0.

105-Doug Englert, Lisbon beat Craig Broderson, North Central (Manly) 6-1.

112-Randy Swoyer, Greenfield beat Randy Nelson, Denver 6-4.

119-Dave Smith, Iowa Valley (Marengo) beat Bruce McClure, Morning Sun 4-2.

126-Steve Deike, Plainfield beat Dave Bierman, Marcus 5-3.

132-Doug Lord, Lisbon beat Mark Schuling, Bondurant-Farrar 11-6.

138-Dennis Boorn, Wilton beat Kevin Frohling, Guthrie Center 7-5.

145-Dick Keith, Reinbeck pinned Gary Carpenter, Plainfield 1-1, 2:47 OT.

155-Jim Mitchell, Riceville beat Chuck Burbridge, West Harrison 5-4.

167-Curt Ballard, Reinbeck beat Mike McKibben, Kingsley-Pierson 5-4.

185-Randy Terpstra, North Mahaska pinned Bill Thompson, Janesville 3:15.

Hwt-Mike Furne, Durant pinned Gary Boecker, Graettinger 5:15.

1974 (March 2)

CLASS AAA

98-Randy Lampe, Fort Madison beat Roy Grant, Cedar Falls 10-6.

105-Dave Muell, Harlan beat Don Hittenmiller, Cedar Rapids Jefferson 3-2.

112-Mike Babcock, Ankeny beat Jeff Hunt, Council Bluffs Jefferson 7-6.

119-Joe Egeland, Mason City beat Mark Sullivan, Bettendorf 14-3.

126-Mike Land, West Dees Moines Valley beat Doug Meyer, Council Bluffs Jefferson 5-3.

132-Mark Rhoades, Cedar Falls beat Jim Anderson, Waterloo East 3-2.

138-Joe Zuspann, Fort Dodge beat Stan Allen, Waterloo East 5-0.

145-Dennis Anderson, Waterloo East beat Gary Vance, Charles City 7-4.

155-Jim Jones, Southeast Polk beat Mike Wardlow, Waterloo Columbus 3-2.

167-Glenn Zenor, Cedar Rapids Kennedy beat Ron Ott, Waterloo West 3-2.

185-Mark Johnson, Des Moines Hoover beat Cassim Igram, Cedar Rapids Jefferson 5-2.

Hwt-John Bowlsby, Waterloo West pinned Doug Benschoter, Waverly-Shell Rock.

CLASS AA

98-Dave Prehm, Eagle Grove beat Dan Boos, New Hampton 6-5.

105-Kevin Braner, Belmond beat Larry Winslow, Glenwood 4-4, 2-2 (referee's decision).

112-Rich Wilson, Belmond beat Brent Hagen, Britt 6-4.

119-Mike Howard, Creston beat Richy Nelson, Britt 4-3.

126-Dave Morgan, Eagle Grove beat Lowell Ewalt, Jesup 7-5.

132-Gary Wood, Centerville beat Lyle Clabaugh, South Hamilton 13-3.

138-Mark Stevenson, Britt beat Mike Woodall, Eagle Grove 3-1.

145-Bob Erickson, Clear Lake beat Keith Poolman, Clarion 5-2.

155-Paul Martin, Algona beat Marv Brown, Adel 6-0.

167-Mark Vogel, Jesup beat Paul Baker, Creston 6-4.

185-Randy Smith, Clarion beat Don Erickson, Clear Lake 6-3.

Hwt-Mike Stensrud, Lake Mills beat Mike Dagel, Sibley 6-1.

CLASS A

98-Kevin Ralston, Grundy Center beat Ron Coleman, Wapello 1-0.

105-Dave Finken, Tri-Center (Neola) beat Bruce Mask, Dysart-Geneseo 5-0.

112-Doug Englert, Lisbon pinned Jeff Billerbeck, Reinbeck 5:32.

119-Steve Hackett, Oakland beat Jim Bennett, Lisbon 2-1.

126-Randy Swoyer, Greenfield beat Bruce McClure, Morning Sun 15-6.

132-John Corcoran, Greenfield beat Kent Lang, Rockwell City 9-2.

138-Marty Bussanmas, Norwalk beat Doug Lord, Lisbon 4-0.

145-Randy Meendering, Rock Valley beat Steve Mullen, Corning 15-0.

155-Mark Haynes, Lenox beat Jim Gravett, Pleasantville 6-4.

167-Dave Stamp, Tri-Center (Neola) pinned Carl Cheesman, Reinbeck :47.

185-Mike McAninch, Norwalk beat Jim Blomme, Belle Plaine 7-4.

Hwt-Rich Juchems, BCL (Conrad) pinned Mike Thurman, Winfield-Mt. Union 1:50.

1975 (March 1)

CLASS AAA

98-Jim Gibbons, Ames beat Dan Glenn, Fairfield 0-0, 0-0 (referee's decision).

105-Kirk Sallis, Waterloo Central beat Dave DeSart, Waterloo West 5-4.

112-Dave Muell, Harlan beat Rob Fogarty, West Des Moines Valley 5-0.

119-Scott Kollings, West Des Moines Dowling beat Dave Brown, Cedar Rapids Kennedy 3-1.

126-Vince Uthoff, Cedar Rapids Prairie beat Kevin Ott, Cedar Falls 5-0.

132-Ray Cole, Waterloo Central beat Doug Meyer, Council Bluffs Jefferson 7-3.

138-Terry Sinclair, Indianola beat Boyd Ethington, Southeast Polk 9-6.

145-Jim Comreid, Cedar Rapids Jefferson beat Mike Sells, Cedar Falls 1-1, 1-1 (referee's decision).

155-Doug Anderson, Ankeny beat Harlan Neuendorf, Waterloo Central 8-7.

167-Dave Schreck, West Des Moines Dowling beat Les Gatrel, Indianola 2-0.

185-Tom Rusk, Dubuque Hempstead beat Robbie Myers, Iowa City High 4-0.

Hwt-Doug Benschoter, Waverly-Shell Rock beat Tom Ingram, Ames 6-2.

CLASS AA

98-Henry Reicks, Turkey Valley beat Roger Meyers, Glenwood 9-2.

105-Dave Prehm, Eagle Grove beat John Walters, Creston 11-3.

112-Dennis Smith, Creston beat Mark Aspenson, Cresco 10-2.

119-Dan Owen, Adel beat Rich Wilson, Belmond 1-1, 1-1 (referee's decision).

126-Jeff Steffen, Cedar Rapids LaSalle beat Wally Miller, Cherokee 4-2.

132-Bruce Kinseth, Decorah beat Dennis Husak, South Tama 12-2.

138-Rich Stillman, Emmetsburg beat Kevin Finch, Eagle Grove 8-5.

145-Kevin Ruhnke, Algona pinned Gary Kayser, Jesup 3:08.

155-Marv Brown, Adel beat Keith Poolman, Clarion 5-1.

167-Mark Harris, Algona beat Dean Heying, Cresco 5-2.

185-Don Erickson, Clear Lake pinned Brett Benson, Algona 1:45.

Hwt-Dick Cuvelier, Turkey Valley beat Kevin Kurth, South Tama 4-0.

CLASS A

98-David Lott, Denver beat Jim Lord, Lisbon 4-0.

105-Chuck LeGrand, Lisbon pinned Kevin Ralston, Grundy Center 2:54.

112-Brent Hagen, Britt beat Jim Makey, Guthrie Center 4-1.

119-Duane Cook, Britt beat Dave Finken, Tri-Center (Neola) 1-0.

126-Jim Einfeldt, Durant beat Gale Johnston, Greenfield 3-0.

132-John Corcoran, Greenfield beat Dwight Evers, West Harrison 6-5.

138-Larry Hommer, Southeast Warren beat Mark Schmitz, Denver 2-0.

145-Mark Stevenson, Britt beat Wayne Driver, Underwood 9-0.

155-John Mohr, Gladbrook beat Dave Hamad, North Linn 6-6, 4-0 OT.

167-Kurt Frisk, Ackley-Geneva beat Mike Bradley, Lenox 12-6.

185-Gary Scott, Corning beat Mike Burgraaf, North Mahaska 8-8, 10-1 OT.

Hwt-Hugh Marsden, Eldora-New Providence beat Pat McHugh, Pekin 2-2, 3-0 OT.

1976 (February 28)

CLASS 3-A

98-Tim Gibbons, Ames beat Chuck Jerkovich, Council Bluffs Jefferson 10-6.

105-Jim Gibbons, Ames beat Jeff Hanson, Indianola 7-0.

112-Bob Logan, Marshalltown beat Tom Chapman, Cedar Rapids Jefferson 9-5.

119-Todd Clayter, Waterloo East beat Rob Fogarty, West Des Moines Valley 7-4.

126-Mitch Stearns, Fort Dodge beat Mike Allen, Grinnell 4-0.

132-Kevin Ott, Cedar Falls beat Scott Harmon, Marshalltown 3-1.

138-Tony Hughes, Waterloo West beat Ray Cole, Waterloo Central 8-4.

145-Mike Sells, Cedar Falls beat Ken Gallagher, Waterloo Columbus 6-4 (OT).

155-Mark Woltz, Waverly-Shell Rock beat Dave Zimmerman, Cedar Rapids Jefferson 8-3.

167-Dave Fitzgerald, Davenport West beat Bob Knipp, Waterloo Columbus 7-1.

185-Mark Thorpe, LeMars beat Mark Waters, West Des Moines Valley 8-4.

Hwt-Mike Willett, Cedar Falls beat Mike Early, Davenport Assumption 5-4.

CLASS 2-A

98-Jeff Kerber, Emmetsburg beat Jeff Hannum, Pleasant Valley 1-0.

105-Tracy Moore, Roland-Story pinned Mark Oxley, Nevada 5:28.

112-Joe Christopherson, St. Ansgar beat Mark Niblo, Winterset 6-0.

119-Dennis Smith, Creston beat Dan Boos, New Hampton 9-2.

126-Rich Wilson, Belmond beat Dan Hanson, Decorah 5-0.

132-Kevin Kauffman, Emmetsburg beat Dan Broulik, Mount Vernon 10-3.

138-John Broulik, Mount Vernon beat Gene Costello, New Hampton 9-0.

145-Rich Stillman, Emmetsburg beat Denny Parker, Chariton 5-1.

155-Dave Hamad, North Linn beat Jack Higley, Emmetsburg 6-2.

167-Brett Benson, Algona pinned Craig Poolman, Clarion :59 (OT).

185-Jim Dreyer, Humboldt beat Paul Gronbach, Algona 7-1.

Hwt-Dick Cuvelier, Turkey Valley beat Dean Phinney, Clear Lake 7-6.

CLASS 1-A

98-Gary Knutson, Lamoni beat Dan Reiter, LaPorte City 5-3.

105-Jim Lord, Lisbon beat Dave Lott, Denver 9-3.

112-Steve Roby, Rockwell City beat Ray Fox, Don Bosco (Gilbertville) 6-5.

119-Jim Kimsey, Underwood beat Bryan Sinn, WACO (Olds) 6-5.

126-Duane Cook, Britt beat Casey Robb, LaPorte City 7-2.

132-Rod Earleywine, West Harrison beat Ron Coleman, Grundy Center 15-3.

138-Jim Einfeldt, Durant beat John Duffy, Belle Plaine 9-2.

145-Paul Geerlings, Northwood-Kensett beat Mark Artist, Guthrie Center 6-4.

155-Brad Blanchard, Belle Plaine pinned Rory Benton, Greenfield 5:41.

167-Mark Helling, Hudson beat Toim Tomkins, Midland (Wyoming) 10-4.

185-Paul Tanis, Dike beat Mike Burgraaf, North Mahaska 12-3.

Hwt-Dave Ehrig, Grundy Center beat Don Petersen, Tripoli 6-5.

1977 (February 26)

CLASS 3-A

98-Chuck Jerkovich, Council Bluffs Jefferson beat Tim Schultz, Charles City 7-2.

105-Randy Clark, Fort Dodge beat Victor Kincaid, Waterloo West 9-2.

112-Jerry Johnson, Cedar Rapids Jefferson beat Jeff Knight, Clinton 3-2.

119-Jim Gibbons, Ames beat Larry Obrecht, Harlan 3-2.

126-Lennie Zalesky, Cedar Rapids Prairie beat Larry Luttrell, Waterloo Central 9-2.

132-Craig Garvin, Waterloo West beat Al Melcher, Fairfield 8-4.

138-David Brown, Cedar Rapids Kennedy beat Dick Marshall, Southeast Polk 5-3.

145-Ken Gallagher, Waterloo Columbus beat Tony Hughes, Waterloo West 5-2.

155-Perry Hummel, West Des Moines Dowling beat Tony Henson, Ames 4-3.

167-Dave Fitzgerald, Davenport West beat Lon Liebergen, Iowa City West 7-6 (OT).

185-Joe Gormally, Sioux City East beat Jay Hilgenberg, Iowa City High 5-2.

Hwt-Brian Neal, West Des Moines Dowling beat Bruce Kittle, Cedar Falls 3-2.

CLASS 2-A

98-Ralph Reicks, Turkey Valley beat John Strohman, Algona 5-0.

105-Roger Meyers, Glenwood beat Jay Ironside, North Linn 8-6.

112-Jeff Kerber, Emmetsburg beat Tracy Moore, Roland-Story 6-2.

119-Pat Vogel, Benton (Van Horne) beat Mark Niblo, Winterset 0-0 (referee's decision).

126-Dan Waid, Cresco beat Mark Nail, Clarion 9-6.

132-Dan Hanson, Decorah beat Kevin Schmidt, Fort Dodge St. Edmond 4-2.

138-John Schaumburg, Eagle Grove beat Al Freeman, Griswold 19-4.

145-Dave Robinson, Winterset beat Brad Blanchard, Belle Plaine 5-1.

155-Rich Stillman, Emmetsburg beat Joel Nelson, Belmond 4-3.

167-Greg Chapman, Clarion beat Jack Higley, Emmetsburg 7-4.

185-Kirk Myers, Algona beat Jay Boelkes, Hampton 8-0.

Hwt-Dean Phinney, Clear Lake beat Mike Appleget, Sigourney 5-0.

CLASS 1-A

98-Scott Morningstar, Lisbon beat Vince Kimm, Iowa Valley (Marengo) 4-2.

105-Scott Taylor, Midland (Wyoming) beat Scott Clark, West Harrison 7-2.

112-Jim Lord, Lisbon pinned Robert Cole, Highland (Riverside) 3:24.

119-Ray Fox, Don Bosco (Gilbertville) beat Steve Roby, Rockwell City 4-2.

126-Tim LeValley, Dallas Center-Grimes beat Mike Olson, Twin Rivers (Bode) 7-5.

132-Mike Patterson, Hudson beat Rob Leeper, Central Decatur 10-2.

138-Bill Butteris, Lisbon beat Don Cox, Bedford 13-5.

145-Rod Earleywine, West Harrison beat Mike Artist, Guthrie Center 6-1 (OT).

155-Mark Artist, Guthrie Center beat Kent Dierks, Gladbrook 3-2.

167-Dave Poppinga, Manson beat Tim Kruger, George 6-2.

185-Steve Hudson, North Polk pinned Steve Blickenderfer, Nora Springs-Rock Falls 3:31.

Hwt-Curt Braby, Mount Ayr beat Scott Schreck, Coon Rapids-Bayard 3-2.

1978 (February 25)

CLASS 3-A

98-Joe Gibbons, Waterloo Columbus beat Tim Schultz, Charles City 3-1.

105-Roger DeSart, Waterloo West beat Bob Hallman, West Des Moines Dowling 8-0.

112-Barry Davis, Cedar Rapids Prairie beat Dennis Christianson, Harlan 7-7, 4-2 OT.

119-Jeff Knight, Clinton beat Lon Imlay, Southeast Polk 11-0.

126-Tim Riley, Iowa City High beat Dave Morkel, Waterloo West 1-1, 3-1 OT.

132-Tim Berrier, Urbandale beat Joel Schintler, Iowa City West 10-4.

138-John Campana, West Des Moines Dowling beat Larry Luttrell, Waterloo Central 4-0.

145-Jim Zalesky, Cedar Rapids Priairie beat Dick Marshall, Southeast Polk 8-6.

155-Jeff Walker, Davenport Central beat Jay Olson, Fort Dodge 3-3, 3-3 (referee's decision).

167-Perry Hummel, West Des Moines Dowling beat Al McCabe, Cresco 9-2.

185-Mike Mann, Marshalltown beat Pete Bush, Davenport Assumption 14-2.

Hwt-Eric Klassen, Iowa City High beat Steve McWhirter, Fairfield 1-0.

CLASS 2-A

98-Mike Schimp, Belmond beat John Strohman, Algona 8-0.

105-Gorden Barker, Osage beat Paul Kreimeyer, Wilton 12-3.

112-Randy Majors, Mount Vernon beat Randy Samuelson, Decorah 9-2.

119-Jeff Kerber, Emmetsburg beat Bill Pfantz, West Marshall 11-3.

126-Clark Yoder, Sigourney beat Scott Johnston, Nashua 14-2.

132-Dan Kauffman, Emmetsburg pinned Scott Mathes, South Tama 1:47.

138-Al Freeman, Griswold beat Robbie Smith, Wilton 7-1.

145-Ross Yoder, Sigourney beat John Schaumburg, Eagle Grove 13-6.

155-Randy Beranek, Solon beat Jeff Huinker, Postville 12-8.

167-Todd Leighton, Griswold beat Brad Phipps, Cherokee 2-1.

185-Dave Poppinga, Manson beat Dan Foley, Maquoketa 7-2.

Hwt-Dave Ehrig, Grundy Center pinned Dave Gunsallus, St. Ansgar 3:31.

CLASS 1-A

98-Kevin Hough, Underwood beat Ben Kresse, Maxwell 7-0.

105-Scott Morningstar, Lisbon beat Duane Grant, Britt 10-5.

112-Scott Taylor, Midland (Wyoming) beat Kevin Grasser, Plainfield 10-5.

119-Kurt Hinschberger, Belle Plaine beat Brian Blinks, Lisbon 2-0.

126-Jim Lord, Lisbon beat Mike Blasberg, Tripoli 28-7.

132-Mark Stevens, Northwood-Kensett beat Wade Finch, Britt 12-2.

138-Mike Paterson, Hudson pinned Dave Stevens, Northwood-Kensett 1:11.

145-Tony Bedard, Don Bosco (Gilbertville) beat Don Cox, Bedford 10-2.

155-Dan Snyder, Midland (Wyoming) pinned Randy Schares, Don Bosco (Gilbertville) 3:32.

167-Matt Schaeffer, Midland (Wyoming) beat Clay Zellmer, Kingsley-Pierson 6-5.

185-Steve Blickenderfer, Nora Springs-Rock Falls beat Don Gerot, Highland (Riverside) 8-6.

Hwt-Tom Brown, Graettinger beat Mark Lloyd, Woodbury Central 4-1.

1979 (February 24)

CLASS 3-A

98-Lewie Massey, Council Bluffs Lewis Central beat Scott Penrod, Cedar Rapids Prairie 7-4.

105-Joe Gibbons, Waterloo Columbus beat Phil Callahan, Clinton 1-0.

112-Bob Hallman, West Des Moines Dowling beat Scott Thomas, Charles City 9-5.

119-Barry Davis, Cedar Rapids Prairie beat Terry McGee, Cedar Falls 9-1.

126-Tim Riley, Iowa City High beat Kurt Ranshaw, Iowa City West 10-5.

132-Dave Morkel, Waterloo West beat Bob Pertzborn, West Des Moines Dowling 11-7.

138-Dan Waid, Cresco beat Drew Waddell, Urbandale 6-4.

145-Jim Zalesky, Cedar Rapids Prairie beat Dave Ewing, Fort Dodge 10-7.

155-Kevin Wedeking, Charles City beat Steve Ross, Ames 9-3.

167-Jay Llewellyn, Cedar Falls beat Joe Ickes, Marion 11-2.

185-Pete Bush, Davenport Assumption beat John Schebler, Davenport Central 13-2.

Hwt-John Kriebs, Dubuque Wahlert beat Steve Wilbur, Indianola 11-4.

CLASS 2-A

98-Greg Randall, Mount Vernon beat John Thorn, Algona 13-11.

105-Tom Bieber, Clear Lake beat Dave Kist, Eagle Grove 6-2.

112-Paul Kreimeyer, Wilton beat Bruce Ralston, North Fayette (West Union) 9-3.

119-Kurt Hinschberger, Belle Plaine beat Dave Mauser, Osage 4-4, 3-1 OT.

126-Jeff Kerber, Emmetsburg pinned Todd Fey, Central (DeWitt) 5:18.

132-Clark Yoder, Sigourney beat Dana Robinson, Humboldt 8-2.

138-Dan Kauffman, Emmetsburg beat Vaun DeJong, Knoxville 11-0.

145-Al Frost, Nashua beat George Snakenberg, Sigourney 7-4.

155-Dave Hagedorn, Jefferson pinned Jim Lenth, Riceville 1:00

167-Curt Pacha, Washington beat Steve Bussey, Glenwood 2-2, 4-1 OT.

185-Paul Hufford, Mount Vernon beat Brian Tucker, West Branch 6-3.

Hwt-Jeff Dreyer, Humboldt beat Scott Dagel, Sibley 4-3.

CLASS 1-A

98-Ricky Cole, Highland (Riverside) beat Al Francis, Don Bosco (Gilbertville) 3-0.

105-Ryan Haines, Winfield-Mount Union beat Todd Staats, Wapello 6-1.

112-Mike Hogan, Don Bosco (Gilbertville) beat Bruce Ball, Clear Creek (Tiffin) 14-6.

119-Scott Morningstar, Lisbon beat Mitch Woosley, BCL (Conrad) 8-4.

126-Clark Ulven, Westwood (Sloan) pinned Robert Cole, Highland (Riverside) 2:56.

132-Mark Stevens, Northwood-Kensett beat Dave Purrell, North Polk 3-1.

138-Gene Hartley, Maxwell beat Kirk Van Rees, Lynnville-Sully 5-2.

145-Don Cox, Bedford pinned Todd Wolverton, Oakland 1:58.

155-Dave Kempena, Rock Valley beat Mike Elson, Bondurant-Farrar 3-0.

167-Reo Straw, Iowa Valley (Marengo) pinned Brian Bedard, Don Bosco (Gilbertville) 2:49.

185-Steve Cory, Coon Rapids beat John Carpenter, New London 9-3.

Hwt-John Simpson, Central Decatur beat Scott Becker, Don Bosco (Gilbertville) 10-9.

1980 (March 1)

CLASS 3-A

98-Tim Klinghammer, Waterloo Central beat Ron Lower, Sioux City Heelan 18-3.

105-Rick DeBartolo, West Des Moines Dowling beat Dion Sproles, Waterloo West 9-8.

112-Pat Pickford, Fort Madison beat Payl Glynn, Bettendorf 5-3.

119-Barry Davis, Cedar Rapids Prairie beat Tommy Thompson, Fort Dodge 14-3.

126-Joe Gibbons, Ames beat Kevin Brown, Cedar Rapids Prairie 9-3.

132-John DiGiacomo, Waterloo West beat Griffin Couch, West Des Moines Valley 7-2.

138-Keith Carman, Cresco beat Jeff Quick, Southeast Polk 4-2.

145-Scott Bouslog, Linn-Mar (Marion) beat Dave Ewing, Fort Dodge 5-2.

155-Steve Ross, Ames beat John Stopperan, Cresco 7-0.

167-Wayne Love, Waterloo Central beat Kirk Hale, Marshalltown 8-2.

185-John Schebler, Davenport Central beat Antione Caldwell, Des Moines East 15-2.

Hwt-Steve Wilbur, Indianola beat Mark Coffin, West Des Moines Dowling 11-1.

S Hwt-Duane Clark, Waverly-Shell Rock pinned Jay Bean, Cedar Falls :52.

CLASS 2-A

98-Al Francis, Don Bosco (Gilbertville) beat Jim Yates, Glenwood 9-2.

105-Scott Jehle, Durant beat Tom Cleavenger, Tri-Center (Neola) 8-5.

112-Greg Randall, Mount Vernon beat John Thorn, Algona 5-3.

119-Paul Kreimeyer, Wilton beat Mike Schimp, Belmond 9-2.

126-Kevin Dresser, Humboldt beat Scott Sesker, Forest City 8-0.

132-Clark Yoder, Sigourney beat Bill Bowers, Mount Vernon 11-0.

138-Mark Baker, Ballard (Huxley) beat Mike Reynolds, Carlisle 10-2.

145-George Snakenberg, Sigourney beat Joe Dunn, Carlisle 4-3.

155-Rick Ruebel, Grundy Center beat Miles Erickson, Mediapolis 4-1.

167-Curt Pacha, Washington beat Jeff Weatherman, Ballard (Huxley) 10-1.

185-Ron Nielsen, Denver beat Tom Cuvelier, Turkey Valley 8-4.

Hwt-Doug Fischer, Sheldon beat Dennis Shannon, Independence 5-2.

S Hwt-Tom Dole, Algona pinned Al Schmitt, Turkey Valley 3:08.

CLASS 1-A

98-Brett Stoneking, Lisbon beat Dennis Johnson, Bedford 7-6.

105-Brian Hall, Lisbon pinned Roy Keough, Nora Springs-Rock Falls 5:36.

112-Glenn Lewis, Lynnville-Sully beat Bill O'Connor, Dike 13-0.

119-Jack Barron, Iowa School of Deaf beat Steve Hiller, Kingsley-Pierson 16-2.

126-Scott Morningstar, Lisbon beat Tim DeLarm,. Midland (Wyoming) 4-3.

132-Mike Johnson, Terril pinned Dave Durrell, North Polk 3:35.

138-Rich Linkenmeyer, Riceville beat Brian Welle, Milford 4-0.

145-Jay Johnson, Morning Sun beat Mike Horstmann, Britt 10-3.

155-Jim Lenth, Riceville beat Tony Mosher, Pleasantville 7-1.

167-Aaron Tolander, WACO (Olds) beat Perry Christensen, West Harrison 3-2.

185-Steve Cory, Coon Rapids beat Dennis Sanderson, Tripoli 4-1.

Hwt-John Carpenter, New London beat Al Schweer, Tripoli 4-3.

S Hwt-Duane Duryee, Riceville beat Jerry Malone, Morning Sun 9-3.

1981 (February 28)

CLASS 3-A

98-Jeff Carter, West Des Moines Dowling pinned Chuck Pearson, Waterloo East 5:40.

105-Rick DeBartolo, West Des Moines Dowling beat Terry Cook, Spencer 4-0.

112-Matt Egeland, West Des Moines Dowling beat Tim Belz, Cedar Falls 15-6.

119-Paul Glynn, Bettendorf pinned David Weaver, Des Moines Lincoln 5:51.

126-Phil Callahan, Clinton beat Lewie Massey, Council Bluffs Lewis Central 12-7.

132-Joe Gibbons, Ames beat Russ Graves, Webster City 13-0.

138-Kurt Ranshaw, Iowa City West beat Mark Olson, Clinton 5-4.

145-Mike Hahesy, Cedar Rapids Prairie beat Tom Hanson, Cedar Rapids Kennedy 4-3.

155-Mike Johnson, Cedar Rapids Jefferson pinned Steve Bass, Charles City 1:56.

167-Fritz Stratton, Muscatine beat Matt Furey, Carroll Kuemper 7-5.

185-Brian McCracken, Bettendorf beat Bill Reed, Fort Dodge 8-6.

Hwt-Hap Peterson, Bettendorf beat Randy McFadden, Muscatine 3-1.

S Hwt-Mark Sindlinger, Charles City beat Terry Rolfs, Oelwein 6-5.

CLASS 2-A

98-Mike Schwab, Osage beat Tom Lensing, Turkey Valley 3-1.

105-Rick Sawyer, Humboldt beat Jeff Coltvet, Eagle Grove 9-4.

112-Terry Cooper, Creston pinned Scott Jehle, Durant 3:40.

119-Robert Burrows, Atlantic beat Jerry Reising, Garner-Hayfield 7-1.

126-Greg Randall, Mount Vernon beat Erickk Strawn, Jefferson 4-3.

132-Kevin Dresser, Humboldt beat Dave Meirick, Turkey Valley 9-7.

138-Steve Randall, Mount Vernon beat Todd Sesker, Forest City 13-5.

145-Bob Kauffman, Emmetsburg beat Bob Kincade, Glenwood 7-2.

155-Mikes Erickson, Mediapolis beat Bud Postma, Central Lyon 3-2.

167-Rollie Kane, Wapsie Valley beat John Hassler, Cherokee 6-4.

185-Todd Smith, Denver beat Kurt Angell, Osage 9-7.

Hwt-Steve Reimers, Humboldt beat Bryon Berner, Maquoketa 4-0.

S Hwt-Tom Dole, Algona beat Larry Kerr, Washington 6-5.

CLASS 1-A

98-Corey Mills, Don Bosco (Gilbertville) beat Kelly Madison, LDF (LeGrand) 4-1.

105-Roy Keough, Nora Springs-Rock Falls beat Brett Stoneking, Lisbon 13-9.

112-Marty Davis, Coon Rapids beat Ben Kresse, Maxwell 17-14.

119-Earl Bryant, Morning Sun beat Jerry Moran, Woodward-Granger 5-3.

126-Royce Alger, Lisbon pinned Rod Hess, Woodward-Granger 5:21.

132-Mark Mangerich, Don Bosco (Gilbertville) beat Jeff Peden, Pekin 5-4.

138-David Durrell, North Polk beat LeRoy Green, Iowa School for the Deaf 5-4.

145-Joel Henning, Lynnville-Sully beat Jeff Beier, Pleasantville 4-1.

155-Doug Cox, Bedford beat Paul Higginbottom, North Polk 6-0.

167-Irv Thome, Don Bosco (Gilbertville) beat Paul Jones, Waukee 6-5.

185-Kim Reis, Coon Rapids beat Kendall Barz, Ackley-Geneva 13-5.

Hwt-Scott Von Stein, Bondurant-Farrar beat Kevin Ortner, Don Bosco (Gilbertville) 9-1.

S Hwt-Jerry Malone, Morning Sun pinned Scott Beenken, Reinbeck 2:22.

1982 (February 27)

CLASS 3-A

98-Dail Fellin, Mason City beat Mickey Bates, Davenport West 5-4.

105-Steve Knight, Clinton beat Jeff Gibbons, Ames 3-2 (OT).

112-Tim Klinghammer, Waterloo West beat Bobby Thompson, Fort Dodge 10-1.

119-Tim Krieger, Mason City beat Brandon Tate, Waterloo Columbus 16-9.

126-Parry Hughes, Clinton beat Mike Seymour, Bettendorf 7-4.

132-Lewie Massey, Council Bluffs Lewis Central beat John Bellig, Bettendorf 10-3.

138-Todd Piper, Mason City beat Stewart Carter, Waterloo Columbus 4-0 OT.

145-Mike Van Arsdale, Waterloo West beat John Hughes, Clinton 4-3.

155-Ted Camamo, Fort Dodge beat Chris Campana, West Des Moines Dowling 5-0.

167-J. D. Lueders, Clinton beat Jim Sturdevant, Fort Dodge 7-3.

185-Brian McCracken, Bettendorf beat Steve Metzger, Ames 7-2.

Hwt-Todd Krieger, Mason City pinned Todd Emsinger, Burlington :56.

S Hwt-Mark Sindlinger, Charles City beat Jim Kisner, Bettendorf 15-6.

CLASS 2-A

98-Mark Schwab, Osage beat Jeff Schmitz, Don Bosco (Gilbertville) 13-4.

105-Corey Mills, Don Bosco (Gilbertville) beat John Regan, Cedar Rapids LaSalle 11-2.

112-Al Francis, Don Bosco (Gilbertville) beat Dave Ludemann, Cresco 5-3.

119-Jeff Coltvet, Eagle Grove beat Mike Brainerd, Emmetsburg 3-0 OT.

126-Eric Strawn, Jefferson beat Marty Williams, Mount Vernon 14-4.

132-Greg Randall, Mount Vernon beat Doug Stumberg, Grundy Center 21-5.

138-Steve Randall, Mount Vernon beat Scott Wilcox, Eagle Grove 14-4.

145-Dave Greenlee, Wasgington beat Steve Pico, Emmetsburg 8-2.

155-Chuck Martens, Cresco beat Jim Fry, Wilton 9-2.

167-Troy Johnson, Eagle Grove beat Mike Oakes, Jefferson 13-5.

185-Rollie Kane, Wapsie Valley beat Todd Snitker, Waukon 7-3.

Hwt-Doyle Naig, Emmetsburg pinned Jon Vrieze, Forest City 5:22.

S Hwt-Jeff Knutson, Cresco beat Larry Kerr, Washington 8-0.

CLASS 1-A

98-Dean Happel, Lisbon beat Mike Hemann, Riceville 3-2.

105-Brett Stoneking, Lisbon pinned David Butler, Dallas Center-Grimes 2:21.

112-Scott Jehle, Durant beat C. T. Campbell, Lisbon 5-3.

119-Marty Davis, Coon Rapids pinned Duane Norton, Bondurant-Farrar :36.

126-Earl Bryant, Morning Sun beat Mike Davis, Woodbury Central 9-4.

132-Courtney Risk, North Tama beat Todd Ahrenstorff, Harris-Lake Park 6-4.

138-Royce Alger, Lisbon beat Craig Schwienebart, BCL (Conrad) 13-7.

145-Keevin Shaffer, Lisbon beat Kelly McGovern, Riceville 16-8.

155-Jim Lee, East Buchanan beat Mitch Hiscocks, Britt 4-0.

167-Aric Birchmeier, Bondurant-Farrar beat Mark Tindall, Greene 3-2.

185-Phil Roehlk, Durant pinned Craig Hassebroek, Bondurant-Farrar 5:01.

Hwt-Myron Keppy, Durant beat Brian Dahl, North Central 12-2.

S Hwt-Scott Beenken, Reinbeck pinned Scott McKinney, Lenox 3:29.

1983 (February 26)

CLASS 3-A

98-John Abadi, Iowa City High beat Mark Burrell, West Des Moines Valley 16-12.

105-Mike Guthrie, West Des Moines Dowling beat Dan Higgins, Council Bluffs Lewis Central 3-1.

112-Steve Knight, Clinton beat Bobby Thompson, Fort Dodge 10-5.

119-Jeff Gibbons, Ames beat Terry Cook, Spencer 4-3.

126-Darnell Sallis, Waterloo East pinned Jeff Castro, Bettendorf 1:14.

132-Tim Krieger, Mason City beat Jeff Walton, Waterloo West 25-7.

138-John Hughes, Clinton beat Johnny Scott, Waterloo East 9-8.

145-David Baird, Iowa City West pinned Steve Stallsmith, Dubuque Wahlert 2:41.

155-Bill Tate, Waterloo Columbus beat Mike Van Arsdale, Waterloo West 3-3, 2-2 (criteria).

167-Jason Roseland, Marshalltown beat Matt Fleckenstein, Cedar Rapids Washington 6-3.

185-Jay Gunther, Council Bluffs Lewis Central beat Dave Toops, Burlington 5-4.

Hwt-Matt Burbach, Dubuque Wahlert pinned Andy Haman, Iowa City High 1:01.

S Hwt-Mark Sindlinger, Charles City pinned Lee Schoon, Fort Dodge 1:08.

CLASS 2-A

98-Scott Mangrich, Don Bosco (Gilbertville) beat Jason Kelber, West Marshall 5-4.

105-Mark Schwab, Osage beat Brian Forgy, Winterset 16-3.

112-John Regan, Cedar Rapids LaSalle beat Jeff Schmitz, Don Bosco (Gilbertville) 12-3.

119-Jason Etherington, Algona beat Mike Schwab, Osage 10-2.

126-Marty Anderson, Clarion beat Jeff Arnold, West Marshall 8-3.

132-Murray Anderson, Clarion beat Jeff Coltvet, Eagle Grove 7-5.

138-Jeff Clutter, Winterset pinned Alan Sigmund, North Polk 4:54.

145-Dave Strohman, Algona pinned Brad Hildebrandt, Griswold 4:51.

155-Ed Neuzil, Iowa City Regina beat Jeff Miner, Jefferson 8-5.

167-Chuck Martens, Cresco beat Darrell Yates, Glenwood 10-2.

185-Roger Baker, Creston beat Eric Willim, Clarion 20-2.

Hwt-Don Salyars, Central (DeWitt) beat Scott Miller, Wapsie Valley 3-1 (OT).

S Hwt-John Nielsen, Lake Mills pinned Darren Chipp, Carlisle 1:56.

CLASS 1-A

98-Kelly Fox, Guthrie Center beat Charlie Luther, SEMCO (Gilman) 6-5.

105-Matt Carl, Corning beat Brian Byers, Harris-Lake Park 12-5.

112-Dean Happel, Lisbon beat Layne Billings, Nora Springs-Rock Falls 5-2.

119-Brad Brosdahl, North Central (Manly) beat Larry Goodell, Harris-Lake Park 5-4.

126-Tim Mahin, Sergeant Bluff-Luton beat Scott Noble, Morning Sun 5-2.

132-Dave Tool, Gilmore City-Bradgate beat Rick Swalla, Stuart-Menlo 8-4.

138-Jack Barron, Iowa School for the Deaf pinned Mark Sexton, Rockwell City 3:24.

145-Craig Schwinebart, BCL (Conrad) beat Ken Dow, South Page 9-5.

155-Dan Burgess, Lisbon pinned Dirk Cowan, Laurens-Marathon 2:34.

167-Royce Alger, Lisbon beat Jeff Hiveley, Harris-Lark Park 15-3.

185-Joel Ralfs, Durant beat Bryan Hoeg, North Tama 12-7.

Hwt-Myron Keppy, Durant beat Ryan Hoeg, North Tama 9-3.

S Hwt-Doren Montgomery, Lisbon beat Scott Silberstein, East Buchanan 7-0.

1984 (February 25)

CLASS 3-A

98-Dan Knight, Clinton beat Paul Huffman, Cedar Falls 16-1.

105-Chuck Hardin, Cedar Rapids Prairie pinned John Abadi, Iowa City High 1:44.

112-Gary McCall, Cedar Rapids Washington beat Mike Guthrie, West Des Moines Dowling 8-6.

119-Chuck Pearson, Waterloo East beat Derrick Woods, Waterloo Columbus 4-0.

126-Jeff Gibbons, Ames beat Jay Barrientes, Mason City 8-4.

132-Chris Bazzocco, West Des Moines Dowling beat Rick Lynch, Charles City 11-7.

138-Taras Stevenson, Waterloo West beat Keith Friess, West Des Moines Valley 3-1 OT.

145-Tim Krieger, Mason City pinned Tim Johnson, Davenport Central 5:46.

155-Mike Flynn, Davenport Assumption beat Johnny Scott, Waterloo East 7-6.

167-Tony Hanson, Waterloo West beat Russell Steven, New Hampton 7-1.

185-Joel Greenlee, Waverly-Shell Rock beat Andy Petersen, Iowa City High 4-2.

Hwt-Andy Haman, Iowa City High beat Kelly Flynn, West Des Moines Dowling 10-2.

S Hwt-Mike Schemmel, Western Dubuque beat Graig Cooper, Newton 17-3.

CLASS 2-A

98-Terry Schmuecker, Benton (Van Horne) beat Skip Steiert, West Marshall, 9-0.

105-Jason Kelber, West Marshall beat John Ites, Iowa Falls 4-3.

112-Mark Schwab, Osage beat Greg Hargrave, Louisa-Muscatine 19-2.

119-John Regan, Cedar Rapids LaSalle beat Doug Streicher, Starmont 18-4.

126-Pat Hamilton, Emmetsburg beat Shawn Voigt, Mount Vernon 6-0.

132-Steve Rogers, Iowa City Regina beat Shawn Ryan, Maquoketa 14-3.

138-Pat Hogan, Don Bosco (Gilbertville) beat Glenn Barker, Osage 8-2.

145-Jeff Kelly, Britt beat Brad Coulon, Algona 7-1.

155-Jeff Coltvet, Eagle Grove beat Doug Rogers, Mount Vernon 11-2.

167-Todd Lappe, Algona beat Mark Emsick, Griswold 3-1 OT.

185-Tim Stanley, Grundy Center beat Jerry Hansel, Cedar Rapids Regis 4-3.

Hwt-Chad Hennings, Benton (Van Horne) beat Mark Zinnel, Humboldt 15-1.

S Hwt-Jeff Schwartz, Sheldon pinned Tim Tietz, Griswold :10.

CLASS 1-A

98-Rod Helgeson, North Central (Manly) beat Vance Light, Lisbon 7-2.

105-Doug Hatch, Dallas Center-Grimes beat Robert O'Connor, Dike 12-7.

112-Daryel Hamlin, Janesville beat Shane Baum, Belmond 6-3.

119-Dean Happel, Lisbon beat Dave Vote, Gilmore City-Bradgate 4-2.

126-Mike Hemann, Riceville beat Todd Peters, Woodbury Central 10-0.

132-Ken Bradley, North Tama beat Wes Andrew, Monroe 10-8.

138-Jim Gribben, Mason City Newman beat Matt Spading, Belle Plaine 4-3.

145-Kevin Kahl, Durant beat Mark Megaard, Rock Valley 3-2.

155-John Cory, Coon Rapids beat Kevin Shedenhelm, Belle Plaine 6-3.

167-Tom Kaufman, North Tama beat Jack Denholm, Parkersburg 14-6.

185-Pat Rule, Parkersburg pinned Brad Baier, Griswold 3:36.

Hwt-Dick Morrison, English Valleys pinned Mike Hanson, New London 3:50.

S Hwt-Danny Stephani, North Central (Manly) pinned Lee Schweer, Tripoli 1:24.

1985 (March 2)

CLASS 3-A

98-Tim Ascherl, Fort Dodge beat Sean Watt, Ames 8-4.

105-Dave Jordan, Cedar Falls beat Jan Kahler, Waverly-Shell Rock 16-3.

112-Dan Knight, Clinton pinned Brent Helmkamp, Fort Dodge 1:38.

119-Gary McCall, Cedar Rapids Washington beat John Moore, Marshalltown 2-1.

126-Ken Lewton, West Des Moines Dowling beat Brian Thomas, Davenport West 9-7.

132-Scott Kline, Bettendorf beat Brian Jeffords, Cedar Rapids Prairie 3-2 OT.

138-Bill Hanson, Bettendorf beat Rick Lynch, Charles City 8-3.

145-Keith Friess, West Des Moines Valley beat Jay Hynek, Cedar Rapids Prairie 8-4.

155-Mike Bowlin, Indianola beat Johnny Scott, Waterloo East 12-11.

167-Maurice Morehead, Waterloo East beat Darrell Long, Cedar Rapids Jefferson 17-11.

185-Randy Ewing, Fort Dodge beat Mark Moody, Waterloo Columbus 8-5.

Hwt-Brooks Simpson, Newton beat Randy Bern, Spencer 16-1.

S Hwt-Jeff Koeppel. Urbandale pinned Rich Metcalf, Fairfield 3:01.

CLASS 2-A

98-Terry Brands, Sheldon beat Jay Soupene, Anamosa 11-4.

105-Jason Kelber, West Marshall beat Tom Brands, Sheldon 10-1.

112-Terry Schmuecker, Benton (Van Horne) beat Randy Vogel, Camanche 2-0.

119-Mark Schwab, Osage pinned Dan Sinnott, Albia 2:40.

126-Steve Hamilton, Emmetsburg beat Mark Reiland, Eagle Grove 8-6.

132-Pat Hamilton, Emmetsburg beat Randy Marlin, Creston 14-7.

138-Shawn Voigt, Mount Vernon beat Steve Rogers, Iowa City Regina 4-3.

145-Bart Chelesvig, Webster City beat Tim Weatherman, Ballard (Huxley) 9-7.

155-Shawn Nessa, Eagle Grove beat Brad Coulon, Algona 4-3.

167-Todd Lappe, Algona beat Roger Koppes, Cascade 4-1 OT.

185-Joe Malecek, Osage beat Tracey Allen, Mount Vernon 3-0.

Hwt-George Moorehead, Winterset beat Tim Leuer, Emmetsburg 5-4.

S Hwt-Bob Nadler, Clarke (Osceola) pinned Dave Saxton, Emmetsburg 1:16.

CLASS 1-A

98-Chris Hoffman, Sigourney beat Matt Otten, North Central (Manly) 7-2.

105-Keith Van Beek, Central Lyon beat Steve Thoma, Don Bosco (Gilbertville) 22-8.

112-Joe Rohrer, Clarion beat Troy Kinyon, Greenfield 5-2.

119-Rod Decker, East Buchanan beat Jerry Ackerman, Clarksville 5-3 OT.

126-Jeff Schmitz, Don Bosco (Gilbertville) beat Jeff Bakken, Northwood-Kensett 12-1.

132-Dave Vote, Gilmore City-Bradgate beat Mark Pogge, Tri-Center (Neola) 8-4.

138-Layne Billings, Nora Springs-Rock Falls beat Gus Roberts, Wapsie Valley 5-3.

145-Rod Frank, Highland (Riverside) pinned Dan Johannes, Pocahontas, 1:59.

155-Jeff Kelly, Britt beat Randy Lenth, Postville 5-3.

167-Darrell Hoogendoorn, Rock Valley beat Mike Rupert, Galva-Holstein 6-0.

185-Devin Embray, Twin Cedars beat Brad Porterfield, Postville 7-0.

Hwt-Mike McNamara, Rock Valley beat Seth Bonnette, Riceville 17-2.

S Hwt-Danny Stephani, North Central (Manly) beat Lee Schweer, Tripoli 4-3.

1986 (March 1)

CLASS 3-A

98-Dave Manchon, Marshalltown beat David Schmidt, Boone 10-6.

105-Baron Hendricks, Clinton beat Doug Knotek, Council Bluffs Lewis Central 11-3.

112-Gary Steffensmeier, Fort Madison beat Brad Bruhl, Fort Dodge 17-5.

119-Brent Helmkamp, Fort Dodge pinned Rob Bennett, Mason City :36.

126-Dan Knight, Clinton won by technical fall over Steve Swanson, Davenport West 27-12, 5:00.

132-Bill Wilson, Ankeny beat Rick Caldwell, Marshalltown 4-1.

138-Pat Waters, Iowa City High beat Toiny Neuzil, Iowa City West 15-8.

145-Rick Novak, Cedar Rapids Prairie beat Terry Dunlay, Waterloo Columbus 10-7.

155-Bob Thompson, Ames beat Kyle Wedeking, Charles City 12-1.

167-Bart Chelesvig, Webster City won by technical fall over Aaron Chambers, Marshalltolwn 17-2, 4:21.

185-Greg Herber, Dubuque Wahnlert beat Kevin Tann, Cedar Rapids Washington 5-2.

Hwt-Paul Weltha, Ames won by injury default over Matt Sindlinger, Charles City 5:36.

S Hwt-Jeff Koeppel., Urbandale beat Kevin Luensmann, Western Dubuque 3-2.

CLASS 2-A

98-Kent Streicher, Starmont beat Bryan Wilcox, Davis County 8-1.

105-Terry Brands, Sheldon beat Brad Gazaway, Eagle Grove 9-1.

112-Tom Brands, Sheldon beat Chad Zaputil, Centerville 8-2.

119-Jason Kelber, West Marshall beat Dan Sinnott, Albia 6-5.

126-Stacey Rice, Storm Lake beat Brent Jennings, Clarinda 11-9.

132-Randy Marlin, Creston won by technical fall over Chris Hupke, Cherokee 21-5, 5:22.

138-Doug Streicher, Starmont beat Steve Hamilton, Emmetsburg 7-2.

145-Mark Reiland, Eagle Grove won by technical fall over Curt Hayek, Cedar Rapids LaSalle 15-0, 4:19.

155-Jym Guyer, North Fayette (West Union) beat Dave Uthe, Osage 9-0.

167-Eric Eggers, West Marshall beat Mark Friesner, Estherville 5-0.

185-Tracey Allen, Mount Vernon beat Rod Lyman, South Tama 4-3.

Hwt-George Moorehead, Winterset beat Paul Wildeman, Cherokee 5-3.

S Hwt-Dave Saxton, Emmetsburg beat Dan Chipp, Carlisle 2-2, 1-1 (criteria).

CLASS 1-A

98-Matt Otten, Noirth Central (Manly) beat Tony Hunt, Central Decatur 8-4.

105-Chad Williams, Lisbon pinned Bobby Short, Central Decatur 2:23.

112-Vance Light, Lisbon beat Mat McClenahan, Sigourney 9-4.

119-Chad Dietze, Iowa Valley (Marengo) beat Gary Hauser, Rock Valley 13-8.

126-Rod Decker, East Buchanan beat Patrick Wilson, Shelby-Tenant 14-6.

132-Vince Miller, Plainfield beat Mike Spading, Belle Plaine 8-2.

138-Randy Kittleson, St. Ansgar beat Todd Luther, SEMCO (Gilman) 13-7.

145-Layne Billings, Nora Springs-Rock Falls pinned Keith Slifka, Grundy Center 4:28.

155-Mike Kelly, Britt beat Chris Charley, Janesville 3-2.

167-John Cory, Coon Rapids-Bayard beat Brian Benning, Ackley-Geneva 6-0.

185-Don Finch, Britt beat Barney Drenth, Central Lyon 15-3.

Hwt-Todd Jackson, Laurens-Marathon pinned Mike Meyer, Belmond :57.

S Hwt-Seth Bonnette, Riceville beat John Brown, Van Buren (Keosauqua) 10-3.

1987 (February 28)

CLASS 3-A

98-Dan Osborn, Cedar Rapids Prairie beat Doug Black, Fort Dodge 1-0 OT.

105-Ken Stecher, Iowa City High beat Brent Laartz, Charles City 13-3.

112-Baron Hendricks, Clinton beat Eddie Lee, Council Bluffs Lincoln 5-3.

119-Gary Steffensmeier, Fort Madison won by technical fall over Tam Ho, Boone 15-0, 5:30.

126-Dan Knight, Clinton pinned Andy Price, Burlington :28.

132-Tim Anderson, West Des Moines Dowling beat Greg Garman, Cedar Rapids Jefferson 10-7.

138-Travis Young, Indianola beat John Hiffernan, Council Bluffs Lincoln 4-3 OT.

145-Keith Linden, Sioux City Heelan beat Kurt McDermott, Newton 7-4.

155-Mike Angrick, Des Moines Roosevelt beat Matt Rechkemmer, Waverly-Shell Rock 3-2.

167-Bart Chelesvig, Webster City won by technical fall over Steve Sparbel, Muscatine 22-6, 4:49.

185-Kurt Rosenberger, West Des Moines Valley won by technical fall over Brad Dinsdale, Webster City 16-1, 5:19.

Hwt-Paul Weltha, Ames beat Jamie Cutler, West Des Moines Dowling 2-1 OT.

S Hwt-Brian Borota, Clinton beat Mike Fontana, Ankeny 2-1 (OT).

CLASS 2-A

98-Todd Frush, LaPorte City won by technical fall over Paul Rush, Dallas Center-Grimes 16-0, 5:14.

105-Kent Streicher, Starmont beat Bryan Wilcox, Davis County 5-3.

112-Troy Budden, Sheldon pinned Cale Sponsler, Johnston 1:18.

119-Chad Zaputil, Centerville beat Terry Brands, Sheldon 2-2, 2-1 OT.

126-Brent Carstensen, Camanche beat Dave Messerly, Eagle Grove 10-9.

132-Mike Moreno, Glenwood beat Curt Bennethum, North Polk 10-2.

138-Steve Hamilton, Emmetsburg won by technical fall over Jim Boehmer, Osage 22-6, 5:46.

145-Doug Streicher, Starmont beat Rick Coltvet, Eagle Grove 7-4.

155-Mark Reiland, Eagle Grove pinned Mike Kane, Cedar Rapids LaSalle 2:55.

167-Jym Guyer, North Fayette (West Union) beat Carson Kyhl, Waukee 14-6.

185-Stacy Hand, South Tama beat Craig Steven, New Hampton 5-2.

Hwt-Paul Wildeman, Cherokee pinned Brad Wymer, North Fayette (West Union) 1:36.

S Hwt-Ed Huff, Sheldon pinned Dan Cox, North Polk 1:35.

CLASS 1-A

98-Shane Light, Lisbon beat Ward Buster, Wapello 2-2, 5-0 OT.

105-Matt Otten, North Central (Manly) pinned C.C. Hoffman, Sigourney 1:15.

112-Bret Moews, Ackley-Geneva beat Tim Griffin, Laurens-Marathon 6-4.

119-Vance Light, Lisbon beat Bruce Obrecht, Underwood 11-3.

126-Chad Dietze, Iowa Valley (Marengo) beat Troy Brenning, Don Bosco (Gilbertville) 11-3.

132-Jim Benda, Don Bosco (Gilbertville) beat David Avila, Corning 8-3.

138-Vince Miller, Plainfield pinned San McIlrath, SEMCO (Gilman) 2:14.

145-Don Finch, Britt beat Kent Purdy, Don Bosco (Gilbertville) 5-3.

155-Dan Kopriva, North Tama beat Greg Hoing, George 4-3.

167-Greg Butteris, Lisbon beat Travis Fiser, Iowa Valley (Marengo) 6-3.

185-Don Finch, Britt won by technical fall over Terry Walter, MFL (Monona) 17-1, 2:54.

Hwt-Pat Kelly, Britt beat Tom Mashek, Don Bosco (Gilbertville) 8-2.

S Hwt-Mike Kilgore, Southeast Warren pinned Rodney Benson, Griswold 1:20.

1988 (February 27)

CLASS 3-A

98-Mike Neuman, West Des Moines Valley beat Randy Rowray, Cedar Rapids Prairie 5-3.

105-Lance Paulson, Cedar Rapids Kennedy beat Doug Black, Fort Dodge 8-2.

112-Doug Knotek, Council Bluffs Lewis Central beat Greg Meyers, Waterloo West 11-4.

119-Brad Bruhl, Fort Dodge beat Eddie Lee, Council Bluffs Lincoln 8-6.

126-Jeff Theiler, West Des Moines Dowling beat Kurt Christensen, Dubuque Hempstead 4-3.

132-Tim Anderson, West Des Moines Dowling beat Rob Watt, Ames 5-4.

138-Steve Hartle, Sioux City East beat John Hiffernan, Council Bluffs Lincoln 12-6.

145-Jamie Byrne, Cedar Rapids Washington beat Kyle Beaird, Keokuk 11-4.

155-Marcus Mangum, Waterloo East beat Shane Yates, Indianola 6-4.

167-Curtis White, West Des Moines Dowling beat James Young, Waterloo West 14-5.

185-Curt Engler, West Des Moines Dowling beat Greg Berg, Southeast Polk 8-2.

Hwt-Brad Schoenfelder, Bettendorf beat Steve Davis, Fort Dodge 5-4.

S Hwt-Chris Stogdill, Charles City beat Terry Alcott, Waterloo West 4-3.

CLASS 2-A

98-Gary McLaughlin, Hampton pinned Mike Needham, West Marshall 7:50 (OT).

105-Ward Buster, Wapello beat Todd Neal, Mount Vernon 5-5, 2-1 OT.

112-Cale Sponsler, Johnston beat Mike Powell, LaPorte City 7-5.

119-Chad Zaputil, Centerville beat Kent Streicher, Starmont 5-5, 3-2 OT.

126-Tracy Tucker, Spirit Lake won by technical fall over Rob Seil, Storm Lake 20-5, 5:22.

132-Stacey Rice, Storm Lake beat Brad Gazaway, Eagle Grove 5-4.

138-Mike Young, Emmetsburg beat Keith Moody, LaPorte City 4-3.

145-Rick Coltvet, Eagle Grove beat Jim Angran, Albia 11-1.

155-Mark McGrauth, Emmetsburg beat Mike Bergan, Cresco 4-4, 5-1 OT.

167-Dave Malecek, Osage beat Mike Beebe, Wilton 8-3.

185-Kent Jay, Grinnell beat Pat Williams, Decorah 3-2.

Hwt-John Oostendorp, West Liberty beat Todd Kinney, Central (DeWitt) 10-0.

S Hwt-Lance Keller, Iowa Falls beat Shawn Bohlmann, Audubon 5-4.

CLASS 1-A

98-Eric Ehlen, Belle Plaine pinned D.J. Wade, Morning Sun 5:37.

105-Tony Norton, Clarksville beat Jon Gilgen, West Harrison 12-10.

112-Shane Light, Lisbon beat Matt Otten, North Central (Manly) 3-1.

119-Tim Griffin, Laurens-Marathon pinned Mat McClenahan, Sigourney 3:28.

126-Bobby Short, Central Decatur beat Lynn Silver, Ackley-Geneva 4-3.

132-Tom Hogan, Don Bosco (Gilbertville) beat John Steckelberg, Stuart-Menlo 2-0.

138-Steve Thoma, Don Bosco (Gilbertville) pinned Pat Hyland, Coon Rapids-Bayard 3:24.

145-Brian Krob, Lisbon beat Tracy Watts, Bellevue 7-6.

155-Greg Hansen, AHST (Avoca) beat Dan Kopriva, North Tama 3-3, 5-2 OT.

167-Brian Benning, Ackley-Geneva beat Nick Lentz, East Buchanan 3-1.

185-Jamie Kamberling, Lisbon beat Mike Hemann, Riceville 10-5.

Hwt-Pat Kelly, Britt beat Tom Mashek, Don Bosco (Gilbertville) 9-4.

S Hwt-Ruel Kirstein, Lincoln (Stanwood) beat Brent James, Akron-Westfield 11-4.

1989 (February 25)

CLASS 3-A

103-Dan Osborn, Cedar Rapids Prairie beat Scott Sams, Ames 9-3.

112-Lance Paulson, Cedar Rapids Kennedy beat Randy Rowray, Cedar Rapids Prairie 8-2.

119-Marc Chase, Cedar Rapids Jefferson pinned Brent Beck, Grinnell 5:06.

125-Doug DeWald, Cedar Falls beat Gary Tucker, Dubuque Hempstead 6-4.

130-Andy Showalter, Waterloo West beat Montrice Anderson, Waterloo East 11-6 OT.

135-Matt Orton, Cedar Rapids Jefferson beat Jeff Dalrymple, Waterloo West 14-12 OT.

140-Jeff Theiler, West Des Moines Dowling beat Jason Welch, West Des Moines Valley 10-3.

145-Doug Kjeldgaard, Council Bluffs Lewis Central beat Troy Crigger, Clinton 7-1.

152-Curt Bennethum, West Des Moines Valley beat Robert Edmonds, Des Moines Roosevelt 9-0.

160-Steve Williams, Charles City beat Curtis White, West Des Moines Dowling 7-5.

171-Cory Manning, West Des Moines Dowling beat Craig Lamont, North Scott 9-0.

189-Glenn Wilder, Waterloo West pinned Tony Burger, Harlan 1:59.

275-Brad Henry, West Des Moines Dowling beat Matt Purdy, Cedar Falls 3-1.

CLASS 2-A

103-Donni Donahue, Clarinda pinned Marty Bolin, Davis County 3:08.

112-Brian Reece, Clarke (Osceola) beat Roger Vogel, Camanche 8-4.

119-Jereme Sutton, Williamsburg beat Kevin Cochran, Centerville 2-1.

125-Kent Streicher, Starmont beat Tim Krouse, Cardinal (Eldon) 9-2.

130-Mark Moorman, Centerville beat Rob Seil, Storm Lake 14-5.

135-Stacey Rice, Storm Lake beat Mike Bonham, Missouri Valley 11-4.

140-Jeremy Ask, St. Ansgar beat Jay Nelson, Dallas Center-Grimes 9-7.

145-John Royer, Marion beat Jason Wedgbury, Hampton-Dumont 8-5.

152-Jeff Jens, Glenwood beat Ryan Kittelson, Decorah 7-2 OT.

160-Mike Vander Woude, Central Lyon pinned Chad Stouder, Glenwood 2:24.

171-Dave Malecek, Osage beat Scott Stogdill, Glenwood 7-1.

189-Tyrone Roberts, South Tama beat Dave Vrba, Eagle Grove 5-4.

275-Lance Keller, Iowa Falls beat Niles Havard, Clarke (Osceola) 7-5.

CLASS 1-A

103-Eric Ehlen, Belle Plaine beat Scott Eppinga, Rock Valley 6-0.

112-Kevin Hogan, Ed-Co beat David Stirling, Clarksville 16-7.

119-Bret McKinney, Belle Plaine beat Tim Stoll, Orient-Macksburg 7-5.

125-Shane Light, Lisbon beat Tim Griffin, Laurens-Marathon 8-7.

130-Todd Griffin, Laurens-Marathon pinned Cody Shay, Mount Ayr 5:19.

135-Steve Stirling, Clarksville won by technical fall over Alex Malcom, Fremont-Mills 21-6, 5:22.

140-Shannon Bucknell, Postville beat Randy Heideman, Janesville 4-2.

145-Steve Brandt, Sumner pinned Joe Kilburg, Bellevue 5:31.

152-Brian Schmitz, Lisbon beat Bruce Kuennen, Turkey Valley 6-2.

160-Troy Rohret, Clear Creek (Tiffin) beat Wes Pargeon, Montezuma 4-2.

171-Tim O'Brien, Stuart-Menlo beat Craig Stork, Anita 6-5.

189-Mike Isaacson, Lake Mills beat Mike Funke, Ed-Co 8-3.

275-Brian Moretz, Northwood-Kensett beat Drew Brandt, Ackley-Geneva 9-4.

1990 (February 24)

CLASS 3-A

103-Jeff McGinness, Iowa City High beat Luke Swarbrick, Cedar Falls 9-4.

112-Jason Jewett, West Des Moines Dowling pinned Brent Paulson, Cedar Rapids Kennedy 5:15.

119-Matt Dickey, Waterloo West beat Scott Munson, Waterloo Columbus 2-1.

125-Ali Igram, Cedar Rapids Jefferson beat Brad Piper, Mason City 4-3.

130-Joe Piazza, West Des Moines Dowling beat Dan Dickey, Waterloo West 3-2 OT.

135-Jarid Downey, Indianola beat Bill Fullhart, Decorah 12-1.

140-Nate Hartle, Sioux City East beat Bert Johnson, Burlington 23-11.

145-Jeff Theiler, West Des Moines Dowling won by technical fall over Jay Cox, Indianola 18-3, 5:29.

152-Ryan Kittelson, Decorah beat Mark Fox, Urbandale 6-3.

160-Ed Miles, Mason City beat Ken McNear, Ankeny 6-1.

171-Casey Hesseltine, Iowa City High pinned Ernest Middleton, Waterloo West 1:05.

189-Jeff Horak, Cedar Rapids Jefferson beat Trent Lyman, Marshalltown 3-0.

275-Justin Greenlee, Waverly-Shell Rock pinned Kevin Weber, Dubuque Hempstead 4:30.

CLASS 2-A

103-Jessie Whitmer, Eagle Grove beat Brian Benitz, Jefferson-Scranton 11-4.

112-Brian Reece, Clarke (Osceola) beat Lim Prim, Grinnell 7-6.

119-Steve Pladsen, Waukon pinned Joe Moorman, Centerville 1:46.

125-Dan Beerman, Norwalk beat Ken Hron, Cresco 11-9.

130-Mike Dombrowski, Hampton-Dumont beat Scott Stickler, Clarinda 3-2.

135-Matt Sesker, Forest City pinned Joe Stephens, Centerville 3:23.

140-Jeremy Ask, St. Ansgar beat Grant Hjortshoj, PCM (Monroe) 12-6.

145-Mark Speltz, New Hampton beat Mike Madden, North Polk 4-2.

152-Jeff Jens, Glenwood beat Chad Thurn, Mount Vernon 17-7.

160-Dan Rule, Parkersburg beat Robbie Brown, Winterset 11-2.

171-Curtis Heideman, New Hampton beat Tony Dammen, Osage 11-4.

189-Greg Dimit, Grinnell beat Dave Vrba, Eagle Grove 6-5 OT.

275-Parker Wildeman, Cherokee beat Matt Carson, Clarke (Osceola) 7-4.

CLASS 1-A

103-Ike Light, Lisbon beat Ron McNichols, Lenox 10-6.

112-Eric Ehlen, Belle Plaine beat Jason Raisty, Greene 8-2.

119-Kevin Hogan, Ed-Co pinned John Smith, North Central (Manly) 2:26.

125-Shane Light, Lisbon pinned Matt Lundquist, Corning 2:19.

130-Brian Stewart, Lisbon beat Travis Moore, Tri-County (Thornburg) 19-12.

135-Daryl Weber, Don Bosco (Gilbertville) beat Zach Light, Lisbon 8-6.

140-Randy Heideman, Janesville beat Rick Wittrock, Okoboji (Milford) 9-0.

145-Damon Loyd, New London pinned Bruce Christopher, North Winneshiek (Decorah) :57.

152-Lynn Johnsen, Logan-Magnolia beat Randy Jimenez, Southeast Warren 6-6, 2-1 OT.

160-Chad Kroeze, Clarksville beat Mike Prehm, Clarion 5-5 OT (criteria).

171-Matt Straight, Logan-Magnolia beat Robby Kamberling, Lisbon 13-8.

189-Mike Isaacson, Lake Mills pinned Tolly Thompson, Janesville 4:23.

275-Brian Moretz, Northwood-Kensett beat Jay Malone, Morning Sun 5-4.

1991 (March 2)

CLASS 3-A

103-Darren Coppock, Council Bluffs Lincoln beat Jeff Bellows, Council Bluffs Lewis Central 9-5.

112-Jeff McGinness, Iowa City High beat Matt Mathiesen, Denison-Schleswig, 15-3.

119-Matt Dickey, Waterloo West beat Tom Smith, Dubuque Wahlert 9-2.

125-Derek Mountsier, Newton beat Manuel Macias, Davenport North 8-6.

130-Tony DeAnda, Sioux City Heelan beat Jesse Reynolds, Muscatine 8-7.

135-Matt Ironside, Cedar Rapids Jefferson beat Dan Lovell, Marshalltown 8-4.

140-Matt Hatcher, Cedar Rapids Prairie beat Bart Horton, Dubuque Wahlert 8-4.

145-Jarid Downey, Indianola beat Mark Wallace, Bettendorf 9-3.

152-Mark Fox, West Des Moines Dowling beat Ben Smith, Southeast Polk 9-3.

160-Sean Scarbrough, Waterloo Columbus pinned Aaron Baugher, Ankeny 1:55.

171-Erik Josephson, Fort Dodge beat Greg Lechtenberg, Bettendorf 4-4 OT (criteria).

189-Erik Stroner, Webster City beat Rusty Van Wetzinga, Pleasant Valley 8-5.

275-Jeff Watts, Linn-Mar (Marion) pinned Matt Purdy, Cedar Falls 5:32.

CLASS 2-A

103-Paul Wilkerson, Wapello beat Brad Meinecke, Jefferson-Scranton 7-2.

112-Jason Nurre, Dyersville Beckman beat Dave Morgan, New Hampton 9-2.

119-Lim Prim, Grinnell beat Brian Howell, Maquoketa 8-4.

125-Cory Christensen, Winterset beat Adam Hutchinson, West Delaware 6-6, 1-0 OT.

130-Daryl Vaske, West Delaware beat Shawn Zimmerman, Clear Lake 10-8.

135-Brian Duckworth, Johnston beat Jason Coy, Parkersburg 5-4.

140-Tony Daugherty, Norwalk beat Corey Johnson, Garner-Hayfield 11-2.

145-Rick Moreno, Glenwood beat Mike Uker, Osage 7-2.

152-Kirk Crawford, Union (LaPorte City) beat Scott Carlton, Winterset 8-5.

160-Jason Wedgbury, Hampton-Dumont pinned John Robinson, New Hampton 3:14.

171-Tony Ersland, Humboldt beat Ryan Furnal, Carlisle 5-5, 4-3 OT.

189-Curtis Heideman, New Hampton beat Rick Sanger, West Hancock 12-5.

275-Brian Moretz, Northwood-Kensett beat Darrin Adams, North Iowa (Buffalo Center) 10-3.

CLASS 1-A

103-Peter Taft, Mason City Newman beat Tony Milcoff, Cedar Rapids LaSalle 3-3, 3-1 OT.

112-Ike Light, Lisbon beat Jamie Cochran, Moravia 5-3.

119-Tracy Dietze, Iowa Valley (Marengo) beat Rob Wadle, Southeast Warren 11-0.

125-Chad Caskey, Carson-Macedonia-Oakland beat Rob Meister, Clarksville 7-6.

130-Ryan Van Den Heuvel, Tri-County (Thornburg) pinned Mark Hood, Westwood (Sloan) 3:31.

135-David Stirling, Clarksville beat Tom Vodraska, Martensdale-St. Marys 14-3.

140-Zach Light, Lisbon beat Tim Novak, Cedar Rapids LaSalle 14-7.

145-Daryl Weber, Don Bosco (Gilbertville) pinned Dannel Ripperger, East Union (Afton) 5:12.

152-Corbon Kinney, Griswold beat Joe Kielman, Clarksville 12-7.

160-Troy Purdy, Don Bosco (Gilbertville) pinned Shon Houdek, Iowa Valley (Marengo) 3:58.

171-Chris Swalla, Stuart-Menlo beat Matt Straight, Logan-Magnolia 6-4.

189-Wade Kroeze, Clarksville beat Tolly Thompson, Janesville 5-3.

275-Ryan Behr, Mason City Newman pinned Russ Frazier, Logan-Magnolia :49.

1992 (February 29)

CLASS 3-A

103-Eric Keller, Indianola beat Troy Yegge, Pleasant Valley 6-2.

112-Darren Coppock, Council Bluffs Lincoln beat Jeff Bellows, Council Bluffs Lewis Central 5-1.

119-Brent Paulson, Cedar Rapids Kennedy beat Tom Smith, Dubuque Wahlert 6-4.

125-Jeff McGinness, Iowa City High beat Jason Proctor, Cedar Rapids Prairie 17-5.

130-Mark Ironside, Cedar Rapids Jefferson beat Courtney Anderson, Fort Dodge 7-2.

135-Chris Coppola, West Des Moines Dowling beat Chad Vance, Charles City 5-5, 2-0 OT.

140-Dan Lovell, Marshalltown beat Terry Vaughn, Iowa City West 10-2.

145-Matt Hatcher, Cedar Rapids Prairie beat Greg Halsor, Cedar Falls 20-9.

152-Bart Horton, Dubuque Wahlert beat Jay Cox, Indianola 6-5.

160-Louis Pelsang, Iowa City High beat Ben Smith, Southeast Polk 7-6.

171-Ernest Middleton, Waterloo West pinned Chad Niles, Charles City 1:57.

189-Rusty Van Wetzinga, Pleasant Valley beat Ryan Reasland, Webster City 3-3, 2-0 OT.

275-Gabe Toft, Spencer beat Mark Mitchell, Iowa City High 8-4.

CLASS 2-A

103-Chad Bennett, Ballard (Huxley) beat Mike Dennis, Iowa Falls 10-3.

112-Doug Titus, Carlisle beat Paul Wilkerson, Wapello 8-4.

119-Brian Howell, Maquoketa beat Aaron Grimes, North Fayette (West Union) 9-6.

125-Dusty Rhodes, Osage beat Tom Harbison, Wapello 3-3, 2-0 OT.

130-Matt Gonshorowski, Washington beat Chad Venz, NC/NK 9-2.

135-Cory Christensen, Winterset beat Brian Fuhrmeister, West Liberty 8-2.

140-Dan Sperry, Independence pinned Lee Klinkenborg, Parkersburg 3:01.

145-Rick Moreno, Glenwood beat Howard Fullhart, Decorah 12-4.

152-Ryan Cummings, Mediapolis beat Cory Jones, Iowa Falls 7-3.

160-Lee Fullhart, Decorah beat Kirk Crawford, Union (LaPorte City) 8-0.

171-Tony Ersland, Humboldt beat Richie Ludwig, Dyersville Beckman 4-4, 2-0 OT.

189-Matt Eckerman, Forest City beat Frank Bachman, Glenwood 1-1, 2-0 OT.

275-Adam Greiner, Mid-Prairie (Wellman) pinned Aaron Klosterman, Vinton-Shellsburg 5:06.

CLASS 1-A

103-Jason Keenan, Ogden beat Travis Johannes, Montezuma 4-2.

112-Marc Schulze, Rock Valley beat Peter Taft, Mason City Newman 3-0.

119-Juan Robles, Wilton beat Tony Milcoff, Cedar Rapids LaSalle 7-3.

125-Ike Light, Lisbon beat Dan Gabrielson, Belmond-Klemme 9-6.

130-Matt Kiger, Audubon beat Josh Jones, Lisbon 4-3.

135-Tom Davis, West Monona beat Chad Ryan, Underwood 6-5.

140-Brian Follman, CAM (Anita) pinned Mike Huitink, West Sioux 3:46.

145-Zach Light, Lisbon beat John DeLeon, West Hancock 19-6.

152-George Robinson, Central City beat Brad Olson, Nashua 2-1.

160-Joe Kielman, Clarksville beat Tim Jager, George-Little Rock 6-2.

171-Kirk Rathjen, Iowa Valley (Marengo) beat Todd Gray, Don Bosco (Gilbertville) 13-7.

189-Wade Kroeze, Clarksville beat Rick Sanger, West Hancock 4-4, 2-0 OT.

275-Matt Sauer, Woodbury Central beat Cary Myer, West Hancock 9-3.

1993 (February 27)

CLASS 3-A

103-Eric Juergens, Maquoketa beat Jason Anderson, Council Bluffs Lewis Central 3-2.

112-Jeff Bellows, Council Bluffs Lewis Central beat Jason Osborn, Sioux City Heelan 6-6, 2-0 OT.

119-Wil Kelly, Dubuque Washlert beat Matt Rial, Fort Dodge 3-0.

125-Zach Geary, Cedar Falls beat Victor Martinez, Fort Madison 9-4.

130-Jeff McGinness, Iowa City High pinned Rod Ergenbright, Newton 4:36.

135-Mark Ironside, Cedar Rapids Jefferson beat Seth Septer, Mason City 27-16.

140-Jon Tornberg, West Des Moines Valley beat Wade Anderson, Waterloo West 4-3.

145-Jason Francois, Dubuque Wahlert beat Mark White, West Des Moines Dowling 15-8.

152-Greg Halsor, Cedar Falls beat Adam Bendorf, Council Bluffs Lewis Central 10-8.

160-Ben Smith, Southeast Polk beat Eric LaGrange, Cedar Rapids Prairie 10-7.

171-Matt Mulvihill, West Des Moines Dowling beat Chris Lensing, Bettendorf 7-5.

189-Tony Wieland, Cedar Falls beat Ryan Reasland, Webster City 1-1, 1-0 OT.

275-Scott Peck, Council Bluffs Jefferson beat Dion Reed, Waterloo East 6-4.

CLASS 2-A

103-Chase Zaputil, Centerville beat Doug Schwab, Osage 7-3.

112-Kelly Seery, New Hampton beat Shane Peterson, Independence 5-1.

119-Doug Titus, Carlisle beat Terry Zuraff, West Lyon 6-5.

125-Mark Brandenburg, Emmetsburg beat Will Smith, NC/N-K 7-5.

130-Jamie Heidt, Humboldt beat Steve Wilbur, Storm Lake 4-2.

135-David Morgan, New Hampton beat Ben Uker, Osage 12-6.

140-Ryan Jensen, Winterset beat Kirk Stansbery, Chariton 10-5.

145-Cory Christensen, Winterset beat Brad Horton, Norwalk 5-3.

152-Ryan Cummings, Mediapolis beat Howard Fullhart, Decorah 9-9, 2-0 OT.

160-Brad Beaman, Johnston beat Mike Cosgrove, Albia 10-2.

171-Lee Fullhart, Decorah beat Robert Armey, West Liberty 4-4, 2-0 OT.

189-Chad Utley, New Hampton beat Chad Koedam, West Lyon 5-2.

275-Adam Greiner, Mid-Prairie (Wellman) beat Cary Myer, West Hancock 11-4.

CLASS 1-A

103-Josh Crain, Southwest (Sidney) beat Jeremy Sprague, Bondurant-Farrar 8-0.

112-Jason Keenan, Ogden beat Todd Kuhse, Ed-Co 10-2.

119-Kirk Eknes, Rock Valley beat Darren Hellman, Don Bosco (Gilbertville) 13-5.

125-Marc Schulze, Rock Valley beat Brad Canoyer, Carson-Macedonia-Oakland 5-4.

130-Dan Gabrielson, Belmond-Klemme beat Chris Jones, Central Decatur 6-3.

135-Chad Stanley, Interstate 35 (Truro) beat Paul Coffelt, Central Decatur 5-3.

140-Corey Starry, Cedar Rapiods LaSalle beat Chad Martin, Belle Plaine 8-4.

145-B. J. Miller, North Iowa (Buffalo Center) beat Kevin Brisker, Lisbon 12-5.

152-Tim Norton, Clarksville beat Rob Wadle, Southeast Warren 3-2.

160-Dan Sweeting, Highland (Riverside) beat Matt Kruger, George-Little Rock 13-6.

171-Matt Hoover, Belle Plaine beat Chris Ortner, Don Bosco (Gilbertville) 10-9.

189-Tait Stamp, Lisbon beat Todd Peach, Bedford 6-5.

275-Mike Christensen, Lenox pinned Clay Bowman, Logan-Magnolia 5:18.

1994 (February 26)

CLASS 3-A

103-Mark Rial, Fort Dodge beat Casey Doyle, West Delaware 11-5.

112-Eric Juergens, Maquoketa beat Jon Vlasek, Cedar Rapids Jefferson 15-10.

119-Eric Keller, Indianola beat Nick Dohrmann, Iowa City West 9-8.

125-Victor Martinez, Fort Madison beat Matt Young, Indianola 8-7.

130-Wil Kelly, Dubuque Wahlert pinned Todd Buckland, Des Moines Lincoln 3:30.

135-David Kjeldgaard, Council Bluffs Lewis Central beat Brad Miller, Pleasant Valley 17-5.

140-Dusty Coufal, Cedar Rapids Prairie beat Seth Septer, Mason City 6-5.

145-Andy Krueger, Sioux City Heelan beat Brant LaGrange, Cedar Rapids Prairie 7-3.

152-Travis Pike, Cedar Rapids Jefferson beat Casey Aldridge, Indianola 1-1, 2-0 OT.

160-Adam Bendorf, Council Bluffs Lewis Central pinned Travis Evans, Iowa City High 2:30.

171-Jason Crooks, Fort Madison beat Todd Scott, Newton 8-7.

189-Tony Wieland, Cedar Falls beat Jeremy Mize, Ames 5-5, 2-0 OT.

275-Dion Reed, Waterloo East beat Jeremy Whalen, Indianola 5-3.

CLASS 2-A

103-Ben Shirk, Wilton beat Ryan Cunningham, Forest City 2-1.

112-Nick Marin, West Liberty beat Jody Beck, Cresco 9-8.

119-Jason Halupnick, Centerville beat Dan Casey, Clarinda 4-0.

125-Will Thomsen, Jefferson-Scranton beat Ben Scorpil, West Liberty 3-3, 2-0 OT.

130-Ben Shane, Iowa Falls beat Mark Brandenburg, Iowa Falls 4-3.

135-Ben Uker, Osage beat Mike Coss, Wilton 6-2.

140-Jamie Heidt, Humboldt beat Ryan Robbins, Carlisle 12-5.

145-Ryan Jensen, Winterset beat Travis Holm, Osage 7-4.

152-Brad Horton, Norwalk beat Ryan Kinsella, Creston 11-6.

160-Tim Duff, Winterset beat David Wimberly, Clarinda 6-3.

171-Damian Moses, Clarinda beat Jake Hayes, Creston 7-5.

189-Lee Fullhart, Decorah beat Josh Dodd, NC/N-K 10-5.

275-Bob Muller, Osage beat Gregg Recker, Dyersville Beckman 12-7.

CLASS 1-A

103-Jeremy Sprague, Bondurant-Farrar pinned Jared Greiner, Pekin 2:59.

112-Mark Van Beek, Rock Valley beat Nick Field, Woodward-Granger 6-2.

119-Jason Keenan, Ogden pinned Don LaGrange, Montezuma 3:05.

125-Kirk Eknes, Rock Valley beat Colby Yoder, Belmond-Klemme 7-2.

130-Chris Jones, Central Decatur beat Tony Milcoff, Cedar Rapids LaSalle 8-2.

135-Jeff Meyer, Sumner beat Darrin Youngblut, Jesup 8-7.

140-Ryan Schweitzberger, Kingsley-Pierson beat Cory Davis, Wapsie Valley 9-4.

145-Chad Dutler, Galva-Holstein beat Aaron Slaymaker, Belle Plaine 9-4.

152-Justin Decker, West Central (Maynard) beat Todd Foster, Riceville 6-0.

160-John Whitmer, Eagle Grove beat Jeff Rhea, Sumner 7-3.

171-Jeff Clark, Lisbon beat Clint Dunlop, Woodbine 6-2.

189-Matt Hoover, Belle Plaine pinned Jesse Moore, Lisbon 1:23.

275-Matt Powelka, Janesville beat Shawn Striegel, Tri-County (Thornburg) 1-1, 2-0 OT.

1995 (February 25)

CLASS 3-A

103-Josh Budke, Cedar Falls won by technical fall over Gabe Capps, Indianola 16-0, 5:00.

112-Chad Wickman, West Delaware pinned Robert Rivas, Des Moines East 4:26.

119-Eric Juergens, Maquoketa beat Mark Rial, Fort Dodge 16-4.

125-Nick Flach, Fort Madison pinned Scott Vance, Charles City 2:25.

130-Willie Crile, Oskaloosa pinned Josh Dorothy, Mount Pleasant 6:22 (OT).

135-Wil Kelly, Dubuque Wahlert beat Chris Lukan, Marshalltown 11-1.

140-David Kjeldgaard, Council Bluffs Lewis Central beat Todd Buckland, Des Moines Lincoln 9-1.

145-Steve Blackford, West Des Moines Dowling pinned Gary Lake, Waterloo East 2:36.

152-Andy Krueger, Sioux City Heelan beat Brad Honnold, Clarinda 11-4.

160-Adam Bendorf, Council Bluffs Lewis Central beat Travis Evans, Iowa City High 6-4.

171-Matt DeRocher, LeMars beat Steve Niles, Charles City 9-4.

189-Jason Crooks, Fort Madison beat Satori Snow, Cedar Rapids Prairie 14-11.

275-Trent Hynek, Cedar Rapids Prairie beat Chad Deal, Council Bluffs Lewis Central 4-1.

CLASS 2-A

103-Kannon Grotegut, Waukon beat Nick Marin, West Liberty 5-1.

112-Chase Zaputil, Centerville beat Tou Vongpanya, Fairfield 6-1.

119-Corey Stanley, Wilton beat Doug Schwab, Osage 6-5.

125-Ben Scorpil, West Liberty beat Jason Halupnick, Centerville 5-2.

130-Justin Jeffs, Winterset beat David Marrah, Union (LaPorte City) 7-6.

135-Greg Breeding, Winterset beat Joey Beaver, Knoxville 8-3.

140-Erik Fitzer, Wilton beat Gavin Bradley, JSPC (Jefferson) 6-2.

145-Ben Jobgen, Davenport Assumption beat Scott Kauffman, Emmetsburg 15-3.

152-Shane Boorn, Wilton beat Marcus Kurtz, Davenport Assumption 13-1.

160-Matt Gravert, Davenport Assumption beat Dave Doebel, Clear Lake 3-2.

171-Dain Lundvall, Glenwood beat Ryan Kinsella, Creston 4-2.

189-Bob Fullhart, Decorah beat Tag Noel, Chariton 5-0.

275-Wes Hand, South Tama beat Nate Wernburg, Marion 19-8.

CLASS 1-A

103-Travis Brant, Interstate 35 (Truro) beat Jay Field, Woodward-Granger 8-2.

112-Jared Greiner, Pekin beat Jason Cassady, Interstate 35 (Truro) 12-2.

119-Jimmy Rodgers, Riverside (Oakland) beat Tim Backer, Clarksville 8-5.

125-Jason Keenan, Ogden pinned Eric Hart, Coon Rapids-Bayard :40.

130-Josh Meier, Denver beat Jerrod Keith, Eldora-New Providence 4-3.

135-Cory Davis, Wapsie Valley beat Fritz Baier, Griswold 11-5.

140-Pat Rupp, Belle Plaine beat Bobby Forseen, New London 8-4.

145-Randy Pugh, Columbus Junction won by injury default over Jeff Kress, East Buchanan :44.

152-Justin Decker, West Central (Maynard) beat Jacobs Knight, Mount Ayr 3-0.

160-Justin Short, East Buchanan beat David Sandhoff, Schaller-Crestland 6-2.

171-Lee Weber, Don Bosco (Gilbertville) beat Paul Jenn, West Hancock 11-6.

189-Calley Kruger, Aplington-Parkersburg pinned Derek Maeder, Corning 5:53.

275-Dan Griffith, Twin Cedars pinned Adam Bucklin, Colfax-Mingo 2:40.

1996 (February 24)

CLASS 3-A

103-Joe Lucchi, Iowa City High beat Cliff Moore, Dubuque Hempstead 4-3.

112-Josh Budke, Cedar Falls beat Gabe Capps, Indianola 3-0.

119-Casey Doyle, West Manchester beat Bob Koenig, Spencer 5-4.

125-Mark Rial, Fort Dodge pinned Ben Barnes, Johnston 2:40.

130-Matt Pence, Cedar Rapids Prairie beat Scott Vance, Charles City 8-7 (2 OT).

135-Nick Flach, Fort Madison beat Troy Thompson, Des Moines Lincoln 21-11.

140-Trent Moore, Dubuque Hempstead beat Keith Weber, Dubuque Senior 6-4.

145-Todd Buckland, Des Moines Lincoln beat Justin Wolfe, Fort Dodge 17-8.

152-David Kjeldgaard, Council Bluffs Lewis Central pinned Todd Gelner, Charles City 3:09.

160-Steve Blackford, West Des Moines Dowling beat Steve Long, Clinton 17-5.

171-Robert Cole, Des Moines North beat Ryan LaGrange, Cedar Rapids Prairie 3-2.

189-Micah Daggy, West Des Moines Dowling beat Aaron Tecklenburg, Marshalltown 7-2.

275-Tony Beminio, Iowa City West beat Justin Galbraith, Waterloo West 2-2, 2-0 OT.

CLASS 2-A

103-Jamie Taxted, Webster City beat Justin Stanley, Wilton 1-0.

112-Nick Marin, West Liberty beat Kevin Bratland, Humboldt 11-3.

119-Mike Pentecost, Independence beat Marc Juergens, Maquoketa 5-1.

125-Eric Juergens, Maquoketa beat Mike Corsiglia, Davenport Assumption 17-6.

130-Doug Schwab, Osage beat Ben Scorpil, West Liberty 13-3.

135-David Marrah, Union (LaPorte City) beat Matt Gogel, Anamosa 10-0.

140-Bobby Gonshorowski, Washington beat Mike Fertig, Webster City 5-3.

145-Matt Hand, South Tama beat Eric Schulte, Independence 1-1, 2-0 OT.

152-Jeff Friedhof, New Hampton beat Steve Schechinger, Harlan 5-2.

160-Chad Rowson, Central (DeWitt) beat Scott Kauffman, Emmetsburg 8-6.

171-Dave Doebel, Clear Lake beat Tyler Abens, Webster City 7-6.

189-Chad Morrison, West Liberty beat Matt Mann, Missouri Valley 8-2.

275-Tom Van Dyke, Clarke (Osceola) beat Josh Liddle, Camanche 2-1.

CLASS 1-A

103-Adam Robertson, Highland (Riverside) beat Kelly Killian, Westwood (Sloan) 6-1.

112-Kyle Canoyer, Riverside (Oakland) beat J. D. Pugh, Columbus Junction 2-1 (2 OT).

119-Tim Backer, Clarksville beat Andy Wollner, Mason City Newman 10-1.

125-Steve Swope, Riverside (Oakland) beat Tim Cory, Bondurant-Farrar 11-7.

130-Travis Morrow, Southern Cal beat Trevor Kruger, George-Little Rock 6-3.

135-Jimmy Rodgers, Riverside (Oakland) beat Matt Stirling, Clarksville 8-6.

140-Troy Pecenka, Don Bosco (Gilbertville) beat Joe Even, Wapsie Valley 7-6.

145-Jeremy Neuhaus, MFL (Monona) beat Daniel Klindt, Riverside (Oakland) 8-8, 2-0 OT.

152-Kyle Sargisson, Kingsley-Pierson beat Tim Kelly, New London 7-2.

160-Mike Cassady, Martensdale-St. Marys beat Brett Harvey, Kingsley-Pierson 9-2.

171-Matt Buskohl, Diuke-New Hartford beat Greg Hammes, Sigourney 4-3.

189-Jason Payne, Columbus Junction pinned Nick Weeks, Cedar Rapids LaSalle 1:44.

275-Luke Sampson, Roland-Story beat Kurt Lowenburg, Pekin 7-3.

1997 (March 1)

CLASS 3-A

103-Keith Edwards, Iowa City West beat Bobby Duggan, Muscatine 7-6.

112-Cliff Moore, Dubuque Hempstead beat Jeremy Hendricks, Marshalltown 13-3.

119-Adam Eichhorn, Cedar Falls pinned David Brown, LeMars 5:50.

125-Josh Budke, Cedar Falls beat Jesse West, Iowa City High 3-1.

130-Eric Sinclair, Cedar Falls pinned Dustin Breckenridge, Newton :41.

135-Toronald Harris, Cedar Rapids Jefferson beat Raymond Luna, Mason City 5-4.

140-Brandon Duncan, Pleasant Valley beat Jake Emerick, Pella 6-5.

145-Drew Kelly, Charles City beat Joe Hargrave, Spencer 11-0.

152-Terry Parham, Glenwood beat Brannon Hilton, Indianola 3-1.

160-Mitch Peyton, West Delaware beat Andy Harrison, West Des Moines Valley 21-11.

171-Creighton Duncan, Pleasant Valley pinned Jessman Smith, Southeast Polk 1:46.

189-Ryan LaGrange, Cedar Rapids Prairie beat Greg Roorda, Southeast Polk 18-7.

275-MacJohn Daggy, West Des Moines Dowling beat Nabeel Yehyawi, Keokuk 1:42.

CLASS 2-A

103-Justin Riddle, Clarinda beat Dylan Long, Creston 5-5, 4-0 OT.

112-Jamie Taxted, Webster City beat Nick Marolf, Columbus Junction 12-4.

119-J. D. Pugh, Columbus Junction beat Marc Juergens, Maquoketa 6-4.

125-Luke Moffitt, Estherville pinned Jeff Dirks, Anamosa 5:54.

130-Brandon Livingood, Decorah beat Tyler McGinnis, Shenandoah 4-2.

135-Frank Marchant, Humboldt beat Rob Hoback, Columbus Junction 14-11.

140-Matt Anderson, Shenandoah beat Casey Gwinn, Chariton 7-3.

145-Bobby Gonshorowski, Washington beat Tim Matthys, Davenport Assumption 3-1.

152-Chay Wood, Chariton pinned Travis Hauser, Grinnell 4:36.

160-Drew Bouwman, West Lyon beat Chris Chambers, Webster City 3-2.

171-Trey Clark, Union (LaPorte City) beat Chris Higgins, Forest City 3-3, 2-0 OT.

189-Jason Payne, Columbus Junction beat Chris Hayworth, Dallas Center-Grimes 7-2.

275-Scott Eddy. Independence beat Andy Kelley, Knoxville 8-8, 2-0 OT.

CLASS 1-A

103-Matt Pasvogel, Wilton beat Kurt Morgan, Eagle Grove 12-2.

112-Justin Stanley, Wilton beat Kaleb McCarty, Guthrie Center 11-2.

119-Ryan Friedrich, Riceville beat Brad Scoles, Underwood 11-11, 2-0 OT.

125-Kyle Canoyer, Riverside (Oakland) beat Eric Wallis, Logan-Magnolia 6-3.

130-Tim Cory, Bondurant-Farrar beat Matt Van Meter, Guthrie Center 12-5.

135-Nate Trees, Greene beat Matt Nason, West Marshall 13-5.

140-Ben Shirk, Wilton beat Jake Munger, West Central (Maynard) 10-2.

145-Jimmy Rodgers, Riverside (Oakland) beat Tyler Nixt,. Greene 13-5.

152-Benji Silver, Central City beat Andy Kiger, Audubon 6-0.

160-Kyle Hansen, Wilton beat Cody Alesch, Graettinger 7-3.

171-Adam Cory, Bondurant-Farrar beat Perry Blanchard, Belle Plaine 6-5.

189-David Reid, Wapello beat Kurt Boustead, Woodbine 1-1 OT (criteria).

275-Jason Gilbertson, Lake Mills beat Mike Steckley, Williamsburg 4-2.

1998 (February 28)

CLASS 3-A

103-Brian Hessenius, LeMars beat Chad Davis, Council Bluffs Lewis Central 17-9.

112-Rice Owens, West Des Moines Valley beat Mark Hangsleben, Urbandale 3-3, 2-0 OT.

119-Cliff Moore, Dubuque Hempstead beat Reggie Monson, Des Moines North 8-4.

125-Kentral Galloway, Waterloo East won by technical fall over Solomon Hughes, Muscatine 19-2, 5:03.

130-Tim Ironside, Cedar Rapids Jefferson beat Cory Tarchinski, Davenport West 6-2.

135-Brandon Livingood, Decorah beat Scott Shover, West Delaware 3-1.

140-Bob Koenig, Spencer beat Austin Coufal, Cedar Rapids Prairie 11-4.

145-Clint Madison, Glenwood beat Jerry Reicks, Sioux City Heelan 9-9, 2-0 OT.

152-Drew Kelly, Charles City beat Dayton Ericson, Cedar Falls 9-1.

160-Andy Harrison, West Des Moines Valley beat Terry Parham, Glenwood 7-1.

171-Jessman Smith, Southeast Polk beat Ted Prier, Cedar Falls 10-0.

189-Paul Hynek, Cedar Rapids Prairie pinned Brant Chambers, West Des Moines Dowling :57.

275-Randy Fulsaas, Decorah beat Jim Farrell, Cedar Falls 7-5.

CLASS 2-A

103-Josh Watts, Davenport Assumption beat Trent Goodale, Osage 8-6.

112-Joe Glissman, Knoxville beat Adam Kramer, New Hampton 6-0.

119-Dylan Long, Creston beat Tim Halligan, Independence 6-0.

125-Andy Thjompson, Clear Lake beat Jesse Zobeck, Crestwood (Cresco) 7-4.

130-Cole Pape, Maquoketa beat Garrett Kurth, Waukon 6-4.

135-Jon Garvin, Davenport Assumption beat Luke Moffitt, Estherville 6-5.

140-Cory Beckman, New HZampton beat Andy Vitzthum, Humboldt 3-0.

145-Matt Anderson, Shenandoah beat Chad Smith, Winterset 17-5.

152-Tim Matthys, Davenport Assumption beat Kurtis Williamson, Eagle Grove 4-2.

160-Mike Claeys, BGM-HLV (Brooklyn) pinned Eric Pettingill, Union (LaPorte City) 1:32.

171-Scott Kauffman, Emmetsburg pinned Lucas Kluever, Maquoketa 1:32.

189-Lance Guyer, North Fayette (West Union) beat Nick Paulsen, Atlantic 5-2.

275-Travis Henning, MFL (Monona) pinned Dan Beitz, Maquoketa Valley 1:32.

CLASS 1-A

103-Jesse Sundell, Ogden beat Joe Reiter, Don Bosco (Gilbertville) 9-5.

112-Jeff Harrison, Westwood (Sloan) beat Scott Burns, Pleasantville 1-1, 2-0 OT.

119-Tony Sweeting, Highland (Riverside) beat Jeremiah Butteris, Lisbon 9-9. 2-0 OT.

125-Tom FZitzer, Wilton beat Chris Wernimont, Pocahontas 8-1.

130-Justin Stanley, Wilton beat Casey Baxa, Lisbon 11-1.

135-Tim Cory, Bondurant-Farrar beat Kurt Nelson, Nashua-Plainfield 12-3.

140-Pat McMillan, Valley (Elgin) beat Chad Eberhart, Diuke-New Hartford 7-2.

145-Rob Hoback, Columbus Junction beat Dustin Destival, Wapsie Valley 11-9.

152-Blu Wahle, Underwood beat Kent Noska, North Linn 16-6.

160-Benji Silver, Central City beat Zeb evans, Lenox 6-2.

171-Jed VanLengen, Janesville beat Brent Meyers, Postville 7-2.

189-Justin Garvey, New London beat Derrick Powers, St. Ansgar 10-6.

275-Tim Helgeson, Lake Mills beat Bill Stuart, Interstate 35 (Truro) 5-1.

1999 (February 27)

CLASS 3-A

103-Dominick Moyer, Nebraska beat Chad Davis, Council Bluffs Lewis Central 5-4.

112-Travis Paulson, Council Bluffs Lewis Central pinned Brian Hessenius, LeMars 3:44.

119-Mark Hangsleben, Urbandale beat Ricky Pence, Cedar Rapids Prairie 8-6.

125-Cliff Moore, Dubuque Hempstead beat Aaron Groves, Newton 16-5.

130-Ryan Heim, Dubuque Hempstead beat Matt Vasey, Des Moines Lincoln 7-0.

135-David Brown, LeMars beat Pat Rial, Fort Dodge 5-0.

140-Dan Reisner, Cedar Rapids Kennedy beat Phil Klees, Burlington 11-5.

145-Eric Weber, Dubuque Senior beat Walker Evans, Iowa City High 8-4.

152-Richard Schroeder, LeMars beat Brandon Lyons, Charles City 4-4, 2-0 OT.

160-Drew Kelly, Charles City pinned Kenyatta Carter, Waterloo West 1:45.

171-Josh Porter, Fort Dodge beat Sean Stender, North Scott 8-4.

189-Randy Fulsaas, Decorah beat Tameem Yehyawi, Keokuk 15-5.

275-Ryan Fulsaas, Decorah beat Mike Novak, Cedar Rapids Prairie 16-5.

CLASS 2-A

103-Joe Honts, Louisa-Muscatine pinned Kellen Kraber, Knoxville 2:58.

112-Trent Goodale, Osage beat J. D. Naig, Emmetsburg/Armstrong-Ringsted 12-3.

119-Adam Kramer, New Hampton beat Dustin Dunton, South Tama 6-6, 2-0 OT.

125-Joe Havig, Osage pinned Cody Townsend, Davis County 2:59.

130-Dylan Long, Creston won by technical fall over Tim Halligan, Independence 21-4, 5:45.

135-Cole Pape, Maquoketa beat Ryan Utterback, New Hampton 6-4.

140-Jon Garvin, Davenport Assumption beat Ryan Sturm, Emmetsburg/Armstrong-Ringsted 3-0.

145-Cory Beckman, New Hampton beat Paul Bradley, South Tama 7-2.

152-Andrew Hayes, Creston beat Nick Thurn, Mount Vernon 8-2.

160-Mike Lester, Clear Lake beat Mike Kennedy, Monticello 8-1.

171-Jason Reicks, New Hampton beat Rex Gray, Clarke (Osceola) 4-2.

189-Trey Clark, Union (LaPorte City) beat Dustin Den Hartog, Clear Lake 5-0.

275-Josh Grube, Crestwood (Cresco) pinned Jake Veach, Maquoketa 5:24.

CLASS 1-A

103-Nick Lee, Columbus Junction beat Joe Reiter, Don Bosco (Gilbertville) 10-10, 2-0 OT.

112-Jesse Sundell, Ogden pinned Keith Simmons, Sidney 4:54.

119-Jeff Harrison, Westwood (Sloan) won by technical fall over Tyler Grieser, Ogden 17-2 6:00.

125-Tysen Christensen, Lenox beat Justin Helgenson, Lake Mills 5-4.

130-Jeremiah Butteris, Lisbon pinned Neal Vanderleest, North Polk 3:33.

135-Eli Sanders, Columbus Junction beat Keith Peyton, Wapsie Valley 3-1.

140-JoeDurick, Underwood beat Justin Slaybaugh, Guthrie Center 14-5.

145-Chad Eberhart, Dike-New Hartford beat Keith Clausen, Underwood 9-5.

152-Kurtis Williamson, Eagle Grove beat Seth Evans, Lenox 2-2 OT (criteria).

160-Blu Wahle, Underwood beat Jacob Feuerbach, Belle Plaine 3-1.

171-Tyler Nixt, Greene beat Adam Cory, Bondurant-Farrar 8-4.

189-Jeremiah Pottebaum, Lawton-Bronson beat Matt Langreck, Turkey Valley 5-3.

275-Scott Webb, Sigourney beat Derrick Schumacher, AHST (Avoca) 3-0.

2000 (February 26)

CLASS 3-A

103-Dominick Moyer, Oskaloosa beat Nick Beuter, Cedar Falls 3-1.

112-Nick Voss, Pleasant Valley beat Gabe Rostermundt, Council Bluffs Lewis Central 4-1.

119-Chad Davis, Council Bluffs Lewis Central beat Anthony Watson, Iowa City High 15-8.

125-Mark Hangsleben, Urbandale pinned Zach Paulson, Cedar Rapids Kennedy 5:19.

130-Cory Connell, Iowa City High beat Adam Olaby, Des Moines Lincoln 11-2.

135-Ryan Heim, Dubuque Hempstead beat Trent Paulson, Council Bluffs Lewis Central 9-4.

140-Brandon Winkey, Ames beat David Weihs, Harlan 9-8.

145-Johnny Galloway Jr., Waterloo East beat Matt Davis, Dubuque Senior 8-6.

152-Blake Anderson, Council Bluffs Lewis Central beat Howard Hughes, Muscatine 7-5.

160-Kenyatta Carter, Waterloo West beat Pat Wilsbacher, Sioux City Heelan 5-2.

171-Ashten Richardson, Iowa City West beat Andy Bollhoefer, Newton 2-1.

189-Sean Stender, North Scott pinned Doug Onstot, Indianola :56.

275-Mike Shedek, Cedar Rapids Xavier beat Ben Foutch, Council Bluffs, Lincoln 3-2.

CLASS 2-A

103-Dusty Pollard, Osage pinned Justin Swafford, Mediapolis 3:20.

112-C. J. Ettelson, Hudson beat Joe Honts, Louisa-Muscatine 14-7.

119-Trent Goodale, Osage beat Brad Stockton, Williamsburg 6-1.

125-Josh Watts, Davenport Assumption pinned Michael Mickey, Clarinda 3:33.

130-Taylor Wood, Chariton beat Mitch Preston, Emmetsburg/Armstrong-Ringsted 12-4.

135-Tim Halligan, Independence beat Dustin Bliven, Louisa-Muscatine 5-2.

140-Bart Mehlert, Union (LaPorte City) beat Dustin Bussanmas, Norwalk 7-5.

145-Keith Pearl, West Liberty beat Mark Sturm, Emmetsburg/Armstrong-Ringsted 8-4.

152-Tyler McGinnis, Shenandoah beat Ryan Sturm, Emmetsburg/Armstrong-Ringsted 4-1.

160-Andrew Hayes, Creston beat Paul Bradley, South Tama 4-3.

171-Jason Reicks, New Hampton beat Cody Hickle, NC-NK 5-3.

189-Trey Clark, Union (LaPorte City) beat Joe Brewer, Dallas Center-Grimes 9-0.

275-Tom Conlon, Humboldt beat Robbie Krominga, Iowa Falls 3-1.

CLASS 1-A

103-Mack Reiter, Don Bosco (Gilbertville) beat Luke Reiland, Eagle Grove 3-3, 2-0 OT.

112-Jesse Sundell, Ogden beat Justin McClintock, Eagle Grove 6-0.

119-Kris Thayer, Odebolt-Arthur beat Brett Shields, Mount Ayr 8-5.

125-Joe Reiter, Don Bosco (Gilbertville) pinned Tysen Christensen, Lenox 5:25.

130-Jeff Harrison, Westwood (Sloan) beat Danny Ebling, Greene 12-2.

135-Nick Cole, Highland (Riverside) beat Garrett Kozik, Belle Plaine 4-1.

140-Jeremiah Butteris, Lisbon pinned Brett Little, Tri-County (Thornburg) 2:19.

145-Chris Wernimont, Pocahontas beat Rick Delagardelle, Don Bosco (Gilbertville) 11-3.

152-Seth Evans, Lenox beat Mark Mueller, Postville 5-4.

160-Keith Clausen, Underwood beat Wade Samo, Lenox 7-4.

171-Jacob Feuerbach, Belle Plaine beat Dan Moulds, Waspie Valley 8-5.

189-Jeremiah Pottebaum, Lawton-Bronson beat Curtis Eben, Central Lyon 14-9.

275-Mark Lander, Underwood beat Brett Christensen, Lenox 5-3.

2001 (February 24)

CLASS 3-A

103-Jake Halvorsen, Iowa City West pinned Brandon McDonough, Des Moines Lincoln 4:32.

112-Ryan Osgood, Mason City beat Nick Beuter, Cedar Falls 3-1.

119-Gabe Rostermundt, Council Bluffs Lewis Central beat Travis Snover, Des Moines Lincoln 7-3.

125-Jeremy Meyer, Newton beat Chad Czerwiec, Muscatine 5-4.

130-Chad Davis, Council Bluffs Lewis Central beat Anthony Watson, Iowa City High 16-9.

135-Brandon Mason, Council Bluffs Lewis Central beat Brett Stedman, Sioux City Heelan 2-0.

140-Trent Paulson, Council Bluffs Lewis Central beat John Tucker, Ames 13-2.

145-Travis Paulson, Council Bluffs Lewis Central beat David Weihs, Harlan 3-1.

152-Johnny Galloway Jr., Iowa City High beat Nathan Specht, Dubuque Senior 3-3, 2-0 OT.

160-Blake Anderson, Council Bluffs Lewis Central beat Caleb Twito, Cedar Falls 5-2.

171-Akeem Carter, Waterloo West pinned Jeff Garrison, Urbandale 3:39.

189-Travis Behrends, Waverly-Shell Rock beat Joe Vedepo, Iowa City High 11-8.

215-Mike Engelmann, Spencer pinned Ryan Groom, Oskaloosa 3:05.

275-Mike Shedek, Cedar Rapids Xavier beat Phil Klein, West Delaware 7-3.

CLASS 2-A

103-Dustin Finer, Emmetsburg/Armstrong-Ringsted beat Albert McNeil, Northeast (Goose Lake) 14-0.

112-Jacob Naig, Emmetsburg/Armstrong-Ringsted beat Justin Swafford, Mediapolis 7-4.

119-C.J. Ettelson, Hudson beat Brady Dolan, Independence 16-4.

125-Trent Goodale, Osage beat Michael Billings, Clear Lake 12-1.

130-Trevor Arbogast, Davenport Assumption beat Michael Wells, Clarinda 7-7, 2-0 OT.

135-Josh Watts, Davenport Assumption beat Eric Bantz, Independence 7-2.

140-Terry Vesey, Davenport Assumption beat Dustin Bussanmas, Norwalk 5-3.

145-Kirk Artist, Glenwood beat Clint Manny, Winterset 14-8.

152-Cole Pape, Maquoketa beat Joe Weiser, Clarke (Osceola) 6-3.

160-Ryan Sturm, Emmetsburg/Armstrong-Ringsted beat Ben Miller, Benton (Van Horne) 7-3.

171-Paul Bradley, South Tama beat Mark Sturm, Emmetsburg/Armstrong-Ringsted 9-6.

189-Travis Hinners, Emmetsburg/Armstrong-Ringsted beat Brian Milbert, Dyersville Beckman 8-4.

215- Joe Brewer, Dallas Center-Grimes pinned Matt Nitchals, Storm Lake 3:55.

275-Adam Prins, Sibley-Ocheyedan beat Justin Heins, North Fayette (West Union) 7-6.

CLASS 1-A

103-Mack Reiter, Don Bosco (Gilbertville) beat Adam Bender, Lenox 13-4.

112-Aaron Helmrich, North Linn beat Corey Kalina, Belle Plaine 14-6.

119-Jesse Sundell, Ogden pinned Chris Helgeson, Lake Mills 3:20.

125-Kris Thayer, Odebolt-Arthur beat Jeremy Johnson, Clarksville 7-2.

130-Layne Greedy, Sidney beat Kyle Burkle, North Linn 5-3.

135-Alex Grunder, Wilton pinned Dusty Martin, Bedford 5:21.

140-Kevin Kurovski, Belle Plaine pinned Bart Little, Tri-County (Thornburg) 2:35.

145-Dustin Bliven, Columbus Junction pinned Brad Asche, Eagle Grove 5:24.

152-Cody Koenig, Underwood beat Adam Benton, Nodaway Valley (Greenfield) 9-7.

160-Garrett South, CAM (Anita) beat Aaron Kaufman, Wapsie Valley 15-3.

171-Mark Mueller, Postville beat Tom Meester, Central Lyon 5-3.

189-Mark Sanger, West Hancock pinned Michael Irvin, Bedford 1:47.

215-Mike Kuecker, Tripoli beat John Gallery, East Buchanan 10-5.

275-Ryan Fuller, Lisbon beat Darin Jacobson, MVAO (Mapleton) 1-1, 1-0 (2 OT).

2002 (February 23)

CLASS 3-A

103-Jay Borschel, Linn-Mar (Marion) pinned Joey Slaton, Cedar Rapids Kennedy 2:55.

112-Adam Gottschalk, Dubuque Hempstead beat Jake Halvorsen, Iowa City West 8-5.

119-Kyle Anson, Iowa City High beat Dominick Moyer, Oskaloosa 6-6 2 OT (criteria).

125-Travis Snover, Des Moines Lincoln beat Josh Marker, Ames 6-2.

130-Brad Stockton, Iowa City West beat Ben Moss, Council Bluffs Lewis Central 7-5.

135-Mike Foster, Oskaloosa beat Pat Allibone, Sioux City Heelan 6-4.

140-Anthony Watson, Iowa City West pinned Christopher Ewing, Ankeny 3:11.

145-Trent Paulson, Council Bluffs Lewis Central beat Jacob Smith, Iowa City High 14-1.

152-Travis Paulson, Council Bluffs Lewis Central won by technical fall over Ben Stedman, Sioux City Heelan 20-4, 5:05.

160-Johnny Galloway Jr., Iowa City High beat Grant Turner, Johnston 16-6.

171-Dan Zepeda, Des Moines Lincoln beat Phil Porter, Linn-Mar (Marion) 4-0.

189-Akeem Carter, Waterloo West beat Jeff Butcher, Sioux City East 11-3.

215-Ryan Phillips, Burlington beat Chris McDonald, Linn-Mar (Marion) 2-1 (2 OT).

275-Kasey Deaver, Indianola pinned Matt Thompson, Southeast Polk 1:52.

CLASS 2-A

103-Justin Brown, Centerville beat Tyler Bjustrom, Algona 10-1.

112-Andre Avila, Davenport Assumption beat Justin Hanson, Humboldt 5-2.

119-Wade Satern, Humboldt beat Brad Gregory, Glenwood 7-2.

125-Justin Swafford, Mediapolis beat Brady Dolan, Independence 4-3.

130-C. J. Ettelson, Hudson beat Chad Hutchinson, Mediapolis 9-4.

135-Michael Wells, Clarinda beat Adam Grell, Central (DeWitt) 7-1.

140-James Lange, Centerville beat Kent Reams, Charles City 6-3.

145-Jared Abel, Winterset beat Joe Uker, Osage 13-4.

152-J. D. Naig, Emmetsburg/Armstrong-Ringsted beat Danny Elsbury, South Tama 7-4.

160-Reed Kuper, Osage beat Nick Ohrtman, Emmetsburg/Armstrong-Ringsted 10-3.

171-Brent Schumacher, Harlan beat Jordan McLaughlin, Belmond-Klemme 12-1.

189-Clint Sellers, Chariton pinned Ben Strandberg, Emmetsburg/Armstrong-Ringsted 4:48.

215-Mike Humpal, New Hampton pinned Matt Ricke, Carroll Kuemper 5:12.

275-Chris Harrison, South Tama beat Aaron Johannsen, GRNT (Reinbeck) 14-1.

CLASS 1-A

103-Dan Davila, Underwood pinned Tony Hager, Ogden 3:06.

112-Mack Reiter, Don Bosco (Gilbertville) pinned Gannon Hjerleid, Wapello 1:50.

119-Dan LeClere, North Linn beat Corey Kalina, Belle Plaine 5-3.

125-Justin Bohlke, Kingsley-Pierson beat Jeremy Johnson, Clarksville 5-5, 2-0 OT.

130-Kyle Burkle, North Linn beat Aaron Wernimont, Pocahontas Area 9-8.

135-Dustin Hinschberger, Belle Plaine beat Dana Vote, Twin River Balley (Bode) 9-0.

140-Luke Reiland, Eagle Grove beat Henry Wahle, Underwood 3-0.

145-Jesse Drahos, Belle Plaine beat Alex Grunder, Wilton 6-1.

152-Scott Linden, Woodbury Central beat Heath Lamp, AHST (Avoca) 3-2.

160-Adam Benton, Nodaway Valley (Greenfield) beat J.J. Cooper, Wilton 3-3, 2-0 OT.

171-Mark Mueller, Postville beat Blake Haugland, Mount Ayr 12-4.

189-Tyler Babb, Wilton beat Matt Ritchey, Interstate 35 (Truro) 2-1.

215-Mike Kuecker, Tripoli beat Matt Fields, North Cedar (Stanwood) 5-4.

275-Ryan Fuller, Lisbon beat Brett Christensen, Lenox 3-2 OT.

2003 (March 1)

CLASS 3-A

103-Derek Moyer, Oskaloosa beat Montell Marion, West Des Moines Valley 6-3.

112-Brandon McDonough, Des Moines Lincoln beat Joey Slaton, Cedar Rapids Kennedy 3-2.

119-Eric Hoffman, Davenport North beat Matt Kelly, Dubuque Hempstead 12-9.

125-Jay Borschel, Linn-Mar (Marion) beat Jake Halvorsen, Iowa City West 11-2.

130-Nick Beuter, Cedar Falls beat Josh Marker, Ames 4-2.

135-Jeremy Meyer, Newton beat Edgar Haynes, Cedar Rapids Washington 11-5.

140-Colby Goetsch, Ankeny beat Brandon Graham, Oskaloosa 1-0.

145-Christopher Ewing, Ankeny beat Willie Leonard, Dubuque Wahlert 9-4.

152-Nick Hayes, Council Bluffs Lewis Central beat Brett Behrends, Waverly-Shell Rock 3-1.

160-Brandon Mason, Council Bluffs Lewis Central beat Omar Maktabi, Iowa City West 1-0.

171-Chase Holmgaard, Fort Dodge beat David Hessel, Pleasant Valley 4-3.

189-Andrew Anderson, Sioux City East beat Dan Peters, Clinton 11-6.

215-Blake Gillis, Spencer pinned Bill Breedlove, West Des Moines Dowling 4:50.

275-Chase Rogers, Marshalltown beat Justin Fah, Pleasant Valley 14-6.

CLASS 2-A

103-T. J. Sebolt, Centerville beat Nick Pickerell, Albia 9-1.

112-Justin Brown, Centerville beat Laramie Shaffer, Winterset 3-2.

119-Aaron Conway, Marion beat Josh Swanson, Knoxville 7-6.

125-Justin Hanson, Humboldt pinned Justin Kerber, Emmetsburg/Armstrong-Ringsted 3:12.

130-Jay Bjustrom, Algona beat Willie Harris, Creston 14-7.

135-Moza Fay, Anamosa beat Tyler Brewer, Carlisle 14-6.

140-Dallas Kuper, Osage beat Mike Piper, Clear Lake 8-8, 2-0 OT.

145-Jacob Naig, Emmetsburg/Armstrong-Ringsted pinned Michael Wells, Clarinda 4:31.

152-Nathan Van Dyke, South Tama beat Brett Hakeman, Union (LaPorte City) 8-0.

160-Jacob Craig, Mount Vernon beat Brady Hakeman, Union (LaPorte City) 3-1.

171-Eric Pedretti, Crestwood (Cresco) beat Chris Loudon, Creston 9-5.

189-Bruce Chyma, South Tama beat Matt Garvin, Davenport Assumption 3-2.

215-Mike Humpal, New Hampton won by injury default over Dane Pape, Maquoketa.

275-Matt Fields, North Cedar (Stanwood) pinned Kyle Lehman, Winterset 2:11.

CLASS 1-A

103-Patrick Makey, Logan-Magnolia beat Tony Hager, Ogden 5-0.

112-Brett Ray, Orient-Macksburg beat Richie Thacker, Sioux Central 3-2.

119-Brandon Bohlke, Kingsley-Pierson beat Andy Ohnemus, Southeast Warren 5-4.

125-Mack Reiter, Don Bosco (Gilbertville) won by technical fall over Dan Helgeson, Lake Mills 19-4, 5:08.

130-Dan LeClere, North Linn beatr Charlie Ettelson, Hudson 6-2.

135-C. J. Ettelson, Hudson beat Kyle Burkle, North Linn 13-2.

140-Ryan Morningstar, Lisbon beat Logan Frescoln, Cardinal (Eldon) 13-3.

145-Aaron Wernimont, Pocahontas Area beat Derek Pike, Nora Springs-Rock Falls 7-5.

152-B. J. Olberding, Council Bluffs St. Albert pinned Matt Johnsen, Logan-Magnolia 1:55.

160-Heath Lamp, AHST (Avoca) beat Scott Hazen, Underwood 5-4.

171-Travis Branson, Melcher-Dallas beat Johnny Walz, Starmont 13-10.

189-Clarke Gerlock, CAM (Anita) beat Wade Hammen, Rockwell City-Lytton 5-2.

215-Mitch Langreck, Turkey Valley beat Dylan White, Ogden 2-2, 2-0 OT.

275-Todd Parish, Lenox pinned Adam Lyons, Central Decatur 5:55.

2004 (February 28)

CLASS 3-A

103-Russell Weakley, Fort Madison beat Dan Klavitter, Dubuque Senior 10-5.

112-Derek Moyer, Oskaloosa beat Montell Marion, West Des Moines Valley 11-10.

119-Joey Slaton, Cedar Rapids Kennedy beat Matt Kelly, Dubuque Hempstead 13-5.

125-Kyle Anson, Iowa City High beat Eric Hoffman, Davenport North 10-3.

130-Mitch Mueller, Iowa City West beat Zach McKray, Iowa City High 7-2.

135-Adam Kurimski, Fairfield beat Tyler Arey, Indianola 7-2.

140-Mike Russell, Cedar Rapids Kennedy beat Brett Blasberg, Waterloo West 4-2.

145-Bryce Carruthers, Council Bluffs Jefferson beat Jimmy Waters, Council Bluffs Lewis Central 4-0.

152-Jay Borschel, Linn-Mar (Marion) pinned Ryan Bixler, Oskaloosa 2:35.

160-Brandon Mason, Council Bluffs Lewis Central pinned Mikel Hansen, Decorah 3:12.

171-Chase Holmgaard, Fort Dodge beat Bret Richardson, Council Bluffs Lincoln 2-1.

189-Andrew Anderson, Sioux City East beat Jason Bowling, Pleasant Valley 13-7.

215-Alex Kanellis, Iowa City West pinned Dan Peters, Clinton 1:16.

275-Shane Spooner, Ankeny pinned Blake Rowland, Cedar Rapids Washington 1:00.

CLASS 2-A

103-T. J. Sebolt, Centerville beat Ben Knight, Sergeant Bluff-Luton 4-1.

112-Zach Kressley, Waterloo Columbus beat Tyler Bjustrom, Algona 7-5.

119-Laramie Shaffer, Winterset beat Andy Schmitt, Clear Lake 3-0.

125-Chris Sandy, Spirit Lake Park beat Kody Blazek, Marion 6-6, 2-0 OT.

130-Robert Struthers, Emmetsburg/Armstrong-Ringsted beat T. J. Moen, Saydel 5-0.

135-Justin Hanson, Humboldt beat Justin Kerber, Emmetsburg/Armstrong-Ringsted 9-5.

140-Daniel Scarbery, Creston/Orient-Macksburg beat Aaron Janssen, Emmetsburg/Armstrong-Ringsted 8-7.

145-Moza Fay, Anamosa beat Darrin Kaisand, Grinnell 9-4.

152-Sam Hansen, Waterloo Columbus beat Dallas Kuper, Osage 1-0.

160-Nick Weber, Clear Lake beat Dane Kuper, Osage 9-2.

171-Jacob Craig, Mount Vernon pinned Ryan Hawn, Spirit Lake Park 3:13.

189-Cody Kroul, Solon beat Jovani Galvan, West Liberty 3-1.

215-Tyler Blum, Atlantic beat Dane Pape, Maquoketa 4-2.

275-Matt Kroul, Mount Vernon beat Ben Dunkelberger, Union (LaPorte City) 3-1.

CLASS 1-A

103-Mark Kist, Eagle Grove beat Jordan Hasenkamp, Twin River Valley (Bode) 10-0.

112-Patrick Makey, Logan-Magnolia pinned Andrew Erdman, Eagle Grove 5:09.

119-Nate Behrendsen, Pocahontas Area beat Zach Ingles, Hudson 7-7, 2-0 OT.

125-Chris Utesch, Akron-Westfield beat Austin Baier, Nodaway Valley (Greenfield) 1-1, 1-0 (2 OT).

130-Jacob Pedersen, Hudson beat Keith Hefley, Prairie Valley (Gowrie) 7-4.

135-Charlie Ettelson, Hudson beat Jacob Hall, Ogden 6-1.

140-Dan LeClere, North Linn beat Mitch Norton, Nashua-Plainfield 11-2.

145-Ryan Bormann, Tipton pinned Matt Klingenberg, MMC (Marcus) 3:19.

152-Ryan Morningstar, Lisbon beat Matt Norton, Nashua-Plainfield 5-4.

160-Zach Bates, Rockwell City-Lytton beat Matt Johnsen, Logan-Magnolia 9-6.

171-Chad Beatty, Wilton beat Craig Kreman, Tipton 5-3.

189-Jordan McLaughlin, Belmond-Klemme pinned Tim DeBoer, Central Lyon 4:51.

215-Michael Bucklin, Colfax-Mingo beat Nathan Ploen, Woodbury Central 15-2.

275-Matt Fields, North Cedar (Stanwood) won by technical fall over Andy Kavanaugh, Southern Cal 17-1, 2:51.

2005 (February 26)

CLASS 3-A

103-Mark Ballweg, Waverly-Shell Rock beat Nate Moore, Iowa City West 11-8.

112-Russell Weakley, Fort Madison beat Kody Pudil, Iowa City West 9-1.

119-Montell Marion, Des Moines Roosevelt beat Matt Kelly, Dubuque Hempstead 3-2.

125-Kyle Anson, Iowa City High pinned Kalen Lenz, West Delaware 4:52.

130-Joey Slaton, Cedar Rapids Kennedy beat Adam Schumacher, Dubuque Senior 11-5.

135-Zach McKray, Iowa City High beat Clint Whitcome, Waverly-Shell Rock 9-3.

140-Matt Ballweg, Waverly-Shell Rock pinned Adam Manz, Council Bluffs Lincoln :34.

145-Brad Lower, Burlington beat Marcus Hollingshead, Oskaloosa 6-0.

152-Mike Stamp, Council Bluffs Lewis Central beat Billy Lewis, Bettendorf 4-4, 2-0 OT.

160-Jimmy Waters, Council Bluffs Lewis Central beat Nick Billups, North Scott 6-2.

171-Jay Borschel, Linn-Mar (Marion) beat Austin Boehm, Urbandale 12-1.

189-Romeo Djoumessi, Waverly-Shell Rock beat Gordon Johnson, Fort Madison 7-0.

215-Jesse Smith, Southeast Polk beat Wes Lane, Waterloo West 4-1.

275-Travis Meade, Iowa City West beat Blake Rowland, Cedar Rapids Washington 1-1 2 OT (criteria).

CLASS 2-A

103-Tyler Halverson, Cherokee beat Kyle Pedretti, MFL (Monona) 7-5.

112-Pat McCaffrey, Centerville beat Ben Knight, Sergeant Bluff-Luton 16-6.

119-T.J. Sebolt, Centerville pinned Quin Leith, Creston/Orient-Macksburg 1:49.

125-Laramie Shaffer, Winterset beat J.J. Krutsinger, Waterloo Columbus 4-2.

130-Nick Pickerell, Albia beat Chris Sandy, Spirit Lake Park 3-1.

135-Luke Satern, Humboldt beat Tony Lovstuen, Centerville 12-6.

140-Travis Eggers, MFL (Monona) beat Kurt Simon, West Liberty 8-3.

145-Justin Kerber, Emmestburg/Armstrong-Ringsted beat Nate Alber, Independence 11-2.

152-Micah Keller, Mediapolis pinned Calvin Barber, Winterset 2:46.

160-Brett Hakeman, Union (LaPorte City) beat Mitch Artist, Glenwood 7-5.

171-Chad Beatty, Wilton beat Jake Madsen, NC/N-K 14-5.

189-Joe Curran, Sioux City Heelan beat Ty Copsey, Glenwood 7-3.

215-Ben Lehman, Independence pinned Adam Kenny, Emmetsburg/Armstrong-Ringsted 3:15.

275-Mike Zimmerly, Independence beat Jordan Limbaugh, Algona 7-4.

CLASS 1-A

103-Dalton Jensen, Missouri Valley won by technical fall over Ridge Kiley, Eagle Grove 15-0, 4:42.

112-Mark Kist, Eagle Grove beat Brady Jacobi, Belle Plaine 3-1.

119-David O'Loughlin, Don Bosco (Gilbertville) beat Patrick Makey, Logan-Magnolia 6-4.

125-Austin Baier, Nodaway Valley (Greenfield) beat Marshall Koethe, Akron-Westfield 3-1.

130-Eric Davis, WACO (Wayland) beat Kelby Ryerson, Eagle Grove 3-2.

135-Charlie Ettelson, Hudson beat Gavin Nelson, Missouri Valley 11-2.

140-Dan LeClere, North Linn beat Brett Rose, Woodbury Central 16-8.

145-Mitch Norton, Nashua-Plainfield beat Kalab Evans, Lenox 9-4.

152-Ryan Morningstar, Lisbon beat Joey Verschoor, Kingsley-Pierson 5-1.

160-Phil O'Loughlin, Don Bosco (Gilbertville) beat Greg Meirick, Turkey Valley 4-2.

171-Scott Hazen, Underwood beat Craig Kreman, Tipton 7-1.

189-Thomas Hess, Bedford beat Alec Bonander, West Lyon 6-4.

215-Rory Miller, Riverside (Oakland) beat Darren Kreiner, South Winneshiek 4-3.

275-Adam Lyons, Central Decatur beat Reid Muxfeldt, Logan-Magnolia 1-0.

2006 (February 25)

CLASS 3-A

103-Dylan Carew, Iowa City west beat Steve Welcher, Newton 7-0.

112-Matt McDonough, Linn-Mar (Marion) won by technical fall over Bret Baumbach, Council Bluffs Lewis Central 18-2, 5:57.

119-James Nicholson, Des Moines Roosevelt beat Nate Moore, Iowa City West 6-4.

125-Jeff Rau, Council Bluffs Lewis Central beat Kyle Doherty, Fort Madison 4-0.

130-Montell Marion, Des Moines Roosevelt pinned Zach Morley, Urbandale 1:18.

135-Derek Moyer, Oskaloosa beat Kody Pudil, Iowa City West 7-6.

140-Phil Sexton, Cedar Rapids Prairie beat Evan Shaw, Iowa City West 3-2

145-Matt Ballweg, Waverly-Shell Rock pinned Nick Keeling, Des Moines Lincoln 3:47.

152-Luke Stamp, Council Bluffs Lewis Central beat Jason Nelson, Linn-Mar (Marion) 10-3.

160-Kevin Kluesner, Western Dubuque beat Grant Gambrall, Iowa City High 8-6.

171-Jimmy Waters, Council Bluffs Lewis Central beat Jesse Swanson, Knoxville 6-3.

189-Gordon Johnson, Fort Madison beat Craig Abrahamson, Boone 8-5.

215-Nick Shandri, Southeast Polk beat Ben Schott, Iowa City West 14-5.

275-Taylor Mansfield, Decorah beat Seth Fischer, LeMars 4-3.

CLASS 2-A

103-Andrew Long, Creston/Orient-Macksburg won by technical fall over Cory Olson, Denver-Tripoli 20-5, 5:40.

112-Tyler Linderman, Creston/Orient-Macksburg beat Dillon Miner, Spirit Lake Park 3-1.

119-Kyle Pedretti, MFL (Monona)/Mar-Mac beat Brad Gustafson, Aurelia/Galva-Holstein 3-1.

125-J. J. Krutsinger, Waterloo Columbus beat Blake Hilmer, Denver-Tripoli 5-4.

130-T. J. Sebolt, Centerville beat Zach McCool, West Delaware 9-3.

135-Nick Pickerell, Centerville pinned Trent Weatherman, Ballard (Huxley) 1:28.

140-T. J. Moen, Saydel beat Chris Sandy, Spirit Lake Park 7-3.

145-Seth Pugh, Columbus Junction beat Brett Rosedale, East Marshall/ GMG 4-2.

152-Aaron Janssen, Emmetsburg/Armstrong-Ringsted beat Ryan Collins, Glenwood 7-0.

160-Justin Kerber, Emmetsburg/Armstrong-Ringsted beat Mitch Artist, Glenwood 7-3.

171-Andy O'Loughlin, Independence beat Vinnie Wagner, Osage 20-9.

189-Ty Copsey, Glenwood beat Blake Suckow, North Fayette (West Union) 3-1.

215-Cory Van Pelt, Winterset pinned Ben Lehman, Independence 3:58.

275-Kyle Slifka, Crestwood (Cresco) beat Blake Rasing, New Hampton 10-6.

CLASS 1-A

103-Bart Reiter, Don Bosco (Gilbertville) pinned Kendall Witt, Tri-Center (Neola) 4:48.

112-Mark Kist, Eagle Grove beat Alex Helmrich, Graettinger-Terril 14-2.

119-Jase Thompson, Mason City Newman beat Travis Taylor, Prairie Valley (Gowrie) 16-4.

125-Marshall Koethe, Akron-Westfield beat Lee Meirick, Turkey Valley 5-5, 2-0 OT.

130-Kelby Ryerson, Eagle Grove beat Ryan Mulnix, North Linn 7-6.

135-Kirk Landon, Audubon beat Cale Hall, Nodaway Valley (Greenfield) 10-0.

140-Brandon Bohlke, Kingsley-Pierson beat Kendall Cole, Highland (Riverside) 8-1.

145-Trevor Kittleson, St. Ansgar beat Nick LeClere, North Linn 7-1.

152-Tyler Burkle, North Linn beat David Hutton, Interstate 35 (Truro) 12-0.

160-Todd Becker, Don Bosco (Gilbertville) pinned Cole Heimer, Nora Springs-Rock Falls 5:14.

171-Ben Becker, Fort Dodge St. Edmond pinned Trevor Gehringer, Martensdale-St. Marys 1:57.

189-Thomas Hess, Bedford beat Mitch Sander, North Cedar (Stanwood) 1-1, 2-0 OT.

215-Darren Kreiner, South Winneshiek beat Jason Courtney, Bondurant-Farrar 3-2.

275-Donovan Grove, Southeast Webster beat Trent Hardin, Van Buren (Keosauqua) 2-2, 1-0 (2 OT).

2007 (February 24)

CLASS 3-A

103-Cruse Aarhus, Cedar Rapids Kennedy beat Wes Shetterly, Linn-Mar (Marion) 5-3.

112-Nick Trizzino, Bettendorf beat Jake Ballweg, Waverly-Shell Rock 10-1.

119-Matt McDonough, Linn-Mar (Marion) beat Tyler Clark, Bettendorf 4-3.

125-Nate Moore, Iowa City West beat Anthony Baccam, Marshalltown 15-7.

130-Nick Moore, Iowa City West won by technical fall over Isaiah Smith, Newton 26-11, 4:24.

135-Derek St. John, Iowa City West beat Alec Hoffman, Davenport North 14-4.

140-Zach McCool, West Delaware beat Logan Edgington, Indianola 6-4.

145-Stew Gilmoor, North Scott beat Blaze Gill, Sioux City North 5-2.

152-Ryan Helenthal, Keokuk pinned Evan Knight, Urbandale 1:41.

160-Robert Kellogg, Sioux City North beat B. J. Brooks, Waterloo West 2-0.

171-Grant Gambrall, Iowa City West beat Dylan Wrage, Waverly-Shell Rock 11-4.

189-Jimmy Waters, Council Bluffs Lewis Central beat Anthony Losasso, Bettendorf 5-3.

215-Eric Thompson, Waverly-Shell Rock beat Matt Sixta, West Des Moines Valley 15-6.

275-Ben Boothby, Clinton beat Alex Petersen, Indianola 7-5.

CLASS 2-A

103-Joe Colon, Clear Lake beat Levi Wolfensperger, Denver-Tripoli 11-9.

112-Andrew Long, Creston/Orient-Macksburg beat Blake Sorensen, Denver-Tripoli 21-7.

119-Dillon Miner, Spirit Lake Park pinned Tanner Burke, Crestwood (Cresco) 3:50.

125-Kyle Pedretti, MFL (Monona)/Mar-Mac beat J. J. Krutsinger, Waterloo Columbus 6-5 OT.

130-Brandon Ball, Columbus Junction beat Bret Kautz, Creston/Orient-Macksburg 8-6.

135-Blake Hilmer, Denver-Tripoli beat Matt Stillman, Emmetsburg/Armstrong-Ringsted 10-7.

140-Cody Stanley, Wilton beat Ben Knight, Sergeant Bluff-Luton 4-1.

145-T. J. Moen, Saydel beat Trent Weatherman, Ballard (Huxley) 6-5.

152-Andrew Sorenson, Forest City pinned Jared Ramsay, Ballard (Huxley) 4:53.

160-Kalab Evans, Creston/Orient-Macksburg beat Jacob Ryan, Mount Vernon 9-3.

171-Ryan Ketelsen, Osage beat Josh Ihnen, Sheldon/South O'Brien 3-2.

189-Vinnie Wagner, Osage beat Luke Stika, Crestwood (Cresco) 5-2.

215-Kyle Simonson, Algona beat John Helgerson, North Fayette (West Union) 6-5.

275-Blake Rasing, New Hampton beat Brian Rodas, MFL (Monona)/ Mar-Mac 3-2.

CLASS 1-A

103-Cole Welter, Don Bosco (Gilbertville) pinned Deric Thomas, Mason City Newman 1:27.

112-Bart Reiter, Don Bosco (Gilbertville) beat Cameron Wagner, Belle Plaine 3-0.

119-Travis Taylor, Prairie Valley (Gowrie) beat Jase Thompson, Mason City Newman 2-2, 2-0 OT.

125-Dalton Jensen, Missouri Valley pinned Brad Exline, West Branch 1:14.

130-Marshall Koethe, Akron-Westfield pinned Mitch Johnson, Interstate 35 (Truro) 1:58.

135-Nate Herda, Central Lyon beat Jordan Hasencamp, Twin River Valley (Bode) 3-3, 2-0 OT.

140-Johnny Siegel, New London/Winfield-Mt. Union won by injury default over Sam Groves, Nodaway Valley (Greenfield) (illegal slam by Groves).

145-Nick LeClere, North Linn beat Matt Terrell, Interstate 35 (Truro) 13-10.

152-Mike Finch, HMS (Hartley) pinned Gavin Nelson, Missouri Valley 4:29.

160-Jordan Gacke, Central Lyon beat Marshall Barney, Logan-Magnolia 3-1.

171-Cole Heimer, Nora Springs-Rock Falls beat Adam Jergens, Twin River Valley (Bode) 11-2.

189-Jared Enderton, Graettinger-Terril beat Sam Baier, Alburnett 3-1.

215-Dillon Heesch, Southeast Webster beat Jadd Dithmart, Ogden 4-1.

275-Donovan Grove, Southeast Webster beat Kyle Kober, West Branch 9-3.

2008 (February 16)

CLASS 3-A

103-Adam Perrin, North Scott beat Chad Ryan, Sioux City North 6-5.

112-Joey Jerkovich, Council Bluffs Lewis Central beat Kevin Hancock, Cedar Falls 5-2.

119-Jake Ballweg, Waverly-Shell Rock beat Cody Swim, Indianola 9-1.

125-Nate Moore, Iowa City West pinned Casey Strub, Indianola 2:50.

130-Matt McDonough, Linn-Mar (Marion) pinned Julian Feikert, Keokuk 3:00.

135-Mark Ballweg, Waverly-Shell Rock beat Bret Baumbach, Council Bluffs Lewis Central 7-0.

140-Nick Moore, Iowa City West beat Alec Hoffman, Davenport North 12-2.

145-Derek St. John, Iowa City West beat Kyven Gadsen, Waterloo East 18-6.

152-John Nicholson, Des Moines Roosevelt beat Michael Moreno, Urbandale 2-1.

160-Evan Knight, Urbandale beat Bryce Skaggs, Newton 5-3.

171-Grant Gambrall, Iowa City West pinned Justin Rau, Council Bluffs Lewis Central 3:15.

189-Dylan Wrage, Waverly-Shell Rock beat Drew Love, Waukee 16-3.

215-Byron Tate, Clinton beat Mickey Sprague, Cedar Rapids Prairie 5-2.

285-Eric Thompson, Waverly-Shell Rock pinned James Ferentz, Iowa City High 1:25.

CLASS 2-A

103-Tanner Schmidt, Charles City beat Christopher Halblom, Center Point-Urbana 11-2.

112-Ridge Kiley, Eagle Grove beat Levi Wolfensperger, Denver-Tripoli 3-2.

119-Tyler Grask, Ballard (Huxley) beat Matt Boyington, Humboldt 2-0.

125-Andrew Long, Creston/Orient-Macksburg won by technical fall over Tanner Weatherman, Ballard (Huxley) 18-3, 4:43.

130-Quin Leith, Creston/Orient-Macksburg beat Tanner Hiatt, Ballard (Huxley) 7-2.

135-Seth Noble, Columbus Junction beat Bret Kautz, Creston/Orient-Macksburg 8-4.

140-Trent Tucker, Creston/Orient-Macksburg beat Theran Goodale, Osage 8-4.

145-Tanner Kampen, Humboldt beat Matt Stillman, Emmetsburg/Armstrong-Ringsted 3-1.

152-Trent Weatherman, Ballard (Huxley) beat Nick Loughlin, Cherokee 17-8.

160-Kalab Evans, Creston/Orient-Macksburg beat Jared Ramsay, Ballard (Huxley) 11-5.

171-Brock Weatherman, Ballard (Huxley) beat Sam Upah, East Marshall/GMG 5-3.

189-Josh Ihnen, Sheldon/South O'Brien won by technical fall over Tomas Lira, West Liberty 21-4, 5:16.

215-Holden Blythe, Williamsburg pinned Patrick Kolker, Clear Lake 5:24.

285-Avery Fuhs, Chariton beat Austin Blythe, Williamsburg 5-1.

CLASS 1-A

103-Klint Stapes, Interstate 35 (Truro) beat Brandon Welter, Don Bosco (Gilbertville) 8-3.

112-Deric Thomas, Mason City Newman beat Adam Hight, Nodaway Valley (Greenfield) 13-6.

119-Jake Demmon, Eddyville-Blakesburg pinned Travis Taylor, Prairie Valley (Gowrie) 5:44.

125-Bart Reiter, Don Bosco (Gilbertville) won by technical fall over Jason Winkler, South Winneshiek 16-0, 3:29.

130-Cody Johnston, Nashua-Plainfield beat Colton Wagner, Belle Plaine 5-3.

135-Nathan McRoberts, Rockford beat Zach Beekman, Pocahontas Area 10-4.

140-Nate Herda, Central Lyon beat Christopher Reil, Guthrie Center 12-4.

145-Clay Welter, Don Bosco (Gilbertville) beat James Houchins, Interstate 35 (Truro) 9-4.

152-Jeret Chiri, New London/Winfield-Mt. Union pinned Jason Frain, Riverside (Oakland) 1:20.

160-Marcus Edgington, Hinton beat Ryan Koolker, CMB (Baxter) 6-3.

171-Jordan Gacke, Central Lyon beat Marshall Barney, Logan-Magnolia 9-6.

189-Jake Lerdal, New London/Winfield-Mt. Union beat Scott Eben, Central Lyon 4-3 OT.

215-Cameron Olson, South Hamilton beat Ryan Schares, Don Bosco (Gilbertville) 7-2.

285-Dillon Heesch, Southeast Webster pinned Tyler Crouse, Pekin 2:40.

2009 (February 21)

CLASS 3-A

103-Cory Clark, Southeast Polk beat Connor Ryan, North Scott 5-0.

112-Brandon Jones, West Des Moines Valley beat Eric DeVos, Waverly-Shell Rock 1-1, 2-0 OT.

119-John Meeks, Des Moines Roosevelt beat Jordan Rinken, Waverly-Shell Rock 5-3.

125-Cody Caldwell, Waverly-Shell Rock beat Dom Chase, Clinton 9-1.

130-Bret Baumbach, Council Bluffs Lewis Central beat Tommy Mirocha, Davenport Central 3-2.

135-Jake Ballweg, Waverly-Shell Rock beat Zach White, Cedar Rapids Prairie 11-0.

140-Dylan Carew, Iowa City West beat Blake Meeks, Des Moines Roosevelt 12-3.

145-Michael Kelly, Cedar Falls beat Chad Lowman, Des Moines Roosevelt 7-1.

152-Nick Moore, Iowa City West beat Josiah South, Urbandale 2-1.

160-John Nicholson, Des Moines Roosevelt beat Michael Moreno, Urbandale 3-2.

171-Kyven Gadsen, Waterloo East beat Jason McCormick, Cedar Rapids Jefferson 3-2.

189-Evan Knight, Urbandale beat Matt Riley, Des Moines Roosevelt 7-3.

215-Cody Krumwiede, Waverly-Shell Rock beat Ethan Bass, Southeast Polk 6-2.

285-Brandon Burrell, Cedar Rapids Washington beat Jacob Crawford, Southeast Polk 2-2, 1-0 (2 OT).

CLASS 2-A

103-Alex Spooner, Forest City beat Dylan Peters, Denver-Tripoli 8-4.

112-Dakota Bauer, Ballard (Huxley) beat Jacob Colon, Clear Lake 8-7.

119-Levi Wolfensperger, Denver-Tripoli beat Willie Miklus, Ballard (Huxley) 18-7.

125-Joe Colon, Clear Lake beat Tyler Grask, Ballard (Huxley) 4-1.

130-Nathan Vaske, West Delaware beat Tucker Weber, Clear Lake 7-2.

135-Tanner Weatherman, Ballard (Huxley) pinned Chris Alber, Independence 5:37.

140-Tanner Hiatt, Ballard (Huxley) beat Seth Noble, Columbus Junction 5-4.

145-Matt Mougin, Columbus Junction beat Ryan Hand, Wilton 5-4.

152-Trent Weatherman, Ballard (Huxley) won by technical fall over Ted Krueger, Sibley-Ocheyedan 19-4, 4:35.

160-Ethan Moorman, Centerville beat T. J. Hiatt, Ballard (Huxley) 3-1.

171-Brock Weatherman, Ballard (Huxley) beat Mikey England, Centerville 3-2.

189-Carl Broghammer, West Delaware beat Tomas Lira, West Liberty 8-5.

215-Bryant Hummel, Clarinda beat Chris Schaudt, Ballard (Huxley) 3-0.

285-Austin Blythe, Williamsburg pinned Javier Rendon, West Liberty 1:50.

CLASS 1-A

103-Sawyer Farris, New London/Winfield-Mt. Union beat Zachh Buch, Belle Plaine 2-2, 2-0 OT.

112-Christopher Halblom, Alburnett beat Brandon Welter, Don Bosco (Gilbertville) 3-2.

119-Deric Thomas, Mason City Newman beat Ben McMahon, Don Bosco (Gilbertville) 6-4.

125-Cole Welter, Don Bosco (Gilbertville) beat Nolan Oviatt, Logan-Magnolia 7-0.

130-Drew Hinschberger, Belle Plaine beat Seth Epling, Woodbury Central 9-4.

135-Bart Reiter, Don Bosco (Gilbertville) beat Cameron Wagner, Belle Plaine 7-1.

140-Colton Wagner, Belle Plaine beat Levi Peters, Twin River Valley (Bode) 8-5.

145-Dmitri Boyer, Eddyville-Blakesburg beat Joseph Atwell, Panorama (Panora) 12-3.

152-Clay Welter, Don Bosco (Gilbertville) beat Andrew Anthofer, Coon Rapids-Bayard 5-2.

160-Joe Sievert, Akron-Westfield beat Blake Faucher, Guthrie Center 14-9.

171-Nate Tool, Twin River Valley (Bode) beat Taylor Kettman, Don Bosco (Gilbertville) 3-3, 2-0 OT.

189-Jake Thome, Don Bosco (Gilbertville) beat Scott Eben, Central Lyon 3-2.

215-Alex Burkle, North Linn beat Jordan Simon, Aplington-Parkersburg 12-5.

285-Kyle Kober, West Branch pinned Cory Becker, Don Bosco (Gilbertville) 2:41.

2010 (February 20)

CLASS 3-A

103-Tyler Willers, Pleasant Valley pinned Colby Knight, Urbandale 5:08.

112-Cory Clark, Southeast Polk beat Connor Ryan, North Scott, 7-0.

119-Eric DeVos, Waverly-Shell Rock beat Kirk Sallis, Waterloo East, 5-3.

125-John Meeks, Des Moines Roosevelt beat Adam Perrin, North Scott, 7-4.

130-Chad Ryan, Sioux City North beat Jordan Rinken, Waverly-Shell Rock, 10-1.

135-Bo Schlosser, Bettendorf beat Gradey Gambrall, Iowa City West, 3-1.

140-Jake Ballweg, Waverly-Shell Rock beat Elijah Sullivan, Council Bluffs Lewis Central, 5-0.

145-Cody Caldwell, Waverly-Shell Rock beat Gustavo Martinez, Marshalltown, 5-2.

152-Michael Kelly, Cedar Falls beat Joey Trizzino, Bettendorf, 8-7 (3 OT).

160-Nick Moore, Iowa City West beat Spencer BeLieu, Indianola, 11-6.

171-Michael Moreno, Urbandale beat Walt Gillmor, North Scott, 12-2.

189-Kyven Gadson, Waterloo East beat Matt Riley, Des Moines Roosevelt, 13-3.

215-Cody Krumwiede, Waverly-Shell Rock beat Josh Lambrecht, Cedar Rapids Prairie, 5-2.

Hwt-Brody Berrie, Bettendorf beat Nolan Proehl, Davenport West, 4-2.

CLASS 2-A

103-Dylan Peters, Denver-Tripoli pinned Colton McCrystal, Sergeant Bluff-Luton, 1:39.

112-Gunnar Wolfensperger, Denver-Tripoli beat Kalen Greiner, Sigourney-Keota, 11-5.

119-Brandon Sorensen, Denver-Tripoli beat Logan Thomsen, Union (LaPorte City), 25-12.

125-Levi Wolfensperger, Denver-Tripoli pinned Tyler Patten, Webster City, 1:50.

130-Jake Marlin, Creston/Orient-Macksburg beat Jake Keller, Columbus Junction, 5-3.

135-Kyle Paulsen, Wilton beat Kyler Risher, Centerville, 4-2.

140-Seth Noble, Columbus Junction beat Blake Meling, East Marshall/GMG, 5-2.

145-Aaron Sorenson, Forest City beat Willie Miklus, Ballard (Huxley), 4-3.

152-Tanner Weatherman, Ballard (Huxley) beat Taylor Berger, Carroll, 11-4.

160-Landon Williams, Davenport Assumption beat Kyle Walker, Algona, 13-1.

171-Mike England, Centerville beat Brock Weatherman, Ballard (Huxley), 1-1, 2-0 OT.

189-Stewart Holloway, West Burlington/Notre Dame beat Trevor Voelker, Dallas Center-Grimes, 5-4.

215-Ryan Fank, Independence beat Slater Poe, Albia, 2-1 (2 OT).

Hwt-Austin Blythe, Williamsburg beat Adam Praska, Crestwood (Cresco) 3-2.

CLASS 1-A

103-Jordan Bremer, Woodbury Central beat Brance Simms, Twin River Valley (Bode), 5-3.

112-Tyler Shulista, Alburnett beat Kody Krenz, Louisa-Muscatine, 12-3.

119-Christopher Halblom, Alburnett beat Ben McMahon, Don Bosco (Gilbertville), 2-1 (ot).

125-Logan Mulnix, North-Linn (Troy Mills) beat Jake Kadel, New London/Winfield-Mount Union, 6-2.

130-Derric Thomas, Mason City Newman beat Brayton Taylor, Prairie Valley (Gowrie), 10-8.

135-Cole Welter, Don Bosco (Gilbertville) beat Ben Huber, Hudson, 17-4.

140-Robert Walker, Martensdale-St. Marys beat Brode Hills, Louisa-Muscatine, 4-3.

145-Justin Hoffman, East Buchanan beat Michael Jensen, Graettinger-Terril, 17-9.

152-Dmitri Boyer, Eddyville-Blakesburg beat Tyler Ogburn, Corning, 4-2.

160-Levi Peters, Twin River Valley (Bode) pinned Jason Frain, Riverside (Oakland), 2:43.

171-Quinn Wilson, Riverside (Oakland) beat Dacoda Ward, Lisbon, 6-0.

189-Taylor Kettman, Don Bosco (Gilbertville) beat Bryce Olson, Eagle Grove, 7-2.

215-Jon Meyers, Coon Rapids-Bayard beat Jordan Simon, Aplington-Parkersburg, 7-2.

Hwt-Caleb Wilken, Nashua-Plainfield beat Dylan Lame, Mount Ayr, 4-2 (2 OT).

2011 (February 19)

CLASS 3-A

103-Phillip Laux, Iowa City West beat Jake Koethe, West Des Moines Valley, 12-3.

112-Colby Knight, Urbandale beat Jake Agnitsch, Ames, 5-4.

119-Cory Clark, Southeast Polk beat Keegan Wakefield, Iowa City West, 5-2.

125-Jack Hathaway, Iowa City West beat Connor Ryan, Bettendorf, 6-1.

130-John Meeks, Des Moines Roosevelt beat Dakota Bauer, Iowa City West, 9-4.

135-Wade Edgington, Indianola beat Jay Hildreth, Council Bluffs Lewis Central, 2-2, 2-0 (OT).

140-Brian Warren, Des Moines North-Hoover beat Jordan Rinken, Waverly-Shell Rock, 1-1, 2-0 (OT).

145-Zach Witte, Cedar Rapids Prairie beat Gabe Moreno, Urbandale, 6-5.

152-Cody Caldwell, Waverly-Shell Rock beat Trey Lewis, West Des Moines Valley, 9-3.

160-Taylor Berger, Carroll pinned Ethan Lara, Sioux City East, 5:22.

171-Willie Miklus, Southeast Polk beat Levi Peters, Fort Dodge, 10-6.

189-Brandon Abernathy, Indianola beat Jared Bartel, Mason City, 3-0.

215-Connor Herman, Cedar Rapids Jefferson beat Ben Nagle, North Scott (Eldridge), 3-3, 2-0 (OT).

Hwt-Cody Krumweide, Waverly-Shell Rock beat Brody Berrie, Bettendorf, 10-0.

CLASS 2-A

103-Doug Miner, Spirit Lake Park beat Zach Less, West Delaware, 7-1.

112-Dylan Peters, Denver-Tripoli beat Colton McCrystal, Sergeant Bluff-Luton,13-4.

119-Topher Carton, Davenport Assumption beat Sawyer Farris, New London/Winfield-Mount Union, 6-2.

125-Jacob Colon, Clear Lake beat Dakota Simmons, Fairfield, 4-0.

130-Brandon Sorenson, Denver-Tripoli beat Josh Perkins, Atlantic, 15-7.

135-Jake Marlin, Creston/Orient-Macksburg beat Tyler Patten, Webster City, 13-4.

140-Kyle Risher, Centerville beat Brad Schwenke, Atlantic, 11-3.

145-Brody Grothus, Davenport Assumption beat Tanner Hiatt, Ballard (Huxley), 2-2, 2-0 (OT).

152-Ryan Valline, East Marshall-GMG beat Chase Skoneczka, Benton (Van Horne), 6-4.

160-Kyle Lux, South Tama beat Nick Fuller, Independence, 13-7.

171-Tanner Weatherman, Ballard (Huxley) beat Colton Vant Hof, Sioux Center, 17-5.

189-Ross Larson, Ballard (Huxley) beat Devin Mitchell, Bondurant-Farrar, 7-3.

215-Kane Seeley, Perry pinned Collin Bevins, Creston/Orient-Macksburg, 2:50.

Hwt-Austin Blythe, Williamsburg pinned Zach Bauer, Dallas Center-Grimes, 5:31.

CLASS 1-A

103-Jordan Bremer, Woodbury Central beat Andrew Foutch, Underwood, 6-2.

112-Brance Simms, Twin River Valley (Bode) beat Nathan Ryan, Woodbury Central, 10-2.

119-Tyler Shulista, Alburnett pinned Jesse Partlow, Manson-Northwest Webster, 1:07.

125-Christopher Halblom, Alburnett beat Kolbi Kohl, Lisbon, 1-1, 1-0 OT.

130-Brennan McNitt, Council Bluffs St. Albert beat Jordan Johnson, Interstate 35 (Truro), 9-4.

135-Drew Proctor, Tipton beat Logan Mulnix, North-Linn (Troy Mills), 6-2.

140-Robert Walker, Martensdale-St. Marys beat Nolan Oviatt, Logan-Magnolia, 5-1.

145-Loren Williams, Tri-Center (Neola) beat Matt Finch, H-M-S (Hartley), 5-4.

152-Dallas Houchins, Interstate 35 (Truro) beat Austin Kessler, Durant-Bennett, 6-4.

160-Austin Even, Jesup beat Brett Roberts, Eddyville-Blakesburg, 4-2.

171-Jake Everts, Aplington-Parkersburg beat Tevin Brinson, Mason City Newman, 7-1.

189-Andrew Nodtvedt, Central Springs (Manly) beat Ethan Calvert, Interstate 35 (Truro), 7-0.

215-Nate Howard, Graettinger-Terril pinned Zach Salisbury, Sumner-Fredericksburg, 2:34.

Hwt-Caleb White, Tri-Center (Neola) beat Joe Koehn, Valley Community (Elgin), 3-3, 2-0 (OT).

IOWA'S STATE CHAMPIONS TO NATIONAL CHAMPIONS SINCE 1928

NCAA DIVISION I

Richard Cole, Ames (105 pounds, 115 pounds 1926, 1927) 135 pounds, Iowa State 1931

Robert Hess, Cresco (135 pounds, 1927) 174 pounds, Iowa State 1932, 1933

Dale Brand, Fort Dodge (105 pounds, 1931) 126 pounds, Cornell College 1937

Dale Hansen, Cresco (85 pounds, 105 pounds 1934, 1935) 128 pounds, Minnesota 1939

Don Nichols, Cresco (95 pounds, 135 pounds 1933, 1935) 175 pounds, Michigan 1940

Gerald Leeman, Osage (105 pounds, 115 pounds, 123 pounds 1939, 1940, 1941) 128 pounds, Iowa State Teachers College 1946

Bill Koll, Fort Dodge (135 pounds, 1941) 145 pounds, 147.5 pounds, Iowa State Teachers College 1946, 1947, 1948

Bill Nelson, Eagle Grove (Heavyweight, 1945) 165 pounds, 155 pounds, Iowa State Teachers College 1947, 1948, 1949

Dick Hauser, Waterloo West (105 pounds, 118 pounds 1944, 1945, 1946) 121 pounds, Cornell College 1947

Lowell Lange, Waterloo West (145 pounds 1945, 1946) 136 pounds, Cornell College 1947, 1949, 1950

Dick Govig, Britt (105 pounds, 1951; 112 pounds, 1952) 123 pounds, Iowa 1954

Simon Roberts, Davenport (133 pounds, 1954) 147 pounds, Iowa 1957

Les Anderson, Clarion (103 pounds, 1954) 130 pounds, 137 pounds, Iowa State 1958, 1960

Ron Gray, Eagle Grove (103 pounds, 120 pounds, 138 pounds 1952, 1953, 1955) 147 pounds, Iowa State 1958, 1959

Gary Kurdelmeier, Cresco (Heavyweight, 1953, 1954) 171 pounds, Iowa 1958

Larry Hayes, D.M. Lincoln (138 pounds Class A, 1957) 137 pounds, 147 pounds, Iowa State 1959, 1960, 1961

Bill Dotson, Waterloo East (133 pounds, 145 pounds Class A, 1957, 1958) 137 pounds, State College of Iowa 1963

Gordon Hassman, New Hampton (120 pounds Class B, 1960) 157 pounds, Iowa State 1964

Tom Peckham, Cresco (127 pounds Class B, 154 pounds Class A, 165 pounds Class B 1960, 1961, 1962) 177 pounds, Iowa State 1965, 1966

Dale Anderson, Waterloo West (120 pounds Class A, 127 pounds Class 2-A 1963, 1964) 137 pounds, Michigan State 1967, 1968

Dan Gable, Waterloo West (95 pounds, 103 pounds, 112 pounds Class AA 1964, 1965, 1966) 130 pounds, 137 pounds, Iowa State 1968, 1969

Dale Bahr, Iowa Falls (145 pounds Class B, 145 pounds Class A 1963, 1964) 145 pounds, Iowa State 1968

Jason Smith, Ankeny (165 pounds Class A, 1966) 167 pounds, Iowa State 1969, 1970

Dave Martin, Algona (145 pounds Class A, 154 pounds Class A 1965, 1966) 158 pounds, Iowa State 1970

Rich Binek, Waterloo West (165 pounds Class 3-A, 1969) 177 pounds, Iowa State 1973

Mike Land, W.D.M. Valley (126 pounds Class 3-A, 1974) 126 pounds, Iowa State 1978

Bruce Kinseth, Decorah (132 pounds, Class 2-A 1975) 150 pounds, Iowa 1979

Jim Gibbons, Ames (98 pounds, 105 pounds, 119 pounds Class 3-A 1975, 1976, 1977) 134 pounds, Iowa State 1981

Pete Bush, Davenport Assumption (185 pounds, Class 3-A 1979) 190 pounds, Iowa 1982

Barry Davis, Cedar Rapids Prairie (112 pounds, 119 pounds Class 3-A 1978, 1979, 1980) 118 pounds, 126 pounds, Iowa 1982, 1983, 1985

Jim Zalesky, Cedar Rapids Prairie (145 pounds, Class 3-A 1978, 1979) 158 pounds, Iowa 1982, 1983, 1984

Joe Gibbons, Waterloo Columbus, Ames (98 pounds, 105 pounds, 126 pounds, 132 pounds Class 3-A 1978, 1979, 1980, 1981) 142 pounds, Iowa State 1985

Kevin Dresser, Humboldt (126 pounds, 132 pounds, Class 2-A 1980, 1981) 142 pounds, Iowa 1986

Royce Alger, Lisbon (126 pounds, 138 pounds, 167 pounds, Class 1-A 1981, 1982, 1983) 167 pounds, 177 pounds, Iowa 1987, 1988

Tim Krieger, Mason City (119 pounds, 132 pounds, 145 pounds Class 3-A 1982, 1983, 1984) 150 pounds, Iowa State 1987, 1989

Mike Van Arsdale, Waterloo West (145 pounds Class 3-A, 1982) 167 pounds, Iowa State 1988

Terry Brands, Sheldon (98 pounds, 105 pounds, Class 2-A 1985, 1986) 126 pounds, Iowa 1990, 1992

Tom Brands, Sheldon (112 pounds, Class 2-A 1986) 134 pounds, Iowa 1990, 1991, 1992

Jason Kelber, West Marshall (105 pounds, 119 pounds Class 2-A 1984, 1985, 1986) 126 pounds, Nebraska 1991

Mark Reiland, Eagle Grove (145 pounds, 155 pounds, Class 2-A 1986, 1987) 167 pounds, Iowa 1991

Jeff McGinness, Iowa City High (103 pounds, 112 pounds, 125 pounds, 130 pounds, Class 3-A 1990, 1991, 1992, 1993) 126 pounds, 142 pounds, Iowa 1995, 1998

Daryl Weber, Don Bosco (Gilbertville) (135 pounds, 145 pounds Class 1-A, 1990, 1991) 167 pounds, Iowa 1996

Lee Fullhart, Decorah (160 pounds, 171 pounds, 189 pounds Class 2-A, 1992, 1993, 1994) 190 pounds, Iowa 1997

Mark Ironside, Cedar Rapids Jefferson (130 pounds, 135 pounds Class 3-A, 1992, 1993) 134 pounds, Iowa 1997, 1998

Jessie Whitmer, Eagle Grove (103 pounds, Class 2-A 1990) 118 pounds, Iowa 1997

Doug Schwab, Osage (130 pounds, Class 2-A 1996) 141 pounds, Iowa 1999

Eric Juergens, Maquoketa (103 pounds Class 3-A, 112 pounds Class 3-A, 119 pounds Class 3-A, 125 pounds Class 2-A 1993, 1994, 1995, 1996) 133 pounds, Iowa 2000, 2001

Cliff Moore, Dubuque Hempstead (112 pounds, 119 pounds, 125 pounds, Class 3-A 1997, 1998, 1999) 141 pounds, Iowa 2004

Trent Paulson, Council Bluffs Lewis Central (140 pounds, 145 pounds Class 3-A 2001, 2002) 157 pounds, Iowa State 2007

Matt McDonough, Linn-Mar (Marion) (112 pounds, 119 pounds. 130 pounds Class 3-A, 2006, 2007, 2008) 125 pounds, Iowa 2010.

Jay Borschel, Linn-Mar (Marion) (103 pounds, 125 pounds, 152 pounds, 171 pounds Class 3-A 2002, 2003, 2004, 2005) 174 pounds, Iowa 2010.

NCAA DIVISION II

Dee Brainerd, Fort Dodge (112 pounds, 120 pounds 1955, 1956) South Dakota State 130 pounds, 1963.

Bill Dotson, Waterloo East (133 pounds, 145 pounds 1957, 1958) State College of Iowa 137 pounds, 1963.

Don Parker, North Fayette (165 pounds, Class B 1963) State College of Iowa 177 pounds, 1966, 1967.

Kent Osboe, Fort Dodge (Heavyweight, Class AA 1964) Northern Iowa heavyweight, 1968, 1969.

Clint Young, Algona (145 pounds, Class A, 1967) Northern Iowa 158 pounds, 1971.

Ken Snyder, Waterloo Columbus (138 pounds, Class AAA 1971) Northern Iowa 142 pounds, 1974, 1975.

Randy Omvig, Eagle Grove (185 pounds, Class AA 1971) Northern Iowa heavyweight, 1975.

Gary Bentrim, Cedar Rapids Jefferson (126 pounds, Class AAA 1973) Northern Iowa 142 pounds and 158 pounds, 1976, 1977, 1978.

Brent Hagen, Britt (98 pounds Class A, 98 pounds Class AA, 112 pounds Class A 1972. 1973, 1975) Mankato State 118 pounds, 1977

Kirk Myers, Algona (185 pounds, Class 2-A 1977) Northern Iowa 190 pounds, 1978, 1979, 1980

Ken Gallagher, Waterloo Columbus (145 pounds, Class 3-A 1977) Northern Iowa 150 pounds, 1980.

Bob Kauffman, Emmetsburg (145 pounds Class 2-A 1981) Edinboro 150 pounds, 1986.

Jeremiah (J.D.) Naig, Emmetsburg/Armstrong-Ringsted (152 pounds, Class 2-A 2002) Nebraska-Omaha 165 pounds, 174 pounds 2005, 2006, 2007.

Ryan Phillips, Burlington (215 pounds Class 3-A 2002) Upper Iowa 197 pounds, 2007.

Travis Eggers, MFL (Monona)/Mar-Mac (140 pounds Class 2-A 2005) Upper Iowa 165 pounds, 2010.

NCAA DIVISION III

Gary Wood, Centerville (Class 2-A 132, 1974) William Penn 150 pounds, 1979.

Dave Jordan, Cedar Falls (Class 3-A 105, 1985), Buena Vista 118 pounds, 1989.

Shawn Voigt, Mount Vernon (Class 2-A 138, 1985) Cornell College 150 pounds, 1990.

Travis Young, Indianola (Class 3-A 138, 1987) Simpson 150 pounds, 1991, 1992.

Tom Hogan, Don Bosco (Gilbertville) (Class 1-A 132, 1988), Wartburg 150 pounds, 1993.

Brian Stewart, Lisbon (Class 1-A 130, 1990) Buena Vista 150 pounds, 1994.

Cory Christensen, Winterset (Class 2-A 125, 1991; Class 2-A 135, 1992; Class 2-A 145, 1993) Simpson 158 pounds, 1996.

Dusty Rhodes, Osage (Class 2-A 125, 1992) Wartburg (134 pounds, 1997).

Ben Shane, Iowa Falls (Class 2-A 130, 1994) 142 pounds, Wartburg 1998

Ryan Schweitzberger, Kingsley-Pierson (140 pounds, Class 1-A 1994) 150 pounds, Buena Vista 1998

Andy Krueger, Sioux City Heelan (Class 3-A 145, 1994; Class 3-A 152, 1995) Buena Vista (157 pounds, 1999).

Jamie Taxted, Webster City (Class 1-A 103, 1996; Class 2-A 112, 1997) 125 pounds, Buena Vista 2002

Wil Kelly, Dubuque Wahlert (Class 3-A 119, 1993; Class 3-A 130, 1994; Class 3-A 135, 1995) 141 pounds, Wartburg 2003

Cody Koenig, Underwood (Class 1-A 152, 2001), Wis.-Stevens Point (174 pounds, 2003).

Bart Mehlert, Union (LaPorte City) (Class 2-A 140, 2000) Wartburg (149 pounds 2004).

Ryan Sturm, Emmetsburg/Armstrong-Ringsted (Class 2-A 160, 2001) Wartburg (184 pounds, 2004).

Dustin Hinschberger, Belle Plaine (Class 1-A 135, 2002) Wartburg (141 pounds, 2004, 2005, 2006).

Akeem Carter, Waterloo West (Class 3-A 171, 2001; Class 3-A 189, 2002) Wartburg 197 pounds, 2004, 2005.

Garrett South, CAM (Anita) (Class 1-A 160, 2001) Luther 165 pounds, 2005.

Blake Gillis, Spencer (Class 3-A 215, 2003) Wartburg heavyweight, 2007.

Jacob Naig, Emmetsburg/Armstrong-Ringsted (Class 2-A 112, 2001; Class 2-A 145, 2003) Wartburg 149 pounds, 2008.

Aaron Wernimont, Pocahontas Area (Class 1-A 145, 2003) Wartburg 157 pounds, 2008, 2009.

Tyler Burkle, North-Linn (Class 1-A 152, 2006), Coe 165 pounds, 2008.

Romeo Djoumessi, Waverly-Shell Rock (Class 3-A 189, 2005) Wartburg 184 pounds, 2008.

Justin Hanson, Humboldt (Class 2-A 125, 2003; Class 2-A 135 pounds, 2004) Wartburg 165 pounds, 2009.

Byron Tate, Clinton (Class 3-A 215 pounds, 2008) Wartburg 197 pounds, 2010.

NAIA

Wade Winters, Bondurant-Farrar (Class A heavyweight, 1964) Heavyweight, Westmar 1968

Jamie Kamberling, Lisbon (Class 1-A 185, 1988) 190 pounds, Western Montana 1993

Rick Moreno, Glenwood (Class 2-A 145, 1991; Class 2-A 145, 1992) 149 pounds, Mount St. Clare 1999

Brad Stockton, Iowa City West (Class 3-A 130, 2002) 149 pounds, Waldorf College 2007

JUNIOR COLLEGE

Rich Mihal, Cedar Rapids Jefferson (Class AA 138, 1965) 160 pounds, Rochester (Minn.) Junior College 1967

Bob Fouts, Waterloo West (Class AAA heavyweight, 1972) Heavyweight, North Iowa Area Community College 1973

Dave Morgan, Eagle Grove (98 pounds, 105 pounds, 126 pounds Class

2-A 1972, 1973, 1974) 142 pounds, Iowa Central Community College 1977

Mark Helling, Hudson (Class 1-A 167, 1976) 190 pounds, Waldorf 1978

John Schaumburg, Eagle Grove (Class 2-A 138, 1977), 158 pounds, Iowa Central Community College 1980

Paul Weltha, Ames (Class 3-A heavyweight, 1986, 1987) Heavyweight, Iowa Central Community College 1989

Erik Josephson, Fort Dodge (Class 3-A 171, 1991) 167 pounds, Iowa Central Community College 1993

Greg Butteris, Lisbon (Class 1-A 167, 1987) 190 pounds, North Idaho Junior College 1989

Matt Ironside, Cedar Rapids Jefferson (Class 3-A 135, 1991) 134 pounds, Iowa Central Community College 1995

Todd Buckland, D.M. Lincoln (Class 3-A 145, 1996) 157 pounds, Waldorf 1998

Luke Moffitt, Estherville (Class 2-A 125, 1997) 141 pounds, Iowa Central Community College 2000

Bart Mehlert, Union (LaPorte City) (Class 2-A 140, 2000) 149 pounds, Ellsworth 2001

Eric Hoffman, Davenport North (Class 3-A 119, 2003) 125 pounds, Iowa Central Community College 2006

Brad Lower, Burlington (Class 3-A 145, 2005) 165 pounds, Iowa Central Community College 2009

Joe Colon, Clear Lake (Class 2-A 103, 2007; 125 2009) 125 pounds, Iowa Central Community College 2010

The author wishes to thank the State Historical Society of Iowa's Library and microfilm collection of newspapers, which proved to be invaluable during research for this book. Special thanks to executive director Rick Wulkow, assistant executive directors Alan Beste and Dave Anderson, information director Bud Legg and communications and marketing director Chad Elsburry of the Iowa High School Athletic Association. Chuck Offenburger, a former colleague, provided terrific advice to a first-time author as well as years of example on how to tell a story. Thanks to Bob Steenlage, Jeff Kerber, Tom Peckham, Bill Nelson, Dan Gable, Dale McDonough, Marv Reiland, Brian Reimers and many others who allowed me into their home or office to learn about their lives in high school wrestling history. Thank you to Bob Siddens, who sat in a training room at Waterloo West High School and gave considerable time and information. I hope you were not late for your grandchildren's game that afternoon, Bob. All in all, thanks to the 159 people who were interviewed face-to-face, by telephone or by e-mail for this book. Many thanks to Jim Gibbons, who braved an ice storm to meet with me about this book. Kudos to Pat, Terry, Tom and Mike who encouraged me to finally move forward with a years-old idea of writing a book about the state wrestling tournament after a career change. Ames Athletic Director Judge Johnston provided much-needed assistance and gets many thanks. John and Mary Doak contributed the debut issue of *The Predicament*. Ray Arnold gets credit for showing a kid the importance of knowing as much of the story and the behind-the-scenes color to write wrestling. A tip of the cap to the coaches who endured highs and lows, often in the same tournament, and to the kids who laced up a pair of "boots" and gave up a lot of free time to compete and create so many lasting memories.

Also, thanks to editorial assistants Oby and Frosty, who slept long enough for chapters to be written before they demanded food. My editor, Diane, did an amazing job trying to comprehend the sport of wrestling and some of its colorful characters while making sure I was sure of my subject and my predicate.